The
PHOSPHATIDES

BY

HAROLD WITTCOFF

Research Dept., General Mills, Inc.

American Chemical Society
Monograph Series

BOOK DIVISION
REINHOLD PUBLISHING CORPORATION
330 WEST FORTY–SECOND STREET, NEW YORK, U.S.A.
1951

Series

Cat. for Chem.

CHEMISTRY

Copyright, 1951, by

REINHOLD PUBLISHING CORPORATION

———

Printed in U. S. A. by
BERWICK & SMITH CO., NORWOOD, MASS.

TO
MY WIFE, MY SONS, MY PARENTS, MY SISTER,
EACH OF WHOM CONTRIBUTED,
THIS BOOK IS DEDICATED

GENERAL INTRODUCTION

American Chemical Society's Series of
Chemical Monographs

By arrangement with the Interallied Conference of Pure and Applied Chemistry, which met in London and Brussels in July, 1919, the American Chemical Society was to undertake the production and publication of Scientific and Technologic Monographs on chemical subjects. At the same time it was agreed that the National Research Council, in cooperation with the American Chemical Society and the American Physical Society, should undertake the production and publication of Critical Tables of Chemical and Physical Constants. The American Chemical Society and the National Research Council mutually agreed to care for these two fields of chemical progress. The American Chemical Society named as Trustees, to make the necessary arrangements of the publication of the Monographs, Charles L. Parsons, secretary of the Society, Washington, D. C.; the late John E. Teeple, then treasurer of the Society, New York; and the late Professor Gellert Alleman of Swarthmore College. The Trustees arranged for the publication of the ACS Series of (a) Scientific and (b) Technological Monographs by the Chemical Catalog Company, Inc. (Reinhold Publishing Corporation, successor) of New York.

The Council of the American Chemical Society, acting through its Committee on National Policy, appointed editors (the present list of whom appears at the close of this sketch) to select authors of competent authority in their respective fields and to consider critically the manuscripts submitted.

The first Monograph of the Series appeared in 1921. After twenty-three years of experience certain modifications of general policy were indicated. In the beginning there still remained from the preceding five decades a distinct though arbitrary differentiation between so-called "pure science" publications and technologic or applied science literature. By 1944 this differentiation was fast becoming nebulous. Research in private enterprise had grown apace and not a little of it was pursued on the frontiers of knowledge. Furthermore, most workers in the sciences were coming to see the artificiality of the separation. The methods of both groups of workers are the same. They employ the same instrumentalities, and frankly recognize that their objectives are common, namely, the search for new knowledge for the service of man. The officers of the Society therefore combined the two editorial Boards in a single Board of twelve representative members.

Also in the beginning of the Series, it seemed expedient to construe rather broadly the definition of a Monograph. Needs of workers had to be recognized. Consequently among the first hundred Monographs appeared works in the form of treatises covering in some instances rather broad areas. Because such necessary works do not now want for publishers, it is considered advisable to hew more strictly to the line of the Monograph character, which means more complete and critical treatment of relatively restricted areas, and, where a broader field needs coverage, to subdivide it into logical subareas. The prodigious expansion of new knowledge makes such a change desirable.

These Monographs are intended to serve two principal purposes: first, to make available to chemists a thorough treatment of a selected area in form usable by persons working in more or less unrelated fields to the end that they may correlate their own work with a larger area of physical science discipline; second, to stimulate further research in the specific field treated. To implement this purpose the authors of Monographs are expected to give extended references to the literature. Where the literature is of such volume that a complete bibliography is impracticable, the authors are expected to append a list of references critically selected on the basis of their relative importance and significance.

PREFACE

The lack of a modern text in English on phosphatide chemistry has provided the inspiration for the present volume. Many centuries elapsed from the time of the Greek philosophers, who considered brain phosphorus necessary for thought processes, until 1719, when Hensing isolated a phosphorus-containing lipide from brain. The literature which has accumulated in the much shorter period since Hensing's discovery, however, is as complex as the compounds it describes; and, unfortunately, many errors have been recorded. An attempt has been made in this book to summarize the accurate literature with emphasis on that which has accumulated in the past two decades since MacLean and MacLean, and Thierfelder and Klenk published their classic works. For complete coverage, chemical, physical, analytical, biochemical and industrial aspects have each been treated in turn. The literature has been covered through 1949, although some data appearing in 1950 have been included. For the sake of convenience, a large number of *Chemical Abstracts* references have been included in the bibliography.

An attempt at interpretation has been made whenever it appears warranted. The present state of knowledge is such, however, that it is often of greater moment to point out a gap which serves to preclude interpretation. Happily, there are competent workers who have accepted the challenge presented by phosphatide investigation and have set about in a systematic way to eliminate some of these gaps. Undoubtedly firmer bases for interpretation will be available for future revisions of this book.

Existing reviews and summaries of specific aspects of phosphatide chemistry have been drawn upon freely, and an earnest attempt was made to accord due credit to these in the text.

It is more than a pleasure to acknowledge the cooperation and inspiration provided by the General Mills Research Laboratory through its director, Dr. Ralph H. Manley.

The encouragement and advice provided by all my colleagues as well as by Mr. Whitney Eastman, Dr. Gustav Egloff and Dr. Byron Riegel is mentioned in gratitude. Numerous people contributed immeasurably by constructive criticism of the book. Dr. Herbert Carter's contribution to the nomenclature section, as well as his critical review of Part I, is gratefully acknowledged. Similarly, thanks are due to Dr. Robert Roach for his review of Part I, to Dr. Irving Klotz for his review of the portion on physical chemistry, to Dr. David Glick for his review of Part II, to Dr. Herbert Barnes for his review of Part III, to Dr. Betty Sullivan for her review of the portion on phosphatides of wheat, to Dr. Cyrus P. Barnum and Dr. W. L. Lundberg for their reviews of Part V, to Dr. A. Gehrke, Mr. W. H. Goss, Mr. Jakob Jakobsen and Mr. William Taylor for their reviews of Part VI and to Mr. Taylor for preparing Table II of Part VI.

The cooperation of Miss Margaret Hilligan and the General Mills, Inc. library staff contributed immeasurably to the preparation of the volume. The typing of numerous drafts was the burden and responsibility of Miss June Whitney and also of Miss Elsie Gustafson. These tireless workers deserve unqualified thanks. To Mrs. Donald Smith are extended sincere thanks for aid in preparing the Author Index.

Finally, to my wife, Dorothy B. Wittcoff, for her inspiration as well as her practical contribution of devoting uncounted hours to copyreading each draft of the manuscript, goes an expression of heartfelt gratitude.

For permission to reproduce much of the tabular material found in the book the author is indebted to the editors and publishers of *Acta Ophthalmologica, Archives of Biochemistry, Biochemical Journal, Bulletin de la société de chimie biologique, Canadian Journal of Research, Fette und Seifen, The Harvey Lectures, Journal of the American Oil Chemists' Society, Journal of Biological Chemistry, Journal of Cellular and Comparative Physiology, Journal für praktische Chemie* and "The German Oilseed Industry" by W. H. Goss.

Notwithstanding these many contributions, the author himself assumes the responsibility for errors both of omission and commission and will appreciate greatly having these called to his attention.

HAROLD WITTCOFF

Minneapolis, Minnesota
January, 1951

CONTENTS

Part I: The Chemistry of the Phosphatides

CHAPTER   PAGE

I   NOMENCLATURE AND CLASSIFICATION OF LIPIDES   3

    Introduction   3
    Generic and Species Names   4
    Classification of the Lipides   5

II   THE STRUCTURE OF LECITHIN   9

    Historical   9
    Structure Proof   9
      Polylecithins   11
      Acid-Base Relationships   12
       Isoelectric Point   14
    The Hydrolysis Products of Lecithin   15
      General   15
      Glycerophosphoric Acid   16
       Isolation   16
       Configuration   16
       Properties   18
       Synthesis   18
       Optically Active α-Glycerophosphoric Acids   19
       Glycerophosphatases   20
      The Fatty Acids of Lecithin   20
       General   20
       Ratio of Saturated to Unsaturated Acids   21
       Degree of Unsaturation   22
      Choline   23
       Structure and Synthesis   23
       Properties   23

III   THE STRUCTURE OF THE CEPHALIN PHOSPHATIDES   25

    Historical   25
    Structure Proof   26
      Phosphatidylserine   28
       Serine   31
      Phosphatidylaminoethyl Alcohol   32
       Acid-Base Relationships   32
       β-Aminoethyl Alcohol   34
      Inositol-containing Phosphatides   35
    The Hydrolysis Products of the Cephalin Phosphatides   36
      General   36
      Fatty Acids   37

IV   THE STRUCTURE OF SPHINGOMYELIN   38

    Historical and Introduction   38
    Sphingosine   39
      Structure   39
      Dihydrosphingosine   41
      Sphingosine Ethers   42
      Properties of Sphingosine   43

CHAPTER   PAGE

Sphingomyelin   43
  Structure   43
    Fatty Acids   44
    Acid-Base Relationships   45
  General Properties of Sphingomyelin   46
    Isolation   46
    Hydrolysis   46
    Related Compounds   47

V   THE STRUCTURE OF THE MINOR PHOSPHATIDES   48

  Phosphatidic Acids   48
    Historical   48
    Structure Proof   48
      Fatty Acids   49
    Origin of Phosphatidic Acids   49
    Cardiolipin   50
  Acetal Phosphatides   51
    Introduction   51
    Structure Proof   51
    Sources of Acetal Phosphatides   53
  Hydrophosphatides   53
    Introduction   53
    Structure Proof   54
  Alleged Phosphatides   54
  Lysophosphatides   55

VI THE PURIFICATION AND THE CHEMICAL PROPERTIES OF THE
    PHOSPHATIDES   56

  Introduction   56
  The Purification and Properties of Lecithin   57
    Purification   57
    The Properties of Lecithin   58
    The Chemical Reactions of Lecithin   59
      Hydrolysis   59
      Hydrogenation of Lecithin   60
      Halogenation of Lecithin   61
      Miscellaneous Reactions   61
  The Purification and Properties of the Cephalin Phosphatides   61
    Purification   61
    The Properties and the Chemical Reactions of the Cephalin
      Phosphatides   63
      Hydrogenation of the Cephalins   63
      Reactions of the Amino Nitrogen Atom   64
  The Purification and Properties of Sphingomyelin   64
    Purification   64
    The Properties of Sphingomyelin   65
  The Purification and Properties of Phosphatidic Acid   65
  The Purification and Properties of the Acetal Phosphatides   66
  The Purification and Properties of the Hydrophosphatides   67
  The Purification and Properties of the Lysophosphatides   67

VII THE PHYSICAL CHEMISTRY OF THE PHOSPHATIDES   68

  Introduction   68
  The Interaction of Lecithin with Water   69
    Monomolecular Films   69
    Myelin Forms   71
  Phosphatide Sols   71
    General Properties of Phosphatide Sols   72
    The Coagulation of Phosphatide Sols   73
    Hydrotropic Action on Lecithin Sols   75

CHAPTER

PAGE

Complex Coacervation 75
Lecithin as a Protective Colloid 76
Effect of Lecithin on Swelling of Gels 77
Phosphatides as Emulsifying Agents 78

VIII PHOSPHATIDE COMPLEXES 81

Introduction 81
Lipoproteins 82
  Introduction 82
  Lipide-Protein Linkages 83
  Occurrence of Lipoproteins 84
    Egg Yolk 84
    Cell Parts 85
    Tissue 86
    Blood Serum 86
    Milk 88
    Bacteria and Yeast 88
    Plants 89
  Synthetic Lipoproteins 90
  Properties of Lipoproteins 91
    Dissociation 91
    Physical Properties 92
Carbohydrate Complexes 93
  Introduction 93
  Occurrence of Carbohydrate Complexes 93
  Synthetic Carbohydrate Complexes 94
Metallic Salt Complexes 94
  Cadmium Chloride Complex 95
    Lecithin-Cadmium Chloride Complex 95
  Platinum Chloride Complex 96
  Other Metallic Complexes 96
Cholesterol-Lecithin Complex 96
Miscellaneous Complexes 97

IX THE LYSOPHOSPHATIDES AND THE LECITHINASES 99

Historical and Nomenclature 99
  Nomenclature 100
The Lysophosphatides 101
  The Preparation of the Lysophosphatides 101
    Lysosphingomyelin 103
  The Structure of the Lysophosphatides 103
  Occurrence of the Lysophosphatides 104
The Lecithinases 105
  Lecithinase A 105
    Occurrence 105
    Properties 106
    The Preparation and Detection of Lecithinase A 108
  Lecithinase B 108
  Lecithinases C and D 110
    The Cholinephosphatase 110
    The Glycerophosphatase 111
  Biological Significance of the Lecithinases 115
  Summary 115

X SYNTHESIS OF THE PHOSPHATIDES 116

Synthesis of the Glycerophosphatides 116
  Baer and Kates' Synthesis of Lecithin 116
  Rose's Synthesis of Phosphatidylaminoethyl Alcohol 117
  Synthesis of Optically Active Phosphatidylaminoethyl Alcohol 119
  Kabashima's Syntheses 119
  Arnold's Synthesis 121

CHAPTER   PAGE

        Obata's Synthesis   121
        Grün's Synthesis   121
        Synthesis of Lysophosphatides   122
        Synthesis of Acetal Phosphatides   124
        Synthesis of Phosphatidic Acids   125

   Part II: The Analytical Determination of the Phosphatides

   XI   EXTRACTION AND DETERMINATION OF TOTAL PHOSPHATIDES   147

        Introduction   147
        Microextraction of Phosphatides   147
          Blood   148
            Red Blood Cells   150
          Tissue   150
          Purification of Ethanol-Ether Extract   151
          Other Methods of Extraction for Blood and Tissue   152
          Extraction of Phosphatides Containing P^{32} 153
        Macroextraction of Phosphatides   154
          Blood and Tissue   154
          Plants   155
          Grain Products   158
          Milk   158
        Determination of Total Phosphatides   159
          Oxidative Method   160
            Precipitation by Halides   161
          Determination from Phosphorus Content   161
            Phosphatide Factor   162
          Determination from Fatty Acid Content   162

   XII DETERMINATION OF INDIVIDUAL PHOSPHATIDES AND RE-
        LATED COMPOUNDS   164

        Determination of Individual Phosphatides   164
          Solubility Procedures   165
          Determination from Hydrolysis Products   165
          Determination by Preferential Hydrolysis   167
          Determination by Isotope Dilution   168
          Determination of the Cephalin Fraction   168
          Determination of Phosphatidylserine   170
          Determination of Sphingomyelin   171
          Determination of Saturated Phosphatides   173
          Determination of Acetal Phosphatides   173
        Determination of Choline   174
        Determination of Aminoethyl Alcohol   177
        Determination of Glycerol   177
        Determination of Fatty Acids   178
        Elementary Analysis   180
          Phosphorus   180
          Nitrogen   181
        Iodine Number   182
        Qualitative Tests   182
        Histochemical Reactions   183

   Part III: Phosphatides from Plant Sources

   XIII INTRODUCTION TO PLANT PHOSPHATIDES   191

   XIV PHOSPHATIDES OF MICROORGANISMS AND LOWER PLANTS   196

        Bacteria   196
          Enteric Bacilli   196
          Phytomonas Tumefaciens   197

CHAPTER   PAGE

    Timothy Bacillus 199
    Lactobacillus Acidophilus 199
    Bacillus Albolactis 200
    Diphtheria Bacillus 200
    Calmette-Guérin Bacillus 200
    Turtle and Smegma Bacilli 201
    Leprosy Bacillus 201
    Tubercle Bacillus 202
      Isolation 203
      Hydrolysis Products 204
      Human Bacilli 205
      Tuberculous Tissue 205
      Avian Bacilli 205
      Bovine Bacilli 206
      Nature of the Phosphatides 207
      Neutral Fat 208
      Fatty Acids 208
      Carbohydrates 211
      Phthiocol 213
  Viruses 213
  Fungi 214
    Yeast 214
  Molds 216
  Pathogenic Fungi 217
    Blastomyces Dermatiditis 217
    Monilia Albicans 218

XV PHOSPHATIDES OF CEREALS, GRAINS AND OIL-PRODUCING
    PLANTS 219

  Introduction 219
  Soybeans 220
    Phosphatide Content 220
    Complex Formation 221
    Fatty Acids 222
    Phosphatide Distribution 223
  Wheat and Wheat Products 224
    Phosphatide Content 224
    Complex Formation 226
    Fatty Acids 226
    Constituent Phosphatides 227
  Cottonseed 227
    Phosphatide Content 228
    Fatty Acids 228
    Constituent Phosphatides 228
  Corn 229
    Phosphatide Content 229
    Fatty Acids 230
    Constituent Phosphatides 230
  Rapeseed 230
  Peanuts 231
  Sunflower Seeds 232
  Rye 232
  Barley 233
  Grain Sorghum 233
  Flaxseed 234
  Oats 234
  Tobacco 234
  Cacao Bean 235
  Sesame Seed 235
  Castor Seeds 235
  Miscellaneous Seeds 235

CHAPTER   PAGE

XVI   PHOSPHATIDES OF VEGETABLES AND MISCELLANEOUS PLANTS   236

Carrots   236
Peas   237
Beans   237
Lupines   238
Beets   238
Cabbage   238
Lettuce   239
Miscellaneous Vegetables   239
Rubber Producing Plants   239
Flowers   240
Fruits   241
Grass   242
Alfalfa   242
Leaves   243
Cactus   243
Sugar Cane   243

Part IV: Phosphatides from Animal Sources

XVII   INTRODUCTION TO ANIMAL PHOSPHATIDES   255

XVIII PHOSPHATIDES OF NORMAL ANIMAL ORGANS AND TISSUES   259

Blood   259
  Human Blood   259
    Isolation   259
    Determination of Total Phosphatides   261
    Determination of Individual Phosphatides   261
    Nature of Phosphatides   268
    Amino Acid-containing Lipides   268
    Summary   268
  Animal Blood   270
  Fatty Acids   273
  Complex Formation   274
Brain and Nervous System   274
  Isolation   275
  Distribution of Phosphatides   276
  Phosphatides of the Nervous System   278
  Serine-containing Phosphatides   279
  Inositol-containing Phosphatides   280
  Acetal Phosphatides   280
  Hydrolecithin   280
  Free Bases   281
  Fatty Acids   281
  Complex Formation   283
  Variation of Phosphatide Content with Age   283
Liver   284
  General   284
  Phosphatide Content   284
  Nature of the Phosphatides   288
  Fatty Acids   289
Lung   292
  Phosphatide Content   292
  Nature of the Phosphatides   293
Kidney   294
Spleen   295
Gall Bladder and Bile   297
Bone Marrow   298
Reproductive System   300
  Distribution of Phosphatides   300

CHAPTER   PAGE

Variation in Phosphatide Content During Reproductive Processes 301
Corpus Luteum 302
Glands 303
Adrenal Glands 303
Pancreas 306
Thymus 306
Miscellaneous Glands 306
Muscle 307
General 307
Distribution of Phosphatides 308
Cardiac Muscle 310
Fatty Acids 310
Nature of the Phosphatides 312
Skin and Mucosa 313
Skin 313
Gums 315
Intestine and Intestinal Mucosa 315
Gastric Mucosa 316
Eyes 316
Tooth Pulp 317
The Entire Animal Organism 317
Vertebrates 317
Marine Animals 317
Cysticercus Fasciolaris 318
Miscellaneous 319

XIX PHOSPHATIDES OF EGGS AND MILK 320

Eggs 320
Phosphatide Content 320
Fatty Acids 321
Complex Formation 322
Milk and Dairy Products 323
Phosphatide Content 323
Distribution of Phosphatides 326
Fatty Acids 326
Rancidity 327

Part V : The Biochemistry and Physiology of the Phosphatides

XX INTRODUCTION TO BIOCHEMISTRY OF THE PHOSPHATIDES 339

Proposed Functions of the Phosphatides 339
The Phosphatides as Structural Elements 341
The Phosphatides as Components of Particulate Portions of Cells 343

XXI GENERAL ASPECTS OF LIPIDE METABOLISM 345

Introduction 345
Lipide Metabolism 345
Digestion of Lipides 345
Absorption of Lipides 346
Transportation and Disposition of Absorbed Lipides 348
The Storage of Lipides 350
The Synthesis of Lipides from Carbohydrate and Protein 351
The Role of the Liver in Fat Transportation and Disposition 354
Dietary Fatty Livers 355
Fatty Livers Produced by Factors Other Than Dietary 357
Degradation of Fatty Acid by the Liver 358
Formation and Role of Ketone Bodies 359
The Complete Oxidation of Fatty Aicds 360

CHAPTER   PAGE

       The Role of Extrahepatic Tissues and Organs in Fat Metab-
          olism   361
          Pancreas   362
          Kidneys   362
          Adrenal Glands   363
          Other Tissues   364
       Excretion of Lipides   364

XXII   THE PHOSPHATIDES AS METABOLIC ELEMENTS   366

       The Role of Phosphatides in Metabolism   366
       Introduction   366
       Labeling Techniques   367
          Elaidic Acid in the Study of Phosphatide Metabolism   367
          Miscellaneous Fatty Acid Labels in the Study of Phosphatide
             Metabolism   369
          Conjugated Acids   369
          Fatty Acids Labeled with Radioactive Atoms   370
          Choline and Aminoethyl Alcohol Labels in the Study of
             Phosphatide Metabolism   370
          Radioactive Phosphorus in the Study of Phosphatide Me-
             tabolism   371
       Metabolic Activity of Phosphatides of Various Organs and
          Tissues   377
       Metabolic Activity of Blood Phosphatides   377
          Effect of Dietary Factors on Blood Phosphatides   377
          Effect of Drugs and Biological Substances on Blood Phos-
             phatides   379
          Effect of Pregnancy and Menstruation on Blood Phos-
             phatides   380
          Turnover of Blood Phosphatides   381
          Origin of Blood Phosphatides   383
       Phosphatides as Transport Agents for Fatty Acids   384
       Metabolic Activity of Liver Phosphatides   385
       Metabolic Activity of the Phosphatides of the Gastroin-
          testinal Tract   389
       Metabolic Activity of Kidney Phosphatides   392
       Metabolic Activity of Muscle Phosphatides   393
       Metabolic Activity of the Phosphatides of the Brain and
          Central Nervous System   395
       Metabolic Activity of the Phosphatides of the Reproductive
          System   396
       Metabolic Activity of the Phosphatides of the Egg and the
          Developing Embryo   397
          The Origin and Behavior of Yolk and Embryo Phosphatides 400
       Metabolic Activity of Milk Phosphatides   401
       Metabolic Activity of Miscellaneous Tissues   403
       Metabolic Activity of Plant Phosphatides   404
       The Synthesis of Phosphatides by Isolated Tissues   407
       The Mechanism of Formation of Phosphatides   408
       The Effect of Radiant Energy on Phosphatides   411

XXIII THE ROLE OF PHOSPHATIDE HYDROLYSIS PRODUCTS IN ME-
       TABOLISM   413

       Choline   413
          Lipotropism   413
          Manifestations of Alipotropism   414
          Transmethylation   415
          The Mechanism of Lipotropism   418
          Other Functions of Choline   419
       Aminoethyl Alcohol, Serine and Sphingosine   420

PAGE

CHAPTER

Glycerophosphoric Acid 421
Inositol-containing Phosphatides 421
Lysophosphatides 421

XXIV   THE ROLE OF THE PHOSPHATIDES IN PATHOLOGICAL CONDI-
       TIONS 424

Lipidoses 424
  Xanthomatoses 425
  Niemann-Pick's Disease 426
  Tay-Sachs' Disease 428
  Gaucher's Disease 428
General Diseases 428
  Diseases of the Liver and Bile Ducts 428
  Diseases of the Kidneys 430
  Diseases of the Pancreas and the Gastrointestinal Tract ... 431
  Diseases of the Blood 432
  Diseases of the Blood Vessels 433
  Diseases of the Central Nervous System 434
  Diabetes 435
  Tumors and Neoplasms 436
  Tuberculosis 438
  Diseases of the Heart 439
  Diseases of the Skin 439
  Avitaminoses 439
  Diseases of the Thyroid Gland 441
  Miscellaneous Diseases 441

XXV   SEROLOGICAL AND OXIDATIVE FUNCTIONS OF THE PHOSPHA-
       TIDES 443

Blood Coagulation 443
  Introduction 443
  The Thromboplastic Factor 444
  The Lipide Constituent of the Thromboplastic Factor ... 445
  Lipide Inhibitors of Thromboplastic Activity ... 446
Antigenic Reactions 447
  Lipide Antigens or Haptens 447
  Bacterial Lipide Antigens 449
  Lipide-containing Antigens in the Detection of Disease ... 450
    Syphilis 450
    Liver Disorders 451
Oxidative Functions of the Phosphatides 452
  The Oxidation of Phosphatides 452
  The Phosphatides as Antioxidants 454

Part VI: The Industrial Aspects of the Phosphatides

XXVI   THE MANUFACTURE OF PHOSPHATIDES 483

Introduction 483
The Isolation of Phosphatides 486
  The Bollman Process 486
  Other Extraction Processes 488
    Isolation of Phosphatides from Oil Residues .. 488
    Isolation of Phosphatides from Soapstock 490
    The Extraction of Phosphatides with Alcohol .. 490
    The Use of Adsorbents for Isolating Phosphatides ... 491
    Miscellaneous Modifications for Precipitating Phosphatides ... 492
    The Role of the Phosphatides During Oil Refining ... 492
    Phosphatides from Miscellaneous Sources 493

CONTENTS

CHAPTER   PAGE

The Refining of Phosphatides   494
  Improvement of Odor and Taste   494
  Improvement of Color   495
  Replacement of the Oil   496
The Modification of Commercial Phosphatides   497
  The Admixture of Phosphatides with Organic Carriers   497
   Mixtures with Sugars and Related Substances   497
   Mixtures with Lactates   498
   Mixtures with Miscellaneous Materials   498
  The Admixture of Phosphatides with Salts, Acids and Bases   499
   Mixtures with Salts   499
   Mixtures with Acids   500
   Mixtures with Bases   500
  Fluidization of Phosphatides   501
  Chemical Modifications of Phosphatides   501
   Sulfonation   501
   Halogenation   502
   Hydrogenation   502
   Hydration   502
   Metallic Complexes   503
   Miscellaneous   503

XXVII THE INDUSTRIAL USES OF PHOSPHATIDES   504

Introduction   504
Food Uses   504
  Chocolate   504
  Margarine   505
  Shortening   507
  Antioxidants   507
  Bakery Goods   510
  Macaroni and Noodles   511
  Candy   512
  Ice Cream   512
  Miscellaneous Food Uses   512
Non-food Uses   514
  Petroleum Derivatives   514
  Textiles   515
  Leather   516
  Protective Coatings   517
  Rubber and Resins   518
  Soaps   519
  Pharmaceutical and Proprietary Articles   520
  Miscellaneous Non-food Uses   521

AUTHOR INDEX   535

SUBJECT INDEX   547

PART I

THE CHEMISTRY OF THE PHOSPHATIDES

CHAPTER I

NOMENCLATURE AND CLASSIFICATION OF LIPIDES

INTRODUCTION

From a chemical point of view the lipides are more difficult to identify and classify than the proteins and the carbohydrates, with which they combine to form still more complex constituents of plant and animal tissue. On the one hand, proteins are composed of amino acids bonded by a specific type of chemical linkage; whatever else may be present, each structural unit must have an amino and a carboxyl group in order that the composite may meet the definition of a protein. With carbohydrates, on the other hand, chemical definition is somewhat more difficult; but the monose, characterized by a hydroxyl group and an actual or potential carbonyl group, is generally considered to be the basic structural entity. However, lipides, with their multiplicity of functional groups, cannot be so neatly classified, for they contain no specific chemical grouping or linkage which is consistently present and which per se places a compound in this important category. Thus, lipides, like amino acids, may contain amino and carboxyl groups; and, like carbohydrates, they may contain hydroxyl groups, although none of these is characteristic. Nor is any one element characteristic of the lipides, since they may contain nitrogen, phosphorus and sulfur in addition to the more usual carbon, hydrogen and oxygen. Thus, the classification of lipides is complicated by lack of specificity and by the presence of more elements and more reactive groups than are found in proteins and carbohydrates.

Since a purely chemical characterization of the lipides is not possible, Bloor (1925) chose to identify them, quite logically, not only on a chemical basis but also on the bases of solubility and biological relationships. Thus lipides have the following characteristics. (1) They are naturally occurring materials which are insoluble in water and soluble in the so-called "fat solvents" such as ether, chloroform and benzene. The solubilities, nevertheless, are by no means absolute, since lecithin disperses in water and sphingomyelin is insoluble in the most characteristic solvent for lipides, ether. In general, however, the lipides differ markedly from the proteins and carbohydrates, the simpler members of which are either soluble or dispersible in water. (2) The lipides

3

are either actual or potential esters of fatty acids. (3) They ordinarily must be utilized by living organisms. This establishes a metabolic relationship of the lipides to the fatty acids in addition to the chemical relationship defined in (2).

GENERIC AND SPECIES NAMES

The foregoing discussion has used the term "lipide" (derived from the Greek *lipos*, fat) as the generic name of the substances whose characteristics include those listed in the preceding paragraphs. This is in accord with the recommendation of the International Congress for Pure and Applied Chemistry. Although the final "e" is often omitted in modern usage, this is not in agreement with the practice of *Chemical Abstracts* or with the recommendation of the Nomenclature, Spelling and Pronunciation Committee of the American Chemical Society (Crane, 1934). The final "e" also enters into the pronunciation which corresponds to "lī'pīd" *. The "-id", ending no doubt reflects the German influence, since in that language an "e" would indicate the plural number. Although Germanisms were once common in American chemical literature, it is likely that they will disappear, now that American standards have become as well defined as they are.

Various other generic terms have been proposed, but they are in the main unsuitable. The word "fat" which was used by Leathes (1913) is obviously inadequate since modern usage applies it to the triglycerides. "Lipoid", which is, of course, a variation of "lipide", has also been used as a generic term. Rewald (1928) has strongly urged its use as a generic term for everything except sterols, which he considered a separate class. Smedley-MacLean (1932) has consistently used "lipoid" to designate the "ether-soluble constituents of tissue". The word, however, has also been used to designate the neutral fats, and its continued usage serves only to create confusion.

"Lipin" was used as a generic term by Thannhauser and Schmidt (1943), since in a review entitled "Chemistry of the Lipins" they discussed fatty acids as well as phosphatides. Leathes (1913, p. 3), however, added a final "e" to the term and used "lipine" to denote indefinite materials supposedly containing nitrogen but not phosphorus. To MacLean and MacLean (1927, p. 3), "lipin" denoted a group containing the two subdivisions, phosphatides and cerebrosides. Thus this word, like "lipoid", is a source of confusion.

* The Nomenclature Committee actually gave preference to the pronunciation "lī'pīd", listing "lī'pīd" as an alternative. Present-day usage, however, seems to favor the short sound for the first "i" as does the fifth edition of Webster's Collegiate Dictionary.

"Phosphatide" will be used in this monograph as the specific term which designates phosphorus-containing lipides. The word was first used in this sense by Thudichum (1901, p. 102). The term "phospholipide" has also come into common usage and is equally satisfactory. "Phosphatide" is given preference here merely because it corresponds to the usage of *Chemical Abstracts*. Leathes (1913, p. 3) suggested the term "phospholipine" for lipides containing phosphorus and nitrogen and MacLean and MacLean (1927) omitted the final "e" to correspond to "lecithin" and "cephalin". Both these variations, however, have gradually fallen into disuse.

The spelling of "cephalin" with a "k" instead of a "c" and its corresponding pronunciation with a hard sound is a Germanism occasionally seen in American chemical literature. The "c" of cephalin should, of course, be accorded a soft sound. The term "cephalin" was used for many years to denote the glycerophosphatide whose basic constituent is β-aminoethyl alcohol. More recently it has been shown (Folch and Schneider, 1941) that serine may be the base as well as aminoethyl alcohol. Still other phosphatides (Folch and Woolley, 1942) which contain inositol have been found in what has previously been considered cephalin. Accordingly, the term "cephalin" in modern usage must denote a mixture of compounds rather than a distinct entity. For the pure compounds it seems wise to accept the suggestion of Folch (1942a) in which the aminoethyl alcohol and serine-containing compounds are termed, respectively, "phosphatidylaminoethyl alcohol" and "phosphatidylserine". Although Folch (1942a) actually suggested the term "phosphatidyl ethanolamine", "aminoethyl alcohol" is used here since it conforms to more consistent organic chemical nomenclature. The other specific terms of lipide nomenclature are noncontroversial and are indicated in the classification which follows.

CLASSIFICATION OF THE LIPIDES

Just as lipide nomenclature has not been standardized by any official society, so has the classification of lipides been neglected in recent years. Classifications were indeed adopted by the ninth conference of the International Union of Pure and Applied Chemistry in London in 1928 and by the National Committee of Great Britain which met in the same year. The first group proposed two divisions, the first to include lipide-like substances containing only carbon, hydrogen and oxygen and the second to include materials with elements other than the above three. Cerebrosides were excluded from the realm of lipides.

The National Committee of Great Britain chose not to classify fatty acids, sterols and higher alcohols as lipides. The remaining compounds were categorized in distinct groups as (1) the glycerides and the esters of higher fatty acids and alcohols and (2) the group of phosphatides and cerebrosides. Neither of these proposals enjoyed wide recognition; and the classification of lipides thus becomes a somewhat arbitrary matter. Bloor (1925, 1943 pp. 1–2) has proposed a classification for lipides which has been widely used in America (e.g., Bull, 1937, p. 2). This classification is both logical and flexible and can be applied to the problems of lipide chemistry. Bloor chose to classify phosphatides as lipides containing both phosphoric acid and a nitrogenous compound. The phosphatidic acids which do not have a nitrogenous constituent were accorded a separate classification. It seems more convenient to classify the phosphatides merely on the basis of the phosphoric acid entity, thus making phosphatidates a subclassification under phosphatides. Indeed, this is in accord with the original wishes of Thudichum (1901, p. 102), who did not make the presence of nitrogen a prerequisite. It is also in harmony with the proposal of Channon and Chibnall (1927), who first isolated the phosphatidates. Likewise, Anderson (1927) classified as phosphatides the compounds which he isolated from the tubercle bacilli, although they contained no nitrogen. With this modification, then, Bloor's classification of lipides as it appears below will be used in this monograph.

LIPIDES

Simple Lipides: Esters of fatty acids with various alcohols.

Fats and Oils (Glycerides): Esters of fatty acids with glycerol.

Waxes: Solid esters of fatty acids with alcohols other than glycerol.

Compound Lipides: Esters of fatty acids with alcohols which contain still an additional group.

Phosphatides: Lipides containing the phosphoric acid residue.

Glycolipides: Compounds, such as the cerebrosides, in which fatty acids, a carbohydrate and a nitrogen compound are combined.

Sulfolipides: Lipides containing the sulfuric acid residue.

Aminolipides and other insufficiently characterized compounds.

Derived Lipides: Compounds derived from the preceding groups which may have the general properties of lipides, although it is not prerequisite that they should have all of these properties.

Fatty Acids

Alcohols: Mostly high molecular weight solids such as the sterols. Glycerol must also be included.

Hydrocarbons: Compounds such as squalene which accumulate in the liver of some animals.

Bases: The nitrogenous constituents of the phosphatides: choline, aminoethyl alcohol, sphingosine, serine.

This Monograph, as its title has already announced, will concern itself with only one facet of this field—the phosphatides. The classification of the phosphatides is somewhat less complex since there are so few compounds which merit admission into this group.

The classifications of the earlier workers are listed by MacLean and MacLean (1927, pp. 7–11). The classical subdivisions are based on the ratio of nitrogen to phosphorus in the molecule, the monoaminophosphatides being those in which $N:P = 1:1$ and the diaminophosphatides those in which $N:P = 2:1$. This is an expedient which developed because early workers did not have at their disposal techniques other than nitrogen and phosphorus analyses for the identification of phosphatides. Modern techniques have caused this method of classification to lose much of its value. Actually, of the specific compounds listed by the earlier workers, well over fifty per cent have been shown by modern research to be impure lecithin, sphingomyelin or the cephalins, or mixtures thereof.

As mentioned above, modern research has shown also that what was classically considered cephalin may be, depending on its source, a mixture of phosphatidylaminoethyl alcohol, phosphatidylserine and the inositol-containing phosphatides. The latter are a group of poorly defined compounds present in both plant and animal sources which contain inositol in place of, or in addition to, glycerol.

It therefore follows that three distinct polyhydric alcohols provide the basic constituents for the various phosphatides. The first of these is glycerol, and the phosphatides containing it may well be termed "glycerophosphatides". Included herein, in addition to lecithin, phosphatidylaminoethyl alcohol and phosphatidylserine, are the acetal phosphatides (see p. 51), the lysophosphatides (see p. 99), the phosphatidic acids (see p. 48) and the phosphatides of the tubercle bacillus (see p. 202). The second polyhydric alcohol is the aminodihydroxy compound, sphingosine, which is the basis not only for the phosphatide, sphingomyelin, but also for the glycolipides. All these compounds based on sphingosine, accordingly, have been termed "sphingolipides" by Carter and co-workers (1947). The third polyhydric alcohol is the above-mentioned inositol, which forms the basis of phosphatides whose structures present a fertile field for chemical investigation.

Compounds have been reported which contain both inositol and glycerol. They provide no problem of classification, however, since their physical characteristics logically place them in the inositol-containing group.

The phosphatide classification proposed here, accordingly, is based on the presence of these three polyfunctional alcohols. It is thus believed to be sufficiently flexible to include the results of future research.

Glycerophosphatides: Phosphorus-containing lipides in which glycerol is the only alcohol present.

    Lecithin

    Cephalins

        Phosphatidylaminoethyl alcohol

        Phosphatidylserine

    Acetal phosphatides

    Lysophosphatides

        Lysolecithin

        Lysophosphatidylaminoethyl alcohol

    Phosphatidic acids

    Phosphatides of the tubercle bacillus

Sphingosine-Containing Phosphatides: Phosphorus-containing lipides in which sphingosine is present.

    Sphingomyelin

Inositol-Containing Phosphatides: Phosphorus-containing lipides in which inositol is present. Other polyhydric alcohols such as glycerol may also be involved, but the presence of inositol is sufficient to place the compounds in this group.

    Phosphatides containing inositol in chemical linkage (structures are yet to be proved).

CHAPTER II
THE STRUCTURE OF LECITHIN

HISTORICAL

That phosphorus is normally a constituent of the brain was probably first discovered by J. T. Hensing in 1719 (quoted by Thudichum, 1901, p. 1), who described his discoveries in a thesis presented to the University of Giessen. An indication of the existence of complex fatty compounds is found in the work of Fourcroy (1793), but to Vauquelin (1812), who worked with brain, is generally attributed the first isolation of phosphorus-containing fatty materials. Other investigators (e.g., Couerbe, 1834; Frémy, 1841; and Frémy and Valencienne, 1857) found similar materials—undoubtedly impure mixtures of phosphatides and other lipides—in various animal sources, and in a remarkably short time the structure of lecithin was deduced from fragmentary data on impure substances. That the occurrence of phosphatides was not limited to animal tissue was shown by Töpler (1861), who found phosphorus-containing fats in plant seeds. Although many years passed before plant and animal phosphatides were proved to be identical, it soon became a tacit and correct assumption that phosphatides are present in all living tissue.

To be sure, there were a few diehards such as Barbieri (1917) who vociferously proclaimed the absence of lecithin in five thousand eggs which he analyzed. The contribution of this school is of historical interest only, the phosphatides having maintained their position as important, although intricate and elusive, constituents of living tissue.

STRUCTURE PROOF

Gobley (1846, 1847) isolated a phosphatide from egg yolk to which he later (1850) gave the name "lecithin" from the Greek *lekithos,* egg yolk. He observed that phosphoric anhydride remained after ashing; and he succeeded in isolating for the first time from a natural source glycerophosphoric acid which was, of course, present in the hydrolysis products. The hydrolysis mixture also provided both a saturated (margaric *) and an unsaturated (oleic) acid, but the means were not at hand which would make possible the isolation and identification of the nitrogenous com-

* This was undoubtedly a mixture of palmitic and stearic acids.

9

ponent. It was not long, however, before both Diakanow (1867, 1868, 1868a) and Strecker (1868) showed that the nitrogen compound was a base which, with chloroplatinic acid, yielded an oxygen-containing compound of the formula $C_5H_{14}NO \cdot Cl \cdot PtCl_2$. The identification of this base was simplified by recognition of the fact that it was the same material which Strecker (1862) had previously isolated from bile and to which he had given the name choline (Greek *cholē*, bile). These workers also showed that at least two molecules of fatty acids were present for every molecule of glycerophosphoric acid and of base in the hydrolysis products.

These observations were made on impure material, and there was no assurance that all the hydrolysis products had been isolated. They were nevertheless sufficient to allow both Diakanow (1868, 1868a) and Strecker (1868) to postulate a formula for lecithin based on the assumption that the fatty acids served to esterify the glycerol portion of the molecule. Thus, lecithin was believed to be a diglyceride, linked through its free hydroxyl group to choline by a phosphoric acid radical. Furthermore, there was recognized at this early date the possibility of the existence of several lecithins which differed only in their fatty acid components. Thus it is seen that a provisional structure of lecithin which served as a point of departure for further work was postulated entirely from the identification of the hydrolysis products.

If phosphoric acid served to link the diglyceride portion of lecithin to choline, it necessarily formed an ester with the glycerol portion of the molecule. This, of course, was confirmed by the isolation of glycerophosphoric acid from the hydrolysis products. The choline, on the other hand, was an alcohol as well as a base and thus could form either an ester or a salt with the phosphoric acid. Strecker (1868), unlike Diakanow (1868, 1868a), held that the choline was attached as an ester, a belief which was later confirmed by Hundeshagen (1883) and Gilson (1888).

Isomers are possible, since the glycerophosphoric acid may exist either in the α- or β-form (see p. 16). A further possible complication arises from the presence of both an acidic group (from the phosphoric acid) and a basic group (from the choline) in the same molecule (see p. 12). Both of these points are discussed in detail later. On the basis of the evidence presented above, however, the α-form of lecithin, the only one which has been shown conclusively to exist (Baer and Kates, 1948a), may be represented by (I) where R and R' are the same or different fatty acid residues. Natural optically active α-lecithins have been shown by Baer and Kates (1950) to possess the L-configuration.

Hence the early workers were able to provide a provisional structure for lecithin which, with minor modifications, is now known to be quite

$$CH_2O—C—R$$
$$\underset{O}{\overset{\parallel}{|}}$$
$$CH—O—C—R'$$
$$\underset{O}{\overset{\parallel}{|}}$$

$$\underset{O}{\overset{\parallel}{|}}$$
$$CH_2—O—P—OC_2H_4—N(CH_3)_3$$
$$\underset{OH}{|}\qquad\underset{OH}{|}$$

(I)

accurate. Of great importance in this early period is the work of Thudichum, who carried on extensive researches on brain chemistry from 1865 to 1882. His contributions are detailed in both an English (1884) and a German (1901) edition of the classic work "Chemical Constitution of the Brain". Thudichum's interesting biography is well presented by Page (1937, chap. 1). This prolific worker (Thudichum, 1901, p. 102 ff.) isolated lecithin from brain and confirmed its structure. In addition, he isolated from brain many other related substances containing varying proportions of nitrogen and phosphorus, and others containing only one of these two elements. In order to categorize this vast array of compounds, he introduced a classification by nitrogen-phosphorus ratio. Thus he described not only mono- and diaminophosphatides but also diaminodiphosphatides, "non-nitrogenized monophosphatides" and "nitrogenized non-phosphorized" lipides. Although his discoveries included "cephalin" and sphingomyelin, it is obvious now that most of Thudichum's compounds were impure mixtures of partially decomposed phosphatides and cerebrosides. The work that followed by such investigators as MacLean in England and Levene in the United States, coupled with some very modern work, has reduced this complicated array to a few more or less well defined substances. Nevertheless, Thudichum's work cannot be underestimated, not only because of the accurate contributions he made, but, more important, because he pioneered and laid the groundwork in a difficult, complex field.

With the basic structure established, more intricate details may now be discussed, such as the possibility for polymeric structures, the relationship of the acidic and basic functions, and the nature of the hydrolysis products—glycerophosphoric acid, the fatty acids and choline.

Polylecithins

As already indicated, the earlier workers had conceived of the possibility of several lecithins which differed because of their fatty acid components. However, experimental evidence did not eliminate the possibility of polylecithins, since a simple molecule with but two fatty acids had never been isolated. In polylecithin the lecithin units would be linked together in a macromolecule which would contain all the various fatty acids. Molecular weight determinations in polar solvents such as alcohol which tend to prevent association (Levene and Simms, 1921; Price and Lewis, 1929) favored the monomer structure; and actual chemical evidence was provided by Levene and Rolf (1925), who found that although lecithin itself could not be separated into simple compounds, the bromo derivatives were amenable to fractionation and subsequent hydrolysis to yield not more than two fatty acids. From soybean lecithin they were able to obtain a hexabromo and a tetrabromolecithin, thus providing important evidence that lecithin exists as a simple molecule with two fatty acids.

Acid-Base Relationships

In lecithin there is present a strongly acidic and a strongly basic group. Thus, some sort of internal neutralization must necessarily be expected. This is demonstrated by the fact that lecithin in solution is substantially neutral and that it has practically no buffering power in the physiological range (Grün and Limpächer, 1927; Rudy and Page, 1930; Fabisch, 1931).

The earliest theory, advanced by Grün and Limpächer (1923, 1926), held that lecithin existed as an inner anhydride or "endo" salt (II), where actual neutralization with the attendant loss of water had taken

$$
\begin{array}{l}
CH_2\!-\!O\!-\!C\!-\!R \\
\qquad\quad \underset{O}{\|} \\[4pt]
CH\!-\!O\!-\!C\!-\!R \\
\qquad\quad \underset{O}{\|} \qquad\qquad (II) \\[6pt]
\qquad\qquad\; O \;\; O\!-\!C_2H_4 \\
\qquad\qquad\;\; \diagdown\!\diagup \qquad | \\
CH_2\!-\!O\!-\!P \\
\qquad\qquad\;\; \diagdown \\
\qquad\qquad\qquad O\!-\!N(CH_3)_3
\end{array}
$$

place between the acidic and basic functions. The synthetic material prepared by these workers (see p. 121) was also believed to have an anhydro structure. This structure is now untenable, since it has been established that nitrogen cannot expand its valence shell to ten. A more logical formula involving a zwitterion or open-dipole structure (III), has been proposed by Jukes (1934).

Jukes (1934) titrated mixtures of lecithin and cephalins electrometrically in 98 per cent ethanol. Since his "cephalin" was obtained from egg yolk, it was probably substantially phosphatidylaminoethyl alcohol. As

$$CH_2-O-C-R$$
$$\quad\quad\quad\;\; \overset{\parallel}{O}$$
$$CH-O-C-R$$
$$\quad\quad\;\; \overset{\parallel}{O}$$
$$\quad\quad\quad\quad\quad\quad\quad\quad (III)$$
$$\quad\quad\;\; \overset{O^-}{}$$
$$CH_2-O-\overset{+}{P^+}-O-C_2H_4-\overset{+}{N}(CH_3)_3$$
$$\quad\quad\quad\;\; \overset{}{O^-}$$

would be expected from their structures, phosphatidylaminoethyl alcohol bound alkali, whereas lecithin did not. Both molecules, however, bound acid at low pH and had pK′ values of 1.1. These observations indicate that lecithin and phosphatidylaminoethyl alcohol exist in zwitterionic forms, although the latter compound, because of the relatively weak amino group, exhibits buffering at a pH close to 9 and can also exist as a neutral molecule, an anion or a cation (cf. Fischgold and Chain, 1935). Further evidence on this score was provided by dielectric constant data. Fürth (1923) measured the dielectric constant of lecithin in water and determined it as 13. Kuhn, Hausser and Bryndówna (1935) measured the dielectric constant of pure lecithin in alcohol and in benzene at 20 to 45°C. and found the material to be dielectrically active in alcohol but not in benzene. The dielectric constant of an alcohol solution was found to be greater than that of the pure solvent, which is further evidence for a zwitterion structure. The situation with benzene is of interest. Here the nonpolar character of the solvent might allow the oppositely charged ends of the lecithin molecule to come together to form a heteropolar ring, as Grün contends. That this is probably not so was shown by molecular weight measurements. As indicated previously, lecithin is monomolecular in polar solvents. In benzene, however, it was found to be highly associated, demonstrating molecular weights of 3000 or even higher (Faure and Legault-Demare, 1950). This had also been observed by Price and Lewis (1929). The high molecular weight may have been derived from association of the fatty acid chains, although it is more likely that it arose from the interaction of the cholinephosphoric acid portions of the molecules with mutual compensation of the dipole moments. This, of course, dispels Grün's arguments which defend the "endo" salt structure on the basis of the monomeric structure of lecithin.

Fischgold and Chain (1935) also concluded that lecithin possessed a zwitterion structure on the basis of their titration experiments. They used a solvent consisting of nineteen volumes of benzene and one of ethanol and titrated a mixture of phosphatides. Like Jukes (1934), they found that lecithin could not bind base but that it could react with one equivalent of hydrogen ion at a low pH.

Isoelectric Point. At the isoelectric point the dissociation of an amphoteric compound, such as lecithin, as an acid and as a base is equal. It is thus the pH at which the net charge is zero. Numerous determinations of the isoelectric point of lecithin have been made, but many of these, unfortunately, must be discounted since they were made on impure or partially decomposed samples.

Fischgold and Chain (1934) calculated that the theoretical isoelectric point of lecithin should be 7.5. The calculations were based on the dissociation constants of the phosphoric acid group, the first having been estimated as 1 and the second as 13.9. Reasonable agreement with this value was obtained experimentally by Chain and Kemp (1934), who measured the change in electrophoretic mobility with pH. Their value proved to be 6.7. They attributed this deviation from the calculated value of 7.5 to decomposition and the presence of acidic impurities even when elaborate precautions were taken. In later work, Fischgold and Chain (1935) noted that electrophoretic mobility increased with a corresponding decrease in isoelectric point with the age of the lecithin suspensions, again due probably to decomposition. Such changes were also noted by Price (1935), who advanced the rather unacceptable idea that aged lecithin is more nearly like the material as it occurs *in situ*.

Still another determination of the isoelectric point of lecithin was made by Bull and Frampton (1936). These workers, realizing the difficulties involved in obtaining chemically pure lecithin, determined the isoelectric points of mixtures of lecithin and cephalin fractions from egg yolk. The concentration of the latter material was determined by analysis of the amino nitrogen, and extrapolation of the experimentally determined values indicated an isoelectric point for pure lecithin of 6.4. This is in fair agreement with the value determined experimentally by Chain and Kemp (1934).

Numerous earlier determinations of the isoelectric point (Feinschmidt, 1912; Fujii, 1924; Remezov, 1930; Sueyoshi and Kawai, 1932; Price and Lewis, 1929, 1933) must be discounted since they were carried out on impure or partially decomposed substances, which caused the values to be low. These low values were explained by Fischgold and Chain (1934), who showed by titration experiments that lecithin decomposed spontaneously, liberating fatty acids but not choline. When a fresh sample was titrated a curve was obtained very similar to the curve for the solvent which in this case was 90 per cent ethanol. In other words, there were no fatty acids to be titrated. Immediate back-titration, however, produced a curve which indicated a buffering effect at pH 7.5, whereas back-titration after 66 hours indicated a very marked buffering action at this pH. Older preparations of lecithin all demonstrated this same phenomenon.

THE HYDROLYSIS PRODUCTS OF LECITHIN

General

Since the elucidation of the structure of lecithin depended on the isolation and identification of the hydrolysis products, it is of interest to describe in some detail the nature of these substances which in chemical union comprise lecithin. Lecithin is hydrolyzed quite readily either by acid or alkali, unlike sphingomyelin which requires more drastic conditions. This difference, as a matter of fact, is sufficient to provide a means for the analytical determination of these compounds (see p. 167). The hydrolysis of lecithin to glycerophosphoric acid, choline and fatty acids proceeds under such mild conditions as the use of normal potassium hydroxide at 37°C. for 16 hours (Hack, 1947). According to Baer and Kates (1950a) the alkaline hydrolysis proceeds mainly by way of glycerylphosphorylcholine and to a lesser extent by way of the phosphatidic acid.

Any of the common basic or acidic reagents are adequate. Thus Moruzzi (1908) hydrolyzed lecithin with 10 per cent sulfuric acid for 4 hours at 100°C. MacLean (1909a) hydrolyzed egg lecithin with aqueous barium hydroxide or with hydrochloric acid. Trier (1913) used dilute sulfuric acid or aqueous barium hydroxide on plant phosphatides. Darrah and MacArthur (1916) used 3 per cent hydrochloric acid or 1.6 to 5 per cent aqueous potassium hydroxide for 15 to 20 hours for phosphatides from brain. Alcoholic reagents are of value because they effect homogeneity and allow the reaction to proceed more rapidly. The use of an atmosphere of inert gas during the hydrolysis is generally considered advantageous, especially when highly unsaturated, unstable fatty acids are present.

The techniques used for isolating and estimating the hydrolysis products are described in Part II. Mention should be made of the fact that in phosphatides from plants and lower organisms, carbohydrates are invariably present, and these are always found in the aqueous portion of the hydrolysate. Except for the inositol-containing phosphatides (see p. 35) there is no evidence that these sugars are chemically part of the phosphatide molecule. As an example of the hydrolysis of phosphatides closely associated with carbohydrates, reference may be made to the work of Pangborn and Anderson (1931) on the phosphatides of the timothy bacillus. These contain no nitrogenous component (see p. 199), for which reason no attempt was made to isolate a base. In this case the hydrolysis was carried out by refluxing about 5 grams of the phosphatide with 120 ml. of 5 per cent sulfuric acid for 8 hours in an atmosphere of carbon dioxide.

Since sugars ordinarily are not chemically a part of lecithin, they will not be considered further here. Techniques for their isolation, however, are of great importance to investigators of plant phosphatides. The three primary hydrolysis products of lecithin will be considered in some detail.

Glycerophosphoric Acid

Isolation. The isolation procedure for glycerophosphoric acid from phosphatides ordinarily involves precipitation as a salt. Since the material is present in the water-soluble portion of the hydrolysis mixture it is isolated in the same way, regardless of whether the hydrolysis is accomplished in acid or basic medium. Folch (1942a) is one of several workers who has described a detailed procedure for the isolation of glycerophosphoric acid from phosphatides.

Configuration. Glycerophosphoric acid possesses two isomeric structures, designated α and β, and indicated by the following formulas. The unsymmetrical or α-form possesses an asymmetric carbon atom which

$$
\begin{array}{cc}
\text{CH}_2\text{OH} & \\
| & \\
\text{CHOH} \quad\quad \text{OH} & \\
| \quad\quad\quad / & \\
\text{CH}_2\text{—O—P}{=}\text{O} & \\
\quad\quad\quad \backslash & \\
\quad\quad\quad \text{OH} &
\end{array}
\qquad
\begin{array}{cc}
\text{CH}_2\text{OH} \quad\quad \text{OH} \\
| \quad\quad\quad\quad / \\
\text{CH—O—P}{=}\text{O} \\
| \quad\quad\quad\quad \backslash \\
\text{CH}_2\text{OH} \quad\quad \text{OH}
\end{array}
$$

α-*Glycerophosphoric acid*   β-*Glycerophosphoric acid*

allows it to exist as optically active stereoisomers. This optical activity is reflected in naturally occurring phosphatides (Ulpiani, 1901; Karrer and Salomon, 1926; Schmidt, Hershman and Thannhauser, 1945; Lesuk and Anderson, 1941; Thannhauser, Benotti and Boncoddo, 1946; Thannhauser and Boncoddo, 1948). Baer and Kates (1950) have recently shown by comparison of physical properties and x-ray diffraction techniques that the synthetic lecithin which they prepared of L-configuration is identical with dextrorotatory dipalmityllecithin isolated from *Cysticercus fasciolaris* by Lesuk and Anderson (1941). Thus it appears that the L-configuration must be assigned to the natural α-lecithins.

Many early investigators (Willstätter and Lüdecke, 1904; Levene and Rolf, 1919; Fourneau and Piettre, 1912; Bailly, 1915, 1916, 1921; Grimbert and Bailly, 1915; Fränkel and Dimitz, 1909; Chibnall and Channon, 1927; Power and Tutin, 1905) attempted to isolate glycerophosphoric acid from the glycerophosphatides and determine its configuration. Actually this work is of little significance, for it has been shown that (1) racemization of α-glycerophosphate occurs under conditions often used for hydrolysis of phosphatides, (2) the racemic forms of barium glycerophosphate do not exhibit optical activity (Baer and Fischer, 1939, 1940, see p. 19 and (3) the hydrolysis of choline from α-glyceryl-phosphorylcholine either with acid or base leads to a migration of the phosphoric acid residue and the formation of an equilibrium mixture of α- and β-compounds (Baer and Kates, 1948a). Subsequently (Baer and Kates, 1950a), this observation was shown to apply to the hydrolysis of synthetic L-α-lecithin. Obviously, then, the configuration of the glycerophosphoric acids in the hydrolysate bears no relation to their configuration in the natural product. α-Phosphatidic acids and α-glycero-phosphoric acid, unlike lecithin, exhibit migratory changes only during acidic hydrolysis and not during basic hydrolysis. Folch (1942) also has provided evidence that the phosphoric acid residue of glycerophosphoric acid migrates reversibly under the influence of acidic and basic reagents, and Bailly and Gaumé (1935) have shown that alkali effects a migration of the phosphoryl group in methyl α- or β-glycerophosphate.

It may be concluded then, as pointed out by Baer and Kates (1948a), that the configuration of the glycerophosphatides cannot be judged from the configurations of the isolated glycerophosphoric acids. Evidence for the occurrence of α-glycerophosphatides has been accumulated by workers (see above) who have isolated optically active phosphatides or phospha-tide derivatives. There is, however, no good evidence for the occurrence of β-isomers.

A group of Japanese workers (Suzuki and Yokoyama, 1930; Nishimoto and Suzuki, 1932; Yokoyama and Suzuki, 1931, 1931a, 1932, 1932a, 1932b; Yokoyama, 1934; Yoshinaga, 1938) contended that α- and β-phosphatides in the form of complexes with metallic salts could be separated by solubility procedures. Burmaster (1946a) reinvestigated these methods and concluded correctly that they do not achieve the isolation of α- and β-phosphatides.

The analysis of mixtures of α- and β-glycerophosphates may be ac-complished by use either of enzymes (Rae, Kay and King, 1934) or of periodic acid (Fleury and Paris, 1933). The first method depends on the observation that the two compounds are attacked by enzymes at dif-ferent rates. In this way it was shown (Rae, 1934) that the brain phos-phatides are predominantly α, whereas egg lecithin is predominantly β, and liver lecithin contains equal amounts of the α- and β-forms.

The use of periodic acid depends on the observation that this reagent cleaves 1,2 glycols quantitatively, but does not react with 1,3 glycols. This method has been refined considerably by Burmaster (1946).

Properties. Free glycerophosphoric acid, regardless of its configuration, is a syrupy liquid which is soluble in alcohol and water and which decomposes on distillation. It may be isolated by the action of hydrogen sulfide on the lead salt. The hydrolysis of glycerophosphoric acid is accomplished by chemical means only with difficulty, despite the fact that glycerol was found very early (Gobley, 1850) in phosphatides from fish eggs and was shown to exist in lecithin in theoretical quantity by Foster (1915). The acid is entirely resistant to the action of concentrated base, whereas it is hydrolyzed very slowly by dilute acid (Plimmer, 1913). Enzymatic hydrolysis has been studied in detail and will be discussed later. Naturally occurring glycerophosphoric acid is usually a mixture of the α- and β-isomers, and this is often the case in the synthetic material due to the facility with which the phosphoric acid radical migrates.

Glycerophosphoric acid is a relatively strong dibasic acid and may be titrated as such. Kiessling (1934) determined the following pK_a values.

	pK_{a1}	pK_{a2}
α-Glycerophosphoric acid	1.40	6.44
β-Glycerophosphoric acid	1.37	6.34

The effect of hydrogen bonding on the strength of these acids is discussed by Kumler and Eiler (1943).

β-Glycerophosphoric acid is, of course, optically inactive. Its barium and calcium salts exist in both amorphous and crystalline forms. The barium salt is quite soluble in both hot and cold water and crystallizes on slow evaporation of the water. It may be precipitated from aqueous solution by alcohol. It forms, in contrast to the α-form, a double salt with barium nitrate which is sparingly soluble in water. This characteristic provides a means for separating the α- and β-acids.

α-Glycerophosphoric acid is optically active. Its barium and calcium salts also exist in amorphous and crystalline forms and possess the unique property of being more soluble in cold than in hot water. Thus a crystalline modification of the barium salt results when an aqueous solution is heated.

Synthesis. Several methods of synthesis for α-glycerophosphoric acid have been published. Most of these are of academic interest only (Bailly, 1916; Tutin and Hann, 1906; Carré, 1909; Zietzsche and Nachmann, 1926). The synthesis of Fischer and Pfähler (1920), which involves the interaction of isopropylideneglycerol and phosphorus oxychloride, has been widely used. Hydrolysis of the isopropylidene residue as well as the chlorine atoms in the initial condensation product provides α-glycerophosphoric acid which may be isolated as the barium salt. A more recent synthesis (Gulland and Hobday, 1940) employs phenylphosphoryl dichloride, $C_6H_5OPOCl_2$, as a phosphorylating agent. The direct inter-action of this compound with glycerol in the presence of pyridine yields phenyl α-glycerophosphate. Thereafter, the phenyl group may be removed by the action of dilute base.

There are fewer methods available for the synthesis of β-glycero-phosphoric acid (Tutin and Hann, 1906; King and Pyman, 1914). Pure barium β-glycerophosphoric acid has been prepared by Obata (1940) by the interaction of 1,3-benzylideneglycerol with phosphorus oxychloride followed by hydrolysis of the chlorine atoms and precipitation as the barium salt.

Optically Active α-Glycerophosphoric Acids. The optically active forms of α-glycerophosphoric acid or its derivatives have been prepared both by resolution and by direct synthesis. The resolution of barium α-glycerophosphate was accomplished by Karrer and Benz (1926) through the quinine salt which, on crystallization from hot water, yielded a levorotatory ($[α]_D = -144.7°$) material. The barium α-glycerophos-phate obtained from this quinine salt, however, did not display optical activity until it was converted to the dimethyl ether, dimethyl ester. This fully methylated derivative showed a specific rotation of $-1.76°$. The resolution of the dimethyl ether of glycerol α-phosphoric acid was next accomplished by Karrer and Benz (1926a) by crystallization of the strychnine or quinine salts from 90 per cent ethanol. Both isomers were obtained, and on conversion to the dimethyl esters they demon-strated specific rotations, $[α]_D$, of $+2.38°$ and $-1.78°$. The lack of rota-tion of the barium salts was later confirmed by the synthetic work of Baer and Fischer (see below).

Enzymic resolution with takaphosphatase was attempted by Rae, Kay and King (1934), who reported unsuccessful results. Meyerhof and Kiess-ling (1933), however, showed that the enzyme of muscle press juice utilized the L-(-)-α-glycerophosphoric acid, leaving the optical antipode intact.

Baer and Fischer (1939, 1940) not only synthesized the enantiomorphic forms of α-glycerophosphoric acid, but also established their absolute configurations by relating them to compounds of known configuration. The method of synthesis which they employed was essentially the same as the previously mentioned method of Fischer and Pfähler (1920, see p. 18), except that optically active materials were used. They were thus able to relate the levorotatory form of α-glycerophosphoric acid to the so-called D-(-)-glyceraldehyde which Baer and Fischer obtained by oxidizing diisopropylidene-D-mannitol with lead tetraacetate. In agreement with the work of Karrer and Benz (1926), these synthetic barium salts did not demonstrate optical activity until converted to suitable derivatives. Thus the synthetic levorotatory diethyl ether of diethyl-α-glycerophosphate possessed a specific rotation, $[\alpha]_D^{19}$, of $-5.31°$. The corresponding value for the dextrorotatory isomer was $+5.94°$. By comparing the rotation of these derivatives with similar derivatives prepared from naturally occurring glycerophosphoric acids, it was possible to demonstrate that the levorotatory α-glycerophosphoric acid was the biologically active enantiomorph.

Glycerophosphatases. Although glycerophosphoric acid is fairly resistant to chemical hydrolysis, enzymatic hydrolysis through the medium of glycerophosphatases proceeds readily. Such an enzyme was detected in yeast by Neuberg and Karczag (1911), and a detailed description of its isolation and purification is given by Schäffner (1940, p. 1667). Although a detailed discussion is beyond the scope of this book, it may be said that glycerophosphatases occur widely in both plant and animal sources. Kay (1928) showed that a glycerophosphatase occurs in the blood. This is of physiological interest, since Brain, Kay and Marshall (1928) believed glycerophosphoric acid to be a possible progenitor of urinary phosphorus. For physiological studies, glycerophosphatases have been isolated from fresh pig kidney and dog feces (Baer and Fischer, 1940).

α-Glycerophosphoric acid is more difficult to hydrolyze enzymatically than the β-isomer (Kay, 1926), and this has formed the basis for an analytical determination of the two.

The Fatty Acids of Lecithin

General. The fatty acids of lecithin formed the subject of part of Thudichum's (1901) research, and in his work many references may be found to a variety of such substances.

In the reaction of phosphatides with hydrolytic agents, the fatty acids seem to hydrolyze first. In basic medium they form soaps which may be reacted with mineral acids to yield free fatty acids, whereas in acidic hydrolysis the free acids are formed directly. In the alcoholysis of phosphatides, esters are obtained. The fatty acids, being water-insoluble, float on the top of the hydrolysis mixture and may be removed either mechanically or by ether extraction. Fatty acids comprise about 70 per cent of the lecithin molecule, variations in this figure resulting from the chain length of the fatty acids involved. The fatty acid content is usually determined gravimetrically by saponifying the phosphatide with alkali and acidifying the isolated soaps. The fatty acid may then be extracted with ether or petroleum ether and recovered and weighed (see, for example, Hanahan and Chaikoff, 1947).

Part II (p. 178) contains a description of the analytical methods used to characterize the fatty acids of phosphatides. Parts III and IV contain detailed descriptions of the fatty acids found in phosphatides from various plant and animal sources. Accordingly, specific fatty acids need be mentioned only briefly here. The role of phosphatide fatty acids in metabolic processes is discussed elsewhere (see p. 345 ff.). Here the fatty acids will be discussed in relation to the structure of lecithin.

Early investigators (Diakanow, 1868a; Strecker, 1868) soon discovered that they could find in the hydrolysis products of a given sample of lecithin more fatty acids than the two required by the accepted lecithin structure. To be sure, their samples were far from pure, but the fact that such a variety of fatty acids was found by various workers made it seem that a given sample of lecithin was not a pure chemical entity, but rather a mixture of lecithins which differed in their fatty acid constituents. It was possible to assume that the fatty acids are distributed more or less in random fashion as they are in the triglycerides. This assumption received further substantiation at the hands of Levene and his collaborators (Levene and Simms, 1921, 1922; Levene and Rolf, 1921, 1921a, 1922, 1922b, 1924, 1925), who were among the first to obtain pure lecithin. Thus, from sources such as brain, liver, egg yolk and soybean they obtained lecithins from which they could isolate palmitic, stearic, oleic, linoleic and arachidonic acids. More recent work has disclosed an even greater variety of fatty acids.

The number of possible lecithins is theoretically limited only by the number of fatty acids available. Actually, in the organism the number of lecithins is limited by the fatty acids ordinarily found in the triglycerides. Although the fatty acids of phosphatides from various sources have been investigated, complete and accurate reports are available only in very few instances, as is indicated in Parts III and IV.

Ratio of Saturated to Unsaturated Acids. The earlier workers put forth the hypothesis that each molecule of lecithin contained one molecule each of saturated and unsaturated acids. Some substantiation for this was derived from the work of Levene and Rolf (1926) on brominated lecithins, but doubt was cast upon it by Contardi and Latzer (1928) who, from their researches on lysolecithin, concluded that both fatty acids of lecithin may be unsaturated. The recent work of Thannhauser, Benotti and Boncoddo (1946) has similarly shown that both fatty acids may be saturated. Sinclair (1935) further showed that the fatty acids from liver phosphatides contained 33 per cent saturated acids, those from muscle 27 per cent and from kidney 26 per cent. Furthermore, by an appropriate diet including a high proportion of unsaturated glycerides, the quantities of unsaturated acids could be increased still further. Snider and Bloor (1933) found 40 per cent of the fatty acids from beef liver phosphatides to be saturated. These are but a few of the data which prove that fatty acid distribution in phosphatides is a random one.

Degree of Unsaturation. In general it may be said that whereas glycerides tend to be stored in as saturated and hence as stable a form as possible, the reverse is true for the phosphatides. Notable examples are available in which highly unsaturated acids are selected from the diet and incorporated into the phosphatide molecule. Of interest in this regard is the work of several investigators (Klenk, 1930, 1931; Klenk and von Schoenbeck, 1931; Brown, 1932; Page and Rudy, 1932) on highly unsaturated, long-chain phosphatide acids. These workers isolated from brain lecithin and cephalin fraction an unsaturated liquid C_{22} acid or mixture of acids which on hydrogenation yielded behenic acid. Such highly unsaturated acids had previously been considered typical only of fish-liver oils. Klenk's work on brain phosphatide showed the presence of a complete series of unsaturated even-numbered fatty acids from C_{16} to C_{24}, with the C_{18} and the C_{24} acids predominating. The saturated acids were represented only by palmitic and stearic acids.

The presence of these highly unsaturated acids was also shown in the liver phosphatides by Klenk and von Schoenbeck (1932) and by Klenk (1935). Here, however, the C_{20} acids were present in larger amount than the C_{22} acids, which is the reverse of the situation obtaining for brain phosphatides. These unsaturated, long-chain acids also occur in the neutral fat, although to a much lesser extent since the glycerides contain a higher percentage of C_{18} unsaturated acids.

In plant as well as animal sources the phosphatides often tend to be more unsaturated than the glycerides, and unsaturated C_{20} and C_{22} acids have been detected in the phosphatides of oil seeds such as cottonseed, peanuts, sunflower seeds and linseeds (Hilditch and Zaky, 1942). Rapeseed phosphatides, according to Hilditch and Pedelty (1937), contain up to 23 per cent of erucic acid (Δ^{12}-docosenic acid). The phosphatides of beef suprarenal glands were found by Ault and Brown (1934) to contain about 22 per cent of arachidonic acid; thus these glands are one of the best natural sources of this unsaturated 20-carbon acid.

Thus, all these observations have led to the conclusion that the fatty acids of phosphatides are generally more unsaturated than those of the corresponding glycerides. More recent data, however, provide certain notable exceptions among which are the fatty acids of the lipides of the corpus luteum, yeast and certain plants.

A discussion of phosphatide fatty acids must necessarily include mention of the saturated liquid acids—tuberculostearic and phthioic acids—which were isolated from the phosphatides of the tubercle bacillus. These are discussed in detail in Part III.

Choline

The basic material found among the water-soluble hydrolysis products of pure lecithin is choline. It comprises about 15 per cent of the lecithin molecule. Its analytical determination has been described in Part II (p. 174) and its biochemistry in Part V (see p. 413). Here the chemistry of this interesting material and its relation to lecithin will be discussed briefly. As will be seen later, it is also an integral part of the sphingomyelin molecule.

Structure and Synthesis. Choline (Greek *cholè*, bile) was first isolated by Strecker (1849) from hog bile, even though it exists there, either free or combined in lecithin, only in very minute quantities. Later (Babo and Hirschbrunn, 1852; Claus and Keesé, 1867) it was isolated from white mustard seed. It was very early shown (Strecker, 1862; Baeyer, 1866, 1867) to be trimethyl-β-hydroxyethylammonium hydroxide, $[HOC_2H_4N^+(CH_3)_3]OH^-$, an alcoholic quaternary ammonium hydroxide to whose plurality of methyl groups great biochemical significance has been attributed (see p. 415).

Early phosphatide literature, particularly the work of Thudichum, is confused by references to "neurine" as the base associated with lecithin. This arises from the work of Liebreich (1865), who isolated by the hydrolysis of brain lecithin a base which he believed to be vinyltrimethylammonium hydroxide, and to which he applied the name "neurine." Actually, as Baeyer (1866) readily suggested, he had obtained choline, and this is the material which some early workers chose to term neurine. Subsequently, vinyltrimethylammonium hydroxide was characterized, and is now known as neurine. It is an extremely poisonous substance which results from choline decomposition. It was first synthesized by Hofmann (1858). Choline and related compounds were later synthesized by Wurtz (1867, 1868), Bode (1892), Krüger and Bergell (1903) and Trier (1912a).

Properties. Choline is extremely hygroscopic, for which reason it is usually obtained as a colorless, viscous liquid. It was obtained in crystalline form by Griess and Harrow (1885) and by Meyer and Hopff (1921). Choline on heating decomposes without melting. It is strongly alkaline (pK = 13.9), liberating ammonia from its salts and precipitating metals as oxides or hydroxides.

Choline reacts with virtually any acidic material to form salts. The reineckate, periodide, phosphotungstate and phosphomolybdate, as well as double salts with gold chloride and mercuric chloride, are water insoluble. Most of the salts, however, such as the chloride, sulfate, nitrate, picrate, borate, carbonate, acetate, oxalate and picrolonate are soluble

in both water and methanol. The chloroplatinate, the acid tartrate and
the monophosphate are soluble in water but not in methanol, whereas
the reverse is true for the double salts with cadmium and zinc chlorides.
The salts of choline are discussed in detail in a monograph by Kahane
and Lévy (1938, p. 15).

CHAPTER III

THE STRUCTURE OF THE CEPHALIN PHOSPHATIDES

HISTORICAL

The cephalin fraction was first isolated from brain tissue and recognized as a distinct entity by Thudichum (1884). Its name is derived from the Greek *kephalē,* meaning head. The material seemed to be insoluble, or at least only slightly soluble, in warm alcohol—a characteristic upon which Thudichum and many subsequent workers depended for its separation from lecithin. As work progressed it became apparent, as pointed out by Koch and Woods (1905), that the cephalin fraction was associated with lecithin in all tissues. Cousin (1906) also found it in brain. Erlandsen (1907) and MacLean (1909) isolated the cephalin fraction from muscle, whereas Stern and Thierfelder (1907) and Mac-Lean (1908) found it in egg yolk. It was found in liver by Baskoff (1908) and in kidney by MacLean (1912).

Thudichum's samples were, of course, quite impure; but nevertheless, as was the case with lecithin, he set about to postulate a structure for "cephalin"—which he believed to be an individual compound—from the hydrolysis products he observed.

Although he isolated the chloroplatinate of what was undoubtedly aminoethyl alcohol, he considered this a decomposition product of choline. Accordingly, he believed that the structure of "cephalin" was identical to that of lecithin, save that one of the acids present was invariably "cephalinic acid"—a 17-carbon acid with 3 oxygen atoms (Thudichum, 1901, p. 150; Falk, 1909; Parnas, 1909). Actually, of course, this material was a mixture of partially oxidized unsaturated acids. Thudichum also advanced an alternate structure in which the fatty acids and glycerol were linked directly to phosphoric acid, whereas the choline was attached to one of the hydroxyl groups of the glycerol.

With these none too well supported assumptions as a point of departure, other workers set about to investigate the structure of cephalin. If lecithin was difficult to isolate in the pure state, "cephalin" was even more so, since nitrogen and phosphorus seemed to have a special affinity for its fatty acids. Elementary analyses were never obtained which checked

25

with any theoretical structure; and in general the problem remained, and in some respects still remains, a challenge. Recent work, however, which will be discussed in detail below, has shown that what pioneer workers believed to be cephalin is actually a mixture of phosphatides and that reasonable structures can be postulated for some of the component compounds.

STRUCTURE PROOF

The first problem associated with the elucidation of the structure of "cephalin" was to determine the structure of the base or bases present. Aminoethyl alcohol, the base of one of the cephalin phosphatides, was difficult to detect in the early work since chloroplatinic acid, which was used as the standard reagent for precipitating nitrogenous bases, yielded a soluble salt of aminoethyl alcohol. That another base was nevertheless present in appreciable quantity was indicated by the early, careful work of MacLean (1908, 1909a), who showed, for example, that only 42 per cent of the nitrogen in heart muscle phosphatides was present as choline when the latter was precipitated as the chloroplatinate. Similar experiments had been conducted by Erlandsen (1907), by Baskoff (1908), and by Parnas (1909), who pointed out quite logically that the base of "cephalin" must be different from that of lecithin.

Trier (1911, 1912, 1913) found aminoethyl alcohol in the phosphatides from the bean, *Phaseolus vulgaris,* and from eggs, and was able to identify the base by the insoluble derivative it forms with gold chloride. He also made the significant observation (Trier, 1913) that when the phosphatides were treated with cadmium chloride in alcohol, one portion formed a relatively insoluble complex, whereas the other portion was soluble. The insoluble material was the cadmium chloride salt of lecithin, and the soluble material was the cephalin fraction complex. This provided an improved procedure for separating the cephalin fraction from the lecithin, and it was by this means that MacLean (1915) isolated a relatively pure sample of lecithin. Although it was not an adequate method for obtaining pure cephalins, it made possible the demonstration (Renall, 1913; Baumann, 1913) that the base in the cephalin fraction was largely aminoethyl alcohol. Eppler (1913), like Trier (1913), found aminoethyl alcohol in egg phosphatides, and MacLean (1915) demonstrated its presence in heart phosphatides.

It was thus established that whatever else might be present, aminoethyl alcohol was definitely a cleavage product of one of the cephalins. On this basis it seemed logical to postulate a structure for "cephalin" analogous to that of lecithin, and thus the α-form may be represented by (IV) where R and R′ are fatty acid residues.

Complete acceptance of this structure was prevented by the fact that elementary analyses were almost invariably lower than the theoretical values. Furthermore, the theoretical percentage of fatty acids was never recovered. It was these discrepancies which led eventually to the discovery of phosphatides other than formula (IV) in the cephalin fraction.

$$
\begin{array}{c}
CH_2O-C-R \\
\quad\quad \| \\
\quad\quad O \\[4pt]
CHO-C-R' \\
\quad\quad \| \\
\quad\quad O \qquad\qquad (IV)\\[4pt]
\quad\quad O^- \\
\quad\quad | \\
CH_2O-P^+-O-C_2H_4NH_3^+ \\
\quad\quad | \\
\quad\quad O^-
\end{array}
$$

The problem was attacked by Levene and West (1916a), who were forced to conclude that certain almost inherent impurities accounted for the discrepant results. They were able (Levene and West, 1916b) to prove the unequivocal presence of an amino group by treating the cephalin fraction with phenyl- or naphthylisocyanate to obtain the expected derivative as indicated by proper elementary analyses. Finally, when the cephalin fraction of egg yolk was hydrogenated, they (Levene and West, 1918) were able to isolate a product whose elementary analyses checked for formula (IV) where the R groups are saturated.

The alcohol-insoluble fraction classically considered "cephalin" was examined in some detail by Gray (1940). The typical analytical figures he observed, as compared to theoretical values for the compound of formula (IV) and for other phosphatides, are shown in Table I.

TABLE I. ANALYTICAL FIGURES FOR "CEPHALIN" AS COMPARED WITH
OTHER LIPIDES (GRAY, 1940)

Material	C	H	N	P
"Cephalin", observed	60.41	9.79	1.67	3.59
"Cephalin", theoretical for stearyl, linoleyl	66.04	10.71	1.88	4.16
Lecithin, theoretical for stearyl, linoleyl	65.75	10.71	1.74	3.86
Sphingomyelin, theoretical for lignoceryl	67.72	11.53	3.37	3.88
Cerebroside, theoretical for nervone	71.13	11.33	1.73	—

An important contribution to the problem was made by Rudy and Page (1930), who actually isolated a pure cephalin. Most previous workers had assumed that the cephalin indicated by formula (IV) was alcohol-insoluble, and the material with which they worked was almost invariably obtained from the portion of the phosphatides which was insoluble in warm ethanol. MacArthur, Norbury and Karr (1917), however, had observed that the alcohol-soluble portion of the phosphatides from heart lecithin contained its nitrogen divided equally between choline and aminoethyl alcohol. This should have caused investigators to realize that the separation by means of alcohol was a very superficial one. Yet the observation bore no fruit until Rudy and Page (1930) showed that from the alcohol-soluble portion of the phosphatides from human brain they could isolate, in addition to lecithin, a phosphatide containing aminoethyl alcohol. This alcohol-soluble material, unlike any cephalin previously isolated, possessed a carbon content in agreement with the theoretical content required by formula (IV). It could be titrated with sodium hydroxide to a phenolphthalein end point in benzene-absolute alcohol solution. Furthermore, the value obtained by this titration agreed fairly well with the Van Slyke amino nitrogen determination carried out after hydrolysis of the phosphatide. It is interesting to note that the amino nitrogen analysis prior to hydrolysis was 10 to 12 per cent too high, due perhaps to the presence of associated substances such as urea.

A similar compound was isolated more recently by Folch (1942a, see p. 29) from brain "cephalin", and he too stressed the point that it was entirely alcohol-soluble. It possessed carbon, hydrogen and amino percentages required by theory. Thus it appears that the classical "cephalin" as represented by the aminoethyl alcohol ester of a diacylglycerophosphoric acid is actually alcohol-soluble and is not the material which is generally called "cephalin" in the older literature, the latter being a mixture characterized by alcohol insolubility. Thus, Folch (1942a) proposed that the material represented by formula (IV) be termed phosphatidylaminoethyl alcohol (see p. 29) rather than cephalin. Cephalin, then, is a general term for a mixture of phosphatidylaminoethyl alcohol, phosphatidylserine and inositol-containing phosphatides. The specific phosphatides of the cephalin fraction are discussed below.

Phosphatidylserine

The older literature (MacLean and MacLean, 1927, p. 51) attempted to account for the discrepancy between the theoretical and calculated analytical values for what was believed to be cephalin, on the basis of the presence of hydrolytic degradation products. This was obviously unsatisfactory. MacLean and MacLean (1927, p. 21), furthermore, described experiments which showed that all the nitrogen of the lecithin fraction was distributed between choline and amino nitrogen, and they proposed that the latter material was probably entirely aminoethyl alcohol. However, from time to time suggestions appeared in the literature that bases other than the above two were present in phosphatides.

Thierfelder and Schulze (1915/16) were of such an opinion, and they pointed out further that the nitrogen in the unknown base was probably amino nitrogen. That "cephalin" might contain an amino acid as one of its basic constituents was first suggested by work of MacArthur (1914), Darrah and MacArthur (1916) and MacArthur, Norbury and Karr (1917). The presence of an amino-containing base in addition to amino-ethyl alcohol was also suggested by the work of Thierfelder and Schulze (1915/16). Further evidence in this direction was not accumulated until Christensen and Hastings (1940) made a study of the electrophoresis and the titration of the cephalin fraction from egg yolk. From this work they concluded that both the instability of the cephalin fraction and its behavior on titration indicate a structure divergent from the generally accepted one. They further made the significant observation that about 0.6 equivalent of alkali metal was bound to each mole of "cephalin", although the idea is generally held now that phosphatidylserine (see p. 320) is not present in the cephalin fraction from egg yolk.

Evidence for the presence of an amino acid in the cephalin fraction of ox brain phosphatides was first provided by Folch and Schneider (1941). Less direct evidence was shortly afterwards provided by Blix (1941). The former workers isolated the cephalin fraction by standard procedures and found that it reacted with ninhydrin to evolve carbon dioxide in a manner similar to α-amino acids. Such analyses on various samples indicated that 40 to 70 per cent of the nitrogen was present as α-amino acids, and after acid hydrolysis of the cephalin an equivalent amount of amino acid was present in the water-soluble hydrolysate. From the ninhydrin reaction, glycolic aldehyde was isolated and identified as its dimedon derivative or as the phenylosazone. The same degradation product resulted from oxidation of the hydrolysate with chloramine-T, whereas oxidation with periodate liberated ammonia, indicating the presence of a hydroxyl group adjacent to an amino group. On the basis of these results it was postulated that the amino acid was serine and that it was attached through the hydroxyl group, since both the amino and the carboxyl groups in the phosphatide molecule were free and available for reaction. In later publications (Folch, 1941a, 1942a), the pure phosphatidylserine was actually isolated, and from it there was obtained on hydrolysis pure L(+)-serine. The serine-containing phosphatide was isolated from the remainder of the cephalin fraction by virtue of the fact that it is more soluble in a mixture of ethanol and chloroform than the inositol phosphatide, and less soluble than phosphatidylaminoethyl alcohol (see p. 62).

The phosphatidylserine isolated by this procedure was in the form of the sodium or potassium salt. The presence of alkali metal in phosphatidylserine recalls the suggestion made long ago by Koch and Pike (1910) that the phosphatides contribute to the maintenance of electrolytic equilibria within the nerve cells.

Folch (1942) points out that the success of his separation depends on the fact that the phosphatidylserine is allowed to remain throughout the isolation procedure as the alkali metal salt. Many previous investigators used hydrochloric acid in order to free the cephalin from its water-soluble impurities. This, of course, released the free acid, and the properties of such a phosphatide are hardly distinguishable from the properties of phosphatidylaminoethyl alcohol.

Further evidence for the structure of phosphatidylserine was advanced by Folch (1948), who showed conclusively that the amino and the carboxyl groups were free since the phosphatide reacted with nitrous acid as well as with ninhydrin. It was proved that the hydroxyl group was in combination, since the phosphatide, unlike the free serine, did not react with periodic acid. Finally, from the hydrolysate, glycerophosphoric acid, serine and fatty acids were isolated in the ratio of 1:1:2. On this basis, the structure may be postulated as the serine ester of a diacylglycerophosphoric acid which occurs naturally as an alkali metal salt. The α-form is shown by (V).

$$
\begin{array}{l}
\quad\quad\quad O \\
\quad\quad\quad \| \\
CH_2O-C-R \\
\quad\quad\quad O \\
\quad\quad\quad \| \\
CHO-C-R' \\
\quad\quad\quad O \\
\quad\quad\quad \| \\
CH_2-O-P-O-CH_2-CH-COOH \\
\quad\quad\quad\quad | \quad\quad\quad\quad\quad | \\
\quad\quad\quad\quad OH \quad\quad\quad\quad NH_2
\end{array}
\qquad (V)
$$

In the product isolated by Folch (1948), the fatty acids were predominantly stearic and oleic, and the bound alkali metal was chiefly potassium. However, Folch points out that other preparations may be obtained in which sodium predominates, and in which the fatty acids may be more unsaturated.

From formula (V) it is obvious that there is one basic group, the amino group; and two acidic groups, the carboxyl and one acidic hydrogen from the phosphoric acid. Thus, at the physiological pH the compound should behave as a monobasic acid, the two remaining functional groups forming a zwitterion. As already indicated, it exists in its natural state as a salt. Folch (1948) was able to show that the alkali metal-phosphorus ratio is 1:1, that the alkali metal may be removed by dilute acid and that from the free acid the original phosphatidylserine may be regenerated by the addition of the theoretical quantity of base.

The elucidation of the structure of phosphatidylserine and the discovery of the inositol phosphatides (see p. 35) have explained the incorrect elementary analyses which the cephalin fraction invariably demonstrated (see p. 27). Table II indicates the elementary analyses obtained by Folch (1948) for a sample of phosphatidylserine which contained 3.76 per cent potassium and 0.51 per cent sodium. The corresponding theoretical values are calculated on the basis that these cations and oleic and stearic acids are present. The third column represents values for the cephalin fraction which have been averaged by Gray (1940). It is interesting to note that Gray (1940) found an appreciable quantity of ash, only a small part of which was phosphorus.

TABLE II. ELEMENTARY ANALYSES OF PHOSPHATIDYLSERINE

Components	Observed	Calculated	Literature values for "cephalin" averaged by Gray (1940)
C	60.8	61.1	60.4
H	9.32	9.59	9.79
N	1.65	1.70	1.67
P	3.75	3.76	3.59

It is obvious that phosphatidylaminoethyl alcohol may be derived from phosphatidylserine by decarboxylation. Folch (1942a), however, offered evidence that phosphatidylaminoethyl alcohol does not arise by post mortem decarboxylation. Thus, the cephalin fraction obtained from dog brain by rapid manipulation at very low temperatures contains the same amount of aminoethyl alcohol and serine as the cephalin fraction prepared in the usual way.

Serine. Serine was first isolated by Cramer (1865) from sericin hydrolysate. Its structure was later proved by Fischer and Leuchs (1902), who also synthesized it. Serine was later synthesized by Leuchs and Geiger (1906), Redemann and Icke (1943), Erlenmeyer and Stoop (1904), Carter and West (1940) and Wood and du Vigneaud (1940).

Serine is found in quantity in proteins such as sericin, gelatin, human serum albumin (Brand, Kassell and Saidel, 1944); in the proteins of cow and human milk (Williamson, 1940); in the proteins of the liver, heart and kidney of pork, beef and lamb and in chicken muscle (Sahyun, 1948, p. 204). Its isolation from sericin was described by Daft and Coghill (1931). During this isolation the material is racemized and an optically inactive mixture obtained. As with all amino acids, the L-form is the naturally occurring one, and Artom, Fishman and Morehead (1945) have shown that the D-form is actually toxic.

Phosphatidylaminoethyl Alcohol

This is the material referred to as "cephalin" in all the work prior to 1940, despite the fact that none of these workers, with the exception of Rudy and Page (1930, see p. 27), had actually isolated the pure material. As already indicated, it is only one constituent of the cephalin fraction which includes phosphatidylserine and the inositol-containing phosphatides, and it is not necessarily the constituent present in greatest amount.

The procedure for the isolation of phosphatidylaminoethyl alcohol has been described by Folch (1942a). Its isolation from a cephalin fraction which has not been treated with acid depends on the fact that it is freely soluble in alcohol. Thus, when a chloroform solution of the mixture is treated with alcohol, the inositol phosphatides which are the least soluble precipitate first. Addition of more alcohol precipitates the phosphatidylserine in the form of its alkali metal salt, whereas the phosphatidylaminoethyl alcohol remains entirely soluble in the mixture of ethanol and chloroform. When the solution is concentrated and treated with acetone, phosphatidylaminoethyl alcohol precipitates.

The product isolated by Folch (1942a) possessed carbon, phosphorus, nitrogen and amino nitrogen contents in good agreement with those re- quired by the formula assigned to "cephalin" in classical biochemistry. On hydrolysis, relatively high yields of aminoethyl alcohol and glycero- phosphoric acid were obtained, and on this basis it is reasonable to postulate that the structure of phosphatidylaminoethyl alcohol corre- sponds to that assigned by the earlier workers to the entire cephalin fraction. The α-form is thus represented by (VI).

$$
\begin{array}{l}
\qquad\qquad\overset{\textstyle O}{\overset{\textstyle \|}{}}\\
CH_2O-C-R\\[4pt]
\qquad\qquad\overset{\textstyle O}{\overset{\textstyle \|}{}}\\
CHO-C-R' \qquad\qquad\qquad (VI)\\[4pt]
\qquad\qquad\qquad O^-\\
\qquad\qquad\qquad |\\
CH_2-O-P^+-OC_2H_4NH_3{}^+\\
\qquad\qquad\qquad |\\
\qquad\qquad\qquad O^-
\end{array}
$$

Acid-Base Relationships. All the work recorded in the literature on the acid-base relationships of the cephalin fraction contains conclu- sions based on the assumption that the material under examination possessed the structure indicated by (VI). This is obviously incorrect in light of recent work, and the need for experiments employing pure samples of phosphatidylserine and phosphatidylaminoethyl alcohol is now indicated.

The presence of the carboxyl group of serine probably accounts for the observation of Fabisch (1931) and of Jukes (1934) that "cephalin" possesses buffering capacity, whereas lecithin does not. Phosphatidylaminoethyl alcohol should be capable of titration by strong alkali since aminoethyl alcohol is a base of intermediate strength. That this is the case was shown by Rudy and Page (1930). Phosphatidylserine, on the other hand, possesses two acidic groups, one of which neutralizes the amino group, leaving the other free to bind cations. Actually, as has already been indicated (see p. 29), it exists as an alkali metal salt. The free acid may be generated from this salt and this too may be titrated with base.

Since aminoethyl alcohol is a relatively weak base compared to choline, it is incapable of compensating for the strong phosphoric acid residue. Accordingly, one would expect phosphatidylaminoethyl alcohol to possess a low isoelectric point. Although the isoelectric point of the pure material has not been determined, some interesting results are recorded in the literature. Bull and Frampton (1936) determined the isoelectric point of a mixture of phosphatides containing lecithin and the cephalin fraction. The value was close to pH = 4. As the cephalin fraction was removed the isoelectric point rose, and by extrapolation it was possible to estimate the true isoelectric point of lecithin. This work showed that the isoelectric point of the cephalin fraction was low, as expected. Bull (1937, p. 122) further pointed out that the difference in isoelectric point between the two substances may lead to the formation of coacervates over a wide range of pH. This may account in part for the difficulty encountered in the separation of lecithin and the cephalin fraction.

A zwitterionic structure for phosphatidylaminoethyl alcohol is necessary, although the weak character of the base might make possible a different relationship in certain instances. Fischgold and Chain (1935) observed that in a solvent of low dielectric constant (19 volumes benzene and 1 volume ethanol) it was possible to titrate quantitatively both the phosphoric acid group and the amino group of the cephalin fraction. This was contrary to the results for lecithin, where it was impossible to titrate the quaternary trimethylammonium group. On this basis they postulated that "cephalin" (for which they visualized structure (VI), although they were probably working with a mixture) exists in water largely as a zwitterion, whereas in solvents of low dielectric constant it may exist as ions or neutral molecules.

Jukes (1934) also provided evidence from titration experiments for the zwitterionic structure of the cephalin fraction. He found that the cephalin fraction bound alkali in 98 per cent ethanol, whereas lecithin did not. Both, however, bound acid at low pH values, demonstrating pK′ values of 1.1. The cephalin fraction, in addition, showed another pK′ value of 8.9 because of its reaction with alkali.

β-**Aminoethyl Alcohol.** This aminoalcohol, which is sometimes called "colamine", is an oily material with a typical amine odor. It is soluble in water, alcohol and chloroform, but demonstrates only slight solubility in ether, benzene and petroleum ether. It boils at 171° C. and distills without decomposition.

Aminoethyl alcohol possesses the structure $NH_2CH_2CH_2OH$, and this was apparent to its discoverer, Wurtz (1859, 1861), who first synthesized it by reacting ammonia with ethylene chlorohydrin or with ethylene oxide. This original procedure is still the most convenient method for preparation, and is the one which is used commercially.

β-Aminoethyl alcohol forms salts of the general formula $CH_2OH-CH_2NH_3X$. These are in general more soluble than the corresponding salts of choline, for which reason the isolation of aminoethyl alcohol from aqueous hydrolysates is more difficult. The well defined salts include the hydrochloride, hydrobromide, nitrate, sulfate, chloroaurate, chloroplatinate, flavianate, oxalate, picrate, picrolonate and the phosphotungstate and silicotungstate (Kahane and Kahane, 1936). With higher fatty acids such as stearic acid, soaps are formed which possess the unique property of solubility in both water and organic solvents. Folch (1942a) described the p-hydroxyazobenzene-p-sulfonate as a derivative useful for isolation purposes. The chloroaurate has also been used for purposes of isolation (Thierfelder and Schulze, 1915/16), and Chargaff (1942a) described the precipitation of aminoethyl alcohol with 3,5-diiodosalicylic acid. Generally, however, it is estimated indirectly by the Van Slyke amino nitrogen method. The amino group may also be titrated with strong acid in the presence of indicators such as methyl orange.

Aminoethyl alcohol reacts both as a primary amine and a primary alcohol. The alcoholic function undergoes the iodoform reaction, and this is one means of identification. The amino group may be methylated by stages with methyl iodide and strong base to yield ultimately the quaternary ammonium compound, choline. The amino group may also be converted to amides; and in the presence of one mole of acid chloride, amide formation takes place in preference to ester formation. Thus, Fourneau and Gonzalez (1921) proposed the formation of the β-naphthalenesulfonamide as a means of separating aminoethyl alcohol from choline in phosphatide hydrolysates. Chargaff (1937) used benzyl chloroformate for a similar purpose.

Inositol-Containing Phosphatides

Inositol (Anderson, 1930) and inositolmonophosphoric acid (Cason and Anderson, 1938) were among the water-soluble constituents resulting from the hydrolysis of the phosphatides of the tubercle bacillus. Klenk and Sakai (1939) also isolated inositol and inositolmonophosphoric acid from the hydrolysate of the cephalin fraction of soybeans. The first evidence that inositol was combined chemically in a phosphatide was advanced by Folch and Woolley (1942) and by Folch (1942a), who found inositol in the cephalin fraction of the phosphatides from brain and spinal cord. These were quite insoluble in ethanol, and when a chloroform solution of the cephalin fraction was treated with ethanol, the inositol compounds precipitated first. The more soluble substances, as already indicated, consisted of phosphatidylserine and phosphatidylaminoethyl alcohol.

In the initial publication (Folch and Woolley, 1942) it was pointed out that the inositol must exist in chemical union with the phosphatide for the following reasons: (1) microbiological assay of the phosphatide for inositol indicated only one-twentieth of the activity of the hydrolytic cleavage products where free inositol existed; (2) added inositol could be removed by dialysis, leaving the inositol content of the phosphatide unchanged and (3) oxidation of the phosphatide with periodic acid indicated no free inositol. The phosphatides isolated contained 6 to 10 per cent inositol which was shown to be in the *meso* form.

The inositol-containing phosphatide fraction was impure, for Folch (1942a) showed the presence of serine which probably came from phosphatidylserine. It was characterized by a low carbon content which helped to explain the difficulties encountered by earlier workers in their attempts to isolate a cephalin compound whose elementary composition checked with theoretical values (see p. 27) required for phosphatidylaminoethyl alcohol. The phosphorus content and the phosphorus-to-nitrogen ratio were high. Glycerophosphoric acid was found among the hydrolysis products indicating the possible presence of two polyhydric alcohols in one molecule.

The inositol-containing phosphatide from brain was investigated by Folch (1946, 1949a), who devised a means for its purification. He termed the compound "diphosphoinositide", since inositol was shown to be present in the molecule as the *meta* diphosphate. All the phosphorus appears to be present in this form; and, as a result of acid hydrolysis, it may be shown that fatty acids, glycerol and inositol metadiphosphate are present in equimolar proportions. The material is acidic, the acid functions arising from each of the phosphoryl radicals. Undoubtedly, it occurs naturally as a salt. The relationship of the glycerol and the fatty acids to the inositol diphosphate remains yet to be determined.

Inositol-containing phosphatides have also been isolated from other sources. Woolley (1943) found soybean lipides to be a rich source, and he named the material which he isolated "lipositol". This material, however, was undoubtedly a gross mixture. More recently, Scholfield and co-workers (1948) have isolated the inositol-containing phosphatide fraction from soybean lipides by use of the "countercurrent distribution" technique. This work indicated the presence of several inositol-containing phosphatides, although it was not highly definitive.

Folch (1947) also isolated the inositol-containing phosphatide fraction from soybeans. He found that it consisted of the mixed calcium, magnesium and potassium salt, and that it contained glycerol in addition to inositol and galactose. He found the following proportions of hydrolysis products: amine, 1; inositol, 2; galactose, 2; glycerol, 2; phosphoric acid, 2 and fatty acids, 3. Olcott (1944) obtained evidence for the presence of inositol-containing phosphatides in cottonseed.

An inositol-containing phosphatide has been isolated from liver by Macpherson and Lucas (1947). De. Sütö-Nagy and Anderson (1947) isolated from the hydrolysis products of the phosphatides of the tubercle bacillus a material which on further hydrolysis yielded both inositolmonophosphoric acid and glycerophosphoric acid. It was not possible to determine the manner in which these two acids were joined or the relationship which existed between the diphosphoric acid and the unhydrolyzed lipides. This work, however, serves to show the complexity of the inositol-containing phosphatides. The biochemistry of inositol has been critically reviewed by Weidlein (1951).

A great deal more work remains to be done on the composition of the inositol-containing phosphatides. What has been done, nevertheless, comprises an extremely important contribution to the explanation of the enigma which previously existed in regard to the composition of the cephalin fraction.

The Hydrolysis Products of the Cephalin Phosphatides

General

The bases associated with the cephalin phosphatides have already been described since their identification was important in the elucidation of structure. As with lecithin, the hydrolysis proceeds readily under the influence of either acid or base; and in the case of phosphatidylserine and phosphatidylaminoethyl alcohol, glycerophosphoric acid is found in the water-soluble portion of the hydrolysate. It may also be present in some of the inositol phosphatides. This substance has already been discussed in some detail in relation to lecithin (see p. 16) and this discussion can be applied also to the cephalin fraction.

Fatty Acids

The fatty acids of lecithin have already been described, and much of the discussion in regard to degree of unsaturation and the ratio of saturated to unsaturated acids applies to the fatty acids of the cephalin fraction. In this fraction, fatty acids arise from the inositol-containing phosphatides as well as from phosphatidylserine and phosphatidylaminoethyl alcohol. Very little work has been done to identify in detail the fatty acids of these recently discovered compounds. Most of the work in the literature on acids from the cephalin fraction concerns the fatty acids of the phosphatide fraction insoluble in alcohol. As has already been pointed out, this solubility fraction does not represent all of the phosphatides in the cephalin fraction. A detailed description of the fatty acids of the cephalin fraction from various sources is found in Parts III and IV.

The identity of cephalinic acid as an impure mixture has already been discussed (see p. 25). The other acids of the cephalin fraction are in general quite similar to the corresponding acids of lecithin, as shown by the work of Cousin (1906, 1907), Parnas (1909, 1913), Levene and West (1913), MacArthur and Burton (1916), Levene and Rolf (1922a), Klenk (1930), Fränkel and Dimitz (1909), Levene and Rolf (1922), Tsujimoto (1920), Brown (1932) and Page and Rudy (1932). These latter workers, who were the first to obtain a pure sample of phosphatidylaminoethyl alcohol, found that 30 per cent of the total acids were stearic, whereas the unsaturated acids possessed chain lengths of 18 and 22 carbon atoms.

CHAPTER IV

THE STRUCTURE OF SPHINGOMYELIN

HISTORICAL AND INTRODUCTION

Sphingomyelin was first isolated by Thudichum (1901, pp. 93, 110, 165), who gave it its name (from the Greek *sphingein*, to bind tight) "in commemoration of the many enigmas which it presented to the enquirer". He obtained the compound from a concentrated alcohol extract of brain tissue whence it precipitated as a white powder which is crystalline when pure. It differed from lecithin and the cephalin fraction in that it appeared quite stable, and a further distinction arose because it contained no glycerol. Thudichum observed that it was a diaminophosphatide, which is to say that the nitrogen-phosphorus ratio was 2:1. His product was contaminated with cerebrosides, but his hydrolysis products, with one exception, were quite accurately identified. Thus he isolated, after hydrolysis with barium hydroxide, two bases, sphingosine and choline (which he termed "neurine"); a fatty acid; the barium salt of what was probably a fatty acid; and phosphoric acid. In addition, he reported an alcohol, sphingol, of empirical formula $C_9H_{18}O$ or $C_{18}H_{36}O_2$ which subsequent workers could not confirm.

Thudichum isolated other substances such as "apomyelin" and "amidomyelin" which were allegedly diaminophosphatides, but which subsequent work has shown to be impure forms of sphingomyelin. Indeed, sphingomyelin is isolated pure only with some difficulty since it is always found in close association with cerebrosides with which it has many properties in common. These mixtures of sphingomyelin and cerebrosides are often referred to as "protagon". Protagon was believed for many years to be an actual chemical entity rather than a mixture, although Thudichum recognized its true nature. The history of protagon and its final evolution as a mixture of brain lipides are well detailed by MacLean and MacLean (1927, p. 124 ff.).

The close physical resemblance of sphingomyelin to the cerebrosides is due to the fact that they are chemically related derivatives of the base, sphingosine. Thus, Carter and co-workers (1947) have termed these substances the "sphingolipides". These may be divided into three categories— the cerebrosides (Thierfelder and Klenk, 1930, pp. 1–60), the gangliosides

(Klenk, 1942) and sphingomyelin. Only the latter material contains phosphorus, for which reason it is classified as a phosphatide. The common structural feature of all three is a fatty acid amide of sphingosine. When this amide is combined by a glycosidic linkage with galactose, cerebrosides result, whereas its combination with the choline ester of phosphoric acid provides sphingomyelin. The second hydroxyl of sphingosine may be esterified with fatty acids in the case of the cerebrosides, but this is not the case with sphingomyelin. The structure of the gangliosides is still somewhat obscure, although the presence of sphingosine as a basic structural unit is well established.

Sphingosine

Sphingosine, from a functional point of view, is analogous to glycerol, since both provide three points for attachment of other chemical groups. In the case of glycerol the three points for attachment are hydroxyl groups, whereas in sphingosine, two are hydroxyl groups and one is an amino group which imparts basic properties to the molecule. Thus it is logical that lipides may be derived from sphingosine just as they are from glycerol. The structure of sphingosine is much more complicated than that of glycerol, for the former contains 18 carbon atoms, a number which immediately brings to mind an association with the most common fatty acids. Since the structure of sphingomyelin depends on the structure of sphingosine, the latter will be discussed first.

Structure

Sphingosine was discovered by Thudichum (1901, p. 187), who isolated it by hydrolyzing the cerebroside, phrenosin. He characterized it incorrectly as a base of empirical composition $C_{17}H_{35}NO_2$, and prepared several of its salts. Early workers (Wörner and Thierfelder, 1900; Levene and Jacobs, 1912) were able to determine that sphingosine is a monounsaturated monoaminodihydroxy alcohol. They reduced sphingosine to dihydrosphingosine and reported, as did Thomas and Thierfelder (1912), the preparation of the triacetyl derivative.

Evidence for the position of the double bond and for other structural features was provided by Lapworth (1913) and by Levene and West (1913/14, 1914) on the basis that chromic acid oxidation of sphingosine yielded a material believed to be a 13-carbon straight chain acid. A similar oxidation of dihydrosphingosine (Levene and West, 1914) yielded *n*-pentadecanoic acid. These results seemed to confirm Thudichum's incorrect postulation that sphingosine possessed 17 carbon atoms. They showed further that a straight chain was present with a double bond between carbons 4 and 5 and with the two hydroxyls and the amino group on the first three carbon atoms. The problem of the arrangement of the three functional groups was attacked by Levene and West (1914), who ozonized sphingosine to obtain a nitrogen-containing fraction which was oxidized further with nitric acid to a substance believed to be *meso*-tartaric acid. On the basis of these data, the formula of sphingosine was incorrectly postulated as (VII).

$$CH_3(CH_2)_{11}CH{=}CH{-}CH{-}CH{-}CH_2$$
$$\underset{\displaystyle OH}{|}\;\;\underset{\displaystyle OH}{|}\;\;\underset{\displaystyle NH_2}{|}\qquad (VII)$$

All this work was reinvestigated by Klenk (1929) and by Klenk and Diebold (1931), who expressed doubt concerning the occurrence of an odd-numbered carbon chain in a natural product. In their work, the chromic acid oxidations of sphingosine and dihydrosphingosine were shown to yield myristic and palmitic acids, respectively, rather than the tri- and pentadecanoic acids previously reported. These data indicated a C_{18} structure for sphingosine, and Klenk (1929) pointed out that the analytical data for triacetylsphingosine and for the salts of dihydro-sphingosine were in closer accord with such a structure.

The nitrogenous fragment from the ozonolysis of triacetylsphingosine was also isolated by Klenk and Diebold (1931). They identified it by removing the acetyl groups, oxidizing the aldehyde to a carboxyl group and reducing the hydroxyl groups with phosphorus and hydroiodic acid. The end product was not identified with absolute certainty, but they believed it to be α-amino-*n*-butyric acid. This led them to the conclusion that the hydroxyl groups were on the two end carbon atoms. This was later shown to be incorrect. Thus they proposed that sphingosine was represented by structure (VIII).

$$CH_3(CH_2)_{12}CH{=}CH{-}CH{-}CH{-}CH_2$$
$$\underset{\displaystyle NH_2}{|}\;\;\underset{\displaystyle OH}{|}\;\;\underset{\displaystyle OH}{|}\qquad (VIII)$$

If the postulations of Klenk and Diebold (1931) were correct, the dihydroxy acid which they obtained after ozonolysis and for which they reported an $[\alpha]_D^{13}$ of $-33.45°$ must have been α-amino-β, γ-dihydroxy-*n*-butyric acid. Niemann and Nichols (1942) synthesized both stereo-isomers of this acid and found that neither was identical with the acid obtained by the earlier workers. At the same time, Carter and co-workers (1942, 1947b) noted that the reduction of triacetylsphingosine to triace-tyldihydrosphingosine proceeded with the uptake of more than the theo-retical quantity of hydrogen and the simultaneous release of an acid. This pointed to the hydrogenolysis of an acetoxy group such as might occur in an allylic system where an acetoxy group was attached to a carbon atom adjacent to a double-bonded carbon atom. In subsequent work (Carter, Greenwood and Humiston, 1950), the expected diacetyl-sphingosine was actually isolated. These same workers observed that neither N-benzoyl nor N-acetyldihydrosphingosine could be oxidized by periodic acid. Since this reagent is specific for α-glycols, it follows that the two hydroxyl groups are not proximal, contrary to prior postulations. With benzaldehyde and zinc chloride, however, a benzylidene derivative resulted. Since this reaction is characteristic only of 1,2 or 1,3 glycols, and since the α-structure was precluded by the results with periodic acid, the two hydroxyl groups must be in the 1,3 position. Thus, Carter and co-workers (1947b) postulated for sphingosine the structure 1,3-dihydroxy-2-aminooctadecene-4 (IX).

$$CH_3(CH_2)_{12}CH{=}CH{-}\underset{\underset{OH}{|}}{CH}{-}\underset{\underset{NH_2}{|}}{CH}{-}\underset{\underset{OH}{|}}{CH_2} \qquad (IX)$$

Further evidence was provided by Carter and co-workers (1947b) from the periodate oxidation of dihydrosphingosine. Although periodic acid will not react with an acylated amino group adjacent to a hydroxyl group, it will react when the amino group is free. Thus, dihydro-sphingosine consumed two moles of periodic acid and yielded equivalent amounts of formic acid, formaldehyde, and ammonia together with an unspecified amount of palmitaldehyde. This reaction proceeds according to the following equation and provides further evidence that sphingosine has 18 carbon atoms and that the three functional groups are on adjacent carbon atoms, one of which must be terminal.

$$CH_3(CH_2)_{14}\underset{\underset{OH}{|}}{CH}{-}\underset{\underset{NH_2}{|}}{CH}{-}\underset{\underset{OH}{|}}{CH_2} \xrightarrow{IO_4^-} CH_3(CH_2)_{14}CHO + HCOOH + NH_3 + HCHO$$

Thus, the structure of sphingosine has been established as (IX), and it is this which forms the basic part of the sphingomyelin molecule.

To gain insight into the configuration of sphingosine Carter, Greenwood and Humiston (1950) oxidized N-benzoylsphingosine to obtain an optically active N-benzoylaminostearic acid. This latter substance, on racemization through the azlactone, was converted to the known dl-benzoyl-α-aminostearic acid. On the basis of studies of optical rotation of acylated amino acids in various solvents, the benzoyl-α-aminostearic acid was tentatively assigned the D-configuration.

Dihydrosphingosine

Recent work has shown that the saturated counterpart of sphingosine, dihydrosphingosine, likewise probably comprises part of the sphingo-myelin molecule. The first isolation of dihydrosphingosine from natural sources was reported by Lesuk and Anderson (1941), who found it in the cerebrosides of *Cysticercus fasciolaris* larvae, an organism which had also yielded lecithin with completely saturated fatty acids.

Carter and Norris (1942) and Carter and co-workers (1947a) reported the isolation of dihydrosphingosine from brain and spinal cord. It was isolated by virtue of the slight solubility of its sulfate in methanol and was identified by its triacetyl derivative. These workers point out that sphingosine, which is difficult to purify and identify, has usually been characterized in the literature as the triacetyl derivative. The melting point of triacetylsphingosine (101–102° C) is very close to the melting point of triacetyldihydrosphingosine (102–103° C.), and very little depression of melting point is observed on mixing. For this reason, many of the products described in the earlier literature may actually have consisted of mixtures of the two substances. Carter and co-workers (1947a) found that optical activity provides a precise method of differentiation since triacetylsphingosine has an $[\alpha]_D^{25}$ of $-11.7°$ (0.1 g. in 10 ml. chloroform) whereas the reduced material demonstrates a corresponding value, $[\alpha]_D^{30}$, of $+18.0°$.

The tribenzoyl derivative of dihydrosphingosine was also prepared by Carter and co-workers (1947a) and was found to melt at 144 to 145° C. The corresponding derivative of sphingosine, on the other hand, could not be obtained pure, as evidenced by its melting range of 118 to 124° C.

The separation of sphingosine from dihydrosphingosine is a difficult process, and these workers point out that brain is preferable to spinal cord for the isolation of sphingosine since dihydrosphingosine occurs to a lesser extent in brain.

Carter and co-workers (1947a) found that dihydrosphingosine is resident in the cerebrosides. Thannhauser and Boncoddo (1948a), influenced by the above findings, showed that it is also present, together with sphingosine, in sphingomyelin from lung and brain.

Sphingosine Ethers

Upon acetylation of the residue remaining from the crystallization of sphingosine sulfate from brain or spinal cord, Niemann (1941a) obtained in addition to triacetylsphingosine, a compound of empirical formula $C_{36}H_{69}NO_4$. Subsequent investigation indicated this compound to be diacetyl-O-tetradecylsphingosine. Thus the material, prior to acetylation, must have been a tetradecyl ether of sphingosine. It was not established which oxygen atom was etherified. The occurrence of such a material in natural sources raises interesting speculation as to the structure of the original sphingolipide of which this was undoubtedly a hydrolysis product.

Properties of Sphingosine

Sphingosine is an alcohol-soluble, water-insoluble base whose salts are likewise, for the most part, soluble in alcohol but insoluble in ether and water. The double bond of sphingosine may be hydrogenated to dihydrosphingosine and brominated to dibromosphingosine.

The sulfate of sphingosine is well known and has been much used in isolation processes. An acetate containing two moles of acetic acid has been prepared, and Levene and West (1916) prepared the picrolonates of sphingosine (m.p. = 87–89° C.) and of dihydrosphingosine (m.p. = 120–121° C.). They also prepared dibromosphingosine sulfate and dihydrosphingosine picrate (m.p. = 88–89° C.) and found that the action of nitrous acid on sphingosine yielded the corresponding triol (m.p. = 54–55° C.).

The configuration of the double bond of sphingosine was investigated by Niemann (1941), who found that the sphingosine sulfate ordinarily isolated from natural sources could be isomerized by treatment with ethanol and a trace of sulfuric acid. The original material, which he designated as α, was soluble in hot ethanol, was readily hydrogenated, and exhibited an intense blue-white fluorescence on irradiation. The isomerized form, which he termed β, was sparingly soluble in ethanol, absorbed hydrogen with difficulty and showed very weak fluorescence upon irradiation. On the basis of these observations, Niemann believed that the α-form is the *cis* isomer and the β-form is the *trans* isomer.

SPHINGOMYELIN

Structure

The structure of sphingomyelin, as of other phosphatides, has been determined from its hydrolysis products. Levene (1914, 1916) was the first to obtain relatively pure sphingomyelin and to report that the hydrolysis products consisted of (1) phosphoric acid, (2) choline, (3) sphingosine and (4) fatty acids, chiefly lignoceric. He also isolated an anhydrosphingosine, but provided evidence that this was a secondary product which formed after the hydrolysis. Levene (1916) was also able to show that the lignoceric acid was present in an amide linkage rather than an ester linkage. Many subsequent workers isolated lignocerylsphingosine after the partial hydrolysis of sphingomyelin (e.g., Thannhauser and Reichel, 1940); and Fränkel and Bielschowsky (1932) and Tropp and Wiedersheim (1933) actually isolated lignocerylsphingosine directly from animal organs. Since the acid is present in amide linkage, the choline and the phosphoric acid must then be distributed between the hydroxyl groups. It is logical to assume, in analogy with the structure of lecithin, that the choline is in ester linkage with the phosphoric acid which in turn esterifies one of the hydroxyls of the sphingosine. There is no evidence to indicate which of the hydroxyls is involved or whether, as with the glycerophosphatides, α- and β-forms are possible. It is hoped that this point will be investigated in current work.

On the basis of these data, and bearing in mind the recently proved structure of sphingosine, the structure of sphingomyelin may be represented by (X).

$$
\begin{array}{cccccc}
CH_3(CH_2)_{12}CH{=}CH-CH-CH\!-\!\!-\!\!-CH_2 \\
\quad\quad\quad\quad\quad | \quad\; | \quad\quad | \\
\quad\quad\quad\quad OH\;\; NH\quad\; O \\
\quad\quad\quad\quad\quad\quad\quad\; | \quad\quad | \\
\quad\quad\quad\quad O{=}C\;\; {}^{-}O-P^{+}\!-O^{-} \quad\quad\quad\quad (X) \\
\quad\quad\quad\quad\quad | \quad\quad\quad | \\
\quad\quad\quad\quad\quad R \quad\quad\; O-C_2H_4\overset{+}{N}(CH_3)_3
\end{array}
$$

As already indicated, this structure may be modified in some cases by the presence of dihydrosphingosine.

Fatty Acids. As may be seen from (X), the structure of sphingomyelin allows for only one fatty acid per molecule. Thudichum (1901, p. 171) isolated an acid isomeric with stearic acid but of lower melting point which he called "sphingostearic acid". This was undoubtedly an impure substance.

Levene (1916) obtained on hydrolysis lignoceric acid, $C_{24}H_{48}O_2$, a normal tetracosanic acid which occurs in widely different natural sources. He obtained in addition a hydroxy acid of low melting point which has not been found by subsequent workers, and which was probably an oxidized unsaturated fatty acid. Merz (1930) described the isolation of stearic acid, lignoceric acid and nervonic acid from sphingomyelin of brain. The latter is an unsaturated counterpart of lignoceric acid possessing the structure $CH_3(CH_2)_7CH \parallel CH(CH_2)_{13}COOH$ where the double bond has the *cis* configuration. Klenk (1933) found lignoceric and stearic acids in sphingomyelin from beef heart.

This work indicates that lignoceric acid is the most predominant acid in sphingomyelin. The presence of several fatty acids shows there are several sphingomyelins, just as there are several lecithins whose structures depend on the fatty acids present. It is interesting to note that the highly unsaturated acids typical of the glycerophosphatides from brain are absent.

In more recent work, Thannhauser, Setz and Benotti (1938) reported that sphingomyelin from the stromata of red blood cells contained chiefly lignoceric acid. On hydrolysis of a highly purified sample of brain sphingomyelin, Thannhauser and Boncoddo (1948a) found stearic, nervonic and lignoceric acids, the latter being present in smallest quantity. They did not find the palmitic acid reported by previous workers (Thannhauser and Reichel, 1940). They believe that this arose from the ether-insoluble dipalmityllecithin (Thannhauser and Boncoddo, 1948, see p. 54) which is often found associated with sphingomyelin.

In visceral organs such as lung and spleen, the fatty acids of sphingomyelin were found by Thannhauser and Boncoddo (1948a) to consist of equal portions of palmitic and lignoceric acids, stearic and nervonic acids being absent.

Acid-Base Relationships. Much of the discussion regarding the acid-base relationships of lecithin (see p. 12) applies here, since sphingomyelin likewise contains a strongly acidic group from the phosphoric acid and a strongly basic group from the choline. The basic character of the sphingosine is not a factor, since the amino group is blocked by an amide linkage which cannot contribute to the electrical properties of the molecule.

Christensen and Hastings (1940) titrated sphingomyelin electrometrically and found that it did not show any buffering action over a wide range of pH. Likewise they failed to find any appreciable combination of sphingomyelin with chloride or sodium ions. This is to be expected, as its strong acidic and basic functions should provide a zwitterion structure. This was borne out by Fischgold and Chain (1935), who developed a method for the determination of the acid- and base-binding capacity of various phosphatides. Thus they titrated sphingomyelin in a solvent consisting of 19 volumes of benzene and 1 volume of ethanol. They found that one equivalent of hydrogen ion was bound only in acid medium. This favors the idea that sphingomyelin is present only as a zwitterion in solution, or else as a cation.

Hausser (1935) explored the dielectric behavior of sphingomyelin. He observed a strong anomalous dispersion which was ascribed to a novel molecular resonator of a low characteristic frequency. The strongly polar group of the sphingomyelin molecule swings like a pendulum under the action of the high frequency field and under the influence of the directing force provided by the long resting arms formed by the two weakly polar chains.

The isoelectric point of sphingomyelin was determined by Chain and Kemp (1934) by use of cataphoretic mobility measurements. This value should be similar to that of lecithin (see p. 14) because of the similarity in structure. These workers found a somewhat lower value, 6.0, due to the presence of an acidic impurity which they could not remove from their sphingomyelin.

General Properties of Sphingomyelin

The best source of sphingomyelin is spinal cord or brain, the latter organ containing about 1 per cent of this lipide (Hunter, 1942) and the former about 1.4 per cent (Carter and co-workers, 1947). It occurs in smaller quantities in kidney, liver, egg yolk, blood, muscle and other organs (see Part IV) and is a characteristic constituent of kidney and spleen during certain pathological conditions (see p. 426).

Sphingomyelin is a white, crystalline compound which is quite stable and nonhygroscopic. It is readily soluble in hot methanol, ethanol, glacial acetic acid and chloroform, and somewhat less soluble in pyridine. It is insoluble in ether and cold acetone. It forms emulsions easily with water. With metallic compounds such as cadmium chloride, lead acetate and chloroplatinic acid, molecular compounds are formed. The compound with Reinecke acid (see Part II) is used for analytical purposes.

Sphingomyelin contains two asymmetric carbon atoms and is therefore optically active. Levene (1916) reported $[\alpha]_D$ values in chloroform-methyl alcohol varying from 7.53 to 8.20.

Isolation. Carter and co-workers (1947) have described a procedure for the isolation of the sphingolipides from brain and spinal cord. The wet organs are thoroughly dehydrated and extracted with acetone. The residue is then extracted well with ether to remove the glycerophosphatides. The resulting material is finally extracted with hot 95 per cent ethanol to obtain a solution from which the sphingolipides precipitate on cooling.

To obtain the sphingomyelin fraction, the ether-insoluble sphingolipides must be treated with acetone in which the cerebrosides and gangliosides are largely soluble and the sphingomyelin insoluble. Thus Thannhauser, Benotti and Boncoddo (1946, 1946a) described a procedure for the isolation of sphingomyelin in which the ether-insoluble lipides are dissolved in petroleum ether-methanol (9:1). Upon the addition of acetone, the sphingomyelin, contaminated with hydrolecithin, precipitates. This mixture is dissolved in glacial acetic acid and is again precipitated with acetone. To remove the saturated glycerophosphatides the mixture is treated with 0.25N sodium hydroxide for several days at 37° C. The hydrolyzed glycerophosphatides may then be removed by appropriate solvents to obtain pure sphingomyelin.

Hydrolysis. Thudichum reported that sphingomyelin was much more resistant to alkali than the glycerophosphatides. This has also been observed by other workers; and Schmidt and co-workers (1946) have devised an analytical procedure for phosphatide determination based on the observation that normal potassium hydroxide at 37° C. completely hydrolyzes the glycerophosphatides without affecting the sphingomyelins (see p. 167). Numerous hydrolytic procedures have been described in the literature (e.g., Klenk and Diebold, 1931) which have employed basic reagents such as barium hydroxide and acidic reagents such as sulfuric acid.

Related Compounds

Reichel and Thannhauser (1940) have esterified lignocerylsphingosine to obtain O-diacetyl, O-dipalmityl, O-distearyl and O-dibenzyllignoceryl-sphingosine. They have pointed out the functional relationship between these compounds and triglycerides.

Booth (1935) reported the isolation from kidney of the choline ester of sphingosinephosphoric acid. This, of course, is sphingomyelin less a fatty acid and is formally analogous to lysolecithin (see p. 99). The same compound was found by King and Small (1939) in pancreas.

CHAPTER V

THE STRUCTURE OF THE MINOR PHOSPHATIDES

PHOSPHATIDIC ACIDS

Historical

Winterstein and Stegmann (1908/09) found substances in *Ricinus* leaves, clover and rhubarb which in the light of modern knowledge must have been phosphatidic acids. Other workers such as Thudichum (1901, p. 130), Stern and Thierfelder (1907), Parnas (1909) and Levene and Komatsu (1919) reported the isolation of phosphatides from egg yolk, heart muscle and other substances which contained calcium in chemical combination. These substances may well have been phosphatidic acids, although there is no modern work to show that these non-nitrogenous phosphatides occur in animal sources. The properties of the phosphatidic acids are very similar to those of lecithin, for which reason the methods of isolation are similar. This similarity also accounts for the fact that they were not recognized as distinct compounds until 1927 when Chibnall and Channon (1927, 1929) reported their isolation from cabbage leaves.

Structure Proof

Chibnall and Channon (1927, 1929) observed that the ether extract from cabbage leaves contained phosphorus and accordingly postulated the presence of phosphatides. When the ether solution was treated with a large excess of acetone, a precipitate resulted, part of which was extractable with hot acetone. The material thus obtained possessed a phosphorus content of 4.6 to 4.9 per cent and a nitrogen content of only 0.22 per cent. The crude product, which was rapidly oxidized by air, yielded 70 per cent of its weight of fatty acids on hydrolysis. Thus its identity as a phosphatide seemed probable, but the very low nitrogen content and the high fatty acid content indicated that it was not one of the known phosphatides. Furthermore, the phosphorus content was higher than would be expected for glycerophosphatides. Since a nitrogen-phosphorus ration of 1:10 did not seem likely, it appeared that the bulk of the acetone-soluble product was nitrogen-free, the small percentage of nitrogen being explained on the basis of minor constituents or impurities.

It was further observed that calcium was present and that the ratio of calcium to phosphorus was close to unity. The metallic ion could be removed by treatment of an ether solution of the phosphatide with dilute hydrochloric acid to obtain a free acid, and this in turn was purified by precipitation as the lead salt. From the pure lead salt, a pure sample of the free acid could be obtained.

The structure of the material was postulated on the basis of the analytical values found for the pure acid and the pure lead salt, and on the basis of the hydrolysis products. The latter (Chibnall and Channon, 1927; Channon and Chibnall, 1927) were found after hydrolysis with barium hydroxide to consist of the barium salt of glycerophosphoric acid, and about 75 per cent fatty acids, the molar ratio of fatty acids to glycerophosphoric acid being approximately 2:1. It thus appeared that the product under investigation was a diacylglycerophosphoric acid which occurred naturally as a calcium salt, and whose α-form is represented by (XI).

$$\begin{array}{l}
\text{CH}_2\text{O}\overset{\overset{\displaystyle O}{\|}}{\text{C}}\text{R} \\[2mm]
\text{CHO}\overset{\overset{\displaystyle O}{\|}}{\text{C}}\text{R}' \qquad \text{(XI)} \\[2mm]
\text{CH}_2\text{O}\underset{\underset{\displaystyle \text{O}}{\|}}{\text{P}}\overset{\displaystyle \text{OH}}{\diagup}_{\diagdown \text{OH}}
\end{array}$$

Fatty Acids. The initial work of Chibnall and Channon (1927) indicated the presence of only a small amount of saturated acid in the phosphatidic acid fraction from cabbage leaf. The unsaturated acids appeared, in initial work, to be oleic, linoleic and linolenic with the latter present in largest quantity. Further investigation on larger quantities of product (Channon and Chibnall, 1927) indicated that the saturated acids were probably stearic and palmitic acids, whereas the unsaturated acids were linoleic and linolenic acids. Oleic acid was not found.

Origin of Phosphatidic Acids

To show that the phosphatidic acid was preformed in the leaf and was not the result of the hydrolysis of glycerophosphatides, Chibnall and Channon (1927) extracted the leaves under mild conditions without the application of heat. The same product was obtained as when more drastic conditions were used.

More recently, Hanahan and Chaikoff (1947a, 1948) have provided some very interesting data which show that the phosphatidic acids may actually result from the enzymic cleavage of glycerophosphatides. They found that phosphatidic acids could be isolated from carrot or cabbage plants by ordinary procedures which, incidentally, were conducive to enzyme action. On the other hand, when the plants were treated with live steam prior to extraction, phosphatides were obtained which possessed nitrogen to phosphorus ratios reasonably close to one. Furthermore, at least part of this nitrogen was shown to be in the form of choline. It thus appeared that the steam treatment inactivated the enzyme responsible for the cleavage of the nitrogen base from the phosphatide. These workers were actually able to isolate the enzyme and to study its properties (see p. 110).

From these results it appears that the phosphatidic acids are actually derived phosphatides whose occurrence depends on the method of isolation rather than on their formation in the plant organism. Nevertheless, they are definite, reproducible materials and as such must be admitted to the family of phosphatides.

Cardiolipin

Pangborn (1942) investigated the factor in alcoholic beef heart extract responsible for the reaction with sera from syphilitic patients. During the course of this work, she obtained a phosphatide-like material which she named "cardiolipin". This substance, admixed with lecithin and cholesterol in proper ratio, gave a specific complement-fixation reaction. It was isolated by extracting with alcohol a petroleum ether suspension of the phosphatides precipitated with cadmium chloride. The active substance remained in the petroleum ether from which it was isolated, and was subjected to further purification. This substance contained no nitrogen and could be titrated as a monobasic acid. On alkaline hydrolysis there was isolated (Pangborn, 1947) oleic and linoleic acids, glycerol, and a polyester of glycerophosphoric acid. The latter substance appears to be either diglycerylphosphoric acid or a larger molecule of the type shown by (XII).

$$
\begin{array}{cccccc}
 & O & & O & & O \\
 & \parallel & & \parallel & & \parallel \\
HG-&P&-G-&P&-G-&P-GH \\
 & | & & | & & | \\
 & OH & & OH & & OH
\end{array} \quad \text{(XII)}
$$

$$G = -OCH_2-CHOH-CH_2O-$$

Pangborn believes that cardiolipin is best classified as a complex phosphatidic acid. This interesting material will bear considerably more investigation.

ACETAL PHOSPHATIDES

Introduction

The presence of a substance in body fluids which was given the name "plasmalogen" was reported by Feulgen and Voit (1924) and by Stepp, Feulgen and Voit (1927), who discovered the material during histo-chemical studies on the staining of tissue by fuchsin-sulfurous acid, a dye which gives a characteristic purple color with aldehydes. This water-insoluble material was soluble in organic solvents and could be extracted from tissues and fluids with alcohol. It was not isolated in pure condition but was characterized by the fact that the action of acid or mercuric chloride liberated another substance termed "plasmal", which appeared to be an aldehyde or a mixture of aldehydes.

Feulgen, Imhäuser and Behrens (1929), working with horse muscle, observed that plasmalogen always accompanied phosphatides and that its solubility and other properties were so similar to those of the phospha-tides that purification was virtually impossible by means of the tech-niques available to them. They investigated plasmal in some detail and found that its hydrolysis from plasmalogen could be effected in 3 hours by 0.1N hydrochloric acid. Mercuric chloride, on the other hand, brought about instantaneous cleavage. The plasmal could be isolated, after cleav-age, either by steam distillation or by saponifying the phosphatides, and extracting the acidified material with ether. The ether solution contained both plasmal and fatty acids, and the latter were removed by alkaline extraction. Thus from 10 kilograms of horse meat they isolated about 2 grams of plasmal, and this formed a thiosemicarbazone. Their substance appeared to be a mixture of palmitic and stearic aldehydes, although they felt that other aldehydes might well be present. Later, Feulgen and Behrens (1938) reported that the plasmal from horse meat consisted of 90 per cent palmitic aldehyde and 10 per cent stearic aldehyde, whereas brain plasmal was much more complex.

Structure Proof

The structure of plasmalogen as a phosphatide containing an aldehyde in acetal linkage was finally elucidated by Feulgen and Bersin (1939), largely from the results of hydrolysis experiments. When beef muscle phosphatides were hydrolyzed with alkali a fraction was obtained which formed an insoluble precipitate with brucine acetate and which yielded aldehydes on treatment with acid. This material could be more com-pletely fractionated since part of it was soluble in acetone and part was not. Furthermore, it was noted that the acetone-soluble portion increased with the time of alkaline hydrolysis. It appeared then that the acetone-insoluble material was plasmalogen, whereas the acetone-soluble substance was a product resulting from plasmalogen on alkaline hydrolysis. The latter material, which was acidic, was named "plasmalogenic acid", and on vigorous acidic hydrolysis it yielded glycerol, phosphoric acid and plasmal or aldehydes. No nitrogenous constituent was present. Thus it was logical to assume that plasmalogenic acid was an acetal of α- or β-glycerophosphoric acid, the α-form of which may be demonstrated by (XIII). The relationship between (XIII) and the phosphatidic acids is obvious.

$$
\begin{array}{l}
CH_2O \\
\qquad\diagdown \\
\qquad\qquad CHR \\
\qquad\diagup \\
CHO \\
\qquad\qquad OH \quad (XIII) \\
\qquad\diagup \\
CH_2OP \\
\qquad\parallel\diagdown \\
\qquad O \quad OH
\end{array}
$$

It remained then to discover the relationship between (XIII) and plasmalogen. By analogy with the phosphatides it could be assumed that plasmalogen is a choline, aminoethyl alcohol or serine ester of (XIII). Examination of the fraction described above which was acetone-insoluble and which was believed to be plasmalogen indicated that acid hydrolysis produced aldehydes and the aminoethyl alcohol ester of glycerophosphoric acid. On this basis Feulgen and Bersin (1939) postulated the structure of plasmalogen as an acetal phosphatide whose α-form is shown by (XIV).

$$
\begin{array}{l}
CH_2O \\
\qquad\diagdown \\
\qquad\qquad CHR \\
\qquad\diagup \\
CHO \\
\qquad\qquad OH \qquad (XIV) \\
\qquad\diagup \\
CH_2OP \\
\qquad\parallel\diagdown \\
\qquad O \quad OC_2H_4NH_2
\end{array}
$$

Feulgen and Bersin (1939) isolated what they believed to be a relatively pure sample of plasmalogen. The isolation is very difficult because of the obvious similarity of properties between the acetal phosphatides and the glycerophosphatides.

Klenk and Schumann (1944) have likewise isolated acetal phosphatides. In their method, ether-soluble brain phosphatides are dissolved in benzene and treated with alcoholic sodium ethoxide. The glycerophosphatides are hydrolyzed, and treatment of the mixture with acetone precipitates a mixture of the sodium salts of the fatty acids and the acetal phosphatides. The former are soluble in methanol whereas the latter are not, which allows the acetal phosphatides to be isolated as pure compounds.

These workers hydrolyzed the acetal phosphatides with methanolic sulfuric acid, and isolated the aldehydes as the dimethyl acetals. The aldehyde fraction was a mixture with an iodine number of 77.3. By conversion to the oximes, stearic aldehyde was identified as well as a small quantity of plamitic aldehyde. Klenk (1945) also oxidized to acids the aldehydes obtained from the acetal phosphatide of brain. He was able to isolate acids corresponding to palmitic, stearic and probably oleylaldehyde.

Sources of Acetal Phosphatides

So far, the presence of acetal phosphatides has never been demonstrated in plant sources. They are identified by staining reactions based on the aldehyde present (see p. 183) and have been shown to be widely distributed in animal tissue. They are most abundant in muscle and brain (Feulgen and Bersin, 1939) and occur to a lesser extent in egg. Pischinger (1941) found acetal phosphatides in practically all the organs of the white mouse except the liver.

HYDROPHOSPHATIDES

Introduction

The hydrophosphatides are produced by the catalytic reduction of glycerophosphatides (see p. 60) or by total synthesis (see p. 116). The first indication of their natural occurrence can probably be attributed to Merz (1931), who isolated an ether-insoluble material from brain phosphatides which on hydrolysis yielded glycerophosphoric acid, choline and a predominance of palmitic acid. His preparation, however, also contained some oleic acid and thus was not pure hydrolecithin. Hydrophosphatides were isolated from natural sources including the tapeworm, *Cysticercus fasciolaris* (Lesuk and Anderson, 1941), and the sphingomyelin fraction of lung, spleen and brain (Thannhauser, Benotti and Boncoddo, 1946; Thannhauser and Boncoddo, 1948). Actually, only lecithin with completely saturated fatty acids has so far been found in natural sources. The material is treated here as a distinct compound since its solubility relationships set it apart from the other glycerophosphatides. Because of its insolubility in ether, special isolation procedures are required, although structurally hydrolecithin differs from ordinary lecithin only in that the fatty acids are completely saturated.

Structure Proof

The product isolated by Lesuk and Anderson (1941) was found in the ether-insoluble lipides of *Cysticercus* larvae. It was separated from the cerebroside fraction by fractional crystallization from pyridine in which the cerebrosides exhibited greater solubility. It was purified by various crystallization techniques, and its structure as dipalmityllecithin was indicated since acidic hydrolysis yielded palmitic acid, glycerophosphoric acid and choline.

The same substance has been isolated more recently from lung by Thannhauser, Benotti and Boncoddo (1946) and from brain and spleen by Thannhauser and Boncoddo (1948). It was found in both instances in the ether-insoluble or so-called "sphingomyelin fraction", and comprised up to 40 per cent of this material. Its presence was detected when a liver enzyme which does not hydrolyze amide linkages was shown to produce palmitic acid from the sphingomyelin fraction. Further investigation indicated the presence of glycerol. The pure phosphatide was isolated by repeated fractional extractions and was identified by its elementary analyses and its hydrolysis products.

It is of interest that palmitic acid is the only saturated acid so far found in the hydrophosphatides and that no saturated components of the cephalin fraction have been discovered in natural sources, although sphingomyelin containing dihydrosphingosine has been observed (see p. 42).

ALLEGED PHOSPHATIDES

The older literature contains many references to a variety of phosphatidic materials of indefinite structure. For the most part, these were impure mixtures or partially oxidized or decomposed phosphatides rather than distinct entities. Thus protagon and carnaubon were shown to be a mixture of cerebrosides and sphingomyelin (Rosenheim and Tebb, 1909, 1910, 1910a; Rosenheim and MacLean, 1915), and cuorin was shown to be an impure cephalin fraction by Levene and Komatsu (1919) and MacLean and Griffiths (1920). Jecorin was identified as a mixture of carbohydrate and lecithin by Meinertz (1905), who was able to remove the sugar by dialysis. Fränkel and Bolaffio (1908), Fränkel and Linnert (1910) and Fränkel and Kafka (1920) reported several new phosphatides which in the light of present knowledge appear to be impure lecithins (Thierfelder and Klenk, 1925). A so-called "acetone-soluble" phosphatide was shown by MacLean (1914) to be a mixture of lecithin and nitrogenous impurities.

Various alleged diaminophosphatides reported in the literature (Hammarsten, 1909; Beumer, 1914; Tamura, 1913) were probably impure sphingomyelin or mixtures of glycerophosphatides with nitrogenous impurities. All these materials are mentioned only in passing, since they are discussed in some detail by MacLean and MacLean (1927, pp. 55, 64, 124–152) and by Thierfelder and Klenk (1930, pp. 134, 157–161).

Water-soluble phosphatides, primarily from vegetable sources, which may be purified by dialysis have been reported by Hansteen-Cranner (1926), Grafe (1925, 1927), Grafe and Horvat (1925), Grafe and Magistris (1925), Magistris and Schäfer (1929), Gutstein (1929), Eisler and Gulaesy (1930) and Bleyer and Diemair (1931). The identity of these materials has not yet been established.

Phosphatides in which betaine (XV), a close relative of choline, com-

$$
\begin{array}{c}
\text{CH}_3 \\
| \quad \diagup \text{CH}_3 \\
\text{N---CH}_3 \quad \text{(XV)} \\
| \diagdown \\
\text{O} \\
\text{CH}_2\text{CO}
\end{array}
$$

prises the basic constituent have been reported to occur in oats (Schulze and Pfenninger, 1911) and in wheat bran (Nottbohm and Mayer, 1935). Here again, confirming experiments are in order.

LYSOPHOSPHATIDES

These compounds are discussed in detail on p. 99 because of their close relationship to the enzymes which effect their formation.

CHAPTER VI

THE PURIFICATION AND THE CHEMICAL PROPERTIES OF THE PHOSPHATIDES

INTRODUCTION

The preparation of pure phosphatides is not a simple matter. In the first place, the amazing instability of phosphatides which contain unsaturated fatty acids must be reckoned with, and every precaution must be taken to prevent the oxidation which sets in almost as soon as a sample of pure glycerophosphatide is exposed to air. In the second place, the danger of contamination by galactolipides, proteins, carbohydrates, decomposition products and other lipides is great, despite many repeated crystallizations and precipitations. However, newer countercurrent solvent extraction techniques now employed in some laboratories may reduce the danger of contamination considerably.

Plant or animal tissue to be used for extraction should be fresh, and should not previously have been subjected to high temperatures or other processes which might cause decomposition. Dehydration, if desired, must be brought about by gentle methods such as treatment with acetone. All operations must be carried out at temperatures which are as low as possible, and caution must be taken to preserve inert atmospheres of carbon dioxide or nitrogen by rigid exclusion of air. Even light should be excluded, and it is advisable to saturate solvents with inert gas. There is no general isolation method for all tissues, as references to Parts II, III and IV will indicate; in every instance the procedure must be fitted to the properties of the tissue at hand.

The various methods which have been used for the extraction of phosphatides will be discussed in Part II, and are included here only where elaboration appears necessary. The preferred solvents for extraction, once the tissue has been dried with acetone, are methyl or ethyl alcohol in combination with ether or petroleum ether. It has long been known that alcohol facilitates the extraction, since it exerts a dissociating effect on the protein-lipide and carbohydrate-lipide complexes.

A more recent method for phosphatide extraction is that advanced by Thornton and Kraybill (1942), in which vegetable oils are subjected to the surface of a solid adsorbent such as aluminum silicate. The ad-

56

sorbed phosphatides may then be recovered in an unaltered condition by extraction of the silicate with organic solvents. In their procedure acetone, ether, absolute ethanol, and 50 per cent ethanol were used successively, and each solvent removed some of the phosphatides. Analysis of layers of the column indicated that the composition of the adsorbed material was constant throughout. This procedure, when applied to oils, obviously serves to refine the oil as well as to separate the phosphatides from it.

The purification of the phosphatides depends in general on their solubility characteristics. They are separated from other lipides, especially sterols and triglycerides, by their insolubility in acetone, and this same characteristic allows them to be separated from water-soluble impurities, since the phosphatides may be precipitated from aqueous suspensions by acetone. They may be separated from other organic impurities by virtue of the fact that they form metallic complexes with salts such as cadmium chloride. The cephalin fraction was separated in classical methods from lecithin because, unlike the latter, it appeared to be insoluble in warm alcohol. Sphingomyelin, in turn, is separated because it is insoluble in ether. But it must be borne in mind at all times that these separations by solvents are not clear-cut. In the presence of impurities a "synergistic solvent effect" may be exerted, as exemplified by the solubility of phosphatides in acetone in the presence of other lipides. Similarly, pure phosphatidylaminoethyl alcohol is freely alcohol-soluble, although in the presence of the inositol-containing phosphatides which comprise a large portion of the cephalin fraction of brain or soybeans, it is apparently partially insolubilized.

The following pages will discuss the methods which are available at present for purifying the various phosphatides, and the properties of these compounds.

THE PURIFICATION AND PROPERTIES OF LECITHIN

Purification

Chemically pure lecithin must possess a nitrogen:phosphorus ratio of 1:1. Nitrogen in the amino form must be lacking; and on saponification theoretical quantities of choline, fatty acids and glycerophosphoric acid should result. Furthermore, these are the only hydrolysis products which should be present. The isoelectric point of the product should be close to neutrality (see p. 14).

A great step forward in the purification of lecithin was made by Mac-Lean (1909a), who showed that an alcoholic solution of crude phosphatides could be treated with cadmium chloride to obtain a precipitate rich in lecithin. The cephalin phosphatides remained in the filtrate. The separation was by no means complete; but a further observation that ether dissolved certain impurities from the lecithin-cadmium chloride complex served to provide relatively pure material. Thus the first pure sample of lecithin was probably prepared by MacLean (1914a, 1915).

This procedure, which depends on the use of cadmium chloride to form a lecithin complex which is more readily separated from the other phosphatides than lecithin itself, was refined by Levene and Rolf (1921, 1927). Their published procedures for the extraction and purification of lecithin from egg, liver and brain have been widely used. Since the original references are readily accessible, the procedures will not be detailed here. Refinements in the purification of the isolated lecithin (Maltaner, 1930) and of the cadmium chloride complex (Pangborn, 1941, 1951) subsequently simplified the preparation. An example of the use of these procedures to obtain pure lecithin from commercial soybean phosphatides may be found in the work of Thornton, Johnson and Ewan (1944).

The purification of lecithin by fractional crystallization is feasible and has been described by Escher (1925) and more recently by Sinclair (1949).

The Properties of Lecithin

Pure lecithin is a white plastic or paraffin-like material which is extremely hygroscopic, forming a soft, sticky mass on exposure to moisture. When entirely dry, lecithin becomes brittle and can be ground into a powder. When the fatty acids of lecithin are unsaturated, the substance displays much greater instability than do the triglycerides of these fatty acids. Thus on exposure to air the material turns brown and becomes disagreeable in odor and taste.

Lecithin has no definite melting point, although it has been reported to soften below 100° C., the softening point depending on the composition of the fatty acids. The melting point, however, is well above 200° C. On continued heating it decomposes.

Lecithin dissolves readily in fat solvents such as methanol, ethanol, benzene and other aromatic hydrocarbons, ether, chloroform, carbon tetrachloride, carbon disulfide, petroleum ether and similar aliphatic hydrocarbons. It is also soluble in pyridine, glycerol, acetic acid and in fact in many organic solvents. It is, however, insoluble in acetone and methyl acetate, although it does dissolve in higher molecular weight ketones and esters. Lecithin containing completely saturated fatty acids is ether-insoluble.

The solubility of an egg lecithin preparation containing 3.94 per cent phosphorus and 2.06 per cent nitrogen in various concentrations of ethanol has been determined by Vita and Bracaloni (1934). At 15° C. the lecithin is completely soluble in 92 volume per cent ethanol.

With water a cloudy colloidal solution is formed from which the phosphatide may be precipitated by acetone, acids or inorganic salts, especially those containing divalent cations.

Natural lecithin is optically active as would be expected if part of the glycerophosphoric acid were present in the α-form (see p. 16).

The Chemical Reactions of Lecithin

Hydrolysis. The chemical hydrolysis of lecithin with acid or base has already been discussed (see p. 15). In summary it may be said that the hydrolysis to yield fatty ·acids, choline and glycerophosphoric acid proceeds more readily than the hydrolysis of glycerides. Thus Paal (1929) observed that an alcoholic solution of lecithin demonstrated signs of hydrolysis on warming to 60 to 70° C. or on exposure to air for a short time, although this would not appear to be the case from the work of Page and Schmidt (1931) and Sato and Wada (1934). The hydrolysis is naturally a function of time, temperature and the concentration of the hydrolytic agent.

Numerous examples may be cited of the use of alkali and acid for the hydrolysis of phosphatides. Barium hydroxide solution has been used extensively (Willstätter and Lüdecke, 1904; MacLean, 1908a; Levene and Rolf, 1919) both on lecithin and its cadmium chloride complex for times varying from 2 to 24 hours at temperatures varying from 20° C. to 100° C. Stronger alkali such as alcoholic potassium hydroxide may also be used (Paal, 1929, Hatakeyama, 1930). Aqueous or alcoholic acid is equally as effective as indicated by Pangborn and Anderson (1931), who used 5 per cent sulfuric acid for 8 hours. Levene and Simms (1921) employed 10 per cent hydrochloric acid for 8–15 hours and Grün and Limpächer (1926a) employed alcoholic hydrogen chloride. When this acid is employed, choline may be isolated as the chloride salt.

The hydrolysis of the glycerophosphoric acid is considerably more difficult, and this has been discussed elsewhere (see p. 18).

A study of the hydrolysis of lecithin at various pH's was reported by Virtanen and Tammelander (1927). They found that the choline seems to split off first under alkaline conditions. The hydrolysis was at a minimum at pH 5.0 to 5.2, and the lecithin molecule appeared as stable in alkali as in acid.

A special type of hydrolysis is represented by the alcoholysis of lecithin wherein the phosphatide is reacted with an alcohol in the presence of an appropriate catalyst. The fatty acids are obtained as esters of the alcohol used, rather than as esters of glycerol. Thus, Rollett (1909) alcoholyzed egg lecithin and Shinowara and Brown (1938) reported the direct alcoholysis of suprarenal phosphatides. They employed methyl, ethyl, propyl, butyl and *n*-amyl alcohols, and obtained the acids as the corresponding esters. These workers found that as much as 5 per cent hydrochloric acid or 7.5 to 12.0 per cent sulfuric acid was necessary as a catalyst, since the choline apparently combined with the acid and lowered its concentration. A large excess of the alcohol was necessary, and refluxing was continued for 36 hours.

Hydrogenation of Lecithin. Phosphatides with fully saturated acids have been found in nature (see p. 53) and have been prepared by total synthesis (see p. 116). They also result from the catalytic reduction of ordinary lecithin. Ordinarily an alcoholic solution of the phosphatide is used and the hydrogenation is allowed to proceed at a low temperature in the presence of a palladium or platinum catalyst. There results a stable, white crystalline, nonhygroscopic compound which is insoluble in methyl and ethyl acetate, ether, acetone and cold alcohol, and in general is less soluble than ordinary lecithin.

The first hydrogenation of phosphatides was carried out by Paal and Oehme (1913) and by Riedel (1911). The former investigators reduced commercial egg lecithin by saturating a 90 per cent aqueous alcohol solution with hydrogen in the presence of colloidal palladium at room temperature. Their product, which probably was not free of cephalins, sintered at 83 to 84° C. and decomposed at 150° C. On hydrolysis it yielded chiefly stearic acid with some palmitic and myristic acids. Ritter (1914) reduced egg lecithin to obtain a product which yielded only stearic acid on hydrolysis. Levene and West (1918a) reduced egg lecithin which contained 10 to 20 per cent cephalin using an alcohol solution containing a small concentration of acetic acid. Their product had a specific rotation of +5.4° and also appeared to contain only stearic acid. Levene and Rolf (1921a, 1926a) reduced brain lecithin and soybean lecithin, and the latter material was also hydrogenated by Shinozaki and Sato (1933). The hydrolecithin from soybeans yielded palmitic and stearic acids on hydrolysis.

The first application of high pressure reduction to lecithin was made by Shinozaki and Sato (1934), who used a nickel catalyst and pressures above 80 atmospheres. Their product possessed only 0.1 per cent amino nitrogen and melted at 84° C. Fujimura (1937) used platinum black as a catalyst at 60 to 70° C. in a 2 per cent alcoholic solution of lecithin. The hydrolecithin precipitated on cooling and was removed by filtration, and the filtrate was hydrogenated further to insure complete reduction. This product, after crystallization from methyl ethyl ketone, turned brown at 100° C., sintered at 200° C. and became liquid at 235° C. It demonstrated a specific rotation of +5.3°.

Halogenation of Lecithin. When lecithin contains unsaturated fatty acids it adds halogens readily, for which reason the iodine number of phosphatides is an analytically reproducible constant (see p. 182). Early investigators attached a therapeutic significance to halogenated phosphatides, and there is an early patent which describes halogenated lecithin for pharmaceutical use (Bergell, 1918). Levene and Rolf (1925, 1926) brominated lecithin from soybeans, egg yolk and liver in order to study the composition of the brominated acids obtained on hydrolysis. Their brominations were carried out in petroleum ether; and since the solubilities of the various brominated lecithins varied, depending on their bromine content, it was possible to obtain some fractionation of the lecithins. On hydrolysis of the brominated soybean lecithin, tetra- and hexabromostearic acids were obtained. Egg lecithin yielded palmitic, stearic and tetrabromostearic acids, and from liver lecithin there were obtained octabromoarachidonic, hexabromostearic, stearic and palmitic acids.

The hydrohalogenation of phosphatides was reported by Richter (1908, 1908a), who added hydrogen bromide and hydrogen iodide to lecithin in carbon tetrachloride solution.

Miscellaneous Reactions. The sulfonation of lecithin has been reported in several patents (see p. 501), although it is difficult to understand how the intact phosphatide can be preserved under conditions usually required for sulfonation. Other reactions to which lecithin has been subjected, primarily for the preparation of materials of possible commercial interest, are described elsewhere (see p. 503).

THE PURIFICATION AND PROPERTIES OF THE CEPHALIN PHOSPHATIDES

Purification

The identity of the cephalin fraction has already been discussed in some detail (see p. 25) and need not be repeated here. As indicated previously, early workers assumed that cephalin was a diacylglycerylphosphorylaminoethyl alcohol. Accordingly, the standards of purity for this compound would require that the nitrogen-phosphorus ratio be 1:1 and that all of the nitrogen be amino nitrogen. Saponification should yield theoretical quantities of aminoethyl alcohol, fatty acids and glycerophosphoric acid. The difficulties encountered in the preparation of such a compound have already been discussed in the light of more modern knowledge.

The first step in the isolation of the cephalin fraction involved its separation from lecithin on the basis of its supposed alcohol insolubility. Thereafter (Renall, 1913), various purification techniques were employed. Levene and Rolf (1927a) published a widely used procedure for obtaining the cephalin fraction from brain. In their method the brain phosphatides were extracted with alcohol, and the insoluble residue—that is, the cephalin fraction—was extracted with ether in which the sphingolipides are insoluble. Modifications of this procedure were suggested by Maltaner (1931) and by Gray (1940). These methods, however, resulted in the isolation of impure mixtures.

As indicated previously (see p. 27), the first pure sample of phosphatidylaminoethyl alcohol was prepared by Rudy and Page (1930), who isolated it from the alcohol-soluble portion of brain phosphatides by numerous successive extractions with ether.

The separation of the cephalin fraction into phosphatidylaminoethyl alcohol, phosphatidylserine and inositol-containing phosphatides and the purification of these substances has been achieved by Folch (1942a, 1949, 1949a, see p. 32). The separation was based on the observation that the three materials have different solubilities in alcohol-chloroform solutions. Thus, by adding alcohol to a chloroform solution of the cephalin fraction from brain, the various fractions were precipitated and subsequently purified. The inositol phosphatides are the most insoluble and precipitate first. This fraction was purified by adding methanol at 4° C. to a chloroform solution of it. The resulting precipitate was dissolved in chloroform and again precipitated; and the precipitation procedure was continued until the supernatant liquid was no longer found to contain material with less than 4.5 per cent phosphorus. The final precipitate is crude diphosphoinositide and is contaminated largely by inorganic phosphates. It may be purified by dialysis against distilled water in the cold for 4 days. The undialyzable material is finally lyophilized. The diphosphoinositide obtained in this way is a white, stable powder.

Phosphatidylserine (Folch, 1948) is the second component to precipitate, on addition of alcohol, to a chloroform solution, whereas phosphatidylaminoethyl alcohol is the most alcohol-soluble and does not precipitate.

The phosphatidylaminoethyl alcohol obtained was a sticky white powder which turned progressively darker even when stored *in vacuo* in the absence of light. It was ash free, and contained 1.7 per cent water. The discoloration did not seem to affect its elementary composition.

Phosphatidylserine is a free-flowing white powder with a tendency to darken. However, if the product is lyophilized it keeps fairly well if stored in the dark under vacuum. Continued storage for long periods of time, according to Folch (1948), does not change the elementary composition but apparently causes some sort of rearrangement, as demonstrated by a decrease in amino nitrogen determined by the ninhydrin method. This does not occur at dry ice temperatures.

Like its aminoethyl alcohol counterpart, the serine compound seems to contain a definite small percentage of water. The material is freely soluble in chloroform, ethyl ether and petroleum ether and is insoluble in ethyl or methyl alcohol and in acetone. The metallic ion which it contains in its natural form may be removed to obtain a compound with a free carboxyl group.

The Properties and the Chemical Reactions of the Cephalin Phosphatides

The properties of the cephalin glycerophosphatides such as hygroscopicity and instability are very similar to those described for lecithin (see p. 58). The inositol-containing phosphatides appear to be somewhat more stable. They are insoluble in dry petroleum ether, dry acetic acid, dry benzene, dry ether and dry chloroform but are soluble in all these except acetic acid in the presence of a small amount of moisture. They are insoluble in acetone and dioxane.

In discussing the chemical reactions of the cephalin phosphatides, reference can be made only to phosphatidylaminoethyl alcohol and its serine analogue, since the structure of the inositol phosphatide is still in doubt. The reactions of these compounds appear to differ from those of lecithin only when the base is involved. Thus, hydrolysis and halogenation of the cephalin phosphatides may be similarly carried out (see p. 61). Likewise, hydrogenation of the cephalin fraction has been reported, although the reaction was found to proceed with difficulty, due probably to the presence of impurities.

Hydrogenation of the Cephalins. The cephalin fraction from egg yolk has been hydrogenated by Levene and West (1918), who purified it by precipitating it with ether from chloroform solution and crystallizing it four times from a mixture of equal parts of chloroform and ethyl acetate and finally from chloroform and ethanol (1:2). In the product so obtained, 93 to 97 per cent of the nitrogen was amino nitrogen, and the compound analyzed properly for the aminoethyl alcohol ester of distearylglycerophosphoric acid.

Salisbury and Anderson (1936) found it necessary to shake an ether solution of cephalin fraction from yeast with platinum oxide under 25 pounds of hydrogen for 96 hours in order to obtain a saturated product. Their material was obtained as a white amorphous solid by precipitation with acetone from moist chloroform.

Gray (1940) reduced brain cephalin fraction by dissolving it (3 grams) in an equal mixture (100 ml.) of cyclohexane and acetic acid and shaking for 7.5 hours with platinum oxide (0.2 gram) in the presence of hydrogen. His product was white and nonhygroscopic and generally less soluble than the unreduced compound. It melted at 156 to 162° C. and was shown to be amorphous by x-ray diffraction.

Reactions of the Amino Nitrogen Atom. Levene and West (1916b) were able to react a cephalin fraction from brain with phenyl- and naphthyl isocyanates in order to obtain what appeared to be the phenyl- and naphthylureido derivatives of phosphatidylaminoethyl alcohol. The products analyzed properly and were hygroscopic, light-colored solids. These same workers, however, could not prepare corresponding acyl derivatives.

Witanowski (1928) has provided indirect evidence that formaldehyde may be used to methylate the aminoethyl alcohol of "cephalin", thus converting the material to lecithin. Similarly, Julian, Meyer and Iveson (1945) have used diazomethane in dry ether or a mixture of formic acid and formaldehyde to methylate the amino groups in a cephalin fraction.

THE PURIFICATION AND PROPERTIES OF SPHINGOMYELIN

Purification

The procedure of Carter and co-workers (1947) is undoubtedly a prefered one for the preparation of the sphingolipides. However, since these workers were not interested in preparing pure sphingomyelin itself, purification procedures must be sought in the work of other investigators. Pure sphingomyelin should show a nitrogen-phosphorus ratio of 2:1 and be free of amino nitrogen and carbohydrates.

Although organs such as normal brain, nerve tissue and spleen are the usual sources of sphingomyelin, the fact must not be overlooked that pathological conditions such as Niemann-Pick's disease are characterized by the accumulation of abnormally large quantities of sphingomyelin in the spleen, liver and brain (Klenk, 1934, 1935).

With sphingomyelin, as with other phosphatides, Levene (1914, 1916) was a pioneer in purification procedures. His method involved the isolation of the ether-insoluble portion of brain phosphatides and the purification thereof by various precipitations and crystallizations.

Merz (1930) purified sphingomyelin through its cadmium chloride salt, whereas Tropp and Eckardt (1936) used alumina to absorb impurities from a petroleum ether-alcohol solution of sphingomyelin. These two techniques were combined by Klenk and Rennkamp (1940) who, in addition, made removal of contaminating glycerophosphatides easier by subjecting them to ester interchange in the presence of a trace of sodium ethoxide. In this way, very pure sphingomyelin was obtained.

Thannhauser and Setz (1936) purified sphingomyelin by precipitating it as the reineckate. They originally sought to prove the existence of a "polydiaminophosphatide". It is now well established that such a compound does not exist, although their work with sphingomyelin reineckate is still of interest.

The purification procedure of Thannhauser and Boncoddo (1948a) depends on the observation that sphingomyelin is more stable in the presence of alkali than are the glycerophosphatides. Accordingly, they hydrolyze the glycerophosphatide impurities with $0.25N$ sodium hydroxide at $37°$ C. for 4 to 5 days. The ether-insoluble material is then further purified to obtain pure sphingomyelin.

The Properties of Sphingomyelin

As the methods for its isolation indicate, sphingomyelin is considerably more stable than the glycerophosphatides, undergoing no change on exposure to air or light. It crystallizes readily, even when not entirely pure; and it does not appear to be hygroscopic. In all these respects it resembles the galactolipides more than it does the phosphatides. In the presence of water it hydrates and emulsifies to form a permanent opalescent suspension which yields a precipitate on treatment with acetone. It melts unsharply above $200°$ C. The solubility of sphingomyelin, as well as some of its other characteristics, have already been recorded (see p. 46).

The chemical reactions of sphingomyelin have been investigated very little. Merz (1930) reported the hydrogenation of sphingomyelin in alcohol over palladium chloride in the presence of a trace of gum arabic and a drop of hydrochloric acid. The reaction was complete in 20 minutes; and the reduced product, precipitated from the alcohol solution by acetone, was crystallized from a mixture of pyridine and alcohol. Merz (1930) acetylated this hydrogenated product by the use of acetic anhydride in the presence of pyridine and chloroform. The hydrolysis of sphingomyelin has been discussed previously (see p. 46).

THE PURIFICATION AND PROPERTIES OF PHOSPHATIDIC ACID

The phosphatidic acids have been shown by Hanahan and Chaikoff (1947a, 1948) to result from the enzymatic cleavage of the base from the glycerophosphatides. They may be isolated from cabbage leaves as originally outlined by Chibnall and Channon (1927) and Channon and Chibnall (1927).

The isolation procedure is a rather complicated one, and in the first step the washed vegetable cytoplasm is extracted for a long period of time with ether. When the material extracted with ether was extracted

with hot acetone, a residue remained which was chiefly calcium phosphatidate. This material could be purified by conversion to a free acid and
precipitation as a lead salt.

The pure free acid is a brownish, sticky mass at room temperature.
It is unstable in air and light and clings tenaciously to traces of solvents.
It is not hygroscopic and is only very slightly soluble in water, but dissolves easily in organic solvents such as acetone and ether. The alcohol
and acetone solutions can be diluted with water without the formation of
an emulsion.

The sodium salt of phosphatidic acid is soluble in water, slightly soluble
in cold alcohol, and insoluble in ether. The barium, calcium and lead
salts are plastic-like substances which are insoluble in water and soluble
in ether from which they can be precipitated by alcohol or acetone. The
salts, like the free acid, are unstable.

Hanahan and Chaikoff (1947) isolated phosphatidic acids from carrots by the following procedure. The fresh carrots were ground and placed
in a round bottom flask with sufficient ether to provide 3 ml. per gram of
carrot. The flask was cooled to below −25° C. by immersion in an alco-
hol-dry ice bath, whereupon the flask with its frozen contents was maintained at 5° C. for 6 hours. During this period melting occurred and the
cell membranes of the carrots were ruptured. The supernatant ether was
decanted and the freezing and thawing process was repeated with more
ether. The combined ether extracts were concentrated and the residue
extracted with petroleum ether several times. The resulting solution was
concentrated and treated with two to three volumes of acetone and several drops of a solution of magnesium chloride in absolute alcohol. The
resulting precipitate was washed repeatedly with acetone and then dissolved in ethyl ether in order that the precipitation procedure might be
repeated.

The Purification and Properties of the Acetal Phosphatides

The simplest procedure for the preparation of acetal phosphatides has
been provided by Klenk and Schumann (1944), who took advantage of
the fact that the acetal linkage is stable in alkaline solution, whereas the
fatty acid ester linkages of the glycerophosphatides are hydrolyzed by
base. Thus, a mixture of phosphatides obtained from human brain by
ether extraction was used as the starting material. This mixture consisted of lecithin, the cephalin fraction, and acetal phosphatides. The
properties of the latter were so similar to those of lecithin that separation had heretofore been achieved only with great difficulty.

When a benzene solution of this mixture was treated with sodium
ethoxide, the glycerophosphatides were hydrolyzed. A mixture of acetal

phosphatides and sodium salts of fatty acids remained, and this mixture could be separated since the sodium salts are soluble in methanol, whereas the acetal phosphatides are not. The product was a solid, white or brown-ish-white substance which was readily pulverizable and which could be dissolved in water to yield a clear solution which gave an alkaline reaction.

Recently Thannhauser, Boncoddo and Schmidt (1951) have described a rather complex procedure for the isolation of crystallized acetal phospha-tides from beef brain. Salient features of the purification process involve removal of the glycerophosphatides by saponification in aqueous emulsion with normal alkali at 37° C. The acetal phosphatides are said to remain intact under these conditions. Another feature of the process is the use of ion exchangers to remove associated cations. The crystalline product decomposed at 205° C., and by controlled hydrolysis it was possible to isolate glycerylphosphorylaminoethyl alcohol. This was shown to have the α configuration, and the corresponding aldehyde was completely saturated. Palmitic aldehyde was present to a larger extent than stearic aldehyde.

The acetal linkage, characteristically stable in alkali, is readily broken by mercuric chloride or by acids, and the resulting aldehyde may be characterized by several reactions typical of this group (see p. 51). The hydrolysis of the acetal phosphatides has already been discussed (see p. 51).

THE PURIFICATION AND PROPERTIES OF THE HYDROPHOSPHATIDES

Naturally occurring hydrophosphatides have escaped detection in most investigations because their ether insolubility made them part of the sphingomyelin fraction. Thannhauser and Boncoddo (1948), however, have recently published a procedure for obtaining hydrolecithin from ether-insoluble beef brain phosphatides. This procedure depends on a differential solubility in acetic acid which exists between sphingomyelin and the hydrophosphatides. The product was a stable, white crystalline powder which was soluble in alcohol and glacial acetic acid, very slightly soluble in acetone, and insoluble in ether. It melted at 238 to 240° C. and demonstrated a specific rotation of +6.25°, the measurement having been made on a 4 per cent solution in a mixture of chloroform-methanol (1:1).

THE PURIFICATION AND PROPERTIES OF THE LYSOPHOSPHATIDES

This subject is discussed on p. 101, where the lysophosphatides are de-scribed in detail. They have been segregated from the other phosphatides because of their close relationship to the enzymes which cause their formation.

CHAPTER VII

THE PHYSICAL CHEMISTRY OF THE PHOSPHATIDES

INTRODUCTION

The physical chemistry of the phosphatides embraces a field of precise measurements which obviously should be made on pure compounds. The difficulties involved in obtaining pure phosphatides are legion, for which reason work of a physicochemical nature has been greatly inhibited. Many of the recorded investigations have been carried out with impure samples; and, although some of this work applies to pure phosphatides, all that can be said for much of it is that the results are characteristic of mixtures consisting of phosphatides and the substances which tend to accompany them.

The glycerophosphatides are strongly hydrophilic colloids, exhibiting characteristic isoelectric points and forming sols with water. Löwe (1922) showed that colloidal solutions may be formed by lecithin and organic solvents. Sphingomyelin swells in water to yield a stiff gel and thus displays a certain amount of hydrophobic character. In this regard the phosphatides differ from the simple glycerides which are not wet by water. The hydrophilic nature of the phosphatides is manifested by their ability to form emulsions; and once the cloudy colloidal solutions have formed, the phosphatides may be precipitated or coagulated by a variety of substances.

The phosphatides form stable combinations with diverse substances such as proteins, carbohydrates and salts; and they exist in tissue, at least in part, as complexes.

It is undoubtedly the colloidal phenomena in which phosphatides participate that relate them so closely to life processes, and it is for this reason that physicochemical investigations are of utmost importance. It is hoped that the volume and the quality of such work will increase as procedures are provided for obtaining pure materials of known chemical constitution.

Certain aspects of the physical chemistry of the phosphatides—acid-base relationships, isoelectric point, titration and dielectric constant—have already been discussed (see pp. 12, 32), since they relate to structure. The remainder of the material will be discussed below.

The Interaction of Lecithin with Water

Monomolecular Films

The ability of lecithin to form a monomolecular film on the surface of water was observed by Leathes (1923, 1925). If a benzene solution of lecithin is dropped on water, the solution spreads on the surface of the water. The benzene quickly evaporates, leaving a thin, continuous, mono-molecular film which depends for its formation on the tendencies of the hydrophilic portion of the molecule to dissolve in the water and the hydrophobic portion to remain aloof from the water. This is simply another example of the orientation of polar molecules at an interface. Desnuelle and Molines (1948) believe that similar orientation takes place at a glyceride-air interface, probably because the polar groups are repelled by the nonpolar solvent.

In these films the lecithin occupies much more area than would be expected from its constituent fatty acids alone, for the other portions of the molecule separate the fatty acid chains and prevent close packing. Thus, Leathes observed that the area occupied by a fatty acid either as an ethyl ester or as a triglyceride was about 21 sq. Å in the condensed film and about 42 sq. Å in the expanded film, the exact values depending on the temperature. This is in good agreement with Adam (1922) and Adam, Berry and Turner (1928). The corresponding value for each fatty acid chain in a purified sample of lecithin was 56.6 sq.Å for the expanded film at 15° C., and this value decreased by only 4 units at 4.5° C. Nor was film condensation observed at low temperatures and high pressures. Accordingly, it appeared that the polar portions of the molecule occupied a much greater space than two carboxyl groups of fatty acids and served to prevent close packing.

Pure hydrolecithin, on the other hand, occupied approximately one-half of the area required by unreduced lecithin, although this area was still greater than that of the simple esters of the fatty acids. Thus it would seem that although the expanded film is in part correlated with the unsaturation of the fatty acids, it is primarily dependent on the polar parts of the lecithin molecule. The net results are that the fatty acid chains are oriented apart from each other, their cohesive force is reduced, and the passage of foreign molecules between the fatty acid chains is made easier.

Cholesterol tends to reduce the surface occupied by lecithin and also by fatty acids. Since the effect is greater with the latter, it would appear that the reduction is a function of the interaction of the cholesterol with the fatty acids rather than with the polar groups of lecithin. This would decrease the weak interactions between fatty acid chains and make the film more permeable.

The area of a monomolecular film of sphingomyelin has been measured by Turner and Watson (1930), who found that the uncondensed film occupied a volume of 60 sq. Å at room temperature. Under pressure, however, the film could be condensed to 42 sq. Å which is what would be expected if the two C_{18} chains of sphingomyelin were lined up side by side in the film. This is amazing since it indicates that the complex polar portions of the molecule did not have the effect of preventing close packing, an effect which was very marked with lecithin.

Hughes (1935a) applied the method of surface potentials (Schulman and Rideal, 1931) to a study of unimolecular films of lecithin, lysolecithin, cholesterol, tripalmitin and triolein. In agreement with previous work, he found the area occupied by each fatty acid of lecithin to be 58 sq. Å. For lysolecithin the value was 108 sq. Å, indicating that this material forms an even more distended film than lecithin. The relative electric moments per molecule were determined as 8.8 for lecithin and 4.3 for lysolecithin, the lower figure in the latter case reflecting the absence of one fatty acid and its corresponding ester linkage.

The films of cholesterol and the triglycerides were unaltered over a pH range of 2 to 11. The lecithin film demonstrated a fall in surface potential at a pH of 3 to 6 due to ionization of the phosphoric acid group. A plateau was reached at a pH of 6 because of the amphoteric nature of the molecule. Lysolecithin behaved similarly, save that the alteration of surface potential was demonstrated over a pH range of 2 to 5, indicating that lysolecithin is a stronger acid than lecithin. Dilute potassium permanganate also lowered the surface potential of lecithin, probably because the unsaturated fatty acids were oxidized. Lysolecithin which supposedly contained no unsaturated acids was acted on more slowly, whereas triolein was affected very slowly since the double bonds of the fatty acids are shielded due to the small surface area.

Force-area relationships for several proteins and for lecithin and lysolecithin were determined at a benzene-water interface by Alexander and Teorell (1939). Their work showed that at low pressures the films were more expanded than at the air-water interface, but at high pressures the areas in the two instances were approximately equal. Cheesman (1946) believes that lecithin films have greater compressibility at a liquid-liquid interface than at an air-water interface. Alexander, Teorell and Åborg (1939) studied the effect of various salts on monolayers of a cephalin fraction at the benzene-water and air-water interface. At the air-water interface there was little effect; but at the benzene-water interface calcium ions as well as strongly acid and alkaline substrates stabilized the phosphatides in the interface, preventing their solution into the benzene phase. In the case of the calcium ions this was due presumably to the formation of the calcium salt of the phosphoric acid group, a substance insoluble in either phase. The stabilization of the film by strong acid or base was explained by the possibility that these substances could increase the hydrophilic nature of the polar portion of the molecule by salt formation.

Sjölin (1943) reported that the surface tension of a lecithin film in a benzene-water interface is greatly increased by salicylic acid. The effect appears to be specific. Lecithin, unlike cholesterol, lowers the interfacial tension at an olive oil-water interface (Blanquet and Duhamel, 1949).

All these observations make possible interesting speculations regarding the role of phosphatides in the living cell, and experiments must be initiated which are intended to show the interrelationship of these physical phenomena with biochemistry.

Myelin Forms

Leathes (1925) confirmed the original observation of Virchow that the interaction of pure lecithin with water, as observed under the microscope, proceeded with the formation of myelin bodies, so called because of their resemblance to medullated nerve fibers. These are oily, thread-like, twisting cylindrical growths, proceeding irregularly in all directions, and are regarded as liquid crystals (Steiger, 1941). They serve to initiate the swelling observed with the naked eye, and depend for their formation on the desire of the polar ends of the molecules to orient themselves at the interface. Calcium ions appeared to inhibit these formations, but this inhibiting effect was nullified by cholesterol. Dervichian and Magnant (1946) have studied the coloration of myelin forms of lecithin with dyes.

Hydrolecithin does not produce myelin bodies in the presence of water; and here, as in the case of film formation, it must be concluded that the unsaturated acids as well as the polar portions of the molecule are factors.

X-ray diffraction studies of myelin forms have been carried out by Palmer and Schmitt (1941).

PHOSPHATIDE SOLS

Because lecithin and the cephalins are hydrophilic colloids, they form markedly lyophilic sols. They possess the ability to make highly polar substances such as sugar soluble in ether because of their ability to combine with these water-soluble materials. Likewise, water-dispersible proteins become soluble in organic solvents in the presence of lecithin.

Porges and Neubauer (1907/08) and Long and Gephart (1909) were among the first to study lecithin sols from a colloidal chemical point of view. Since their studies were made with very impure samples of lecithin, their results cannot be considered very accurate. In general, however, they showed that aqueous colloidal suspensions formed which could be precipitated by a variety of substances including acids and salts. The former workers believed that the efficiency of the flocculation depended on the valence of the cation, whereas the latter workers attributed the efficiency to the degree of dissociation of the salt. Particle size in lecithin sols was studied by Bechhold and Neuschlosz (1921) by means of ultra-filtration, and Hattori (1921) demonstrated the presence of Brownian movement.

Since the time of these investigators, considerably more work has been done, and Keeser (1924), Remezov (1930), Jong, Verberg and Wester-kamp (1935) and Remezov and Karlina (1937) have provided procedures for the preparation of clear, concentrated lecithin sols. The physical properties of these sols and the aging which they undergo have been described by Spiegel-Adolf (1932a).

General Properties of Phosphatide Sols

Lyophilic sols are generally quite viscous, the addition of a small quantity of electrolyte producing a marked decrease in viscosity. Spiegel-Adolf (1932) has shown that potassium bromide depresses the viscosity of a lecithin sol, and that the depression is more marked with this salt than with the chloride, thiocyanate, d-tartrate or borate of potassium. The effect was even more marked in the presence of protein.

The surface tension of lyophilic sols is often, but not universally, lower than that of pure water at the air-liquid interface. This appears to be the case for lecithin. The effect of electrolytes on the surface tension of lecithin sols has been studied by Neuschlosz (1920, 1920a), who pointed out that the surface tension of a lecithin sol passes through a maximum and then slowly decreases with increasing concentrations of the chlorides of alkali metals, alkaline earths and aluminum. Different results have been reported by Boutaric and Berthier (1940), who studied the effect of sodium, barium, aluminum and thorium chlorides on lecithin sols. Salt cencentrations of 10^{-4} to $10^{-1}N$ and 0.5 per cent lecithin sols were employed. From this work it appears that the surface tension is increased with increasing concentrations of salts. Jones and Lewis (1932) found that the surface tension of dispersions of lecithin in water varied with pH, reaching a maximum at pH 2.6. They believed that this coincided with the isoelectric point, although later work showed that the isoelectric point was much closer to neutrality (see p. 14). Cholesterol had no effect on the capillary activity of the dispersions as a function of pH, but shifted the position of the maximum from pH 2.6 to 4.0. Their determinations were made by the Sugden maximum bubble pressure method.

The work of Okunev (1928) showed that lecithin is adsorbed at a water-benzene or water-olive oil interface and serves to lower the surface tension at the interface. Lecithin is much more active in this regard than cholesterol, the effect having been observed when the lecithin concentration was 1:400,000.

The osmotic pressure of a 1 per cent lecithin sol was measured by Thomas (1915). He found that the osmotic pressure was decreased by dilute concentrations of electrolytes in the following order: HCl, NaI, NaBr, NaCl and NaOH. When the concentrations of sodium hydroxide and hydrochloric acid were increased considerably, an increase in osmotic pressure was noted.

Schmitt and Palmer (1940) studied phosphatide sols by means of x-ray diffraction. The patterns they obtained showed that lecithin and cephalin fraction sols had spacings as high as 120 Å, thus indicating the presence of water between the leaflets at the polar interfaces since the spacing in the dry substances were much smaller. Wet sphingomyelin demonstrated maximum spacings of 80 Å, which indicated its lyophobic character. All three phosphatides showed diffraction lines corresponding to spacings between 4.22 to 4.65 Å, whereas lecithin and the cephalin fraction also showed spacings at 46 Å. This latter value was believed to be characteristic. Spiegel-Adolf and Henny (1941, 1942) made similar studies and found the results to vary not only with the lipides themselves but with the origin of the lipides. Purification was reflected in the diffraction pattern, as was denaturation of the phosphatides.

Heffels (1940) measured the absorption of a solution of commercial egg lecithin in benzene in the region of 10.5 to 20 meter waves. When concentration was plotted against the reciprocal of the square of the wave length, a straight line resulted.

Breusch (1937) has observed that aqueous lecithin sols which dialyze slowly themselves increase the rate of dialysis of sodium glycocholate three to five times, but do not affect the diffusion of soaps. Possibly, the degree of aggregation of the glycocholate is decreased.

The Coagulation of Phosphatide Sols

Lyophilic sols are coagulated by substances which reduce the zeta potential and effect dehydration. This may be done by using large quantities of electrolytes which thus "salt out" the dispersed phase, or else a combination of dehydrating solvents such as acetone or alcohol and small quantities of electrolytes which affect the electrical properties.

Some work has been carried out on the coagulation of lecithin sols which shows that they behave somewhat like protein sols.

Remezov (1930) studied both cholesterol and lecithin sols. The former are lyophobic and had a coagulation threshold of pH 3.8–4.0, regardless of the buffer employed or the concentration of the sol. Glucose shifted the pH to 5.3 to 5.8. The coagulation threshold for lecithin was at pH 5.6 and for hydrolecithin at pH 6.2. Lecithin sols had an optimum flocculation zone at pH 2.0 to 2.8. Many substances affected the values, glucose shifting the threshold value to pH 7.4. Proteins, as had previously been shown by Feinschmidt (1912), shift the coagulation threshold, due perhaps to complex formation. Similarly, alkaloids have been shown by Zain (1929) to shift the precipitation zone to less acid regions. The order of effectiveness of the alkaloids is: morphine $<$ cocaine $<$ atropine $<$ strychnine $<$ quinine.

The effect of cations and anions on lecithin sols was studied with impure materials, as has already been indicated, by Porges and Neubauer (1907/08). Höber (1908) performed a similar study. The former workers proposed the following lyotropic series of anions, arranged in order of their effectiveness, for the precipitation of lecithin sols: $SO_4 > C_2H_3O_2 > F > Cl > NO_3 > Br > I > CNS$. The following series of Höber (1908) is quoted by Thierfelder and Klenk (1930, p. 135): $C_2H_3O_2 > Cl > NO_3,Br > CNS > I$. Porges and Neubauer (1907/08) proposed the following two series of alkali and alkaline earth metals: $Li > Na > NH_4 > K$ and $Ba > Sr > Ca > Mg$. Höber (1908) listed the following cations in order of their effectiveness: $Na > Cs > Li > Rb > NH_4,K$. The anion series was the same for sodium, ammonium and potassium salts. Chlorides were used in the cation series. The above series is somewhat similar to the Hofmeister series for the coagulation of proteins, although some of the ions seem displaced if size is a consideration. Two notable exceptions have been observed, however. Spiegel-Adolf (1932) observed that bromides are twice as effective as chlorides in some instances in effecting precipitation. Likewise, alkaline earth salts appear to be very effective in precipitating lecithin sols. Malquori (1933) stated that calcium salts are unique in that small quantities flocculate lecithin sols, intermediate concentrations peptize them, and still larger concentrations cause flocculation again.

As indicated above (see p. 72), Long and Gephart (1908) found no correlation between valence and coagulation and proposed that the degree of dissociation of the salt was the important factor. Kakiuchi (1922), Rona and Deutsch (1926) and Iguchi and Sato (1934), on the other hand, showed that trivalent cations were more effective than bivalent cations in the precipitation of lecithin sols. It was shown by Jong, Verberg and

Westerkamp (1935a) that lecithin sols are coagulated by bivalent and trivalent chlorides but not by sodium chloride. Furthermore, the addition of univalent halide prevented the coagulation by multivalent halides, the amount of univalent salt required decreasing with the increasing valence of the anion used. Similar antagonisms had previously been observed by Rona and Deutsch (1926).

A dependence of the velocity of the precipitation of lecithin sols on temperature was shown by Lepeshkin (1923).

According to Remezov (1930), alcohols are strong coagulating agents, isobutyl alcohol being the most effective. Propyl and ethyl alcohols were next and methyl alcohol was least effective. The alcohol, in addition to exerting a dehydrating effect, appears to lower the dielectric constant of the medium and thus to cause a discharge of the sol particles.

A microscopic procedure for measuring the discharge concentrations of hydrophilic sols has been devised by Jong and Teunissen (1935), who thus measured the discharge concentrations of lecithin sols by calcium, lithium and sodium chlorides.

Hydrotropic Action on Lecithin Sols

The hydrotropic action of various substances on lecithin sols has been studied by Valette (1936, 1937). He has shown that sodium ricinoleate is effective in clearing opalescent sols at pH 7.4–8.0 in concentrations of 50 to 150 milligram per cent. Sodium oleate has a similar effect at pH 9.8. Other sodium soaps of both saturated and unsaturated fatty acids behave similarly. The sodium salts of bile acids are even more effective than the corresponding fatty acid derivatives. In mixtures of lecithin and cholesterol which have a ratio of the former to the latter of 1.5 or more, soaps and bile salts are effective hydrotropic agents at pH 7.4 to 9.2.

Complex Coacervation

Coacervation is a phenomenon observed in lyophilic colloids which is similar to coagulation, save that the sol separates into two liquid phases rather than into a solid and a liquid phase. It was first observed by Jong and Kruyt (1930), who termed the liquid aggregate the coacervate. The coacervates appear to form most readily when two hydrophilic sols carrying opposite charges are mixed in suitable quantities. Although the tightly bound shells of water molecules surrounding the particles prevent them from coalescing, the coulombic attraction holds a number of particles together. If the effect is great enough, macroscopic droplets or coacervates form. They may be redispersed by the addition of ions which bring about hydration of the particles or by multivalent ions which diminish the zeta potential of either sol.

Since lecithin sol carries a negative charge, it has been possible to produce a coacervate with a positively charged protein sol by bringing the two sols together at a pH range between their respective isoelectric points. It was suggested (Horvath, 1937) that this may be the mode of union of proteins and phosphatides in natural sources. Bull (1937, p. 133) expressed doubt on this score, since at the pH of tissue (*ca.* 7) most proteins are negatively charged. If the lecithin also has a negative charge, coacervation would not be possible.

Complex coacervation involving lecithin sols has been studied extensively by Jong and his co-workers. Numerous coacervates have been prepared and the effect of ions has been studied. For example, Jong and Saubert (1936) prepared a coacervate by treating a lecithin sol with sodium arabinate and lanthanum nitrate. This coacervate contained not only two oppositely charged colloids, but also a crystalloidal cation which associated itself with the negative end of the zwitterion (lecithin), whereas the negatively charged sodium arabinate associated itself with the positive end of the zwitterion.

In a system composed of soybean phosphatide and carogeen, most cations did not enter into coacervate formation, but served to precipitate the colloids. The order of efficiency of the cations was $Cd > Ca > Mg > Ag > Sr > Ba > Li$. Sodium and potassium were apparently capable of forming part of the coacervate in aqueous solution but not in 25 per cent ethanol solution (Jong and Rering, 1942).

Lecithin as a Protective Colloid

As a lyophilic colloid, lecithin would be expected to exert a protective action on various substances. It appears to do this in a general way with glycerides, preventing the separation of constituent compounds and causing a mixture of liquid fats to solidify to a homogeneous mass.

Rona and Deutsch (1926) studied the protective action of lecithin on cholesterol sol but used very impure lecithin. A similar study was made by Jong and Joukovsky (1936), who used purified soybean lecithin. They attempted to determine the concentration of lecithin necessary to coat the cholesterol particles with a film, by measuring the concentration of calcium chloride necessary for reversal of the charge on the particles. Their results were inconclusive. When titanium oxide was substituted for the cholesterol, the protective action of the lecithin was clearly demonstrated, a film forming around the particles when the lecithin concentration was 0.001 per cent.

The work of Spiegel-Adolf (1935) indicated that the cephalin fraction from human brain is ten times more effective than lecithin in protecting cholesterol sol against precipitation by salts or proteins. Likewise, her cephalin preparation was three to four times as effective as lecithin in protecting colloidal gold from flocculation by neutral salts. Inaba, Kitagawa and Sato (1934) found that lecithin is inferior to ordinary sodium soaps as a protective colloid for colloidal gold solutions.

Certain industrial uses of phosphatides are said to depend on the ability of these substances to behave as protective colloids. Lecithin, according to Eichberg (1941), stabilizes leaded gasoline, preventing cloud formation, color change and aluminum corrosion. Its use in the stabilization of Vitamin A (Stanley, 1942) and in the homogenization of milk (Pässler, 1940) has also been reported.

Lecithin, according to Damerell and Urbanic (1944) and Damerell and Mattson (1944), was the most effective of several surface active agents tested in maintaining carbon and calcium carbonate dispersed in organosols in which xylene was the solvent. The lecithin increased the degree of dispersion as indicated by sedimentation rate and ultramicroscopic examination.

According to Beck (1925), positively charged ferric oxide sol may be rendered more sensitive to precipitation by electrolytes by the addition of a small amount of positive lecithin sol. This phenomenon is well known when the substances which are mixed are opposite in charge. The desensitization described above is observed when the two colloids are of the same charge or when the lyophilic colloid is present in a relatively large amount.

Effect of Lecithin on Swelling of Gels

Bamberger (1933, 1934) has shown that lecithin increases the swelling capacity of gelatin gels 12 to 15 per cent, regardless of the pH. The increase in the water uptake is apparently due to the effect of the lecithin on the gel structure and is not related to the "bound" water which actually decreases in the presence of lecithin. The lecithin influences the elasticity of the gels, for the elastic modulus of twisting and of shearing and resistance to fatigue are decreased, whereas the capability of plastic deformation is increased. Cholesterol shows the opposite effect, since it decreases the swelling capacity of gelatin gels and increases the bound water.

Exactly opposite results were reported by Moraczewski and Sadowski (1935), who showed that cholesterol promoted and lecithin inhibited the swelling of gelatin. They also showed that when the gelatin is suspended in a salt solution containing sodium, calcium and potassium in the ratio of 10:1:1, the amount of swelling is slightly decreased by lecithin and greatly increased by cholesterol. Calabék and Morávek (1930) had previously reported that the effect of lecithin and cholesterol on the swelling of gels may be antagonistic or additive depending on the proportions in the mixture and the pH of the swelling solution. Thus it is seen that the results are highly discrepant. The experiments should be repeated with very pure lecithin, for the results are of importance in interpreting the actions of cells and other physiological phenomena. In this regard it is interesting to note that Pyenson and Dahle (1938) reported that the "bound" water of milk and cream is in part due to the phosphatides present.

The rate of diffusion of surface active substances such as caprylic acid and octyl alcohol in gelatin gels was increased by the presence of lecithin, as was the rate of diffusion of alkaloids and drugs such as cocaine, novocaine, tutocaine, alypine and eucaine (Yumikura, 1925). Affonskiï (1928) described experiments which showed that the diffusion of acids and alkalies into gels was inhibited by lecithin and facilitated by cholesterol. The latter effect was weaker than the former and was reversed by high concentrations of cholesterol. The same conclusions were reached by Magistris (1932) for both gelatin and agar gels. The origin of the lecithin appeared to affect its action. Organic acids diffused more readily into the gels than mineral acids, and alkali hydroxides diffused more easily than alkaline earth bases.

PHOSPHATIDES AS EMULSIFYING AGENTS

The ability of phosphatides to act as emulsifying agents is of practical as well as theoretical interest, since many of the commercial applications of lecithin depend on this property (see p. 504). Lecithin has long been known to be an efficient emulsifier for fatty substances (see, for example, Pick, 1929). Tristram (1942) has postulated that lecithin is responsible for stable latex emulsions; and Nagel, Becker and Milner (1938) suggest that the lecithin of soybean meal may be responsible for the ease and completeness with which soybean protein disperses in water. Bull (1937, p. 125) is of the opinion that the emulsifying powers of phosphatides are due not to the pure compounds but to the complexes which exist between phosphatides and carbohydrates or proteins. A protein-lecithin combination was reported by Sell, Olsen and Kremers (1935) to be a better emulsifier than pure lecithin.

Lecithin is generally believed to favor oil-in-water emulsions, whereas cholesterol causes the formation of the opposite type (Seifriz, 1923). The effect of a mixture of lecithin and cholesterol on emulsification was studied by Corran and Lewis (1924), who observed that the mixture lowered the interfacial tension between oil and water. The effect was additive, despite the fact that the two agents favored opposite types of emulsions. When the combination was in the aqueous phase of an olive oil-water emulsion, inversion of the emulsion occurred where the ratio of lecithin to cholesterol was 8:1 by weight. When lecithin was in the water phase and cholesterol in the oil phase at the start, the inversion ratio was between 1:1 and 2:1.

The ability of lecithin to form dual types of emulsions was demonstrated by Woodman (1932), who determined emulsion type by the drop method. He found that aqueous dispersions of lecithin formed dual emulsions with fat solvents such as benzene, toluene, carbon tetrachloride and chloroform and with linseed oil, cresylic acid, phenol and hexalin. With oleic acid, the water-in-oil type formed, whereas oil-in-water emulsions were formed with bases such as dimethylaniline, xylidene, toluidine and aniline.

More extensive work on samples of lecithin from different sources and at various ages produced similar results. Woodman (1935) proposed that a possible explanation for this phenomenon might reside in the presence of impurities which favored the formation of emulsion types opposite to that favored by lecithin. This work was done with commercial lecithin, as was most of the work described here. Measurements with purified samples of the various phosphatides would be of great interest. In this regard, Puchkovskiĭ (1937) has pointed out that impure lecithin extracted from soybean flour was a better emulsifier than the partially purified product. On the other hand, Inaba, Kitagawa and Sato (1934) have reported that pure lecithin increased the stability of fatty oil-water emulsions to a greater extent than impure lecithin from soybeans. These conflicting reports demonstrate the need for exacting work with compounds of reproducible purity.

A physiological difference in the use of commercial and purified soybean phosphatides has been observed by McKibben and co-workers (1945). When corn oil emulsions prepared with the commercial product were infused into dogs, hemolysis and urticaria were produced. A similar emulsion with the purified product produced only minor changes.

The ability of lecithin to form "double emulsions" when used as an emulsifying agent for benzene and water was described by Vishnevskaya and Kniga (1933). In this phenomenon the emulsion drop of the external emulsion appears to contain still smaller drops of an internal emulsion.

The effect of lecithin concentration on the stability of sunflower oil-water emulsions was studied by Spranger (1929) and Puchkovskiĭ and Strukova (1934). They found that the lecithin concentration was critical for stability. The latter workers also pointed out that the character of the emulsion depends on the proportion of water and oil, for slight amounts of oil yield oil-in-water emulsions and small quantities of water yield water-in-oil emulsions.

King and Mukherjee (1940) studied emulsions stabilized by hydrophilic colloids including lecithin. Most of these emulsions were coarser but more stable than corresponding compositions prepared with soap. The emulsions, with the exception of those containing lecithin, deteriorated by gradual growth of the dispersed oil droplets by coalescence without the separation of free oil. The lecithin emulsions, on the other hand, aged in the same way as the soap-stabilized emulsions with the separation of free oil.

CHAPTER VIII

PHOSPHATIDE COMPLEXES

INTRODUCTION

The literature contains a multiplicity of references to combinations and complexes of phosphatides with proteins, carbohydrates, glycosides, enzymes, dyes, cholesterol and other substances. Some of these have been prepared in the laboratory and others have been shown to occur naturally. Complexes with carbohydrates and proteins are readily demonstrated in natural sources by the fact that ether and other fat solvents extract only small quantities of the phosphatides. In the presence of alcohol, however, which has a dissociating influence on the complexes, the extraction is more nearly complete. Actually, this solvent is employed in virtually all work where complete extraction is necessary.

The present state of knowledge does not, in most cases, make it possible to determine whether these materials are true molecular compounds, adsorption complexes due to local interaction at the surfaces, or merely mechanical mixtures. Some of the older workers (e.g., Loewe, 1912) held that these combinations are adsorption complexes. A more complete discussion of the possible types of linkages involved will be included later. It must be realized, however, that different types of linkages may be responsible for the complexes depending on whether the substance involved is a protein, a carbohydrate, a metallic salt or an organic material.

The general term "complex" has been adopted in this discussion because it is widely used and generally understood, although it does not require an exact understanding of the types of linkages involved. Willstätter and Rohdewald (1934) reserved "complex" for the Werner type of chemical compound, and coined the word "symplex" to describe substances bound together by accessory valences. Macheboeuf (1937) objected to this term on the basis that it implied simplicity of structure and substituted *cénapse* ("synapse" in English). Because of the unfamiliarity of this word it seems wise not to adopt it but to retain the use of the term "complex" until such time as the structure of these substances is more clearly defined.

Introduction

The existence of phosphatide protein complexes, usually termed "lipoproteins", was recognized early by Hoppe-Seyler (1867), by Weyl (1877/78), and later by Osborne and Campbell (1900), who isolated protein-lipide complexes from egg yolk. They observed that the phosphatides could not be extracted from the complexes with ether, but that alcohol split the complexes and dissolved the lipides. McClendon (1909/10) isolated a lipoprotein from cells by simple centrifugation. Alcohol served to decompose this material also, making possible the isolation of vitellin and a phosphatide. Attempts to synthesize lipoproteins are also recorded in the early literature. The preparation of complexes of lecithin and serum albumin or egg albumin was attempted by Liebermann (1893), Mayer and Terroine (1907) and Galeotti and Giampalmo (1908). The latter workers also interacted lecithin with zein.

The importance of the lipoproteins is demonstrated by the fact that they probably occur in every living cell. They are also important factors in blood coagulation and in the formation and reaction of antibodies (see p. 447). Nevertheless, the chemistry of these substances is still quite obscure. A lipoprotein need not necessarily contain phosphatides, and there are, of course, a great variety of proteins with which the lipides may be linked. The purity and structure of most of the lipoproteins described in the literature is questionable, for which reason an exact nomenclature is not feasible at this time. If the lipide and protein present were known with certainty, the names of each could be combined to give an accurate description of the substance, as, for example, lecithoalbumin.

The structure and purity of these substances depends, however, not only on the chemical identity of the two components involved, but also on the definition of the linkages which bind them together. As Chargaff (1944, p. 2) indicates in his excellent review on this subject, chemical purity has always made the implicit demand that a pure compound possess types of linkages which are clearly defined by chemical knowledge. In materials of biological interest such as enzymes, viruses and lipoproteins, the types of linkages are quite obscure, although the specificity of their biological functions confers upon them a homogeneity quite beyond the scope of chemical purity. As science progresses to the point where these linkages may be explained, it is quite likely that the difference between chemical and biological purity will appear to be an artificial one.

Notwithstanding this present lack of knowledge, the point must be made that the term "lipoprotein" refers to a substance whose biological and physical properties differ from the sum of the properties of its constituents.

Lipide-Protein Linkages

The possible linkages which may exist between lipides and proteins have been discussed by Chargaff (1944, p. 3 ff.). He points out the possible existence of three types of compounds: (1) covalent compounds, (2) electrostatic compounds, (3) secondary valence compounds.

Covalent compounds could form by ester or amide formation between proteins and the carboxyl group of fatty acids or phosphatidylserine; the phosphoric acid groups of lecithin, phosphatidylaminoethyl alcohol, phosphatidylserine or sphingomyelin; the hydroxyl group of glyceryl mono- or diesters, sphingomyelin or the galactolipides; and the amino group of phosphatidylaminoethyl alcohol or phosphatidylserine.

Electrostatic compounds (salts) could form by the interaction of the proteins and the carboxyl groups of fatty acids or phosphatidylserine; the phosphoric acid groups of lecithin, phosphatidylaminoethyl alcohol, phosphatidylserine or sphingomyelin; and the amino or substituted amino groups of lecithin, phosphatidylaminoethyl alcohol, phosphatidylserine or sphingomyelin.

Secondary valence compounds could form by the interaction of the proteins with any of the lipides. These and electrostatic compounds are not mutually exclusive.

The covalent compound is perhaps the least probable, although there are instances where it would be difficult to differentiate between it and electrostatic compounds. The electrostatic or salt-like compounds could form in pH ranges which make available the groups necessary for interaction. Most of the synthetic lipoproteins (see p. 90) are probably of this nature. Reference to the discussion on acid-base relationships of the phosphatides (p. 12) will indicate that at the physiological pH, lecithin and sphingomyelin are probably essentially neutral and would not enter into salt formation as readily as acidic substances such as phosphatidylaminoethyl alcohol, phosphatidylserine and the phosphatidic acids.

Chargaff (1944, p. 5) concludes that most naturally occurring lipoproteins must perforce be classified as secondary valence complexes in which van der Waal's forces have been brought into play. He points out also the possibility of solid solutions of lipides such as glycerides dissolved in the lipide portions of lipoproteins. Again, it is sometimes difficult to distinguish between van der Waal compounds and electrostatic compounds, since electrically charged groups may provide the points of attachments in both instances. Similar possibilities for the structure of lipoproteins had previously been considered by Przylecki (1939).

A theory advanced by Macheboeuf and Sandor (1932) is of interest. They propose that the hydrophobic or lipophilic parts (nonpolar portions) of the proteins and lipides exert mutual attraction, or at least a lesser repulsive effect than do the polar portions, so that the lipides are oriented on the protein. The hydrophilic groups of both the proteins and the lipides, which may even be hydrated, are directed outward and are eager to combine with water or polar solvents such as alcohol. This would explain the inertness of the lipoproteins to ether, since the nonpolar portions are masked by the polar portions. Alcohol, on the other hand, would have ready access to the polar portions of the molecule, which would account for its dissociating influence.

Occurrence of Lipoproteins

As indicated above, lipoproteins are probably constituents of every living cell, although much of the experimental work in this field is indefinite because of the unavailability of proper techniques for isolation and examination of the complexes.

Egg Yolk. The lipoprotein of hen's egg yolk is perhaps the best known, for which reason it will be discussed first. It was first isolated by Hoppe-Seyler (1867) and was studied by other workers including Osborne and Campbell (1900). Until recently it was believed (Jukes and Kay, 1932) that only the vitellin of the egg yolk protein was associated with phosphatides. However, Fevold and Lausten (1946) have been able to show the presence in egg yolk of a lipoprotein different from lipovitellin. The new product, which they named "lipovitellinin", contains more than twice as much lipide as does lipovitellin. It was separated by a centrifugation procedure carried out on the diluted egg yolk. The greater fat content of the lipovitellinin increased its dispersibility in the egg yolk fat emulsion and prevented its precipitation on centrifugation. The lipovitellin, on the other hand, precipitated readily because of its lower fat content. The new lipoprotein possessed 36 to 41 per cent lipide and comprised 40 per cent of the total lipoprotein of egg yolk.

When lipoprotein (Jukes and Kay, 1932) is emulsified with water, the protein is slowly liberated and becomes increasingly less soluble in salt solutions. Thus, the globulin nature of the lipoprotein appears to depend on the phosphatide present. Sell, Olsen and Kremers (1935) were of the opinion that the emulsifying power of egg yolk is due to the phosphatide which is present in complex formation with the protein.

Blackwood and Wishart (1934) studied the action of enzymes on the lipoprotein of egg and from the rate of enzyme attack concluded that there must be present two unlike phosphorus-containing complexes.

Chargaff (1942a, 1942b) studied the lipovitellin of egg yolk in some detail. The lipovitellin complex was isolated and purified by a procedure, the details of which may be found in the original reference. Chargaff believes that only 18.8 per cent of the egg yolk phosphatides was firmly bound to the protein. Fevold and Lausten (1946), however, have postulated on the basis of their above-described, new lipoprotein that one-half of the total phosphatides of egg yolk are bound. The lipovitellin had the following elemental composition: P, 1.5 per cent, N, 13.0 per cent, S, 0.9 per cent and ash, 3.7 per cent. The complex contained 23 per cent lipides of which 17.9 per cent was phosphatides. The bound and the free phosphatides possessed the same composition and consisted almost entirely of lecithin and phosphatidylaminoethyl alcohol. Unlike brain phosphatides, phosphatidylserine was absent. This same observation had been made by other workers (see p. 320). Chargaff (1942b) was also able to show by use of radioactive phosphorus tracers that the bound and the free phosphatides formed at the same rate and were in equilibrium.

Cell Parts. As indicated previously, lipoproteins are probably present in all living cells, although rigid proof of this statement is lacking. In addition to the egg cell, which is the most common source, lipoproteins have been found in the various structural portions of other cells. The occurrence of phosphatides in cell particulates is discussed elsewhere (see p. 343). For the most part they are not well characterized compounds. The possibility that the cell membrane may consist of a complex of lipides and proteins has been much discussed in biochemical theory. Because of the difficult techniques involved, there is not much evidence on this score (see, e.g., Schmitt and Palmer, 1940). Jong and Hartkamp (1939) have provided evidence that the membrane surrounding the unicellular *Paramecium caudatum* contains phosphatides. Parpart and Dziemian (1940) were able to show that 40 to 60 per cent of the red blood cell membrane could be extracted by ether only when alcohol was present. Sigurdsson (1943) found lipides in hemolyzed red blood cells isolated from stroma. Obviously a great deal more work remains to be done on the composition of cell membranes.

Evidence for the presence of lipoproteins in the cell nucleus was advanced by Stoneburg (1939) and by Dounce (1943). The latter worker extracted the lipides from cell nuceli with alcohol-ether and estimated that lipides comprise about 11 per cent of the nucleus. The former worker carried out microanalyses on the lipides extracted from cell nuclei with alcohol. He concluded that both phosphatides and cholesterol were present and that the phosphatides probably contained saturated fatty acids.

Evidence for the presence of lipides in mitochondria (see p. 343) was advanced by Bensley (1942) and by Chargaff (1942a). On the basis of evidence obtained by microscopic observation, lipides have been postulated in the Golgi apparatus (Kirkman and Severinghaus, 1938). Claude (1943) found 22–24 per cent lipides in the secretory glands of liver. This same worker (Claude, 1941) found 40 to 50 per cent lipides in the heavy, submicroscopic particles isolated from chicken tumor tissue. Most of the lipides appeared to be phosphatides, some of which were possibly similar to the acetal phosphatides (see p. 51).

Tissue. The presence of lipoproteins in tissue was recognized early, as is evidenced by the issuance of a patent to Adler (1913) for the aqueous extraction of "lecithalbumin" from fish. Of great interest is the presence of lipoproteins in living tissue which possess high thrombo-plastic activity (see, e.g., Mills, 1921). Recent work of this nature has been carried out largely by Chargaff and his co-workers. Thus, Cohen and Chargaff (1940, 1941) obtained a thromboplastic lipoprotein from beef lung by precipitating it at its isoelectric point of pH 5.1. The substance contained about 18 per cent bound lipides that could be removed only by the dissociating influence of alcohol. Unlike mixtures of lecithin and the cephalin fraction, the lipoprotein did not move in the electric field of an electrophoresis apparatus, even in a basic medium. Once the lipides were removed, the remaining protein was without thromboplastic activity. The phosphatide fraction included sphingomyelin and yielded the following isolable products on hydrolysis: palmitic, stearic and unsaturated acids; choline; aminoethyl alcohol and glycerophosphoric acid.

Chargaff, Moore and Bendich (1942) obtained a more homogeneous product by ultracentrifugal fractionation of beef lung saline extracts. It possessed 8 to 9 per cent nitrogen and 1.3 per cent phosphorus, and was extremely thromboplastic.

Blood Serum. The lipides of blood plasma (see p. 272) are complex in nature and heterogeneous in chemical behavior. Thus, whereas cholesterol, cholesterol esters, fatty acids and neutral fat may be hydrophobic in nature, lecithin and the cephalin phosphatides are strongly hydrophilic colloids. It is immediately obvious, then, why so little is known about the method of occurrence of plasma lipides. Most of the studies on the physical state and distribution of the lipides have led only to the rather obvious conclusion that lipides associate themselves with certain fractions of the plasma proteins.

Both globulin (Hardy, 1905) and euglobulin (Chick, 1914) have been shown to be associated with phosphatides in serum. Cholesterol likewise enters into complex formation, particularly with globulin and fibrinogen (Gardner and Gainsborough, 1927; Macheboeuf, 1929). Thus, Went and

Goreczky (1931) showed that when serum was separated by ultrafilters of different porosities, the lipide content of the serum filtrate was largely dependent on its protein content. Cholesterol decreased as the protein content diminished, and phosphatides decreased sharply when euglobulin was no longer present. Turner and Gibson (1932) fractionated plasma and serum by salt precipitation methods. They found that about one-half of the total lipides were associated with the proteins, and that the globulins contained more phosphatides than either fatty acids or cholesterol. Macheboeuf (1929a) also fractionated serum by salt precipitation procedures and reported the isolation of a lipoprotein of constant composition, which contained 59.1 per cent proteins, 22.7 per cent phosphatides and 17.9 per cent cholesterol esters. As might be expected, the complex was dissociated by hot alcohol, but not by other solvents. Similar work is reported in later publications by Macheboeuf and Sandor (1932a) and Macheboeuf and Januszkiewicz (1937).

Adair and Adair (1943/44) isolated a globulin fraction of low density from human serum by precipitation with ammonium sulfate between 0.5 and 0.6 saturation. This fraction consisted of 8.5 per cent phosphatides, 16.5 per cent cholesterol and 20.4 per cent fatty acids. The molecular weight as determined by osmotic pressure was 370,000.

The validity of such experiments has been questioned by Sörensen (1930), who pointed out that the addition of an electrolyte to serum might cause association or dissociation of the various components and precipitation of insoluble complexes which bear no relationship to the original composition or method of occurrence of the lipides initially associated with the proteins.

The behavior of lipoproteins in an electrical field gives some insight into the true situation, although the method is hampered by the extreme difficulty accompanying the isolation of any component in high purity. Thus, Blix, Tiselius and Svensson (1941) fractionated human serum electrophoretically into albumin and α-, β- and γ-globulins. Each of these fractions was then analyzed for cholesterol and lipide phosphorus. Although lipides were present in all the fractions, they appeared to be concentrated in the α- and β-globulin fractions and were not affected by repeated electrophoresis. From the β-globulin fraction, Pedersen (1945, p. 32) isolated a lipoprotein which he termed "X-protein" and which other workers (Edsall, 1947, p. 450) have called "β_1-lipoprotein". Pedersen believed it to be a complex of albumin, globulin and lipides with a total particle weight of the order of 10^6. Edsall has stated that it contains 75 per cent lipide which, nevertheless, does not prevent it from dissolving to the extent of 10 per cent in dilute aqueous salt solutions. This material has been investigated in detail by Pedersen (1947); Oncley and co-workers (1949); Oncley, Gurd and Melin (1950) and Gofman, Lindgren and Elliott (1949).

That the lipide-protein complex of serum is a weak one is indicated by several observations. It is disrupted by heat, and Blix (1941) found that the acetone-ether extraction at low temperature of acetone-precipitated human serum proteins removed all the cholesterol and about three-fourths of the phosphatides. The unextracted phosphatides which were presumably in complex formation belonged to the cephalin fraction. McFarlane (1942a) reported that the freezing (−25° C.) and subsequent thawing of an ether-serum mixture caused most of the lipides to dissolve in the ether fraction.

Milk. The presence of lipoproteins in milk and cream has been postulated by several workers. Wiese and Palmer (1932) and Palmer and Wiese (1933) studied the film which appears to form a stabilizing membrane around the fat globules of milk and cream. They concluded that phosphatides, together with certain proteins, are invariably present as the stabilizing material which serves to maintain the colloidal system. The composition of the lipoprotein of the film appears to be somewhat variable (Rimpila and Palmer, 1935) and has not yet been established. The electrophoretic experiments of Moyer (1940), however, show that the proteins of the complex which forms the membrane are different from ordinary milk proteins.

Tayeau (1940) has shown that part of the lipoprotein of milk is dissociated by soap, making it possible to extract the lipides with ether. The remainder of the lipides become ether soluble once the proteins are coagulated by boiling alcohol.

Bacteria and Yeast. The observations of Anderson and his co-workers (see p. 202) that some of the lipides of acid-fast bacteria were "firmly bound" have already been described. These bound lipides could be extracted with fat solvents only after the partially defatted bacteria were treated with a dilute solution of alcoholic hydrochloric acid. Anderson, Reeves and Stodola (1937) actually isolated from the tubercle bacillus lipide complexes, although it was not possible to tell whether the lipides were bound to proteins or carbohydrates.

The reversal of the antimicrobial activity of various proteins by phosphatides has been reported by several workers. This may well be due to the formation of inactive lipoproteins at the cell surface, although most of the work has shown that the phosphatide employed does not affect the results. This is not in accord with the theoretical considerations (see p. 83), which cast doubt on the ability of lecithin to enter into complex formation, at least by the commonly postulated mechanisms. Woolley and Krampitz (1942) showed that the action of a bacteriostatic protein from wheat was inhibited by lecithin, phosphatidyl-serine and an inositol-containing phosphatide. Duboss and Hotchkiss (1942) found that phosphatidylserine and phosphatidylaminoethyl alcohol counteracted the effect of gramicidin, and Baker and co-workers (1941) reported that lecithin, phosphatidylaminoethyl alcohol, phosphatidylserine and sphingomyelin were antagonistic to the effect of detergents on gram-positive bacteria.

The presence of lipoprotein in the yeast *Saccharomyces cervisiae* has been reported by Nyman and Chargaff (1949). The material contained 22 to 26 per cent lipides.

Plants. Most of the evidence supports the presence in plants of carbohydrate-lipide complexes rather than lipoproteins. Nevertheless, Horvath (1937) has pointed out the possibility of phosphatide-protein complexes in soybeans. Olcott and Mecham (1947) have shown that the lipide and protein of wheat flour form a lipoprotein during the wetting and "doughing" of flour. Thus, whereas 70 per cent of the lipides of a given flour could be extracted by ether prior to interaction with water, only 40 per cent could be extracted after wetting and drying, and only 6 per cent after "doughing". The phosphatides seemed to be bound preferentially and largely accompanying the gluten fraction.

Antener and Högl (1947) conducted studies which show that the lipides of wheat germ, and particularly the phosphatides, occur in complex formation with both carbohydrates and proteins. Treatment of the complexes with solvents such as trichlorethylene split the lipide-carbohydrate link entirely, but affected only slightly the lipide-protein link. Conversely, short treatment with boiling alcohol split quantitatively the lipide-protein linkage but left the lipide-carbohydrate linkage intact. The carbohydrate participating in the complex formation was identified as sucrose. The phosphatide consisted of a mixture of lecithin, the cephalin fraction and magnesium phosphatidate.

The mode of linkage of lipide and carbohydrate could not be determined, although excellent evidence was provided to demonstrate the presence of a strong complex rather than a loose association. Thus the ratio of sugar to phosphorus was approximately constant in all the experiments. Attempts to enrich the phosphorus content by fractionation led also to enrichment of the sugar content; and the sugar could not be extracted with water as it could be in artificially prepared complexes.

Some evidence exists to confirm the presence of lipoproteins in the chloroplasts, chromoplasts and leucoplasts of plant cells (Frey-Wijssling, 1937/38), although Menke (1938) has shown that most of the lipides could be extracted with ether. Considerably more investigation is indicated in this field.

Synthetic Lipoproteins

Numerous reports are contained in the literature which describe the formation of complexes between phosphatides and proteins. Some workers reported unsuccessful results (e.g., Handovsky and Wagner, 1911), due probably to the use of phosphatides which were predominantly lecithin; for this, as has already been pointed out, is a neutral material probably incapable of participating in complex formation. Many of these studies have involved the interaction of phosphatides with serum or egg albumin. Thus Fujii (1924) showed that an impure lecithin in the presence of albumin was no longer water-dispersible, but rather that the two substances formed an ether-soluble product. Similar experiments of Hofer (1938) showed that egg albumin and phosphatides combined at pH 3 to yield a complex. Galeotti and Giampalmo (1908) reacted phosphatides with zein. Chick (1914) explored the interaction of phosphatides with serum pseudoglobulin, and Parsons (1928) of phosphatides with caseinogen. Spiegel-Adolf (1932a, 1935) studied the interaction of lecithin sol with serum-albumin and pseudoglobulin and has described optimum concentrations and the effect of aging. Wagner-Jauregg and Arnold (1938) found that phosphatidic acids, as would be expected from their acidic nature, form complexes with clupein, globulin, pseudoglobulin and serum albumin.

That lecithin and the cephalins behave differently in complex formation was shown by Wadsworth, Maltaner and Maltaner (1930), who were able to obtain complexes between proteins and a cephalin fraction, but not between proteins and unhydrolyzed lecithin. A more extensive study of a similar nature was carried out by Chargaff (1938). When the highly basic protamine, salmine, was treated with an emulsion of the cephalin fraction of brain, a precipitate which could not be re-emulsified in water formed. The cephalin fraction presumably was a mixture of phosphatidylaminoethyl alcohol and phosphatidylserine, either of which is acidic. The inability of the precipitate to be reëmulsified is evidence that mere flocculation had not taken place. The water-insoluble products formed over pH ranges of 2 to 11, the isoelectric point of salmine being 12. The dried products had nitrogen-phosphorus ratios of 4:1 or 5:1 and swelled in water to rubber-like masses. They contained about 80 per cent phosphatide and could be recrystallized from ethyl acetate. Ether solutions could be treated with dilute acids or with acetone without changing the composition of the solute. Products prepared in this manner are presumably salts. With pure lecithin the results differed in that no compound formation took place in the physiological range, although in highly alkaline solutions of pH 10 to 11, compound formation was observed. Similar results were obtained in experiments with sphingomyelin.

The cephalin fraction formed salts with egg albumin at pH's of 2 to 4 which would be expected since egg albumin has an isoelectric point of 4.8. With this acidic protein, lecithin did not form salts at any pH.

In further work, Chargaff and Ziff (1939) found that a cephalin fraction of brain reacted with histone from calf thymus and with globin from cattle hemoglobin at pH's of 2 to 7 in the former instance, and at pH's below 4 in the latter. Lecithin reacted with histone at pH's between 7 to 8, but not with globin. These complexes of phosphatides and basic proteins may likewise be considered salts. Their composition varied with pH, as might be expected, since the number of basic groups in the protein available for reaction is a function of pH. The compounds with histone and globin, unlike those with protamine, were insoluble in organic solvents.

Insight into the relative stabilities of oxyhemoglobin and the complex formed from globin and brain cephalin fraction was obtained from experiments of Chargaff, Ziff and Hogg (1939). These workers showed that the brain cephalin fraction disrupted the hemoglobin linkage in both oxyhemoglobin and carbon monoxide hemoglobin at pH 7 to form a complex of cephalin-globin with the release of hematin:

$$\text{oxyhemoglobin} + \text{cephalin} \rightleftharpoons \text{cephalin-globin} + \text{hematin}.$$

The cephalin fraction referred to in these experiments was a mixture of phosphatidylaminoethyl alcohol and phosphatidylserine. Reduced hemoglobin did not react with the cephalins.

X-ray studies of cephalin-protein complexes were made by Palmer, Schmitt and Chargaff (1941), who suggested that the complexes consist of thin protein layers intercalated between bimolecular leaflets of phosphatide.

Properties of Lipoproteins

Dissociation. References have already been made to the dissociating influence of alcohol on lipoproteins. The practical use of this reagent in the extraction of phosphatides has been described in Part II. As an example may be mentioned the work of Grigaut (1935), who treated samples of blood serum with mixtures of ethanol-water, the ethanol content having been varied from zero to 100 per cent. This was followed by ether extraction of each sample in order to determine the dissociating effect of various concentrations of alcohol.

More detailed studies were carried out by Delsal (1949) and by Macheboeuf (1929b). The latter worker determined the effect of alcohol concentration, pH and time on aqueous solutions of lipoproteins. He found that the initial precipitate produced by addition of alcohol dissolves when more water or alcohol is added. This first precipitate is rich in lipides which dissolve when the mixture is allowed to stand. The proteins, on the other hand, become progressively more denatured, and the denaturation is accelerated by acid and high temperatures. Macheboeuf and Sandor (1932) found that 8 to 12 per cent of alcohol by volume is optimum for the decomposition of the lipoproteins of serum, as indicated by the amounts of lipides which become ether soluble. Delage (1935) found that methyl, propyl, butyl and isoamyl alcohols exerted a dissociating effect equal to that of ethyl alcohol on lipoproteins.

The use of alcohol to dissociate lipoproteins is limited in some instances by the fact that the proteins are invariably denatured. If denaturation is harmful in a given investigation, it may in part be circumvented by the use of soaps. Macheboeuf and Tayeau (1938, 1938a) studied the effect of sodium oleate, and sodium or potassium plamitate or dibromostearate at various pH's and concentrations. They found that soap split lipoglobulins completely but that lipoalbumins, which were readily dissociated by alcohol, resisted the action of soap. Tayeau (1939) compared the efficacy of various soaps in the liberation of lipides from lipoproteins, and found that the effectiveness of sodium soaps decreased as follows: ricinoleate, linoleate, dibromostearate, oleate, undecylenate, undecylate and sebacate.

Heparin has been found by Chargaff, Ziff and Cohen (1940) and by Chargaff (1942a) to liberate lipides from certain lipoproteins. Thus, heparin reacted with the thromboplastic lipoprotein of lung to yield lipides and a heparin-protein complex. Lipoproteins including lipovitellin, mitochondria and a synthetic cephalin-histone compound all reacted with heparin to yield heparin-lipoprotein complexes without the liberation of lipides.

Physical Properties. Chargaff, Moore and Bendich (1942) have determined some of the physical properties of the thromboplastic protein of lung. The lipoprotein was isolated by fractional ultracentrifugation. From the sedimentation rate ($s_{20} = 330S$), diffusion measurements ($D_{20} = 0.38 \times 10^{-7}$), and partial specific volume ($V_{27} = 0.87$), the particle weight was calculated as 167,000,000. Electron micrographs showed these large particles to be spherical with diameters of 80 to 120 mμ.

The electrophoretic mobility at pH 8.6 was 8.4 cm.^{2}/volt/sec. $\times 10^{-5}$. Edsall (1947, p. 400) has pointed out that the lipide content of lipoproteins does not affect the electrophoretic mobility of the protein, since the lipoprotein components of α- and β-globulins have been shown to have the same electrophoretic behavior as the lipide-free globulin.

Electrophoresis and ultracentrifuge studies have also been carried out by Macheboeuf and co-workers (1943).

Introduction

The observation that phosphatides, due to their colloidal nature, form with glucose combinations of indefinite composition which are ether soluble, was made very early by Bing (1899) and was confirmed by Mayer (1906). That carbohydrate complexes occur in nature was shown by Winterstein and Hiestand (1906). These workers showed that the hydrolysis of plant phosphatides yielded carbohydrates in addition to the usual hydrolysis products, and that these sugars accounted in some instances for as much as 16 per cent of the product. Among the sugars identified by early workers in the hydrolysis products were glucose, galactose, pentose and methylpentose; and their affinity was demonstrated by the fact that complete hydrolysis did not result unless the complex was subjected to the action of boiling dilute sulfuric acid (Schulze, 1907). The identity of the carbohydrates is discussed in some detail in Part IV where it is concluded that they occur probably as di- and polysaccharides rather than as simple sugars.

The occurrence of carbohydrate-phosphatide complexes seems to be limited to plant sources, although this is by no means definitely established. The inositol-containing phosphatides (see p. 35), in which the inositol is actually in chemical union in the phosphatide molecule, occur in both plant and animal sources. Although very little can be said about the mode of union in the carbohydrate-lipide complexes of vegetable origin, it is safe to say that the majority of these complexes are not true chemical entities as appears to be the case with the inositol phosphatides. That carbohydrates are present in virtually every phosphatide of plant origin is well illustrated by reference to Part IV. Despite the early recognition of these complexes, present knowledge is not sufficient for a satisfactory discussion of them at this time. Considerably more research in this difficult field is indicated.

Occurrence of Carbohydrate Complexes

As indicated above, the occurrence of carbohydrates associated with phosphatides in plant sources will be detailed in Part IV and need not be described at length here. Typical of the many observations is that of Nottbohm and Mayer (1934), who found 26 per cent carbohydrates associated with the phosphatides of wheat flour. Lockwood (1938) also observed the presence of these complexes in flour, cacao and similar materials. The association of lipides with cornstarch was proved by Taylor and Lehrman (1926). Although phosphatides could not be detected in their lipide fraction, they may have been destroyed during the hydrolysis procedure.

The acid-fast bacteria are excellent sources of carbohydrate-lipide complexes. The extremely complex carbohydrates found in the lipide fraction of the tubercle bacillus by Anderson and his co-workers have been described elsewhere (see p. 211). Carbohydrate-lipide complexes from the tubercle bacillus with antigenic properties have been reported (e.g., Heidelberger and Menzel, 1935), although there is no evidence here that the lipide fractions contain phosphatides.

The inositol-containing phosphatides which are compounds containing carbohydrates in actual chemical linkage have likewise already been discussed (see p. 35).

Synthetic Carbohydrate Complexes

The literature records a few instances where carbohydrates have been combined in complex formation with phosphatides. Evidence from boiling point rise for the formation of a compound between phosphatides and glucose was obtained by Scott (1917). Przylecki and Majmin (1935) added phosphatides to starch and similar compounds, and reported that a combination resulted with as many as fifty molecules of lecithin per molecule of starch. The reactants were mixed in aqueous solution and precipitated by the addition of acid, sometimes in the presence of electrolytes. The compositions of the precipitates varied over a wide range according to the conditions of precipitation and the proportions of the reactants.

There are several patents relating to possible commercial products consisting of phosphatides combined with sugars which are supposed to have a stabilizing effect (see p. 497).

METALLIC SALT COMPLEXES

Phosphatides possess the ability to form combinations with salts of various heavy metals. Some of these, like the cadmium chloride salt, are insoluble and have proved valuable in the purification of lecithin. Reference to its use for this purpose has already been made (see p. 26). Again, very little can be ventured about the linkage which exists between the phosphatides and the salt. These are generally stated to be addition compounds, although McKinney, Jamieson and Holton (1937) are of the opinion that with cadmium chloride, salt formation may actually take place between the cadmium ion and the phosphoric acid radical.

Cadmium Chloride Complex

Strecker (1868) was the first investigator to prepare a phosphatide-cadmium chloride complex. This worker mixed alcoholic solutions of the two reagents to obtain a white, flocculent precipitate of uncertain cadmium content. Similar results were reported by Ulpiani (1901), Erlandsen (1907) and Eppler (1913). These preparations contained mixtures of phosphatides which accounted for their indefinite composition.

Lecithin-Cadmium Chloride Complex. The observation of MacLean (1909a) that the cadmium chloride complex of lecithin is less soluble than the corresponding complex of the cephalin phosphatides has already been mentioned (see p. 26). The application of this observation to the purification of lecithin, which incidentally requires the purification of the cadmium complex, has also been discussed (see p. 57). The general procedure of Levene and co-workers mentioned there for purifying the complex by extracting its impurities repeatedly with ether has been used extensively.

Although the lecithin-cadmium chloride complex is insoluble in ether, it is soluble in a mixture of carbon disulfide and ether or alcohol and in hot alcohol alone or in xylene. It crystallizes readily from the last two solvents.

Baer and Kates (1950) have prepared a cadmium chloride complex of synthetic lecithin, and have shown that two molecules of lecithin are present for three molecules of cadmium chloride. The results of Levene and Komatsu (1919) point to the presence of two moles of cadmium chloride in the complex per mole of lecithin, whereas Contardi and Latzer (1927) prepared a complex containing 22.37 per cent cadmium chloride. This calculates to be more than one mole of salt per lecithin molecule but less than two.

A variety of basic materials are known to split the lecithin-cadmium chloride complex. Ulpiani (1901) decomposed an alcohol suspension of the complex with lead or silver oxide and Cousin (1906) decomposed a petroleum ether solution with silver oxide. A better reagent is ammonium carbonate, first used by Bergell (1900), who added it slowly to a suspension of the complex in boiling alcohol. Ammonium carbonate was also used by Levene and West (1918b), whereas Levene and Simms (1921) and Levene and Rolf (1927) in their procedures for the purification of lecithin used a methanolic solution of ammonia.

Cadmium chloride complexes with the phosphatides of the cephalin fraction have not been well characterized.

Platinum Chloride Complex

A phosphatide-platinum chloride complex was first prepared by Strecker (1868), who showed that it analyzed for two moles of platinum chloride per mole of phosphatide. His lipides were undoubtedly a mixture of lecithin and the cephalin fraction. His analyses were confirmed by other early workers (Hammarsten, 1902; Lüdecke, 1905). The complex is insoluble in alcohol but is soluble in ether, carbon disulfide, chloroform and benzene. Solutions of the complex on standing yield a precipitate of the platinum chloride salt of choline due, apparently, to the hydrolytic effect of the acidic salt.

Other Metallic Complexes

Lecithin forms a complex with numerous other metallic salts. Bing (1901) described a complex with mercuric chloride which was soluble in ether, alcohol and acetone. He also prepared an ether-soluble sodium chloride complex which was virtually insoluble in alcohol and acetone. A complex with ammonium molybdate was reported by Ehrenfeld (1908).

Complexes of phosphatides with lead salts are well known and are exemplified by the ether-insoluble material prepared by Welch (1945) by reacting the cephalin fraction from various tissues with basic lead acetate. Tompsett (1934) has shown that ferric but not ferrous salts form complexes with phosphatides. He was unable to show the formation of copper complexes, although a patent issued to Linden, Meissen and Strauss (1913) claims the formation of an ether-soluble complex from cupric chloride and lecithin. Liebrecht (1930) prepared, purportedly for therapeutic use, complexes of lecithin with high molecular weight bismuth salts.

Christensen and Hastings (1940) have reviewed the literature on the ability of phosphatides to form complexes with chloride ions. On the basis of their own work, they conclude that complex formation does not take place.

CHOLESTEROL-LECITHIN COMPLEX

The complex between lecithin and cholesterol is of great interest biochemically. Several early workers (e.g., Berczeller, 1914) reported that complex formation took place between these two substances. Complex formation between cholesterol, polycyclic hydrocarbons and phosphatides have been postulated by Davis, Krahl and Clowes (1940). There is as yet, however, no evidence to establish the type of union between cholesterol and lecithin in the absence of a third substance.

Jones and Lewis (1932) found that the addition of cholesterol to a lecithin dispersion did not disturb the capillary behavior of lecithin as a function of pH. It did, however, shift the position of the maximum surface tension from a pH of 2.6 to a pH of 4, thus indicating some sort of union. Price (1933) found that cholesterol did not change the pH of the isoelectric point of a lecithin dispersion. He pointed out, accordingly, that the union of cholesterol and lecithin does not involve the amphoteric groups of the lecithin or the groups on which ion adsorption may have taken place. He concluded that the cholesterol and the lecithin probably exist as an adsorption complex.

From measurements of interfacial tensions, Guastalla (1949) concluded that a lecithin-cholesterol-gelatin complex may exist at the interface of an aqueous solution of gelatin and a benzene solution of lecithin-cholesterol.

MISCELLANEOUS COMPLEXES

Complexes between phosphatides and a variety of miscellaneous substances have been reported. With most of these it is impossible to differentiate between true molecular compounds, adsorption complexes or mere mechanical mixtures. The formation of a complex between lecithin and bile acid salts was reported by Hammarsten (1905). His material was soluble in ether, chloroform and benzene. This product was further investigated by Fürth, Breuer and Herrmann (1934). Bing (1901) mentioned the preparation of complexes of phosphatides with glycosides and with alkaloids. Cruickshank (1920) found that lecithin combined with quinine and strychnine, but not with codeine and morphine. Boas and Rosenbloom (1911) prepared a complex with caffeine and reported that a complex with strychnine dialyzed partially. These latter workers also prepared complexes with urea, creatine and creatinine which did not dialyze. Complexes with digitonin and salicin dialyzed partially.

The digitonin complex was investigated more recently by McEwen and MacLachlan (1941), who found that digitonin renders phosphatides from blood plasma or egg yolk insoluble in petroleum ether.

A complex of a cephalin fraction and streptomycin has been prepared by Rybak and Gros (1948). Lecithin did not form a complex under similar conditions.

Complexes with invert soaps of the quaternary ammonium type have been described by Beck and Meier (1947). Weissman and Graff (1947) have observed that lecithin neutralizes the bactericidal effect of a quaternary ammonium detergent known as "Zephiran", due probably to complex formation.

The association of lecithin and oleic acid is suggested since a monomolecular film of the two occupies less than the calculated amount of space (Dervichian and Pillet, 1944).

The adsorption of dyes by phosphatides is of interest, especially for histochemical purposes. So far (see p. 182), adequate histochemical techniques for the determination of phosphatides have not been evolved. Chargaff and Ziff (1939) showed that the cephalin fraction reacts with basic dyes such as methylene blue and thionine, whereas lecithin does not. Their cephalin preparation probably contained phosphatidylserine and was acidic, whereas lecithin is essentially neutral. The older work on dye adsorption was undoubtedly carried out on impure lecithin preparations which contained some of the cephalin fraction, and thus the preference for complex formation with basic dyes was observed. Loewe (1912) was among the first to report the formation of complexes between lecithin and dyestuffs. Cruickshank (1920) found that lecithin adsorbed many basic dyes but that acidic dyes were only slightly adsorbed. A similar observation was made by Hansteen-Cranner (1927).

CHAPTER IX

THE LYSOPHOSPHATIDES AND THE LECITHINASES

HISTORICAL AND NOMENCLATURE

Probably the first indication of the existence of enzymes which hydrolyze phosphatides was obtained by Bókay (1877), who observed that the action of pancreatic juice on lecithin yielded glycerophosphoric acid, fatty acids and choline, a finding which was later confirmed by Mayer (1906). Contrariwise, Stassano and Billon (1903) and Kalabankoff and Terroine (1909) were of the opinion that such enzymes did not exist. In the meantime, Kyes (1903, 1907) and Kyes and Sachs (1903) reacted an aqueous solution of cobra poison with a chloroform solution of lecithin and were able to extract a product which they named "Cobralecithid". This product differed from its parent compound in its stability and solubility characteristics and possessed the unique property of being able to hemolyze red blood cells.

This observation was of great importance since it was related to the biologically important problem of the mechanism of snake poisoning. It was known that such poisoning was accompanied by hemolysis of the red blood cells and the subsequent liberation of hemoglobin. Flexner and Noguchi (1902), however, had observed that cobra venom did not hemolyze red blood cells which had been carefully washed and suspended in physiological saline solution. Their work further showed that the prerequisite for hemolysis was the presence of a small amount of serum which apparently contained a substance which served as a complement to the snake venom. This complement, in view of Kyes' (1903, 1907) work, appeared to be lecithin, and it became of interest to determine the composition of the hemolytic "Cobralecithid". Subsequent workers, incidentally, have not all adhered to this theory of snake poisoning, and in any case it certainly cannot be considered as the complete or exclusive mechanism. Thus, Gronchi (1936a) has provided evidence which he believes shows that the toxicity of venom is not caused by the lecithinase present.

Lüdecke (1905) and Willstätter and Lüdecke (1904) observed that the interaction of lecithin and cobra venom was accompanied by the liberation of oleic acid, for which reason they proposed that the hemolytic product was a "de-oleo-lecithin". Other workers such as Dungern and Coca

(1908) and Neuberg and Rosenberg (1907) were of a similar opinion. Delezenne and Ledebt (1911, 1912), Delezenne and Fourneau (1914) and Fourneau (1920) showed unequivocally that the hemolytic "Cobralecithid" was merely lecithin from which one fatty acid had been removed; and it appeared that the fatty acid which was hydrolyzed off was invariably unsaturated. Thus the structure of lysolecithin may be represented by (XVI), in which the position of the fatty acid and the configuration of the glycerophosphoric acid are arbitrarily designated.

$$
\begin{array}{l}
CH_2OCR \\
\quad \| \\
\quad O \\
CHOH \\
\quad\quad\quad\quad O \\
\quad\quad\quad\quad \| \\
CH_2\!-\!O\!-\!P\!-\!OC_2H_4\!-\!N(CH_3)_3 \\
\quad\quad\quad\quad | \quad\quad\quad | \\
\quad\quad\quad\quad OH \quad\quad OH
\end{array}
\qquad (XVI)
$$

It was of interest to the early workers to determine whether the enzymes which attacked phosphatides were independent and specific substances. Clementi (1910) observed that pancreatic juice hydrolyzed both phosphatides and neutral fats. Wohlgemuth (1912), on the other hand, showed that after pancreatic juice had been stored at low temperature it lost its lipase activity on monobutyrin, whereas its ability to hydrolyze phosphatides remained unimpaired. Thus it appeared that lecithinases were independent substances and distinct from lipases. Similar evidence was provided by Friedemann (1909), Manwaring (1910) and Brunius (1930).

Nomenclature

Delezenne and Fourneau (1914) gave to the substance indicated by (XVI) the name "lysocithin", which was a name compounded from lysin and lecithin and which signified the chief property as well as the origin of the material. *Chemical Abstracts* lists as variants of lysocithin, "lysocytin" and "lysozithin". These terms have been used widely in the literature as a general classification for the compounds which result when one fatty acid is removed from a glycerophosphatide. Lysocithin has also been used synonymously with the specific term "lysolecithin", which it resembles closely in both spelling and pronunciation. To avoid such confusion it is proposed here that the term "lysophosphatide" be used to designate the primary product of enzymatic phosphatide hydrolysis— that is, the product which results from the removal of one fatty acid from a phosphatide. This term has been used previously by Page (1937, p. 57). The specific lysophosphatides may then be named, as is already common practice, by attaching the prefix "lyso" to the name of the phosphatide—e.g., lysolecithin, lysocephalins. Such terms as lysophosphatidyl-aminoethyl alcohol and lysophosphatidylserine may also be used justifiably. The products which result on further enzymatic hydrolysis, such as after the removal of both fatty acids from the glycerophosphatides or the choline from lecithins, may be designated by their systematic chemical names.

The enzymes which act on phosphatides have been widely designated as "lecithases" or "lecithinases". Belfanti, Contardi and Ercoli (1936, p. 213) entitled their excellent review "Lecithases". Udagawa (1935) suggested that the enzymes be called "phosphatidolipase", and Ogawa (1936) suggested the term "phospholipase". Delezenne and Fourneau (1914) offered the logical designation "phosphatidase". Although the term "lecithinase" is obviously somewhat less logical as a general designation, its use in the literature is well entrenched, and it should not be too strongly opposed since the enzymes which attack lecithin appear to be the same ones which attack the other glycerophosphatides. This fact makes unnecessary a term such as "cephalinase" which was proposed by Dunn (1934). Accordingly, the enzymes which effect the hydrolysis of phosphatides will be referred to as "lecithinases" in this review. The term "phosphatidase" with its obvious meaning, however, need not be discarded.

Four lecithinases have been described. Two of these, known as lecithinase A and lecithinase B, possess lipolytic activity, lecithinase A freeing one fatty acid from a glycerophosphatide and lecithinase B freeing the second fatty acid from the lysophosphatide. Of the other two enzymes, one possesses choline esterase action and frees choline, whereas the other has phosphatase action and splits the glycerophosphoric acid linkage. These will be discussed in detail below.

THE LYSOPHOSPHATIDES

A discussion of the lysophophatides is necessarily limited to the primary enzymatic hydrolysis products of lecithin and of what was classically considered to be cephalin. Very little, if anything, is known about the action of the lecithinases on sphingomyelin (see p. 103) or on the yet ill-defined inositol-containing phosphatides. The phosphatidic acids, as has been seen (see p. 49), are now thought to be the result of the action of lecithinases on glycerophosphatides *in vivo*.

The Preparation of the Lysophosphatides

Delezenne and Fourneau (1914) prepared lysophosphatides by allowing an emulsion of egg yolk to react with cobra poison for one-half to three days, depending on the amount of venom present. The vacuum-dried reaction mixture was then treated with a large excess of acetone and the insoluble material dissolved in various solvents and subsequently precipitated. This was followed by numerous crystallizations from alcohol, chloroform and alcohol-petroleum ether mixtures. A crystalline product was obtained which was insoluble in acetone and, unlike the parent material, insoluble in ether and quite soluble in warm water. The acids present were completely saturated. That the product, despite its crystallinity, was not pure, however, was shown by the fact that hydrolysis yielded less than the theoretical amount of choline for lysolecithin. Accordingly, it appeared that another base, probably aminoethyl alcohol, was present. That this was actually the case was shown by Levene and Rolf (1923), who prepared the lysophosphatides from egg yolk and showed that on hydrolysis, choline and aminoethyl alcohol were formed as well as palmitic and stearic acids. These workers assumed, therefore, that their lysophosphatides consisted of a mixture of lysolecithin and lysophosphatidylaminoethyl alcohol. The latter material they termed "lysocephalin" since the other components of the cephalin phosphatides were unknown to them.

The separation of lysolecithin and the lysocephalin was accomplished by Levene, Rolf and Simms (1924), since the cadmium chloride complex of the lysocephalin fraction proved to be less soluble in organic solvents than the corresponding complex of lysolecithin. The products gave elementary analyses in accord with the theoretical values of lysolecithin and lysophosphatidylaminoethyl alcohol. The lysocephalin fraction on hydrolysis yielded only stearic acid, whereas the lysolecithin yielded both stearic and palmitic acids. It is apparent from this work that the lecithinases hydrolyze both lecithin and the cephalins.

The lysolecithin obtained by these workers was found to be more soluble in organic solvents than the lysocephalin fraction and could be crystallized from chloroform, acetic acid, pyridine and methyl or ethyl alcohol. It softened at 100° C., and melted with decomposition at 263° C. It was insoluble in ether and acetone and was very hygroscopic. In acetic acid the material demonstrated a specific rotation of +0.8°. In pyridine the value increased to +1.2°, and in chloroform it was −2.6°. The lysophosphatidylaminoethyl alcohol prepared by these workers was not hygroscopic and could be crystallized from chloroform and from pyridine to yield needles which melted at 212–213° C. In acetic acid the compound exhibited a specific rotation of +2°.

The above work was carried out on egg yolk rather than on the isolated phosphatides. Chargaff and Cohen (1939) reacted snake venom with pure lecithin obtained from beef brain, pig brain or egg yolk. In each case, a small (15 to 50 per cent) yield of lysolecithin was readily obtained. The lysolecithins were purer than the parent lecithins since they contained almost no amino nitrogen, whereas the parent lecithin in each case contained a small amount. The iodine numbers of the lyso-lecithin preparations were below 6, indicating that the fatty acids were virtually completely saturated. An attempt to increase the yield of prod-uct by emulsifying the lecithin in egg white was not successful. The lower yields with the isolated lecithin are not readily explained.

In contrast to the work with lecithin, Chargaff and Cohen (1939) found it impossible to prepare a lysocephalin by the action of snake venom on the isolated cephalin fraction. This is indeed an interesting observation, from which speculation may arise as to the state in which the phosphatides occur in their natural sources. Chargaff and Cohen (1939) also pointed out that the amount of phosphatides which can be isolated from egg yolk in the form of their lyso compounds is much greater than the amount isolated as true phosphatides. In view of these results with the cephalin fraction, mention must be made of the earlier work of Dunn (1934) and of Storm van Leeuwen and Szent-Györgi (1923), who had reported that snake venom reacted with the isolated cephalin fraction to yield a lysocephalin.

Lysosphingomyelin. According to Magistris (1929), wasp poison reacts with sphingomyelin to liberate lignoceric acid and form a lysosphingo-myelin. Ercoli (1940, p. 480) believes these results to be questionable, and here, too, further investigation is indicated.

The Structure of the Lysophosphatides

As has already been indicated, it is well established that the lysophos-phatides are structurally different from the glycerophosphatides in that one fatty acid is removed. From formula (XVI) for lysolecithin it is apparent that the phosphoric ester linkage might involve either an α- or a β-hydroxyl group. Evidence on this score is lacking. In the event that the phosphoric acid group occupies an α-position, there are then two positions available for the attachment of the fatty acid. Here again it is not known whether the α- or the β-position is the preferred one or whether the distribution is random. Levene and Mehltretter (1937) car-ried out experiments designed to shed light on the position of the fatty acid, but could not draw conclusive results from their data.

Lüdecke (1905), on the basis of his original work on the structure of the lysophosphatides, advanced the concept that the fatty acid which was removed was invariably unsaturated, whereas the acid which re-mained was saturated. Latzer (1927) was of the opinion that this is not necessarily the case. The former view, however, was apparently con-firmed by many workers including Delezenne and Fourneau (1914); and Belfanti, Contardi and Ercoli (1936, p. 217) mentioned the existence of newer evidence which confirms this idea. It was these observations which were in part responsible for the view that the glycerophosphatide molecule contains precisely one saturated and one unsaturated fatty acid. However, it is now known that the distribution of saturated and unsaturated acids in phosphatides is random rather than specific (see p. 21), so that considerably more or less than 50 per cent of saturated fatty acids may be present. If this is the case, it does not seem feasible that the enzyme would limit its activity to unsaturated acids, especially since lysophosphatide formation in some instances has been reported to be quantitative. On the other hand, the evidence available indicates that the fatty acids in purified lysophosphatides consist either of palmitic or stearic acids, although this point is worthy of further investigation. The lecithinases which hydrolyze phosphatides completely, liberating inorganic phosphorus compounds, do not distinguish between saturated and unsaturated acids. Thus, King (1934) has shown that hydrolecithin prepared by the catalytic reduction of natural lecithin is attacked as rapidly as the parent compound. Accordingly, it must be concluded that further investigation must be designed to determine the composition of the acids which are liberated and the acids which remain during lysophosphatide formation.

Occurrence of the Lysophosphatides

The presence of lysophosphatides in the animal body was shown for the first time by Belfanti (1924), who isolated lysolecithin from the pancreas and salivary glands of horses and cattle. This, of course, pointed to the presence of a lecithinase in these organs, which was actually shown to be the case (see p. 106). Pighini and Delfini (1931) found lysolecithin in the brain of the guinea pig and in egg yolk. Iwata (1930) reported the presence of lysolecithin in the alcoholic extracts of polished rice, and Francioli (1935) found it in only one of many poisonous and edible fungi examined, *Lycoperdon giganteum*. Hirao (1931) examined various food plants and found lysolecithin in rice, millet, barley, wheat and rye. Chargaff (1942b) provided evidence for the possible presence of lysophosphatides in the mitachondria from rabbit liver.

Francioli (1934) observed that various air-dried organs contained lysolecithin due to the presence of a lecithinase which became active during the treatment of the organs. If, however, the organ was autoclaved first in order to inactivate the lecithinase, no lysolecithin was found. This situation is entirely analogous to that discovered by Hanahan and Chaikoff (1948), who showed that the phosphatidic acids of cabbage leaves probably are formed during isolation by an enzymatic action which could be inhibited by initial steam treatment (see p. 50).

The Lecithinases

The preceding discussion has concerned itself with the lysophosphatides which are formed by the enzymatic removal of one fatty acid molecule. The specific enzyme responsible for this activity has been named lecithinase A, and this is the enzyme which has been studied the most extensively. Obviously in lecithin, as well as in what was classically considered cephalin, there are three other points of attachment (ester linkages), in addition to the linkage attacked by lecithinase A, which should prove susceptible to enzymatic attack. These comprise the second fatty acid linkage, the phosphoric acid-glycerol linkage and the amino-alcohol-phosphoric acid linkage. That such enzymes did indeed exist was shown in the results of several early workers (Slowtzoff, 1905; DaCruz, 1928; Page and Schmidt, 1931), who found that enzymatic action freed choline from phosphatides. Other workers such as Akamatsu (1923), Kay (1926) and King, King and Page (1930) have shown that enzymatic hydrolysis of phosphatides leads to the liberation of phosphoric acid. Accordingly, it seemed logical to postulate the existence of lecithinases corresponding to each of the ester linkages of lecithin. As the following discussion will indicate, the presence of such enzymes has actually been proved. These are defined as follows:

Lecithinase A: An enzyme which removes one fatty acid from lecithin.

Lecithinase B: An enzyme which removes the remaining acid from lysolecithin.

Lecithinase C: An enzyme with cholinephosphatase activity capable of splitting choline from lecithin (and presumably the nitrogenous bases from the cephalin phosphatides).

Lecithinase D: An enzyme with glycerophosphatase activity which separates lecithin at its ester linkage between glycerol and phosphoric acid.

Lecithinase A

The term lecithinase A was applied by Contardi and Ercoli (1933) and by Belfanti (1933) to the enzyme which removes one fatty acid from lecithin. Presumably it acts similarly on the constituents of the cephalin fraction which are structurally analogous to lecithin.

Occurrence. As already indicated, lecithinase A was originally found in cobra venom where it was detected because it reacted with lecithin to yield a hemolytic substance. This enzyme, as indicated by Belfanti (1924a, 1925a), occurs not only in the venom of various types of cobras but also in reptiles of the viper family (*Vipera russelli, V. aspis, V. ammodytes*) and the *Crotalus* family (*Crotalus terrificus, Lachesis alternata,*

L. atrox, L. lanceolata, Bothrops jararaca, B. jararacussu). Ghosh (1940) isolated lecithinase A from *Boa fasciatus* and *Echis carinata*. In general, the enzyme seems to be present in the salivary secretions of all poisonous snakes and may, to some extent at least, be correlated with the toxicity of the secretions. Slotta and Szyszka (1938) found that the venom of *C. terrificus* contained large quantities of the lecithinase, whereas the venom from the various species of *Bothrops* contained relatively little of the enzyme. The enzyme was also found by Belfanti (1925a, 1926) in the poison of bees and scorpions. He observed (1924, 1925) that many of these poisons yielded lytic substances with egg yolk and brain but not with slurries in physiological saline of heart muscle, lung, kidney, spleen or liver. Apparently the phosphatides in these substances were not available for enzymatic attack without prior treatment.

Belfanti (1924, 1925) found lysolecithin in the salivary glands of horses and cattle and in pancreas, indicating that lecithinase A must also occur in these sources. Later, Belfanti and Arnaudi (1932) separated lecithinase A from other enzymes in the pancreas, and Nikuni (1932) also showed that pancreas extract converted lecithin to lysolecithin. Gronchi (1933) likewise found lecithinase A in pancreas as well as in the adrenal cortex. Gronchi (1936) showed that pancreas extract or pancreatin contained other enzymes which could be inactivated by heat, leaving unchanged the heat-stable lecithinase A.

That this enzyme probably occurs in most animal organs was shown by Francioli (1934), who found lysolecithin in dried heart, liver, spleen, muscle, brain, suprarenals, thymus and prostate. The fresh organs, on the other hand, contained only lecithin, indicating that the lecithinase A was in some manner held in check in the fresh organ by other enzymes or protective substances. These materials were apparently inactivated during the drying process, leaving the lecithinase A free to act on the lecithin.

Scheff and Awny (1949) found that the lecithinase A content of spleen increased in patients with thrombocytopenia purpura, splenic neutropenia and congenital hemolytic icterus.

Lecithinase A is also found in certain substances of vegetable origin, although its occurrence is apparently not as wide here as in the animal kingdom. Iwata (1930, 1931) found it in polished rice, and Francioli (1935) obtained evidence for its occurrence in a fungus, *Lycoperdon giganteum*. The occurrence of lecithinase in *Bacillus cereus* has been suggested by Colmer (1948).

Properties. The heat stability of lecithinase A, which was early observed by Flexner and Noguchi (1902), has already been mentioned. It was because of this property that Gronchi (1936) was able to isolate the enzyme from commercial pancreatin, since heating for 30 minutes at 90° C. inactivated all the enzymes except lecithinase A. The enzyme so isolated has been shown to be incapable of degrading lecithin still further, thus indicating its very specific activity (Latzer, 1927).

Lecithinase A is sensitive to pH and was found by Levene, Rolf and Simms (1924), who worked with cobra poison, to be inactivated at a pH of 8 or above. These workers conducted their experiments at a pH of 7.0 ± 0.5. Other workers have reported similar values for optimum activity, e.g., Belfanti and Arnaudi (1932) reported 6.8 to 7.0 for lecithinase A from horse pancreas at 37° C. Their enzyme was inactivated at 58 to 60° C. Hughes (1935) measured the rate of hydrolysis of lecithin to lysolecithin by the change in surface potential of a surface film. He employed venoms from the black snake, black tiger, copperhead, daboia and cobra, and in each instance found the optimum pH to be 7.3. He observed that the enzyme was stable when boiled at a pH of 5.9 but was destroyed by boiling in alkaline solutions.

Lecithinase A has been observed (Contardi and Latzer, 1928) to attack the cadmium chloride complex of lecithin, yielding the corresponding complex of lysolecithin. Latzer (1927) obtained similar results with the zinc chloride complex of lecithin. The metallic complexes of lysolecithin, as might be expected, are hemolytic.

The enzyme appears to be activated by various substances such as calcium salts (Delezenne and Fourneau, 1914; Kudicke and Sachs, 1916). It has long been known that a higher yield of lysophosphatides is obtained from egg yolk than from previously isolated phosphatides. Belfanti, Contardi and Ercoli (1936, p. 216) pointed out that the highly emulsified condition of the phosphatides in their natural state may contribute to this, as well as the activating influence of the calcium salts present.

The activity of lecithinase A was observed by Kyes (1903) to be inhibited by cholesterol which appeared to form a nonhemolytic molecular complex with lysophosphatides. This was also observed by Delezenne and Fourneau (1914) and Delezenne and Ledebt (1911, 1912). Hughes (1935) likewise observed that the addition of cholesterol to a lecithin surface film markedly decreased the rate of hydrolysis of the lecithin by snake venom. Belfanti, Contardi and Ercoli (1936, p. 220) pointed out, contrary to the opinion of Césari and Bouquet (1937), that snake poison serum is a specific inactivator of lecithinase A. Thus they were able to show that when snake poison is "neutralized" with the exact amount of serum, lysophosphatide formation will not proceed. Belfanti and Arnaudi (1932) observed that sodium chloride inhibited the enzyme to a very slight extent.

Ogawa (1936) observed that calcium chloride, potassium cyanide and sodium fluoride did not impair the activity of the enzyme. Levene, Rolf and Simms (1924) noted that large quantities of various antiseptics inhibited the enzymic action, although small quantities sufficient to retard putrefactive processes did not. Francioli (1937) found that physostigmine did not produce an adverse effect on the enzyme.

Contardi and Latzer (1928) found that cobra venom did not hydrolyze the synthetic distearyllecithin of Grün and Limpächer (1926), thus casting some doubt on the identity of the material. Saturated lecithin prepared by catalytic reduction of lecithin was found by Ogawa (1936) to be hydrolyzed by lecithinase A from pancreas.

The Preparation and Detection of Lecithinase A. Various methods for isolating lecithinase A have been discussed by Francioli and Ercoli (1940, p. 1686). For isolation from pancreas, an unpublished procedure of Belfanti and Arnaudi is described in which the tissue is repeatedly frozen with dry ice and thawed rapidly in order to rupture the cell membranes. The material is then extracted with 90 per cent ethanol to obtain a mixture of lysolecithin and lecithinase A which is separated by treating an aqueous solution with barium oxide. The precipitated lysolecithin is filtered quickly, and the enzyme is recovered from the filtrate.

For isolation of lecithinase from pancreatin, the method of Gronchi (1936) may be used in which the other enzymes are inactivated by heating an aqueous suspension for one-half hour at 80 to 90° C. The water-insoluble portion is then extracted with 95 per cent alcohol for 4 hours at 45° C. in order to obtain the enzyme.

Gronchi (1936a) also provided a procedure for the isolation of lecithinase A from venoms which involves a simple alcohol extraction. Ordinarily, however, the venoms are used without purification. Ghosh (1941) has described the isolation of a lecithinase-containing hemolysin from cobra venom by precipitation with sodium chloride and subsequent purification. A lecithinase from the venom of *Crotalus t. terrificus* was crystallized by Slotta and Fraenkel-Conrat (1938).

Lecithinase A is detected by its activity on phosphatides. Egg yolk may be used conveniently. The lysolecithin produced may in turn be detected by its hemolytic properties. Thus, laking will occur when the lysolecithin-containing material and phosphate buffer of pH 7.0 to 7.1 are mixed with defibrinated blood. These techniques are discussed in detail by Francioli and Ercoli (1940, p. 1687).

Lecithinase B

The information regarding lecithinase B is quite incomplete, and a great deal more investigation is indicated. On the basis of existing data, however, it may be said that lecithinase B, like the better known lecithinase A, does have a separate and distinct existence. Like lecithinase A it is lipolytic, but differs in that it possesses the ability to remove the remaining fatty acid from lysolecithin. It probably demonstrates similar activity with phosphatidylaminoethyl alcohol (Fairbairn, 1948) and phosphatidylserine and their corresponding lyso compounds.

It had been observed by numerous workers that lecithin or lysolecithin may be hydrolyzed enzymatically to choline, glycerophosphoric acid and fatty acids. Light was shed on the specificity of the enzymes involved by Contardi and Ercoli (1933), who observed that an enzyme existed in old rice bran hulls which destroyed the hemolytic activity of lysolecithin. Coincident with the disappearance of the hemolytic properties, a fatty acid separated. Unlike the results of previous investigations, the water-soluble products did not consist of choline and inorganic phosphate. Instead, the intact choline ester of glycerophosphoric acid could be isolated, although in a rather impure form. Pure α-glycerylphosphorylcholine was later isolated from incubated beef pancreas by Schmidt, Hershman and Thannhauser (1945). This indicated the presence of a new enzyme which was called lecithinase B. The enzyme could be precipitated from aqueous extracts of rice polishings by lead acetate and was shown to be present in takadiastase and in *Aspergillus oryzae*. Torboli (1945) extracted a lecithinase from rice hulls with water and toluene. The enzyme was precipitated with ammonium sulfate and the residue, after centrifuging, was dialyzed to provide a lecithinolytic material. It is not clear whether or not this is relatively pure lecithinase B.

The enzyme appears to be present in higher fungi, in most animal organs such as pancreas (LeBreton and Pantaleon, 1947), heart, liver, spleen and brain, and also in blood (Belfanti, Contardi and Ercoli, 1936, p. 223; Rezek, 1945). The pH for the optimum activity of lecithinase B was determined by Contardi and Ercoli (1933) by noting the value at which the hemolytic activity of lysolecithin disappeared most rapidly. The value proved to be 3.5, which is quite different from the neutral value found to be optimum for lecithinase A. The enzyme is activated by calcium salts, as is lecithinase A, but it is probably less heat-stable.

Fairbairn (1948) found lecithinase B in extracts of *Penicilium notatum* and reported that it acted only on lysophosphatides, since no reaction at all was obtained with phosphatides. From the reaction products he was actually able to isolate glycerylphosphorylcholine and glycerylphosphorylaminoethyl alcohol. Maximum activity, in fair accord with the above results, was found to exist at a pH of 4. These data are the first to prove that lecithinase B acts specifically on lysophosphatides but not on phosphatides.

Lecithinases C and D

It was apparent to early workers that enzymes existed which degraded phosphatides completely, liberating phosphoric acid, and, in the case of lecithin, choline. Indications of the specificity of these enzymes was derived from the work of Thiele (1913) and of Porter (1916), who found that an enzyme exists in blood which can split phosphatides but not ordinary glycerides. Enzymes which release the bases from the cephalin phosphatides have received practically no study. Presumptive evidence, however, that an enzyme exists which hydrolyzes serine from phosphatidylserine may be gained from the work of Rose (1950).

Phosphatide-splitting enzymes with cholinephosphatase and glycerophosphatase activity were found in a variety of sources such as pancreas (Bókay, 1877, Wohlgemuth, 1912); mucous membrane of the digestive tract (Schumoff-Simonowski and Sieber, 1906); intestinal juice (Bergell, 1901, Clementi, 1910); meconium (Schmidt, 1914); castor bean lipase and wasp poison (Contardi and Latzer, 1928). They have also been observed in kidney extracts (Kay, 1926); blood and pus leucocytes (Fiessinger and Clogne, 1917); in takadiastase (Akamatsu, 1923); and after autolysis in organs such as pancreas (Kutscher and Lohmann, 1903), brain (Stamm, 1926), and liver (Artom, 1925). More recently, Rezek (1946) found in the Weinberg snail (*Helix pomatia*) a combination of enzymes which not only released the fatty acids from lecithin, but also hydrolyzed the choline and released inorganic phosphate and glycerol. Felsenfeld (1944) has reported lecithinases in the cholera bacteria, *Vibrio comma* and *El Tor Vibrio*, which hydrolyze lecithin completely. An enzyme preparation liberating phosphate from phosphatides has been found in *Clostridium bifermentans* by Miles and Miles (1948).

The Cholinephosphatase. Reference has already been made to older work which recorded the liberation of choline from lecithin by enzymic action. The existence of an enzyme which demonstrated such specific activity was postulated by Contardi and Ercoli (1933, 1935) and referred to by them (1933a) as lecithinase C. Contardi and Ravazzoni (1934) and Francioli (1937) were of the opinion that this cholinephosphatase was different from ordinary cholineesterase. This was also the opinion of Yoshinaga (1936), who found that takadiastase contained an enzyme which split the maximum amount of choline from lecithin at pH 4.0 Recently, Hanahan and Chaikoff (1947) verified the original postulation.

The first evidence of a separate choline-splitting enzyme was obtained when Hanahan and Chaikoff (1947) made certain observations regarding carrot phosphatides. They showed that the phosphatide which could be extracted by alcohol-ether mixtures from raw carrots was characterized by a low nitrogen content and by a virtual absence of choline. The same extraction, when applied to steam-treated carrots, provided a more conventional phosphatide with a nitrogen-phosphorus molar ratio of 0.89. The product extracted from raw carrots appeared to be similar to the phosphatidic acids; and it seemed logical, in view of the effect of prior treatment with steam, to postulate the presence of an enzyme which split the nitrogenous base from the phosphatide during the isolation process unless first inactivated.

This was substantiated in further work by Hanahan and Chaikoff (1947a), who were able to isolate from carrots an enzyme extract which possessed no cholineesterase activity, but which split the ester linkage between the nitrogenous base and the phosphoric acid grouping in phosphatides obtained from carrots and soybeans. Furthermore, it was shown that the activity of the enzyme was not limited to choline, since more nitrogen was liberated from the phosphatides than could be accounted for by loss in choline nitrogen. The enzyme exerted its maximum activity at a pH range of 5.2 to 5.9 in a 0.05 molar phosphate buffer. It showed a high degree of heat stability since it was not completely inactivated when exposed to a temperature of 95° C. for 15 minutes.

A similar enzyme was shown to be present in cabbage leaves (Hanahan and Chaikoff, 1948), and, as in the case of carrots, a normal phosphatide could be isolated only after the cabbage leaves had been subjected to steam treatment. From the fresh leaves, phosphatidic acids were isolated; and thus this work sheds considerable light on the origin of the phosphatidic acids (see p. 49), since the usual isolation procedure provides conditions favorable to enzyme action.

The enzyme in cabbage leaves exhibited its maximum activity in the same pH range as the carrot enzyme, and adhered to first order reaction kinetics at 25° C. between 0.5 and 2 hours. It, too, was quite thermostable.

The Glycerophosphatase. The enzyme which hydrolyzes lecithin at the glycerol and phosphoric acid ester linkage may be referred to as lecithinase D.

This enzyme, according to present available data, must be considered to be distinct from the phosphatase which acts on glycerophosphoric acid. This latter ester is formed by the action of lecithinases A, B and C on lecithin, since these hydrolyze the fatty acids and the choline. Once this ester is formed, its phosphoric acid may, of course, be liberated by an ordinary phosphatase. The enzyme, however, which splits lecithin (and presumably lysolecithin and the choline ester of glycerophosphoric acid) to yield the choline ester of phosphoric acid is a distinct substance.

The isolation of phosphoric acid was reported in much of the older work. It must be assumed that the phosphoric acid was liberated either by the action of lecithinase D to produce the choline ester of phosphoric acid followed by the action of a phosphatase or by the action of lecithinases A, B and C to produce a glycerophosphoric acid which in turn was hydrolyzed by a phosphatase.

Kay (1926) observed in kidney extract an enzyme which had a weak action in freeing phosphoric acid from lecithin. On the basis of its behavior King, King and Page (1930) concluded that this enzyme was different from ordinary bone phosphatase. Although the material was probably a mixture, substances of similar activity were found in numerous tissues. The order of decreasing glycerophosphatase activity in various tissues was found by King (1931, 1934) and King and Dolan (1933) to be as follows: kidney, small intestine, spleen, liver, testis, pancreas, large intestine, brain, ovary, bone, suprarenal, lung, blood vessel, cardiac muscle and skeletal muscle.

These workers showed that lysolecithin was hydrolyzed more readily than lecithin, although a lack of specificity was indicated by the fact that bone phosphatase, which is relatively inactive against lecithin, also hydrolyzed lysolecithin. It was further shown (King, 1934) that the cephalin fraction and phosphatidic acids are attacked at the same rate as lecithin. Synthetic lecithin of Grün and Limpächer (1926) was attacked so slowly that doubt is again cast on the structure of the synthetic product. Brominated lecithin was hydrolyzed ten times faster than the natural substance. The enzyme demonstrated its optimum reactivity with lecithin at a pH of 7.5. Here it differed from kidney phosphatase whose optimum value was 8.9. It was stable in neutral solutions but was destroyed by either acid or alkali at 38° C.

What appears to be the true lecithinase D * was found by Macfarlane and Knight (1941) in *Clostridium welchii*. The enzyme appears to be a component of the bacterial toxin elaborated by this organism. When the toxin was allowed to react with egg yolk phosphatides, it was possible to isolate all the phosphorus in the form of an organic compound which was identified as the choline ester of phosphoric acid. On treatment of this compound with bone phosphatase, the phosphorus was rapidly and completely hydrolyzed to inorganic phosphate. The ether-soluble material remaining after enzymic hydrolysis was shown by physical constants and hydrolysis experiments to be a diglyceride. Thus, it appears that the enzyme hydrolyzed lecithin to produce a diglyceride and the choline ester of phosphoric acid, and that this decomposition occurred to the extent of over 90 per cent. An optimum pH of 7.0–7.6

* Macfarlane and Knight (1941) designate their enzyme as lecithinase C. It is termed D here in accord with the classification of Contardi and Ercoli (1933a), who reserved C for the choline-splitting enzyme.

was observed for the hydrolysis, and it was activated by calcium ion. The enzyme is relatively heat-stable, but is inactivated by surface denaturation and by detergents such as sodium dodecyl sulfate. It is inhibited by fluoride, citrate and phosphate, and is specifically inhibited by serum which is antitoxic for *Clostridium welchii* (type A). It is of interest that this lecithinase is probably identical with the specific α-toxin present in type A *C. welchii* filtrates.

Lecithinase D from *C. welchii* appears to be inactive toward a brain cephalin fraction (Macfarlane, 1942, 1948), as well as toward phosphatidylaminoethyl alcohol and phosphatidylserine. Sphingomyelin, on the other hand, is hydrolyzed easily, although somewhat slower than lecithin (Macfarlane, 1948). With a crude sample, approximately 90 per cent of the lipide phosphorus was converted to the choline ester of phosphoric acid, whereas the phosphorus-free material appeared to be an impure form of lignocerylsphingosine. As with lecithin, the activity of the enzyme was increased by calcium ions and inhibited by sodium fluoride.

Further investigations by Macfarlane (1948a) revealed that lecithinase D also occurred in *C. oedematiens*. Although this material was similar in its biochemical reactions to the enzyme from *C. welchii*, it was immunologically distinct as evidenced by its behavior toward homologous and heterologous antitoxic sera.

Mention should be made of the diphosphatase found by Udagawa (1935) in takaphosphatase. This material, like lecithinase D, split the cholinephosphoric acid from lecithin. It was, however, not recognized as a lecithinase by its discoverer. Udagawa reported a pH of 4 to 5 for optimum activity. This is considerably lower than the value 7.0 to 7.6 found by Macfarlane and Knight (1941) for their lecithinase D, a fact which throws doubt on the identity of the two substances. The phosphatases which may concern lecithin are discussed in greater detail by Folley and Kay (1936, pp. 159–212).

The activity of the lecithinase D may be measured by a manometric procedure devised by Zamecnik, Brewster and Lipmann (1947). The method depends on the fact that the liberated choline ester of phosphoric acid displaces carbon dioxide from a sodium bicarbonate-carbon dioxide buffered medium. The liberated gas is measured directly.

Lecithinase D was shown by Nagler (1939) and by Macfarlane and Knight (1941) to release lipide from human blood serum. Petermann (1946) studied the effect of this enzyme from *C. perfringens* on various serum-protein fractions and found that the release of lipide from serum paralleled the action of lecithinase on the so-called "X-protein" complex. However, the amount of phosphorus released from the various serum fractions bore no relation to the amount of lipide set free. The experi-

THE LECITHINASES

$$
\begin{array}{l}
\overset{\displaystyle O}{\overset{\|}{CH_2OCR}} \\
\overset{\displaystyle O}{\overset{|}{CHOCR'}} \\
\qquad\quad\; \overset{\displaystyle O}{\|} \\
CH_2O-P-OC_2H_4N(CH_3)_3 \\
\qquad\;\; | \qquad\quad | \\
\qquad\;\; OH \qquad\;\; OH
\end{array}
$$

Lecithin

R′COOH* ←———— Lecithinase A
Fatty acid
+

$$
\begin{array}{l}
\overset{\displaystyle O}{\overset{\|}{CH_2OCR}} \\
\overset{|}{CHOH} \\
\quad\;\; \overset{\displaystyle O}{\|} \\
CH_2OP-OC_2H_4N(CH_3)_3 \\
\quad\; | \qquad\quad | \\
\quad\; OH \qquad\;\; OH
\end{array}
$$

———— Lecithinase B ————→

$$
\begin{array}{l}
CH_2OH \\
\overset{|}{CHOH} \\
\quad\;\; \overset{\displaystyle O}{\|} \\
CH_2O-P-OC_2H_4N(CH_3)_3 \\
\qquad\; | \qquad\quad | \\
\qquad\; OH \qquad\;\; OH
\end{array}
$$

Lysolecithin — Choline ester of glycerophosphoric acid

Lecithinase D ↓ ↓ Lecithinase C ——— Lecithinase D ↓ ↓ Lecithinase C

$[HOC_2H_4\overset{+}{N}(CH_3)_3]OH^-$
Choline
+

$$
\begin{array}{l}
\overset{\displaystyle O}{\overset{\|}{CH_2OCR^{**}}} \\
\overset{|}{CHOH} \\
CH_2OH \\
\text{Monoglyceride} \\
+ \\
\overset{\displaystyle O}{\overset{\|}{[HOP-OC_2H_4\overset{+}{N}(CH_3)_3]OH^-}} \\
\quad | \\
\quad OH
\end{array}
$$

Choline ester of phosphoric acid

$$
\begin{array}{l}
\overset{\displaystyle O}{\overset{\|}{CH_2OCR^{**}}} \\
\overset{|}{CHOH} \\
\quad\;\; \overset{\displaystyle O}{\|} \\
CH_2OP-OH \\
\qquad\; | \\
\qquad\; OH
\end{array}
$$

Mono fatty acid ester of glycerophosphoric acid

$$
\begin{array}{l}
CH_2OH \\
\overset{|}{CHOH} \\
CH_2OH \\
\text{Glycerol} \\
+ \\
\overset{\displaystyle O}{\overset{\|}{[HOPOC_2H_4\overset{+}{N}(CH_3)_3]OH^-}} \\
\quad | \\
\quad OH
\end{array}
$$

Choline ester of phosphoric acid

$[HOC_2H_4\overset{+}{N}(CH_3)_3]OH^-$
Choline
+

$$
\begin{array}{l}
CH_2OH \\
\overset{|}{CHOH} \\
\quad\;\; \overset{\displaystyle O}{\|} \\
CH_2OP-OH \\
\qquad\; | \\
\qquad\; OH
\end{array}
$$

Glycerophosphoric acid

↓ Phosphatase

H_3PO_4+$[HOC_2H_4\overset{+}{N}(CH_3)_3]OH^-$
Phosphoric　　Choline
acid

↓ Phosphatase

$$
\begin{array}{l}
\overset{\displaystyle O}{\overset{\|}{CH_2OCR}} \\
\overset{|}{CHOH} + H_3PO_4 \\
CH_2OH \quad \text{Phosphoric} \\
\qquad\qquad \text{acid}
\end{array}
$$
Monoglyceride

↓ Phosphatase

$[HOC_2H_4\overset{+}{N}(CH_3)_3]OH^-$
Choline
+
H_3PO_4
Phosphoric
acid

↓ Phosphatase

$$
\begin{array}{l}
CH_2OH \\
\overset{|}{CHOH} \\
CH_2OH \\
\text{Glycerol} \\
+ \\
H_3PO_4 \\
\text{Phosphoric} \\
\text{acid}
\end{array}
$$

↓ Lipase

$$
\begin{array}{l}
CH_2OH \\
\overset{|}{CHOH} + RCOOH \\
CH_2OH \quad \text{Fatty acid}
\end{array}
$$
Glycerol

*R′ is presumably unsaturated.
**The fatty acid in this molecule may presumably be hydrolyzed by a lipase.

ments were not conducted in such a way that it could be concluded with certainty that all the phosphorus was released by lecithinase action.

Biological Significance of the Lecithinases

The role of the lecithinases in normal and pathological conditions as well as in cell metabolism presents an interesting challenge to biological investigators. Interesting observations have been made which must be followed up and correlated. Thus Gerstl, Tennant and Pelzman (1945) showed that mouse liver enzymes split 90 per cent of the phosphatides of the tubercle bacillus (see p. 202) in 48 hours, and that liver enzymes from immunized rabbits split the phosphatides much more readily than enzymes from untreated rabbits. Öhman (1945) has shown that lysolecithin inhibits plasma division in newly fertilized sea urchin eggs, and Trager (1948) found that lysolecithin inhibited the growth of *Lactobacillus casei* cultured on a medium which was normal except that subminimal amounts of biotin were present. When the biotin was replaced with oleic acid, the lysolecithin no longer exerted an inhibiting effect.

Zamecnik and Lipmann (1947) have shown that lecithin inhibits the reaction between *Clostridium welchii* toxin, which is a lecithinase, and the corresponding antitoxin. They suggest that this is due to a competition between the lecithin and the antitoxin for the lecithinase; and this may account, in part, for the failure of the antitoxin in certain instances. Such observations may indeed prove to be of extreme value in the understanding of the mechanisms of diseases and their subsequent therapy.

The widespread occurrence of lecithinases in animal organs points to a relationship between the enzymes and lipide metabolism. Likewise, the stepwise activity of the lecithinases and the hemolytic action of the lysophosphatides appear to be portions of an uncorrelated biological phenomenon which awaits for its unravelling the ingenuity and perseverance of researchers.

Summary

Present knowledge regarding the lecithinases is summarized in the preceding chart. It must be remembered that the mode of production of free choline (other than by lecithinase C) or free phosphoric acid has not been determined experimentally.

CHAPTER X

SYNTHESIS OF THE PHOSPHATIDES

SYNTHESIS OF THE GLYCEROPHOSPHATIDES

Various attempts have been made to synthesize lecithin and phosphatidylaminoethyl alcohol. The syntheses of the former compound by Baer and Kates (1950) and of the latter compound by Rose (1947) have been the most successful and will be discussed first. The literature contains no references to attempted synthesis of sphingomyelin, although the work of Carter, Norris and Rockwell (1947) gives promise that dihydrosphingosine will be synthesized. Here, indeed, lies a fertile field for the imaginative organic chemist.

Baer and Kates' Synthesis of Lecithin

An elegant synthesis of enantiomeric α-lecithins has been announced by Baer and Kates (1950). Their procedure (p. 117) involves the phosphorylation with monophenylphosphoryl dichloride of a D-α,β-diglyceride (I). This optically active material had previously been prepared by Sowden and Fischer (1941). The phosphorylation effected in the presence of one mole equivalent of pyridine gave rise largely to the expected compound, (II), and to some of the bis compound, (III). This mixture, when treated with choline chloride in excess pyridine, yielded (IV), together with unreacted (III). (IV) was converted into lecithin, isolated, and purified by precipitation as a reineckate, which in turn was converted to a sulfate. Catalytic hydrogenolysis served to remove the protective phenyl group, whereas the sulfate ion was precipitated with barium carbonate. There resulted an L-α-lecithin (V) in which the R groups, depending on the diglyceride originally used, were stearoyl, palmitoyl or myristoyl. Racemic mixtures were also prepared in this way.

The L-α-lecithin in which the R groups were stearic acid residues sintered at 84 to 90° C. and formed a meniscus at 230.5 to 231.5° C. The value varied with the rate of heating. The molecular rotation, $[M]_D$, was +49.3°.

Rose's Synthesis of Phosphatidylaminoethyl Alcohol

The starting material for Rose's (1947) excellent synthesis of phosphatidylaminoethyl alcohol was a diglyceride. He employed a simple pro-

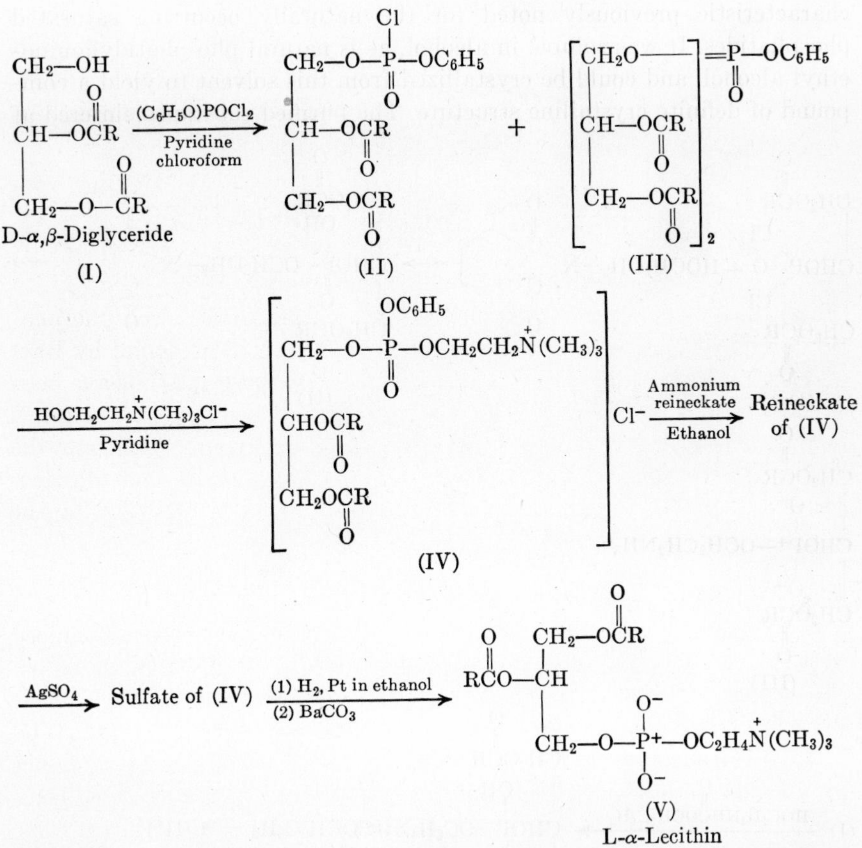

CH$_2$—OH
|
CH—OCR
|
CH$_2$—O—CR
D-α,β-Diglyceride
(I)

$\xrightarrow[\text{Pyridine chloroform}]{(C_6H_5O)POCl_2}$

CH$_2$—O—P—OC$_6$H$_5$
|
CH—OCR
|
CH$_2$—OCR
(II)

+

$\left[\begin{array}{c} CH_2O \\ | \\ CH—OCR \\ | \\ CH_2—OCR \end{array} \right]_2$ =P—OC$_6$H$_5$

(III)

$\xrightarrow[\text{Pyridine}]{HOCH_2CH_2\overset{+}{N}(CH_3)_3Cl^-}$

$\left[\begin{array}{c} OC_6H_5 \\ | \\ CH_2—O—P—OCH_2CH_2\overset{+}{N}(CH_3)_3 \\ \| \\ O \\ | \\ CHOCR \\ \| \\ O \\ | \\ CH_2OCR \\ \| \\ O \end{array} \right]$ Cl$^-$

(IV)

$\xrightarrow[\text{Ethanol}]{\text{Ammonium reineckate}}$ Reineckate of (IV)

$\xrightarrow{AgSO_4}$ Sulfate of (IV) $\xrightarrow[\text{(2) BaCO}_3]{\text{(1) H}_2, \text{Pt in ethanol}}$

RCO—CH
|
CH$_2$—OCR
|
CH$_2$—O—P$^+$—OC$_2$H$_4$N(CH$_3$)$_3$

(V)
L-α-Lecithin

cedure for the synthesis of α,γ-dipalmitin, since he found that a pure product resulted from the direct acylation of glycerol with a theoretical quantity of palmitoyl chloride. The interaction of the dipalmitin with phosphorus oxychloride yielded dipalmitylglycerophosphoryl chloride (I) which was converted to the desired phosphatidylaminoethyl alcohol by the two routes indicated below (p. 118).

In both syntheses, (I) was reacted with a derivative of β-aminoethyl alcohol in which the amino group was blocked to prevent its reaction. Carbobenzoxyaminoethyl alcohol and β-hydroxyethylphthalimide were prepared by standard procedures and were condensed with (I) in pyridine and chloroform. The removal of the carbobenzoxy residue from (IV) was accomplished by use of phosphonium iodide—catalytic hydrogenation and the use of sodium in liquid ammonia having proved inadequate. The amino group in (II) was cleaved in good yield by use of hydrazine.

The dipalmityl compound (III) was extremely insoluble in ether, a characteristic previously noted for the naturally occurring saturated phosphatides. It was soluble in alcohol, as is natural phosphatidylaminoethyl alcohol, and could be crystallized from this solvent to yield a compound of definite crystalline structure. The purified substance sintered at

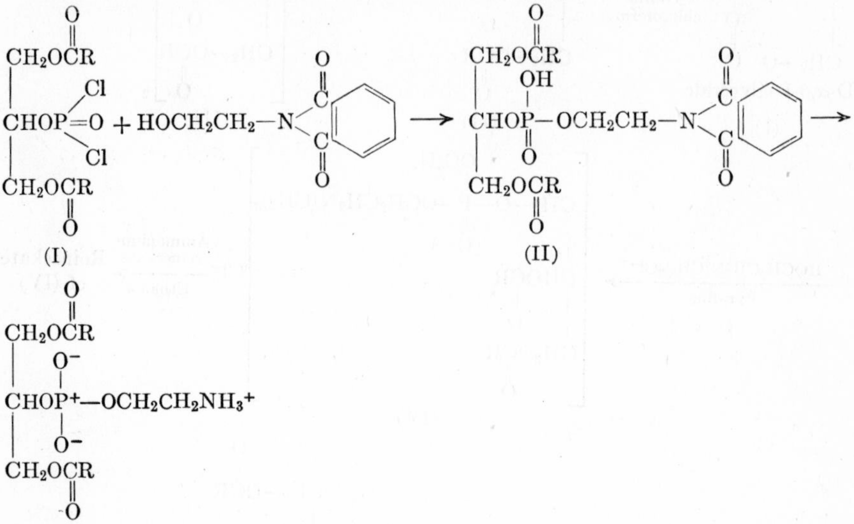

$$
\begin{array}{c}
O \\
\parallel \\
CH_2OCR \\
\mid \quad Cl \\
CHOP{=}O + HOCH_2CH_2{-}N{\big<}_C^{C} \\
\mid \quad Cl \\
CH_2OCR \\
\parallel \\
O \\
(I)
\end{array}
\longrightarrow
\begin{array}{c}
O \\
\parallel \\
CH_2OCR \\
\mid \quad OH \\
CHOP{-}OCH_2CH_2{-}N{\big<}_C^{C} \\
\mid \quad O \\
CH_2OCR \\
\parallel \\
O \\
(II)
\end{array}
\longrightarrow
$$

$$
\begin{array}{c}
O \\
\parallel \\
CH_2OCR \\
\mid \quad O^- \\
CHOP^+{-}OCH_2CH_2NH_3{}^+ \\
\mid \quad O^- \\
CH_2OCR \\
\parallel \\
O \\
(III)
\end{array}
$$

$$
(I) \xrightarrow{\ HOC_2H_4NHCOCH_2C_6H_5\ }
\begin{array}{c}
O \\
\parallel \\
CH_2OCR \\
\mid \quad OH \\
CHOP{-}OC_2H_4NHCOCH_2C_6H_5 \\
\mid \quad O \\
CH_2OCR \\
\parallel \\
O
\end{array}
\longrightarrow (III)
$$

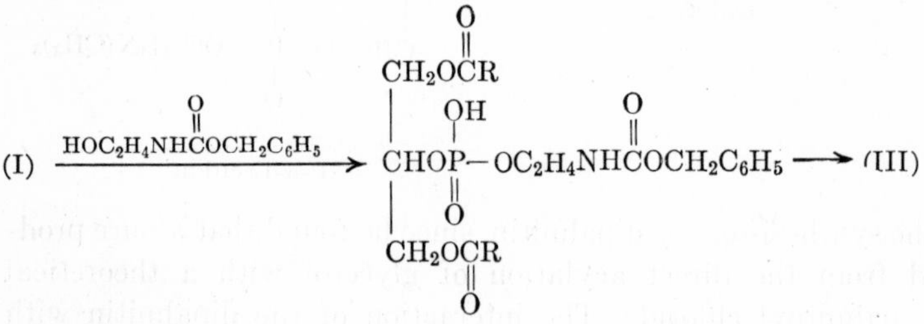

$$R = CH_3{-}(CH_2)_{13}{-}CH_2{-} \qquad (IV)$$

187° C. and melted at 192 to 193° C. or 195 to 198° C., depending on the rate of heating. This melting point was much higher than that reported by prior workers (see below). The reduced cephalin fraction of brain was reported by Gray (1940) to melt at 155 to 162° C. It was slightly soluble in ether and insoluble in alcohol. These different solubility characteristics may have been due to the phosphatidylserine which was undoubtedly present in Gray's brain cephalin fraction.

The equivalent weight of Rose's compound could be determined by titration in neutral alcohol. The amino group yielded a 3,5-dinitrobenzamide with 3,5-dinitrobenzoyl chloride and was replaced with a hydroxyl group by the action of nitrous acid.

Rose's synthesis employing the phthalimido derivative was employed by Hunter, Roberts and Kester (1948) to prepare a symmetrical phosphatidylaminoethyl alcohol containing two myristic acid groups and an unsymmetrical one containing erucic and stearic acid residues. The preparation of the first compound required as a starting material α,γ-dimyristin, which was prepared by Rose's method for α,γ-dipalmitin. The diglyceride needed for the unsymmetrical phosphatide was prepared by a new method in which the stearic acid ester of glycidol was reacted with erucic acid.

$$CH_2-CH-CH_2OC-C_{17}H_{35} + C_{21}H_{41}COOH \longrightarrow \begin{array}{l} CH_2OOC_{17}H_{35} \\ | \\ CHOH \\ | \\ CH_2OOC_{21}H_{41} \end{array}$$

The dimyristo compound melted at 173 to 174° C., whereas the erucostearo compound melted at 163.5 to 164° C.

Synthesis of Optically Active Phosphatidylaminoethyl Alcohol.
Baer, Maurukas & Russell (1951) have recently described briefly their synthesis of three enantiomeric α-phosphatidylaminoethyl alcohols. Their starting material comprised an α,β-diglyceride which was phosphorylated with phenylphosphoryl dichloride, $C_6H_5OPOCl_2$, in the presence of pyridine. The reaction product was treated, without isolation, with carbobenzoxyaminoethyl alcohol, $HOC_2H_4NH-\overset{\overset{\textstyle O}{\|}}{C}O-CH_2C_6H_5$. The resulting product was isolated and was subjected to catalytic hydrogenolysis in order to remove both the protective phenyl and carbobenzoxy groups.

L-α-distearylphosphatidylaminoethyl alcohol sintered at 83° C. and formed a meniscus at 172 to 175° C. Its molecular rotation, M_D, was +44.5°. The corresponding dipalmityl compound sintered at 88° C. and formed a meniscus at 172 to 175° C. Its M_D was +43.5°. The dimyristoyl compound sintered at 88° C. and melted with meniscus formation at 175 to 177° C. Its M_D was +42.5°.

Kabashima's Syntheses

Kabashima and Suzuki (1932) and Kabashima (1938, 1938a) reported syntheses of both lecithin and phosphatidylaminoethyl alcohol. The starting material for these syntheses was the dipalmityl ester of β-glycerophosphoric acid, prepared by the acylation of β-glycerophosphoric acid with palmitoyl chloride by the Schotten-Baumann procedure. Rose (1947), incidentally, reported difficulty in the preparation of the starting material by this method. The monosilver salt of the diacylglycerophosphoric acid was heated with the picrate of β-bromoethylamine to produce phosphatidylaminoethyl alcohol, and with bromocholine picrate to yield lecithin. The reactions for the preparation of the two compounds are indicated below.

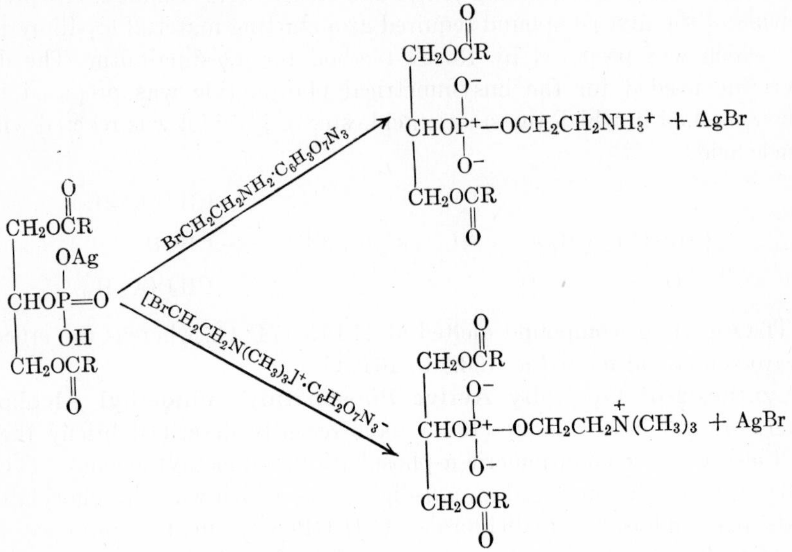

$$
\begin{array}{c}
\text{O} \\
\| \\
\text{CH}_2\text{OCR} \\
| \quad\quad \text{O}^- \\
| \\
\text{CHOP}^+\!-\!\text{OCH}_2\text{CH}_2\text{NH}_3^+ \;+\; \text{AgBr} \\
| \quad\quad \text{O}^- \\
\text{CH}_2\text{OCR} \\
\| \\
\text{O}
\end{array}
$$

$$
\begin{array}{c}
\text{O} \\
\| \\
\text{CH}_2\text{OCR} \\
| \quad \text{OAg} \\
| \\
\text{CHOP}\!=\!\text{O} \\
| \quad \text{OH} \\
\text{CH}_2\text{OCR} \\
\| \\
\text{O}
\end{array}
$$

BrCH₂CH₂NH₂·C₆H₃O₇N₃

[BrCH₂CH₂N(CH₃)₃]⁺·C₆H₂O₇N₃⁻

$$
\begin{array}{c}
\text{O} \\
\| \\
\text{CH}_2\text{OCR} \\
| \quad\quad \text{O}^- \\
| \\
\text{CHOP}^+\!-\!\text{OCH}_2\text{CH}_2\overset{+}{\text{N}}(\text{CH}_3)_3 \;+\; \text{AgBr} \\
| \quad\quad \text{O}^- \\
\text{CH}_2\text{OCR} \\
\| \\
\text{O}
\end{array}
$$

Kabashima (1938a) reported the cephalin compound to melt at 77° C. and the lecithin compound at 81° C. Although these syntheses are probably feasible, they proceed with much less ease than those of Rose (1947) or of Baer, Maurukas and Russell (1951). Rose tried to repeat Kabashima's synthesis of phosphatidylaminoethyl alcohol. He found it impossible to obtain the monosilver salt shown above, for in every instance the disilver salt resulted. In one experiment he reacted the crude reaction product of silver nitrate and the monosodium salt of dipalmitoglycerophosphoric acid with bromoethylamine picrate. There resulted a small yield of crude product which, when purified, proved to be phosphatidylaminoethyl alcohol. Its melting point, however, was 191 to 193° C. rather than 77° C. as reported by Kabashima.

Kabashima (1938a) also described the synthesis of phosphatidylaminoethyl alcohol of the α- rather than the β-configuration. The starting material was distearylglycerol-α-phosphoric acid, prepared by phosphorylating α,β-isopropylidineglycerol. Thereafter the acetone residue was removed and the free hydroxyl groups were acylated with stearoyl chloride. The remainder of the synthesis is identical with that described above. This product melted at 175° C.

Arnold's Syntheses

Arnold (1940) prepared lecithin-like compounds containing chaulmoogric and hydnocarpic acid residues in the hope that these would prove valuable in leprosy therapy. Unfortunately they were not of great value. The starting materials for Arnold's syntheses were obtained by acylating glycerophosphoric acid with hydnocarpic or chaulmoogric acids. Then the acid was converted to a silver salt which Arnold believed to be the disilver salt contaminated with the monosilver salt. This compound in turn was reacted with trimethyl-(β-bromoethyl)-ammonium bromide, as indicated in the following equations. Since the starting material was prepared using chaulmoogra oil acids which are a mixture of chaulmoogric and hydnocarpic acids, one of each is indicated in the formula below.

The product melted at 170 to 175° C. and was readily soluble in ether. It was soluble in ethanol, warm methanol and warm acetone.

Obata's Synthesis

A synthesis for lecithin reported by Obata (1943) depends on the acylation with palmitoyl chloride of the choline ester of β-glycerophosphoric acid. The abstract which was available gave no indication of how the choline ester was prepared, although this compound was previously reported by Arnold (1940), by Rávazzoni and Fenaroli (1940) and by Jeney, Mihalik and Uri (1942). The synthetic lecithin softened at 84° C., became transparent at 160° C. and liquefied at 185° C.

Grün's Syntheses

All of the above-outlined syntheses have involved the interaction of a glycerophosphoric acid or a derivative thereof with a derivative of choline or aminoethyl alcohol in which the amino group was prevented from entering into the reaction. This was also the approach used in the early attempts of Hundeshagen (1883) and Gilson (1888). The former worker prepared a choline salt of distearylglycerophosphoric acid on the assumption that the base was present in salt rather than in ester linkage. Gilson (1888) obtained what he believed to be distearylglycerophosphoric acid by the careful hydrolysis of natural lecithin. He reacted this with ethylene oxide and trimethylamine in an attempt to prepare lecithin. This partial synthesis failed, probably because the hydrolysis of lecithin did not yield pure distearylglycerophosphoric acid.

The syntheses of the α- and β-forms of both lecithin and phosphatidylaminoethyl alcohol advanced by Grün and his co-workers were of a different nature, in that the bases were used as salts rather than as derivatives which would prevent interaction of the amino groups. Thus, Grün and Limpächer (1926a, 1927a) heated a diglyceride with phosphorus pentoxide for a few minutes, after which choline bicarbonate was added. From the reaction mixture they isolated what they believed to be lecithin, together with some choline ester of phosphoric acid. For the preparation of phosphatidylaminoethyl alcohol these workers (Grün and Limpächer, 1927) substituted aminoethyl alcohol for choline.

The products were reported to be very hygroscopic, although reduced lecithin (Gray, 1940) was not. They were soluble in ethanol, but insoluble in ether. Both the lecithin and the phosphatidylaminoethyl alcohol sintered at about 80° C. to translucent droplets which formed a meniscus in the region of 180° C.

Considerable doubt has been expressed as to the identity of these products. The α,β-diglycerides used in some of the work were undoubtedly products which had rearranged to the more stable α,α-configuration. The method of synthesis did not prevent reaction of the amino group of aminoethyl alcohol or of the substituted amino group of choline with the phosphatidic acid, for the bicarbonate ion would not be expected to mask these under the conditions of the reaction. Thus, salt formation undoubtedly occurred, as has recently been demonstrated by Baer (1951). In addition, several other side reactions could be postulated. Contardi and Latzer (1928) reported that Grün's lecithin, unlike the natural material, was not converted to lysolecithin by snake poison. Similarly, King (1934) found that it was attacked more slowly than natural lecithin by an enzyme from intestinal mucosa.

Synthesis of Lysophosphatides

Lysolecithin was prepared by Kabashima (1938b) by his procedure described above for the synthesis of lecithin. The monoglyceride, α-monopalmitin, was converted to the corresponding phosphoric acid by the use of phosphoryl chloride. The silver salt of this acid was then reacted with bromocholine picrate to yield a lysolecithin. The synthesis is demonstrated by the following equation.

$$
\begin{array}{c}
\underset{\|}{\text{O}} \\
\text{CH}_2\text{OCR} \\
|\\
\text{CHOH} \qquad\qquad \xrightarrow[\text{H}_2\text{O}]{[\text{BrCH}_2\text{CH}_2\text{N}(\text{CH}_3)_3]^+ \cdot \text{C}_6\text{H}_2\text{O}_7\text{N}_3{}^-} \\
|\quad\;\;\text{OH} \\
\text{CH}_2\text{OP}{=}\text{O} \\
\qquad\text{OAg}
\end{array}
\qquad
\begin{array}{c}
\underset{\|}{\text{O}} \\
\text{CH}_2\text{OCR} \\
|\\
\text{CHOH} \\
|\qquad\quad \text{O}^- \\
\text{CH}_2\overset{+}{\text{O}}\text{P}{-}\text{O}^- \\
\qquad \overset{+}{\text{OCH}_2\text{CH}_2\text{N}}(\text{CH}_3)_3
\end{array}
\;+\; \text{AgBr}
$$

The product sintered at 109° C. and melted with decomposition at 260 to 262° C. It was insoluble in acetone and ether, and soluble in chloroform, pyridine, methanol and ethanol. It possessed about one-fourth of the hemolytic activity demonstrated by lysolecithin prepared by the action of pancreas enzyme on egg lecithin.

Arnold (1940) prepared a lysolecithin containing hydnocarpic acid by the same synthesis which he used to prepare lecithin (see above). The starting material consisted of the monohydnocarpic acid ester of glycerophosphoric acid which was prepared by the direct acylation of the glycerol derivative. The following equation demonstrates the synthesis.

$$
\begin{array}{c}
\underset{\|}{\text{O}} \\
\text{CH}_2\text{OC}{-}\text{-}(\text{CH}_2)_{10}{-}\!\!\big\langle\!\!\big\rangle \\
|\qquad \text{OAg} \\
\text{CHOP}{=}\text{O} \\
|\qquad \text{OAg} \\
\text{CH}_2\text{OH}
\end{array}
\;
\begin{array}{c}
\text{Br}{-}\text{N}(\text{CH}_3)_3 \\
\quad\backslash\text{CH}_2 \\
\text{Br}{-}\dot{\text{C}}\text{H}_2 \\
\xrightarrow{\text{H}_2\text{O}}
\end{array}
\;
\begin{array}{c}
\underset{\|}{\text{O}} \\
\text{CH}_2\text{OC}{-}\text{-}(\text{CH}_2)_{10}{-}\!\!\big\langle\!\!\big\rangle \\
|\qquad\quad \text{O}^- \\
\text{CHOP}{-}\text{O}^- \\
|\qquad\quad\backslash \overset{+}{\text{O}}{-}\text{CH}_2\text{CH}_2\overset{+}{\text{N}}(\text{CH}_3)_3 \\
\text{CH}_2\text{OH}
\end{array}
\;+\; 2\text{AgBr}
$$

The water-soluble product was not obtained in crystalline form.

Arnold (1940) also prepared the choline ester of β-glycerophosphoric acid by the interaction of trimethyl-(β-bromoethyl)-ammonium bromide and the disilver salt of β-glycerophosphoric acid. This is the compound which results from the action of lecithinase B on lysolecithin. The product was very hygroscopic and melted at 104 to 105° C. It was soluble in methanol and ethanol, but insoluble in ether, acetone, chloroform, benzene and pyridine. This ester was also syntheized by Ravazzoni and Fenaroli (1940), who employed the above method as well as an alternative route involving the interaction of monosilver glycerophosphate with bromocholine picrate. These workers found that their compound was hydrolyzed by the enzymes found in snake venom and in extracts of rice husks. Jeney, Mihalik and Uri (1942) reported the synthesis of the choline ester of glycerophosphoric acid by the direct interaction of free choline and free glycerophosphoric acid.

A very elegant synthesis of the choline ester of α-glycerophosphoric acid has recently been reported by Baer and Kates (1948), who prepared both the racemic mixture and the optically active L-form. The synthesis is very similar to their synthesis of lecithin (see p. 116). D-Isopropylideneglycerol, which provided the starting material for the optically active product, was treated with the phosphorylating agent, monophenylphosphoryl dichloride. This reaction product—the monophenyl ester of isopropylideneglycerophosphoric acid—was esterified directly with choline in the presence of pyridine, and the resulting ester was isolated as an alkali-insoluble reineckate. This salt was purified by crystallization from ethyl acetate and converted to its sulfate, whereupon the protective phenyl group was removed by hydrogenolysis in ethanol over platinum. Removal of the isopropylidene residue by acid and the sulfate groups by barium carbonate provided L-α-glycerylphosphorylcholine as a viscous liquid with a rotation, $[a]_D^{23}$, of —2.85° in water. The above order of removal of the protective group was found mandatory in order to prevent liberation of the choline and migration of the phosphoric acid group to the β-position.

Synthesis of Acetal Phosphatides

An acetal phosphatide in which the base is aminoethyl alcohol and the acetal is derived from palmitaldehyde or stearaldehyde was synthesized by Bersin and co-workers (1941) by the series of reactions demonstrated below:

$$
\begin{array}{l}
CH_2OH \\
| \\
CHOH + C_{15}H_{31}CHO \xrightarrow{\text{sulfosalicylic acid}} \\
| \\
CH_2OH
\end{array}
\qquad
\begin{array}{l}
CH_2O \\
\quad \diagdown CHC_{15}H_{31} \\
CHO \diagup \\
| \\
CH_2OH
\end{array}
$$

$$
\xrightarrow[\substack{H_2O \\ AgNO_3}]{POCl_3}
\begin{array}{l}
CH_2O \\
\quad \diagdown CHC_{15}H_{31} \\
CHO \diagup \\
| \quad\; OAg \\
CH_2OP{=}O \\
\qquad\quad OAg
\end{array}
\xrightarrow{BrCH_2CH_2NH_3Br}
\begin{array}{l}
CH_2O \\
\quad \diagdown CHC_{15}H_{31} \\
CHO \diagup \\
| \qquad O^- \\
CH_2OP{-}O^- \\
\qquad\; OCH_2CH_2NH_3{}^+
\end{array}
+ 2AgBr
$$

In the last step special precautions were necessary to exclude oxygen in order to prevent peroxide formation with the ether oxygen atoms. The product was readily hydrolyzed to aminoethyl alcohol and the corresponding glycerophosphoric acid, for which reason purification by crystallization was not advisable.

Synthesis of Phosphatidic Acids

Several syntheses of phosphatidic acids, the diacylglycerophosphoric acids, have been reported. Recently Baer (1951) has described a generally applicable synthesis for the enantiomeric forms of fully saturated α-phosphatidic acids. In his procedure the D- or L-isomer of an α,β-diglyceride is phosphorylated with diphenylphosphoryl chloride, $(C_6H_5O)_2POCl$, in the presence of pyridine. Catalytic hydrogenolysis of the protective phenyl groups provides the corresponding α-phosphatidic acid. In this study distearoyl-, dipalmityl- and dimyristoyl-L-α-phosphatidic acids were prepared and their properties compared with those of their choline and aminoethyl alcohol salts and esters.

Practically all of the above-described syntheses of phosphatides employed phosphatidic acids or their derivatives as intermediates. Thus, Rose (1947) used the acid dichloride (XVII) obtained by reacting a

$$
\begin{array}{l}
\quad\quad\; \overset{\text{O}}{\overset{\|}{}} \\
\text{CH}_2\text{OCR} \\
|\quad\quad\;\; \text{Cl} \\
\quad\quad\;\; / \\
\text{CHOP}\!\!=\!\!\text{O} \quad \text{(XVII)} \\
|\quad\quad\;\; \backslash \\
\quad\quad\quad \text{Cl} \\
\text{CH}_2\text{OCR} \\
\quad\;\; \| \\
\quad\;\; \text{O}
\end{array}
$$

diglyceride with phosphorus oxychloride. Kabashima's (1938, 1938a) syntheses involved a silver salt (XVIII) prepared by acylating glycerophosphoric acid and converting the resulting compound to the silver salt. Arnold (1940) was of the opinion that the salt prepared in this way was

$$
\begin{array}{l}
\quad\quad\; \overset{\text{O}}{\overset{\|}{}} \\
\text{CH}_2\text{OCR} \\
|\quad\quad\;\; \text{OAg} \\
\quad\quad\;\; / \\
\text{CHOP}\!\!=\!\!\text{O} \quad \text{(XVIII)} \\
|\quad\quad\;\; \backslash \\
\quad\quad\quad \text{OH} \\
\text{CH}_2\text{OCR} \\
\quad\;\; \| \\
\quad\;\; \text{O}
\end{array}
$$

chiefly the disilver salt with only a small amount of the mono salt as an impurity. Rose (1947) also could not prepare the monosilver salt. Wagner-Jauregg and Arnold (1937) prepared the lead salt of phosphatidic acid by reacting a diglyceride with phosphorus oxychloride, hydrolyzing the resulting product and treating an ether solution of it with acidified lead acetate. The diglyceride in this instance was prepared from glycerol α,γ-bromohydrin and the sodium salt of chaulmoogric acid.

In these syntheses the intermediate phosphatidic acids were used without purification. Hunter, Roberts and Kester (1948) found that the isolation of a pure, free phosphatidic acid was virtually impossible. The half quinolinium salt, however, which contained two molecules of phosphatidic acid combined with one of quinoline, was stable and capable of purification. Arnold (1941) prepared the sodium and barium salts of α-acyl-β-glycerophosphoric acid by acylating β-glycerophosphoric acid with a theoretical quantity of the acyl halide.

Baer, Cushing and Fischer (1943) prepared the *levo*-form of the potassium salt of α-benzoyl-β-glycerophosphoric acid. The starting material was optically active isopropylidineglycerol, which was first acylated. The acetone residue was removed to obtain a monoglyceride, which was converted to α-acyl-γ-tritylglycerol. This compound was phosphorylated with phosphorus oxychloride and thence converted to the potassium salt. The triphenylmethyl ether group was removed to obtain potassium *l*-α-benzoyl-β-glycerophosphate. The product was somewhat impure. Further acylation of it would, of course, yield a phosphatidic acid.

The use of triphenylmethyl ether as blocking groups in the synthesis of phosphatidic acids has been discussed by Verkade (1938). He pointed out that the use of this reagent should make it possible to obtain α- or β-phosphatidic acids in which the fatty acids may be the same or different.

BIBLIOGRAPHY—PART I

Adair, G. S., and Adair, M. E., *J. Physiol.*, 102, 17P (1943/44); *C. A.*, 39, 536 (1945).
Adam, N. K., *Proc. Roy. Soc. (London)*, 101A, 452 (1922); *C. A.*, 16, 4107 (1922).
——, Berry, W. B., and Turner, H. A., *Proc. Roy. Soc. (London)*, 117A, 532 (1928).
Adler, R., U. S. Pat. 1,057,316, March 25, 1913; *C. A.*, 7, 1786 (1913).
Affonskiĭ, S. I., *Biochem. Z.*, 195, 387 (1928); *C. A.*, 22, 4548 (1928).
Ajazzi-Mancini, M., and Donatelli, L., *Boll. ist. sieroterap. milan.*, 20, 307 (1941); *C. A.*, 38, 2391 (1944).
Akamatsu, S., *Biochem. Z.*, 142, 184, 186 (1923); *C. A.*, 18, 1839 (1924).
Alexander, A. E., and Teorell, T., *Trans. Faraday Soc.*, 35, 733 (1939); *C. A.*, 33, 5721 (1939).
——, ——, and Åborg, C. G., *Trans. Faraday Soc.*, 35, 1200 (1939); *C. A.*, 33, 9085 (1939).
Altmann, R., *Arch. Anat. u. Physiol.*, *Physiol. Abt.*, 524 (1889).
Anderson, R. J., *J. Biol. Chem.*, 74, 525, 537 (1927).
——, *J. Am. Chem. Soc.*, 52, 1607 (1930); *C. A.*, 24, 2490 (1930).
——, Reeves, R. E., and Stodola, F. H., *J. Biol. Chem.*, 121, 649 (1937).
Antener, I., and Högl, O., *Mitt. Gebiete Lebensm. Hyg.*, 38, 207, 226 (1947).
Arnd, O., and Hafner, E. A., *Biochem. Z.*, 167, 440 (1926).

Arnold, H., *Ber.*, **71**, 1505 (1938).

——, *ibid.*, **73**, 87, 90 (1940); *C. A.*, **34**, 2789 (1940)

——, *ibid.*, **74**, 1736 (1941); *C. A.*, **37**, 2346 (1943).

Artom, C., *Bull. soc. chim. biol.*, **7**, 1099 (1925); *C. A.*, **20**, 1656 (1926).

——, Fishman, W. H., and Morehead, R. P., *Proc. Soc. Exptl. Biol. Med.*, **60**, 284 (1945).

Ault, W. C., and Brown, J. B., *J. Biol. Chem.*, **107**, 607 (1934).

Babo, L., and Hirschbrunn, M., *Ann. Chem. Pharm.*, **84**, 10 (1852).

Baer, E., *J. Biol. Chem.*, **189**, 235 (1951).

——, and Fischer, H. O. L., *J. Biol. Chem.*, **128**, 491 (1939).

——, ——, *ibid.*, **135**, 321 (1940).

——, and Kates, M., *J. Am. Chem. Soc.*, **70**, 1394 (1948).

——, ——, *J. Biol. Chem.*, **175**, 79 (1948a).

——, ——, *J. Am. Chem. Soc.*, **72**, 942 (1950).

——, ——, *J. Biol. Chem.*, **185**, 615 (1950a).

——, Cushing, I. B., and Fischer, H. O. L., *Can. J. Research,* **21B**, 119 (1943); *C. A.*, **37**, 4692 (1943).

——, Maurukas, J., and Russell, M., *Science*, **113**, 12 (1951).

Baeyer, A., *Ann. Chem. Pharm.*, **140**, 306 (1866).

——, *ibid.*, **142**, 322 (1867).

Bailly, M. C., *Compt. rend.*, **206**, 1902 (1938); *C. A.*, **32**, 7018 (1938).

——, *ibid.*, **208**, 443, 1820 (1939); *C. A.*, **33**, 2884, 6243 (1939).

Bailly, O., *Compt. rend.*, **160**, 395 (1915); *C. A.*, **9**, 1745 (1915).

——, *Ann. chim.*, **6**, 96 (1916); *C. A.*, **10**, 3069 (1916).

——, *ibid.*, **6**, 215 (1916a); *C. A.*, **11**, 331 (1917).

——, *Compt. rend.*, **172**, 689 (1921); *C. A.*, **15**, 1884 (1921).

——, and Gaumé, J., *Bull. soc. chim.* [5], **2**, 354 (1935); *C. A.*, **29**, 3981 (1935).

Baker, Z., and co-workers (Harrison, R. W., Miller, B. F., and Wexler, R.), *J. Exptl. Med.*, **74**, 621 (1941); *C. A.*, **36**, 1060 (1942).

Bamberger, P., *Biochem. Z.*, **266**, 175 (1933); *C. A.*, **28**, 792 (1934).

——, *ibid.*, **270**, 366 (1934); *C. A.*, **28**, 5089 (1934).

Barbieri, N. A., *Gazz. chim. ital.*, **47** I, 1 (1917); *C. A.*, **12**, 1198 (1918).

Baskoff, A., *Z. physiol. Chem.*, **57**, 395 (1908); *C. A.*, **3**, 1880 (1909).

Baumann, A., *Biochem. Z.*, **54**, 30 (1913); *C. A.*, **8**, 142 (1914).

Bechhold, H., and Neuschlosz, S. M., *Kolloid Z.*, **29**, 81 (1921); *C. A.*, **16**, 1892 (1922).

Beck, G. E., and Meier, R., *Experientia,* **3**, 371 (1947); *C. A.*, **42**, 5245 (1948).

Beck, W., *Biochem. Z.*, **156**, 471 (1925); *C. A.*, **19**, 3190 (1925).

Belfanti, S., *Biochem. Z.*, **154**, 148 (1924); *C. A.*, **19**, 1431 (1925).

——, *Boll. ist. sieroterap. milan,* **5**, 265 (1924a).

——, *Z. Immunitätsforsch.*, **44**, 347 (1925); *C. A.*, **20**, 1268 (1926).

——, *Rend. adunanza accad. med. fis. fiorentina; Sperimentale,* **79**, 932 (1925a); *C. A.*, **20**, 1465 (1926).

——, *Rend. ist. lomb. sci. lett. II,* **59**, 591 (1926).

——, *Fisiol. e med.* (*Rome*), **12**, 821 (1933).

——, and Arnaudi, C., *Boll. soc. intern. microbiol. Sez. ital.*, **4**, 399 (1932); *C. A.*, **27**, 2460 (1933).

——, Contardi, A., and Ercoli, A., "Ergebnisse der Enzymforschung," Vol. 5, Leipzig, R. Weidenhagen, Akademische Verlagsgesellschaft M. B. H., 1936.

Bensley, R. R., *Science,* **96**, 389 (1942); *C. A.*, **37**, 1171 (1943).

Berczeller, L., *Biochem. Z.*, **66**, 218 (1914) ; *C. A.*, **8**, 3447 (1914).

Bergell, P., *Chem. Ber.*, **33**, 2, 2584 (1900).

——, *Zentr. Path.*, **12**, 633 (1901).

——, Ger. Pat. 307,490 (1918) ; *C. A.*, **13**, 1127 (1919).

Bersin, T., and co-workers (Moldtmann, H. G., Nafziger, H., Marchand, B., and Leopold, W.), *Z. physiol. Chem.*, **269**, 241 (1941) ; *C. A.*, **36**, 6499 (1942).

Beumer, H., *Arch. exptl. Path. Pharmakol.*, **77**, 304 (1914) ; *C. A.*, **8**, 3461 (1914).

Bing, H. J., *Skand. Arch. Physiol.*, **9**, 336 (1899).

——, *ibid.*, **11**, 166 (1901).

Blackwood, J. H., and Wishart, G. M., *Biochem. J.*, **28**, 550 (1934) ; *C. A.*, **28**, 6163 (1934).

Blanquet, P., and Duhamel, J., *Bull. soc. chim. biol.*, **31**, 716 (1949) ; *C. A.*, **44**, 1551 (1950).

Bleyer, B., and Diemair, W., *Biochem. Z.*, **238**, 197 (1931) ; *C. A.*, **25**, 5690 (1931).

Blix, G., *J. Biol. Chem.*, **137**, 495 (1941).

——, *ibid.*, **139**, 471 (1941a).

——, Tiselius, A., and Svensson, H., *J. Biol. Chem.*, **137**, 485 (1941).

Bloch, K., *Z. physiol. Chem.*, **244**, 1 (1936) ; *C. A.*, **31**, 1066 (1937).

Bloor, W. R., *Chem. Rev.*, **2**, 243 (1925) ; *C. A.*, **19**, 3278 (1925).

——, *J. Biol. Chem.*, **80**, 443 (1928).

——, "Biochemistry of the Fatty Acids and Their Compounds, the Lipids," New York, Reinhold Publishing Corp., 1943.

Boas, E., and Rosenbloom, J., *Proc. Soc. Exptl. Biol. Med.*, **8**, 132 (1911) ; *C. A.*, **5**, 3588 (1911).

Bode, J., *Ann. Chem. Pharm.*, **267**, 268 (1892).

Bókay, A., *Z. physiol. Chem.*, **1**, 157 (1877).

Booth, F. J., *Biochem. J.*, **29**, 2071 (1935) ; *C. A.*, **30**, 125 (1936).

Boutaric, A., and Berthier, P., *Compt. rend.*, **211**, 100 (1940) ; *C. A.*, **35**, 7803 (1941).

Brain, R. T., Kay, H. D., and Marshall, P. G., *Biochem. J.*, **22**, 628 (1928) ; *C. A.*, **22**, 4158 (1928).

Brand, E., Kassell, B., and Saidel, L. J., *J. Clin. Invest.*, **23**, 437 (1944) ; *C. A.*, **38**, 5934 (1944).

Breusch, F. L., *Biochem. Z.*, **293**, 280 (1937) ; *C. A.*, **32**, 410 (1938).

Brown, J. B., *J. Biol. Chem.*, **97**, 183 (1932).

Brunius, E., *Arkiv. Kemi, Mineral. Geol.*, **10A**, No. 8, 1–13 (1930) ; *C. A.*, **24**, 3050 (1930).

Bull, H. B., "The Biochemistry of the Lipides," New York, John Wiley & Sons, Inc., 1937.

——, and Frampton, V. L., *J. Am. Chem. Soc.*, **58**, 594 (1936) ; *C. A.*, **30**, 3299 (1936).

Bülow, M., and Page, I. H., *Z. physiol. Chem.*, **205**, 25 (1932) ; *C. A.*, **26**, 3551 (1932).

Bungenberg de Jong, see Jong, H. G. B. de

Burmaster, C. F., *J. Biol. Chem.*, **164**, 233 (1946).

——, *ibid.*, **165**, 565 (1946a).

——, *ibid.*, **165**, 577 (1946b).

Calábek, J., Morávek, V., *Kolloid Z.*, **50**, 141 (1930) ; *C. A.*, **24**, 1782 (1930).

Carré, P., *Compt. rend.*, **154**, 220 (1909) ; *C. A.*, **6**, 1132 (1912).

Carter, H. E., and co-workers (Glick, F. J., Norris, W. P., and Phillips, G. E.), *J. Biol. Chem.*, **142**, 449 (1942).

——, —— (Haines, W. J., Ledyard, W. E., and Norris, W. P.), *J. Biol. Chem.*, **169**, 77 (1947).

Carter, H. E., and co-workers (Norris, W. P., Glick, F. S., Phillips, G. E., and Harris, R.), *J. Biol. Chem.,* **170,** 269 (1947a).

——, —— (Glick, F. J., Norris, W. P., and Phillips, G. E.), *J. Biol. Chem.,* **170,** 285 (1947b).

——, and Norris, W. P., *J. Biol. Chem.,* **145,** 709 (1942).

——, and West, H. D., *Org. Syntheses,* **20,** 81 (1940); *C. A.,* **34,** 5052 (1940).

——, Greenwood, F. L., and Humiston, C. G., *Federation Proc.,* **9,** 159 (1950).

——, Norris, W. P., and Rockwell, H. E., *J. Biol. Chem.,* **170,** 295 (1947).

Cason, J., and Anderson, R. J., *J. Biol. Chem.,* **126,** 527 (1938).

Césari, E., and Bouquet, P., *Ann. inst. Pasteur,* **58,** 6 (1937); *C. A.,* **31,** 7105 (1937).

Chain, E., and Kemp, I., *Biochem. J.,* **28,** 2052 (1934); *C. A.,* **29,** 2555 (1935).

Channon, H. J., and Chibnall, A. C., *Biochem. J.,* **21,** 1112 (1927); *C. A.,* **22,** 1790 (1928).

——, and Foster, C. A. M., *Biochem. J.,* **28,** 853 (1934); *C. A.,* **28,** 6735 (1934).

——, and Smith, J. A. B., *Biochem. J.,* **30,** 115 (1936); *C. A.,* **30,** 3480 (1936).

Chargaff, E., *J. Biol. Chem.,* **118,** 417 (1937).

——, *ibid.,* **125,** 661 (1938).

——, *ibid.,* **144,** 455 (1942).

——, *ibid.,* **142,** 491 (1942a).

——, *ibid.,* **142,** 505 (1942b).

——, in Anson, M. L., and Edsall, J. T., "Advances in Protein Chemistry," Vol. I, New York, Academic Press, Inc., 1944.

——, and Cohen, S. S., *J. Biol. Chem.,* **129,** 619 (1939).

——, and Ziff, M., *J. Biol. Chem.,* **131,** 25 (1939).

——, Moore, D. H., and Bendich, A., *J. Biol. Chem.,* **145,** 593 (1942).

——, Ziff, M., and Cohen, S. S., *J. Biol. Chem.,* **136,** 257 (1940).

——, Ziff, M., and Hogg, B. M., *J. Biol. Chem.,* **131,** 35 (1939).

Cheesman, D. F., *Arkiv. Kemi, Mineral. Geol.,* **B22,** No. 1 (1946); *C. A.,* **41,** 898 (1947).

Chibnall, A. C., and Channon, H. J., *Biochem. J.,* **21,** 225, 233 (1927); *C. A.,* **21,** 2489 (1927).

——, ——, *ibid.,* **23,** 176 (1929); *C. A.,* **23,** 4242 (1929).

Chick, H., *Biochem. J.,* **8,** 404 (1914); *C. A.,* **9,** 90 (1915).

Christensen, H. N., and Hastings, A. B., *J. Biol. Chem.,* **136,** 387 (1940).

Claude, A., *Cold Spring Harbor Symposia Quant. Biol.,* **9,** 263 (1941); *C. A.,* **38,** 988 (1944).

——, *Science,* **97,** 451 (1943); *C. A.,* **37,** 4413 (1943).

Claus, A., and Keesé, C., *J. prakt. Chem.,* **102,** 24 (1867).

Clementi, A., *Arch. fisiol.,* **8,** 399 (1910); *C. A.,* **5,** 3085 (1911).

Cohen, S. S., and Chargaff, E., *J. Biol. Chem.,* **136,** 243 (1940).

——, ——, *ibid.,* **140,** 689 (1941).

Colmer, A. R., *J. Bact.,* **55,** 777 (1948); *C. A.,* **42,** 6409 (1948).

Contardi, A., and Ercoli, A., *Biochem. Z.,* **261,** 275 (1933); *C. A.,* **27,** 4258 (1933).

——, ——, *Gazz. chim. ital.,* **63,** 37 (1933a); *C. A.,* **27,** 3488 (1933).

——, ——, *Arch. sci. biol. (Italy),* **21,** 1 (1935); *C. A.,* **29,** 8018 (1935).

——, and Latzer, P., *Rend. ist. lombardo sci.,* 847 (1927); *C. A.,* **23,** 1655 (1929).

——, ——, *Biochem. Z.,* **197,** 222 (1928); *C. A.,* **23,** 201 (1929).

——, and Ravazzoni, C., *Rend. ist. lombardo sci.,* **67,** 503 (1934).

Corran, J. W., and Lewis, W. C. M., *Biochem. J.,* **18,** 1364 (1924); *C. A.,* **19,** 1144 (1925).

Couerbe, *Ann. chim. phys.,* **56,** 160 (1834).

Cousin, H., *J. pharm. chim.* [6], **24,** 101 (1906).

——, *Compt. rend. soc. biol.,* **62,** 238 (1907); *C. A.,* **1,** 1437 (1907).

Cramer, E., *J. prakt. Chem.,* **96,** 76 (1865).

Crane, E. J., *Ind. Eng. Chem., News Ed.,* **12,** 202 (1934); *C. A.,* **28,** 3947 (1934).

Cruickshank, J., *J. Path. Bact.,* **23,** 230 (1920); *C. A.,* **14,** 3678 (1920).

DaCruz, A., *Compt. rend. soc. biol.,* **99,** 1530 (1928).

Daft, F. S., and Coghill, R. D., *J. Biol. Chem.,* **90,** 341 (1931).

Damerell, V. R., and Mattson, R., *J. Phys. Chem.,* **48,** 134 (1944); *C. A.,* **38,** 3532 (1944).

——, and Urbanic, A., *J. Phys. Chem.,* **48,** 125 (1944); *C. A.,* **38,** 3532 (1944).

Darrah, J. E., and MacArthur, C. G., *J. Am. Chem. Soc.,* **38,** 922 (1916); *C. A.,* **10,** 1199 (1916).

Daubert, B. F., and King, C. G., *J. Am. Chem. Soc.,* **61,** 3328 (1939); *C. A.,* **34,** 985 (1940).

Davis, W. W., Krahl, M. E., and Clowes, G. H. A., *J. Am. Chem. Soc.,* **62,** 3080 (1940); *C. A.,* **35,** 363 (1941).

Delage, B., *Bull. soc. chim. biol.,* **17,** 927 (1935); *C. A.,* **29,** 6913 (1935).

Delezenne, C., and Fourneau, E., *Bull. soc. chim.* [4], **15,** 421 (1914); *C. A.,* **8,** 3591 (1914).

——, and Ledebt, E., *Compt. rend.,* **153,** 81 (1911); *C. A.,* **5,** 3093 (1911).

——, ——, *ibid.,* **155,** 1101 (1912); *C. A.,* **7,** 1752 (1913).

Delsal, J. L., *Bull. soc. chim. biol.,* **31,** 122 (1949); *C. A.,* **43,** 8420 (1949).

Dervichian, D., and Magnant, C., *Compt. rend. soc. biol.,* **140,** 94 (1946); *C. A.,* **41,** 3494 (1947).

——, and Pillet, J., *Bull. soc. chim. biol.,* **26,** 454 (1944); *C. A.,* **40,** 1891 (1946).

Desnuelle, P., and Molines, J., *Biochem. et Biophys. Acta,* **2,** 124 (1948); *C. A.,* **42,** 5934 (1948).

de Sütö-Nagy, G. I., and Anderson, R. J., *J. Biol. Chem.,* **171,** 761 (1947).

Diakanow, C., *Hoppe-Seyler Med. Chem. Untersuch.,* **2,** 221 (1867).

——, *Zentr. Med. Wissensch.,* **2,** 97, 434 (1868)

——, *Hoppe-Seyler Med. Chem. Untersuch.,* **3,** 405 (1868a).

Dounce, A. L., *J. Biol. Chem.,* **147,** 685 (1943).

Duboss. R. J., and Hotchkiss, R. D., *Trans. Coll. Physicians Phila.,* **10,** 11 (1942).

Dungern, E., and Coca, A. F., *Biochem. Z.,* **12,** 407 (1908); *C. A.,* **3,** 809 (1909).

Dunn, E. E., *J. Pharmacol.,* **50,** 393 (1934); *C. A.,* **28,** 5540 (1934).

Edsall, J. T., in Anson, M. L., and Edsall, J. T., "Advances in Protein Chemistry," Vol. **III,** New York, Academic Press, Inc., 1947.

Ehrenfeld, R., *Z. physiol, Chem.,* **56,** 89 (1908); *C. A.,* **3,** 336 (1909).

Eichberg, J., *News Ed., (Am. Chem. Soc.),* **19,** 575 (1941); *C. A.,* **35,** 5682 (1941).

Eisler, M., and Gulaesy, Z. v., *Zentr. Bakt. Parasitenk., Abt. I,* **117,** 500 (1930); *C. A.,* **25,** 137 (1931).

Eppler, J., *Z. physiol. Chem.,* **87,** 233 (1913); *C. A.,* **8,** 351 (1914).

Ercoli, A., "Lecithasen" in Nord, F. F., and Weidenhagen, R., "Handbuch der Enzymologie," Leipzig, Akademische Verlagsgesellschaft Becker und Erler Kom.-Ges., 1940.

Erlandsen, A., *Z. physiol. Chem.,* **51,** 71 (1907); *C. A.,* **1,** 1576 (1907).

Erlenmeyer, E., *Ber.,* **13,** 1077 (1880).

——, and Stoop, F., *Ann.,* **337,** 236 (1904).

Escher, H. H., *Helv. Chim. Acta,* **8,** 686 (1925); *C. A.,* **20,** 431 (1926).

Fabisch, W., *Biochem. Z.*, **242**, 121 (1931) ; *C. A.*, **26**, 1308 (1932).

Fairbairn, D., *J. Biol. Chem.*, **173**, 705 (1948).

Falk, F., *Biochem. Z.*, **16**, 187 (1909) ; *C. A.*, **3**, 1308 (1909).

Faure, M., and Legault-Demare, J., *Bull. soc. chim. biol.*, **32**, 509 (1950) ; *C. A.*, **45**, 679 (1951).

Feinschmidt, J., *Biochem. Z.*, **38**, 244 (1912) ; *C. A.*, **6**, 1011 (1912).

Felsenfeld, O., *J. Bact.*, **48**, 155 (1944) ; *C. A.*, **38**, 6324 (1944).

Feulgen, R., and Behrens, M., *Z. physiol. Chem.*, **256**, 15 (1938) ; *C. A.*, **33**, 1351 (1939).

——, and Bersin, Th., *Z. physiol. Chem.*, **260**, 217 (1939) ; *C. A.*, **33**, 8635 (1939).

——, and Voit, K., *Arch. ges. Physiol. (Pflügers)*, **206**, 389 (1924) ; *C. A.*, **19**, 1155 (1925).

——, Imhäuser, K., and Behrens, M., *Z. physiol. Chem.*, **180**, 161 (1929) ; *C. A.*, **23**, 1912 (1929).

Fevold, H. L., and Lausten, A., *Arch. Biochem.*, **11**, 1 (1946) ; *C. A.*, **40**, 7244 (1946).

Fiessinger, N., and Clogne, R., *Compt. rend.*, **165**, 730 (1917) ; *C. A.*, **12**, 705 (1918).

Fischer, E., *Ber.*, **53**, 1621 (1920).

——, and Leuchs, H., *Ber.*, **35**, 3787 (1902).

——, and Pfähler, E., *Ber.*, **53**, 1606 (1920) ; *C. A.*, **15**, 686 (1921).

Fischgold, H., and Chain, E., *Biochem. J.*, **28**, 2044 (1934) ; *C. A.*, **29**, 2555 (1935).

——, ——, *Proc. Roy. Soc. (London)*, **117B**, 239 (1935) ; *C. A.*, **29**, 5465 (1935).

Fleury, P., and Paris, R., *Compt. rend.*, **196**, 1416 (1933) ; *C. A.*, **27**, 3915 (1933).

Flexner, S. and Noguchi, H., *J. Exptl. Med.*, **6**, 277 (1902).

Folch, J., *J. Biol. Chem.*, **139**, 973 (1941a).

——, *ibid.*, **146**, 31 (1942).

——, *ibid.*, **146**, 35 (1942a).

——, *Federation Proc.*, **5**, 134 (1946).

——, *ibid.*, **6**, 252 (1947).

——, *J. Biol. Chem.*, **174**, 439 (1948).

——, *ibid.*, **177**, 497 (1949).

——, *ibid.*, **177**, 505 (1949a).

——, and Schneider, H. A., *J. Biol. Chem.*, **137**, 51 (1941).

——, and Woolley, D. W., *J. Biol. Chem.*, **142**, 963 (1942).

Folley, S. J., and Kay, H. D., "Ergebnisse der Enzymforschung," R. Weidenhagen, Vol. **5**, Leipzig, Akademische Verlagsgesellschaft M. B. H., 1936; *C. A.*, **30**, 5242 (1936).

Foster, M. L., *J. Biol. Chem.*, **20**, 403 (1915).

Fourcroy, A., *Ann. chim.*, **16**, 282 (1793).

Fourneau, E., *Bull. soc. chim. biol.*, **2**, 67 (1920) ; *C. A.*, **15**, 1142 (1921).

——, and Gonzalez, A., *Anales soc. españ. fís. y quím.*, **19**, 151 (1921) ; *C. A.*, **15**, 2891 (1921).

——, and Piettre, *Bull. soc. chim., Mém.*, **2**, 249 (1905).

——, ——, *Bull. soc. chim.*, **11**, 805 (1912) ; *C. A.*, **7**, 803 (1913).

Fränkel, E., and Bielschowsky, F., *Z. physiol. Chem.*, **213**, 58 (1932) ; *C. A.*, **27**, 527 (1933).

——, and Pollanz, A., *Z. physiol. Chem.*, **218**, 153 (1933) ; *C. A.*, **27**, 4263 (1933).

Fränkel, S., and Bolaffio, C., *Biochem. Z.*, **9**, 44 (1908) ; *C. A.*, **2**, 2565 (1908).

——, and Dimitz, L., *Biochem. Z.*, **21**, 337 (1909) ; *C. A.*, **5**, 716 (1911).

——, ——, *ibid.*, **28**, 295 (1910) ; *C. A.*, **5**, 525 (1911).

——, and Kafka, F., *Biochem. Z.*, **101**, 59 (1920) ; *C. A.*, **14**, 2002 (1920).

Fränkel, S., and Linnert, K., *Biochem. Z.*, 24, 268 (1910); *C. A.*, 4, 1501 (1910).
Francioli, M., *Fermentforschung*, 14, 241 (1934); *C. A.*, 28, 6739 (1934).
——, *ibid.*, 14, 493 (1935); *C. A.*, 29, 8010 (1935).
——, *Enzymologia*, 3, 200, 204 (1937); *C. A.*, 31, 8566 (1937).
——, and Ercoli, A., in "Die Methoden der Fermentforschung," compiled by Bamann, E. and Myrbäck, K., Leipzig, Georg Thieme, 1940.
Frémy, E., *Ann. chim. phys.* [3], 2, 463 (1841); *J. pharm.*, 27, 453 (1841); *Ann. Chem. Pharm.*, 39, 69 (1841).
——, and Valencienne, *Ann. chim. phys.* [3], 50, 127 (1857).
Frey-Wijssling, A., *Protoplasma*, 29, 279 (1937/38); *C. A.*, 32, 3786 (1938).
Friedemann, U., *Arch. Hyg.*, 69, 106 (1909); *C. A.*, 3, 1546 (1909).
Fujii, N., *J. Biochem.* (*Japan*), 3, 393 (1924); *C. A.*, 18, 3606 (1924).
Fujimura, S., *J. Biochem.* (*Japan*), 25, 595 (1937).
Fürth, O., Breuer, J. and Herrmann, H., *Biochem. Z.*, 271, 233 (1934); *C. A.*, 29, 2185 (1935).
Fürth, R., *Ann. Physik*, 70, 63 (1923); *C. A.*, 17, 1579 (1923).
Galeotti, G., and Giampalmo, G., *Arch. fisiol.*, 5, 503 (1908).
Gardner, J. A., and Gainsborough, H., *Biochem. J.*, 21, 141 (1927); *C. A.*, 21, 2278 (1927).
Gerstl, B., Tennant, R., and Pelzman, O., *Yale J. Biol. Med.*, 17, 455 (1945); *C. A.*, 39, 1457 (1945).
Ghosh, B. N., *Oesterr. Chem. Ztg.*, 43, 158 (1940); *C. A.*, 35, 469 (1941).
Gilson, E., *Z. physiol. Chem.*, 12, 585 (1888).
Gobley, M., *J. pharm. chim.* [3], 9, 1, 81, 161 (1846).
——, *ibid.*, 11, 409 (1847); 12, 1 (1847).
——, *ibid.*, 17, 401 (1850).
Gofman, J. W., Lindgren, F. T., and Elliott, H., *J. Biol. Chem.*, 179, 973 (1948).
Grafe, V., *Biochem. Z.*, 159, 444 (1925); *C. A.*, 20, 923 (1926).
——, *Naturwissenschaften*, 15, 513 (1927); *C. A.*, 21, 2912 (1927).
——, and Horvat, V., *Biochem. Z.*, 159, 449 (1925); *C. A.*, 20, 931 (1926).
——, and Magistris, H., *Biochem. Z.*, 162, 366 (1925); *C. A.*, 20, 1831 (1926).
Gray, E. L., *J. Biol. Chem.*, 136, 167 (1940).
Griess, P., and Harrow, G., *Ber.*, 18, 717 (1885).
Grigaut, A., *Bull. soc. chim. biol.*, 17, 1031 (1935); *C. A.*, 29, 6913 (1935).
Grimbért, L., and Bailly, O., *Compt. rend.*, 160, 207 (1915); *C. A.*, 9, 1309 (1915).
Gronchi, V., *Biochim. e terap. sper.*, 20, 562 (1933); *C. A.*, 28, 3432 (1934).
——, *Sperimentale*, 90, 223 (1936); *C. A.*, 31, 1831 (1937).
——, *ibid.*, 90, 262 (1936a); *C. A.*, 31, 1832 (1937).
Grün, A., in Hefter-Schönfeld, "Chemie und Technologie der Fette und Fettprodukte," Vol. I, Vienna, Julius Springer, 1936.
——, and Limpächer, R., *Chem. Umschau*, 30, 246 (1923); *C. A.*, 18, 536 (1924).
——, ——, *Ber.*, 59, 1345 (1926); *C. A.*, 20, 3013 (1926).
——, ——, *ibid.*, 59, 1350 (1926a); *C. A.*, 20, 3014 (1926).
——, ——, *ibid.*, 60, 151 (1927); *C. A.*, 21, 1659 (1927).
——, ——, *ibid.*, 60, 147 (1927a); *C. A.*, 21, 1659 (1927).
Guastalla, L., *Research* (*London*), *Suppl., Surface Chemistry*, 153 (1949); *C. A.*, 43, 8800 (1949).
Guerrini, G., *Z. Immunitätsforsch*, 45, 249 (1925); *C. A.*, 20, 1268 (1926).
Gulland, J. M., and Hobday, G. I., *J. Chem. Soc.*, 746 (1940); *C. A.*, 34, 6640 (1940).
Gutstein, M., *Biochem. Z.*, 207, 177 (1929); *C. A.*, 23, 3241 (1929).

Hack, M. H., *J. Biol. Chem.*, **169**, 137 (1947).

Hammarsten, O., *Z. physiol. Chem.*, **36**, 525 (1902).

——, *Erg. Physiol.*, **4**, 1 (1905).

——, *Z. physiol. Chem.*, **61**, 454 (1909).

Hanahan, D. J., and Chaikoff, I. L., *J. Biol. Chem.*, **168**, 233 (1947).

——, ——, *ibid.*, **169**, 699 (1947a).

——, ——, *ibid.*, **172**, 191 (1948).

Handovsky, H., and Wagner, R., *Biochem. Z.*, **31**, 32 (1911); *C. A.*, **5**, 1609 (1911).

Hansteen-Cranner, B., *Planta*, **2**, 438 (1926).

——, *Meldinger Norg. Landbrukshøgskole*, **7**, 611 (1927); *C. A.*, **22**, 2186 (1928).

Hardy, W. B., *J. Physiol.*, **33**, 251 (1905).

Hatakeyama, T., *Z. physiol. Chem.*, **187**, 120 (1930); *C. A.*, **24**, 1873 (1930).

Hattori, K., *Biochem. Z.*, **119**, 45 (1921); *C. A.*, **15**, 3309 (1921).

Hausser, I., *Sitzber. heidelberg. Akad. Wiss., Math. naturw. Klasse*, No. 6 (1935); *C. A.*, **30**, 7134 (1936).

Heffels, J., *Ann. Physik.*, **37**, 477 (1940); *C. A.*, **35**, 976 (1941).

Heidelberger, M., and Menzel, A. E. O., *Proc. Soc. Exptl. Biol. Med.*, **32**, 1150 (1935).

Hilditch, T. P., "The Chemical Constitution of Natural Fats," London, Chapman and Hall, Ltd., 1947.

——, and Pedelty, W. H., *Biochem. J.*, **31**, 1964 (1937); *C. A.*, **32**, 2572 (1938).

——, and Zaky, Y. A. H., *Biochem. J.*, **36**, 815 (1942); *C. A.*, **37**, 2201 (1943).

Hirao, S., *J. Agr. Chem. Soc. Japan*, **7**, 364 (1931); *C. A.*, **25**, 5681 (1931).

Höber, R., *Beitr. chem. Physiol. (Hofmeister)*, **11**, 35 (1908); *C. A.*, **2**, 2261 (1908).

Hofer, E., *Acta Biol. Exptl. (Warsaw)*, **12**, 70 (1938); *C. A.*, **33**, 6351 (1939).

Hofmann, A. W., *Compt. rend.*, **47**, 558 (1858).

Hoppe-Seyler, F., *Med. chem. Untersuch.*, **1**, 162 (1866).

——, *ibid.*, **2**, 215 (1867).

Horvath, A. A., *Chemistry & Industry*, **56**, 735 (1937); *C. A.*, **31**, 8065 (1937).

Hughes, A., *Biochem. J.*, **29**, 437 (1935); *C. A.*, **29**, 5138 (1935).

——, *ibid.*, **29**, 430 (1935a); *C. A.*, **29**, 5137 (1937).

Hundeshagen, F., *J. prakt. Chem. N. F.*, **28**, 219 (1883).

Hunter, F. E., *J. Biol. Chem.*, **144**, 439 (1942).

Hunter, I. R., Roberts, R. L., and Kester, E. B., *J. Am. Chem. Soc.*, **70**, 3244 (1948).

Iguchi, T., and Sato, M., *J. Soc. Chem. Ind. Japan*, **37**, Suppl. binding 198 (1934); *C. A.*, **28**, 5479 (1934).

Inaba, T., Kitagawa, K., and Sato, M., *J. Soc. Chem. Ind. Japan*, **37**, Suppl. binding 595 (1934); *C. A.*, **29**, 1273 (1935).

Iwata, M., *Biochem. Z.*, **224**, 430 (1930); *C. A.*, **24**, 5318 (1930).

——, *Proc. Imp. Acad. (Tokyo)*, **7**, 96 (1931); *C. A.*, **25**, 3732 (1931).

Jackson, D. T., and King, C. G., *J. Am. Chem. Soc.*, **55**, 678 (1933); *C. A.*, **27**, 1324 (1933).

Jeney, A. v., Mihalik, I., and Uri, W. J., *Arch. exptl. Path. Pharmakol.*, **199**, 99 (1942); *C. A.*, **37**, 4137 (1943).

Jones, R., and Lewis, W. C. M., *Biochem. J.*, **26**, 633 (1932); *C. A.*, **26**, 5583 (1932).

Jong, H. G. B. de, and Hartkamp, J. L. L. F., *Protoplasma*, **31**, 550 (1939); *C. A.*, **33**, 6967 (1939).

——, and Joukovsky, N. I., *Compt. rend. soc. biol.*, **123**, 299, 303 (1936); *C. A.*, **31**, 924 (1937).

——, and Kruyt, H. R., *Kolloid Z.*, **50**, 39 (1930); *C. A.*, **24**, 1782 (1930).

Jong, H. G. B. de, and Rering, C. H., *Proc. Nederland. Akad. Wetensch.*, **45**, 697 (1942); *C. A.*, **38**, 5712 (1944).

——, and Saubert, S. S. P., *Biochem. Z.*, **288**, 1, 13 (1936); *C. A.*, **31**, 592 (1937).

——, and Teunissen, P. H., *Rec. trav. chim.*, **54**, 460 (1935); *C. A.*, **29**, 5338 (1935).

——, Verberg, H. G., and Westerkamp, R. F., *Kolloid Z.*, **71**, 184 (1935); *C. A.*, **29**, 7751 (1935).

——, ——, ——, *ibid.*, **71**, 194 (1935a); *C. A.*, **29**, 7751 (1935).

Jordan, R. C., and Chibnall, A. C., *Ann. Botany*, **47**, 163 (1933); *C. A.*, **27**, 4269 (1933).

Jukes, T. H., *J. Biol. Chem.*, **107**, 783 (1934).

——, and Kay, H. D., *J. Nutrition*, **5**, 81 (1932); *C. A.*, **26**, 5613 (1932).

Julian, P. L., Meyer, E. W., and Iveson, H. T., U. S. Pat. 2,373,686; *C. A.*, **39**, 3093 (1945).

Kabashima, I., *Ber.*, **71**, 76 (1938); *C. A.*, **32**, 2138 (1938).

——, *ibid.*, **71**, 1071 (1938a); *C. A.*, **32**, 5850 (1938).

——, *ibid.*, **71**, 1073 (1938b); *C. A.*, **32**, 5851 (1938).

——, and Suzuki, B., *Proc. Imp. Acad. (Tokyo)*, **8**, 492 (1932); *C. A.*, **27**, 1634 (1933).

Kahane, E., and Kahane, M., *Bull. soc. chim.* [5], **3**, 621 (1936); *C. A.*, **30**, 5521 (1936).

——, and Lévy, J., "Biochemie de la Choline et de ses Dérivés. I. Choline-Neurine," Paris, Hermann and Cie, 1938.

Kakiuchi, S., *J. Biochem. (Japan)*, **1**, 165 (1922); *C. A.*, **16**, 1597 (1922).

Kalabankoff, L., and Terroine, E. F., *Compt. rend. soc. biol.*, **66**, 176 (1909); *C. A.*, **3**, 1181 (1909).

Karrer, P., and Benz, P., *Helv. Chim. Acta*, **9**, 23 (1926); *C. A.*, **20**, 1219 (1926).

——, ——, *ibid.*, **9**, 598 (1926a); *C. A.*, **21**, 57 (1927).

——, and Salomon, H., *Helv. Chim. Acta*, **9**, 3 (1926); *C. A.*, **20**, 1218 (1926).

Kay, H. D., *Biochem. J.*, **20**, 791 (1926); *C. A.*, **21**, 421 (1927).

——, *ibid.*, **22**, 855 (1928); *C. A.*, **22**, 4543 (1928).

Keeser, E., *Biochem. Z.*, **154**, 321 (1924).

Kiessling, W., *Biochem. Z.*, **273**, 103 (1934); *C. A.*, **29**, 25 (1935).

King, A., and Mukherjee, L. N., *J. Soc. Chem. Ind.*, **59**, 185 (1940); *C. A.*, **35**, 950 (1941).

King, E. J., *Biochem. J.*, **25**, 799 (1931); *C. A.*, **25**, 5903 (1931).

——, *ibid.*, **28**, 476 (1934); *C. A.*, **28**, 6163 (1934).

——, and Dolan, M., *Biochem. J.*, **27**, 403 (1933); *C. A.*, **27**, 3728 (1933).

——, and Small, C. W., *Biochem. J.*, **33**, 1135 (1939); *C. A.*, **33**, 8223 (1939).

King, H., and Pyman, F. L., *J. Chem. Soc.*, **105**, 1238 (1914); *C. A.*, **8**, 3023 (1914).

——, King, E. J., and Page, I. H., *Z. physiol. Chem.*, **191**, 234 (1930); *C. A.*, **25**, 118 (1931).

Kirkman, H., and Severinghaus, A. E., *Anat. Record*, **70**, 413, 557; **71**, 79 (1938).

Klenk, E., *Z. physiol. Chem.*, **185**, 169 (1929); *C. A.*, **24**, 859 (1930).

——, *ibid.*, **192**, 217 (1930); *C. A.*, **25**, 120 (1931).

——, *ibid.*, **200**, 51 (1931); *C. A.*, **25**, 5439 (1931).

——, *ibid.*, **221**, 67 (1933); *C. A.*, **28**, 184 (1934).

——, *ibid.*, **229**, 151 (1934); *C. A.*, **29**, 482 (1935).

——, *ibid.*, **232**, 47 (1935); *C. A.*, **29**, 2980 (1935).

——, *ibid.*, **235**, 24 (1935a); *C. A.*, **29**, 6942 (1935).

——, *Ber.*, **75**, 1632 (1942).

——, *Z. physiol. Chem.*, **282**, 18 (1945); *C. A.*, **42**, 8777 (1948).

Klenk, E., and Diebold, W., *Z. physiol. Chem.*, **198**, 25 (1931); *C. A.*, **25**, 4278 (1931).
——, and Rennkamp, F., *Z. physiol. Chem.*, **267**, 145 (1940); *C. A.*, **35**, 3225 (1941).
——, and Sakai, R., *Z. physiol. Chem.*, **258**, 33 (1939); *C. A.*, **33**, 4610 (1939).
——, and von Schoenbeck, O. *Z. physiol. Chem.*, **194**, 191 (1931); *C. A.*, **25**, 1541 (1931).
——, ——, *ibid.*, **209**, 112 (1932); *C. A.*, **26**, 4614 (1932).
——, and Schumann, E., *Z. physiol. Chem.*, **281**, 25 (1944); *C. A.*, **40**, 6526 (1946).
——, and Schuwirth, K., *Ann. Rev. Biochem.*, **6**, 120 (1937).
Koch, W., *Z. physiol. Chem.*, **36**, 134 (1902).
——, and Pike, F., *J. Pharmacol.*, **2**, 245 (1910); *C. A.*, **5**, 2263 (1911).
——, and Woods, H. S., *J. Biol. Chem.*, **1**, 203 (1905).
Krüger, M., and Bergell, P., *Ber.*, **36**, 2901 (1903).
Kudicke, R., and Sachs, H., *Biochem. Z.*, **76**, 359 (1916); *C. A.*, **11**, 1204 (1917).
Kuhn, R., Hausser, I., and Brydówna, W., *Ber.*, **68**, 2386 (1935); *C. A.*, **30**, 1813 (1936).
Kumler, W. D., and Eiler, J. J., *J. Am. Chem. Soc.*, **65**, 2355 (1943); *C. A.*, **38**, 908 (1944).
Kutscher, F., and Lohmann, *Z. physiol. Chem.*, **39**, 159 (1903).
Kyes, P., *Berlin. klin. Wochschr.*, **40**, 956, 982 (1903).
——, *Biochem. Z.*, **4**, 99 (1907); *C. A.*, **1**, 2263 (1907).
——, and Sachs, H., *Berlin. klin. Wochschr.*, **40**, 57 (1903).
Lapworth, A., *J. Chem. Soc.*, **103**, 1029 (1913); *C. A.*, **7**, 3121 (1913).
Latzer, P., *Boll. chim. farm.*, **66**, 353, 385 (1927); *C. A.*, **21**, 3630 (1927).
Leathes, J. B., "The Fats," London, Longmans, Green & Co., 1913.
——, *J. Physiol.*, **58**, Proc. VI (1923).
——, *Lancet*, **208**, 853, 957, 1019 (1925); *C. A.*, **19**, 2964 (1925); *21*, 130 (1927).
LeBreton, E., and Pantaleon, J., *Arch. sci. physiol.*, **1**, 63 (1947); *C. A.*, **42**, 2296 (1948).
Lepeshkin, V. V., *Kolloid Z.*, **32**, 166 (1923); *C. A.*, **18**, 1600 (1924).
Lesuk, A., and Anderson, R. J., *J. Biol. Chem.*, **139**, 457 (1941).
Leuchs, H., and Geiger, W., *Ber.*, **39**, 2644 (1906).
Levene, P. A., *J. Biol. Chem.*, **15**, 153 (1913).
——, *ibid.*, **18**, 453 (1914).
——, *ibid.*, **24**, 69 (1916).
——, and Ingvaldsen, T., *J. Biol. Chem.*, **43**, 359 (1920).
——, and Jacobs, W. A., *J. Biol. Chem.*, **11**, 547 (1912).
——, and Komatsu, S., *J. Biol. Chem.*, **39**, 83, 91 (1919).
——, and Mehltretter, C. L., *Enzymologia*, **4**, 232 (1937); *C. A.*, **31**, 8513 (1937).
——, and Rolf, I. P., *J. Biol. Chem.*, **40**, 1 (1919).
——, ——, *ibid.*, **46**, 193 (1921).
——, ——, *ibid.*, **46**, 353 (1921a).
——, ——, *ibid.*, **51**, 507 (1922).
——, ——, *ibid.*, **54**, 91 (1922a).
——, ——, *ibid.*, **54**, 99 (1922b).
——, ——, *ibid.*, **55**, 743 (1923).
——, ——, *ibid.*, **60**, 677 (1924).
——, ——, *ibid.*, **62**, 759 (1924/25).
——, ——, *ibid.*, **65**, 545 (1925).
——, ——, *ibid.*, **67**, 659 (1926).
——, ——, *ibid.*, **68**, 285 (1926a).

Levene, P. A., and Rolf, I. P., *ibid.*, **72,** 587 (1927).
——, ——, *ibid.*, **74,** 713 (1927a).
——, and Simms, H. S., *J. Biol. Chem.*, **48,** 185 (1921).
——, ——, *ibid.*, **51,** 285 (1922).
——, and West, C. J., *J. Biol. Chem.*, **16,** 419 (1913).
——, ——, *ibid.*, **16,** 549 (1913/14).
——, ——, *ibid.*, **18,** 481 (1914).
——, ——, *ibid.*, **24,** 63 (1916).
——, ——, *ibid.*, **24,** 41 (1916a).
——, ——, *ibid.*, **25,** 517 (1916b).
——, ——, *ibid.*, **35,** 285 (1918).
——, ——, *ibid.*, **33,** 111 (1918a).
——, ——, *ibid.*, **34,** 175 (1918b).
——, Rolf, I. P., and Simms, H. S., *J. Biol. Chem.*, **58,** 859 (1924).
Liebermann, L., *Arch. ges. Physiol.* (*Pflügers*), **54,** 573 (1893).
Liebrecht, A., U. S. Pat. 1,777,173, Sept. 30, 1930; *C. A.*, **24,** 5939 (1930).
Liebreich, O., *Ann. Chem. Pharm.*, **134,** 29 (1865).
Linden, G. M. von, Meissen, E., and Strauss, A., U. S. Pat. 1,072,745, Sept. 9, 1913; *C. A.*, **7,** 3640 (1913).
Lockwood, H. C., *Analyst*, **63,** 705 (1938); *C. A.*, **33,** 246 (1939).
Loewe, S., *Biochem. Z.*, **42,** 150, 205 (1912); *C. A.*, **6,** 2627 (1912).
Long, J. H., and Gephart, F., *J. Am. Chem. Soc.*, **30,** 895 (1908); *C. A.*, **2,** 2704 (1908).
Löwe, S., *Biochem. Z.*, **127,** 231 (1922); *C. A.*, **16,** 1783 (1922).
Lüdecke, K., Dissertation, University of München. (1905).
MacArthur, C. G., *J. Am. Chem. Soc.*, **36,** 2397 (1914); *C. A.*, **8,** 3801 (1914).
——, and Burton, L. V., *J. Am. Chem. Soc.*, **38,** 1375 (1916); *C. A.*, **10,** 2222 (1916).
——, Norbury, F. G., and Karr, W. G., *J. Am. Chem. Soc.*, **39,** 768 (1917); *C. A.*, **11,** 1682 (1917).
McClendon, J. F., *Am. J. Physiol.*, **25,** 195 (1909/10).
McEwen, H. D., and MacLachlan, P. L., *Proc. Soc. Exptl. Biol. Med.*, **48,** 195 (1941); *C. A.*, **36,** 566 (1942).
McFarlane, A. S., *Nature*, **149,** 439 (1942a); *C. A.*, **36,** 5192 (1942).
Macfarlane, M. G., *Biochem. J.*, **36,** iii (1942).
——, *ibid.*, **42,** 587 (1948); *C. A.*, **42,** 8872 (1948).
——, *ibid.*, **42,** 590 (1948a); *C. A.*, **42,** 8872 (1948).
——, and Knight, B. C. J. G., *Biochem. J.*, **35,** 884 (1941); *C. A.*, **36,** 3823 (1942).
Macheboeuf, M. A., *Bull. soc. chim.*, **45,** 662 (1929); *C. A.*, **24,** 417 (1930).
——, *Compt. rend.*, **188,** 109 (1929a); *C. A.*, **23,** 2743 (1929).
——, *Bull. soc. chim. biol.*, **11,** 485 (1929b); *C. A.*, **24,** 1653 (1930).
——, "Etat des Lipides dans la Matière Vivante," Paris, Herman et Cie, 1937; *C. A.*, **31,** 5003 (1937).
——, and co-workers (Delsal, J. L., Lepine, P., and Giuntini, J., *Ann. inst. Pasteur*, **69,** 321 (1943); *C. A.*, **38,** 5565 (1944).
——, and Januskiewicz, M., *Bull. soc. chim. biol.*, **19,** 694 (1937); *C. A.*, **31,** 6262 (1937).
——, and Sandor, G., *Bull. soc. chim. biol.*, **14,** 1168 (1932); *C. A.*, **27,** 327 (1933).
——, ——, *Compt. rend.*, **194,** 1102 (1932a); *C. A.*, **26,** 3551 (1932).
——, and Tayeau, F., *Compt. rend.*, **206,** 860 (1938); *C. A.*, **32,** 5005 (1938).
——, ——, *Compt. rend. soc. biol.*, **129,** 1181 (1938a); *C. A.*, **33,** 2917 (1939).

McKibben, J. M., and co-workers (Pope, A., Thayer, S., Ferry, R. M., and Stare, F. J.), *J. Lab. Clin. Med.*, **30**, 488 (1945); *C. A.*, **39**, 3817 (1945).

McKinney, R. S., Jamieson, G. S., and Holton, W. B., *Oil & Soap*, **14**, 126 (1937); *C. A.*, **31**, 5191 (1937).

MacLean, H., *Z. physiol. Chem.*, **57**, 296, 304 (1908).

——, *ibid.*, **55**, 360 (1908a); *C. A.*, **2**, 2565 (1908).

——, *Biochem. J.*, **4**, 38, 168 (1909); *C. A.*, **3**, 1186 (1909).

——, *Z. physiol. Chem.*, **59**, 223 (1909a); *C. A.*, **4**, 221 (1910).

——, *Biochem. J.*, **6**, 333 (1912); *C. A.*, **7**, 369 (1913).

——, *ibid.*, **8**, 453 (1914); *C. A.*, **9**, 636 (1915).

——, *J. Path. Bact.*, **18**, 490 (1914a); *C. A.*, **9**, 1341 (1915).

——, *Biochem. J.*, **9**, 351 (1915); *C. A.*, **10**, 345 (1916).

——, and Griffiths, W. J., *Biochem. J.*, **14**, 615 (1920); *C. A.*, **15**, 241 (1921).

——, and MacLean, I. S., "Lecithin and Allied Substances," London, Longmans, Green & Co., 1927.

Macpherson, L. B., and Lucas, C. C., *Federation Proc.*, **6**, 273 (1947).

Magistris, H., *Biochem. Z.*, **210**, 85 (1929); *C. A.*, **23**, 4956 (1929).

——, *ibid.*, **253**, 81 (1932); *C. A.*, **27**, 111 (1933).

——, and Schäfer, P., *Biochem. Z.*, **214**, 401 (1929); *C. A.*, **24**, 1136 (1930).

Malquori, G., *Atti IV congr. nazl. chim. pura applicata, 1932*, **752** (1933); *C. A.*, **29**, 3355 (1935).

Maltaner, F., *J. Am. Chem. Soc.*, **52**, 1718 (1930); *C. A.*, **24**, 2467 (1930).

——, *ibid.*, **53**, 4019 (1931); *C. A.*, **26**, 493 (1932).

Manwaring, W. H., *Z. Immunitätsforsch.*, **6**, 513 (1910); *C. A.*, **4**, 2679 (1910).

Mayer, A., and Schaeffer, G., *Compt. rend.*, **157**, 156 (1913); *C. A.*, **7**, 3512 (1913).

——, and Terroine, E. F., *Compt. rend. soc. biol.*, **62**, 398 (1907); *C. A.*, **1**, 1435 (1907).

Mayer, P., *Biochem. Z.*, **1**, 39 (1906).

Meinertz, J., *Z. physiol. Chem.*, **46**, 376 (1905).

Menke, W., *Z. physiol. Chem.*, **257**, 43 (1938); *C. A.*, **33**, 2180 (1939).

Merz, W., *Z. physiol. Chem.*, **193**, 59 (1930); *C. A.*, **25**, 306 (1931).

——, *ibid.*, **196**, 10 (1931); *C. A.*, **25**, 3040 (1931).

Meyer, K. H., and Hopff, H., *Ber.*, **54**, 2274 (1921); *C. A.*, **16**, 1220 (1922).

Meyerhof, O., and Kiessling, W., *Biochem. Z.*, **264**, 40 (1933); *C. A.*, **27**, 5350 (1933).

Miles, E. M., and Miles, A. A., *J. Gen. Microbiol.*, **1**, 385 (1948); *C. A.*, **42**, 5500 (1948).

Mills, C. A., *J. Biol. Chem.*, **46**, 135 (1921).

Moraczewski, W. v., and Sadowski, T., *Biochem. Z.*, **276**, 388 (1935); *C. A.*, **29**, 4238 (1935).

Moruzzi, G., *Z. physiol. Chem.*, **55**, 352 (1908); *C. A.*, **2**, 2565 (1908).

Moyer, L. S., *J. Biol. Chem.*, **133**, 29 (1940); *C. A.*, **34**, 3384 (1940).

Nagel, R. H., Becker, H. C., and Milner, R. T., *Cereal Chem.*, **15**, 766 (1938); *C. A.*, **33**, 1049 (1939).

Nagler, F. P. O., *Brit. J. Exptl. Path.*, **20**, 473 (1939); *C. A.*, **34**, 2408 (1940).

Neuberg, C., and Karczag, L., *Biochem. Z.*, **36**, 60 (1911); *C. A.*, **6**, 380 (1912).

——, and Rosenberg, E., *Berlin. klin. Wochschr.*, **44**, 54 (1907); *C. A.*, **1**, 745 (1907).

Neuschlosz, S. M., *Kolloid Z.*, **27**, 292 (1920); *C. A.*, **15**, 1237 (1921).

——, *Arch. ges. Physiol. (Pflügers)*, **181**, 17 (1920a); *C. A.*, **15**, 1734 (1921).

Niemann, C., *J. Am. Chem. Soc.*, **63**, 1763 (1941); *C. A.*, **35**, 5460 (1941).

——, *ibid.*, **63**, 3535 (1941a); *C. A.*, **36**, 1013 (1942).

——, and Nichols, P. L., Jr., *J. Biol. Chem.*, **143**, 191 (1942).

Nikuni, J., *Proc. Imp. Acad. (Tokyo)*, **8**, 300 (1932); *C. A.*, **26**, 5978 (1932).

Nishimoto, U., *Proc. Imp. Acad. (Tokyo)*, **10**, 578 (1934); *C. A.*, **29**, 1830 (1935).

——, and Suzuki, B., *Proc. Imp. Acad. (Tokyo)*, **8**, 424, 428 (1932); *C. A.*, **27**, 989 (1933).

Norris, F. A., *Oil & Soap*, **17**, 257 (1940); *C. A.*, **35**, 924 (1941).

Nottbohm, F. E., and Mayer, F., *Z. Untersuch. Lebensm.*, **67**, 369 (1934); *C. A.*, **28**, 3489 (1934).

——, ——, *ibid.*, **69**, 289 (1935); *C. A.*, **29**, 7507 (1935).

Nyman, M. A., and Chargaff, E., *J. Biol. Chem.*, **180**, 741 (1949).

Obata, Y., *J. Agr. Chem. Soc. Japan*, **16**, 175 (1940); *C. A.*, **34**, 4727 (1940).

——, *Bull. Inst. Phys. Chem. Research (Tokyo)*, **22**, 115 (1943); *C. A.*, **42**, 522 (1948).

Ogawa, K., *J. Biochem. (Japan)*, **24**, 389 (1936); *C. A.*, **31**, 3078 (1937).

Ohman, L. O., *Arkiv Zool.*, **36A**, No. 7, 1 (1945); *C. A.*, **42**, 687 (1948).

Okunev, N., *Biochem. Z.*, **198**, 296 (1928); *C. A.*, **23**, 400 (1929).

Olcott, H. S., *Science*, **100**, 226 (1944); *C. A.*, **38**, 6334 (1944).

——, and Mecham, D. K., *Cereal Chem.*, **24**, 407 (1947); *C. A.*, **42**, 1671 (1948).

Oncley, J. L., and co-workers (Melin, M., Richert, D. A., Cameron, J. W., and Gross, P. M., Jr.), *J. Am. Chem. Soc.*, **71**, 541 (1949).

——, Gurd, F. R. N., and Melin, M., *J. Am. Chem. Soc.*, **72**, 458 (1950).

Osborne, T. B., and Campbell, G. F., *J. Am. Chem. Soc.*, **22**, 413 (1900).

Paal, C., and Oehme, H., *Ber.*, **46**, 2, 1297 (1913); *C. A.*, **7**, 2569 (1913).

Paal, H., *Biochem. Z.*, **211**, 244 (1929); *C. A.*, **23**, 5205 (1929).

Page, I. H., "Chemistry of the Brain," Baltimore, Charles C. Thomas, 1937.

——, and Bülow, M., *Z. physiol. Chem.*, **194**, 166 (1931); *C. A.*, **25**, 1541 (1931).

——, and Rudy, H., *Z. physiol. Chem.*, **205**, 115 (1932); *C. A.*, **26**, 3395 (1932).

——, and Schmidt, E., *Z. physiol. Chem.*, **199**, 1 (1931); *C. A.*, **25**, 4562 (1931).

Palmer, K. J., and Schmitt, F. O., *J. Cellular Comp. Physiol.*, **17**, 385 (1941); *C. A.*, **35**, 5920 (1941).

——, ——, and Chargaff, E., *J. Cellular Comp. Physiol.*, **18**, 43 (1941); *C. A.*, **35**, 7429 (1941).

Palmer, L. S., and Wiese, H. F., *J. Dairy Sci.*, **16**, 41 (1933); *C. A.*, **27**, 1954 (1933).

Pangborn, M. C., *J. Biol. Chem.*, **137**, 545 (1941).

——, *ibid.*, **143**, 247 (1942).

——, *ibid.*, **168**, 351 (1947).

——, *ibid.*, **188**, 471 (1951).

——, and Anderson, R. J., *J. Biol. Chem.*, **94**, 465 (1931).

Parnas, J., *Biochem. Z.*, **22**, 411 (1909); *C. A.*, **4**, 475 (1910).

——, *ibid.*, **56**, 17 (1913); *C. A.*, **8**, 923 (1914).

Parpart, A. K., and Dziemian, A. J., *Cold Spring Harbor Symposia Quant. Biol.*, **8**, 17 (1940); *C. A.*, **38**, 558 (1944).

Parsons, T. R., *Biochem. J.*, **22**, 800 (1928); *C. A.*, **22**, 4543 (1928).

Pässler, J., Ger. Pat. 697,440, Sept. 19, 1940; *C. A.*, **35**, 6688 (1941).

Pedersen, K. O., "Ultracentrifugal Studies on Serum and Serum Fractions," Uppsala, 1945.

——, *J. Phys. Colloid Chem.*, **51**, 156 (1947); *C. A.*, **42**, 262 (1948).

Petermann, M. L., *J. Biol. Chem.*, **162**, 37 (1946).

Pick, L., *Allgem. Oel-u. Fett-Ztg.*, **26**, 577 (1929); *C. A.*, **24**, 740 (1930).

Pighini, G., and Delfini, D., *Biochim. e terap. sper.*, **18**, 56 (1931); *C. A.*, **25**, 3711 (1931).

Pischinger, A., *Klin. Wochschr.*, **20**, 25 (1941); *C. A.*, **36**, 6603 (1942).

Plimmer, R. H. A., *Biochem. J.*, **7**, 72 (1913); *C. A.*, **7**, 2382 (1913).

Porges, O., and Neubauer, E., *Biochem. Z.*, **7**, 152 (1907/08); *C. A.*, **2**, 1290 (1908).

Porter, A. E., *Biochem. J.*, **10**, 523 (1916); *C. A.*, **11**, 1456 (1917).

Power, F. B., and Tutin, F., *J. Chem. Soc.*, **87**, 249 (1905).

Price, C. W., *Biochem. J.*, **27**, 1789 (1933); *C. A.*, **28**, 3087 (1934).

——, *ibid.*, **29**, 1021 (1935); *C. A.*, **29**, 5869 (1935).

——, and Lewis, W. C. M., *Trans. Faraday Soc.*, **29**, 775, 1181 (1933); *C. A.*, **28**, 952 (1934).

Price, H. I., and Lewis, W. C. M., *Biochem. J.*, **23**, 1030 (1929); *C. A.*, **24**, 870 (1930).

Przylecki, S. J., *Proc. Roy. Soc. (London)*, **127B**, 26 (1939); *C. A.*, **33**, 3823 (1939).

——, and Majmin, R., *Biochem. Z.*, **280**, 413 (1935); *C. A.*, **30**, 122 (1936).

Puchkovskiï, B. S., *Colloid J. (U.S.S.R.)*, **3**, 643 (1937); *C. A.* **32**, 6766 (1938).

——, and Strukova, J. P., *Bull. inst. colloides Voronège, No. 1*, 93 (1934); *C. A.*, **32**, 3851 (1938).

Pyenson, H., and Dahle, C. D., *J. Dairy Sci.*, **21**, 169 (1938); *C. A.*, **32**, 4232 (1938).

Rae, J. J., *Biochem. J.*, **28**, 152 (1934); *C. A.*, **28**, 4082 (1934).

——, Kay, H. D., and King, E. J., *Biochem. J.*, **28**, 143 (1934); *C. A.*, **28**, 4082 (1934).

Fränkel, S., and Bolaffio, C., *Biochem. Z.*, **9**, 44 (1908); *C. A.*, **2**, 2565 (1308). 1765 (1941).

Redemann, C. E., and Icke, R. N., *J. Org. Chem.*, **8**, 159 (1943); *C. A.*, **37**, 3737 (1943).

Reichel, M., and Thannhauser, S. J., *J. Biol. Chem.*, **135**, 15 (1940).

Remezov, I., *Biochem. Z.*, **218**, 86, 134 (1930); *C. A.*, **24**, 2480, 2481 (1930).

——, and Karlina, M. I., *Biokhimiya*, **2**, 337 (1937); *C. A.*, **31**, 7914 (1937).

Renall, M. H., *Biochem. Z.*, **55**, 296 (1913); *C. A.*, **8**, 1129 (1914).

Rezek, A., *Veterinarski Arkiv*, **15**, 161 (1945); *C. A.*, **42**, 5925 (1948).

——, *Enzymologia*, **12**, 59 (1946).

Richter, G., Ger. Pat. 223,594 (1908); *C. A.*, **4**, 3121 (1910).

——, Brit. Pat. 28,011 (1908a); *C. A.*, **4**, 86 (1910).

Riedel, J. D., Ger. Pat. 256,998 (1911).

Rimpila, C. E., and Palmer, L. S., *J. Dairy Sci.*, **18**, 827 (1935); *C. A.*, **30**, 1133 (1936).

Ritter, F., *Ber.*, **47**, 530 (1914); *C. A.*, **8**, 1436 (1914).

Rollett, A., *Z. physiol. Chem.*, **61**, 210 (1909); *C. A.*, **4**, 597 (1910).

Rona, P., and Deutsch, W., *Biochem. Z.*, **171**, 89 (1926); *C. A.*, **20**, 3303 (1926).

Rose, W. G., *J. Am. Chem. Soc.*, **69**, 1384 (1947); *C. A.*, **41**, 6530 (1947).

——, *Food Technol.*, **4**, No. 6, 230 (1950).

Rosenheim, O., and MacLean, H., *Biochem. J.*, **9**, 103 (1915); *C. A.* ,**9**, 1789 (1915).

——, and Tebb, M. C., *J. Physiol.*, **38**, Proc. 51 1 (1909).

——, ——, *ibid.*, **41**, Proc. 1 (1910).

——, ——, *Biochem. Z.*, **25**, 151 (1910a).

Rubow, V., *Arch. exptl. Path. Pharmakol.*, **52**, 173 (1905).

Rudy, H., and Page, I. H., *Z. physiol. Chem.*, **193**, 251 (1930); *C. A.*, **25**, 718 (1931).

Rybak, B., and Gros, F., *Experientia*, **4**, 396 (1948); *C. A.*, **43**, 2668 (1949).

Sahyun, M., "Proteins and Amino Acids in Nutrition," New York, Reinhold Publishing Corp, 1948.

Salisbury, L. F., and Anderson, R. J., *J. Biol. Chem.*, **112**, 541 (1936).

Sato, M., and Wada, N., *J. Soc. Chem. Ind. Japan*, **37**, Suppl. binding 717–8 (1934); *C. A.*, **29**, 1209 (1935).

Schäffner, A., in Bamann, E., and Myrbäck, K., "Die Methoden der Fermentforschung," Leipzig, Georg Thieme, 1940.

Scheff, G. J., and Awny, A. J., *Am. J. Clin. Path.*, **19**, 615 (1949); *C. A.*, **43**, 7571 (1949).

Schmidt, G., and co-workers (Benotti, J., Hershman, B., and Thannhauser, S. J.), *J. Biol. Chem.*, **166**, 505 (1946).

——, Hershman, B., and Thannhauser, S. J., *J. Biol. Chem.*, **161**, 523 (1945).

Schmidt, R., *Biochem. Z.*, **63**, 287 (1914); *C. A.*, **8**, 3585 (1914).

Schmitt, F. O., and Palmer, K. J., *Cold Spring Harbor Symposia, Quant. Biol.*, **8**, 94 (1940); *C. A.*, **38**, 561 (1944).

Scholfield, C. R., and co-workers (Dutton, H. J., Tanner, F. W., Jr., and Cowan, J. C.), *J. Am. Oil Chemists' Soc.*, **25**, 368 (1948).

Schulman, J. H., and Rideal, E. K., *Proc. Roy. Soc. (London)*, **130A**, 259 (1931); *C. A.*, **25**, 3217 (1931).

Schulze, E., *Z. physiol, Chem.*, **52**, 54 (1907); *C. A.*, **1**, 2900 (1907).

——, and Pfenninger, U., *Z. physiol. Chem.*, **71**, 174 (1911); *C. A.*, **5**, 2118 (1911).

Schumoff-Simonowski, C., and Sieber, N., *Z. physiol. Chem.*, **49**, 50 (1906); *C. A.*, **1**, 65 (1907).

Scott, E. L., *Proc. Soc. Exptl. Biol. Med.*, **14**, 34 (1917); *C. A.*, **11**, 1840 (1917).

Seifriz, W., *Am. J. Physiol.*, **66**, 124 (1923); *C. A.*, **17**, 3513 (1923).

Sell, H. M., Olsen, A. G., and Kremers, R. E., *Ind. Eng. Chem.*, **27**, 1222 (1935); *C. A.*, **29**, 7515 (1935).

Sharpless, G. R., *Proc. Soc. Exptl. Biol. Med.*, **45**, 487 (1940); *C. A.*, **35**, 784 (1941).

Shinowara, G. Y., and Brown, J. B., *Oil & Soap*, **15**, 151 (1938); *C. A.*, **32**, 5860 (1938).

Shinozaki, S., and Sato, M., *J. Agr. Chem. Soc. Japan*, **9**, 728 (1933); *C. A.*, **27**, 5563 (1933).

Shinozaki, Y., and Sato, M., *J. Soc. Chem. Ind. Japan*, **37**, Suppl. binding 432 (1934); *C. A.*, **28**, 7566 (1934).

Sigurdsson, B., *J. Exptl. Med.*, **77**, 315 (1943); *C. A.*, **37**, 3156 (1943).

Sinclair, R. G., *J. Biol. Chem.*, **82**, 117 (1929).

——, *ibid.*, **92**, 245 (1931).

——, *ibid.*, **97**, XXXIV (1932).

——, *ibid.*, **95**, 393 (1932a).

——, *ibid.*, **111**, 261, 275, 515 (1935).

——, *Can. J. Research*, **12**, 777 (1949); *C. A.*, **43**, 3868 (1949).

Sjölin, S., *Biochem. Z.*, **314**, 82 (1943); *C. A.*, **37**, 4950 (1943).

Slotta, K. H., and Fraenkel-Conrat, H. L., *Ber.*, **71**, 1076 (1938); *C. A.*, **32**, 7946 (1938).

——, and Szyszka, G., *Ber.*, **71**, 258 (1938); *C. A.*, **32**, 3435 (1938).

Slowtzoff, B. J., *Hofmeister's Beitr. z. Chem. Physiol. u. Pathol.*, **7**, 508 (1905); *Chem. Zentr.*, **I**, 575 (1906).

Smedley-MacLean, I., *Ann. Rev. Biochem.*, **1**, 135 (1932); *C. A.*, **27**, 3729 (1933).

Smith, J. A. B., and Chibnall, A. C., *Biochem. J.* **26**, 1345 (1932); *C. A.*, **27**, 521 (1933).

Snider, R. H., and Bloor, W. R., *J. Biol. Chem.*, **99**, 555 (1933).

Sörensen, S. P. L., *Kolloid-Z.*, **53**, 306 (1930); *C. A.*, **25**, 861 (1931).

Sowden, J. C., and Fischer, H. O. L., *J. Am. Chem. Soc.*, **63**, 3244 (1941); *C. A.*, **36**, 1013 (1942).

Spiegel-Adolf, M., *Klin. Wochschr.*, **11**, 185 (1932); *C. A.*, **26**, 3528 (1932).

——, *Biochem. J.*, **26**, 2183 (1932a); *C. A.*, **27**, 3229 (1933).

——, *J. Am. Chem. Soc.*, **57**, 1431 (1935); *C. A.*, **29**, 7747 (1935).

——, and Henny, G. C., *J. Biol. Chem.*, **140**, CXXII, CXXIII (1941).

Spiegel-Adolf, M., and Henny, G. C., *Radiologica Clinica*, 11, 154 (1942).

Spranger, W., *Biochem. Z.*, 208, 164 (1929); *C. A.*, 23, 4253 (1929).

Stamm, W., *Arch. exptl. Path. Pharm.*, 111, 133 (1926); *C. A.*, 20, 2023 (1926).

Stanley, J., *Food Inds.*, 14, 69 (1942); *C. A.*, 36, 4923 (1942).

Stassano, H., and Billon, F., *Compt. rend. soc. biol.*, 55, 482 (1903).

Steiger, A., *Mikrokosmos*, 35, 54 (1941); *C. A.*, 37, 3648 (1943).

Stepp, W., Feulgen, R., and Voit, K., *Biochem. Z.*, 181, 284 (1927); *C. A.*, 21, 2000 (1927).

Stern, M., and Thierfelder, H., *Z. physiol. Chem.*, 53, 370 (1907); *C. A.*, 2, 139 (1908).

Stoneburg, C. A., *J. Biol. Chem.*, 129, 189 (1939).

Storm van Leeuwen, W., and Szent-Györgyi, A. v., *J. Pharmacol.*, 21, 85 (1923); *C. A.*, 17, 2015 (1923).

Strecker, A., *Ann. Chem. Pharm.*, 70, 149 (1849).

——, *ibid.*, 123, 353 (1862).

——, *ibid.*, 148, 77 (1868).

Sueyoshi, Y., *J. Biochem.* (*Japan*), 13, 145 (1931); *C. A.*, 25, 4295 (1931).

——, and Furukubo, T., *J. Biochem.* (*Japan*), 13, 155 (1931); *C. A.*, 25, 4018 (1931).

——, and Kawai, K., *J. Biochem.* (*Japan*), 15, 277 (1932); *C. A.*, 26, 5589 (1932).

Suzuki, B., and Maruyama, T., *Proc. Imp. Acad.* (*Tokyo*), 6, 67 (1930); *C. A.*, 24, 2770 (1930).

——, and Nishimoto, U., *Proc. Imp. Acad.* (*Tokyo*), 6, 262 (1930); *C. A.*, 24, 5309 (1930).

——, and Yokoyama, Y., *Proc. Imp. Acad.* (*Tokyo*), 6, 341 (1930); *C. A.*, 25, 530 (1931).

Tamura, S., *Z. physiol. Chem.*, 87, 85 (1913); *C. A.*, 8, 727 (1914).

Tayeau, F., *Compt. rend. soc. biol.*, 130, 1027 (1939); *C. A.*, 33, 5467 (1939).

——, *Lait*, 20, 129 (1940); *C. A.*, 34, 4169 (1940).

Taylor, T. C., and Lehrman, L., *J. Am. Chem. Soc.*, 48, 1739 (1926); *C. A.*, 20, 2310 (1926).

Thannhauser, S. J., and Boncoddo, N. F., *J. Biol. Chem.*, 172, 135 (1948).

——, ——, *ibid.*, 172, 141 (1948a).

——, and Reichel, M., *J. Biol. Chem.*, 135, 1 (1940).

——, and Schmidt, G., *Ann. Rev. Biochem.*, 12, 233 (1943); *C. A.*, 37, 6682 (1943).

——, and Setz, P., *J. Biol. Chem.*, 116, 527 (1936).

——, Benotti, J., and Boncoddo, N. F., *J. Biol. Chem.*, 166, 669 (1946).

——, ——, ——, *ibid.*, 166, 677 (1946a).

——, Boncoddo, N. F., and Schmidt, G., *J. Biol. Chem.*, 188, 417, 423, 427 (1951).

——, Setz, P., and Benotti, J., *J. Biol. Chem.*, 126, 785 (1938).

Thiele, F. H., *Biochem. J.*, 7, 275, 287 (1913); *C. A.*, 8, 1816, 1817 (1914).

Thierfelder, H., and Klenk, E., *Z. physiol. Chem.*, 145, 221 (1925); *C. A.*, 19, 2676 (1925).

——, ——, "Die Chemie der Cerebroside und Phosphatide," Berlin, Julius Springer, 1930.

——, and Schulze, O., *Z. physiol. Chem.*, 96, 296 (1915/16); *C. A.*, 10, 914 (1916).

Thomas, A., *J. Biol. Chem.*, 23, 359 (1915).

Thomas, K., and Thierfelder, H., *Z. physiol. Chem.*, 77, 511 (1912); *C. A.*, 6, 2085 (1912).

Thornton, M. H., Johnson, C. S., and Ewan, M. A., *Oil & Soap*, 21, 85 (1944); *C. A.*, 38, 2228 (1944).

——, and Kraybill, H. R., *Ind. Eng. Chem.*, 34, 625 (1942); *C. A.*, 36, 3379 (1924).

Thudichum, J. L. W., "A Treatise on the Chemical Constitution of the Brain," London, Baillière, Tindall & Cox, 1884.

——, "Die Chemische Konstitution des Gehirns des Menschen und der Tiere," Tübingen, Franz Pietzcker, 1901.

Thunberg, T., *Skand. Arch. Physiol.*, **43**, 275 (1923); *C. A., 18,* 110 (1924).

Tompsett, S. L., *Biochem. J.*, **28**, 1802 (1934); *C. A.*, **29**, 1841 (1935).

Töpler, *Landw. Vers. Sta.*, **3**, 85 (1861).

Torbolí, A., *Boll. soc. ital. biol. sper.*, **20**, 843 (1945), *C. A.*, **40**, 6531 (1946).

Trager, A., J. *Bact.*, **56**, 195 (1948); *C. A.*, **42**, 8254 (1948).

Trier, G., *Z. physiol. Chem.*, **73**, 383 (1911); *C. A.*, **6**, 375 (1912).

——, *ibid.*, **76**, 496 (1912); *C. A.*, **6**, 1446 (1912).

——, *ibid.*, **80**, 409 (1912a); *C. A.*, **7**, 800 (1913).

——, *ibid.*, **86**, 1, 141, 153 (1913); *C. A.*, **8**, 947 (1914).

Tristram, G. R., *Biochem. J.*, **36**, 400 (1942); *C. A.*, **36**, 7070 (1942).

Tropp, C., and Eckardt, B., *Z. physiol. Chem.*, **243**, 38 (1936); *C. A.*, **31**, 156 (1937).

——, and Wiedersheim, V., *Z. physiol. Chem.*, **222**, 39 (1933); *C. A.*, **28**, 785 (1934).

Tsujimoto, M., *J. Chem. Ind.* (*Japan*), **23**, 1007 (1920); *C. A.*, **15**, 1227 (1921).

Turner, K., and Watson, M. M., *Biochem. J.*, **24**, 113 (1930); *C. A.*, **24**, 5203 (1930).

Turner, M. E., and Gibson, R. B., *J. Clin. Investigation,* **11**, 735 (1932); *C. A.*, **27**, 124 (1933).

Tutin, F., and Hann, A. C. O., *J. Chem. Soc.*, **89**, 1749 (1906); *C. A.*, **1**, 555 (1907).

Udagawa, H., *J. Biochem.* (*Japan*), **22**, 323 (1935); *C. A.*, **30**, 6767 (1936).

Ulpiani, C., *Gazz. chim. ital.*, **31**, [2], 47 (1901).

Valette, G., *Compt. rend. soc. biol.*, **122**, 150 (1936); *C. A.*, **30**, 5651 (1936).

——, *Bull. soc. chim. biol.*, **19**, 1676 (1937); *C. A.*, **32**, 3818 (1938).

——, and Cavier, R., *Bull. soc. chim. biol.*, **20**, 1256 (1938); *C. A.*, **33**, 1349 (1939).

Vauquelin, *Ann. chim.*, **81**, 37 (1812).

Verkade, P. E., *Fette u. Seifen,* **45**, 457 (1938); *C. A.*, **33**, 423 (1939).

——, Stoppelenburg, J. C., and Cohen, W. D., *Rec. trav. chim.*, **59**, 886 (1940); *C. A.*, **35**, 4738 (1941).

Vickery, H. B., and co-workers (Smith, E. L., Hubbell, R. B., and Nolan, L. S.), *J. Biol. Chem.*, **140**, 613 (1941).

Virtanen, A. I., and Tammelander, R., *Ann. acad. sci. Fennicae*, **26A**, no. 9, 3 (1927); *C. A.*, **21**, 2708 (1927).

Vishnevskaya, G. R., and Kniga, A. G., *Schriften zentral. biochem. Forsch. Inst. Nahr. u. Genussmittelind.* (*U.S.S.R.*), **3**, 392 (1933); *C. A.*, **28**, 2970 (1934).

Vita, G., and Bracaloni, L., *J. pharm. chim.*, **20**, 22 (1934); *C. A.*, **28**, 7426 (1934).

Wadsworth, A., Maltaner, F., and Maltaner, E., *Am. J. Physiol.*, **91**, 423 (1930); *C. A.*, **24**, 4818 (1930).

Wagner-Jauregg, T., and Arnold, H., *Ber.*, **70**, 1459 (1937); *C. A.*, **31**, 6621 (1937).

——, ——, *Biochem. Z.*, **299**, 274 (1938); *C. A.*, **33**, 1772 (1939).

Weidlein, E. R., Jr., "The Biochemistry of Inositol," Pittsburgh, Mellon Institute, Bibliographic Series, Bull. No. 6, 1951.

Weissman, N., and Graff, L. H., *J. Infectious Diseases,* **80**, 145 (1947); *C. A.*, **41**, 7444 (1947).

Welch, E. A., *J. Biol. Chem.*, **161**, 65 (1945).

Went, I., and Goreczky, L., *Biochem. Z.*, **239**, 441 (1931); *C. A.*, **26**, 205 (1932).

Weyl, Th., *Z. physiol. Chem.*, **1**, 72 (1877/78).

Wiese, H. F., and Palmer, L. S., *J. Dairy Sci.*, **15**, 371 (1932); *C. A.*, **26**, 6028 (1932).

Williamson, M. B., *J. Biol. Chem.*, **156**, 47 (1940).

Willstätter, R., and Lüdecke, K., *Ber.,* **37**, 3753 (1904).

——, and Rohdewald, M., *Z. physiol. Chem.,* **225**, 103 (1934) ; *C. A.,* **225**, 103 (1934).

Winterstein, A., and Stein, G., *Z. physiol. Chem.,* **220**, 247, 263 (1933) ; *C. A.,* **28**, 391 (1934).

Winterstein, E., and Hiestand, O., *Z. physiol. Chem.,* **47**, 496 (1906).

——, and Stegmann, L., *Z. physiol. Chem.,* **58**, 527 (1908/09) ; *C. A.,* **3**, 1994 (1909).

Witanowski, W. R., *Acta Biol. Exptl., (Warsaw),* **2**, 61 (1928) ; *C. A.,* **23**, 2192 (1929).

Wohlgemuth, J., *Biochem. Z.,* **39**, 302 (1912) ; *C. A.,* **6**, 1630 (1912).

Wood, J. L., and du Vigneaud, V., *J. Biol. Chem.,* **134**, 413 (1940).

Woodman, R. M., *J. Soc. Chem. Ind.,* **51**, 95T (1932) ; *C. A.,* **26**, 3164 (1932).

——, *ibid.,* **54**, 70T (1935) ; *C. A.,* **29**, 3575 (1935).

Woolley, D. W., *J. Biol. Chem.,* **147**, 581 (1943).

——, and Krampitz, L. O., *J. Biol. Chem.,* **146**, 273 (1942).

Wörner, E., and Thierfelder, H., *Z. physiol. Chem.,* **30**, 542 (1900).

Wurtz, A., *Compt. rend.,* **49**, 898 (1859).

——, *ibid.,* **53**, 338 (1861).

——, *ibid.,* **65**, 1015 (1867).

——, *ibid.,* **66**, 772 (1868).

Yokoyama, Y., *Proc. Imp. Acad. (Tokyo),* **10**, 582 (1934) ; *C. A.,* **29**, 1830 (1935).

——, and Suzuki, B., *Proc. Imp. Acad. (Tokyo),* **7**, 12 (1931) ; *C. A.,* **25**, 1836 (1931).

——, ——, *ibid.,* **7**, 226 (1931a) ; *C. A.,* **25**, 5432 (1931).

——, ——, *ibid.,* **8**, 183 (1932) ; *C. A.,* **26**, 4834 (1932).

——, ——, *ibid.,* **8**, 358 (1932a) ; *C. A.,* **27**, 1374 (1933).

——, ——, *ibid.,* **8**, 361 (1932b) ; *C. A.,* **27**, 1374 (1933).

Yoshinaga, T., *J. Biochem. (Japan),* **24**, 21 (1936) ; *C. A.,* **30**, 8265 (1936).

——, *ibid.,* **27**, 1, 81 (1938) ; *C. A.,* **32**, 5018, 5019 (1938).

Yumikura, S., *Biochem. Z.,* **157**, 359, 371 (1925) ; *C. A.,* **20**, 427 (1926).

Zain, H., *Arch. exptl. Path. Pharmakol.,* **146**, 78 (1929) ; *C. A.,* **24**, 3803 (1930).

Zamecnik, P. C., and Lipmann, F., *J. Exptl. Med.,* **85**, 395 (1947) ; *C. A.,* **41**, 4540 (1947).

——, Brewster, L. E., and Lipmann, F., *J. Exptl. Med.,* **85**, 381 (1947) ; *C. A.,* **41**, 4533 (1947).

Zietzsche, F., and Nachmann, M., *Helv. Chim. Acta,* **9**, 708 (1926) ; *C. A.,* **21**, 2461 (1927).

PART II
THE ANALYTICAL DETERMINATION OF THE PHOSPHATIDES

CHAPTER XI

EXTRACTION AND DETERMINATION OF TOTAL PHOSPHATIDES

Introduction

Because of the complex nature of the phosphatides, the problems associated with their analysis are great. Quantitative phosphatide analysis may be divided into three parts. (1) The extraction of the phosphatides from plant or animal sources by either micro- or macrotechniques. Not only must the extraction be complete, but ideally these delicate compounds must be obtained as nearly as possible as they exist in the living tissue without denaturation, oxidation, or other change which will interfere with proper analysis. Also, extraneous phosphorus-containing material must be absent. (2) The determination of the total phosphatides in this phosphatide-containing extract. (3) The division of the total phosphatides, either directly or indirectly, into the component compounds and the determination of the amounts of these.

Although these problems of analytical determination are still controversial, great progress has been made, and the important work which has been carried out is summarized here. Closely associated problems which must be considered include methods for the determination of the hydrolysis products of phosphatides as well as for the determination of the chemical elements which comprise phosphatides. The iodine number of phosphatides is the only commonly determined physical constant, for which reason it, too, is discussed here. Finally, mention is made of various attempts to detect phosphatides qualitatively and histochemically.

Microextraction of Phosphatides

It very soon became apparent that if physiological investigations were to be practical, micromethods for the determination of phosphatides would have to be discovered for the sake of convenience as well as for conservation of material. The quantitative isolation of a phosphatide fraction which in some instances consists of only a few milligrams is an extremely difficult process. Nevertheless, adequate procedures are available, and these are discussed before the macromethods because there is greater interest among most modern workers in microtechniques.

The ultimate refinements in the difficult field of phosphatide micro-analysis will not be made for many years to come. Great strides have been made, however, due in large part to the continued efforts of Bloor and his co-workers. The microprocedure used by these investigators is described in Bloor's monograph (1943, pp. 44–47) and, as the following discussion will indicate, it has been used extensively with various modifications by many workers.

Blood

The efficacy of ethanol (Kumagawa and Suto, 1908) or methanol (Fourneau and Piettre, 1913) for the extraction of phosphatides from blood was early recognized. In Bloor's (1914, 1915) procedure for the isolation of lipides from blood, freshly distilled ethanol was combined with peroxide-free ether in the ratio of three to one. A measured volume of blood or fluid was added slowly to an excess of the solvent and the proteins were thus precipitated in a finely divided form. This fine state of division, combined with the excess solvent, allows the extraction and distribution process to proceed rapidly, making it necessary only to bring the solvents to the boiling point for complete extraction. Alternatively, the mixed materials may be allowed to stand at room temperature for a longer period of time. Bloor pointed out that the dissociating influence of alcohol was combined with the great solvent power of ether to provide a solvent mixture capable of complete extraction and distribution. In addition, the gentle heating was believed to be a sufficiently mild treatment, thus avoiding extensive decomposition of the phosphatides.

The proteins were next removed by filtration and the filtrate used for lipide analysis. It is obvious that extraction must be complete only in the sense that no phosphatides must be left associated with the proteins. Otherwise, all that is required is that the mixture of solvent and the blood components including phosphatides be homogeneous. In order to obtain the phosphatide fraction in Bloor's procedure, the solvent is carefully removed and the residue is extracted with petroleum ether. From this solution the phosphatide fraction may be precipitated by the addition of excess acetone containing a small amount of an alcoholic solution of magnesium chloride. The phosphatide content of this fraction is then determined by procedures to be discussed in detail later. Bloor (1918) described the application of his method to whole blood, plasma and corpuscles, at the same time outlining procedures for the determination of total phosphate and acid-soluble, phosphorus-containing materials in blood.

Taurog, Entenman and Chaikoff (1944) have modified Bloor's procedure by extracting the precipitated proteins further with ether for six to twelve hours. Other investigators, too, have seen fit to extend the time of extraction and to employ higher temperatures and auxiliary solvents in order to insure complete removal of the lipides. The various arguments and their validity in the face of experimental evidence have been reviewed by Boyd (1936). The original procedure published by Bloor (1914, 1915) recommended the addition of 3 ml. of blood slowly to 70 to 80 ml. of freshly distilled ethanol (3 parts) and ether (1 part). The mixture was shaken, heated to boiling, cooled, diluted to 100 ml. and filtered. Subsequently, Bloor, Pelkan and Allen (1922) employed the lower dilution of 1 part of blood in 15 parts of solvent, and in subsequent publications (Bloor, 1928, 1932) dilutions varied from 1:12.5 to 1:50. Still another publication (Bloor, 1929) mentioned the use of 95 per cent ethanol in the analysis of whole blood rather than the alcohol-ether mixture previously used.

Man and Gildea (1932/33, 1937), however, in the belief that the short heating period recommended by Bloor was not adequate, refluxed the mixture of blood and solvent for one hour. By this modification they found it possible to extract 5 to 31 per cent more lipide. This same modification was adopted by Kirk, Page and Van Slyke (1934), as well as by other investigators.

Stewart and Hendry (1935), on the other hand, are of the opinion that an alcohol-ether mixture extracts phosphatides from blood completely without heating. That extraneous material is not extracted was indicated by the fact that the solvent did not extract other phosphorus-containing material added to the blood.

Boyd (1936) investigated in some detail the limitations of Bloor's procedure. He concluded that for serum or plasma at least 20 volumes of solvent must be used, whereas with whole blood 30 to 35 volumes are required. When the extracts were diluted to this extent, refluxing for as long as two hours did not increase the yield of lipide. Nor did cold extraction for two days increase the yield over that obtained by an extraction period of less than 15 minutes. Continued heating was found, in addition, to effect solution of colored substances which caused high results in the analyses. The percentages of alcohol and ether in the solvent could be varied widely without altering the results.

Of importance is the fact that aliquots of serum below 3 ml. require proportionately greater quantities of solvents for complete extraction, and even then erratic results may be obtained. This limitation is not a serious one. Boyd's procedure has been used with slight modifications by Weil and Russell (1942).

The effect of anticoagulants on blood plasma is important, for Schmidt (1935) found about 12 per cent more phosphatides in heparinized plasma than in oxalated plasma. Boyd (1936) also observed that oxalated plasma had a lower lipide content than defibrinated plasma, although his results were subject to considerable variation.

Red Blood Cells. The estimation of lipides in red blood cells presents special problems which were investigated and reviewed by Boyd (1936a). His procedure involved centrifugation of oxalated blood until the red blood cell layer became translucent. An aliquot of the red blood cells obtained well below the surface of the sample was then hemolyzed with an equal volume of water. The extraction of the lipides was carried out with 25 to 30 volumes of ethanol-ether per volume of aliquot. Elevated temperatures were found to be undesirable. The extract was then filtered, the residue was washed, and an aliquot of filtrate and washings was analyzed for phosphatides. This work also showed that lipide values are higher in cells from oxalated than from defibrinated blood.

Tissue

Bloor's method of phosphatide extraction for blood may also be applied to tissue with appropriate modifications which take into consideration the difference in the physical state of the two materials. The earlier workers' belief that drying is essential was discussed by MacLean and MacLean (1927, pp. 76–78). Drying by means other than the use of solvents is now considered undesirable, however, because of the danger of oxidation and degradation of the lipides, and because of possible denaturation of the proteins which would make subsequent separation of the lipides almost impossible. Bloor (1943, p. 45) points out that vacuum drying of frozen tissue is desirable. Although this method is limited by the rather elaborate equipment necessary, it has been used by some workers.

It was originally recommended by Bloor (1929) that undried, finely ground tissue be extracted in a continuous extraction apparatus with hot alcohol. After completion of the extraction the solvent may be removed and, as in the case of blood, the lipides are extracted with ether or petroleum ether and the phosphatides are precipitated by use of acetone and alcoholic magnesium chloride. The procedure is elaborated and somewhat modified in Bloor's monograph (1943, pp. 45–6), where it is indicated that a finer state of division may be obtained by mixing the tissue intimately with sand. The tissue in this form does not need extensive extraction, the recommended procedure requiring three short extractions with boiling alcohol followed by two with ether.

Thannhauser and Setz (1936) advocated the extraction of lipides from both blood and tissue by the use of equal portions of methanol and chloroform. Much less of this mixture is required than of alcohol-ether, and they believed also that a better extraction of sphingomyelin was effected, leading ultimately to more accurate analyses.

The uses of ethanol-ether and chloroform-methanol solutions for the extraction of phosphatides from blood and tissue were compared by Erickson and co-workers (1940). In their opinion, both were adequate.

Fries and co-workers (1941) obtained phosphatides for analysis from brain and nervous tissue by successive extractions with 95 per cent alcohol, ethyl ether and petroleum ether.

Artom and Fishman (1943) extracted tissue which had been dehydrated with cold alcohol, with boiling alcohol and then with alcohol-ether (2:1). The extracts were evaporated, dried under nitrogen and reëxtracted with hot chloroform. The efficiency of this method was demonstrated by the fact that a maximum of two per cent of fatty acids remained in the extracted tissue.

Purification of Ethanol-Ether Extract

The complexity of blood or tissue is such that any one organic solvent or combination of solvents could hardly be expected to extract lipides in preference to all the other compounds present. This is especially true when one considers the polar nature of alcohol, which must necessarily be used, and the solubilizing effect of lipides on carbohydrates and inorganic material. Accordingly, rectification of some sort is necessary after the initial extraction. Bloor recommended the use of petroleum ether to extract the residue left after concentration of the alcohol-ether solution. The efficacy of this reëxtraction has been the subject of some controversy in the literature. Thus, Erickson and co-workers (1940) reported that lecithin and sphingomyelin were refractory to reëxtraction with petroleum ether. Accordingly, this step was eliminated in their work. It seems likely, however, that their results were largely due to the oxidation and subsequent insolubilization which phosphatides are prone to undergo during manipulation. It is thus important to stress the point that all manipulation must be carried out in inert atmospheres so far as is possible. High temperatures must be avoided, for which reason solvents must be evaporated under reduced pressures. If an ebullition tube is used in these evaporations, it should be attached to a reservoir of inert gas. Some investigators even saturate the solvents with inert gas, and it is, of course, obvious that the solvents must be pure and free from peroxides.

Although these precautions were not mentioned in Bloor's earlier work (1929), a later publication (Bloor, 1937) indicated that they were being observed in his laboratory.

Ellis and Maynard (1937), who were interested in determining the phosphatide content of bovine blood, observed that petroleum ether reëxtraction was feasible as long as the solvent from the alcohol-ether extract was removed *in vacuo.* The same conclusion was reached by Man (1937).

Although a considerable amount of rectification is undoubtedly effected by petroleum ether, it has nevertheless been shown that this solvent, like alcohol and ether, is not specific for phosphatides. Although Kirk, Page and Van Slyke (1934) postulated that low-boiling petroleum ether was specific for lipides, later work from the same laboratory (Folch and Van Slyke, 1939, 1939a) showed that the use of petroleum ether yielded high nitrogen-to-phosphorus ratios due to the extraction of urea and amino acids. Thus, the lipides cause these materials, which are ordinarily insoluble in petroleum ether, to be solubilized. These same observations were made concurrently by Christensen (1939), who was actually able to isolate crystalline urea from petroleum ether solutions of blood phosphatides. In addition, he found that in some instances alkali halides were present to the extent of 40 per cent of the phosphatides. These observations emphasize the necessity for washing the petroleum ether solutions with water prior to the precipitation of the phosphatides with acetone and magnesium chloride.

Other Methods of Extraction for Blood and Tissue

To eliminate the use of petroleum ether, Folch and Van Slyke (1939a) proposed an entirely different procedure for the extraction of phosphatides from blood. Use was made of "colloidal" iron to precipitate both proteins and lipides, after which the latter were extracted according to a prescribed procedure by alcohol-ether.

Artom (1941) pointed out that erratic values for phosphatide content often result either from incomplete or irregular phosphatide recovery due largely to the incorrect use of petroleum ether and to the presence of contaminants which behave like choline in analyses for the individual phosphatides. Accordingly, he compared the results of the following four procedures when applied to blood. (1) The whole blood was extracted in a Kumagawa-Suto type of apparatus with cold and hot ethanol in turn. The solvents were removed and the residue was reëxtracted with chloroform. (2) The protein-lipide complex was precipitated with 55 per cent aqueous ammonium sulfate at an apparent pH of 3. The precipitate was then washed with the salt solution and extracted as in the first procedure. (3) The protein-lipide complex was precipitated with the "colloidal" iron of Folch and Van Slyke (1939a) in combination with magnesium sulfate. The precipitate, having been washed with saline solution, was extracted with cold alcohol-ether. The solvent was then removed and the residue extracted with chloroform. (4) The third procedure was repeated, except that the final extraction with chloroform was omitted.

From the resulting data Artom concluded that adequate extraction occurred in each case. The washing with aqueous saline solution was of definite advantage in removing substances ordinarily calculated as choline, whereas the final purification with chloroform served to eliminate extraneous matter which increases the phosphorus content.

McKibbin and Taylor (1949) have found it possible to obtain pure phosphatide extracts by treating tissue first with alcohol-ether and then with chloroform. Subsequently, a chloroform solution of the extract is washed, in an emulsified state, with $0.25M$ magnesium chloride. The lipides thus removed can actually be estimated from the fatty acid content of the washings. This technique, it is believed, removes contaminating, nonlipide phosphorus and nitrogen.

Still another type of extraction for blood and tissue (Fawaz, Lieb and Zacherl, 1937; Norberg and Teorell, 1933) makes use of trichloroacetic acid to precipitate the protein-lipide complex and to keep in solution the so-called acid-soluble phosphorus. Then the precipitate may be extracted with alcohol and ether to obtain the phosphatides.

The use of methylal, the formal of methyl alcohol, was advocated by Delsal (1944) for extracting phosphatides and cholesterol from blood serum. The proteins are precipitated at the same time. The serum may be treated with either a large or a small excess of methylal, but in the latter case the precipitated proteins must be washed with the solvent. After evaporation of the methylal the phosphatides may be determined in the residue by any of the known procedures. Absolute ethanol is said by Egsgaard (1948) to be a suitable solvent for extraction since the proteins are precipitated simultaneously and no inorganic phosphorus passes into the extract.

Extraction of Phosphatides Containing P^{32}

The quantitative isolation of phosphatides containing isotopic phosphorus is of great importance in modern tracer work. In general, the same microtechniques are employed as with unlabeled phosphatides but, as pointed out by Hevesy (1948, p. 280), care must be taken to remove extraneous phosphorus-containing material. This is best done by washing ether extracts of the phosphatides with $0.1N$ hydrochloric acid. For the separation of choline and noncholine-containing phosphatides, Hevesy recommends a slightly modified version of the adsorption procedure of Taurog and co-workers (1944, see p. 169).

MACROEXTRACTION OF PHOSPHATIDES

Although microtechniques for phosphatide extraction demonstrate an advantage from the point of view of time and the small quantities of material needed, macroprocedures may sometimes, although by no means invariably, be more accurate. They are necessary, furthermore, in instances where a quantitative analysis of fatty acids is to be carried out.

Blood and Tissue

The problem of dehydrating tissue is the same here as with samples for microanalysis (see p. 150), and again it must be concluded that most drying procedures are undesirable because of the adverse effect on the phosphatides. Bloor (1943, pp. 39–40) recommended the use of ethanol as a solvent for removing the water as well as extracting the lipides from finely ground tissue. As indicated previously, alcohol has the advantage of dissociating protein-lipide and other complexes and is known to effect a more complete lipide extraction than any other common solvent. Naturally, the same precautions against oxidation and chemical changes must be observed here as in microprocedures.

Bloor's (1943, pp. 40–42) procedure for extraction involves a preliminary treatment of the fresh, finely ground tissue with an excess of 95 per cent ethanol. After several hours the solution, which has been stirred intermittently, is filtered. The filtrate is saved and the residue is extracted with hot alcohol in an extractor described by Bloor. Fresh alcohol is provided every hour for three hours. Thereafter, the combined solutions are concentrated *in vacuo* and the residue is rectified by ether. The ether solution is then concentrated somewhat and the phosphatides are precipitated either from the entire solution or from an aliquot by the addition, as in the microprocedure, of acetone and alcoholic magnesium chloride. Purification of the phosphatides may be effected by repeated solution and precipitation.

The application of this macroprocedure to blood (Bloor, 1924) as well as to tissue such as beef heart muscle (Bloor, 1926) has been described in detail.

The use of ether, as advocated by Bloor, is subject to some criticism when applied to substances such as brain and nervous tissue where sphingomyelin and cerebrosides are important constituents. These, as well as the recently discovered hydrophosphatides are ether-insoluble. A portion of them would probably be solubilized by the other lipides, but the distinct possibility that some of them would remain insoluble detracts from the quantitative nature of the procedure. In such cases, the substitution of chloroform for purposes of rectification of the original extract may be advisable.

Once the tissue has been extracted with alcohol, it is sometimes wise to extract it further with fat solvents such as chloroform or ether. When the lipides are particularly resistant to extraction, the residue after several extractions may be treated with hydrochloric acid and then extracted further. Such a procedure was used in some cases by Anderson and co-workers in their investigations of the lipides of the tubercle bacilli (see p. 202). Obviously, however, less strenuous procedures are desirable if the lipides are to be obtained as they exist in the living organs.

Salisbury and Anderson (1939) used an extraction procedure for the larva of the tapeworm, *Cysticercus fasciolaris,* similar to that used by Anderson (1927) for the tuberculosis bacilli. The dried larvae, ground to a powder, were extracted for periods of from one to three days at room temperature as follows: twice with acetone, three times with ethanol-ether (1:1) and once with chloroform. The solvents were removed at temperatures not exceeding 35° C. and the combined residues were extracted with ether. The lipides obtained by removal of the ether were then analyzed for phosphorus content.

The extraction of phosphatides from feces for analysis has been described by Monasterio and Gigli (1947).

Plants

So far, the discussion has been limited largely to procedures for extracting phosphatides for quantitative analysis from blood and animal tissue. The determination of phosphatides in seeds, cereals, other plant sources and dairy products is likewise important. The methods which have been used are far from exact and are complicated very often by the presence of large quantities of extraneous substances such as carbohydrates and inorganic salts whose solubilities are aggravatingly changed by their close association with the lipides. This, coupled with the fact that phosphatides are often present in only small quantities, makes quantitative isolation a difficult matter. Here, as with blood and tissue, alcohol is most generally used as the initial solvent either alone or in combination with ether. The time required for complete extraction is variable, but the material to be extracted must, of course, be in as fine a state of division as possible. Some workers have been content to assume that the phosphorus content of the material obtained in the initial extraction is a measure of the phosphatides present. Others, as will be seen in the following discussion, have resorted to rectification by various solvents and to precipitation of the phosphatides with acetone and magnesium chloride. It should be noted that in extraction procedures for plant phosphatides only the solubilities of the glycerophosphatides need be considered since sphingomyelin is absent.

As indicated above, many investigators of plant phosphatides have used only alcohol for purposes of extraction. Thus Sokolov (1940), who studied the determination of lipide and other types of phosphorus in plants, concluded that ethanol extraction of the dried sample was an adequate means for obtaining the phosphatides quantitatively. Drying the material before analysis, as with animal tissue, is of doubtful value because of the danger of insolubilizing the phosphatides.

Jamieson and McKinney (1935) have extracted phosphatides from soybeans, for analysis, by use of 95 per cent ethanol.

Some of the difficulties involved in phosphatide analyses in soybeans were investigated by Earle and Milner (1938). The chief problem arises from the presence of phytins, nucleic compounds including phosphoproteins and nucleic acid derivatives, and inorganic materials such as potassium acid phosphates. The solubilities of such mixtures are not clear-cut, nor are the solubilities of the compounds necessarily the same in mixtures as they are in the pure state. These complicating factors are typical in plant analyses.

Eichgorn, Milskii and Kalashnikov (1931) analyzed soybeans for phosphatide content by extracting first with ethanol and then with ether. The combination of these two solvents has been used by many investigators since ether is an excellent solvent for lipides once alcohol has exerted its dissociating influence.

In one of the first quantitative investigations of the total phosphatide content of seeds, Guerrant (1926) extracted the ground material with ethanol-ether (4:1) for extended periods of time. After removal of the solvent, the lipide phosphorus was determined in the residue.

Andrews and Bailey (1932) used this same solvent combination for the determination of lipide phosphorus in wheat bran and germ. Gorbach (1944a) used benzene-ethanol or ethanol alone as a solvent for the extraction of phosphatides from oil seeds.

Hanahan and Chaikoff (1947) have described the extraction of phosphatides from carrots and have shown that practically quantitative results may be obtained by extracting twice with alcohol-ether (3:1) at 55 to 60° C. for 18 to 24 hours. The solvent was then removed and the residue was reëxtracted with petroleum ether. From this solution, the phosphatides were precipitated with acetone and magnesium chloride.

Still another procedure worthy of note was used by these same investigators. The carrots were ground and a slush was made with ether which was frozen at − 25° C. This frozen mass with additional ether was placed in a room at 5° C. for 6 hours and allowed to melt. The freezing process ruptured the membranes of the cell, freeing the lipides which then dissolved in the ether. The ether solution thus obtained was decanted and the process repeated. The phosphatides could be isolated from the ether solution as in the above procedure.

Reiser (1947) has described a procedure for the extraction of phosphatides from commercial feeds by the use of several portions of alcohol-ether (3:1) as well as ether alone. This worker found reëxtraction with petroleum ether to be impractical, due probably to oxidation of the phosphatides during manipulation.

An entirely different procedure has been proposed by Roth and Schuster (1940), who extracted phosphatides from plant sources with boiling 50 per cent methanol for 2 hours. The solution was then diluted with an equal quantity of water and the phosphatides were adsorbed on lead sulfide prepared *in situ*. Methanol saturated with hydrogen sulfide served to elute the phosphatide fraction, whose phosphorus content could then be determined.

Schramme (1939) used benzene as an auxiliary solvent with alcohol. The extraction was carried out in a continuous apparatus with two portions of solvent. The residue from the concentration of the lipide solution was then rectified by reëxtraction with ether and the phosphatides were estimated from the phosphorus content of the ether-soluble fraction.

These two preceding methods were reinvestigated by Gorbach (1944), who found that they gave comparable results.

Benzene-ethanol (1:4) was also used by Rewald (1937a) for the initial extraction of lipides from oil-bearing sources. He followed this by a second extraction with 96 per cent ethanol. Unlike Reiser (1947), Rewald found it quite feasible to rectify the lipides with petroleum ether, after which the phosphorus was determined in the petroleum ether-soluble fraction. Rewald saw fit to stress the point, however, that no exact method for phosphatide determination in plant material is yet known.

The extraction of phosphatides from fruits and vegetables is complicated by their very small lipide content and the high water content. Arbenz (1919) was among the first to propose an analytical procedure for the determination of phosphatides in fruits and vegetables. In his method, the material was dried and powdered at 36° C. and then extracted continuously for 10 hours with ethanol and ether to yield an extract whose phosphorus content was determined.

Although phosphatides are insoluble in acetone, they may be made somewhat soluble in this solvent by the presence of other lipides and proteins. In chlorophyll-containing substances, the use of acetone is advantageous, and Rewald (1928) found it suitable for the extraction of phosphatides from lettuce and cabbage. More recently, Rewald (1944) analyzed for the phosphatide content of dried grass by successive extraction with acetone, petroleum ether and ethanol-benzene (1:4). The latter solvent combination served to extract most of the phosphatides, as would be expected, although some extraneous phosphorus-containing material was also present.

Nielsen and Bohart (1944) also provided evidence to show that acetone can extract phosphatides from plant sources such as soybeans and corn. The samples were comminuted prior to extraction in a "Waring Blendor" or similar type of apparatus. In this method, rectification of the extract with petroleum ether was used.

Grain Products

The estimation of total lipide and of lipide phosphorus in grain products such as egg noodles was studied by Rask and Phelps (1925). This is often important for purposes of food control. In their procedure the total lipides are extracted with ammoniacal alcohol and the phosphorus content of this extract is then determined.

The analysis of phosphatides in cereals, macaroni, egg noodles and similar products is also described in the official methods of the A.O.A.C. (Lepper, 1945, pp. 249, 265). The procedures involve extraction of the product with alcohol, ether and petroleum ether in the presence of hydrochloric acid.

Milk

Bloor's (1915) procedure for the extraction of phosphatides from blood was applied to milk by Hess and Helman (1925). The milk was treated with about eight volumes of ethanol-ether (3:1), which served to extract the lipides whose phosphorus content was then determined. More recently, Buruiana and Furtunesco (1941) made use of this same procedure.

Brodrick-Pittard (1914) also used alcohol-ether, employing an extraction time of 6 hours. This worker, however, believed a reëxtraction with chloroform to be necessary. His observation was confirmed by Holm, Wright and Deysher (1936), who pointed out that alcohol and ether in combination extract from milk not only phosphatides, but also inorganic phosphates which lead to high results. Accordingly, they too resorted to reëxtraction with chloroform. Holwerda (1936) has also pointed out the possibility for error due to contaminating phosphates.

Grossfeld and Ziesset (1943) believe that ethyl or isopropyl alcohol and benzene mixtures are best for the extraction of phosphatides from dairy materials.

Rewald (1937) proposed a method for determining phosphatides in milk which involved first of all the conversion of milk to whole milk powder. This was extracted with acetone to remove neutral fat, and it was shown that none of the phosphatides were removed in this step. The phosphatides were obtained, however, by extraction with alcohol, and the residue was further extracted with alcohol and benzene. The soluble material consisted of a mixture of glycerides and phosphatides from which pure phosphatides could be obtained by the use of acetone.

Various investigators have employed the Mojonnier modification of the Roese-Gottlieb procedure for the extraction of phosphatides together with other lipides from milk products (e.g., Perlman, 1935). This procedure involves treatment of the milk with ammonium hydroxide followed by successive extraction with alcohol, ethyl ether and petroleum ether. The lipides thus obtained are ashed according to specified conditions in order to determine the phosphorus content. This procedure is described in the official methods of the A.O.A.C. (Lepper, 1945, p. 309). It was used by Wiese, Nair and Fleming (1932) for the determination of the phosphatide content of cream and by Crane and Horrall (1942, 1943) in an extensive study of the phosphatides of various dairy products.

DETERMINATION OF TOTAL PHOSPHATIDES

Once the phosphatide fractions have been obtained from their various sources by any of the procedures indicated in the foregoing discussion, the problem of determining the actual phosphatide content arises. The phosphatides may exist in solution in ether, petroleum ether, chloroform, alcohol or other solvents; or they may have been precipitated by the addition of acetone and alcoholic magnesium chloride. The obvious procedure of weighing the precipitated phosphatides was resorted to by earlier workers and by investigators whose problems do not require quantitative methods. Clearly, the possibility of error is great in such a gravimetric method because of the great difficulties attached to the preparation of pure compounds. Accordingly, three indirect procedures have been devised which are especially valuable in micro-estimation.

The first of these, known as Bloor's (1929) method, since it was largely devised and exploited by him and his students, is an oxidative procedure. By the use of potassium dichromate in strong acid the phosphatide molecule is completely oxidized and either the resulting gaseous products are accurately measured or else the quantity of oxidizing agent consumed is estimated. This procedure has been widely used and should theoretically be quite accurate since the analysis is based on the bulk of the molecule rather than on an individual element comprising only a small percentage of the molecule. The second procedure for the determination of total phosphatides has been used most extensively, largely because of its relative simplicity. It involves the determination of the amount of lipide phosphorus, which may then be translated to total phosphatides by the application of a suitable factor. The presence of extraneous phosphorus is, of course, a threat to the accuracy of the method. The third procedure makes use of the fatty acid content as an index of the total phosphatide content. The acids are obtained by saponification and can be determined either by titration or else by oxidation and measurement of the gaseous oxidation products. Artom (1932) has been the chief proponent of this method.

Oxidative Method

The oxidative procedure as proposed by Bloor (1929) was based on early observations by Bang (1918). The phosphatides for analysis were isolated as already described (see p. 148), the final step involving precipitation with acetone and a saturated alcoholic solution of magnesium chloride. The latter is used to the extent of about 1 drop per mg. of phosphatide believed to be present. For about 2 ml. of phosphatide solution, Bloor used 7 ml. of acetone. The sample for analysis ordinarily contains 4 to 6 mg. of phosphatide and may contain as little as 2 mg. With quantities less than this, the precipitation is not quantitative and erratic results are obtained, as shown both by Boyd (1931) and by Kirk, Page and Van Slyke (1934).

The precipitated phosphatides are washed with acetone and dissolved in moist ether for analysis. The possibility for error here because of the fact that sphingomyelin even in combination with other phosphatides may be partially ether-insoluble (see Kirk, Page and Van Slyke, 1934) has already been discussed (see p. 150). The ether solution, having been centrifuged, is evaporated to dryness. The oxidation is accomplished by the addition of excess standard potassium dichromate solution and so-called silver reagent which is a solution of silver dichromate in concentrated sulfuric acid. The silver serves as a catalyst for oxidation which is completed at elevated temperatures in about 30 minutes. Back titration with sodium thiosulfate is a measure of the dichromate consumed. For the calculations it is assumed that no sphingomyelin is present and that the fatty acids are divided equally between oleic and palmitic. These assumptions are ordinarily valid within the limits of experimental error. On this basis the oxidation proceeds, according to Boyd (1931), in the following manner:

$$2C_{42}H_{84}O_9NP + 118O_2 + H_2SO_4 \longrightarrow 84CO_2 + 78H_2O + 2H_3PO_4 + (NH_4)_2SO_4.$$

It may then be shown that 3 ml. of $O.1N$ dichromate solution are equivalent to 1 mg. of phosphatide.

A somewhat similar oxidative procedure was advanced by Kirk, Page and Van Slyke (1934) in which the carbon dioxide produced is taken as a measure of the phosphatide content. They believed that this procedure has advantage over Bloor's (1929) method in that the magnesium chloride present in the total precipitate liberates hydrochloric acid. This in turn may reduce some dichromate, introducing an error in the titration. This objection, of course, does not hold where the titrimetric method is applied only to the ether-soluble portion of the precipitate. Furthermore, Bloor (1929) in his original article showed that this error was compensated for by a blank determination.

Precipitation by Halides. The use of alkaline earth halides together with acetone in order to insure complete precipitation of phosphatides is a technique of long standing—alcoholic magnesium chloride having been used by Nerking in 1910. Katsura, Hatakeyama and Tajima (1934) showed that calcium chloride may be used in a procedure similar to Bloor's (1929) for determining total phosphatides, whereas Kroeker, Strong and Peterson (1935) believed strontium chloride to be a more efficient precipitant than magnesium chloride.

Determination from Phosphorus Content

Probably the most common procedure for determining total phosphatides is by analyzing the phosphatide fraction for phosphorus. Numerous procedures for phosphorus analysis are available, and these are discussed in detail later. The phosphorus analysis may be carried out on an aliquot of an alcohol-ether extract. Some workers, however, employ rectification with ether or petroleum ether, analyzing the material which dissolves in these solvents. Still other workers prefer to determine the phosphorus content of the precipitate obtained by the use of acetone and magnesium chloride.

The stage of purification at which the analysis takes place depends largely on the possible contaminants in the original source of the phosphatides—the chief danger, of course, arising from the presence of inorganic phosphorus-containing compounds. In fats where there are no extraneous phosphorus compounds, the phosphorus content is a direct indication of the quantities of phosphatides present (Thaler and Just, 1944). Such is not the case with blood, however. Thus, Stewart and Hendry (1935) believed that the phosphorus extracted from blood by alcohol-ether is derived entirely from lipides, making further purification unnecessary. On the other hand, LeBreton (1921) pointed out that the ether-soluble lipide phosphorus may include phosphorus-containing materials other than phosphatides. In tissues such as muscle, liver and kidney these may account for 10 to 20 per cent of the phosphorus content. Similar observations were reported by May (1930) and Artom (1932). These conclusions were reached largely because the material obtained by alcohol-ether extraction was in part insoluble in solvents such as petroleum ether which should normally dissolve phosphatides. However, Man (1937) pointed out that these observations were made on samples from which the solvent had been evaporated in air. The ability of oxygen to insolubilize phosphatides is well known. It is entirely feasible, however, that this criticism of the determination of total phosphatides from phosphorus content is partially valid. In any case, a generalization cannot be made because the contaminants in the various source materials differ. The logical procedure in any given investigation, and one which has been used by many workers, is to compare the results obtained from phosphorus-content determination with the results from the oxidative procedure. In every case, caution must be exerted to prevent oxidation and insolubilization of the phosphatides during isolation.

Phosphatide Factor. Once the phosphorus content has been determined, it must be converted to total phosphatides by multiplication by a factor. Since the phosphorus content of glycerophosphatides and sphingomyelin is about 4 per cent, most investigators have multiplied the lipide phosphorus content by a value very close to 100/4 or 25. (See e.g., Jamieson and McKinney, 1935.) Because of other sources of inaccuracy in the analyses, this is usually adequate.

A factor of 23.5 was determined experimentally by Kirk, Page and Van Slyke (1934), whereas Artom and Fishman (1943) used a different procedure to obtain a value of 22.7. Neither of these determinations could arrive at an absolute value, however, since certain assumptions were necessarily employed.

Determination from Fatty Acid Content

The determination of total phosphatides from the fatty acid content is the third method under consideration. It is discussed in detail by Artom (1932), and according to him it is capable of good accuracy. His method is applicable to 10 to 20 mg. of fatty acids, such as would be found in 1 gram of tissue, and it is accurate within 5 parts per 100. To obtain the fatty acids for titration, the precipitated phosphatides may be saponified with alkali, acidified with mineral acid and isolated by extraction with ether. The total phosphatides are then calculated from the theoretical fatty acid content. Here, as with the preceding methods, accuracy is impaired by inability to obtain an exact empirical formula for the mixture of phosphatides.

Epshteïn (1942) applied electrometric and conductimetric techniques to the determination of phosphatides by titration. He was able to titrate not only the phosphatides directly but also the hydrolysis products. For the determination of total phosphatides from the hydrolysis products, the alcohol-ether extract is saponified and either the fatty acids are titrated with alkali or else the barium salt of glycerophosphoric acid is titrated with hydrochloric acid. Comparable results are obtained when the unhydrolyzed phosphatides are titrated directly with sodium hydroxide which reacts, according to Epshteïn, with the acidic functions of lecithin and phosphatidylaminoethyl alcohol.

CHAPTER XII

DETERMINATION OF INDIVIDUAL PHOSPHATIDES AND RELATED COMPOUNDS

DETERMINATION OF INDIVIDUAL PHOSPHATIDES

Until comparatively recently, analytical techniques for phosphatide determination ended at the point where total phosphatides were determined. The determination of the individual phosphatides present in the phosphatide fraction seemed, because of their solubility characteristics and their resistance to purification, to defy ordinary quantitative techniques. Although the functions of the individual phosphatides in the body are not yet known with certainty, it was realized that the glycerophosphatides performed duties different from the sphingolipides. From the metabolic point of view, analyses for the individual phosphatides are thus of prime importance. Although various workers have resolved phosphatide mixtures by solubility techniques, these are precarious methods, especially when microquantities are employed. A fair separation between lecithin and the cephalin fraction can be made by adding absolute alcohol to an ether solution of these. The cephalin fraction, being insoluble, precipitates. By repeating this procedure several times, fairly pure lecithin may be obtained. The purification of the cephalins, however, is considerably more difficult. This procedure is described by Bloor (1926, 1943, p. 42), and it has been used by many investigators, including Erickson and co-workers (1937). It should be pointed out that this method is far from quantitative, especially in view of the observation by Folch (1942) that pure aminoethyl alcohol-containing phosphatides are freely soluble in alcohol.

The amino group of phosphatidylaminoethyl alcohol seemed a logical point of attack for the determination of this phosphatide in a mixture, but this was complicated by the presence of amino-containing impurities. The determination of sphingomyelin by precipitation with Reinecke salt has been used to separate sphingolipides from glycerophosphatides. However, data are available to show that there are serious sources of error in this method. In general, the best procedures for the determination of individual phosphatides depend on analyses of the hydrolysis products. The more important methods will be discussed here, but again it must be stated that much work remains to be done.

Solubility Procedures

One of the first procedures for the microdetermination of individual phosphatides was an approximate one advanced by Kirk (1938, 1938a). Since his method was based on solubility characteristics it has been subjected to considerable criticism; for, as has already been indicated, the solubilities of these complex substances in mixtures may differ markedly from their solubilities in the pure state. In Kirk's method, the phosphatides are precipitated by acetone and magnesium chloride and this mixture is extracted with moist ethyl ether on the assumption that the glycerophosphatides will dissolve and the sphingomyelin will remain insoluble. Kirk recognized, however, that other phosphatides may be present in the ether-insoluble portion, although he did not believe that this interfered inherently with the accuracy of the method. That the ether-insoluble material was not primarily sphingomyelin but rather a portion of all the phosphatides present was shown later by Sinclair and Dolan (1942). These workers also showed that such ether insolubility is merely a function of the amount of magnesium chloride present during the acetone precipitation. Criticisms of a similar nature were advanced by Thannhauser, Benotti and Reinstein (1939) and by Ramsay and Stewart (1941), both groups of workers stressing the fallacy involved in applying solubility procedures to small quantities of phosphatides.

The second portion of Kirk's procedure (1938a) provided for the determination of lecithin from the choline content of the ether-soluble portion. This, of course, is basically sound and has been used by numerous investigators, except that in this instance some of the lecithin was undoubtedly in the ether-insoluble portion. The cephalin fraction was calculated by difference between the lecithin and the total ether-soluble phosphatides which were determined gasometrically.

A similar procedure on a macro scale was employed by both Chargaff (1939) and Hevesy and Hahn (1940), who used cold petroleum ether instead of moist ethyl ether to extract the glycerophosphatides from a phosphatide mixture. There is no reason to believe, however, that petroleum ether would be any more effective than moist ether in separating the two types of phosphatides.

The cephalins were separated from the lecithin because of their supposed insolubility in ethanol. It should be mentioned, however, that the nature of the experiments carried out by the above workers did not require rigidly quantitative separations.

Determination from Hydrolysis Products

As mentioned previously, the most satisfactory methods for the determination of the individual phosphatides depend on the analysis of certain hydrolysis products. The following tabulation indicates the distribution of hydrolysis products between the common phosphatides.

	Phosphorus	Choline	Aminoethyl alcohol	Serine	Glycerol
Lecithin	1	1			1
Phosphatidyl-aminoethyl alcohol	1		1		1
Phosphatidyl-serine	1			1	1
Sphingomyelin	1	1			

Thus it is readily seen that choline determination measures the total lecithin and sphingomyelin; glycerol determination the total glycerophosphatides; aminoethyl alcohol determination the phosphatidylaminoethyl alcohol; and serine determination the phosphatidylserine. In plant phosphatides where sphingomyelin has never been proved to be present, the choline is, of course, a direct measure of the lecithin. The determination of phosphorus, the three bases and the total phosphatides should provide a means for calculating the quantities of the individual phosphorus-containing lipides. Still another tool is available and has been used extensively, although it is of questionable accuracy: the determination of sphingomyelin by precipitation as the reineckate. The specific, analyses will be discussed later. In practice, most investigators have preferred not to determine all these quantities, and to calculate one of the phosphatides by difference.

As an example, Erickson and co-workers (1940), who were interested in determining the individual phosphatides in blood and tissue, determined the total phosphatide content from the lipide phosphorus, and the choline-containing phosphatides from the choline content of the hydrolysate. The total phosphatides multiplied by the molecular ratio of choline to phosphorus served as a means of estimating the choline-containing phosphatides. The difference between the latter and the total phosphatides was a measure of the cephalins present. Then the sphingomyelin was determined separately as the reineckate, and the difference between this and the total choline-containing phosphatides accounted for the lecithin present. Thus, two of the phosphatides were measured by difference. It is obvious that glycerol determination would have provided a check for the total glycerophosphatides, whereas the determination of serine and aminoethyl alcohol or lipide amino nitrogen would provide a check on the cephalin fraction content. Actually, these workers did check their method by estimating the amino nitrogen (Folch and Van Slyke, 1939a).

They found this value to be proportional to the cephalin fraction content determined indirectly.

Similar procedures have been published by Thannhauser, Benotti and Reinstein (1939), Artom and Fishman (1943) and Marenzi and Cardini (1943a). All of these workers were interested in the determination of blood phosphatides, and the procedures differ only in analytical details.

A variation of this general procedure was published by Ramsay and Stewart (1941), who worked out an analytical procedure for glycerol applicable to a phosphatide hydrolysis mixture (see p. 165). This, combined with the determination of total phosphatides and choline, made possible the calculation of the amounts of each of the individual phosphatides. In most of this work, phosphatidylserine was not recognized as a component of the cephalin fraction.

Determination by Preferential Hydrolysis

The recent work of Hack (1947) has provided an entirely different approach to the problem of individual phosphatide analysis. He observed that the choline of lecithin under certain conditions may be hydrolyzed quantitatively while leaving sphingomyelin intact. This observation, combined with the previously observed fact that sphingomyelin remains unhydrolyzed under conditions which hydrolyze glycerophosphatides entirely (see p. 46), makes possible the estimation of lecithin, the cephalin fraction and sphingomyelin. The estimation requires 15 ml. of blood for duplicate determinations and has been applied to both blood and plasma. The sample, having been dried *in vacuo* while frozen, was extracted continuously with methanol and chloroform for 6 hours, and total phosphorus was determined in this extract. The extracted material was hydrolyzed with potassium hydroxide under specified conditions which did not affect the sphingomyelin. This mixture was then acidified and filtered to remove the unreacted sphingomyelin, and the phosphorus content of the filtrate was determined. This latter phosphorus content indicates the total lecithin and cephalins present, and the difference between this and the original phosphorus content is a measure of the sphingomyelin present.

The basic solution also contains all of the choline from the lecithin, and this may be determined as the reineckate. Thus, the lecithin is determined directly, whereas the other two constituents are determined indirectly.

The critical step of the procedure—the hydrolysis with caustic—was tested on purified samples of lecithin, phosphatidylaminoethyl alcohol, inositol-containing phosphatides, acetal phosphatides and sphingomyelin.

In every case except the last, practically all the phosphorus and the choline, where present, was liberated by normal potassium hydroxide at 37° C. for 16 hours. It is of great significance, however, that with sphingomyelin reineckate both phosphorus and choline were liberated under these conditions, indicating that the reineckate contains lecithin and cephalin fractions as impurities.

Determination by Isotope Dilution

For macroquantities of phosphatides, the method of isotope dilution used by Chargaff, Ziff and Rittenberg (1942) is worthy of note as a means of determining phosphatide composition by analysis of the nitrogenous constituents. It serves further to indicate, with reservations, the presence of possible new phosphatides. Thus, pure choline and aminoethyl alcohol, containing isotopic nitrogen, were added to a hydrolyzed tissue phosphatide mixture. The pure bases were later isolated, and the amount of isotope dilution therein served as a measure of the amounts originally present in the phosphatides. The total nitrogen, as well as the amino and amino acid nitrogen, was determined in the original material. The aminoethyl alcohol and the choline were isolated as the 3,5-diiodo-salicylate and the mercuric chloride double salt, respectively. These were easily purifiable derivatives, containing no nitrogen other than that of the base.

These results are quite interesting, for with beef brain phosphatides it was possible to account for all the amino nitrogen in the form of aminoethyl alcohol and amino acid, the latter, in view of Folch and Schneider's work (1941, see p. 29), being serine. Of the nonamino nitrogen, however, only 50 per cent was present as choline. With pig liver phosphatides, on the other hand, all the nonamino nitrogen was present as choline, whereas only 64 per cent of the amino nitrogen could be accounted for by aminoethyl alcohol and amino acid. It cannot, as the authors point out, be assumed without further data that unaccountable nitrogen represents hitherto undiscovered phosphatides.

Determination of the Cephalin Fraction

The determination of the cephalin fraction, either directly or indirectly, has occupied the attention of many workers. Rudy and Page (1930) pointed out quite early that in uncontaminated phosphatide samples, phosphatidylaminoethyl alcohol can be titrated in benzene solution with absolute alcoholic sodium hydroxide to a phenolphthalein end point. This same observation was made by Epshteïn (1942), who found it possible to titrate the amino group of phosphatidylaminoethyl alcohol, as well as the methylated amino group of lecithin.

The estimation of the cephalins from the α-amino nitrogen content of blood and tissue lipides was attempted by Schmitz and Koch (1930) and by Kirk, Page and Van Slyke (1934). Later, however, Van Slyke and co-workers (1935) found this unsatisfactory because of the presence of amino-containing impurities which led to high results. However, the observation that urea is the chief contaminant in phosphatides extracted with petroleum ether (Christiansen, 1939; Folch and Van Slyke, 1939, 1939a), together with the subsequent procedure proposed for the removal of the urea (see p. 152), has made possible the direct estimation of the cephalins by the determination of amino nitrogen. This procedure was used by Erickson and co-workers (1940) with good results, since the values they obtained agreed with those calculated by difference. In the determination of amino nitrogen, however, it is possible that the nitrous acid reagent used reacts with unsaturated linkages which may be present, to liberate nitrogen. This naturally leads to high results. Folch, Schneider and Van Slyke (1940) found this to be the case, as did Chargaff (1942). Thus, the amino nitrogen determination procedure as a measure of cephalin content must be used with caution.

The determination of the cephalin fraction by difference is a relatively simple matter, involving the determination of total phosphatides and choline-containing phosphatides. Among the first workers to take advantage of such a method were Lintzel and Fomin (1931) and Lintzel and Monasterio (1931). These workers determined choline by treating the phosphatides with strong alkali. This procedure liberated trimethylamine, which was estimated by formalin titration. Thus the combined lecithin and sphingomyelin could be calculated. The difference between these and the total phosphatides provided a means for estimating the cephalin fraction. Essentially the same procedure was employed by Williams and co-workers (1938) and by Artom (1941).

An entirely different procedure was advanced by Taurog and co-workers (1944), who employed adsorption for resolving phosphatide mixtures into choline- and noncholine-containing compounds. These workers extracted the tissue with alcohol and prepared a petroleum ether solution of the extract. This was treated with magnesium oxide in order to adsorb all the phosphatides. The mixture of phosphatides and magnesium oxide was then treated with methanol, which served to elute only the choline-containing compounds whose quantity could be estimated by choline and phosphorus analyses. The difference between these and the total phosphatides was a measure of the cephalin fraction present. Alternatively, the phosphatides in methanol solution may be treated with magnesium oxide, which adsorbs only the noncholine-containing phosphatides, leaving the lecithin and sphingomyelin in solution.

Determination of Phosphatidylserine

Since the discovery of phosphatidylserine, methods have been evolved for the determination of this amino acid-containing compound. Where large quantities of the serine-containing phosphatide are present, the amino acid nitrogen may be determined by the ninhydrin method. Thus, Chargaff, Ziff and Rittenberg (1942) identified phosphatide mixtures isolated from tissue in terms of nonamino, amino, and amino acid nitrogen.

The quantitative estimation of serine-containing phosphatides was studied by Artom (1945). He contrived the ingenious scheme of separating the serine in the phosphatide hydrolysate from the chemically similar aminoethyl alcohol by "Permutit", the latter being adsorbed quantitatively and the serine not at all. The aminoethyl alcohol is subsequently eluted with concentrated salt solution, and the quantities of each of the amino alcohols may then be individually estimated from the amount of ammonia liberated during periodate oxidation. The analysis of aminoethyl alcohol by periodate oxidation had previously been investigated by Ramsay and Stewart (1941), who did not find it applicable to lipide hydrolysates. Artom, however, was able to analyze quantitatively both aminoethyl alcohol and serine when these were added to lipide extracts. He made the significant observation that barium hydroxide when used as a hydrolytic agent causes appreciable destruction of both amino alcohols, whereas alcoholic hydrogen chloride does not. Choline, urea, glycerol and galactose, all of which are common products of lipide hydrolysis, did not affect the analysis, although Artom points out that sphingosine would undoubtedly interfere.

By combining this procedure with analyses for choline and total phosphatides, Artom (1945) was able to determine the distribution in tissues of the choline-containing phosphatides, as well as of the aminoethyl alcohol and serine-containing phosphatides.

Serine- and aminoethyl alcohol-containing phosphatides were estimated somewhat differently by Burmaster (1946). The total ammonia liberated from oxidation with periodate of both serine and aminoethyl alcohol was determined by a microdiffusion technique employing potassium metaborate. The serine nitrogen was then determined independently by the ninhydrin technique which is standard for α-amino acids. The difference between the two values is a measure of the aminoethyl alcohol present. The use of periodate for determination of amino groups adjacent to hydroxyl groups presents an advantage in that urea does not interfere as it does in the nitrous acid procedure.

Determination of Sphingomyelin

The determination of sphingomyelin is important in the analysis of phosphatides of the brain and nervous system where this sphingolipide is fairly abundant. It has already been noted that procedures based on the alleged insolubility of sphingomyelin in petroleum ether or moist ethyl ether (see p. 165) are not capable of great accuracy. The indirect procedure of Ramsay and Stewart (1941) based on the determination of total phosphatides, choline and glycerol in the phosphatide hydrolysis products is worthy of note (see p. 167) since it is probably a very accurate one.

Most workers, however, have analyzed for sphingomyelin directly by precipitating it as the reineckate. This procedure was used on a macro scale by Thannhauser, Benotti and Reinstein (1939), who extracted the phosphatides from dried tissue or blood with chloroform-methanol (1:1). The extracted phosphatides were then dissolved in methanol and treated with hydrochloric acid and Reinecke salt, $Cr(NH_3)_2(SCN)_4NH_4$. The resulting precipitate, according to Erickson and co-workers (1940), has the formula $C_{45}H_{91}N_8PO_7S_4Cr$, although it has been proved that it is not a homogeneous substance. In Thannhauser's procedure, the precipitate was weighed and the weight converted to sphingomyelin by use of the factor 0.788 which was determined from the phosphorus content of the precipitate. It soon became apparent, however, that the weight of the precipitate was not an accurate measure of the sphingomyelin since the precipitate was not homogeneous. Accordingly, the phosphorus content was taken as a better indication of the sphingomyelin content.

Both Erickson and co-workers (1940) and Hunter (1942) proposed microprocedures based on the above original method of Thannhauser, Benotti and Reinstein (1939). In Erickson's test experiments it was shown that 102 per cent of sphingomyelin could be recovered when added to lipide extracts of red blood cell stroma. In Hunter's method somewhat larger quantities of materials are used, although it is still a micromethod. Washing of the precipitate is important and must be done carefully. Although Erickson and co-workers (1940) advocated extensive washing with methanol and ether, Marenzi and Cardini (1943a) are of the opinion that such washing leads to low results. Artom and Fishman (1943), however, suggest washing with chloroform instead of ether in order to remove any partially oxidized glycerophosphatides which may be present. All these workers agree that washing with acetone is advisable.

The factor arbitrarily used for the conversion of the phosphorus content of the precipitate to sphingomyelin is 25. Hunter (1942) proposed a factor of 26 in deference to the fact that the phosphorus content of purified sphingomyelin is usually below the theoretical value of 4 per cent.

Marenzi and Cardini (1943a) studied in some detail the determination of the sphingomyelin of blood as the reineckate. Since it was known that the weight of the precipitate was not a true index of the sphingomyelin present, they investigated colorimetry of the precipitate which likewise did not yield satisfactory results. Determination of the phosphorus, choline and chromium content of the reineckate showed that only the phosphorus existed in theoretical quantity, and that this element, as noted above, is a satisfactory basis for the determination of the sphingomyelin content.

Hack (1946) made a critical study of the determination of sphingomyelin as the reineckate. He found, first of all, in accord with other workers, that nitrogen determinations by the method of Kjeldahl were always variable and low, due probably to the choline which is known to resist this type of analysis. By the Dumas method, higher and more consistent results were obtained.

Similarly, analyses of sphingomyelin for choline obtained either by basic or acidic hydrolysis were low, due probably to the known resistance of phosphorylcholine linkages to hydrolysis. This is an important observation in view of the fact that many analyses of phosphatides depend on the determination of choline in the hydrolysis products. This resistance to hydrolysis is, of course, the basis for the analytical procedure of Schmidt, Benotti and Thannhauser (1946), and the feasibility of this method was confirmed by Hack (1946).

Of great interest is the observation by this latter worker that sphingomyelin reineckates contained glycerol and hexoses, indicating that lipides other than sphingomyelin may be precipitated. Further work showed that a fraction of cephalin soluble in methanol yielded a reineckate as did the galactolipides, phrenasin and kerasin. Obviously, then, there is the danger of high values when the precipitation procedure is employed. In the face of these observations it is not surprising that only a low recovery of pure sphingomyelin from the reineckate was possible. Hack (1946) concluded that the determination of sphingomyelin by direct isolation leads to low results, whereas its determination as the reineckate leads to high results.

The determination of sphingomyelin by a method which circumvents the difficulties of the reineckate procedure was proposed by Schmidt, Benotti and Thannhauser (1946) and by Schmidt and co-workers (1946). This method is based on selective saponification, for it has long been known that the glycerophosphatides are less resistant to the action of alkali than is sphingomyelin. This has some advantage over solubility and precipitation procedures in that interfering substances which influence these two techniques do not influence the selective hydrolysis. The authors point out a further advantage in that the fully saturated glycerophosphatides whose solubility characteristics are practically the same as those of sphingomyelin are hydrolyzed in their procedure. The phosphorus content of the unsaponified material is a measure of the sphingomyelin present. When combined with the determination of total lipide phosphorus, the sphingomyelin determination provides an indirect means for the estimation of total glycerophosphatides. Hack (1947) modified the method still further to include the determination of the individual glycerophosphatides.

The determination of micromole quantities of sphingosine has been described by McKibbin and Taylor (1949). The analysis is based on the observation that sphingosine may be extracted practically quantitatively from aqueous lipide hydrolysates with chloroform. The nitrogen content of the extract is a measure of the sphingosine present.

Determination of Saturated Phosphatides

The estimation of saturated phosphatides, which are now known to occur naturally, was described by Thannhauser, Benotti and Boncoddo (1946). The method is based on the fact that these compounds are ether-insoluble but will nevertheless hydrolyze with base under specific conditions in preference to sphingomyelin. Thus, the unsaturated glycerophosphatides are first of all removed by use of ether. The phosphorus content of the remainder is determined, and this residue is then subjected to selective hydrolysis. The phosphorus content of the unhydrolyzed portion is a measure of the sphingomyelin present, and the difference between the total ether-insoluble phosphatides and the sphingomyelin is a measure of the saturated phosphatides. More directly, the acid-soluble phosphorus obtained after the selective saponification is a measure of the saturated phosphatides, since it originates entirely from this source. This method, however, is based on solubility procedures, and is probably subject to the same difficulties discussed previously (see p. 165).

Determination of Acetal Phosphatides

The estimation of the acetal phosphatides depends on the quantitative evaluation, colorimetrically, of the Schiff reaction which is undergone by the aldehyde group of these lipides. Such a procedure was outlined by Feulgen and Grünberg (1938) and was later modified by Anchel and Waelsch (1944). Recently Ehrlich, Taylor and Waelsch (1948) have cast doubt on the accuracy of this determination, since color development in the Schiff test appears to be inhibited by certain naturally occurring lipides. Accordingly, more definitive work is indicated.

DETERMINATION OF CHOLINE

The determination of choline is important, not only in the field of phosphatides, but also in the general field of plant and animal biochemistry and physiology (Lucas and Best, 1943, p. 9 ff.). Choline determination has generally been based on the formation of slightly soluble salts such as the bismuth iodide, chloroplatinate, picrate, picrolonate, chloroaurate, periodide and reineckate. Of these, the last two have received the most attention. Besides this, the methods of acetylation followed by biological assay and the determination of the trimethylamine resulting from the decomposition of choline have been used.

For the determination of the choline in a phosphatide hydrolysate, it is essential that complete hydrolysis be effected. Williams and co-workers (1938) proposed that the phosphatides be hydrolyzed with barium hydroxide. Thannhauser, Benotti and Reinstein (1939) objected to this procedure on the basis that it effected only partial splitting of the sphingomyelin. They proposed an alternative technique involving the use of an anhydrous solution of hydrogen chloride in methanol. Erickson and co-workers (1940), repeating both procedures, were able to obtain almost identical results when the sphingomyelin comprised approximately 25 per cent of the total phosphatides. When it exceeded 50 per cent, however, the acidic method of hydrolysis yielded results which were about 10 per cent higher.

The precipitation of choline as the reineckate has been used extensively. This is based on the fact that, whereas most basic substances may be precipitated at various pH's as reineckates, only quaternary bases without carboxyl groups yield reineckates insoluble at a pH of 12 to 13. This does not preclude its precipitation at lower pH's where contaminating bases are absent. Street, Kenyon and Watson (1946) point out, however, that the precipitate is tractable only when it is not contaminated with other basic substances.

Kapfhammer and Bischoff (1930) were the first to determine choline by precipitating it with Reinecke acid. Beattie (1936) then adapted this procedure to a microcolorimetric determination based on the observation that an acetone solution of the reineckate develops a deep red color. Beattie (1936) used a saturated aqueous solution of ammonium reineckate and stated that the precipitation was complete in 10 minutes at temperatures as high as 60° C. A modification by Jacobi, Baumann and Meek (1941) involved the use of a 2 per cent solution of ammonium reineckate in methanol in order to increase the concentration of the precipitating agent. A further modification was proposed by Entenman, Taurog and Chaikoff (1944), who increased the concentration of ammonium reineckate still more by dissolving it in 1.2N hydrochloric acid. In their method, precipitation was complete within 30 minutes at room temperature, and they were able to show that their method was quantitative for concentrations of choline as low as 1 mg.

Glick (1944, 1945) applied a photoelectric method to the determination of the intensity of the color of choline reineckate in acetone solution. He pointed out the advantage of precipitation in an alkaline medium and was the first to propose the use of propanol as a wash liquid in which the precipitate is entirely insoluble.

Hack (1947) has also determined choline reineckate spectrophotometrically, as have Winzler and Meserve (1945) and Fleury and Guitard (1948). Hack stresses the importance of using fresh ammonium reineckate solutions in order to obtain quantitative results, and he is of the opinion that ethanol is as effective a wash liquid as propanol.

Earle and Milner (1938) reported in the course of the analysis of soybean phosphatides that this color reaction for choline is not specific, since it is developed by other amino compounds as well. Marenzi and Cardini (1943, 1943a) pointed out, in this connection, that the reineckate procedure for choline is adaptable to colorimetric techniques only when fairly concentrated solutions are available. They proposed a procedure based on the colorimetric determination of the chromium content of the precipitate, which in their work was shown to exist in the amount required by theory. The procedure was accurate for samples containing as little as 15 gamma of choline.

The original micromethod of Roman (1930) for the determination of choline as the enneaiodide, $C_2H_5(CH_3)_3NOI_9$, has also been used for the analysis of choline-containing phosphatides. Roman found that with considerable precaution it was possible to estimate 0.005 to 5.0 mg. of choline with an error of ±5 per cent. The iodine consumption was measured by titrating the unreacted iodine with thiosulfate. Street, Kenyon and Watson (1946) pointed out, however, that the achievement of quantitative yields may be difficult and that the precipitate is unstable and may vary in composition. Earle and Milner (1938) earlier believed that this was the most satisfactory means for the determination of choline in soybean phosphatides. The precipitation of choline with iodine can be effected in the presence of aminoethyl alcohol, for which reason phosphatidylaminoethyl alcohol is not a complicating factor. Crane and Horrall (1942) found Roman's method applicable to the determination of choline in milk phosphatides.

This method was also used by Kirk (1938) in his procedure for the analysis of phosphatides in blood and tissue. He mentioned that precautions must be taken against loss of iodine which he, like Roman (1930), determined by titration with thiosulfate. Erickson and coworkers (1940) also studied this method and suggested the use of immersion filter sticks in washing the precipitate. This makes possible the maintenance of a low temperature during the manipulation. Still another innovation which they proposed involved the oxidation of the iodide to iodate with bromine, thus providing a soluble material which required a sixfold increase of the thiosulfate in the titration. Artom and Fishman (1943) also found this method applicable to the analysis of tissue.

Other salts have been used to precipitate choline by various investigators. Chargaff (1942) determined choline by converting it to the hydrochloride and precipitating the choline hydrochloride·$HgCl_2$ double salt. The picrate, the picrolonate and the chloroplatinate were used extensively by earlier workers (see, e.g., Thierfelder and Schulze, 1916; Levene and Ingvaldsen, 1920; Thierfelder and Klenk, 1930, p. 98).

Of considerable interest is the method for determining choline based on the observation that alkaline potassium permanganate oxidizes it with the quantitative liberation of trimethylamine. This method proved successful in the hands of Lintzel and Fomin (1931) and Lintzel and Monasterio (1931), who treated an alkaline solution of the water-soluble phosphatide hydrolysis products with potassium permanganate. This liberated not only trimethylamine from choline, but also ammonia from aminoethyl alcohol and other nitrogen-containing substances. On treatment of the mixture of gases with formaldehyde, the ammonia reacts, allowing the estimation of the trimethylamine by titration.

Street, Kenyon and Watson (1946) adapted the procedure of Lintzel and Monasterio (1931) to derivatives of choline such as the hydrochloride, reineckate and mercurichloride. The method may be used for quantities of choline nitrogen ranging from 0.7 to 3.2 milligrams with a mean deviation of ± 2 per cent. The method is quite specific and is thus valuable in instances where other bases are present; for, when combined with a preliminary Reinecke salt precipitation, the interference of other bases is practically eliminated, according to the proponents of the method.

Microbiological techniques have frequently been applied to the determination of choline (e.g., Carayon-Gentil, Corteggiani and Pelou, 1941; Fletcher, Best and Solandt, 1935). The phosphatides are hydrolyzed and the liberated choline is acetylated. The resulting acetylcholine may be determined by its action on tissues such as eserinized, denervated leech muscle or isolated rabbit intestine.

Horowitz and Beadle (1943) described a new microbiological technique based on the observation that a mutant of the mold, *Neurospora crassa*, required choline for normal growth. This method was used by Hodson (1945) and was modified slightly by Siegel (1945).

Chargaff, Levine and Green (1948) have recently applied the technique of paper chromatography to the demonstration of phosphatide constituents such as choline, serine and aminoethyl alcohol. Quantitative estimations, based on this technique, may be evolved in the future.

For the conversion of choline to lecithin where sphingomyelin is absent or negligible or has already been accounted for, factors of 6.65 to 6.68 (Artom and Freeman, 1940; Kirk, 1938) have been used.

DETERMINATION OF AMINOETHYL ALCOHOL

The methods for the determination of aminoethyl alcohol as a hydrolysis product of phosphatides are limited. Levene and Ingvaldsen (1920), following a procedure used by Thierfelder and Schulze (1916), separated aminoethyl alcohol from choline by extraction with acetone and then converted it to the gold chloride salt. For the most part, however, aminoethyl alcohol-containing phosphatides have been determined, as has been seen above, by direct titration of the amino group, by analysis of amino nitrogen or, indirectly, by difference between the total and the choline-containing phosphatides. Of great importance is the estimation by periodate oxidation, which has already been discussed (see p. 170).

Chargaff (1942) found that 3,5-diiodosalicylic acid is a good precipitant for aminoethyl alcohol, and that it may be used in the presence of choline. Although it is a derivative which is easily isolated and readily purified, it does not, like many other reagents, lead to entirely quantitative results. The advisability of a good precipitation method is shown by Chargaff's (1942) work in which the diiodosalicylate accounted for only 44 per cent of what had previously been determined by nitrous acid as amino nitrogen in the unhydrolyzed phosphatide mixture. This discrepancy probably arises from the fact that unsaturated linkages in the intact phosphatide can react with nitrous acid, causing false amino nitrogen values.

The estimation of aminoethyl alcohol by distillation from a phosphatide hydrolysis mixture is described by Blix (1940). The amino alcohol is distilled into acid and determined titrimetrically. Choline and urea do not affect the analysis, and it may be carried out on a micro scale in an apparatus described by Blix (1940).

DETERMINATION OF GLYCEROL

The presence of glycerol in phosphatide hydrolysis mixtures is an indication of glycerophosphatides, and its estimation provides a measure of these compounds. However, glycerol determination has not been used extensively in phosphatide analysis, probably because glycerophosphoric acid is fairly resistant to hydrolysis; and once hydrolysis has been effected, the quantitative isolation or determination of glycerol is difficult.

Blix (1937) provided a microdetermination for the glycerol of lipides which is applicable to both neutral fats and phosphatides. The lipide is hydrolyzed and the glycerol, without being isolated, is converted by red phosphorus and hydroiodic acid to isopropyl iodide which may be recovered by distillation and estimated from its iodine content.

Ramsay and Stewart (1941) determined glycerol in a mixture of phosphatide hydrolysis products, also without prior isolation. The method depends on the oxidation of glycerol with periodic acid and the subsequent analysis, by a colorimetric procedure, of the formaldehyde which is formed. Interfering sugars are first removed in this procedure by use of copper sulfate and calcium hydroxide.

Cahn, Houget and Agid (1948) have described a procedure for the determination of glycerophosphoric acid which may be applied to phosphatides.

DETERMINATION OF FATTY ACIDS

The nitrogen-containing bases and glycerol or glycerophosphoric acid are the water-soluble parts of the phosphatide molecule which are obtained on hydrolysis. The water-insoluble material consists of fatty acids which result as such from acid hydrolysis and as soaps from basic hydrolysis. If the phosphatides are subjected to alcoholysis procedures, the acids are converted directly to esters. The determination of total phosphatides by estimation of the fatty acid content either by titrimetric or oxidative procedures has already been discussed (see p. 162).

Of great interest and importance are the qualitative and quantitative analyses of the individual fatty acids present in phosphatides. Since this is accomplished by more or less standard procedures used for all lipides, a detailed discussion is not in order here. The experimental details are well outlined by Hilditch (1947, p. 464 ff.) in his text on fats and in other prior texts mentioned there. In general, the lipide is saponified by base to obtain soaps. If low molecular weight acids are present—although this is rare in phosphatides—they may be removed by distillation. The acids are usually separated into saturated and unsaturated fractions by virtue of the differential solubility of the metallic soaps of these fractions in organic solvents. Very commonly, the fatty acids are converted to lead soaps, whereupon the unsaturated fraction may be dissolved in ether or alcohol while the saturated fraction remains insoluble. Whereas older workers used ether for the resolution, recent investigators have preferred alcohol. Highly branched chain saturated acids such as those found in the phosphatides of the tubercle bacillus (see p. 208) behave like unsaturated acids in this procedure. Lithium soaps have also been used, especially where long-chain polyunsaturated acids are involved, since the lithium salts of these are soluble in acetone. The acetone-insoluble fraction, consisting of ordinary chain length saturated and unsaturated acids, may then be separated by the usual lead soap-ethanol method. An excellent example of this latter technique is found in the work of Klenk (1932), who investigated the fatty acids of brain and liver phosphatides, many of which possess long carbon chains with multiple unsaturation.

The soaps, separated by these methods, are converted to methyl esters and are fractionally distilled *in vacuo*. Many types of apparatus have been devised for this purpose, some of which are described by Hilditch. Diemair and Schmidt (1937) described an apparatus which is especially applicable to the fractional distillation of C_{15} to C_{20} phosphatide fatty acids. From the molecular weights (neutralization equivalents), iodine numbers, and boiling ranges of the various fractions, the fatty acid composition is estimated. Typical data and their treatment are discussed by Hilditch.

Fitelson (1950) has described a method for the estimation of saturated fatty acids in a mixture which involves the oxidation of the unsaturated acids with performic acid.

Solid derivatives such as di- and tetrahydroxystearic acids for mono- and diunsaturated acids, and polybromides for di- and polyunsaturated acids are of value in identifying the component acids. In general, however, the usual solid derivatives for acids are of little value, since these derivatives of higher fatty acids indicate little differentiation in melting points.

Newer techniques have also been applied in a few instances to the analysis of phosphatide fatty acids. Thus, Halden and Schauenstein (1943) used absorption spectra to detect and measure conjugated fatty acids in rye phosphatides, and by this means were able to identify 9,11-linoleic acid.

In some instances, especially where the acids are highly unsaturated, low temperature crystallization from organic solvents is a feasible means for separating some of the components.

An excellent example of the application of most of the methods discussed above to the fatty acids of egg-yolk lecithin is found in the work of Riemenschneider, Ellis and Titus (1938).

ELEMENTARY ANALYSIS

Phophorus

As indicated previously in this chapter, the determination of lipide phosphorus provides an indirect means for the determination of total phosphatides. Numerous procedures have been suggested, including gravimetric, nephelometric, gasometric, titrimetric and colorimetric methods. Of these, colorimetric procedures are generally preferred because of their rapidity and adaptibility to micro work.

The first step, regardless of the method, is the fusion or the ashing of the lipides in order to convert the lipide phosphorus to phosphoric acid. This is discussed in detail in standard analytical texts. A typical method of ashing is that of Krasnow and co-workers (1935) in which nitric and sulfuric acids are used in combination with potassium chlorate and sodium and potassium nitrates in order to insure complete oxidation. The destruction of organic matter is also discussed by Fiske and Subbarow (1925).

Most colorimetric procedures for phosphorus depend on the conversion of phosphoric acid to phosphomolybdic acid, and the reduction of this by a suitable reagent to blue molybdic oxide. Bell and Doisy (1920) proposed the use of hydroquinone for this purpose. Their procedure has been used quite extensively, usually with certain modifications (see, e.g., Randles and Knudson, 1922; Whitehorn, 1924/25; Chopra and Roy, 1936; Roe, Irish and Boyd, 1926). Recently, Beveridge and Johnson (1949); have used a molybdate-hydrazine sulfate reagent for the development of color which is said to be very stable and to adhere strictly to Beer's law over a range of 0 to 65 gammas of phosphorus. Molines and Desnuelle (1948) have described a procedure employing molybdate which may detect 0.01 milligram of phosphorus.

Based on the method of Bell and Doisy (1920), Fiske and Subbarow (1925) advanced a procedure for the colorimetric determination of phosphorus which has found wide application in the field of lipides. This method employs 1-amino-2-hydroxynaphthalene-4-sulfonic acid as the reducing agent. This compound is considerably more active than hydroquinone, quickly yielding an intense, stable color. Certain micro-modifications have been suggested by Stewart and Hendry (1935) and by Krainick (1938). Both the latter worker and Horecker, Ma and Haas (1940) have used the photoelectric spectrophotometer whereby as little as one gamma of phosphorus can be determined. This latter modification was also employed successfully by Hack (1947).

The use of stannous chloride as a reducing agent was proposed by Kuttner and Cohen (1927).

An entirely different colorimetric procedure was worked out by Lieboff (1928) in which the phosphate is precipitated with uranium acetate. The uranium phosphate is then dissolved in trichloroacetic acid and reacted with potassium ferrocyanide in order to develop a color which may be compared with a known standard.

A nephelometric procedure for phosphorus has been described by Bloor (1915) in which the phosphoric acid was precipitated as silver phosphate in slightly alkaline solution. Nephelometric comparison of the amount of precipitate with known standards provided a measure of the phosphorus content.

A microgasometric procedure for the indirect determination of phosphorus has been devised by Kirk (1934). The phosphoric acid is precipitated as strychnine phosphomolybdate (Koch, 1930) which is washed, dissolved in acetone, filtered, and recovered by evaporation. Thereafter, the precipitate is oxidized with a mixture of chromic, sulfuric and phosphoric acids, according to the method of Van Slyke, Page and Kirk (1933), in order to determine the carbon content from the carbon dioxide which is liberated.

The titrimetric determination of lipide phosphorus is exemplified by the procedure of Fiandaca and Capizzi (1934). The phosphoric acid is precipitated as ammonium phosphomolybdate, and the amount of this precipitate is estimated by dissolving it in excess standard base and back-titrating with acid. Such a procedure is also discussed by Grant (1946, p. 112).

The microgravimetric procedure for the determination of phosphorus as the phosphomolybdate was first advanced by Pregl (1935, p. 156).

Nitrogen

The carbon, hydrogen and nitrogen contents of phosphatides are determined by standard procedures. The Kjeldahl analysis for nitrogen is usually carried out in the presence of metallic selenium which aids in the digestion of the fatty acids. Kirk, Page and Van Slyke (1934) described a micro-Kjeldahl procedure for lipide nitrogen in which the liberated ammonia is measured gasometrically. Kurtz (1933) pointed out that nitrogen and phosphorus may be determined in the same sample. Thus the sample is digested with selenium, potassium sulfate and sulfuric acid and the nitrogen is determined by the usual Kjeldahl method. From the residue of this determination, the phosphorus may be precipitated as ammonium phosphomolybdate.

The determination of nitrogen in vegetable oils has been described by McGuire, Earle and Dutton (1947). Practically all of this nitrogen arises from phosphatides and is thus a rough measure of the phosphatide content of the oil. The nitrogen is made water-dispersible by the action of alcoholic hydrochloric acid, which under specified conditions hydrolyzes the phosphatides but not the glycerides. The nitrogen-containing component may then be extracted with water and digested by the Kjeldahl procedure. When the ammonia is determined by Nessler's method, as little as 0.1 mg. of nitrogen can be measured. Procedures of this sort are important in order to check the efficiency of refining processes intended to remove the phosphatides from oils.

IODINE NUMBER

Most of the standard macroprocedures for iodine number determination have been adapted to micromethods which may—often with some difficulty—be applied to phosphatides. Thus, Gibson and Howard (1923) used an adaptation of the Hanus method on blood lipides. Yasuda (1931/32), on the other hand, found that this method was not generally applicable. He devised a procedure using the Rosenmund-Kuhnhenn reagent, pyridine dibromide. Boyd (1933) found this procedure to yield erratic results as did MacLachlan (1944), who attributed the discrepant data to the presence of magnesium chloride in the chloroform solution. Boyd (1933) accordingly determined the iodine number of the fatty acids subsequent to saponification. However, MacLachlan (1944) is of the opinion that blood and tissue phosphatides contain unsaponifiable or difficultly saponifiable materials which would invalidate a procedure based on saponification. MacLachlan (1944) was, moreover, able to obtain consistent results by extracting the precipitated phosphatides twice with chloroform rather than once as advocated by Yasuda (1931/32). This apparently removed all of the magnesium chloride.

QUALITATIVE TESTS

Several qualitative color tests for phosphatides have been advanced which are based primarily on the fact that phosphorus is present. By far the best known is the Pettenkofer Reaction (Thudichum, 1901, pp. 121, 142) in which a purple color results when phosphatides are brought into contact with sugar and concentrated sulfuric acid. The reaction studied by Casanova (1911, 1926) involves treatment of an ether solution of phosphatides with ammonium molybdate and concentrated sulfuric acid. At the zone of contact a red color is said to develop which changes to green and blue. Sterols apparently do not interfere. Other color reactions were advanced by Ekkert (1928), Migliacci (1928) and Fernández and Folch (1932). All the above tests, however, were criticized by Diemair, Schloemer and Täufel (1933) on the basis that they are not specific, as many of these reactions are given by oleic and other unsaturated acids.

HISTOCHEMICAL REACTION

Various workers have attempted to devise staining techniques which would make possible the detection of phosphatides in tissue. This work up to 1936 is well summarized by Lison (1936, p. 189ff.). Dyes such as Sudan III and IV and Nile blue have been shown not to give specific reactions with phosphatides, since any lipide will give a stain. Colors are very often due to unsaturation in the lipides rather than to a specific substance and, in general, it may be said that no satisfactory procedure has been evolved. The difficulties may in part be due to the complexes which exist between the phosphatides and proteins of tissue. Of possible interest is the method of Romieu (1927) in which lecithin is treated with dilute hydrochloric acid and a concentrated solution of iodine in potassium iodide. The lecithin assumes a mahogany-brown color which is also characteristic of glycogen under the same conditions. However, when the test material is warmed with 10 per cent hydrochloric acid the glycogen dissolves, whereas the lecithin remains.

Several methods have been proposed based on the acetone-insolubility of the phosphatides (Shapiro, 1927; Ciaccio, 1931), but these have not proved satisfactory. More recently Alsterberg (1940) has published a reaction based on the use of cyanogen iodide in combination with silver or palladium salts which is said to be specific for phosphatides.

Unlike the more common phosphatides, the acetal phosphatides (see p. 51) may be detected by staining techniques because of the presence of the aldehyde entity. Feulgen and Voit (1924) found that the so-called "Schiff Reaction" for aldehydes employing sulfurous acid and fuchsin dye gave a slow positive reaction with acetal phosphatides, due probably to the fact that the reagent liberated the aldehyde. When the acetal phosphatide was hydrolyzed first, the staining reaction was immediate. The same test, however, is provided by desoxyribonucleic acid. The situation is discussed in detail by Glick (1949, p. 65).

BIBLIOGRAPHY—PART II

Alsterberg, G., *Arkiv Zool.*, **32A**, No. 2, Contrib. No. 12, 13 pp. (1940); *C. A.*, **35**, 7433 (1941).

Anchel, M., and Waelsch, H., *J. Biol. Chem.*, **152**, 501 (1944).

Anderson, R. J., *J. Biol. Chem.*, **74**, 525 (1927).

Andrews, J. S., and Bailey, C. H., *Ind. Eng. Chem.*, **24**, 80 (1932); *C. A.*, **26**, 1639 (1932).

Arbenz, E., *Mitt. Lebensm. Hyg.*, **10**, 93 (1919); *C. A.*, **14**, 81 (1920).

Artom, C., *Bull. soc. chim. biol.*, **7**, 1099 (1925); *C. A.*, **20**, 1656 (1926).

——, *ibid.*, **14**, 1386 (1932); *C. A.*, **27**, 1023 (1933).

——, *J. Biol. Chem.*, **139**, 65 (1941).

——, *ibid.*, **157**, 585, 595 (1945).

——, and Fishman, W. H., *J. Biol. Chem.*, **148**, 405 (1943).

——, and Freeman, *J. Biol. Chem.*, **135**, 59 (1940).

Bang, I., *Biochem. Z.*, **91**, 86, 235 (1918); *C. A.*, **13**, 2226, 2228 (1919).

Beattie, F. J. R., *Biochem. J.*, **30**, 1554 (1936); *C. A.*, **31**, 729 (1937).

Bell, R. D., and Doisy, E. A., *J. Biol. Chem.*, **44**, 55 (1920).

Beveridge, J. M. R., and Johnson, S. E., *Can. J. Research*, **27E**, 159 (1949); *C. A.*, **43**, 8424 (1949).

Blix, G., *Mikrochim. Acta*, **1**, 75 (1937); *C. A.*, **31**, 5721 (1937).

——, *Biochem. Z.*, **305**, 129 (1940); *C. A.*, **35**, 471 (1941).

Bloor, W. R., *J. Biol. Chem.*, **17**, 377 (1914).

——, *ibid.*, **22**, 133 (1915).

——, *ibid.*, **36**, 33 (1918).

——, *ibid.* **59**, 543 (1924).

——, *ibid.*, **68**, 33 (1926).

——, *ibid.*, **77**, 53 (1928).

——, *ibid.*, **82**, 273 (1929).

——, *ibid.*, **95**, 633 (1932).

——, *ibid.*, **119**, 451 (1937).

——, "Biochemistry of the Fatty Acids and Their Compounds, The Lipids," New York, Reinhold Publishing Corp., 1943.

——, Pelkan, K. F., and Allen, D. M., *J. Biol. Chem.*, **52**, 191 (1922).

Boyd, E. M., *J. Biol. Chem.*, **91**, 1 (1931).

——, *ibid.*, **101**, 323 (1933).

——, *ibid.*, **114**, 223 (1936).

——, *ibid.*, **115**, 37 (1936a).

Brodrick-Pittard, N. A., *Biochem. Z.*, **67**, 382 (1914); *C. A.*, **9**, 639 (1915).

Burmaster, C. F., *J. Biol. Chem.*, **165**, 1 (1946).

Buruiana, L., and Furtunesco, A., *Lait*, **21**, 8 (1941); *C. A.*, **38**, 3029 (1944).

Cahn, T., Houget, J., and Agid, R., *Bull. soc. chim. France*, **666** (1948); *C. A.*, **42**, 8860 (1948).

Carayon-Gentil, A., Corteggiani, E., and Pelou, A., *Compt. rend. soc. biol.*, **135**, 1077 (1941); *C. A.*, **38**, 2980 (1944).

Casanova, C., *Boll. chim. farm.*, **50**, 309 (1911); *C. A.*, **6**, 1013 (1912).

——, *Arch. chim. sci. ind.*, **31**, 282 (1926); *C. A.*, **22**, 1826 (1928).

Chargaff, E., *J. Biol. Chem.*, **128**, 587 (1939).

——, *ibid.*, **142**, 491 (1942).

——, Levine, C., and Green, C., *J. Biol. Chem.*, **175**, 67 (1948).

——, Ziff, M., and Rittenberg, D., *J. Biol. Chem.*, **144**, 343 (1942).

Chopra, R. N., and Roy, A. C., *Indian J. Med. Research*, **24**, 479 (1936); *C. A.*, **31**, 4688 (1937).

Christensen, H. N., *J. Biol. Chem.*, **129**, 531 (1939).

Ciaccio, C., *Boll. soc. ital. biol. sper.*, **6**, 301 (1931); *C. A.*, **25**, 4570 (1931).

Crane, J. C., and Horrall, B. E., *J. Dairy Sci.*, **25**, 651 (1942); *C. A.*, **36**, 7158 (1942).

——, ——, *ibid.*, **26**, 935 (1943); *C. A.*, **38**, 3028 (1944).

Delsal, J. L., *Bull. soc. chim. biol.*, **26**, 99 (1944); *C. A.*, **39**, 3560 (1945).

Diemair, W., and Schmidt, W., *Biochem. Z.*, **294**, 348 (1937); *C. A.*, **32**, 1735 (1938).

——, Schloemer, A., and Täufel, K., *Z. physiol. Chem.*, **220**, 86 (1933); *C. A.*, **27**, 5356 (1933).

Earle, F. R., and Milner, R. T., *Oil & Soap*, **15**, 41 (1938); *C. A.*, **32**, 2769 (1938).

Egsgaard, J., *Acta Physiol. Scand.*, **16**, 171 (1948); *C. A.*, **43**, 4320 (1949).

Ehrlich, G., Taylor, H. E., and Waelsch, H., *J. Biol. Chem.*, **173**, 547 (1948).

Eichgorn, G., Milskii, A., and Kalashnikov, E., *Masloboĭno Zhirovoe Delo*, **11**, 26 (1931); *C. A.*, **26**, 4411 (1932).

Ekkert, L., *Pharm. Zentralhalle*, **69**, 135 (1928); *C. A.*, **22**, 1651 (1928).

Ellis, G., and Maynard, L. A., *J. Biol. Chem.*, **118**, 701 (1937).

Entenman, C., Taurog, A., and Chaikoff, I. L., *J. Biol. Chem.*, **155**, 13 (1944).

Epshteĭn, Ya. A., *Biokhimiya*, **7**, 69 (1942); *C. A.*, **37**, 4417 (1943).

Erickson, B. N., and co-workers (Williams, H. H., Hummel, F. C., and Macy, I. G.), *J. Biol. Chem.*, **118**, 15 (1937).

——, and co-workers (Avrin, I., Teague, D. M., and Williams, H. H.), *J. Biol. Chem.*, **135**, 671 (1940).

Fawaz, G., Lieb, H., and Zacherl, M. K., *Biochem. Z.*, **293**, 121 (1937); *C. A.*, **32**, 607 (1938).

Fernández, O., and Folch, R., *Anales soc. españ. fís. y quím.*, **30**, 849 (1932); *C. A.*, **27**, 245 (1933).

Feulgen, R., and Grünberg, H., *Z. physiol. Chem.*, **257**, 161 (1938); *C. A.*, **33**, 3407 (1939).

——, and Voit, K., *Arch. ges. Physiol. (Pflüger's)*, **206**, 389 (1924); *C. A.*, **19**, 1155 (1925).

Fiandaca, S., and Capizzi, I., *Boll. soc. ital. biol. sper.*, **9**, 809 (1934); *C. A.*, **29**, 1448 (1935).

Fiske, C. H., and Subbarow, Y., *J. Biol. Chem.*, **66**, 375 (1925).

Fitelson, J., *J. Am. Oil Chemists' Soc.*, **27**, 1 (1950).

Fletcher, J. P., Best, C. H., and Solandt, O. M., *Biochem. J.*, **29**, 2278 (1935); *C. A.*, **30**, 1827 (1936).

Fleury, P., and Guitard, H., *Ann. pharm. franç.*, **6**, 252 (1948); *C. A.*, **43**, 5344 (1949).

Folch, J., *J. Biol. Chem.*, **146**, 35 (1942).

——, and Schneider, H. A., *J. Biol. Chem.*, **137**, 51 (1941).

——, and Van Slyke, D. D., *J. Biol. Chem.*, **129**, 539 (1939).

——, ——, *Proc. Soc. Exp. Biol. Med.*, **41**, 514 (1939a); *C. A.*, **33**, 8652 (1939).

——, Schneider, H. A., and Van Slyke, D. D., *J. Biol. Chem.*, **133**, XXXIII (1940).

Fourneau, E., and Piettre, *Bull. soc. chim.*, **11**, 805 (1913); *C. A.*, **7**, 803 (1913).

Fries, B. A., and co-workers (Entenman, C., Changus, G. W., and Chaikoff, I. L.), *J. Biol. Chem.*, **137**, 303 (1941).

Gibson, R. B., and Howard, C. P., *Arch. Intern. Med.*, **32**, 1 (1923); *C. A.*, **17**, 3700 (1923).

Glick, D., *J. Biol. Chem.*, **156**, 643 (1944).

——, *Cereal Chem.*, **22**, 95 (1945); *C. A.*, **39**, 2342 (1945).

——, "Techniques of Histo- and Cytochemistry," New York, Interscience Publishers, Inc., 1949.

Gorbach, G., *Fette u. Seifen*, **51**, 53 (1944); *C. A.*, **41**, 1469 (1947).

——, *ibid.*, **51**, 93 (1944a); *C. A.*, **41**, 775 (1947).

Grant, J., "Quantitative Organic Microanalysis," Philadelphia, The Blakiston Co., 1946.

Grossfeld, J., and Zeisset, A., *Z. Untersuch. Lebensm.,* **85,** 321 (1943); *C. A.,* **38,** 2402 (1944).

Guerrant, N. B., *J. Am. Chem. Soc.,* **48,** 2185 (1926); *C. A.,* **20,** 3021 (1926).

Hack, M. H., *J. Biol. Chem.,* **166,** 455 (1946).

——, *ibid.,* **169,** 137 (1947).

Halden, W., and Schauenstein, E., *Fette u. Seifen,* **50,** 78 (1943); *C. A.,* **38,** 5315 (1944).

Hanahan, D. J., and Chaikoff, I. L., *J. Biol. Chem.,* **168,** 233 (1947).

Hess, A. F., and Helman, F. D., *J. Biol. Chem.,* **64,** 781 (1925).

Hevesy, G., "Radioactive Indicators," New York, Interscience Publishers, Inc., 1948.

——, and Hahn, L., *Kgl. Danske Videnskab. Selskab Biol. Medd.,* **15,** No. 5 (1940); *C. A.,* **36,** 138 (1942).

Hilditch, T. P., "The Chemical Constitution of Natural Fats," London, Chapman and Hall, Ltd., 1947.

Hodson, A. Z., *J. Biol. Chem.,* **157,** 383 (1945).

Holm, G. E., Wright, P. A., and Deysher, E. F., *J. Dairy Sci.,* **19,** 631 (1936); *C. A.,* **31,** 164 (1937).

Holwerda, B. J., *Verslag. Landbouwk. Onderzoek., No. 42, C,* 335 (1936); *C. A.,* **31,** 165 (1937).

Horecker, B. L., Ma, T. S., and Haas, E., *J. Biol. Chem.,* **136,** 775 (1940).

Horowitz, N. H., and Beadle, G. W., *J. Biol. Chem.,* **150,** 325 (1943).

Hunter, F. E., *J. Biol. Chem.,* **144,** 439 (1942).

Jacobi, H. P., Baumann, C. A., and Meek, W. J., *J. Biol. Chem.,* **138,** 571 (1941).

Jamieson, G. S., and McKinney, R. S., *Oil & Soap,* **12,** 70 (1935); *C. A.,* **29,** 3541 (1935).

Kapfhammer, J., and Bischoff, C., *Z. physiol. Chem.,* **191,** 179 (1930); *C. A.,* **25,** 127 (1931).

Katsura, S., Hatakeyama, T., and Tajima, K., *Biochem. Z.,* **257,** 22 (1933); *C. A.,* **27,** 1652 (1933).

——, ——, ——, *ibid.,* **269,** 231 (1934); *C. A.,* **28,** 4093 (1934).

Kirk, E., *J. Biol. Chem.,* **106,** 191 (1934).

——, *ibid.,* **123,** 623 (1938).

——, *Acta Med. Scand., Suppl.,* **89,** 178 (1938a); *C. A.,* **33,** 195 (1939).

——, Page, I. H., and Van Slyke, D. D., *J. Biol. Chem.,* **106,** 203 (1934).

Klenk, E., *Z. physiol. Chem.,* **206,** 25 (1932); *C. A.,* **26,** 3523 (1932).

Koch, K., *Biochem. Z.,* **227,** 334 (1930); *C. A.,* **25,** 532 (1931).

Krainick, H. G., *Klin. Wochschr.,* **17,** 706 (1938); *C. A.,* **32,** 7944 (1938).

Krasnow, F., and co-workers (Rosen, A. S., Phar, D., and Porosowska, Y.), *J. Lab. Clin. Med.,* **20,** 1090 (1935); *C. A.,* **29,** 7369 (1935).

Kroeker, E. H., Strong, F. M., and Peterson, W. H., *J. Am. Chem. Soc.,* **57,** 354 (1935); *C. A.,* **29,** 1853 (1935).

Kumagawa, M., and Suto, K., *Biochem. Z.,* **8,** 212 (1908); *C. A.,* **2,** 2560 (1908).

Kurtz, F. E., *Ind. Eng. Chem., Anal. Ed.,* **5,** 260 (1933); *C. A.,* **27,** 4190 (1933).

Kuttner, T., and Cohen, H. R., *J. Biol. Chem.,* **75,** 517 (1927).

LeBreton, E., *Bull. soc. chim. biol.,* **3,** 539 (1921); *C. A.,* **16,** 722 (1922).

Lepper, H. A., "Methods of Analysis of the A. O. A. C.," 6th ed., Washington, D. C., 1945.

Levene, P. A., and Ingvaldsen, T., *J. Biol. Chem.,* **43,** 355 (1920).

Lieboff, S. L., *J. Biol. Chem.,* **80,** 211 (1928).

Lintzel, W., and Fomin, S., *Biochem. Z.*, **238**, 452 (1931); *C. A.*, **25**, 5686 (1931).
——, and Monasterio, G., *Biochem. Z.*, **241**, 273 (1931); *C. A.*, **26**, 749 (1932).
Lison, L., "Histochimie Animale," Paris, Gauthier-Villars, 1936.
Lucas, C. C., and Best, C. H., in "Vitamins & Hormones," Vol. I, New York, Academic Press, Inc., 1943.
McGuire, T. A., Earle, F. R., and Dutton, H. J., *J. Am. Oil Chemists' Soc.*, **24**, 359 (1947); *C. A.*, **42**, 777 (1948).
McKibbin, J. M., and Taylor, W. E., *J. Biol. Chem.*, **178**, 17, 29 (1949).
MacLachlan, P. L., *J. Biol. Chem.*, **152**, 97 (1944).
MacLean, H., and MacLean, I. S., "Lecithin and Allied Substances the Lipins," London, Longmans, Green and Co., Ltd., 1927.
Man, E. B., *J. Biol. Chem.*, **117**, 183 (1937).
——, and Gildea, E. F., *J. Biol. Chem.*, **99**, 43 (1932/33).
——, ——, *ibid.*, **122**, 77 (1937).
Marenzi, A. D., and Cardini, C. E., *J. Biol. Chem.*, **147**, 363 (1943).
——, ——, *ibid.*, **147**, 371 (1943a).
May, R. M., *Compt. rend.*, **190**, 1150 (1930); *Bull. soc. chim. biol.*, **12**, 934 (1930); *C. A.*, **25**, 1562 (1931).
Meurice, C., *Ing. chim.*, **20**, 36 (1936); *C. A.*, **31**, 3577 (1937).
Migliacci, D., *Boll. chim. farm.*, **67**, 324 (1928); *C. A.*, **22**, 4719 (1928).
Molines, J., and Desnuelle, P., *Bull. Mens. ITERG*, No. 2, 1 (1948); *C. A.*, **42**, 4493 (1948).
Monasterio, G., and Gigli, G., *Rass. fisiopatol. clin. e terap.* (*Pisa*), 19, No. 11/12, 33 pp. (1947); *C. A.*, **43**, 2658 (1949).
Nerking, J., *Biochem. Z.*, **23**, 262 (1910); *C. A.*, **4**, 612 (1910).
Nielson, J. P., and Bohart, G. S., *Ind. Eng. Chem., Anal. Ed.*, **16**, 701 (1944); *C. A.*, **39**, 761 (1945).
Norberg, B., and Teorell, T., *Biochem. Z.*, **264**, 310 (1933); *C. A.*, **27**, 5769 (1933).
Perlman, J. L., *J. Dairy Sci.*, **18**, 113 (1935); *C. A.*, **29**, 3054 (1935).
Pregl, F., "Die Quantitative Organische Mikroanalyse," Revised by Roth, H., Berlin, Julius Springer, 1935.
Ramsay, W. N. M., and Stewart, C. P., *Biochem. J.*, **35**, 39 (1941); *C. A.*, **35**, 6645 (1941).
Randles, F. S., and Knudson, A., *J. Biol. Chem.*, **53**, 53 (1922).
Rask, O. S., and Phelps, I. K., *Ind. Eng. Chem.*, **17**, 187, 189 (1925); *C. A.*, **19**, 864 (1925).
Reiser, R., *J. Am. Oil Chemists' Soc.*, **24**, 199 (1947).
Rewald, B., *Biochem. Z.*, **202**, 399 (1928); *C. A.*, **23**, 3240 (1929).
——, *Lait*, **17**, 225 (1937); *C. A.*, **31**, 6354 (1937).
——, *J. Soc. Chem. Ind.*, **56**, 77T (1937a); *C. A.*, **31**, 3826 (1937).
——, *Oil & Soap*, **21**, 50 (1944); *C. A.*, **38**, 2226 (1944).
Riemenschneider, R. W., Ellis, N. R., and Titus, H. W., *J. Biol. Chem.*, **126**, 255 (1938).
Roe, J. H., Irish, O. J., and Boyd, J. I., *J. Biol. Chem.*, **67**, 579 (1926).
Roman, W., *Biochem. Z.*, **219**, 218 (1930); *C. A.*, **24**, 3029 (1930).
Romieu, M., *Compt. rend.*, **184**, 1206 (1927); *C. A.*, **21**, 2712 (1927).
Roth, H., and Schuster, P., *Angew. Chem.*, **53**, 273 (1940); *C. A.*, **35**, 493 (1941).
Rudy, H., and Page, I. H., *Z. physiol. Chem.*, **193**, 251 (1930); *C. A.*, **25**, 718 (1931).
Salisbury, L. F., and Anderson, R. J., *J. Biol. Chem.*, **129**, 505 (1939).
Schmidt, G., Benotti, J., and Thannhauser, S. J., *Federation Proc.*, **5**, 152 (1946).

Schmidt, G., and co-workers (Benotti, J., Hershman, B., and Thannhauser, S. J.), *J. Biol. Chem.*, 166, 505 (1946).

Schmidt, L. H., *J. Biol. Chem.*, 109, 449 (1935).

Schmitz, E., and Koch, F., *Biochem. Z.*, 223, 257 (1930); *C. A.*, 24, 5062 (1930).

Schramme, A., *Fette u. Seifen*, 46, 635 (1939); *C. A.*, 34, 7783 (1940).

Shapiro, S., *Arch. Path. Lab. Med.*, 3, 661 (1927); *C. A.*, 21, 2151 (1927).

Siegel, L., *Science*, 101, 674 (1945); *C. A.*, 39, 3804 (1945).

Sinclair, R. G., and Dolan, M., *J. Biol. Chem.*, 142, 659 (1942).

Sokolov, A. V., *Chemisation Socialistic Agr. (U.S.S.R.) No. 10*, 36–8 (1940); *C. A.*, 37, 4986 (1943).

Stewart, C. P., and Hendry, E. B., *Biochem. J.*, 29, 1683 (1935); *C. A.*, 29, 7360 (1935).

Street, H. E., Kenyon, A. E., and Watson, G. M., *Biochem. J.*, 40, 869 (1946).

Taurog, A., and co-workers (Entenman, C., Fries, B. A., and Chaikoff, I. L.), *J. Biol. Chem.*, 155, 19 (1944).

——, Entenman, C., and Chaikoff, I. L., *J. Biol. Chem.*, 156, 385 (1944).

Thaler, H., and Just, E., *Fette u. Seifen*, 51, 55 (1944); *C. A.*, 42, 1069 (1948).

Thannhauser, S. J., and Setz, P., *J. Biol. Chem.*, 116, 533 (1936).

——, Benotti, J., and Boncoddo, N. F., *J. Biol. Chem.*, 166, 669 (1946).

——, ——, and Reinstein, H., *J. Biol. Chem.*, 129, 709 (1939).

Thierfelder, H., and Klenk, E., "Die Chemie der Cerebroside und Phosphatide," Berlin, Julius Springer, 1930.

——, and Schulze, O., *Z. physiol. Chem.*, 96, 296 (1916); *C. A.*, 10, 914 (1916).

Thudichum, J. L. W., "Die chemische Konstitution des Gehirns des Menschen und der Tiere, Tübingen, Franz Pietzcker, 1901.

Thurston, L. M., and Petersen, W. E., *J. Dairy Sci.*, 11, 270 (1928); *C. A.*, 22, 3238 (1928).

Van Slyke, D. D., and co-workers (Page, I. H., Kirk, E., and Farr, L. E.), *Proc. Soc. Exptl. Biol. Med.*, 32, 837 (1935).

——, Page, I. H., and Kirk, E., *J. Biol. Chem.*, 102, 635 (1933).

Weil, L., and Russell, M. A., *J. Biol. Chem.*, 144, 307 (1942).

Whitehorn, J. C., *J. Biol. Chem.*, 62, 133 (1924/25).

Wiese, H. F., Nair, J. H., and Fleming, R. S., *Ind. Eng. Chem., Anal. Ed.*, 4, 362 (1932); *C. A.*, 26, 6029 (1932).

Williams, H. H., and co-workers (Erickson, B. N., Avrin, I., Bernstein, S. S., and Macy, I. G.), *J. Biol. Chem.*, 123, 111 (1938).

Winzler, R. J., and Meserve, E. R., *J. Biol. Chem.*, 159, 395 (1945).

Yasuda, M., *J. Biol. Chem.*, 94, 401 (1931/32).

PART III
PHOSPHATIDES FROM PLANT SOURCES

CHAPTER XIII

INTRODUCTION TO PLANT PHOSPHATIDES

It is indeed an odd commentary that although a member of the plant kingdom, the soybean, serves as a commercial source of phosphatides, there has been relatively little fundamental work done on phosphatides from plant sources. The lack of interest in phosphatides from plants derives in part from the mechanical difficulties involved in isolation and purification. For, although all phosphatide work is beset with problems, special difficulties are inherent in the isolation and purification of plant phosphatides. Not only do they ordinarily occur in small quantities, but also they are given to complex formation with proteins and carbohydrates which serves to alter their solubility characteristics and practically precludes the preparation of analytically pure material. Indeed, chemically pure plant phosphatides are museum specimens which very few workers have had the privilege of encountering. Any discussion of plant phosphatides would not be complete without mention of the careful and exhaustive studies carried out by Anderson and co-workers (see p. 202) on the phosphatides of the acid-fast bacteria. This work is discussed in some detail in this chapter and is a keen example of the fact that excellent work, capable of repetition, may be done despite the difficulty of the field.

The history of plant phosphatides is by no means a recent one for Knop (1859) and Töpler (1861) isolated from plant sources a phosphorus-containing material soluble in certain fat solvents. That phosphorus-containing lipides were of general occurrence in plant seeds and other vegetable sources was shown by early investigators such as Hoppe-Seyler (1877, p. 57) and Heckel and Schlagdenhauffen (1886); and a few years later Jacobson (1889) was able to show that choline was a hydrolysis product of the phosphatides from various seeds. Schulze and Likiernik (1891) isolated not only choline from the hydrolysis products of plant phosphatides, but also glycerophosphoric acid and fatty acids.

On the basis of these results it was assumed through the years that lecithin was the characteristic plant phosphatide. Yet recent work has shown that the cephalin fraction probably predominates in the phosphatides of soybean, rapeseed, linseed, peanuts and sunflower seeds. There was also a school of thought which postulated a vast difference between

191

plant and animal phosphatides, and as late as 1927 MacLean and Mac-Lean in their monograph were careful to point out that existing data did not allow one to conclude with certainty that phosphatides from plant and animal sources were identical. This identity has now been well established, although it must be noted the sphingomyelin occurs, as far as is known, only in animal sources.

The establishment of the structure of plant phosphatides was pioneered by Levene and his associates (see p. 58), who were the first to isolate pure lecithin from soybeans. They were able to prove the presence of more than one phosphatide by the simple expedient of demonstrating that lecithin is soluble in warm alcohol, whereas the cephalin fraction is not. Thus a means was provided for a crude separation.

The phosphatide content of plants is generally small. In vegetables, where the water content is high, these two factors combine to make the isolation procedure quite difficult. Although data are scarce, chlorophyll-containing materials seem to have very low phosphatide contents, whereas flowers have somewhat larger amounts. Even in the oil-bearing seeds where the lipide content is relatively high, the phosphatides may amount to only 0.1 to 0.2 per cent of the glycerides. Obvious exceptions, of course, are legumes such as soybeans, where phosphatide contents as high as 3 per cent have been reported. Cereals contain considerably less. It is interesting to note that whereas many of the higher forms of plant life are characterized by low phosphatide contents, bacteria possess relatively large amounts of phosphatides.

The close association of phosphatides with carbohydrates and proteins gave rise to a considerable amount of confusion among the early workers. Not only did ether, the standard fat solvent, serve to extract only small quantities of phosphatides from plants, but once extracted these phosphatides possessed phosphorus contents far below the theoretical value. In addition, the nitrogen-phosphorus ratios deviated from the value of 1:1 which would be expected for the glycerophosphatides. Jacobson (1889) was probably the first investigator to point out that better extractions were obtained with alcohol, an observation which practically all investigators have made use of since his time. Although Jacobson believed that the higher results were due to the extraction by alcohol of other phosphorus-containing materials, the work of Schulze and Steiger (1889) and Maxwell (1891) served to elucidate the concept that plant phosphatides occurred, at least in part, in combination with other substances and that alcohol exerted a dissociating influence on these complexes. In many investigations it has been shown that alcohol is not an adequate solvent for extraction of all of the bound phosphatides, and that some of these become soluble in organic solvents only after treatment of the extracted residue with hydrolytic agents such as base or acid. Naturally such vigorous treatment is detrimental to the phosphatide and may complicate the interpretation of the results.

It is, of course, to be expected that complex formation, even of a physical nature, will change the solubility characteristics of the various components. Although phosphatides are characterized by insolubility in acetone, they may become soluble under the influence of proteins. Similarly, carbohydrates ordinarily insoluble in organic solvents may be solubilized by the influence of phosphatides. Thus, commercial samples of phosphatides obtained from soybeans may contain as much as 25 per cent carbohydrates even though the phosphatides come from oil extracted from the bean by hydrocarbon solvents. Winterstein and Hiestand (1906, 1908) were among the first investigators to find carbohydrates in the water-soluble products of phosphatide hydrolysis. Furthermore, they observed that a low phosphorus content was generally associated with a high carbohydrate content, although Schulze (1907) pointed out that there were other causes for a low phosphorus content.

The nature of these complexes is discussed in detail elsewhere (see p. 221) and it is pointed out that most of them are not chemical combinations. Rewald (1929a, 1936b, 1937) has shown that proper solvents disengaged the phosphatides from the carbohydrates. Woolley (1943), however, has obtained evidence for the presence of a new phosphatide (see p. 35) which may be isolated from soybeans and which consists of inositol in actual chemical combination with galactose, aminoethyl tartrate, phosphoric acid and fatty acids. The phosphatide-protein association has already been discussed (see p. 82). It is of greatest importance in animal sources.

The nature of the carbohydrates which associate with the lipides is somewhat obscure because of the difficulties encountered in their purification. Ordinarily they are complex mixtures which may contain glycosides and carbohydrate phosphoric acids as well as mono-, di- and polysaccharides. Whether the monosaccharides exist as such or whether they form during the isolation and hydrolysis of the phosphatides is still another point which cannot be discussed with complete clarity. Rewald (1929a) has shown that monosaccharides are not present in phosphatide emulsions prepared under conditions which eliminated hydrolysis. Likewise, from the work of Anderson and Roberts (1930, 1930a, 1930b) on the lipides of the tubercle bacillus, there is reason to infer that the monosaccharides obtained were hydrolysis products of more complex carbohydrates. The nature of the sugars found, so far as they have been investigated, are discussed in relation to the individual phosphatides later in the chapter. Extensive work has been done, however, only in the case of the tubercle bacillus. The exact nature of the other impurities associated with phosphatides from plant sources has yet to be determined.

Of the characterized phosphatides, lecithin and phosphatidylaminoethyl alcohol have been found in plant sources. Sphingomyelin has never been shown to be present, and although it may not be entirely lacking it is certainly not of any quantitative importance in the plant kingdom. Austin (1924) indicated that sphingomyelin is absent in yeast. The recently described serine-containing phosphatides (see p. 28) as well as the acetal phosphatides (see p. 51) have come entirely from animal sources, and there is no evidence to indicate that they have been sought after in the plant kingdom. The phosphatidic acids (see p. 48), on the other hand, first described by Chibnall and Channon (1927) who found them in cabbage leaves, seem to occur only in plant sources.

The phosphatidic materials isolated by Anderson and co-workers from the acid-fast bacilli differ from the usual phosphatides in that an organic base seems to be lacking. Bloch (1936, 1936a) has presented evidence which relates these compounds to the phosphatidic acids.

The inositol-containing phosphatides have been found not only in soybeans but also in animal sources such as nerve tissue and in brain. These, however, are not yet well characterized, and there is no assurance of the identity of the products from the two sources.

The supposedly water-soluble phosphatides from plant sources have already been mentioned (see p. 55).

The fatty acids of phosphatides from plant sources are varied and provide subject matter for profitable study. Thus Anderson and co-workers isolated from the phosphatides of acid-fast bacteria certain saturated, branched-chain, liquid acids chief of which are tuberculostearic and phthioic acids. The structure of the former has been determined as 10-methylstearic acid, and thus it has been shown to defy convention by possessing an uneven number of carbon atoms. The structure of the latter acid is still questionable. However, it possesses the important physiological property of inducing cell-proliferation with the formation of typical tuberculous lesions. In this regard it is interesting to note that yeast phosphatides are characterized by relatively simple fatty acids, although yeast is likewise an organism of low order. These acids are discussed in detail later in the chapter.

Aside from this work, systematic investigations of the fatty acids of plant phosphatides, especially of a quantitative nature, are lacking with the exception of the work of Hilditch and co-workers on the fatty acids of oil-seed phosphatides (see p. 219). In general, it may be said that the fatty acid composition of plant phosphatides corresponds qualitatively to the fatty acid composition of the related glycerides. The chief exception arises from the fact that the phosphatides may contain a greater variety of unsaturated acids. Thus highly unsaturated C_{20} and C_{22} acids have been found in the phosphatides but not in the glycerides of materials such as sunflower seeds. Likewise, in cocksfoot grass and in *Hevea* latex the fatty acids of the phosphatides are more unsaturated than those of the glycerides. Also, hexadecenoic acid, which is rare in glycerides, has been found in phosphatides.

As would be expected, palmitic acid is the most predominant saturated acid. Stearic acid is usually present to a lesser extent and arachidonic acid has also been reported. Oleic acid is almost universally present, although Smith and Chibnall (1932) and Channon and Chibnall (1927) could not find it in the phosphatides of cocksfoot grass or cabbage. Oleic together with linoleic acid are the chief unsaturated components, and the latter often predominates. Linolenic acid may also be present, especially in phosphatides derived from drying oil sources. Rapeseed phosphatides have been reported to contain a large quantity of erucic acid.

Quantitative data on the phosphatide content of plants are meager, as indicated above, because of the difficulty involved in isolation. Generally, the usual procedure of extracting the lipides with alcohol or an alcohol-containing solvent mixture is followed. Thereafter the solvent is removed, and the residue is extracted with ether. The phosphorus content of the ether extract is taken as an index of the phosphatide content. However, this phosphorus content very often varies with the source and the history of the material. Furthermore, if the work has not been conducted with the utmost of care, the phosphorus may not all be lipide in nature. Conversely, because of complex formation, all the lipide phosphorus may not have been extracted. Finally, the multiplication of the phosphorus content by an arbitrary factor in order to convert it into phosphatide content is a source of inconsistency, since all investigators have not used the same factor. Data, especially for correlative purposes, would be of greater value if expressed in terms of lipide phosphorus. Thus, practically all of the phosphatide contents found in the literature are subject to some error, and this should be borne in mind when attempting to draw conclusions and arrive at generalizations.

Finally, the point must be stressed that the reported phosphorus and nitrogen contents of some plant phosphatides are so much lower than theoretical that very little can be concluded about the nature of the phosphatides.

The very early literature concerning plant phosphatides has been reviewed by Czapek (1913, pp. 763–783).

CHAPTER XIV

PHOSPHATIDES OF MICROORGANISMS AND
LOWER PLANTS

BACTERIA

Bacteria, particularly those which are acid-fast, contain large amounts of lipides (up to 40 per cent), a portion of which is practically always in the form of phosphatides. The total amount as well as the composition of the lipides has been found to vary markedly with the composition of the growth medium and particularly with its carbohydrate content (Cramer, 1893; Lyons, 1897; Dawson, 1919), the age of the culture, and the strain and virulence of the organism. The method of extraction likewise influences the results, for although simple extraction removes most of the lipides, there are some which are closely associated with the cell membranes and with other cell constituents. For complete extraction these associations must first be broken by alkali or acid, after which the lipides are available for removal by ordinary fat solvents.

Typical of the early researches on bacterial lipides is the work of Nishimura (1893). The most important contributions to the field have been made by R. J. Anderson and his associates in numerous publications to which reference will be made later. Chargaff (1933, p. 92), who was a member of Anderson's school, has presented an excellent outline in Abderhalden's treatise of the means by which bacterial lipides may be isolated and fractionated. It is unfortunate that lack of well correlated work on the phosphatides from many other sources prevents the accumulation of similar well outlined procedures of technique.

Bacterial phosphatides, unlike those from some of the higher vegetable sources, have low iodine numbers and are characterized by the absence of highly unsaturated fatty acids.

Enteric Bacilli

Nicolle and Allilaire (1909) found that 9 to 16 per cent, on a dry basis, of some enteric bacteria grown on potato agar was lipide material. Although positive tests for phosphorus pointed to the presence of phosphatides, they did not investigate their extracts further.

Eckstein and Soule (1931) grew the enteric bacillus, *Escherichia coli*,

196

on a synthetic medium containing alanine in one case and the sulfur-containing cystine in the other. In the former case the lipide content amounted to 7.8 per cent of the dry cells, whereas in the latter case it amounted to only 3.6 per cent. Likewise, in the former case 17.4 per cent of the lipide material was phosphatides, whereas only traces of phosphatides were obtained from the latter product. Since the iodine number of the total lipides was low (25.6 and 31.0) and since no solid bromides could be obtained from the fatty acids, the authors assumed that there were no fatty acids present more highly unsaturated than oleic.

An interesting study was carried out by Williams, Bloor and Sandholzer (1939) on nine strains of gram-negative enteric bacilli which included *E. coli, E. communior, E. aerobacter,* and *Shigella paradysenteriae.* The lipides were extracted by hot ethanol and ether, and the oxidative method of Bloor (1928) was used for determining the phosphatides. The total lipide content of the organisms varied from 4.3 to 7.9 per cent of the dry weight. Phosphatides represented about 60 per cent of these bacterial lipides, varying from 4.4 to 5.7 per cent of the total weight of the organism. The nitrogen-phosphorus ratios were determined in each case. In one sample, which was isolated from a strain of *E. coli,* nitrogen was lacking entirely just as it is in the phosphatides of tubercle and related bacilli. In the other cases, the phosphorus content was somewhat lower than theoretical, whereas the nitrogen content was somewhat higher. The nitrogen-phosphorus ratio, however, approximated 1 for the most part. The iodine numbers of the fatty acids of the total lipides varied from 42 to 82, whereas the iodine values for the fatty acids of the phosphatides varied from 32 to 86. Generally, however, the iodine numbers were low, indicating the absence of highly unsaturated acids. The structures of the acids present were not determined.

Williams, Sandholzer and Van Voorhis (1940) found that both the phosphatide and nucleoprotein fractions of *E. coli* incorporated radioactive phosphorus which was present in the culture medium.

Phytomonas Tumefaciens

Chargaff and Levine (1936, 1938) studied the lipide fraction of *Phytomonas tumefaciens,* an organism which causes a certain type of abnormal tissue elaboration in plants which is known as crown gall disease. Such an investigation was important in order that the lipides might be compared with those from the tubercle bacillus. In this case the phosphatides were shown to consist of lecithin and phosphatidylaminoethyl alcohol since choline and aminoethyl alcohol were found among the hydrolysis products. Thus they are normal phosphatides, unlike those of the tubercle bacillus. It is interesting to note, however, that here, as with the tubercle bacillus, high molecular weight liquid, saturated, fatty acids were present which presumably possessed branched-chain structures and, together with the phosphatide fraction, were responsible for the physiological activity.

The total lipides constituted 7.0 to 8.1 per cent of the dry bacteria, whereas 1.6 to 3.2 per cent of the bacteria was phosphatides. The phosphatides had a nitrogen-phosphorus ratio close to 1 and on hydrolysis yielded fatty acids with an iodine number of 35.8. The acetone soluble fat, on the other hand, had an iodine value of 108.5 and contained besides stearic, palmitic and oleic acids, higher acids which were both saturated and unsaturated. Ordinarily, the more unsaturated acids are found in the phosphatide fraction, particularly in animal sources.

Geiger and Anderson (1939) carried out a similar study in which the phosphatides were examined more thoroughly. They found, as might be expected, that the lipide content varied with the composition of the media upon which the bacteria were grown. Thus, the bacteria from a glycerol-containing medium yielded only 2 per cent lipides of which about 44 per cent was phosphatides. When the medium contained sucrose, the lipide content rose to 6 per cent of which 64 per cent was phosphatides. The isolation procedures were similar to those of Chargaff and Levine (1936, 1938), save that the alcohol-ether extracted bacteria were extracted further with chloroform to obtain still more lipide material. Acidic hydrolysis of the phosphatides yielded glycerophosphoric acid, fatty acids, choline and aminoethyl alcohol, the quantities of the bases indicating that lecithin and phosphatidylaminoethyl alcohol were present in approximately equal quantities. The media used for growth of the bacteria seemed also to influence the fatty acid composition of the phosphatides. From the phosphatide grown on the glycerol medium, there was obtained a fraction of liquid acids with an iodine number of 34, whereas a similar fraction from the phosphatides grown on a sucrose medium possessed an iodine value of 76. In the former case, there was present a small amount of unsaturated acid which was probably chiefly oleic, together with a large amount of liquid saturated acids of high molecular weight. In the latter case the situation was reversed. Similar liquid saturated fatty acids had been found in the glyceride portion of the lipides by Chargaff and Levine (1938).

The acetone-soluble fat was found by Velick and Anderson (1944) to contain palmitic acid, unsaturated acids which yielded chiefly stearic acid and a small amount of palmitic acid on reduction, and phytomonic acid, a liquid saturated acid whose probable empirical structure was $C_{20}H_{40}O_2$.

Timothy Bacillus

The phosphatides of the nonpathogenic timothy bacillus, *Mycobacterium phlei*, were investigated by Chargaff, Pangborn and Anderson (1931) and Pangborn and Anderson (1931). This bacterium is acid-fast and resembles the tubercle bacillus. In general, the timothy bacillus contains less lipides than the tubercle bacillus, but the character of the lipides from each is quite similar. The phosphatides amounted to 0.59 per cent of the bacillus, which is a considerably lower percentage than was found in the various tubercle bacilli. The phosphatides contained 2.80 per cent phosphorus and 0.22 per cent nitrogen. This low nitrogen content is typical of the phosphatides of acid-fast bacteria.

Acidic hydrolysis yielded fatty acids, glycerophosphoric acid, and various carbohydrate-like materials. The fatty acids were separated into a solid and a liquid portion, the former consisting almost entirely of palmitic acid, and the latter containing unsaturated acids which on reduction yielded what was probably a mixture of palmitic and stearic acids. In the liquid portion, likewise, there was a saturated liquid acid whose structure was not determined, but which was similar in physical properties to the liquid saturated fatty acids isolated from the bovine and the avian tubercle bacillus.

The acetone-soluble fat was not a glyceride since no glycerol resulted on hydrolysis (Pangborn, Chargaff and Anderson, 1932). The hydroxyl-containing material which was probably a carbohydrate was not identified in this case. This absence of a true glyceride is characteristic of the acetone-soluble lipides of the tubercle bacillus. The fatty acids of the acetone-soluble lipide included palmitic acid, an optically active hydroxy acid, C_{16} unsaturated acids which yielded palmitic acid on reduction, and a liquid fatty acid similar to tuberculostearic acid.

Lactobacillus Acidophilus

The phosphatides of *Lactobacillus acidophilus* were studied by Crowder and Anderson (1934). The lipides were extracted in the usual manner with ethanol-ether and comprised about 7 per cent of the dry material. The phosphatides were precipitated with acetone from an ether solution of the lipides and were purified by many reprecipitations. The phosphatides comprised about 32 per cent of the lipide fraction and possessed a very low phosphorus content (1.42 per cent) due to the presence of about 21 per cent carbohydrate material, calculated as glucose. Acidic hydrolysis yielded glycerophosphoric acid, fatty acids and choline together with the above-mentioned carbohydrate which proved to be a polysaccharide. Although the amount of choline isolated accounts for only a small part of the total nitrogen, no aminoethyl alcohol was found. The fatty acids were divided into solid and liquid fractions. The former contained palmitic and stearic acids, a trace of an acid lower than palmitic, and a higher acid which was probably a tetracosanic acid. The liquid fraction contained unsaturated C_{16} and C_{18} acids which on reduction yielded palmitic and stearic acids together with an unidentified acid which gave an ether-soluble lead salt.

Bacillus Albolactis

The lipides of *Bacillus albolactis* were investigated by Verna (1935). From the bacteria grown on a glucose medium, he isolated 24 per cent lipides on a dry basis, whereas from bacteria grown on lactose medium he obtained 14.6 per cent lipides. The phosphatide contents were only 0.2 and 0.06 per cent, respectively.

Diphtheria Bacillus

The lipides of the diphtheria bacteria were isolated by Chargaff (1931, 1933b) according to the standard procedure of ethanol-ether extraction. From an ether solution of the lipides, which comprised about 4 per cent of the bacteria, the phosphatides were isolated by precipitation with ethyl acetate. From 293 grams of dry bacteria, 1.17 grams of phosphatide (0.41 per cent) was isolated with a phosphorus content of 1.42 per cent, a nitrogen content of 0.8 per cent and a nitrogen-phosphorus ratio of approximately 1. Acid hydrolysis of the phosphatides indicated an association with carbohydrates and with an unidentified high molecular weight material. Despite the relatively high nitrogen content, which may have been due to impurities, an organic base was present only as a trace, if at all. Palmitic acid was the only solid acid whereas the liquid acids, which had an iodine number of 92.6 and an equivalent weight of 471, contained an acidic material which analyzed approximately for $C_{50}H_{100}O_4$. This was given the name "corynin".

Calmette-Guérin Bacillus

Chargaff (1933a) also investigated the lipides of the Calmette-Guérin bacillus and found them to exist in greater quantity than the lipides of the tubercle bacillus. The phosphatide fraction had a nitrogen-phosphorus ratio of 1:1.8, although a nitrogenous base was not identified. The chief acid of the phosphatides was palmitic and there was close association with a carbohydrate which was probably d-mannose. A liquid acid with 21 carbon atoms and an iodine number of 13 was isolated together with other impure, high molecular weight, low-melting acids.

Chargaff and Schaefer (1935) found that only the phosphatide portion of the lipides of the Calmette-Guérin bacillus was antigenic, and they

believe that this property is inherent in the phosphatides and is not due
to an impurity.

Turtle and Smegma Bacilli

Chargaff (1931a) investigated the lipide content of the nonpathogenic,
acid-fast turtle and smegma bacteria. The phosphatide of the turtle
bacillus, which made up 2.0 per cent of the dry bacteria, contained 3.16
per cent phosphorus and 0.39 per cent nitrogen. Thus, in its low nitrogen
content it resembled the phosphatides of the tubercle bacillus. Evidence
for the presence of the high molecular weight liquid saturated acids
characteristic of the lipides of the tubercle bacillus was found in the
acetone-soluble fat, which was partly glyceride and partly the fatty
acid ester of a carbohydrate.

The lipides of the smegma bacteria, which are found in the fat secretions of saprophytes, were found to be very similar, except that the phosphatide content was higher (4.0 per cent), and the acetone-soluble fat
content was lower (7.1 per cent). The phosphatide contained 2.36 per
cent phosphorus and 0.39 per cent nitrogen.

Leprosy Bacillus

Mycobacterium leprae, the organism associated with leprosy, was investigated by Uyei and Anderson (1932) and Anderson and Uyei (1932).
The extraction procedure developed for the tubercle bacillus was employed here. The bacteria consisted of 18.7 per cent lipides, the phosphatides constituting 2.3 per cent of the organism on a dry basis. The
phosphatide contained a high ash content, 1.75 per cent phosphorus and
practically no nitrogen.

This phosphatide was unexpectedly resistant to hydrolysis, unlike the
phosphatides from other acid-fast bacteria. For complete hydrolysis it
was necessary to employ alkali. The chief saturated solid acid was found
to be palmitic, although a small amount of an unidentified high molecular
weight, saturated fatty acid was found which had not been previously
noted in other acid-fast bacteria. The unsaturated fatty acids on reduction yielded palmitic and stearic acids. In addition, there was obtained
an optically inactive acid which was similar to or perhaps even identical
with tuberculostearic acid. The presence of glycerophosphoric acid was
demonstrated. Likewise, there was close association with a polysaccharide
which on acidic hydrolysis yielded mannose, inositol and a reducing
hexose which was probably invert sugar or fructose.

Comparison of the phosphatides of the tubercle bacilli with those of
other acid-fast bacteria discussed above are given in Tables I, II, and III
(see pp. 204, 206).

Tubercle Bacillus

It was observed by early investigators (Hammerschlag, 1889; Auclair and Paris, 1907, 1908; Baudran, 1906; Kresling, 1901; Aronson, 1910; Bürger, 1916; Goris, 1920) that the lipides extracted with ether from tubercle bacilli contained phosphorus. Accordingly, they postulated and in some instances actually proved the presence of phosphatides. Agulhon and Frouin (1919) described a phosphatide preparation which on hydrolysis yielded fatty acids, glycerophosphoric acid and a base analogous to choline. Carbohydrate was also present. The reference to the base was undoubtedly inaccurate. Koganei (1922) isolated material from tubercle bacilli which he identified incorrectly. The report of Hecht (1935) that the hydrolysis products of the phosphatides of human and bovine tubercle bacilli yielded choline chloroplatinate is also belied by the more extensive work of Anderson.

In the work of Anderson and his co-workers, the lipides of the bacilli were shown to be present to the extent of 20 to 40 per cent and to consist of a mixture of wax, esters and phosphatides in addition to some unsaponifiable matter. However, inexplicably enough, no sterols have ever been found in the lipides of the tubercle bacillus. Anderson's material was grown on Long's synthetic medium under controlled conditions capable of duplication.

The lipides of the tubercle bacillus are quite different from those isolated from higher plants or animals. The acetone-soluble fat contains fatty acid esters of trehalose, whereas the phosphatides, as has been noted, contain no identifiable nitrogenous constituent. A large proportion of the lipides are waxy materials which cannot be discussed here, but which have been excellently reviewed by Anderson (1941). Carbohydrates are closely associated with the lipides and are invariably found in the alcohol-ether extract of the lipides. In addition, the bacillus, together with other acid-fast bacteria, contains certain ether-soluble constituents which are firmly "bound" in the cellular structure. These can be extracted by neutral solvent only after treatment of the bacillary masses with alkali and acid. These likewise are discussed by Anderson (1941). Furthermore, each of the lipide fractions is characterized by acids with a low degree of unsaturation, and by peculiar high molecular weight, branched-chain, liquid, saturated acids to which is attributed certain physiological action such as the formation of the characteristic lesions of tuberculosis. These will be discussed in detail later.

It must be borne in mind throughout the following discussion that not only the quantity of lipides but also the actual chemical constituents themselves vary with the composition of the culture medium, the strain of the bacteria and the age and virulence of the organism. Accordingly, the absolute percentage of lipides which is often given is meaningless unless accompanied by a description of the exact conditions employed in the investigation.

Isolation. The method for the extraction of the lipides and for the isolation of the phosphatides which was outlined by Anderson (1927) in his first paper on this subject has become general for this type of work, and has been used with slight modifications by many other investigators. Use of temperatures higher than 35 to 40° C. was avoided, whereas the possibility of oxidation was reduced by saturating all the solvents with carbon dioxide and by maintaining an atmosphere of carbon dioxide during all of the manipulations such as filtering or extracting.

The moist living bacilli were extracted with a mixture of ethanol and ether (1:1) by agitating the bacteria with this solvent for about four weeks. By this means the glycerides, phosphatides, polysaccharides, a small amount of wax and some basic material were extracted. The bacterial residue from this extraction was then extracted twice with chloroform by allowing digestion to proceed for four weeks in the first case and one week in the second case. By this means, most of the wax was extracted.

Removal of most of the solvent from the alcohol-ether extract yielded a suspension from which the lipide was extracted with ether. The aqueous residue contained carbohydrate material.

The ether solution on treatment with acetone yielded a gummy precipitate of crude phosphatide, whereas the supernatant liquid contained the glycerides. The phosphatides were purified by numerous reprecipitations from ether by means of acetone. In this way a product was obtained which contained 2.66 per cent phosphorus, and only 0.41 per cent nitrogen. In subsequent preparations products were obtained with as much as 3.5 per cent phosphorus. A strain of human tubercle bacilli was used in this instance and the purified material amounted to about 5 per cent of the dry bacilli.

The method for precipitation of the phosphatides proved to be quite important. If acetone was added to an ethereal solution of the phosphatides, a sticky mass resulted. If, however, the reverse procedure was employed, the product after drying was a white or straw-colored, nonhygroscopic powder. Like ordinary phosphatides, they formed colloidal solutions with water. Typical preparations darkened at 200° C. and melted to a dark brown liquid at 210° C. In addition to being soluble in ether, they dissolved readily in chloroform or benzene from which they could be precipitated by acetone, methanol or ethanol. Likewise, concentrated aqueous solutions were precipitated or coagulated by the addition of acids or salts. The phosphatides were found to be invariably associated with carbohydrates, and no claim to chemical purity in the ordinary sense can be made for them. Anderson (1940) summarizes his extraction results for acid-fast bacilli in Table I.

TABLE I. LIPIDE FRACTIONS OBTAINED FROM ACID-FAST BACILLI
(ANDERSON, 1940)

Type of organism	Human	Avian	Bovine	Timothy	Leprosy
No. of cultures	2000	2000	1700	1600	3000
Age of culture (weeks)	6	4	8	4	6
Phosphatide (%)	6.54	2.26	1.55	0.59	2.20
Acetone-soluble fat (%)	6.20	2.19	3.34	2.75	6.47
Total wax (%)	11.03	10.79	8.52	4.98	9.98
Total lipides (%)	23.78	15.26	13.40	8.37	18.70
Bacterial residue (grams)	2902.0	2942.7	3370.1	2783.1	3389.8
Bacterial mass per culture (grams)	1.928	1.757	2.318	1.982	1.488

Hydrolysis Products. The phosphatides in one of the early investigations were hydrolyzed by continued refluxing with 5 per cent sulfuric acid (Anderson, 1927a), after which the fatty acids were extracted from the aqueous mixture with ether. The water-soluble products, which comprised 33 to 40 per cent of the hydrolysate, contained what appeared to be glycerophosphoric acid and carbohydrate; and it was later shown that a portion of the phosphorus was present as a phosphorylated polysaccharide or glycoside (Anderson, Lathrop and Creighton, 1938). More recently, de Sütö-Nagy and Anderson (1947) have studied the phosphatides in the tubercle bacilli residues from the preparation of tuberculin. Here they found among the hydrolysis products glycerophosphoric acid, as well as complex carbohydrate phosphoric acids. No nitrogen-containing base was present, although it was possible to show that at least a portion of the small amount of nitrogen present existed as ammonia or as ammonium salts. It is entirely logical to assume, therefore, that nitrogen found in the elementary analyses was due to impurities from the culture medium. Thus it was immediately evident from Anderson's early work that the phosphatides of the tubercle bacillus differ from the phosphatides ordinarily isolated from plant and animal sources. The lack of nitrogen calls to mind the phosphatidic acids isolated from certain vegetables by Chibnall and Channon (1927), and as will be seen later, Bloch (1936a) has offered evidence that the phosphatides of the tubercle bacillus are actually salts of phosphatidic acids.

The fatty acids comprised 66 to 67 per cent of the phosphatides and possessed a very low iodine number of about 18. The chief saturated acid was palmitic and the chief unsaturated acid was oleic since it yielded stearic acid on reduction. In addition, there was an appreciable quantity of high molecular weight, liquid, saturated acids, some of which were optically active. These will be discussed in detail later.

Human Bacilli. Since all of the work indicated above had been carried out on an old strain of tubercle bacillus from humans, Crowder and co-workers (1936) studied for comparative purposes four different cultures of bacilli which had just been isolated from human cases of tuberculosis. Despite the fact that the bacteria were grown under identical conditions, and the same analytical procedures were employed for each, great variations were found in the amount of the lipide fractions and to some extent in their chemical constants. Thus the amount of phosphatide varied from 0.8 to 6.5 per cent. All the phosphatides, however, contained the characteristic low nitrogen content, and all yielded the same products on hydrolysis. It is interesting to note that the phosphorus content of the phosphatides from the new strains was somewhat higher (3.30 to 3.76 per cent) than that from the old strain (2.95 per cent).

The remarkable influence which the medium exerts on the lipides formed was shown by Creighton, Chang and Anderson (1944). The human strain of tubercle bacillus was grown on a medium in which the glycerol was replaced by dextrose. As would be expected, the lipide fraction increased considerably, and amounted to 30.6 per cent. Amazingly enough, no phosphatide whatsoever was found, the lipide fraction consisting of low melting wax and the esters of a carbohydrate.

Tuberculous Tissue. In an interesting study, Anderson and co-workers (1943) examined human tuberculous lung tissue for certain of the specific chemical compounds which were found repeatedly in human strains of tubercle bacilli grown on synthetic media. Not a trace of compounds such as phthioic acid, tuberculostearic acid, phthiocol, or the characteristic polysaccharides was found. That isolation was possible was proved by incorporating these compounds into lung tissue and again isolating them. Thus the tissue did not destroy them in any way. It is, of course, possible that different products are elaborated under synthetic conditions, or else that an insignificant number of bacilli are present in diseased lung tissue in relation to the infected area.

Avian Bacilli. For comparative purposes, the lipides of the avian type of tubercle bacillus were also investigated (Anderson and Roberts, 1930a, 1930b). Here the lipide constituents were found to be quite similar to those from the human type of bacillus, the chief difference arising from the fact that a smaller amount of total lipides was obtained by simple extraction.

Bovine Bacilli. By the above-outlined procedure Anderson and Roberts (1930c) investigated the lipides of the bovine type of tubercle bacilli. By extraction, 13.4 per cent lipides were obtained which were quite similar to those obtained from the human and the avian species. About 1.5 per cent of the bacillus was phosphatidic material. In the avian strain the phosphatides comprised 2.3 per cent of the bacillus, whereas the human strain consisted of 6.5 per cent phosphatides. The possible variations due to the age of the culture and the composition of the medium must, however, be borne in mind.

It was observed that the phosphatides from the bovine strain (Anderson and Roberts, 1930d) were considerably more resistant to hydrolysis than the previous preparations. From the mixture of water-soluble cleavage products which were contaminated by a mucilaginous substance not observed previously, there was isolated what appeared to be glycerophosphoric acid, mannitol and inactive inositol. The fatty acid portion of the hydrolysis products contained palmitic and oleic acids together with a liquid saturated acid which was optically inactive and which seemed to be similar to tuberculostearic acid which will be discussed later.

In Table II, Anderson (1940) has described the composition of the phosphatides isolated from acid-fast bacteria. Table III (Anderson, 1940) describes the fatty acid composition of these phosphatides.

TABLE II. COMPOSITION OF THE PHOSPHATIDES FROM ACID-FAST BACTERIA
(ANDERSON, 1940)

Strain of bacilli	Human	Bovine	Avian	Timothy	Leprosy
Melting point	210°	208°	210°	190°	231°
Phosphorus (%)	2.30	1.87	2.18	2.80	1.75
Nitrogen (%)	0.36	1.00	0.48	0.22	Trace
Water-soluble material (%)	33–34	43–44	46–47	40	38
Fatty acids (%)	66–67	55–57	55–56	60	62

TABLE III. FATTY ACID COMPOSITION OF PHOSPHATIDES FROM ACID-FAST
BACTERIA (ANDERSON, 1940)

Strain of bacilli	Human	Bovine	Avian	Timothy	Leprosy
Solid saturated acids, mainly palmitic (%)	30.5	26.7	16.7	20.0	24.8
Wax-like acids (%)	None	6.5	8.3	6.0	11.2
Liquid acids (%)	36.1	25.7	34.4	23.6	29.2
Iodine number of liquid acids	31.0	12.1	36.8	26.2	55.0
Solid reduced acids (%)	12.8	6.6	17.7	5.6	17.0
Liquid saturated acids (%)	20.9	15.5	16.7	18.0	10.8
Molecular weight of liquid saturated acids	313	306	303	380	295

Nature of the Phosphatides. The phosphatides of the tubercle bacillus isolated by Anderson and his co-workers were likewise investigated by Bloch (1936, 1936a). The phosphatide isolated by him was a solid, pulverizable substance which sintered at 90 to 100° C. and melted with decomposition at 150 to 200° C. It was entirely free of nitrogen and contained 2.2 per cent phosphorus and 0.8 per cent magnesium. Thus the ratio of phosphorus to magnesium was 1:0.47. By treating this phosphatide fraction with warm acetone he isolated an unsaponifiable substance which contained neither phosphorus nor nitrogen, and which was probably a wax alcohol. Also, he was able to dissociate from the phosphatide a carbohydrate which on hydrolysis appeared to yield mannose.

Bloch believed that the magnesium was organically bound to the phosphatide molecule. By the action of dilute hydrochloric acid under conditions which did not effect complete hydrolysis, he was actually able to remove the magnesium. This pointed strongly to the salts of phosphatidic acid; and it is entirely possible, on the basis of Bloch's work, that the phosphorus-containing lipides of the tubercle bacillus are salts of polyol phosphoric acids.

After removal of the magnesium, there resulted an oil which solidified on cooling. Bloch believed this to be impure phosphatidic acid. Accordingly, he dissolved it in ether and precipitated it as the lead salt. The salt had a phosphorus content slightly in excess of the theoretical, due possibly to low molecular weight, phosphorus-containing impurities. From the lead salt, however, he was able to obtain what he believed to be pure phosphatidic acid which contained the theoretical quantity of phosphorus. It was soluble in all fat solvents, acetone and alcohol, and was strongly acid to litmus. Its molecular weight by titration was 851 as compared to a theoretical value of 806, calculated from the hydrolysis products. The high molecular weight indicates the presence of certain of the high molecular weight acids isolated by Anderson.

Phosphatidic acids have, of course, been isolated from vegetable sources (Chibnall and Channon, 1927), which adds to the possibility of their presence elsewhere in the vegetable kingdom. However, the fact must be borne in mind that the glycerophosphoric acid group has not been found consistently in the phosphatides from the tubercle bacillus. Macheboeuf and Faure (1939) isolated from the tubercle bacillus what they believed to be phosphatidic acids. They obtained evidence that the glycerophosphoric acid is combined chemically with carbohydrates as well as with fatty acids.

Bloch (1936a) likewise studied the phosphatides from the bovine organism and was able to prepare a product with a phosphorus content of 3.2 per cent. This may have been purer than Anderson and Roberts' (1930d) product which contained only 1.9 per cent phosphorus.

Neutral Fat. The acetone-soluble fat of the tubercle bacillus, which was investigated extensively by Anderson and his co-workers (with Newman, 1933, 1933a; with Chargaff, 1929, 1929a; Burt and Anderson, 1931/32) proved to be a mixture of free fatty acids and neutral fat. It soon became apparent that the neutral fat was not a glyceride for, on hydrolysis, glycerol was never found. Instead, the water-soluble constituent in the case of the human strain proved to be the disaccharide, trehalose. This is likewise the case for the leprosy bacillus. Probably this same situation exists in the case of the avian and bovine strains of tubercle bacillus and in other acid-fast bacilli, although it has not yet been proved. It is indeed curious that organisms growing on a medium in which the chief source of carbon is glycerol should synthesize a complex carbohydrate such as trehalose with which to combine the fatty acids to form a neutral fat.

Fatty Acids. The fatty acids of the various lipide fractions of the tubercle bacillus are interesting and important because some of them possess the unique physiological property of causing the formation of typical tuberculous tissue (Sabin and Doan, 1927). Since the acetone-soluble fat was the most abundant, most of the studies were made on fatty acids from this source. Unquestionably, however, many of these acids are likewise components of the phosphatides, and as such, they merit discussion.

All of the lipide fractions isolated from the human strain of the tubercle bacillus, including the phosphatides, contained optically active mixtures of higher saturated fatty acids which are liquids under ordinary conditions (Anderson, 1927a, 1929, 1930, 1932). As would be expected, the lead salts of these acids are ether-soluble, thus providing a means for their isolation. In one investigation the methyl esters were prepared and fractionated (Anderson and Chargaff, 1929, 1929a). A low boiling fraction was obtained which on saponification yielded a liquid saturated acid which at first was believed to be isomeric with stearic acid. Accordingly, it was named "tuberculostearic acid". There was likewise a higher boiling fraction which will be discussed later.

Tuberculostearic acid was optically inactive. Likewise, it displayed no obvious physiological activity, although its presence was indicated in practically every lipide isolated from any strain of tubercle bacillus.

The structure of tuberculostearic acid was established through classical procedures by the excellent work of Spielman (1934). This same investigator likewise confirmed his structure by synthesis of the product. Although analytical values were usually too high, tuberculostearic acid was originally assumed to be isomeric with stearic acid because of the reluctance to attribute to a naturally occurring higher fatty acid a formula with an uneven number of carbon atoms. The existence of such a product is indeed a chemical rarity. Spielman (1934) first of all showed by determination of the neutral equivalent on highly purified samples, and by analysis of the free acid, the silver salt, the amide, and the tribromoanilide that the empirical formula was $C_{19}H_{38}O_2$ instead of $C_{18}H_{36}O_2$. This pointed immediately to a methylstearic acid, and after vigorous oxidation with chromic acid he isolated and characterized methyl-*n*-octyl ketone and azelaic acid. Likewise, caprylic acid was formed as a secondary oxidation product of the ketone. As the following equation indicates, these degradation products could result only from 10-methylstearic acid. Accordingly, this structure was attributed to tuberculostearic acid.

$$CH_3\text{-}(CH_2)_7\text{-}\underset{\underset{CH_3}{|}}{CH}\text{-}(CH_2)_8\text{-}COOH \xrightarrow{(O)} CH_3\text{-}(CH_2)_7\text{-}\underset{\underset{CH_3}{|}}{C}{=}O + HOOC\text{-}(CH_2)_7\text{-}COOH$$

$$CH_3\text{-}(CH_2)_6\text{-}COOH$$

The synthesis of the racemic form of the acid was accomplished through the intermediate 10-ketostearic acid by the following series of reactions:

$$CH_3\text{—}(CH_2)_7\text{—}ZnCl + ClCO(CH_2)_8\text{—}COOC_2H_5 \longrightarrow$$

$$CH_3\text{—}(CH_2)_7\text{—}CO\text{—}(CH_2)_8\text{—}COOH \longrightarrow Barium\ Salt \xrightarrow{CH_3MgI}$$

$$CH_3\text{—}(CH_2)_7\text{—}\underset{\underset{CH_3}{|}}{CH}(OH)\text{—}(CH_2)_8\text{—}COOH \xrightarrow[\substack{then \\ H_2,PtO_2}]{-H_2O} CH_3\text{—}(CH_2)_7\text{—}\underset{\underset{CH_3}{|}}{CH}\text{—}(CH_2)_8\text{—}COOH$$

Although the synthetic and the natural acids yielded identical derivatives and the same peculiar type of lead salt, they differed in melting point by 10°. This, Spielman pointed out, may well be due to the fact that the natural acid, despite its optical inactivity, may not be a racemic form, since certain optically active materials are known to have rotations too `small to measure. Resolution of the synthetic acid would, of course, offer a clue to this discrepancy.

Further evidence on this score was advanced by Velick (1944a), who studied the x-ray diffraction patterns of tuberculostearamide and of the synthetic, racemic 10-methylstearamide. His studies support the hypothesis that the natural acid is optically active despite its lack of optical rotation, and also support the structure of tuberculostearic acid as advanced by Spielman. This was confirmed definitely by Prout, Cason and Ingersoll (1948), who were able to synthesize both optical isomers of

10-methyloctadecanoic acid as well as the racemic mixture by an independent method. Spielman's initial hypothesis was shown to be accurate since the racemic mixture melted at 25.4 to 26.1° C., whereas the optical isomers melted at 13.0 to 13.5° C. and demonstrated a specific rotation of 0.05–0.09°. The synthetic optical isomers, when mixed, melted at 21.0 to 25.8° C. These synthetic isomers and their derivatives were compared with the natural tuberculostearic acid and its derivatives. From these comparisons it was concluded that the natural acid was levorotatory 10-methyloctadecanoic acid.

Still another synthesis of tuberculostearic acid has been reported recently by Schmidt and Shirley (1949), as indicated by the following series of reactions:

$$CH_3-(CH_2)_7-\underset{\underset{CH_3}{|}}{CH}-ZnCl \xrightarrow{C_2H_5OCO(CH_2)_7COCl} CH_3-(CH_2)_7-\underset{\underset{CH_3}{|}}{CH}-CO(CH_2)_7-COOC_2H_5$$

$$\xrightarrow{Zn, Hg, HCl} CH_3(CH_2)_7-\underset{\underset{CH_3}{|}}{CH}-CH_2(CH_2)_7-COOC_2H_5 \xrightarrow[C_2H_5OH]{NaOH}$$

$$CH_3-(CH_2)_7-\underset{\underset{CH_3}{|}}{CH}-(CH_2)_8-COOH$$

It was mentioned previously that in the earlier investigations (Anderson, 1929; Anderson and Chargaff, 1929, 1929a) an appreciable quantity of a still higher molecular weight liquid saturated acid was found. This contained at least 20 carbon atoms and was optically active. In addition, it possessed the interesting physiological property of inducing cell proliferation (Sabin, Doan and Forkner, 1930). Because of this property it was named "phthioic acid" (Anderson, 1931) from the Greek *phthio*, relating to phthisis or tuberculosis. This higher boiling fraction proved to be a mixture. By careful fractionation of the methyl esters (Anderson and Chargaff, 1929a), however, it was possible to isolate pure phthioic acid which possessed the empirical formula $C_{26}H_{52}O_2$, and thus was isomeric with cerotic acid. Various other similar acids have been found together with phthioic acid. These, however, seem to vary with the strain of bacteria, the composition of the media and other variables. Phthioic acid, nevertheless, has been found in practically every investigation; and it together with tuberculostearic acid may be considered characteristic of the lipides of the tubercle bacillus.

Spielman and Anderson (1936) prepared highly purified samples of phthioic acid by careful distillation of the methyl esters. They confirmed the empirical formula as a hexacosanic acid and established the melting point as 20 to 21° C. and the specific rotation as +12.56°. The determination of the structure of this acid was attempted by various techniques including the Barbier-Wieland degradation and vigorous oxidation. Although some evidence was obtained which would indicate the presence of methyl groups on the *alpha* and on the eleventh carbon atoms, the structure of phthioic acid remains yet to be determined. Cason and Sumrell (1950) have recently shed more light on the structure of phthioic acid. They believe that the acid present to the greatest extent in a phthioic acid fraction has 28 carbon atoms. Ultraviolet absorption indicates the presence of one double bond in the α,β position. There appear to be four terminal methyl groups, three of which may be at the α,β and γ positions.

In one investigation (Anderson, 1932), a levorotatory acid was isolated during the purification of phthioic acid. This material melted at 48 to 50° C. and indicated a composition which agreed approximately with the formula $C_{30}H_{60}O_2$. This acid was an irritant but did not possess cell-stimulating properties. Still other acids were found by Ginger and Anderson (1944) in the acetone soluble fat from an unidentified strain of tubercle bacillus grown for the production of tuberculin protein. From the methyl esters they obtained by careful fractionation not only phthioic acid, but also three other acids whose formulas correspond to $C_{24}H_{48}O_2$, $C_{25}H_{50}O_2$ and $C_{27}H_{54}O_2$. All were dextrorotatory, and analyses for C-methyl groups by the Kuhn-Roth procedure indicated the presence of at least three terminal methyl groups in each acid.

The bacterial residues from the manufacture of tuberculin provided an abundant source of phosphatides for fatty acid investigation (Peck and Anderson, 1941). The acids were isolated by distillation of the methyl esters. As would be expected from previous work, the solid saturated acids consisted mainly of palmitic acid with traces of stearic and mycolic acid. The chief unsaturated acid was oleic. The characteristic liquid saturated acids were also present, and tuberculostearic acid was readily isolated. However, no pure phthioic acid was found, although there were present some higher branched-chain dextrorotatory acids.

Various synthetic acids have been prepared with the intent of duplicating either the structure or the physiological activity of phthioic acid. (See, e.g., Stenhagen and Ställberg, 1941; Polgar and Robinson, 1943; Cason, 1942; Cason and co-workers, 1944; Cason and Prout, 1944; Chargaff, 1932; Birch and Robinson, 1942; Schneider and Spielman, 1942.) Various branched-chain acids have been prepared by Buu-Hoi and Cagniant (1943), who found that the physiological activity of α,α-dimethylmyristic acid, α,α-dimethylpalmitic acid and α,α-dimethylstearic acid was similar to that of phthioic acid.

Carbohydrates. The carbohydrates associated with the phosphatides of the tubercle bacillus have been investigated extensively. They are always present in the alcohol-ether extracts, and although their association with the lipides is very close, the exact nature of the bond is not known.

From the carbohydrate fraction obtained by hydrolysis of the phosphatides from the human tubercle bacillus, there was isolated mannose and inactive inositol (Anderson and Renfrew, 1930) together with a reducing sugar similar to invert sugar (Anderson and Roberts, 1930e). Inositol and mannose were likewise found in the aqueous portion of the hydrolysate of the phosphatides from the avian and bovine types.

Since prolonged boiling with acid was necessary before reducing sugars appeared, it seemed fairly certain that the reducing sugars were present originally in firm chemical combination. Thus on basic hydrolysis of the phosphatide fraction from the human strain of tubercle bacillus (Anderson and Roberts, 1930), there resulted a complex organic phosphoric acid which yielded a reducing sugar on hydrolysis. In addition, there was a neutral carbohydrate which on acidic hydrolysis yielded inositol, mannitol and phosphoric acid. Later work (Anderson, Lathrop and Creighton, 1938) showed that this latter carbohydrate, which was given the name "manninositose phosphoric acid", could be hydrolyzed with ammonia to phosphoric acid and a glycoside which was named "manninositose". This latter product on acidic hydrolysis yielded two moles of mannose and one mole of inositol.

The former carbohydrate proved to be a glyceroldiphosphoric acid to which mannose was linked, probably through the free hydroxyl. This product yielded a water-insoluble lead salt.

Surprisingly enough, the carbohydrates associated with the phosphatides from bacillary residues which result from tuberculin manufacture did not yield cleavage products identical to those of the carbohydrates obtained from the live bacteria (Anderson, Peck and Creighton, 1940). The carbohydrates may have changed in some way during the production of the tuberculin; or else the bacillus, influenced by the composition of the medium, may be capable of synthesizing various carbohydrates. This, however, is a good example of the difficulties and inconsistencies with which the systematic investigator in this difficult field must cope.

Chargaff and Anderson (1930) later found in the carbohydrate fraction obtained by alkali saponification of the total crude lipides of the tubercle bacilli a polysaccharide or mixture of polysaccharides which on acidic hydrolysis yielded mannose, inositol, d-arabinose, and d-galactose. The authors point out that the occurrence of d-arabinose is noteworthy, since it is usually the l-isomer which occurs naturally.

Gough (1932) isolated the carbohydrate from the human tubercle bacillus and found that on hydrolysis it yielded mannose, d-arabinose and galactose. In addition, there resulted a mixture of acids which on prolonged hydrolysis partially lose their acidic nature and yield mannose. It was possible that some glycolic acid was also present.

Phthiocol. A discussion of Anderson's work would not be complete without mention of the pigment phthiocol (Anderson and Newman, 1933a, 1933b) which was isolated from the human strain of tubercle bacillus. This possessed the structure 2-methyl-3-hydroxy-1,4-naphthoquinone, and was synthesized by several procedures (Anderson and Newman, 1933b; Newman, Crowder and Anderson, 1934; Anderson and Creighton, 1939). It has since been shown to possess Vitamin K activity.

VIRUSES

Although the chemistry of viruses is still obscure, it is well established that they consist largely of nucleoprotein. The larger ones show certain resemblances to the bacterial cell in that they may contain lipides, polysaccharides and even enzymes. Both Weineck (1940) and Boivin (1940) have observed the presence of lipides in viruses, and other investigators (Lauffer and Stanley, 1944; Taylor, 1944) have reported close to 1 per cent phosphorus in various viruses.

Although the lipides may be impurities, it was shown by McFarlane and McFarlane (1939) that complete removal of the lipides, unlike the removal of cholesterol (Hoagland, Smadel and Rivers, 1940), inactivates vaccinia virus. This is strong evidence that the lipides are an integral part of the virus.

The lipides of vaccinia virus have been investigated by Smadel and Hoagland (1942) and by McFarlane and co-workers (1939). They found 1.4 per cent cholesterol, 2.2 per cent phosphatide, and 2.2 per cent neutral fat.

Taylor (1944) has shown that influenza virus contains about 1 per cent phosphorus, half of which is in the form of phosphatide and the remainder of which is associated with the protein. In swine influenza virus he found considerably less phosphatide. Elementary analysis of the phosphatides showed a nitrogen-phosphorus ratio of 2:1. In view of the small quantities of materials, however, this is probably not significant.

The role of the phosphatides in viruses is still unknown, although Hoagland (1943) raises the possibility that they may be present in the limiting membrane of the virus and may be involved in its osmotic responses.

FUNGI

Yeast

Phosphatides are probably components of many fungi. Francioli (1937) reported choline in many species of fungi, and it is not too unreasonable to believe that this material may arise, at least in part, from lecithin.

The phosphatides of yeast, which have been investigated more thoroughly than those of any other fungi, are somewhat less complex than those from other sources in that they possess fewer constituent fatty acids. Furthermore, highly unsaturated acids are not present and the iodine number of the fatty acids of the phosphatides is somewhat lower than the corresponding constant for the yeast glycerides.

Hoppe-Seyler (1879), Koch (1903), Austin (1924), Sedlmayr (1903) and Daubney and MacLean (1927) were among the first workers to investigate the phosphatides of yeast.

Newman and Anderson (1933) isolated the lipide material from living yeast cells by extraction with alcohol and ether. By this method, 6.0 per cent of the yeast, on a dry basis, proved to be lipides. By further extraction with alcohol containing 1 per cent hydrochloric acid they were able to isolate 0.86 per cent more lipides. The phosphatides were separated from the rest of the lipides by precipitation from ether by the addition of acetone. About 1.3 per cent of the yeast on a dry basis proved to be phosphatides. These were purified by repeated precipitation with acetone from ether solution and possessed a phosphorus content of 4.22 per cent and a nitrogen content of 1.78 per cent. Thus the nitrogen-phosphorus ratio was 1:1.07. Acid hydrolysis of this phosphatide mixture yielded glycerophosphoric acid, choline, aminoethyl alcohol, fatty acids and saturated hydrocarbons. In this work the presence of carbohydrates could not be shown. From the ratio of amino nitrogen to total nitrogen, the authors concluded that the ratio of lecithin to the cephalin fraction is about 4:1. The fatty acid fraction, which possessed an iodine number of 79.5, was separated into 14 per cent solid saturated acids, and 86 per cent liquid acids with an iodine number of 84.9. The saturated portion was composed of equal portions of palmitic and stearic acids, whereas the unsaturated portion consisted of oleic and palmitoleic acids as evidenced by the fact that catalytic reduction yielded a mixture of palmitic and stearic acids. The low iodine number probably precluded the presence of acids more highly unsaturated than oleic. A small amount of lauric acid was also present.

It is interesting to note that the acids which characterize the phosphatides of acid-fast bacteria such as tuberculostearic or phthioic are absent, and the phosphatides seem to be similar to those found in higher plant organisms.

In a later publication, Salisbury and Anderson (1936) separated the yeast phosphatides into lecithin and the cephalin fraction and gave directions for the preparation of the pure materials. Both products on hydrolysis yielded 64 per cent fatty acids of which 14 to 16 per cent were solid and 84 to 86 per cent were liquid in agreement with the previous work. The composition of the acids from both compounds was substantially the same, the solid acids consisting of 43 to 44 per cent palmitic and 56 to 57 per cent stearic, whereas the unsaturated acids on reduction yielded 58 to 63 per cent palmitic acid and 37 to 42 per cent stearic acid. One interesting difference that was observed was that the glycerophosphoric acid from the lecithin demonstrated optical activity indicating the presence of the α-isomer, whereas the same acid from the cephalin fraction was optically inactive.

Soden (1942) has reported that about 4.5 per cent of the non-spore forming yeast, *Torula utilis*, on a dry basis, is phosphatidic material. This yeast was also investigated by Diemair and Koch (1948) and by Dirr and Ruppert (1948). The latter workers reported the presence of 16 per cent saturated acids and 84 per cent unsaturated acids. The former were largely palmitic and stearic, whereas the unsaturated acids were largely oleic and linoleic acids in the ratio 3:1. Both choline and aminoethyl alcohol were present, and Diemair and Poetsch (1949) have shown that there is three times as much choline as aminoethyl alcohol. These latter workers have devised an adsorption procedure for the purification of the phosphatides.

Rewald (1943) investigated the phosphatide content of vinegar yeast, of ordinary dried brewer's yeast, of brewer's yeast which had been debittered by washing with weak alkali, and of brewer's yeast which had been autolyzed at 58° C. His procedure involved three extractions. The first was carried out with petroleum ether, the second with benzenealcohol (4:1) and the third with acidic alcohol. As would be expected, the second extraction produced the largest amount of phosphatides. These extractions yielded other lipide material which was separated from the desired substances by acetone extraction. His rather surprising results are indicated in Table IV.

TABLE IV. PHOSPHATIDE CONTENT OF DIFFERENT TYPES OF YEAST
(REWALD, 1943)

	Brewer's yeast	Vinegar yeast	Debittered yeast	Autolyzed yeast
Total extract (%)	2.97	7.73	4.79	7.00
Oil (%)	1.16	7.40	1.89	4.83
Phosphatides (%)	0.82	0.26	2.22	2.00

It is difficult to explain why vinegar yeast which has the highest lipide content should have the lowest phosphatide content. Vinegar yeast is, of course, unique in that it grows in a strongly acidic medium.

Obviously, the debittering process and the autolysis of the brewer's yeast serve to make the lipides which are there more available for extraction. The fact that there is still a high phosphatide content after autolysis would indicate that active lecithinases are not present.

The phosphorus content of some of these products was high, due either to the presence of nonrelated phosphorus-containing materials or else to glycerophosphates formed by decomposition of phosphatides.

By means of alcohol solubility, Rewald was able to determine in some cases that the ratio of lecithin to the cephalin fraction was of the order of 70:30. This is in fair agreement with the results of Newman and Anderson (1933). Seed phosphatides, on the other hand, very often contain a predominance of cephalin phosphatides.

The yeast-like organisms *Geotrichoides langeron* and *Geotrichoides talice* were investigated by Turpeinen (1936). In order to estimate fairly accurately the yield of lipide, the organisms were extracted with ether after they had been treated with hydrochloric acid to release any so-called "bound" lipides which might be present. The yield of lipides varied from 5.1 to 37.8 per cent on a dry weight basis, depending on the conditions of growth. These increased with the age of the culture, reaching a maximum when the sugar content of the medium was the lowest. Thus, in accord with other observers, it was noted that increased sugar content in the medium leads to increased lipide content in the organisms. The phosphatides constituted about 36 per cent of the total lipide fraction and possessed a nitrogen-phosphorus ratio of 1. Association with carbohydrates was noted. The fatty acids of the glycerides were found to consist of palmitic, stearic, oleic and linoleic acids and it may be expected that these were also present in the phosphatides.

Rewald (1930), by means of alcohol extraction, isolated the phosphatides from *Ost-Hefe* and from *Braasch-Hefe*. The former contained 1.3 per cent phosphatides on the basis of the fresh substance, whereas the latter contained 1.4 per cent. The former yielded 49.1 per cent fatty acids and the latter 58.0 per cent. These were not further investigated.

The presence of phosphatides in saké yeast was noted by Sagara (1930), whose assumption that sphingomyelin was present was probably incorrect.

MOLDS

The presence of phosphatides in molds has been noted by various investigators (Aso, 1900; Takata, 1929; Thomas, 1930). The first systematic investigation was undertaken by Strong and Peterson (1934) and by Woolley and co-workers (1935), who investigated the phosphatides of *Aspergillus sydowi*, a mold which grows readily and possesses a fairly high lipide content. In their study, the mold was extracted with ethanol or with ethanol-ether (1:1). An ether solution of the lipide material obtained in this way was then treated with a large volume of acetone to precipitate the phosphatides. In one case, magnesium chloride was used to aid in the precipitation. Purification was effected by the usual procedure of acetone precipitation to obtain products with a nitrogen-phosphorus ratio of nearly 1.

Acidic hydrolysis yielded glycerophosphoric acid, choline, aminoethyl alcohol and fatty acids. Thus the presence of both lecithin and phosphatidylaminoethyl alcohol was established. The chief unsaturated acid was oleic acid, although traces of a more unsaturated acid were present. Stearic and palmitic acids composed the saturated portion of the fatty acids. Approximately 0.4 to 0.7 per cent phosphatides was isolated. A much higher percentage of phosphatides was shown by Kroeker, Strong and Peterson (1935) to be present in *Penicillium aurantio-brunneum*.

Grafe and Magistris (1925) isolated phosphatide-like products from *Aspergillus oryzae* by dialysis.

PATHOGENIC FUNGI

Blastomyces Dermatiditis

The phosphatides and lipides of certain pathogenic fungi were investigated by Peck and Hauser (1938, 1939, 1940), who hoped to discover to which components pathogenicity might be attributed. Unlike the lipides of the tubercle bacillus, sterols were present and liquid saturated acids were lacking. They investigated first of all *Blastomyces dermatiditis* which was grown on a synthetic medium and which yielded 8.5 to 9 per cent lipides soluble in alcohol-ether and 0.5 to 0.7 per cent soluble in chloroform on a dry basis. Of this material, 24 to 34 per cent proved to be phosphatides which contained 3.89 per cent phosphorus and 1.78 per cent nitrogen and which on hydrolysis yielded 65 per cent fatty acids, 3.0 per cent unsaponifiables and 32.0 per cent water-solubles. The latter was a mixture of glycerophosphoric acid, choline and aminoethyl alcohol, proving the presence of both lecithin and phosphatidylaminoethyl alcohol. The fatty acids were separated into 12.4 per cent solid acids which were chiefly palmitic and stearic, and 52.6 per cent liquid acids which were shown to be oleic and linoleic acids. Similar acids were found in the neutral glycerides. The unsaponifiable material was carbohydrate in nature.

Monilia Albicans

Subsequently, these same investigators (Peck and Hauser, 1939) reported on the lipides of *Monilia albicans*. Using a similar method of extraction, they obtained from the dried cells 5.3 per cent lipides of which 3.4 per cent was phosphatides and 96.6 per cent a mixture of glycerides and ergosterol and other nonsaponifiable material. Because of the small quantity of phosphatides, the fatty acids and the nitrogenous bases resulting on saponification were not identified. Glycerophosphoric acid, however, was isolated and identified. The phosphatide possessed a nitrogen-phosphorus ratio of 1.2:1, the high nitrogen content resulting probably from impurities. A positive Molisch test indicated the presence of carbohydrate in the phosphatide.

The fatty acids of the glycerol esters consisted of palmitic, stearic, oleic and linoleic acids, and it may be assumed that these were likewise components of the phosphatide fraction.

More lipide material was obtained from *B. dermatiditis* than from *M. albicans*, due possibly to the differences in the conditions under which the two were grown. The phosphatides from the two organisms, however, seem comparable on the basis of the available data.

When the dried cells which had been extracted as described above were treated with hot acidic alcohol, still more phosphatide was obtained. This was obviously material which was closely associated with proteins or carbohydrates, and it is interesting to note that a considerably larger percentage of phosphatide was obtained by this means from *M. albicans* than from *B. dermatiditis*.

Complete extraction (Peck and Hauser, 1940) of the "bound" lipide material was accomplished in three steps which involved the use of boiling neutral alcohol, alcohol containing hydrolytic agents such as 1 per cent hydrochloric acid or 2 per cent potassium hydroxide, and finally ether which was used to extract the cells after they had been dissolved in hydrochloric acid. By this means, *B. dermatiditis* yielded 5.7 per cent more lipides and *M. albicans* 8.6 per cent more lipides. Only the boiling neutral alcohol served to extract more phosphatide which, however, was contaminated with carbohydrates.

CHAPTER XV

PHOSPHATIDES OF CEREALS, GRAINS, AND OIL-PRODUCING PLANTS

Introduction

All cereals, grains, and oil-producing plants contain phosphatides. The literature on this phase of phosphatide chemistry is not voluminous and is characterized, as is much of the literature on phosphorus-containing lipides, by inconsistencies and by conclusions drawn from the behavior of impure compounds. There is much room here for consistent and correlated research.

Much of this work has been done on the seeds of the various plants. The phosphatide content of seeds is generally low, and for the most part is less than 0.5 per cent of the total seed. As indicated previously, the pioneer work in the field of seed phosphatides was carried out by Levene and Rolf (1925, 1925a, 1926) on the soybean. Whereas it previously had been assumed that plant phosphatides were primarily lecithin, they were able to show the presence of the cephalin fraction and were able likewise to identify palmitic, stearic, oleic, linoleic and linolenic acids.

According to Lishkevich (1937a), the phosphatide content of the oil seeds which he investigated decreased in the following order: cottonseed, soybean, sunflower seed, flaxseed, castor bean, and peanut. The soybean is, of course, the largest commercial source of phosphatides, although a small amount of cottonseed phosphatides is also available commercially. According to Lishkevich (1937a), 52 to 76 per cent of the phosphorus in the above oil seeds is present as phytin, whereas 1.4 to 8.3 per cent is present as phosphatides.

When the oil is removed from seeds either by extraction or by mechanical means, most of the phosphatides are carried along with the oil. The sludge which sometimes forms when oils are allowed to stand is composed largely of phosphorus-containing lipides. Table V, taken from a review by Kaufmann (1941), indicates the quantities of phosphatides in crude oils from various vegetable sources. Naturally, no such value could be exact, for it varies with the history of the oil and especially with such factors as the species of plant from which it was derived, the method of extraction and the degree of refinement. The results serve only to show on a relative basis the amounts of phosphatides in various oils.

TABLE V. THE PHOSPHATIDE CONTENT OF VARIOUS OILS (KAUFMANN, 1941)

Oil	Phosphatide (%)
Barley	3.4–4.2
Soybean	Up to 3.2 (usually *ca.* 1.8)
Rye germ	1.3–4
Oat	1
Rice	0.5
Linseed	.3
Millet	.2
Rapeseed	.1
Sesame seed	.1
Wheat germ	.08–2
Cacao	.01

Soybeans

Phosphatide Content. Although the apparent phosphatide content of the soybean varies with the extraction procedure employed, it ranges in general from a minimum of 1.5 per cent to a maximum of 2.5 to 3.2 per cent, the latter figures comparing favorably with the phosphatide content of eggs which were formerly the source of commercial phosphatides. The quantitative estimation of soybean phosphatides is difficult. Nottbohm and Mayer (1932), who determined nitrogen, phosphorus and choline in various samples of commercial phosphatides from soybeans, showed that the value for the phosphatide content depended on which of these it was calculated from. The exact quantitative determination is complicated here as in other less well-investigated sources by the fact that the phosphorus of soybeans is distributed among phytins, nucleic compounds including phosphoproteins and nucleic acid derivatives, inorganic salts and phosphatides. Earle and Milner (1938), incidentally, have suggested a procedure for separating these compounds.

Likewise, the phosphatide content varies with the source of the soybean. Jamieson and McKinney (1935) found that the phosphatide content of soybeans from North Carolina and Virginia (2.0–3.8 per cent) was in general higher than that of soybeans from Illinois, Indiana and Ohio (2.0–2.9 per cent). Horel (1934) reported 1.5–2.0 per cent phosphatides in Czechoslovakian soybeans, whereas a sample of German soybeans (Riede and Rewald, 1930) was reported to contain 1.0–2.5 per cent phosphatides. Webster (1928) reported a study in which soybeans were analyzed for total phosphorus, phytin and phosphatide phosphorus.

Practically all the phosphorus content of the oil is derived from the phosphatides, whereas these are present in the seed portion only in minute quantities. Belozerskiï and Kornov (1937) found the oil droplets of the embryos of soybeans to contain 3.2 per cent phosphatides, whereas the oil droplets of the cotyledons contained 2.1 per cent. Rewald (1929c) found that five-week-old soybean plants had practically the same amount of total phosphatide as the original bean, and that the green parts of the plant had the largest portion of the phosphatide, the roots and cotyledons having only a small amount.

Complex Formation. In the soybean, the phosphatides are found in union with other substances. This is readily demonstrated by the fact that hydrocarbon solvents extracted only a maximum of 0.55 per cent phosphatides from raw soybeans (Bredemann and Kummer, 1934). At least some of the phosphatides exist as a protein complex (Grafe and Ose, 1927) just as they do in most other natural sources. These yield to the dissociating influence of alcohol. Other phosphatides are combined with the carbohydrates of the soybean in a complex which dissociates only partially under the influence of alcohol.

Carbohydrates occur in soybeans as complex mixtures of cellulose, glycosides, pentosans, hexosans, free di- and polysaccharide sugars, and probably still in other forms which may possibly include starch. The complexity of the mixtures has so far precluded for the most part the isolation and identification of pure carbohydrates. Likewise, relatively little is known about the percentage of carbohydrates in soybeans. Winterstein and Hiestand (1908) reported the presence in soybean phosphatides of up to 25 per cent of a polysaccharide comprised of glucose, galactose, pentose and methylpentose. Piper and Morse (1923, p. 109) have stated that the carbohydrate content of the entire bean is 22 to 29 per cent. Shollenberger and Goss (1945) have found 6 to 8 per cent carbohydrates in soybean phosphatides. It has been reported (Iwasa, 1937; Okano, Ohara and Kato, 1936) that soybean phosphatides are associated with sugars such as glucose, fructose, galactose, rhamnose, arabinose, glucuronic acid, sucrose and stachyose. Rewald (1929a), however, showed rather conclusively that the monosaccharides do not occur as such in association with the phosphatides, but result from hydrolysis during isolation. Thus soybean phosphatide emulsions under conditions which eliminated hydrolysis gave negative tests for reducing sugars. Hydrolysis yielded chiefly glucose.

From a so-called purified soybean cephalin fraction, Klenk and Sakai (1939) isolated, after hydrolysis, inositol and the brucine salt of inositol monophosphoric acid together with other phosphoric acid esters. This, however, indicates the difficulty involved in the separation of phosphatides from carbohydrates and carbohydrate-like substances. Indeed, this would be expected from the complex nature of the carbohydrates and from the similarity of their solubility relations in water, alcohol, acetone and other organic solvents to those of the phosphatide.

There has been reported (McKinney, Jamieson and Holton, 1937) a phosphatide beta-glucoside complex, the glucoside consisting of a monosaccharide in combination with a dibasic dihydroxy acid. This work would imply that a chemical combination exists between the carbohydrate and the phosphatide, as would the observation of older investigators that it is necessary to boil the complex with 5 per cent sulfuric acid for several hours in order to effect dissociation. Rewald (1929a, 1936b, 1937), however, believes that the carbohydrate-phosphatide complex is not a chemical union since it yields to the dissociating influence of the proper solvents. Thus, when an aqueous suspension of the complex is treated with trichloroethylene or methylene chloride, the phosphatide enters the organic phase, whereas the carbohydrates remain in the aqueous phase.

Actually, the chemical history of the complexes under discussion must be the same before definite conclusions can be drawn concerning the chemical state of the carbohydrate. There is undoubtedly true chemical combination with the carbohydrates in the inositol-containing phosphatides isolated from soybeans by Klenk and Sakai (1939), Woolley (1943) and Scholfield and co-workers (1948, see p. 36).

Fatty Acids. The fatty acids of soybean phosphatides were first investigated extensively by Levene and Rolf (1925, 1925a, 1926), who showed that there were present palmitic, stearic, oleic, linoleic and linolenic acids. The low proportion of saturated fatty acids serves to distinguish soybean phosphatides from egg phosphatides, for the iodine number of the former lies between 90 and 100 whereas the iodine number of the latter rarely exceeds 65. Suzuki and Nishimoto (1930) found in the cephalin fraction of soybeans about 50 per cent stearic acid and a mixture of approximately equal parts of linoleic and linolenic acids. Belozerskiĭ and Kornov (1937) isolated from soybean lecithin oleic, linoleic and linolenic acids and found the latter two acids to be present in greater amounts in the lecithin from the cotyledon than in the lecithin from the embryo.

Hilditch and Pedelty (1937) likewise studied the fatty acids of soybean phosphatides. Their work indicates that the phosphatides contain all of the fatty acids present in the glycerides, although there is a higher proportion of saturated acids in the phosphatides than in the glycerides. These investigators divided the phosphatides into alcohol-soluble and alcohol-insoluble fractions which approximate lecithin and the cephalin fraction, respectively. These are not, of course, to be considered pure samples by any means. Their results are indicated in Table VI. The authors indicated that the alcohol-soluble fraction oxidized rapidly, for which reason the analyses may not be entirely accurate.

TABLE VI. THE FATTY ACIDS OF SOYBEAN PHOSPHATIDES (HILDITCH AND
PEDELTY, 1937)

Acid	Alcohol-insoluble		Alcohol-soluble	
	Weight (%)	Mole (%)	Weight (%)	Mole (%)
Palmitic	11.7	13.1	17.3	18.6
Stearic	4	4	—	—
Arachidic	1.4	1.3	—	—
Hexadecenoic	8.6	9.6	5.5	6
Oleic	5.5	5.7	19	18.5
Linoleic	63.3*	61.5	53	52
Linolenic	—	—	3.7	3.6
C_{20} Unsaturated	5.5	4.8	1.5	1.3

* Includes small amounts of linolenic acid, not over 4% of total fatty acids.

Thornton, Johnson and Ewan (1944) isolated practically pure lecithin from commercial soybean phosphatides and determined the fatty acid composition. They likewise found a higher percentage of saturated acids in the phosphatide than in the glyceride. Their results are indicated in Table VII.

TABLE VII. THE FATTY ACIDS OF SOYBEAN LECITHIN (THORNTON, JOHNSON, AND EWAN, 1944)

Acid	Weight (%)
Palmitic	15.77
Stearic	6.30
Arachidic	0
Oleic	12.98
Linoleic	62.92
Linolenic	2.02

Phosphatide Distribution. The change in the phosphatide content of the soybean plant during ripening has been investigated by various workers (Rewald and Riede, 1933; Duftschmid and Halden, 1942; Halden and Hinrichs, 1942). Apparently, the phosphatide content of the roots, stems, leaves and pods decreases during maturation, whereas the phosphatide content of the bean does not change appreciably during ripening.

Lee and Li (1938) studied the distribution of total phosphorus, lipide phosphorus and acid-soluble phosphorus in the germinating soybean. They found that the lipide phosphorus in the total seedling and in the cotyledon decreased rapidly at the beginning of the germination, and the total amount actually diminished. The amount in the embryo, however, which is the actively growing part, increased gradually. The total and acid-soluble phosphorus remained constant, although transference of these occurs from the cotyledons to the embryo.

Wheat and Wheat Products

Phosphatide Content. The presence of phosphatides in wheat and wheat products was recognized by various early investigators (Schulze and Steiger, 1889; Schulze and Frankfurt, 1894; Bitte, 1894), who reported the presence of about 0.6 per cent phosphatides in wheat, 1.6 per cent in bran (Schulze and Frankfurt, 1894), and 1.6 per cent in wheat germ (Frankfurt, 1896). Bernardini and Chiarulli (1909) found 0.4 per cent phosphatides in the wheat kernel, two-thirds of which was "combined". Thus the tendency of phosphatides to form complexes was recognized in these pioneer investigations. Winterstein and Smolenski (1909) and Smolenski (1909) were among the first to isolate phosphatides from wheat flour and wheat germ. The rather extensive early literature on this subject is reviewed by Nottbohm and Mayer (1934). The isolation and estimation of phosphatides of wheat is hampered here as it is in the case of soybeans and other vegetable sources by the fact that the phosphorus of wheat is distributed between phytin, nucleoprotein, phosphatides and inorganic salts. Furthermore, carbohydrate and protein complexes serve further to complicate the situation. Accordingly, the work of the early investigators is largely qualitative.

As late as 1940, Hanke (1940) criticized earlier methods for the determination of phosphatides in flour on the basis of incomplete extraction or extraction of phosphorus-containing substances other than lipides. He showed that varied experimental conditions could lead to a wide range of results. From this work, he evolved a so-called "normal" procedure for the analysis of phosphatides in flour and reported an average value from twenty-five determinations of 0.047 per cent lipide phosphorus in wheat flour. This would naturally vary with the history of the flour. Nottbohm and Mayer (1934) reported the average phosphatide content of six flour samples to be 1.4 per cent. For the grits or middlings, they found a value of 1.8 per cent. Sinclair and McCalla (1937) similarly determined the average phosphatide content of flour as 1.5 per cent. Geoffroy (1934) investigated the phosphatide content of flours milled from various portions of the wheat. He reported 0.2 per cent phosphatides in the flours from the center of the grain and from the median zone, and 0.3 per cent in the flour from the cortical zone. His results in view of the previous ones are low, although it is possible that the higher results are due to the presence of phosphorus-containing impurities. It must, however, be borne in mind that the phosphatide content of flour must perforce vary with the degree of extraction of the flour. Geoffroy's results were in accord with those of Glick (1945), who analyzed for the choline content of flour of various degrees of extraction. On the basis of a parallelism between the amount of choline which he found and the amount of lipide phosphorus reported by Sullivan and Near (1928), which is likewise low in the face of the above-cited results, Glick concluded that practically all the choline is present as lecithin. This of course does not preclude the presence of the cephalin fraction, which Rewald (1936a) found to be present to the extent of about 20 per cent.

The lipide phosphorus content of five samples of wheat was determined by Guerrant (1927) as 0.027 to 0.033 per cent. This is in agreement with Webster (1928), who reported 0.028 per cent lipide phosphorus. Knowles and Watkin (1932) analyzed for lipide phosphorus in nine stages during the development of the wheat plant from seven weeks before ear emergence until harvest. They found the value to be fairly constant (0.30 to 0.50 per cent P_2O_5, 0.065 to 0.11 per cent P) until the emergence of the ear. Thereafter there was a sharp decline, and the value remained constant (0.12 to 0.13 per cent P_2O_5, 0.026 to 0.028 per cent P) until maturity. They likewise analyzed for phytin and inorganic phosphorus and found, interestingly enough, that the highest percentage of the total phosphorus was in lipide form in the period of most active growth. At the time of harvest, 80 per cent of the lipide phosphorus together with 75 per cent of the phytin phosphorus and all of the inorganic phosphorus was in the ear. Diemair, Bleyer and Schmidt (1937) reported that the phosphatide content of wheat is 0.1 per cent.

The phosphatide content of wheat germ was determined by Geoffroy (1934) as 1.3 per cent, and by Rewald (1936a) as 0.6 per cent. Andrews and Bailey (1932), in closer agreement with the higher value, reported 0.07 per cent lipide phosphorus in wheat germ, whereas Sullivan and Near (1928) reported a median value of 0.043 per cent lipide phosphorus. Halden (1947) reported that the phosphatide content of wheat and rye germ was 1.2 to 1.3 per cent. Although in disagreement, these results serve to show qualitatively that the greatest portion of the phosphatide of wheat is present in the germ. Friese and co-workers (1942) were able to isolate by methanol extraction 2.5 per cent phosphatides from wheat germ which had a nitrogen-phosphorus ratio of 1.2:1. It is not clear why their results are so much higher. However, these discrepant results might well be due to differences in purity of the germ, and to differences in the particular wheat mix from which the germ was milled.

Andrews and Bailey (1932) reported 0.028 per cent lipide phosphorus in wheat bran, in agreement with Sullivan and Near's (1928) value of 0.025 per cent. These results are in fair agreement with Geoffroy's (1934) determination of 0.50 per cent phosphatide. The changes in lipide phosphorus content during the storage of wheat and wheat products were investigated by Sullivan and Near (1933) and by Sinclair and McCalla (1937).

The phosphatide content of gluten, which is quite high, was determined by Sullivan and Near (1927, 1927a, 1928) to be 8.5 to 11.1 per cent. These workers found that the phosphatide content was higher in glutens from less refined flours with poor baking qualities. Working (1924) had previously observed that lower grade flours had a higher phosphatide content than better grades, and that the quality of gluten could be improved by the removal of the phosphatides by washing with water. Rewald (1936a) and Kühl (1935), on the other hand, showed that the addition of approximately 0.05 per cent phosphatides to flour acts as a baking improver and serves to better the qualities of "soft" wheat. These statements are not necessarily in conflict, for the adverse effect of the naturally occurring phosphatide may be due to its presence in quantities which exceed the optimum amount. Likewise, the phosphatide-protein complex in the gluten may for some obscure reason exert an unfavorable effect. It may also be that lecithin is an improver for soft wheat, whereas the cephalin fraction is not. Here again, more definitive investigations are necessary. The complex problem of gluten-phosphatide relationship is discussed by Sullivan (1940) and by Sinclair and McCalla (1937).

Complex Formation. The high phosphatide concentration in the gluten of the wheat indicates here as in other plant sources a close association with proteins (Working, 1924; Rewald, 1936a). Furthermore, the phosphatides also exist in combination with carbohydrates (Nottbohm and Mayer, 1934) from which it is difficult to free them (Sullivan, 1940). Rewald (1936a) found that 63 per cent of the phosphatides of wheat exists in combination with carbohydrates and proteins. He, as well as Sullivan and Bailey (1936), isolated but did not identify a carbohydrate associated with the phosphatides. Rewald (1936a) found that it was a nonreducing polysaccharide which yielded reducing sugars on hydrolysis. Antener and Högl (1947) identified saccharose as a constituent of the sugar-phosphatide complex of wheat germ.

Fatty Acids. The fatty acids of wheat phosphatides were identified by Diemair, Bleyer and Schmidt (1937), who found the saturated acids to consist of myristic, lauric, stearic and palmitic acids, the latter in predominance. The unsaturated acids consisted chiefly of linoleic acid with a small amount of oleic acid. Diemair and Bleyer (1935) had previously found palmitic and linoleic acids to be the chief fatty acid constituents. Sullivan and Bailey (1936) examined an alcohol-ether extract of wheat germ which contained 1.23 per cent phosphorus and was accordingly a mixture of glycerides and phosphatides. They found that palmitic acid was the chief saturated acid together with some stearic and lignoceric acids. In the unsaturated series linoleic acid predominated, followed by oleic and linolenic acids. It is interesting to compare these findings with the following fatty acid composition of wheat germ oil determined by Hilditch (1935): palmitic, 13.8 per cent; stearic, 1.0 per cent; oleic, 30.0 per cent; linoleic, 44.1 per cent; and linolenic, 10.8 per cent.

Webster (1929) reported the iodine value of wheat phosphatide fatty acids to be 81.5.

Constituent Phosphatides. Various investigators (Nottbohm and Mayer, 1934; Diemair and Bleyer, 1935) have reported the isolation of both choline and aminoethyl alcohol from wheat phosphatides, indicating the presence of both lecithin and phosphatidylaminoethyl alcohol. The nitrogen-phosphorus ratio is close to 1:1 (Diemair, Bleyer and Schmidt, 1937; Sullivan, 1940) for germ phosphatides. Rewald (1936a), as mentioned above, found that approximately 80 per cent of the phosphatides was lecithin and 20 per cent was cephalins.

On the basis of the percentage of nitrogen, phosphorus, ash and fatty acid in the phosphatides isolated from wheat germ, Channon and Foster (1934) concluded that in addition to lecithin and the cephalins there is also present, to the extent of 42 per cent of the total phosphatide, phosphatidic acid (see p. 48) as the calcium, magnesium and potassium salts. The presence of this material in wheat germ oil was likewise proved by Barton-Wright (1938), and Antener and Högl (1947) found phosphatidic acids in wheat germ. Although this material may represent an intermediate stage in the synthesis of phosphatides in living tissue, its possible presence as a degradation product, either biological or otherwise, must likewise not be overlooked.

Hirao (1931) found lysolecithin in wheat, although this may well have been a degradation product formed during the isolation procedure rather than an actual constituent.

Cottonseed

The phosphatides of cottonseed are similar in many respects to those of soybeans (Olcott, 1944). Thus, as in soybeans, they are associated with carbohydrates and proteins (Olcott, 1944; Rewald, 1942), and, as in soybeans, their analytical determination is complicated by the presence of other phosphorus-containing compounds. Cottonseed phosphatides, however, are considerably more stable than soybean phosphatides, due in part to the fact that they possess a lower iodine number. Thus, Thurman (1937, 1940a) reported an iodine value of 60 to 70 for commercial cottonseed phosphatides, whereas soybean phosphatides have iodine values of the order of 90.

Phosphatide Content. Lishkevich (1937) reported the presence of 0.80 to 0.99 per cent phosphorus in the cottonseed kernel, only 5 to 6 per cent of which is present as phosphatides. About 75 per cent is present as phytin, and the remainder is present in phosphoproteins and inorganic substances. Guerrant (1927) found about 3.6 per cent phosphatides in cottonseed, whereas in cottonseed oil obtained by pressing, Goldovskiĭ and Lishkevich (1939) found 1.5 to 1.8 per cent phosphatides. In oil obtained by extraction, the upper limit was somewhat lower.

A procedure for the removal of phosphatides from cottonseed soap-stock has been patented by Thurman (1937, 1940). Another patent (Thurman, 1939) describes the isolation of phosphatides from cottonseed oil by the addition of water or salt solution. This is similar to the method used for the extraction of phosphatides from soybean oil.

The isolation of cottonseed phosphatides has been described by Rewald (1942), Hilditch and Zaky (1942) and Olcott (1944). None of these investigators obtained pure preparations. Olcott's product, which was prepared from commercial phosphatides, had an ash content of 10 to 11 per cent which could not be readily removed. Spectral analysis indicated the presence of boron and magnesium in quantity and of calcium, sodium, potassium and silicon in lesser amounts. This suggests the presence of the salts of phosphatidic acid. In addition, Olcott suggests that there is present an inositol-containing phosphatide similar to that isolated from soybeans by Woolley (1943).

Fatty Acids. The fatty acid composition of cottonseed phosphatides as determined by Hilditch and Zaky (1942) is presented in Table VIII. The values for the unsaturated C_{20-22} acids may be somewhat in error.

TABLE VIII. THE COMPONENT ACIDS OF COTTONSEED PHOSPHATIDES (HILDITCH AND ZAKY, 1942)

Acid	Weight (%)	Mole (%)
Palmitic	17.3	18.9
Stearic	7.3	7.1
Arachidic	2.8	2.5
Hexadecenoic	1.5	1.7
Oleic	20.3	20
Linoleic	44.4	44.2
Unsaturated C_{20-22}	6.4	5.6

Constituent Phosphatides. Olcott (1944), on the basis of differential solubility in hot alcohol, found 15 to 20 per cent lecithin in commercial cottonseed phosphatides. After hydrolysis of the phosphatides, 41 per cent of the nitrogen was in the amino form, indicating here as with soybean phosphatides the presence of a substantial quantity of the cephalin fraction. Rewald (1942), who extracted cottonseed phosphatides from both the oil and the corresponding presscake with a mixture of ethanol and benzene (1:4), separated these roughly into lecithin and cephalins, and found 29 per cent of the former and 71 per cent of the latter.

Lishkevich (1939) reported that cottonseed phosphatides could be separated into three fractions on the basis of solubility. The alcohol-soluble portion (76.5 per cent) contained somewhat more lecithin than cephalins. The acetone-soluble portion (16.5 per cent) contained somewhat more cephalins than lecithin, whereas the benzene-soluble fraction (7.0 per cent) was entirely lecithin.

Lishkevich (1937a) found a higher percentage of phosphatides in cottonseed than in soybeans. Furthermore, he found that there is more lecithin in cottonseed phosphatides than in the phosphatides of soybean, sunflower seed, flaxseed, castor bean or peanut. He likewise investigated cottonseed (Lishkevich, 1939a) during the period from the 25th to the 70th day of growth. Although the phosphorus content decreased during this period, the phosphatide phosphorus increased from 0.98 to 1.53 per cent. The phytin content, on the other hand, decreased.

Corn

Phosphatide Content. The phosphatides of corn and its products have not been investigated thoroughly, although they represent a minor source of the commercial product in this country. Weeks and Walters (1946) found that 2.5 to 4.5 per cent of the phosphorus of corn is in the form of phosphatides. Guerrant (1927) found in six different varieties of corn 0.013 to 0.016 per cent lipide phosphorus. This is considerably lower than the values of 0.035 per cent lipide phosphorus reported by Webster (1928) for yellow corn, and 0.049 per cent for white corn. Alpers (1918) had previously reported 1.3 per cent phosphatide in corn embryo using a procedure involving extraction with 95 per cent ethanol. He showed that the phosphatide content of corn oil varied with the method of extraction of the oil. Thus, expressed oil contained 0.04 per cent phosphatides, whereas oil extracted with ether contained 0.5 per cent and oil extracted with gasoline 0.4 per cent phosphatides. Anderson (1923) isolated from corn pollen a phosphatide which contained 4.09 per cent phosphorus. Evans and Briggs (1941) found 0.65 per cent lipide in corn starch of which 0.7 per cent was phosphatides. Thus, only a very small portion of the phosphorus in corn starch is present as phosphatide.

The best solvents for the extraction of neutral fat and phosphatides from either corn or soybeans, according to Reznichenko and Poptzova (1934), are mixtures of ethanol and benzene or methylene chloride and benzene, the latter in the ratio of 3:2. Generally, however, alcohol is considered necessary because of its dissociating influence. A patent issued to Kraybill, Brewer and Thornton (1944) describes the use of an adsorbent such as sodium aluminum silicate in order to remove the phosphatides from corn oil.

Schmalfuss (1941) has found that the phosphatide content of the corn grain decreased during ripening and then increased again in the period between maturation and harvesting. Although phosphorus-containing fertilizer did not influence this behavior, it did increase the inorganic phosphorus content. Rogers, Pearson and Pierre (1940) have shown that corn plants absorb both phosphatides and phytin from nutrient solutions, although the latter is absorbed much more rapidly. Neither is hydrolyzed by root enzymes.

Fatty Acids. The fatty acids of corn phosphatides have not yet been investigated. The fatty acid analysis of corn oil, however, has been carried out by Baughman and Jamieson (1921) and by Longenecker (1939). Both investigations proved that palmitic was the chief saturated acid and that linoleic was the chief unsaturated acid, followed closely by linolenic acid. It is likely, therefore, that these fatty acids would predominate in the phosphatides, for which reason they should possess a relatively high iodine number. Thurman (1940a) in a patent reported the iodine values of corn phosphatides to be as low as 40, although it is likely that such a low value may have been determined on deteriorated or partially oxidized samples. Webster (1929) reported the iodine value of phosphatides from corn to be 65.3.

Constituent Phosphatides. Scholfield, McGuire and Dutton (1950) separated corn phosphatides into alcohol-soluble and alcohol-insoluble fractions, and then examined each of these by the countercurrent distribution technique. The alcohol-soluble portion contained lecithin and a small quantity of phosphatidylaminoethyl alcohol. Inositol-containing phosphatides were found, and there appeared to be two major types just as had previously been observed by these workers for soybeans.

Rapeseed

Rewald (1937c) examined rapeseed phosphatides and found them to be associated with a polysaccharide. On the basis of alcohol solubility, he postulated the presence of 60 per cent cephalins, 20 per cent lecithin and 20 per cent of a material which was soluble in hot alcohol, but insoluble in cold alcohol. This may have been a mixture of phosphatide and impurities, or a partially decomposed phosphatide. The nitrogen-phosphorus ratio of each fraction was 1:1.

Contrary to the findings of Rewald (1937c), Heiduschka and Neumann (1938) did not find carbohydrate material associated with rapeseed phosphatide. This result, however, is unlikely. They likewise found a predominance of cephalins over lecithin on the basis of alcohol solubility. Both fractions were hydrolyzed and analyzed for fatty acids. Their results are indicated in Table IX.

TABLE IX. THE FATTY ACIDS OF RAPESEED PHOSPHATIDES

Fatty acid	Wt. (%) in cephalin fraction, Hilditch and Pedelty (1937)	Wt. (%) in cephalin fraction, Heiduschka and Neumann (1938)	Wt. (%) in lecithin, Heiduschka and Neumann (1938)
Myristic	0.8	—	—
Palmitic	8.3	18.21	15.88
As Behenic	1.5	—	—
Hexadecenoic	2.1	—	—
Oleic	22.4	28.09	26.67
Linoleic	42.2	—	—
α-Linoleic	—	44.83	43.23
β-Linoleic	—	11.03	12.63
Linolenic	Trace	—	—
Erucic	22.7	—	—

Rapeseed phosphatides were likewise examined by Hilditch and Pedelty (1937), who in accord with previous investigators found the cephalins to be the predominant constituent. Their nitrogen-phosphorus ratio in each case was not quite 1:1, indicating the presence of impurities. They analyzed the fatty acid constituents of the alcohol-insoluble portion, but did not have sufficient material to analyze the alcohol-soluble portion. They were able to show qualitatively, however, that the component fatty acids of the two phosphatides were the same. Their results are likewise contained in Table IX.

Bleyer, Diemair, and Weiss (1939) analyzed rapeseed phosphatide which had been exposed to the air and which undoubtedly had undergone oxidation. In this impure product they found oleic acid to be the only unsaturated acid and palmitic to be the chief saturated acid. The other unsaturated acids had apparently undergone extensive oxidation which made their isolation and identification impossible. Their material, likewise, was associated with carbohydrates. Rapeseed phosphatides were actually produced commercially in Europe during World War II.

Peanuts

Peanut phosphatides were examined by Hilditch and Zaky (1942). The acetone-insoluble material which they isolated as a brown powder had an iodine number of 52.0, indicating considerably less unsaturation than is found in soybean and cottonseed phosphatides. The component fatty acids of their product are indicated in Table X.

TABLE X. FATTY ACIDS OF PEANUT PHOSPHATIDES (HILDITCH AND ZAKY, 1942)

Acid	Weight (%)	Mole (%)
Palmitic	16.2	17.8
Stearic	2.8	2.8
Saturated C_{20}, C_{22}, C_{24}	4.6	3.9
As C_{26} saturated	2.5	1.8
Oleic	47.1	47.2
Linoleic	22.7	22.8
Unsaturated C_{20-22}	4.1	3.7

Rewald (1942), on the basis of difference in alcohol solubility, reported peanut phosphatides to consist of 35.7 per cent lecithin and 64.3 per cent cephalins. Guerrant (1927) found 0.088 per cent lipide phosphorus in the peanut.

Sunflower Seeds

Skipin, Engel and Zorabyan (1940) indicate that the foots of sunflower seed oil have a phosphatide content sufficiently high to serve as a commercial source. This is also discussed by Raspopina (1936).

Hilditch and Zaky (1942) analyzed for the component fatty acids in sunflower seed phosphatides. These are indicated in Table XI. The same workers found all of these acids except the unsaturated C_{20-22} acids in sunflower seed oil. In the oil, however, there was considerably less palmitic and more linoleic acid.

TABLE XI. FATTY ACIDS OF SUNFLOWER SEED PHOSPHATIDES (HILDITCH AND ZAKY, 1942)

Acid	Weight (%)	Mole (%)
Palmitic	14.7	16.1
Stearic	5.1	5
Arachidic	9.5	8.6
Oleic	19.3	19.2
Linoleic	45.9	46.3
Unsaturated C_{20-22}	5.5	4.8

The phosphatides of sunflower seeds, like those from similar sources, occur largely in combination with proteins and carbohydrates.

Rewald (1942), on the basis of alcohol solubility, found that sunflower seed phosphatides consisted of 38.5 per cent lecithin and 61.5 per cent cephalin.

Rye

The phosphatide content of rye embryo was found by Alpers (1918) to be 2.4 per cent. The crude oil from the rye embryo contained 3 per cent phosphatides. Friese and co-workers (1942) used methanol to extract 83 grams of phosphatides from 3 kilograms of rye germ. The product had a phosphorus content of 2.80 per cent and a nitrogen content of 1.5 per cent.

Hanke (1940) reported an average value of 0.052 per cent lipide phosphorus for three rye flours.

Ihde and Schuette (1941) found that rye phosphatides in common with most other seed phosphatides are associated with carbohydrates. They point out that the possibility of any chemical union such as a glycoside linkage is obviated by the presence of a nonreducing carbohydrate.

Webster (1928) found that rye which was 75 per cent germinated contained 0.033 per cent lipide phosphorus on a dry weight basis.

Barley

The phosphatide content of barley was found by Diemair, Bleyer and Schmidt (1937) to be 0.16 per cent. They found only lecithin to be present, and the phosphorus contents of their products were low. Analysis of the fatty acids obtained by hydrolysis indicated that palmitic and stearic acids are the saturated constituents, whereas linoleic acid and a small amount of oleic acid constitute the unsaturated portion.

Arney (1939), in an analysis of barley seedlings for all the various phosphorus-containing components, found that the phosphatides were present in greater quantity in the shoot of the seedling than in the root.

Burgevin and Guyon (1933) found that phosphorus-containing fertilizer causes the lipide phosphorus of barley to increase to as much as 10 per cent of the total P_2O_5.

The lipide phosphorus content of barley which was 72 per cent germinated, according to Webster (1928), was 0.022 per cent. Guerrant (1927) reported a considerably higher value of 0.044 per cent.

Grain Sorghum

Webster (1928) found that common kaffir (62 per cent germinated) contained 0.021 per cent lipide phosphorus. This is somewhat lower than Guerrant's (1927) prior determination of 0.036 per cent lipide phosphorus. Similarly, the former investigator reported 0.023 per cent lipide phosphorus for Darso (64 per cent germinated), whereas the latter reported a higher value of 0.031 to 0.039 per cent. The following values were all determined by Guerrant (1927): Red kaffir, 0.042 to 0.045 per cent lipide phosphorus; White kaffir, 0.033 to 0.046 per cent; White milo, 0.036 to 0.037 per cent; Feterita, 0.026 to 0.036 per cent; Yellow milo, 0.042 to 0.051 per cent; Sorgo, 0.037 per cent; Reed's kaffir, 0.033 to 0.034 per cent; Hegari, 0.036 per cent; and Sunrise kaffir, 0.035 per cent. He arrived at an average value of 0.038 per cent.

Yamamoto and Ninomiya (1936) found 3.7 per cent of the total phosphorus to be lipide phosphorus in kaoliang grains, which are varieties of *Sorghum vulgare*. This product consisted of about 73 per cent cephalin and 27 per cent lecithin. The saturated fatty acids included palmitic and myristic acids.

Flaxseed

The fatty acids from linseed phosphatides were investigated by Hilditch and Zaky (1942). Their results are indicated in Table XII.

TABLE XII. FATTY ACIDS OF LINSEED PHOSPHATIDES (HILDITCH AND ZAKY, 1942)

Acid	Weight (%)	Mole (%)
Palmitic	11.3	12.3
Stearic	10.6	10.4
Hexadecenoic	3.5	3.8
Oleic	33.6	33.1
Linoleic	20.4	20.4
Linolenic	17.4	17.4
Unsaturated C_{20-22}	3.2	2.8

Rewald (1942) found 36.2 per cent of linseed phosphatides to be lecithin, as indicated by solubility in hot alcohol.

Oats

The phosphatide content of oats was found by Diemair, Bleyer and Schmidt (1937) to be 0.14 per cent. Here, as with the phosphatides of barley, they found lecithin to be the only constituent. They found the saturated fatty acids to consist of myristic, lauric, palmitic and stearic acids, whereas linoleic acid was the chief unsaturated acid. Oleic acid was present in small amount.

Webster (1928) found 0.029 per cent lipide phosphorus in oats which were 98 per cent germinated. Guerrant (1927) reported a higher value of 0.035 to 0.039 per cent.

The iodine value of the mixed fatty acids from the phosphatides of oats was reported by Webster (1929) as 88.8.

Tobacco

Tobacco seeds were found by Shabanov (1937) to contain not less than 0.5 per cent phosphatides of which 50 to 60 per cent was lecithin. He found a similar quantity of phosphatides in the seeds of *Nicotiana rustica* (Shabanov, 1939), which is a shrub of the same genus to which the common tobacco plant belongs. Here only 20 per cent of the phosphatide was lecithin. Of the fatty acids present, he was able to demonstrate only the presence of palmitic acid.

Cacao Bean

The phosphatide content of many samples of cacao beans was found by Rewald and Christlieb (1931, 1931a) to vary from 0.02 to 0.3 per cent with an average value of 0.1 per cent. They indicated that the phosphatide is associated with protein, and that it is not affected by roasting or alkali treatment of the cacao bean. They also described a procedure for determination of phosphatide from this source.

Sesame Seed

Sesame seed phosphatides according to Rewald (1942) consist of 52.2 per cent lecithin and 40.6 per cent cephalins. This is a considerably higher proportion of lecithin than is found in many similar oil seed phosphatides.

Castor Seeds

According to Gupta (1948), phosphatides comprise 0.47 per cent of the oil which is obtained by ethanol extraction of the castor bean. The phosphatides deposit as a sludge in the oil, and were found to contain 2.84 per cent phosphorus and 1.20 per cent nitrogen.

Miscellaneous Seeds

The seeds of red currants, raspberries and plums were examined for phosphatides by Rewald (1943a). He extracted the oil from the crushed seeds with petroleum ether. In this extraction practically no phosphorus-containing material was obtained. Thereafter, he extracted the residue with a mixture of ethanol and benzene, evaporated the solution to dryness, and extracted the residue with petroleum ether. By analyzing this material for phosphorus and assuming that phosphatides contain 3.8 per cent phosphorus, he found that red currant seeds contain 0.76 per cent phosphatides, raspberry seeds 0.55 per cent, and plum seeds 0.31 per cent. These results are reported on a wet basis. Rewald and Schweiger (1933) had previously reported 0.41 per cent phosphatides for plum seeds.

Schulze (1907) isolated phosphatides from the seeds of *Vicia sativa*, which is a type of climbing herb more commonly known as "Spring Vetch". He likewise isolated phosphatides from the seeds of *Pinus cembra*, a variety of pine tree. Trier (1913) isolated from the seeds of the black spruce a phosphatide which was associated with galactose.

The phosphatides, as well as other constituents of the germinating black walnut seed, were investigated by McClenahan (1913), who found that the large amount of phosphatide in the earlier stages of development decreases as maturity is approached.

About 0.1 per cent phosphatide was found in coffee bean oil by Bengis and Anderson (1934). Rewald (1946) has found that the phosphatide of the unroasted coffee bean contains 3.39 per cent phosphorus.

CHAPTER XVI

PHOSPHATIDES OF VEGETABLES AND MISCELLANEOUS PLANTS

Carrots

Early work (von Euler and Bernton, 1922; Grafe and Magistris, 1926a; Bleyer and Diemair, 1931) demonstrated the presence of phosphatides in carrots, although the products were not well characterized.

Carrot phosphatides have recently been reinvestigated by Hanahan and Chaikoff (1947), who point out that the isolation procedures are complicated by the low lipide content of the vegetable. Their results differed with the isolation procedure employed, thus demonstrating the care which must be taken before conclusions are reached. In the raw carrot they found a very low nitrogen content and the virtual absence of choline. In carrots initially treated with steam, however, sufficient nitrogen and choline were present so that the nitrogen-phosphorus ratio approximated 1:1. A possible explanation for this, they point out, is the presence in the raw carrot of a lecithinase which splits the choline from the phosphatide to yield a material similar to the phosphatidic acids.

When they employed dehydrated carrots they observed a close association of the phosphatide with a carbohydrate, which accounted, at least in part, for the low phosphorus and nitrogen content. The sugar reacted positively to Molisch and Fehling reagents and yielded an osazone whose crystal structure resembled that of glucosazone. The various extraction procedures had a marked effect on the iodine numbers of the phosphatide. Thus, the product obtained from the raw carrot at low temperature had an iodine number of 86.0–90.0. This same material extracted at 55 to 60° C gave a product which in three different analyses possessed iodine numbers of 196, 144 and 59. The product from steam treated carrots had a value of 54 whereas that from steam treated, dehydrated carrots had a value of 38. These workers also showed that complete extraction of the phosphorus-containing lipides could be effected with ethanol-ether mixtures.

Peas

Halász (1918) analyzed various varieties of peas for phosphatides by means of alcohol extraction and found that the phosphatide content varied from 1.1 to 2.3 per cent. He found a larger percentage in the green varieties than in the yellow ones.

Trier (1913) isolated 8.5 grams of phosphatides from 1 kilogram of peas by alcohol extraction. His product was associated with galactose and consisted of both lecithin and the cephalin fraction.

Grafe and Magistris (1926) studied the phosphatides of Norwegian Peas (*Pisum arvense unicolor*). Hydrolysis of the phosphatides obtained by extraction yielded glycerophosphoric acid, choline, aminoethyl alcohol, and palmitic and oleic acids. There was likewise a close association with carbohydrates.

Guerrant (1927) reported the following lipide phosphorus percentages for several varieties of peas: Black Eye, 0.078; Whippoorwill, 0.073; New Era, 0.078; Scotch, 0.072; and Golden Vine, 0.078.

Beans

Trier (1913) isolated phosphatides from beans by extraction of the lipide material with acetone in which the phosphatides were insoluble. He found the phosphatides to be associated with carbohydrates and to consist of mixtures of lecithin and cephalins.

Jordan and Chibnall (1933) analyzed the seed cotyledons, embryo axes, young germinating plants, prophylls and pinnate leaves of the runner bean (*Phaseolus multiflorus*) for phosphatides. They found lecithin and cephalins present in all the organs in progressively smaller amounts from the cotyledons to the pinnate leaves. They also reported the presence of a small amount of the magnesium salts of phosphatidic acid in the cotyledons and embryo axes. On germination, the amount of this salt seems to increase, and the magnesium is slowly replaced by calcium until calcium phosphatidate is the chief phosphatide of the mature prophylls and pinnate leaves.

The phosphatides of the bean, *Vicia faba*, were studied by Magistris and Schäfer (1929), who postulated the presence of both lecithin and cephalins. Palmitic and perhaps stearic acid were found, together with oleic and linoleic acids. The products were associated with carbohydrates, and a considerable quantity of metals such as magnesium, calcium, barium and potassium was demonstrated.

Guerrant (1927) reported the following lipide phosphorus percentages for various varieties of beans: Mung bean, 0.105; Velvet Georgia, 0.083; Velvet Tracys, 0.083; Navy bean, 0.045. Webster (1928) found 0.040 per cent lipide phosphorus in the fully germinated Mung bean.

Lupines

The phosphatides of lupines were investigated by many early investigators (Schulze, 1907; Winterstein and Stegmann, 1909), since the seeds of *Lupinus albus* have long been used in Europe as a staple food.

Töpler (1861), in a very early investigation, reported 0.29 per cent lipide phosphorus in lupine seeds, although his extraction procedure was incomplete since he used only ether. Jacobson (1889) later used alcohol and ether to obtain the higher value of 1.92 per cent. Schulze (1908) reported 2.2 per cent phosphatides in *Lupinus angustifoliics*.

More recently, Diemair and Weiss (1939) isolated a lupine phosphatide which consisted of three-fourths lecithin and one-fourth cephalin fraction. The saturated acids consisted of palmitic with traces of arachidic, whereas the unsaturated acids consisted of 61 per cent oleic, 37.1 per cent linoleic and 1.9 per cent linolenic. As with other plant phosphatides, there is a close association with carbohydrates according to Winterstein and Stegmann (1909). These authors found that the analytical values varied with the method of extraction. Using various mixtures of ethanol-benzene, they obtained values varying from 0.6 to 1.1 per cent. The authors believed 0.8 per cent to be an accurate estimation of the amount of phosphatides in the air-dried seed. These calculations were all made on the basis of a distearyllecithin.

Beets

Lippmann (1887) originally showed the presence of phosphatides in the roots of sugar beets. A so-called water-soluble phosphatide was isolated by Grafe and Horvat (1925) and by Magistris and Schäfer (1929a). Rewald (1929b) isolated phosphatides from beets in quantities of 0.7 per cent based on the dry material. Arbenz (1919) previously had reported only 0.01 per cent.

Cabbage

The phosphatides of cabbage were investigated by Channon and Chibnall (1927). They found very little lecithin or cephalin fraction. Instead they believed the chief constituent to be the calcium salt of phosphatidic acid. From 220 kilograms of cabbage leaves they isolated 60 grams of this material by ether extraction. The work is open to criticism, however, on the basis that phosphatides which are in physical association with carbohydrates or proteins are ordinarily insoluble in ether. They showed that the saturated acids present were probably stearic and palmitic, whereas the unsaturated ones were linoleic and linolenic. Strangely enough, they could find no oleic acid, although it may well have been present. The iodine value of the mixed acids was 143. Arbenz (1919) previously had reported 0.008 per cent phosphatides in cabbage.

Lettuce

Rewald (1928) found that it was impractical to extract phosphatides from chlorophyll-containing substances with alcohol because the lipides so obtained are badly contaminated with colored substances. Accordingly, he extracted lettuce with acetone. Some of the phosphatides were extracted by this solvent because of their association with other substances. It was impossible, despite attempted purification with ethanol and ethanol-benzene, to obtain an entirely pure product by this procedure. He, likewise, applied this method to the isolation of phosphatides from cabbage.

Miscellaneous Vegetables

Tomato plants, according to Rogers, Pearson and Pierre (1940) and Pearson and Pierre (1940) may possibly absorb phosphatides from a nutrient solution containing them. Phytin was absorbed at a fairly rapid rate.

Rewald (1929b) isolated phosphatides from potatoes and obtained 0.17 per cent based on the dry substance. Arbenz (1919) reported 1.9 per cent phosphatides in lentils. Jackson and Kummerow (1949) have investigated the phosphatides of alfalfa leaf meal.

Rubber Producing Plants

Phosphatides were first observed in *Hevea* latex by Belgrave and Bishop (1923). Later, Beumée-Nieuwland (1929) likewise described the presence of phosphatides in latex. Phosphatides were first isolated from latex in quantity by Rhodes and Bishop (1930). These workers coagulated the latex with ethanol. Then they separated the serum, concentrated it under reduced pressure, and extracted the residue with ether. Since it was possible to process only about one and one-half liters of latex at a time, and since the yields were very small, they repeated the procedure 52 times to obtain 151.6 grams of ether-soluble product from 72.8 liters of latex. On this basis, they assumed the average lipide content of latex to be 0.2 per cent. Their extraction procedure, however, may have been incomplete since it employed only ether. These workers purified their product further by extracting the nonphosphatidic materials with acetone. Elementary analyses indicated that the product was impure. They observed a close association with carbohydrates and a great predominance of unsaturated fatty acids over saturated ones.

Their work was extended by Altman and Kraay (1940), who described a relatively simple procedure for the isolation of phosphatides from *Hevea* latex based on the observation that the sludge resulting from centrifugation contains an oily substance in which the phosphatides are concentrated. In their work, ammoniated latex was used, although they recognized the possibility of hydrolysis of the phosphatides in basic medium. The lipides were obtained by alcohol extraction of the sludge, and the alcohol extract was in turn extracted with ether. The phosphatides were precipitated with acetone.

An investigation of the fatty acids revealed the presence of oleic and linoleic acids together with palmitic, stearic and arachidic acids. The only organic base whose presence could be demonstrated was choline, thus indicating the absence of cephalins. As in most phosphatides from vegetable sources, a close association with carbohydrates was found and a crystalline glycoside was isolated.

The phosphatides present in the latex from *Hevea Brasiliensis* were isolated by Tristram (1942) according to the original procedure of Rhodes and Bishop (1930). Using the fractionation procedure of Channon and Foster (1934), he was able to isolate lecithin in an impure state together with phosphatidic acid in the form of the lead salt. In accord with previous work, practically no phosphatidylaminoethyl alcohol was found, as indicated by the absence of aminoethyl alcohol. Tristram (1942), on the basis of the high calcium content of the crude material, believes that the phosphatidic acid is present in the original latex and that it is not a degradation product.

The fatty acids of the phosphatides, which included oleic and linoleic acids, possessed an iodine value of 90 to 112 and were somewhat more saturated than the fatty acids of the corresponding glycerides whose iodine value was 135 to 148. Smith and Chibnall (1932) had made a similar observation in the case of cocksfoot grass.

Tristram (1942) points out that it is entirely possible that the phosphatides which occur in rubber are responsible for the maintenance of latex as a stable emulsion. Altman (1948) has shown that the organic bases of the phosphatides present in latex act as natural vulcanization accelerators in the processing of rubber.

Flowers

Rewald (1944a) estimated the amount of phosphatides in the stamens and petals of various flowers. The preliminary extraction of the flower parts was effected with 96 per cent alcohol. Evaporation of the solvent yielded a mixture of carbohydrates, pigments, glycerides and phosphatides, the latter material being removed by petroleum ether extraction.

To insure complete extraction of the phosphatides, the original material was extracted further with a mixture of ethanol and benzene. The products consisted of mixtures of lecithin and cephalins, and as would be expected, they were in close association with carbohydrates. The proportion of lipide material which was phosphatide was surprisingly high, reaching 43.6 per cent in the case of tulip stamens and 52.1 per cent in the case of rose petals.

The phosphatide content of the various materials examined are given in Table XIII. The calculations are made on the assumption of 3.8 per cent phosphorus in the phosphatides.

TABLE XIII. THE PHOSPHATIDE CONTENT OF FLOWER PARTS (REWALD, 1944a)

Flower part	Phosphatide in dry material (%)
Rose petals	0.52
Daffodil petals	1.36
Dandelion petals	2.97
Dandelion stamens	2.86
Tulip petals	1.76
Tulip stamens	2.22
Poppy petals	0.69
Poppy stamens	1.4
Poppy seeds (unripe and with associated tissue)	2.77

Fruits

Arbenz (1919) found the following amounts of phosphatides in various fruits: raspberries, 0.13 per cent; whortleberries, 0.09 per cent; apples, 0.06 per cent; grapes, 0.08 per cent; strawberries, 0.06 per cent. His results may be somewhat high. Grafe (1928) found an incompletely characterized phosphatide in the fig which contained palmitic and oleic acids.

Rewald and Schweiger (1933) investigated the phosphatide content of the skin and the meat of apples, pears, plums and peaches. The extraction was made with ethanol-benzene after which the phosphatides were precipitated with acetone from an ether solution of the lipides. Their results based on the dry substance indicated 0.07 per cent phosphatides in the meat of the apple and 0.06 per cent in the skin; 0.09 per cent in meat of the pear and 0.1 per cent in the skin; 0.1 per cent in the meat of the plum and 0.26 per cent in the skin; 0.2 per cent in the meat of the peach and 0.16 per cent in the skin. The seed of the plum contained 0.59 per cent phosphatides, whereas the seed of the peach contained 0.41 per cent. All of these results are on a dry basis. It may be seen that the amounts in the skin and the meat do not differ markedly.

Grass

Smith and Chibnall (1932) analyzed dry cocksfoot grass (*Dactylis glomerata*) for phosphatides. From 22 kilograms of grass they obtained by ether extraction 56 grams of phosphatides. They found this material to be associated with carbohydrates as would be expected, and to consist in part of lecithin and cephalins. In addition, they found phosphatidic acid to be present as the calcium or magnesium salt. On hydrolysis they found linoleic and linolenic acids, but no oleic acid. The absence of this latter acid is surprising. The saturated acids, which were probably palmitic and stearic, constituted about one-third of the total fatty acids whose iodine number was of the order of 125 to 145.

Rewald (1944) pointed out that ether extraction such as was used by Smith and Chibnall (1932) is apt not to extract phosphatides completely. This is obviously the case when the phosphatides are in association with proteins or carbohydrates. Rewald isolated phosphatides from ordinary grass by a three-step extraction. In the first step he extracted with acetone in order to free the material from colored products such as chlorophyll and carotin and to extract some of the glycerides. Only a negligible amount of phosphatides was extracted by this means, although phosphatides in the presence of other substances are sometimes soluble in acetone. The second extraction was carried out with petroleum ether to obtain glycerides and phosphatides not associated by physical means with other materials. The final extraction with ethanol-benzene (1:4) yielded wax and phosphatides with part of the associated carbohydrates. Rewald expresses some doubt in regard to the presence of the salts of phosphatidic acid, pointing out that the magnesium may have been due, at least in part, to chlorophyll. By these combined extractions he showed that over 7 per cent of grass is lipide material and that about 0.5 per cent is phosphatide.

Fritsch (1919) observed that when grass is stored in silos most of the phosphatides present decompose.

Alfalfa

Rewald (1936) isolated a phosphatide from dried alfalfa which was in close combination with carbohydrates and which contained 4.92 per cent phosphorus. This high figure was probably due to impurities which contained phosphorus. His extraction procedure involved the use of trichloroethylene.

In a later publication Rewald (1937b) describes the extraction with ethanol-benzene of the residue left from the petroleum ether extraction of alfalfa. The petroleum ether extract yielded a product similar to that described above. From the ethanol-benzene extract it was possible to isolate by the usual procedure a phosphatide with a nitrogen-phosphorus ratio of 1:1. There was likewise close association with a polysaccharide. Rewald points out that the "bound" phosphatides in green substances are more abundant than the "free" ones and that both consist of mixtures of lecithin and cephalins.

Guerrant (1927) found 0.017 per cent lipide phosphorus in German millet, 0.043 per cent in timothy and 0.051 per cent in clover.

Leaves

The work of Echevin (1934) brought forth the interesting observation that the phosphatides in leaves disappear after autumnal coloration sets in. He lists the following phosphatide contents for various green leaves: *Castanea vulgaris*, 0.028 per cent; *Aesculus hippocastanum*, 0.047 per cent; *Ampelopsis hederacea*, 0.036 per cent; *Fagus silvatica*, 0.028 per cent; *Prunus laurocerasus*, 0.020 per cent; *Acer platanoïdes*, 0.054 per cent.

Cactus

Working (1922/23) showed that phosphatides are present in the cactus, *Opuntia discata*. However, he was not able to obtain a material which was sufficiently pure to merit extensive investigation. By hydrolysis he was able to show the presence of glycerol, phosphoric acid, choline, and saturated and unsaturated acids.

Sugar Cane

Shorey (1898) isolated a phosphatide from sugar cane which yielded on hydrolysis oleic, stearic and palmitic acids. A Russian patent (Troitskiǐ, 1935) describes a procedure whereby phosphatides and other materials may be precipitated from molasses solutions with copper sulfate. This would indicate that phosphatides occur in sugar cane in fairly appreciable quantities. They are recovered from the precipitate by extraction with methanol.

BIBLIOGRAPHY—PART III

Agulhon, H., and Frouin, A., *Bull. soc. chim. biol.*, 1, 176 (1919); *C. A.*, 14, 3439 (1920).
Alpers, E., *Chem. Ztg.*, 42, 37 (1918); *C. A.*, 13, 2389 (1919).
Altman, R. F. A., *Ind. Eng. Chem.*, 40, 241 (1948); *C. A.*, 42, 3612 (1948).
——, and Kraay, G. M., *Rubber Chem. Tech.*, 13, 750 (1940); *C. A.*, 35, 3479 (1940).
Anderson, R. J., *J. Biol. Chem.*, 55, 611 (1923).
——, *ibid.*, 74, 525 (1927).

Anderson, R. J., *J. Biol. Chem.*, **74**, 537 (1927a).

——, *ibid.*, **83**, 169 (1929).

——, *ibid.*, **83**, 505 (1929a).

——, *ibid.*, **85**, 327 (1930).

——, *Am. Rev. Tuberc.*, **24**, 746 (1931); *C. A.*, **26**, 2482 (1932).

——, *J. Biol. Chem.*, **97**, 639 (1932).

——, *Harvey Lectures*, **35**, 271 (1940); *C. A.*, **36**, 5191 (1942).

——, *Chem. Revs.*, **29**, 225 (1941); *C. A.*, **36**, 1633 (1942).

——, and Chargaff, E., *J. Biol. Chem.*, **84**, 703 (1929).

——, ——, *ibid.*, **85**, 77 (1929a).

——, and co-workers (Reeves, R. E., Creighton, M. M., and Lathrop, W. C.), *Am. Rev. Tuberc.*, **48**, 65 (1943); *C. A.*, **37**, 6324 (1943).

——, and Creighton, M. M., *J. Biol. Chem.*, **130**, 429 (1939).

——, and Newman, M. S., *J. Biol. Chem.*, **101**, 499 (1933).

——, ——, *ibid.*, **101**, 773 (1933a).

——, ——, *ibid.*, **103**, 405 (1933b).

——, and Renfrew, A. G., *J. Am. Chem. Soc.*, **52**, 1252, 1607 (1930); *C. A.*, **24**, 2158 (1930).

——, and Roberts, E. G., *J. Am. Chem. Soc.*, **52**, 5023 (1930); *C. A.*, **25**, 521 (1931).

——, ——, *J. Biol. Chem.*, **85**, 509 (1930a).

——, ——, *ibid.*, **85**, 519 (1930b).

——, ——, *ibid.*, **85**, 529 (1930c).

——, ——, *ibid.*, **89**, 599 (1930d).

——, ——, *ibid.*, **89**, 611 (1930e).

——, and Uyei, N., *J. Biol. Chem.*, **97**, 617 (1932).

——, Lathrop, W. C., and Creighton, M. M., *J. Biol. Chem.*, **125**, 299 (1938).

——, Peck, R. L., and Creighton, M. M., *J. Biol. Chem.*, **136**, 211 (1940).

Andrews, J. S., and Bailey, C. H., *Ind. Eng. Chem.*, **24**, 80 (1932); *C. A.*, **26**, 1639 (1932).

Antener, I., and Högl, O., *Mitt. Gebiete Lebensm. Hyg.*, **38**, 226 (1947); *C. A.*, **42**, 292 (1948).

Arbenz, E., *Mitt. Gebiete Lebensm. Hyg.*, **10**, 93 (1919); *C. A.*, **14**, 81 (1920).

Arney, S. E., *Biochem. J.*, **33**, 1078 (1939); *C. A.*, **33**, 8243 (1939).

Aronson, H., *Berl. klin. Woch.*, **47**, 1617 (1910); *Chem. Zentr.*, II, 1491 (1910).

Aso, K., *J. Tokyo Chem. Soc.*, **20**, 921 (1900); *Chem. Zentr.*, II, 53 (1900).

Auclair, J., and Paris, L., *Arch. med. exp.*, **19**, 129 (1907); *C. A.*, **1**, 2002 (1907).

——, ——, *ibid.*, **20**, 736 (1908); *C. A.*, **3**, 929 (1909).

Austin, W. C., *J. Biol. Chem.*, **59**, Lii (1924).

Barton-Wright, E. C., *Cereal Chem.*, **15**, 723 (1938); *C. A.*, **33**, 1048 (1939).

Baudran, G., *Compt. rend.*, **142**, 657 (1906); *Chem. Zentr.*, I, 1281 (1906).

Baughman, W. F., and Jamieson, G. S., *J. Am. Chem. Soc.*, **43**, 2696 (1921); *C. A.*, **16**, 1329 (1922).

Belgrave, W. N. C., and Bishop, R. O., *Malayan Agric. Bull.*, **11**, 371 (1923); **13**, 373 (1925); *C. A.*, **18**, 3738 (1924).

Belozerskiĭ, A. N., and Kornev, I. S., *Biokhimiya*, **2**, 894 (1937); *C. A.*, **32**, 7957 (1938).

Bengis, R. O., and Anderson, R. J., *J. Biol. Chem.*, **105**, 139 (1934).

Bernardini, L., and Chiarulli, G., *Staz. sper. agrar. ital.*, **42**, 97 (1909); *C. A.*, **4**, 1870 (1910).

Beumée-Nieuwland, N., *Arch. Rubbercult.*, **13**, 555 (1929); *C. A.*, **24**, 523 (1930).

Birch, A. J., and Robinson, R., *J. Chem. Soc.*, 488 (1942); *C. A.*, 37, 603 (1943).

Bitte, B., *Z. physiol. Chem.*, 19, 488 (1894).

Bleyer, B., and Diemair, W., *Biochem. Z.*, 235, 243 (1931); *C. A.*, 25, 4912 (1931).

——, ——, *ibid.*, 238, 197 (1931a); *C. A.*, 25, 5690 (1931).

——, ——, and Weiss, K., *Biochem. Z.*, 302, 167 (1939); *C. A.*, 34, 3316 (1940).

Bloch, K., *Biochem. Z.*, 285, 372 (1936); *C. A.*, 30, 8291 (1936).

——, *Z. physiol. Chem.*, 244, 1 (1936a); *C. A.*, 31, 1066 (1937).

Bloor, W. R., *J. Biol. Chem.*, 77, 53 (1928).

Boivin, A., *Presse méd.*, 48, 95, 976 (1940); *C. A.*, 37, 3458 (1943).

Boquet, A., and Négre, L., *Compt. rend. soc. biol.*, 89, 138 (1923); *C. A.*, 18, 98 (1924).

Bredemann, G., and Kummer, H., *Fettchem. Umschau*, 41, 81 (1934); *C. A.*, 28, 4926 (1934).

Bürger, M., *Biochem. Z.*, 78, 155 (1916); *C. A.*, 11, 825 (1917).

Burgevin, H., and Guyon, G., *Compt. rend. acad. agr. France*, 19, 929 (1933); *C. A.*, 28, 2099 (1934).

Burt, M. L., and Anderson, R. J., *J. Biol. Chem.*, 94, 451 (1931/32).

Buu-Hoi, N. P., and Cagniant, P., *Z. physiol. Chem.*, 279, 76 (1943); *Ber.*, 76, 689 (1943); *C. A.*, 38, 2314, 2929 (1944).

Cason, J., *J. Am. Chem. Soc.*, 64, 1106 (1942); *C. A.*, 36, 4094 (1942).

——, and co-workers (Adams, C. E., Bennett, Jr., L. L., and Register, U. D.), *J. Am. Chem. Soc.*, 66, 1764 (1944); *C. A.*, 39, 276 (1945).

——, and Prout, F. S., *J. Am. Chem. Soc.*, 66, 46 (1944); *C. A.*, 38, 952 (1944).

——, ——, *ibid.*, 70, 879 (1948); *C. A.*, 42, 3320 (1948).

——, and Sumrell, G., *ibid.*, 72, 4837 (1950).

Channon, H. J., and Chibnall, A. C., *Biochem. J.*, 21, 1112 (1927); *C. A.*, 22, 1790 (1928).

——, and Foster, C. A. M., *Biochem. J.*, 28, 853 (1934); *C. A.*, 28, 6735 (1934).

Chargaff, E., *Z. physiol. Chem.*, 201, 191 (1931); *C. A.*, 26, 493 (1932).

——, *ibid.*, 201, 198 (1931a); *C. A.*, 26, 494 (1932).

——, *Ber.*, 65, 745 (1932); *C. A.*, 26, 3775 (1932).

——, in Abderhalden, E., "Handb. d. biologischen Arbeitsmethoden," Berlin and Vienna, Urban und Schwarzenberg, 1939, Abt. XII, Teil 2, (1933).

——, *Z. physiol. Chem.*, 217, 115 (1933a); *C. A.*, 27, 3497 (1933).

——, *ibid.*, 218, 223 (1933b); *C. A.*, 28, 3437 (1934).

——, and Anderson, R. J., *Z. physiol. Chem.*, 191, 172 (1930); *C. A.*, 25, 128 (1931).

——, and Levine, M., *Proc. Soc. Exptl. Biol. Med.*, 34, 675 (1936).

——, ——, *J. Biol. Chem.*, 124, 195 (1938).

——, and Schaefer, W., *Ann. inst. Pasteur*, 54, 708 (1935); *C. A.*, 30, 3494 (1936).

——, Pangborn, M. C., and Anderson, R. J., *J. Biol. Chem.*, 90, 45 (1931).

Chibnall, A. C., and Channon, H. J., *Biochem. J.*, 21, 233, 1112 (1927); *C. A.*, 21, 2489 (1927).

Cramer, E., *Arch. Hyg.*, 16, 151 (1893); *Chem. Zentr.*, I, 543 (1893).

Creighton, M. M., Chang, L. H., and Anderson, R. J., *J. Biol. Chem.*, 154, 569 (1944).

Crowder, J. A., and Anderson, R. J., *J. Biol. Chem.*, 104, 399, 487 (1934).

——, and co-workers (Stodola, F. H., Pangborn, M. C., and Anderson, R. J.), *J. Am. Chem. Soc.*, 58, 636 (1936); *C. A.*, 30, 4536 (1936).

Czapek, Fr., "Biochemie der Pflanzen," 2 Aufl., Vol. I, Jena, Gustav Fischer, 1913.

Daubney, C. G., and MacLean, I. S., *Biochem. J.*, **21**, 373 (1927); *C. A.*, **21**, 2722 (1929).

Dawson, A. I., *J. Bact.*, **4**, 133 (1919); *C. A.*, **13**, 1717 (1919).

de Sütö-Nagy, G. I., and Anderson, R. J., *J. Biol. Chem.*, 171, 749 (1947).

Diemair, W., and Bleyer, B., *Biochem. Z.*, 275, 242 (1935); *C. A.*, **29**, 2575 (1935).

——, and Koch, J., *Angew. Chem.*, **A60**, 155 (1948); *C. A.*, **43**, 718 (1949).

——, and Poetsch, W., *Biochem. Z.*, 319, 571 (1949); *C. A.*, **44**, 2075 (1950).

——, and Weiss, K., *Biochem. Z.*, 302, 112 (1939); *C. A.*, **34**, 3316 (1940).

——, Bleyer, B., and Schmidt, W., *Biochem. Z.*, 294, 353 (1937); *C. A.*, **32**, 1754 (1938).

Dirr, K., and Ruppert, A., *Biochem. Z.*, 319, 163 (1948); *C. A.*, **43**, 5126 (1949).

Duftschmid, H., and Halden, W., *Fette u. Seifen*, **49**, 348 (1942); *C. A.*, **37**, 5760 (1943).

Earle, F. R., and Milner, R. T., *Oil & Soap*, **15**, 41 (1938); *C. A.*, **32**, 2769 (1938).

Echevin, R., *Compt. rend.*, **198**, 1254 (1934); *C. A.*, **28**, 4770 (1934).

Eckstein, H. C., and Soule, M. H., *J. Biol. Chem.*, **91**, 395 (1931).

Evans, J. W., and Briggs, D. R., *Cereal Chem.*, **18**, 443 (1941); *C. A.*, **35**, 6828 (1941).

Foyn, E., *J. pharm. chim.*, **13**, 465 (1931); *C. A.*, **26**, 2334 (1932).

Francioli, M., *Boll. ist. sieroterap. milan.*, **16**, 825 (1937); *C. A.*, **34**, 6674 (1940).

Frankfurt, E., *Landw. Ver. Stat.*, **47**, 449 (1896); *Chem. Zentr.*, II, 1000 (1896).

Friese, H., and co-workers (Benze, R., Pommer, H., and Wiebeck, R.), *Ber.*, **75**, 1996 (1942); *C. A.*, **38**, 1544 (1944).

Fritsch, R., *Z. physiol. Chem.*, **107**, 165 (1919); *C. A.*, **14**, 1701 (1920).

Geiger, W. B., Jr., and Anderson, R. J., *J. Biol. Chem.*, **129**, 519 (1939).

Geoffroy, R., *Bull. soc. botan. France*, **81**, 17 (1934).

Ginger, L. G., and Anderson, R. J., *J. Biol. Chem.*, **156**, 443 (1944).

Glick, D., *Cereal Chem.*, **22**, 95 (1945); *C. A.*, **39**, 2342 (1945).

Goldovskiĭ, A., and Bozhenko, A., *Masloboĭno-Zhirovoe Delo No. 10*, 21 (1932); *C. A.*, **27**, 3498 (1933).

——, and Lishkevich, M. I., *Trudy VNIIZh*, 118 (1939); *C. A.*, **36**, 4728 (1942).

Goris, A., *Ann. inst. Pasteur*, **34**, 497 (1920); *C. A.*, **15**, 1148 (1921).

Gough, G. A. C., *Biochem. J.*, **26**, 248 (1932); *C. A.*, **26**, 3538 (1932).

Grafe, V., *Beitr. Biol. Pflanz.*, **16**, 129 (1928); *C. A.*, **26**, 4358 (1932).

——, *Biochem. Z.*, 205, 256 (1929); *C. A.*, **23**, 2741 (1929).

——, and Horvat, V., *Biochem. Z.*, 159, 449 (1925); *C. A.*, **20**, 931 (1926).

——, and Magistris, H., *Biochem. Z.*, 162, 366 (1925); *C. A.*, **20**, 1831 (1926).

——, ——, *ibid.*, 176, 266 (1926); *C. A.*, **21**, 1275 (1927).

——, ——, *Z. wiss. Biol.*, Abt. E. *Planta*, **2**, 429 (1926a); *C. A.*, **22**, 3903 (1928).

——, and Ose, K., *Biochem. Z.*, 187, 102 (1927); *C. A.*, **21**, 3384 (1927).

Guerrant, N. B., *J. Agr. Research*, **35**, 1001 (1927); *C. A.*, **22**, 1177 (1928).

Gupta, A. C., *J. Proc. Inst. Chemists (India)*, **20**, 41 (1948); *C. A.*, **42**, 6554 (1948).

Halász, P., *Biochem. Z.*, 87, 104 (1918); *C. A.*, **13**, 2903 (1919).

Halden, W., *Monatsh.*, **77**, 197 (1947); *C. A.*, **42**, 7393 (1948).

——, and Hinrichs, H., *Fette u. Seifen*, **49**, 697 (1942); *C. A.*, **37**, 6003 (1943).

Hammerschlag, A., *Monatsh.*, **10**, 9 (1889).

Hanahan, D. J., and Chaikoff, I. L., *J. Biol. Chem.*, **168**, 233 (1947).

Hanke, U., *Mühlenlab.*, **10**, 33 (1940); *C. A.*, **36**, 6677 (1942).

Hansteen-Cranner, B., *Ber. deut. botan. Ges.*, 37, 380 (1919); *C. A.*, **16**, 3497 (1922).

——, *Planta*, **2**, 438 (1926).

Hecht, E., *Biochem. Z.*, **279,** 157 (1935) ; *C. A.*, **29,** 8048 (1935).

Heckel, E., and Schlagdenhauffen, F., *Compt. rend.*, **103,** 388 (1886).

Heiduschka, A., and Neumann, W., *J. prakt. Chem.*, **151,** 1 (1938) ; *C. A.*, **32,** 7076 (1938).

Hilditch, T. P., *Chemistry & Industry*, 54 (1935) ; *C. A.*, **29,** 2765 (1935).

——, and Pedelty, W. H., *Biochem. J.*, **31,** 1964 (1937) ; *C. A.*, **32,** 2572 (1938).

——, and Zaky, Y. A. H., *Biochem. J.*, **36,** 815 (1942) ; *C. A.*, **37,** 2201 (1943).

Hirao, S., *J. Agr. Chem. Soc. Japan*, **7,** 364 (1931) ; *C. A.*, **25,** 5681 (1931).

Hoagland, C. L., *Ann. Rev. Biochem.*, **12,** 622 (1943).

——, Smadel, J. E., and Rivers, T. M., *J. Exptl. Med.*, **71,** 737 (1940) ; *C. A.*, **34,** 4799 (1940).

Hofer, E., *Acta Biol. Exp. (Warsaw)*, **12,** 70 (1938) ; *C. A.*, **33,** 6351 (1939).

Hoppe-Seyler, F., "Physiologische Chemie," Berlin, August Hirschwald, 1877.

——, *Z. physiol. Chem.*, **3,** 374 (1879).

Horel, J., *Chem. Obzor*, **9,** 66 (1934) ; *C. A.*, **28,** 5147 (1934).

Horvath, A. A., *Chemistry & Industry*, **56,** 735 (1937) ; *C. A.*, **31,** 8065 (1937).

——, *Proc. Pacific Sci. Congr., Pacific Sci. Assoc.*, **6,** 449 (1943).

Ihde, A. J., and Schuette, H. A., *J. Am. Chem. Soc.*, **63,** 2486 (1941) ; *C. A.*, **35,** 7472 (1941).

Iwasa, Y., *J. Agr. Chem. Soc. Japan*, **13,** 225 (1937) ; *C. A.*, **31,** 5607 (1937).

Jackson, A. H., and Kummerow, F. A., *J. Am. Oil Chemists' Soc.*, **26,** 26 (1949) ; *C. A.*, **43,** 1999 (1949).

Jacobson, H., *Z. physiol. Chem.*, **13,** 32 (1889).

Jamieson, G. S., and McKinney, R. S., *Oil & Soap*, **12,** 70 (1935) ; *C. A.*, **29,** 3541 (1935).

Jordan, R. C., and Chibnall, A. C., *Ann. Botany*, **47,** 163 (1933) ; *C. A.*, **27,** 4269 (1933).

Kaufmann, H. P., *Fette u. Seifen*, **48,** 53 (1941) ; *C. A.*, **36,** 1202 (1942).

Klenk, E., and Sakai, R., *Z. physiol. Chem.*, **258,** 33 (1939) ; *C. A.*, **33,** 4610 (1939).

Knop, W., *Landw. Ver. Stat.*, **1,** 26 (1859).

Knowles, F., and Watkin, J. E., *J. Agr. Sci.*, **22,** 756 (1932) ; *C. A.*, **27,** 1910 (1933).

Koch, W., *Z. physiol. Chem.*, **37,** 181 (1903).

Koganei, R., *J. Biochem. (Japan)*, **1,** 353 (1922) ; *C. A.*, **16,** 4244 (1922).

Kraybill, H. R., Brewer, P. H., and Thornton, M. H., U. S. Pat. 2,353,571, July 11 (1944) ; *C. A.*, **38,** 6121 (1944).

Kresling, K., *Centr. Bakt. Parasitenk., I Abt.*, **30,** 897 (1901).

Kroeker, E. H., Strong, F. M., and Peterson, W. H., *J. Am. Chem. Soc.*, **57,** 354 (1935) ; *C. A.*, **29,** 1853 (1935).

Kühl, H., *Die Mühle*, **72,** 177 (1935) ; *C. A.*, **29,** 6960 (1935).

Lauffer, M. A., and Stanley, W. M., *J. Exptl. Med.*, **80,** 535 (1944) ; *C. A.*, **39,** 556 (1945).

Lee, W. Y., and Li, S. L., *Chinese J. Physiol.*, **13,** 257 (1938) ; *C. A.*, **33,** 2942 (1939).

Levene, P. A., and Rolf, I. P., *J. Biol. Chem.*, **62,** 759 (1925).

——, ——, *ibid.*, **65,** 545 (1925a).

——, ——, *ibid.*, **68,** 285 (1926).

Lippmann, E. O., *Ber.*, **20,** 3201 (1887).

Lishkevich, M. I., *Masloboino Zhirovoe Delo*, **13,** No. 4, 20 (1937) ; *C. A.*, **32,** 820 (1938).

——, *ibid.*, No. 6, 9 (1937a) ; *C. A.*, **32,** 4366 (1938).

——, *ibid.*, No. 2, 6–8 (1939) ; *C. A.*, **33,** 9692 (1939).

Lishkevich, M. I., *Trudy VNIIZh,* 106 (1939a); *C. A.,* **36,** 4546 (1942).

Longenecker, H. E., *J. Biol. Chem.,* **129,** 13 (1939).

Lyons, R. E., *Arch. Hyg.,* **28,** 30 (1897); *Chem. Zentr.,* **I,** 116 (1897).

McClenahan, F. M., *J. Am. Chem. Soc.,* **35,** 485 (1913); *C. A.,* **7,** 3144 (1913).

McFarlane, A. S., and co-workers (Macfarlane, M. G., Amies, C. R., and Eagles, G. H.), *Brit. J. Exptl. Path.,* **20,** 485 (1939); *C. A.,* **34,** 2408 (1940).

——, and Macfarlane, M. G., *Nature,* **144,** 376 (1939); *C. A.,* **33,** 8785 (1939).

Macheboeuf, M. A., and Faure, M., *Compt. rend.,* **209,** 700 (1939); *C. A.,* **34,** 2407 **(1940).**

McKinney, R. S., Jamieson, G. S., and Holton, W. B., *Oil & Soap,* **14,** 126 (1937); *C. A.,* **31,** 5191 (1937).

MacLean, H., and MacLean, I. S., "Lecithin and Allied Substances," London, Longmans, Green and Co., Ltd., 1927.

Magistris, H., and Schäfer, P., *Biochem. Z.,* **214,** 401 (1929); *C. A.,* **24,** 1136 (1930).

——, ——, *ibid.,* **214,** 440 (1929a); *C. A.,* **24,** 1137 (1930).

Maxwell, W., *Am. Chem. J.,* **13,** 13 (1891).

Newman, M. S., and Anderson, A. J., *J. Biol. Chem.,* **102,** 219, 229 (1933).

——, Crowder, J. A., and Anderson, R. J., *J. Biol. Chem.,* **105,** 279 (1934).

Nicolle, M., and Allilaire, E., *Ann. inst. Pasteur,* **23,** 547 (1909); *C. A.,* **3,** 2825 (1909).

Nishimura, T., *Arch. Hyg.,* **18,** 318 (1893); *Chem. Zentr.,* II, 1007 (1893).

Nottbohm, F. E., and Mayer, F. M., *Chem. Ztg.,* **56,** 881 (1932); *C. A.,* **27,** 560 (1933).

——, ——, *Z. Untersuch. Lebensm.,* **67,** 369 (1934); *C. A.,* **28,** 3488 (1934).

Okano, K., Ohara, I., and Kato, J., *J. Agr. Chem. Soc. Japan,* **12,** 714 (1936); *C. A.,* **31,** 1238 (1937).

Olcott, H. S., Science, **100,** 226 (1944); *C. A.,* **38,** 6334 (1944).

Pangborn, M. C., and Anderson, R. J., *J. Biol. Chem.,* **94,** 465 (1931).

——, Chargaff, E., and Anderson, R. J., *J. Biol. Chem.,* **98,** 43 (1932).

Parrozzani, A., *Staz. sper. agrar. ital.,* **42,** 890 (1909).

Pearson, R. W., and Pierre, W. H., *Iowa Agr. Expt. Sta., Ann. Rept.,* 95–6 (1940); *C. A.,* **36,** 5940 (1942).

Peck, R. L., and Anderson, R. J., *J. Biol. Chem.,* **138,** 135 (1941).

——, and Hauser, C. R., *J. Am. Chem. Soc.,* **60,** 2599 (1938); *C. A.,* **33,** 681 (1939).

——, ——, *ibid.,* **61,** 281 (1939); *C. A.,* **33,** 3421 (1939).

——, ——, *J. Biol. Chem.,* **134,** 403 (1940).

Piper, C. V., and Morse, W. J., "The Soybean," New York, McGraw-Hill, 1923.

Polgar, N., and Robinson, R., *J. Chem. Soc.,* 615 (1943); *C. A.,* **38,** 1469 (1944).

——, ——, *ibid.,* 389 (1945); *C. A.,* **39,** 4587 (1945).

Prout, F. S., Cason, J., and Ingersoll, A. W., *J. Am. Chem. Soc.* **70,** 298 (1948); *C. A.,* **42,** 3318 (1948).

Raspopina, A., *Masloboïno Zhirovoe Delo,* **12,** 239 (1936); *C. A.,* **30,** 7371 (1936).

Rewald, B., *Biochem. Z.,* **202,** 399 (1928); *C. A.,* **23,** 3240 (1929).

——, *ibid.,* **211,** 199 (1929a); *C. A.,* **23,** 5205 (1929).

——, *ibid.,* **216,** 11 (1929b); *C. A.,* **24,** 1664 (1930).

——, *ibid.,* **216,** 15 (1929c); *C. A.,* **24,** 1664 (1930).

——, *ibid.,* **218,** 481 (1930); *C. A.,* **24,** 3034 (1930).

——, *Chem. Ztg.,* **57,** 373 (1933); *C. A.,* **27,** 3777 (1933).

——, *Biochem. Z.,* **289,** 73 (1936); *C. A.,* **31,** 2240 (1937).

——, *Chemistry & Industry,* 1002 (1936a); *C. A.,* **31,** 1504 (1937).

——, *Food,* **6,** 7 (1936b); *C. A.,* **31,** 5409 (1937).

Rewald, B., *Cong. intern. tech. et chim. ind. agr., Compt, rend. V. Congr.*, **2,** 400 (1937) ; *C. A.*, **32,** 3429 (1938).

——, *Enzymologia*, **3,** 10 (1937a) ; *C. A.*, **31,** 8607 (1937).

——, *J. Soc. Chem. Ind.*, **56,** 77T (1937b) ; *C. A.*, **31,** 3826 (1937).

——, *ibid.*, **56,** 403T (1937c) ; *C. A.*, **32,** 1963 (1938).

——, *Biochem. J.*, **36,** 822 (1942) ; *C. A.*, **37,** 2202 (1943).

——, *Oil & Soap*, **20,** 151 (1943) ; *C. A.*, **37,** 5998 (1943).

——, *ibid.*, **20,** 212 (1943a) ; *C. A.*, **38,** 273 (1944).

——, *ibid.*, **21,** 50 (1944) ; *C. A.*, **38,** 2226 (1944).

——, *ibid.*, **21,** 93 (1944a) ; *C. A.*, **38,** 2227 (1944).

——, *ibid.*, **23,** 19 (1946) ; *C. A.*, **40,** 1332 (1946).

——, and Christlieb, H., *Chem. Ztg.*, **55,** 393 (1931) ; *C. A.*, **25,** 4323 (1931).

——, ——, *Z. Untersuch. Lebensm.*, **61,** 520 (1931a) ; *C. A.*, **26,** 535 (1932).

——, and Riede, W., *Biochem. Z.*, **260,** 147 (1933) ; *C. A.*, **27,** 3500 (1933).

——, and Schweiger, A., *Biochem. Z.*, **257,** 289 (1933) ; *C. A.*, **27,** 1956 (1933).

Reznichenko, M., and Poptzova, A., *Sci. Inst. Cereal Research (U.S.S.R.)*, **13,** 35 (1934) ; *C. A.*, **29,** 543 (1935).

Rhodes, E., and Bishop, R. O., *J. Rubber Research Inst. Malaya*, **2,** 125, 136 (1930) ; *C. A.*, **25,** 3512–3 (1931).

Riede, W., and Rewald, B., *Landw. Vers. Sta.*, **110,** 291 (1930) ; *C. A.*, **25,** 2207 (1931).

Rogers, H. T., Pearson, R. W., and Pierre, W. H., *Soil Sci. Soc. Am. Proc.*, **5,** 285 (1940) ; *C. A.*, **36,** 3607 (1942).

Sabin, F. R., and Doan, C. A., *Proc. Natl. Acad. Sci.*, **13,** 552 (1927) ; *C. A.*, **21,** 3678 (1927).

——, ——, and Forkner, C. E., *J. Exp. Med.*, **52,** Supplement No. 3, 1, (1930).

Sagara, J., *J. Biochem. (Japan)*, **12,** 459 (1930) ; *C. A.*, **25,** 1545 (1931).

Salisbury, L. F., and Anderson, R. J., *J. Biol. Chem.*, **112,** 541 (1936).

Sauton, B., *Compt. rend.* **155,** 860 (1912).

Schmalfuss, K., *Bodenkunde u. Pflanzenernähr.*, **20,** 151 (1941) ; *C. A.*, **37,** 4767 (1943).

Schmidt, G. A., and Shirley, D. A., *J. Am. Chem. Soc.*, **71,** 3804 (1949).

Schneider, A. K., and Spielman, M. A., *J. Biol. Chem.*, **142,** 345 (1942).

Scholfield, C. R., and co-workers (Dutton, H. J., Tanner, Jr., F. W., and Cowan, J. C.), *J. Am. Oil Chemists' Soc.*, **25,** 368 (1948) ; *C. A.*, **43,** 331 (1949).

——, McGuire, T. A., and Dutton, H. J., *J. Am. Oil Chemists' Soc.*, **27,** 352 (1950).

Schulze, E., *Z. physiol. Chem.*, **52,** 54 (1907) ; *C. A.*, **1,** 2900 (1907).

——, *ibid.*, **55,** 338 (1908) ; *C. A.*, **2,** 2565 (1908).

——, and Frankfurt, E., *Landw. Vers. Sta.*, **43,** 307 (1894) ; *Chem. Zentr.*, **I,** 434 (1894).

——, and Likiernik, A., *Z. physiol. Chem.*, **15,** 405 (1891).

——, and Steiger, E., *Z. physiol. Chem.*, **13,** 365 (1889).

——, ——, and Maxwell, W., *Landw. Vers. Sta.*, **39,** 269 (1891).

Sedlmayr, T., *Z. ges. Brauw.*, **26,** 381 (1903) ; *Chem. Zentr.*, **II,** 258 (1903).

Shabanov, I. M., *Vsesoyuz. Inst. Tabach. i Makhoroch. Prom. im. A. I. Mikoyana No. 133,* 78 (1937) ; *C. A.*, **32,** 5444 (1938).

——, *Vsesoyuz. Nauch. Issledovatel'. Inst. Tabach. i Makhoroch. Prom. im A. I. Mikoyana No. 140,* 92 (1939) ; *C. A.*, **34,** 4862 (1940).

Shollenberger, J. H., and Goss, W. H., *U. S. Dept. Agr., Northern Regional Research Laboratory, AIC-74,* p. 8 (1945) ; *C. A.*, **39,** 3605 (1945).

Shorey, E. C., *J. Am. Chem. Soc.*, **20,** 113 (1898).

Sinclair, A. T., and McCalla, A. G., *Can. J. Research,* **C15,** 187 (1937); *C. A.,* **31,** 5047 (1937).

Skipin, A. I., Engel, I. A., and Zorabyan, A. I., *Masloboĭno Zhirovaya Prom.,* **16,** No. 5/6, 1 (1940); *C. A.,* **35,** 5335 (1941).

Smadel, J. E., and Hoagland, C. S., *Bact. Revs.,* **6,** 79 (1942); *C. A.,* **37,** 678 (1943).

Smith, J. A. B., and Chibnall, A. C., *Biochem. J.,* **26,** 218, 1345 (1932); *C. A.,* **27,** 521 (1933).

Smolenski, K., *Z. physiol. Chem.,* **58,** 522 (1909); *C. A.,* **3,** 1994 (1909).

Soden, O. v., *Z. Volksernähr,* **17,** 267 (1942); *C. A.,* **38,** 2685 (1944).

Spielman, M. A., *J. Biol. Chem.,* **106,** 87 (1934).

——, and Anderson, R. J., *J. Biol. Chem.,* **112,** 759 (1936).

Stenhagen, E., and Ställberg, S., *J. Biol. Chem.,* **139,** 345 (1941).

Strong, F. M., and Peterson, W. H., *J. Am. Chem. Soc.,* **56,** 952 (1934); *C. A.,* **28,** 3105 (1934).

Sullivan, B., *Cereal Chem.,* **17,** 661 (1940); *C. A.,* **35,** 526 (1941).

——, and Bailey, C. H., *J. Am. Chem. Soc.,* **58,** 383 (1936); *C. A.,* **30,** 3027 (1936).

——, and Near, C., *Ind. Eng. Chem.,* **19,** 159 (1927); *C. A.,* **21,** 779 (1927).

——, ——, *ibid.,* **19,** 498 (1927a); *C. A.,* **21,** 1503 (1927).

——, ——, *Cereal Chem.,* **5,** 163 (1928); *C. A.,* **22,** 2797 (1928).

——, ——, *Ind. Eng. Chem.,* **25,** 100 (1933); *C. A.,* **27,** 783 (1933).

Suzuki, B., and Nishimoto, U., *Proc. Imp. Acad. (Tokyo),* **6,** 262 (1930); *C. A.,* **24,** 5305 (1930).

Takata, R., *J. Soc. Chem. Ind. Japan,* **32,** Suppl. Binding 171B (1929); *C. A.,* **23,** 4748 (1929).

Tamura, S., *Z. physiol. Chem.,* **87,** 85 (1913); *C. A.,* **8,** 727 (1914).

Taylor, A. R., *J. Biol. Chem.,* **153,** 675 (1944).

Thomas, R. C., *Am. J. Botany,* **17,** 779 (1930).

Thornton, M. H., Johnson, C. S., and Ewan, M. A., *Oil & Soap,* **21,** 85 (1944); *C. A.,* **38,** 2228 (1944).

Thurman, B. H., U. S. Pat. 2,078,428, April 27 (1937); *C. A.,* **31,** 4410 (1937).

——, U. S. Pat. 2,150,732, March 14 (1939); *C. A.,* **33,** 4808 (1939).

——, U. S. Pat. 2,182,767, December 5 (1940); *C. A.,* **34,** 2200 (1940).

——, U. S. Pat. 2,201,061, May 14 (1940a); *C. A.,* **34,** 6470 (1940).

——, U. S. Pat. 2,201,064, May 14 (1940b); *C. A.,* **34,** 6470 (1940).

Töpler, *Landw. Vers. Sta.,* **3,** 85 (1861).

Trier, G., *Z. physiol. Chem.,* **86,** 1,407 (1913); *C. A.,* **8,** 947 (1914).

Tristram, G. R., *Biochem. J.,* **36,** 400 (1942); *C. A.,* **36,** 7070 (1942).

Troitskiĭ, N. V., Russian Pat. 42,551, April 30 (1935); *C. A.,* **31,** 7280 (1937).

Turpeinen, O., *Ann. Acad. Sci. Fennicae,* **A46,** 110 pp. (1936); *C. A.,* **31,** 3097 (1937).

Uyei, N., and Anderson, R. J., *J. Biol. Chem.,* **94,** 653 (1932).

Velick, S. F., *J. Biol. Chem.,* **152,** 533 (1944).

——, *ibid.,* **154,** 497 (1944a).

——, and Anderson, R. J., *J. Biol. Chem.,* **152,** 523 (1944).

Verna, L. C., *Anales farm. y bioquím. (Buenos Aires),* **6,** 90 (1935); *C. A.,* **30,** 5250 (1936).

von Euler, H., and Bernton, A., *Arkiv Kemi, Mineral Geol.,* **8,** No. 21 (1922); *C. A.,* **17,** 3527 (1923).

Webster, J. E., *Oklahoma Agr. Expt. Sta. J. Agr. Research,* **37,** 123 (1928); *C. A.,* **23,** 1665 (1929).

——, *Ohio J. Sci.,* **29,** 39 (1929); *C. A.,* **23,** 3116 (1929).

Weeks, M. E., and Walters, A., *Soil Sci. Soc. Am., Proc.,* **11**, 189 (1946); *C. A.,* **42**, 2382 (1948).

Weineck, E., *Z. Immunitätsforsch,* **98**, 463 (1940); *C. A.,* **38**, 3344 (1944).

Williams, C. H., Bloor, W. R., and Sandholzer, L. A., *J. Bact.,* **37**, 301 (1939); *C. A.,* **33**, 4286 (1939).

——, Sandholzer, L. A., and Van Voorhis, S. N., *J. Bact.,* **39**, 19 (1940); *C. A.,* **34**, 2017 (1940).

Winterstein, E., and Hiestand, O., *Z. physiol. Chem.,* **47**, 496 (1906).

——, ——, *ibid.,* **54**, 288 (1908); *C. A.,* **2**, 1574 (1908).

——, and Smolenski, K., *Z. physiol. Chem.,* **58**, 506 (1909); *C. A.,* **3**, 1994 (1909).

——, and Stegmann, L., *Z. physiol. Chem.,* **58**, 500 (1909); *C. A.,* **3**, 1994 (1909).

Woolley, D. W., *J. Biol. Chem.,* **147**, 581 (1943).

——, and co-workers (Strong, F. M., Peterson, W. H., and Prill, E. A.), *J. Am. Chem. Soc.,* **57**, 2589 (1935); *C. A.,* **30**, 1418 (1936).

Working, E. B., *Carnegie Inst. Wash. Yearbook,* **22**, 43 (1922/23); *C. A.,* **20**, 2181 (1926).

——, *Cereal Chem.,* **1**, 153 (1924); *C. A.,* **18**, 3436 (1924).

Yamamoto, R., and Ninomiya, M., *J. Agr. Chem. Soc. Japan,* **12**, 29 (1936); *C. A.,* **30**, 3673 (1936).

PART IV

PHOSPHATIDES FROM ANIMAL SOURCES

CHAPTER XVII

INTRODUCTION TO ANIMAL PHOSPHATIDES

That phosphorus-containing lipides were first isolated from animal sources follows logically from the fact that they occur in relative abundance in such materials as eggs, brain and nerve tissue. Thus Vauquelin (1812) noted their presence in brain and Gobley (1846, 1847) obtained a substance from egg yolk to which he gave the name lecithin. For many years thereafter, egg yolk was the most important source of phosphatides for both scientific and commercial purposes. And it was not until relatively recent times that soybeans were shown to be a more economical source of commercial phosphatides.

Because phosphatides of animal origin were more plentiful than those from plant sources, the early literature was predominantly concerned with the former. The difficulties involved in isolating pure phosphatide fractions and separating these fractions into pure compounds are manifold; and many of the observations in both the older and the modern literature are invalid because they were made on impure products.

Although phosphatides from animal sources have been known for well over a century, there are still many gaps to be filled before an entirely coherent story can be told. However, the concept that phosphatides occur in every living cell became apparent very early and no good evidence has ever been produced to dispute it. Thus, phosphatides are present in every organ and tissue in the animal body. They exist in amounts which vary with the organs or the tissues, and they comprise varying proportions of the total lipides. Likewise, the relative amounts of the individual phosphatides vary, and a variety of fatty acids have been isolated from the hydrolysis products. These variable factors seem to be concerned with the functional significance of the materials in which the phosphatides occur, with metabolism, or with general body activity. But the relationships are obscure and are only now beginning to yield to the insistence of modern research techniques. Indeed, interest in phosphatides from the point of view of metabolism and physiology is recent, for which reason data are relatively scarce.

As has been indicated above, phosphatides occur throughout the entire animal organism. They comprise the bulk of the fatty substances of the brain whose total lipide content may be as high as 13 per cent (Krause, 1943). There is roughly twice as much phosphatide in the brain as in the liver and the kidney, and about three times as much as in cardiac muscle. Likewise, phosphatides are the chief lipides of the liver, the kidneys, and perhaps the lungs. In blood, phosphatides occur in amounts equal to the cholesterol present and in excess of the neutral fat. In most of the other organs and tissues they constitute lesser amounts of the total lipides, and, as will become apparent from the remainder of the chapter, these have been studied in varying degrees. In practically every case, however, there is still need for careful, well-integrated work.

Lecithin and the cephalin fraction are by far the most predominant phosphatides from most animal sources. In most of the less careful studies, lecithin and the cephalin fraction were estimated by means of alcohol solubility, the latter remaining insoluble in warm alcohol. On this basis lecithin and the cephalin fraction are present practically in equal quantities in organs such as liver, lung, spleen and kidney. In the brain the cephalin fraction predominates. In the plasma and serum of the blood, lecithin is quantitatively the most important phosphatide, whereas it exists only in very small amounts in the corpuscles where the cephalin fraction and sphingomyelin are the major constituents.

Sphingomyelin is present in varying amounts in most and perhaps all of the animal organs and tissues. In this respect phosphatides from animal sources differ from those of plant origin, for the presence of sphingomyelin has never been proved in plant phosphatides. Sphingomyelin differs from the more common phosphatides in that it is ether-insoluble.

Sphingomyelin is present in greatest quantity in the soft organs of the body (Kaucher and co-workers, 1943) whereas it exists in smallest quantity in the skeletal muscles and in eggs. It is present in relatively large quantities in organs which include the brain, lung, kidney and intestines. Likewise, it is an important constituent of blood, and here it has been observed to exist in much more constant amounts than the cephalin fraction or lecithin. The blood corpuscles are one of the few places where sphingomyelin exists in quantities equal to the glycerophosphatides, for some investigators have shown it to be present here in about the same proportion as the cephalin fraction. In lung and brain, on the other hand, where it exists in large quantities compared to other organs, it comprises only 23 and 19 per cent, respectively, of the total phosphatides (Kaucher and co-workers, 1943).

Of great interest is phosphatidylserine (see p. 28) (Folch and Schneider, 1941; Chargaff and Ziff, 1941), whose distribution in the organism has been studied by Artom (1945). The material was first isolated from brain where it comprises perhaps one-fourth of the total phosphatides. Artom found phosphatidylserine in all the organs and tissues which he analyzed, although it was present only in small amount, rarely exceeding one-tenth of the total phosphatides. This work, then, shows that it is probably a small but constant component of most phosphatides of animal origin. Although phosphatidylserine might readily be postulated as a progenitor of phosphatidylaminoethyl alcohol, there is evidence (Folch, 1942) which indicates that this is not the case.

Somewhat less well-investigated is the inositol-containing phosphatide (see p. 35) first described by Folch and Woolley (1942). This material was found in relatively large quantity in the cephalin fraction of brain, and evidence was advanced to show that inositol was actually in chemical union with the other components generally considered characteristic of phosphatides. Although it has not been isolated from other animal sources, it has been found in soybeans, indicating that it is not exclusively characteristic of the animal kingdom.

Likewise present in the brain are the acetal phosphatides (see p. 51) of Feulgen and Bersin (1939). These also are interesting materials which will bear a considerable amount of further investigation.

Of interest as a phosphatide from animal sources is the dipalmityl-lecithin found by Lesuk and Anderson (1941) in the tapeworm, and by Thannhauser, Benotti and Boncoddo (1946) in brain, lung and spleen. This unique material shows that the distribution of phosphatide fatty acids need not necessarily be random as it is generally supposed to be with glycerides. This hydrolecithin is characterized by extreme ether insolubility, for which reason it is found in the sphingomyelin fraction.

Phosphatides of animal origin, like plant phosphatides, are prone to form complexes (see p. 81). Association with carbohydrates is, of course, much less common; although, as indicated above, a phosphatide has been isolated from brain in which inositol is actually a chemical component. Association with proteins is quite common, however, and the dissociating influence of a solvent like alcohol is necessary in order for the extraction to approach completion.

A variety of interesting fatty acids have been identified among the hydrolysis products of phosphatides from animal sources. Although such exciting substances as tuberculostearic and phthioic acids seem to be limited to the plant kingdom, there have been found in animal phosphatides long-chain, highly unsaturated acids whose presence gives rise to much interesting speculation.

The early work on the phosphatide fatty acids from animal sources was carried out largely by Levene and his colleagues (Levene and Rolf, 1921, 1922, 1922a, Levene and Simms, 1921, 1922), who found in sources such as brain and liver palmitic, stearic, oleic and arachidonic acids.

The most predominant saturated acid in animal phosphatides is, of course, palmitic acid. Stearic acid is also present; and, to a lesser extent, arachidic acid. In the phosphatides of the tapeworm Salisbury and Anderson (1939) found a saturated acid of higher molecular weight than arachidic, but this was not identified.

The unsaturated acids present vary with the source of the phosphatide. Thus the phosphatide fatty acids from blood are not ordinarily highly unsaturated, and are believed to be representative of the lipides which have been most recently ingested. Organs such as the brain and the liver, on the other hand, contain highly unsaturated phosphatide acids. Klenk (1929, 1930, 1931, 1932) has shown that an uninterrupted series of even-numbered unsaturated fatty acids from C_{16} to C_{24} exists in brain phosphatides. The C_{18} and the C_{22} acids seemed to predominate. The presence of highly unsaturated long-chain acids is considered quite unusual, for these are characteristic of marine animal oils and have been found in very few other sources. The C_{20} acids were both trienoic and tetraenoic, whereas the C_{22} acids probably contained four and five double bonds.

These highly unsaturated acids are not limited to brain, for their presence has been proved in the heart, spleen, corpus luteum, liver and adrenal glands. Milk and eggs likewise contain highly unsaturated acids, and Klenk and Dittmer (1936) believe that C_{20} and C_{22} acids always exist together although one or the other may predominate. Thus, whereas the C_{22} acids are quantitatively more important in brain, the C_{20} acids occur to a greater extent in liver.

Lignoceric acid is ordinarily found in sphingomyelin.

A great deal of profitable investigation remains to be done on the fatty acids of phosphatides from organs and tissues. In general it may be said that the fatty acid composition of the phosphatides is similar to that of the corresponding glycerides, although in the face of the above observations, it is obvious that the phosphatides tend to be more unsaturated. This situation likewise prevails in the phosphatides from many plant sources.

Quantitative procedures for the estimation of phosphatides from animal sources are for the most part still inadequate. Artom (1941) investigated the usual procedures for the estimation of blood phosphatides and found he was able to obtain fairly quantitative results only by the application of correction factors. The usual precautions must be exerted to guard against incomplete extraction of the lipide phosphorus-containing material, and against the extraction of extraneous phosphorus-containing substances. As with plant phosphatides, alcohol is necessary to dissociate the lipide-protein complexes, and the alteration in solubility effected by these complexes must be taken into consideration.

CHAPTER XVIII

PHOSPHATIDES OF NORMAL ANIMAL ORGANS AND TISSUES

BLOOD

The determination of phosphatides in blood and in the individual constituents of blood is extremely important since herein is to be found an important factor in the solution of the complex problem of intermediary lipide metabolism. In a normal animal in the so-called postabsorptive state, the bulk of the data indicate that there are present in the blood relatively large amounts of lecithin and the cephalin fraction with varying amounts of sphingomyelin. In the plasma and serum, lecithin predominates, whereas in the corpuscles the cephalin fraction and sphingomyelin constitute the bulk of the phosphatides. Most workers have found the phosphatide content to be greater in red blood cells than in the plasma, and these constitute 60 to 65 per cent of the total lipides of these cells. The total blood contains between 0.2 to 0.3 per cent phosphatides. This figure seems to be fairly constant under comparable conditions. However, the point must be stressed that the nature of blood allows wide variation not only within a species but also within a given individual. Whereas phosphatides and cholesterol and other unsaponifiables are the chief lipides of the corpuscles, there is to be found in addition in the remainder of the blood very small quantities of neutral fat and possibly some free fatty acids. The phosphatides of the blood contain fatty acids which appear not to be highly unsaturated and, in all probability, at least a portion of them are in combination with blood protein. The range of concentration of the various lipides of the blood have been tabulated by Peters and Van Slyke (1946, p. 469).

Human Blood

Isolation. There is a large amount of literature on phosphatide determination in blood. Although much of it is concerned with lower animals, human blood has likewise undergone considerable investigation. These will be considered separately. The earlier workers often employed solvent extraction for obtaining the phosphatides which they actually determined gravimetrically. Obviously, such a procedure, unless carried out under carefully controlled conditions, is fraught with error when applied to compounds which are so difficult to purify as phosphatides. Later workers have used other procedures, one of which being the widely used method of analyzing for total phosphatide by determining the phosphorus content of the isolated phosphatides. The individual phosphatides are then determined by analyzing for the hydrolysis products of these phosphatides and applying suitable mathematical manipulations. Even here, however, as in all phosphatide determinations, one must proceed cautiously, for as early as 1921 LeBreton (1921) showed that in ether-alcohol extracts phosphorus compounds other than phosphatides may be present in some organs to the extent of 20 per cent. Likewise, the intersolubility of phosphatides with other lipides causes these to be present almost universally as impurities which serve to complicate isolation and analytical procedures. As will be indicated later, other procedures have been introduced which circumvent some of these difficulties.

The worker in the field must weigh carefully the various procedures which have been advanced, utilizing the one which seems most applicable to the particular problem at hand. Since comparative data are usually desired, sampling conditions as well as analytical procedures must be standard and unvarying. It should be noted that in the study of blood lipides, samples should ordinarly be taken in the so-called postabsorptive state. This is desirable since the quantity of blood lipides must necessarily change as the blood proceeds to carry out its function of transporting raw materials and the products of cellular metabolism to and from immobile tissues. The postabsorptive state is that theoretical condition in which no food is entering the blood stream from the intestine, and in which the fasting state when blood stores are removed has not yet started. Although the actual time chosen is generally arbitrary, sixteen to eighteen hours after the last meal is often considered to approximate the postabsorptive state.

In general, the phosphatides are best obtained from blood by extraction with a mixture of ether-ethanol. From the residue remaining after evaporation of the solvents, the lipides may be extracted with petroleum ether. Acetone and magnesium chloride serve to precipitate the phosphatides from the petroleum ether solution. As will be indicated later, however, the concentration of the magnesium chloride must be carefully controlled for accurate results. Furthermore, Artom (1941) believes that the variable results obtained by different investigators for the phosphatide content of normal blood may be due to the presence of contaminants assumed to be choline. He studied various extraction procedures, none of which proved to be highly satisfactory for exact analytical work. However, he outlined several which may be used for more or less routine work.

He believes that procedures are preferable in which the blood is treated with ammonium sulfate solution or with "colloidal" iron and magnesium sulfate to obtain a protein-lipide precipitate. This must be washed with saline solution to remove substances otherwise computed as choline. The precipitate may then be extracted continuously with hot ethanol or with cold ethanol-ether in order to isolate the phosphatides. This is essentially the procedure which had been proposed by Folch and Van Slyke (1939a), save that these investigators did not wash their precipitate with saline solution. Recently, Delsal (1944) has proposed the use of methylal or a mixture of methanol and methylal as an extraction solvent for blood serum phosphatides. Both the cholesterol and the phosphatides are extracted by this solvent, whereas the proteins are precipitated.

Determination of Total Phosphatides. Once the extraction has been accomplished, three procedures which are in general use are available for the determination of total phosphatides. The first of these, and one which has been used extensively for the determination of phosphatides in tissues and fluids such as blood, is the oxidative method of Bloor (1929) (see p. 159).

A second procedure for accomplishing the same purpose depends on the determination of the total phosphorus in the extracted mixture of phosphatides. This, for example, may be done colorimetrically (Fiske and Subbarow, 1925), nephelometrically (Bloor, 1918) or microgravimetrically (Pregl, 1924, p. 47). This method has been used most extensively of all for determination of phosphatides from all sources. It is subject to the error mentioned above which arises from the presence of phosphorus from nonlipide sources. Stewart and Hendry (1935), however, have offered evidence that the phosphorus present in the alcohol-ether extract of blood is an accurate measure of the phosphatides present when controlled conditions are followed.

Still a third procedure for determination of total phosphatides is to estimate the fatty acids resulting from the hydrolysis of the phosphatides. These may be determined either by oxidation as described above for the total phosphatide, or by titration. This method, which has been used less extensively than the other two, is capable of good accuracy and is described by Artom (1932).

These procedures with various slight modifications are the ones which are employed for the determination of total phosphatides by practically all the investigators who have concerned themselves with the phosphatides of tissue.

Determination of Individual Phosphatides. Kirk (1938) has outlined a procedure for the estimation of individual blood phosphatides based on solubility differences. The phosphatides, precipitated by acetone and magnesium chloride, are treated with moist ether to dissolve the glycerophosphatides. Lecithin is estimated in this mixture by choline analysis and the cephalin fraction is estimated by calculating the difference between the lecithin and the total ether-soluble phosphatides. The sphingomyelin in turn is calculated from the phosphorus content of the ether-insoluble phosphatides. Kirk indicates that his method is only approximately quantitative, although he obtained good results with synthetic mixtures of known concentration. His method, on the other hand, is criticized by Ramsay and Stewart (1941), who believe justifiably that a solubility procedure cannot be applied quantitatively to small amounts of phosphatides which in such analyses are of the order of one milligram.

Kirk (1938) applied his method not only to heparinized plasma but also to isolated red blood cells. He found in normal human plasma as an average of twenty determinations 145 milligram per cent total phosphatides of which lecithin comprised 13 per cent of the total. The cephalin fraction comprised 47 per cent of the total and sphingomyelin made up 40 per cent of the total phosphatides. It should be noted that he did not find much difference between the total phosphatide content of the red blood cells (0.196 per cent) and the plasma (0.145 per cent). Actually the bulk of evidence indicates that there is a considerably greater concentration of phosphatides in the red blood cells than in the plasma. Kirk found as an average of twenty determinations that lecithin comprises 16 per cent of the total phosphatides of the red blood cells, whereas the cephalin fraction comprises 60 per cent and sphingomyelin 24 per cent. These results, in accord with those of other workers, show that lecithin is quantitatively the minor constituent of the red blood cell phosphatides.

Kirk's (1938) procedure was modified by Boyd (1938), who varied the concentration of magnesium chloride employed for the initial precipitation. Sinclair and Dolan (1942) also found that the amount and concentration of magnesium chloride solution used has a great effect on the accuracy and significance of the results. Kirk (1938), in his method, assumed that the choline and lecithin were contained in the moist ether extract, whereas the sphingomyelin was the chief constituent of the ether-insoluble phosphatides. Actually, Sinclair and Dolan (1942) showed that the ether-insoluble phosphatides were merely a mixture of all those present, and that the quantity of this material was practically a linear function of the concentration of magnesium chloride added. Likewise, they found the source of the phosphatides to influence ether insolubility, for the ether-insoluble phosphatides of the blood plasma may consist of 90 to 100 per cent of the total, whereas they rarely exceed 20 per cent of the total phosphatide of various other tissues. Thus, it may be seen that analytical procedures involving precipitation of the phosphatides are subject to great inaccuracies when it is necessary to determine individual phosphatides. Sinclair and Dolan (1942) were able to show, however, that precipitation was an adequate means of determining total phosphatides since quantitative precipitation could be effected by the use of specified quantities of acetone and magnesium chloride. Thus, the method may be used safely only when it is desired to estimate the total phosphatide content.

A procedure for the estimation of the individual phosphatides of blood was investigated carefully by Ramsay and Stewart (1941). This method is based on the determination of lipide phosphorus, choline and glycerol by microprocedures which they outline in detail. From these data, it is possible to calculate the amount of lecithin, cephalin fraction and sphingomyelin present, since phosphorus is present in all three, whereas choline is present only in lecithin and sphingomyelin, and glycerol is present only in lecithin and the cephalin fraction.

They applied their procedure to twelve samples of whole blood obtained from twelve healthy men, most of whom were under twenty-five years of age. Their results, which are given in detail in Table I, indi-

TABLE 1. CONCENTRATION OF PHOSPHATIDES IN WHOLE BLOOD
(RAMSAY AND STEWART, 1941)

Sample	Lecithin		Cephalin fraction		Sphingomyelin	
	Millimol. per 100 ml.	% of total phosphatides	Millimol. per 100 ml.	% of total phosphatides	Millimol. per 100 ml.	% of total phosphatides
1	0.028	6	0.148	35	0.250	59
2	.110	33	.039	11	.184	56
3	.054	15.5	.055	15.5	.246	69
4	.071	23	.053	14	.212	63
5	.034	13	.085	25	.211	62
6	.043	11	.095	26	.228	63
7	.052	16	.059	19	.204	65
8	.035	14	.092	26	.192	60
9	.031	9	.077	22	.244	69
10	.000	0	.104	30	.245	70
11	.017	5	.086	25	.244	70
12	.025	9.5	.078	20.5	.267	70
Mean		13		22		64

cate the rather surprising fact that sphingomyelin is quantitatively the most important constituent, and that the cephalin fraction is present in greater concentration than lecithin. Likewise, the proportion of sphingomyelin is relatively constant, ranging between 56 to 70 per cent of the total phosphatide with an average value of 64 per cent. Cephalin phosphatides account for an average of 22 per cent of the total, whereas lecithin comprises an average of 13 per cent, although the individual variation in the case of lecithin and the cephalin fraction are so great that an average is of little significance. Indeed, it will be noted in one case that lecithin was completely lacking. These workers, unfortunately, do not indicate the physiological condition of the individuals from which the samples were taken. The table is included, however, because it is an example of the fact that even with careful work it is difficult to obtain data which check sufficiently for generalization.

Still another method for the determination of the individual phosphatides in blood and other body fluids and tissues has been advanced by Thannhauser and Setz (1936) and Thannhauser, Benotti, and Reinstein (1939). In their procedure, sphingomyelin is determined as the reineckate. The total choline is determined and this value is transformed by a suitable factor into the combined amount of lecithin and sphingomyelin present. The difference between this value and the total phosphatides is the amount of cephalin fraction present. The lecithin, obviously, may be determined by difference. According to Ramsay and Stewart (1941), this method has the disadvantage of requiring large amounts of sample in order for sphingomyelin precipitation to be complete. When this method was applied to normal human blood serum, the average results of six determinations showed 226 milligrams per 100 ml. of phosphatides present. This figure is somewhat higher than Kirk's (1938) results. Of this amount, 10.1 per cent was sphingomyelin, 42.4 per cent was cephalin fraction, and the remainder (47.3 per cent) was lecithin. Here, as in the results of Ramsay and Stewart (1941) for whole blood, it was noted that the sphingomyelin concentration was much more constant than that of the other two constituents, for, whereas it varied from approximately 15 to 35 milligram per cent, the cephalin fraction varied from 50 to 130 and the lecithin from 50 to 200 milligram per cent.

Sinclair and Dolan (1942) found this method inapplicable in a study of the phosphatide content of blood under various conditions. Marenzi and Cardini (1943), however, were able to apply this general procedure to blood plasma, using their own procedure for choline. They found further that the reineckate of sphingomyelin was not precipitated as a pure material. Accordingly, it is somewhat more accurate to estimate the sphingomyelin from the phosphorus content of the precipitate. Their results indicated 204 milligram per cent of phosphatides in blood plasma, which is somewhat higher than the results of other investigators. Of this total, lecithin comprised 61.5 per cent, cephalin fraction 21.5 per cent and sphingomyelin 17.1 per cent.

Artom (1941), using his method (described above) in which the protein-lipide complex was precipitated, found 152 ± 16 milligram per cent of total phosphatides in blood plasma of fasting individuals. This is an average of sixteen determinations, and the individual variations are quite small in comparison with results of other investigators. He made no attempt to separate the lecithin and sphingomyelin since he does not believe, and rightly so, that any of the analytical procedures for sphingomyelin are accurate. Thus, he merely analyzed for the choline-containing phosphatides, and from the choline content and the total phosphorus content the cephalin fraction was calculated by difference. His results for fasting individuals indicated 122 ± 14 * milligram per cent of combined lecithin and sphingomyelin, and 30 ± 9.5 milligram per cent of cephalin fraction. For persons in the absorptive state, the results were somewhat higher, especially for the cephalin fraction.

Williams and co-workers (1938) provided a method for the determination of lecithin and cephalin fraction in blood and tissues which was based on the determination of the choline-phosphorus ratio of the glycerophosphatides which were precipitated with acetone and magnesium chloride. The cephalin fraction was estimated by difference. Their procedure, however, was criticized by Thannhauser, Benotti and Reinstein (1939) on the basis that the hydrolytic procedure employed to free the choline for analysis was incomplete. Ramsay and Stewart (1941) likewise point out that the precipitation of the choline may have been carried out in too acidic a medium for quantitative results. Their work, nevertheless, showed, in general agreement with other workers, that the cephalin fraction was a major component of red blood cell phosphatides and a lesser component of plasma phosphatides. Their individual analyses, on the other hand, showed a wide variation.

A micromethod for the determination of the individual phosphatides in blood is described by Erickson and co-workers (1940). Thus, sphingomyelin was precipitated as the reineckate and the amount of sphingomyelin present was calculated from the phosphorus content of the precipitate. Total choline was determined as well as total phosphatide, thus providing sufficient data to calculate the quantities of each compound present. These workers determined the phosphatides in blood plasma as well as in the red blood cells and in red blood cell stroma. They found 189 milligram per cent of total phosphatides in plasma, 317 milligram per cent in red blood cells and 10 milligram per cent in the dried stroma. Their results for plasma are in fair agreement with the above-cited results of Thannhauser, Benotti and Reinstein (1939) and Thannhauser and Setz (1936). However, although both groups of workers found that

---

* Unless otherwise indicated, the expression $x \pm y$ represents an average plus or minus a standard deviation.

lecithin was the chief component of plasma phosphatides, Erickson and co-workers found considerably less cephalin fraction than did the previous workers. Both agreed that sphingomyelin was quantitatively the minor constituent. Erickson's results for the red blood cells are much higher than those of Kirk's (1938), the discrepancy probably arising from the precipitation procedure employed by Kirk. Both sets of data showed, however, that over one-half of the total phosphatides of the red blood cells is present as cephalin fraction, whereas the remainder is divided fairly evenly between the other two components.

Hack (1947) has applied his procedure for phosphatide analysis (see p. 167) to the components of human blood sampled after three and fifteen hours of fasting. The average results are listed in Table II in millimoles per liter.

TABLE II. PHOSPHATIDES OF HUMAN BLOOD (HACK, 1947)

Material	No. of samples	Hours of fasting	Total phospha-tide	Lecithin	Cephalin fraction	Sphingomyelin
Blood	2	3	3.38	1.71	0.80	0.72
	2	15	3.35	1.80	.80	.75
Cells	2	3	3.89	0.95	1.94	1.01
	2	15	3.93	1.32	1.50	1.11
Plasma	2	3	2.97	2.33	0.14	0.50
	2	15	2.86	2.24	.18	.44
Serum	8	3	2.79	2.26	.17	.39
	8	15	2.69	2.12	.14	.43

This work confirms the conclusions of Taurog, Entenman and Chaikoff (1944, see below) that the bulk of the phosphatides of plasma are choline-containing. This is likewise the case for serum, whereas most of the cephalin fraction is found in the cells. The distribution of phosphatides in the serum and the plasma is shown by this work to be approximately equal.

Blix (1940) developed a microprocedure for the determination of phosphatidylaminoethyl alcohol which depends on the fact that aminoethyl alcohol may be distilled quantitatively under certain specified conditions from a mixture of the hydrolysis products of phosphatides. In blood serum he found 229 milligram per cent of total phosphatides of which 60 per cent was lecithin, 27 per cent was phosphatidylaminoethyl alcohol and 13 per cent was sphingomyelin. The latter was determined indirectly from the total phosphatide, fatty acid and glycerol contents. These results are in fair agreement with other workers. Kirk, Page and Van Slyke (1934) had estimated the cephalin fraction by determination of the amino nitrogen in petroleum ether solutions of extracts of plasma. Later, however, they (Van Slyke and co-workers, 1934/35) showed that the nitrogen in the petroleum ether extract of blood plasma contained more amino and nonamino nitrogen than could be accounted for by the phosphatides present. Folch and Van Slyke (1939) showed that significant amounts of urea and amino acids were present which caused high results for the cephalin fraction estimated in this way. Although Ramsay and Stewart (1941) had not been able to estimate aminoethyl alcohol quantitatively by periodate oxidation, Artom (1945) applied this oxidative determination to a mixture of serine and aminoethyl alcohol. By this procedure he was able, as will be indicated later, to show the presence of serine-containing phosphatides in the cephalin fraction of human blood plasma.

Hunter (1942) found the blood plasma of the cat to contain 0.18 ± 0.2 per cent total phosphatides of which 0.03 ± 0.1 per cent was sphingomyelin as determined by precipitation of the reineckate. The cells contained 0.49 ± 0.03 per cent total phosphatides and 0.12 ± 0.02 per cent sphingomyelin.

Brante (1940), who was primarily interested in studying the change in blood phosphatides during lipemia, found 185 milligram per cent of total phosphatides in blood serum of which 22 per cent was cephalin fraction and 78 per cent was choline-containing phosphatides. His method was similar to that of Erickson and co-workers (1940).

Izzo and Marenzi (1944) found that plasma phosphatides are somewhat reduced in tuberculous individuals and that the lecithin fraction decreased the most. Their average values in milligram per cent for twelve normal individuals are: total phosphatides, 165.3 ± 53.2; cephalin fraction, 95.9 ± 31.3; lecithin, 61.9 ± 39.9; sphingomyelin, 7.4 ± 4.3.

The phosphatide content of the white blood cells has been studied by Boyd (1936c). He found that so-called active leucocytes contained larger percentages of phosphatide than inactive ones. This is formally analogous to the observations that active glands and muscles are richer in phosphatides than inactive ones. In his publication, Boyd outlines his procedure for isolating the white cells. The phosphatides are extracted from them by conventional procedures and estimated by the oxidative procedure (Boyd, 1931). Analyses on twenty-two normal individuals yielded an average value of 844 ± 241 milligram per cent of phosphatides in the white blood cells. This is the only instance in which the phosphatide content of the leucocytes has been investigated.

Erickson and co-workers (1939) studied the lipides of blood platelets and found that they were composed, on a dry basis, of 12 per cent phosphatides, of which 68 per cent was cephalin fraction.

Lipide distribution in the blood of children has been studied extensively by Macy (1942, p. 217).

Nature of Phosphatides. Taurog, Entenman and Chaikoff (1944) studied the phosphatides of both dog and human blood plasma. On the basis of the choline-phosphorus ratio they arrived at the surprising conclusion that the plasma of neither the dog nor man contained appreciable amounts of the cephalin fraction, but rather that all the phosphatides are choline-containing. They did not, however, analyze for the presence of aminoethyl alcohol or serine. Their evidence, however, is good and is in agreement with Hack (1947, see above). This work was corroborated also by Sinclair (1948).

Other investigators have reported instances in which the cephalin fraction was absent from blood phosphatides. Artom and Freeman (1940) found this to be the case at times in rabbits who had been fed oil, and Williams and co-workers (1941) found no cephalin fraction in the blood plasma of dogs suffering from anemia caused by propyl disulfide. The samples analyzed by Taurog and co-workers, however, were from normal individuals or animals and were taken during the postabsorptive state. In view of this work, serious doubt is placed on the older results which show appreciable quantities of cephalin fraction in human plasma.

Amino Acid-containing Lipides. Artom (1945) has recently shown that serine-containing phosphatides are co-existent with aminoethyl alcohol-containing phosphatides, and has demonstrated the presence of these in human blood plasma. Accordingly, as stated in Part I, the term "cephalin fraction" is used here to designate a mixture of these phosphatides, even though the earlier workers were not aware of the presence of phosphatidylserine in what they termed "cephalin". Artom found 197 micromoles per 100 milliliters of plasma of which 66.5 per cent were choline-containing phosphatides. The aminoethyl alcohol-containing phosphatides comprised 21.4 per cent and the serine-containing phosphatides 6.6 per cent of the total. The remainder was not accounted for. In a check analysis in which the sphingomyelin was precipitated as the reineckate, it was found that there was 55 per cent lecithin, 12 per cent sphingomyelin, 21 per cent phosphatidylaminoethyl alcohol and 7 per cent serine-containing phosphatides. This is in excellent agreement with the previous results. This work cannot at the present time be made compatible with the observations that human plasma contains only choline-containing phosphatides.

Summary. Table III indicates the results obtained by representative investigators for the phosphatide content of human blood.

In analyses of this sort an observation of Schmidt (1935) must be borne in mind. He has shown that the phosphatide content of oxalated plasma is 10 to 12 per cent lower than that of heparinized plasma and that this difference is due to alterations in cell and plasma volumes pro-

TABLE III. THE PHOSPHATIDE CONTENT OF HUMAN BLOOD

Investigator	Serum, plasma or corpuscles	Number of subjects	Total phosphatides (Mg. %)	Lecithin (% of total)	Cephalin fraction* (% of total)	Sphingomyelin (% of total)	Choline phosphatides (% of total)	Dietary state of subject
Thannhauser, Benotti & Reinstein (1939)	Serum	6	226	47	42	11	58	Postabsorptive
Brante (1940)	Serum	12	185		22		78	Postabsorptive
Blix (1940)	Serum	2	229	60	27	13	73	Not stated
Erickson & co-workers (1940)	Plasma	4	189	52	29	19	71	Not stated
Marenzi & Cardini (1943)	Plasma	Not stated	204	61	22	17	78	Not stated
Artom (1941)	Plasma	16	152		20		80	Postabsorptive
Kirk (1938)	Plasma	20	145	13	47	40	53	Fasting
Taurog, Entenman & Chaikoff (1944)	Plasma	11	235	55	3		97	Postabsorptive
Artom (1945)	Plasma	Not stated	153		28	12	67	Not stated
Schmitz & Koch (1930)	Serum	2	184		59			Not stated
Erickson & co-workers (1940)	Erythrocytes	4	317	24	60	50	74	Not stated
Kirk (1938)	Erythrocytes	20	196	16	60	24	40	Fasting
Erickson & co-workers (1940)	Erythrocyte Stroma	4	10					Not stated
Boyd (1936c)	Leucocytes	22	844 ± 241	20	50	30	50	Not stated

* This figure includes serine-containing phosphatides.

duced by the oxalate, and not to the precipitation of phosphatides. In his experiments he used heparin concentrations of 0.04 per cent and potassium oxalate concentrations of 0.1 to 0.8 per cent. Boyd (1936b), in addition, has shown that oxalate increases the apparent lipide content of the red blood cells because it serves to decrease their volume by dehydration.

Animal Blood

The phosphatide content of the blood of animals has concerned many workers. In general, the literature indicates that there are wide variations in the values of different species, and lesser although definite variations between individuals of the same species. The methods of analyses for the most part are similar to those indicated for human blood and will not be described in detail.

Some of the earliest reliable values were obtained by Abderhalden (1911), whose results, indicated in Table IV, are valuable for comparative purposes. He does not describe the dietary state of the animals. The remarkable constancy of Abderhalden's results is worthy of comment. This constancy among different species has not been observed to such a great extent by other workers.

TABLE IV. PHOSPHATIDE CONTENT OF BLOOD OF VARIOUS ANIMALS ACCORDING TO ABDERHALDEN (1911)

(Values are parts per thousand parts by weight)

Animal	Phosphatide in blood	Phosphatide in serum	Phosphatide in corpuscles
Cow	2.349	1.675	3.748
Bull	2.197	1.869	2.850
Sheep	2.220	1.709	3.379
Sheep	2.417	1.599	4.163
Goat	2.466	1.727	3.856
Horse	2.913	1.720	3.973
Horse	2.982	1.746	4.855
Pig	2.309	1.426	3.456
Rabbit	2.827	1.760	4.627
Dog	2.052	1.699	2.568
Dog	1.994	1.755	2.296
Cat	2.325	1.716	3.119

Mayer and Schaeffer (1913) made similar determinations, estimating the phosphatide content from the ether-soluble phosphorus. These are listed in Table V.

In these results it is seen that the variations in the corpuscle values are much narrower than in the values for serum. This has been found

TABLE V. PHOSPHATIDE CONTENT OF BLOOD OF VARIOUS ANIMALS ACCORDING
TO MAYER AND SCHAEFFER (1913)

Animal	Phosphatide in dry serum (mg./100 gms.)	Phosphatide in moist serum (mg./100 cc.)	Phosphatide in dry corpuscles (mg./100 gms.)
Guinea pig	253	15	902
Rabbit	704	45	1,573
Sheep	704	48	1,045
Horse	1,463	130	836
Cow	1,100	93	726
Hen	3,685	240	1,364
Dog	3,245	275	957
Pig	803	68	1,199
Eel	10,241	883	
Muraena eel	308		

generally true for many species of animals, and for lipides other than
phosphatides.

One of the first investigators to use microprocedures was Horiuchi
(1920), who analyzed the blood of rabbits for phosphatides. He found
that neither a low nor a high fat diet varied the results, there being
210 milligram per cent of total phosphatides in the whole blood,
110 milligram per cent in the plasma and 380 to 400 milligram per cent
in the corpuscles. The phosphatide values determined by Bloor (1921)
for the blood of various animals are listed in Table VI. These are average
values in which considerable individual variations were demonstrated.
The value for man is included for comparative purposes. Again it will
be noted that the values for corpuscles vary much less than the values for
the plasma.

TABLE VI. PHOSPHATIDE CONTENT OF BLOOD OF VARIOUS ANIMALS ACCORDING
TO BLOOR (1921)

Animal	No. of samples	Phosphatide in plasma (mg. %)	Phosphatide in corpuscles (mg. %)
Man	21	192	448
Dog	5	240	440
Beef	3	144	400
Calf	4	72	400
Cat	3	144	600
Rabbit	19	92	544
Hen	2		496

Boyd (1942, 1944) used the method of Bloor (1929) for the determination of phosphatides in the blood plasma of various animals. His results
are indicated in Table VII. It is interesting to note that in bullfrog
plasma no neutral fat whatsoever was found. Dog plasma had the greatest

TABLE VII. PHOSPHATIDE CONTENT OF BLOOD OF VARIOUS ANIMALS
ACCORDING TO BOYD (1942, 1944)

Animal	No. of samples	Phosphatides in plasma (mg. % ± standard deviation)	Per cent of total lipides
Man	118	165 ± 28	31
Guinea pig	10	51 ± 12	29
Bullfrog	10	52 ± 16	25
Albino rat	116	83 ± 24	36
Rabbit	89	78 ± 33	32
Cow	3	84 ± 21	24
Cat	27	132 ± 53	35
Cockerel	22	155 ± 34	30
Dog	15	242 ± 80	41

amount of total lipides of any animal investigated and, as will be noted in the table, the dog possessed the greatest percentage of phosphatides. Boyd (1942, 1944) also determined the phosphatide content of the red blood cells from oxalated blood of various animals. He found the following results in milligram per cent for various animals: bullfrog, 201 ± 32; rabbit, 259 ± 35; guinea pig, 347 ± 48.

Dziemian (1939), using the procedures of Kirk (see p. 165), analyzed for the individual phosphatides of the red blood cells of various animals. His results, as in the case of man, indicate a predominance of cephalin fraction as shown in Table VIII.

TABLE VIII. PHOSPHATIDE CONTENT OF THE RED BLOOD CELLS OF VARIOUS
ANIMALS ACCORDING TO DZIEMIAN (1939)

Animal	Lecithin (mg./cc. of red blood cell)	Cephalin fraction (mg./cc.of red blood cell)	Ether-insoluble phosphatides (mg./cc. of red blood cell)
Rabbit	0.57	2.06	0.20
Rat	.64	3.82	.38
Beef	.31	3.32	.42
Macaque monkey	1.87	2.91	

Cardini and Serantes (1942) found that the plasma of adult female albino rats contained 0.086 per cent lecithin, 0.019 per cent cephalin fraction and 1.11 per cent sphingomyelin; whereas the whole blood contained 1.04 per cent lecithin, 0.105 per cent cephalin fraction and 4.13 per cent sphingomyelin. The high sphingomyelin content is questionable.

Chaikoff and Entenman (1946) have studied carefully the total lipide and phosphatide content of turtle blood. The male blood contained 195 ± 43 (standard error) milligrams of phosphatide per 100 ml., whereas the female blood contained 195 ± 45 to 246 ± 52 milligrams per 100 ml., depending on the ovarian activity of the animal.

Erickson and co-workers (1938) analyzed for the lipides of red blood cells, with and without stroma, from cows, sheep, horses, chicken, turkey and man. Their results indicated that the lipide content is related to the characteristic size of the cell, for the large avian cell demonstrated a high lipide content in contrast to the small sheep cell. Correspondingly, the human and bovine cells were both intermediate in size and in lipide content. The type and composition of the lipides, however, were essentially the same except in the case of avian blood. In both the stroma and the red blood cells, the phosphatides comprised about 60 per cent of the total lipides, whereas the remainder was divided between free cholesterol (30 per cent) and a mixture of cholesterol esters and neutral fat (10 per cent). The cephalin fraction was the chief constituent, accounting for about 50 per cent of the total. In the avian blood, phosphatides accounted for about 75 per cent of the lipides of the red blood cells.

A recent study of Ranney, Entenman and Chaikoff (1949) on the phosphatide content of the plasma of the fowl has indicated that about 21 per cent of the phosphatides are cephalins. This is in marked contrast to previous results obtained by these workers with mammals, since non-choline-containing phosphatides were virtually absent in the plasma of man, dog, pig and beef. In fowl, lecithin comprised 65 per cent of the plasma phosphatides, and sphingomyelin 14 per cent. Sinclair (1948), similarly, found 16 to 20 per cent cephalin fraction in the serum of the turkey.

Fatty Acids

As indicated previously, little is known about the fatty acids of blood phosphatides. Sinclair (1936) believes that the fatty acids of blood plasma phosphatides are largely those of the fat which has been most recently absorbed. The fatty acids are ordinarily fairly saturated and seem to be very similar to the free fatty acids and to those of the neutral fat in the blood. Schaible (1932), however, found that the fatty acids of plasma phosphatides of cows are less saturated than those of both cholesterol esters and neutral fat. For the fatty acids of the phosphatides of normal human plasma, Bloor, Blake and Bullen (1938) observed an iodine number of 125 as compared to 102 for the neutral fat and 158 for the cholesterol esters. Page, Pasternak and Burt (1930) found the iodine numbers of the phosphatides from human blood to vary from 52 to 103. The iodine number of the fatty acids of beef plasma has been determined as 71 (Bloor, 1923, 1924, 1925; Channon and Collinson, 1929). The similar constant for the pig is 80 (Bloor, 1923, 1924, 1925), and for the dog is 89 (Bloor, 1923, 1924, 1925).

Wilson and Hansen (1936) obtained some evidence for the presence of 20- or higher carbon acids in blood lipides together with the predominant unsaturated C_{18} acids. The iodine values of their fatty acids varied from 99 to 113.

Thannhauser, Setz and Benotti (1938) isolated sphingomyelin from the stromata of red blood cells and found the chief acid present to be lignoceric acid. Palmitic and stearic acids were probably also present in smaller quantity.

Complex Formation

Evidence has been advanced by Roche and Marquet (1935) and by Macheboeuf (1929, 1929a, 1929b, 1929c) which indicates that blood phosphatides occur to a large extent in the form of protein complexes. Water-soluble protein, phosphatide and cholesterol combinations, which are apparently compounds, have been obtained by Macheboeuf (1929) from blood plasma. Macheboeuf and Sandor (1932) found that an appreciable amount of phosphatide is not ether-extractable from serum until alcohol is added. In the latter case, 50 per cent of the material may be extracted. The lipides removed in this way are associated with globulin, whereas the albumin complexes remain resistant to extraction. Turner and Gibson (1932) found that about one-half of the total lipides of human and dog plasma and of horse serum was carried along during precipitation of the proteins; and the globulins were in combination with the greater part of the lipides. It is undoubtedly this tendency for complex formation which accounts for many of the physiological properties of blood phosphatides.

BRAIN AND NERVOUS SYSTEM

The brain is a rich source of phosphatides and, together with the spinal cord, probably possesses the highest phosphatide content of any of the organs, a fact to which great significance was attributed by earlier workers. It contains roughly twice as much phosphatide as does liver and kidney, and about three times as much as heart muscle. The chief phosphatide of the brain is the cephalin fraction which has now been shown to include the inositol phosphatides and phosphatidylserine, as well as phosphatidylaminoethyl alcohol. Much of the brain phosphatide is contained in the myelin sheaths where sphingomyelin is prominent (Johnson, McNabb and Rossiter, 1949), although the cells themselves likewise contain representative amounts. The phosphatide content of the brain increases with age to a certain point of its own accord (Schuwirth, 1940), but it appears very difficult to alter the amount by external means such as diet. Disease, on the other hand, especially if concerned with demyelinating processes, may effect marked changes.

Isolation

The isolation of the phosphatides from brain has been carried out by many workers similarly to the isolation of phosphatides from other tissues (see p. 150). The situation, however, is somewhat complicated by the presence in brain of cerebrosides and organic phosphorus compounds such as adenylic pyrophosphate, phosphocreatine and adenylic acid. Fawaz, Lieb and Zacherl (1937) proposed a microisolation procedure for phosphatides which makes use of the standard solvent, trichloracetic acid, to extract the extraneous phosphorus-containing material. The residue is then extracted with alcohol and the lipide phosphorus is determined in the alcohol extract.

The analytical determination of brain phosphatides may be carried out according to any of the procedures indicated in the discussion of blood phosphatides with appropriate modifications which arise from the different physical nature of the two substances. The procedure used by most investigators for the determination of total phosphatides is to analyze for the phosphorus of the phosphatide fraction and apply suitable calculations. The individual phosphatides are determined by analyzing quantitatively for the hydrolysis products. There is a surprising amount of agreement in the literature for the values of the phosphatide content of brain, even though a wide variety of analytical procedures have actually been used. Most of the data are derived from analyses of animal brains, although a representative amount of work is also concerned with the human brain. Although phosphatides in brain were first detected by Gobley (1847), the first extensive investigations of brain phosphatides were carried out by Thudichum (1901), to whom a great deal of credit is due for the careful work he was able to accomplish without the benefit of modern analytical techniques. This worker found in the brain, lecithin, the cephalin fraction and sphingomyelin which he isolated and characterized.

It is interesting to note, however, that Schuwirth (1940) could find no sphingomyelin in the fetal brain or in the brain of the new-born child, although he mentions the presence of "ether-insoluble glycerophosphatides".

The brain phosphatides are characterized by highly unsaturated acids which will be discussed later. These, however, in many cases have not been fully characterized, and more work remains to be done here as in other aspects of phosphatide chemistry.

The phosphatides of the nervous system have not been explored extensively, no doubt because of the difficulty involved in isolating nerve tissue. The work which has been done, however, will be included in this discussion.

Distribution of Phosphatides

Despite the contrary results of Thudichum (1901), there seems to be a greater quantity of phosphatide in the white matter of the brain than in the grey matter. Thus, Smith (1912/13) reported the dry white matter of brain to contain about 23 per cent and the grey matter about 15 per cent phosphatides. According to Yasuda (1937), the phosphatide contents of the grey and white matter of brain are fairly constant and characteristic for each. The fresh white matter contains 12.5 per cent phosphatide, which is almost three times as much as that contained by the grey matter (4.4 per cent). This difference, however, decreases markedly when analyses are made on dry material. Thus, the dry white matter contained 39.3 per cent and the dry grey matter 25.2 per cent phosphatide. The white matter also contains a greater proportion of cholesterol. The iodine numbers of the phosphatides of the two fractions likewise differ considerably, and Randall (1938), who also reported a higher percentage of phosphatide in the white matter, found that the fatty acids of the phosphatides of the white matter of human brain had an iodine number of 84. The corresponding value for the acids of the grey matter was 129. Likewise, he noted that the grey tissue had a higher sphingomyelin content than the white tissues.

A comparison of the concentration of the various phosphatides in the brains of infants and adults has been made by Johnson, McNabb and Rossiter (1949).

Erickson and co-workers (1940) applied their micromethod of analysis (see p. 265) to the phosphatides of dog brain. They found, as an average of four determinations on dry tissue, 20 per cent total phosphatides of which 20 per cent was lecithin, 60 per cent was cephalin fraction, and 20 per cent was sphingomyelin. This approximates the results of Thannhauser and co-workers (1939), who employed a macroprocedure on human brain. They found as an average of two determinations on dry brain 31 per cent phosphatides of which 16 per cent was lecithin, 65 per cent was cephalin fraction and 19 per cent was sphingomyelin.

Carayon-Gentil and Corteggiani (1942) extracted the free choline of beef brain with an acetone solution of magnesium chloride. From the brain residue they obtained the glycerophosphatides by petroleum ether extraction and the sphingomyelin by extraction with a methanol-chloroform mixture. The separation by such a procedure is undoubtedly not entirely quantitative. Their results, calculated from the choline contents of the extracts, indicated 6 to 29 milligrams of free choline per gram of fresh brain, 8 to 15 milligrams of lecithin per gram and 5.8 to 6.3 milligrams of sphingomyelin per gram.

Cardini and Serantes (1942) analyzed the brain of adult female albino rats for the constituent phosphatides. Their procedure involved the determination of choline and sphingomyelin as the reineckates (pp. 171, 174). They found 11.2 per cent lecithin, 2.0 per cent cephalin fraction, and 0.51 per cent sphingomyelin. These results are indeed strange, for it is generally agreed that the cephalin fraction is the chief constituent of the brain phosphatides.

The phosphatides of composite samples of beef brain were determined by Kaucher and co-workers (1943). By determining the total amount of choline and sphingomyelin present, it was possible to calculate the amounts of the individual phosphatides. Thus their method was in principle similar to that of Cardini and Serantes (1942), although their results are more in accord with the accepted values. They obtained the following results for two analyses. The figures are per cent of dry weight.

Total phosphatide	Cephalin fraction	Lecithin	Sphingomyelin
24.27	12.57	6.65	5.05
28.48	16.14	7.46	4.88

Hunter (1942) found 1.25 ± 0.19 per cent sphingomyelin in the brain of the cat. This is on a wet basis and comprises approximately one-fourth of the total phosphatides.

There have been various studies which have been induced by a desire to correlate the function of a given portion of the brain or nervous system with its composition. Thus Gorodisska (1925) studied the variation in concentration of the lipides in various parts of the brain. Cholesterol exhibited the greatest amount of variation, followed by the saturated phosphatides and cerebrosides. The unsaturated phosphatides were somewhat more constant. In general, the amount of protein exceeded the amount of lipide in the more important and more active portions of the nervous system. The peripheral nerves contained the highest lipide content, the spinal cord contained less and the brain contained least of all. These studies likewise showed that the white matter contained more lipides than the grey matter, for lipide constituted two-thirds of the former and one-third of the latter.

Randall (1938) also determined the phosphatide content of the various portions of the brain. He used both the oxidative procedure (Bloor, 1929) and the procedure whereby lipide phosphorus is determined. The former values were practically always higher than the latter because in the oxidative method the cerebrosides were also included since they are acetone-insoluble. The results are listed in Table IX.

TABLE IX. PHOSPHATIDE CONTENT OF BRAIN PORTIONS (RANDALL, 1938)

Portion of brain	% Phosphatide (mean values) Oxidative method	From lipide phosphorus	Iodine numbers of fatty acids
Corona radiata	40.33 ± 2.42	30.80 ± 2.17	84 ± 6.6
Frontal white	38.54 ± 2.33	29.79 ± 2.11	84 ± 5.6
Parietal white	40.86 ± 4.81	29.90 ± 2.29	84 ± 6.8
Brain stem	38.59 ± 2.54	30.42 ± 2.22	88 ± 6.7
Thalamus	33.86 ± 2.06	29.26 ± 1.62	95 ± 9.4
Caudate nucleus	24.12 ± 3.21	25.95 ± 3.15	116 ± 12.2
Frontal cortex	24.17 ± 1.57	25.24 ± 2.15	129 ± 10.6
Parietal cortex	24.71 ± 1.22	25.15 ± 1.74	129 ± 12.3

Fries and co-workers (1941) likewise studied the total phosphatide content of various divisions of the rat brain. They found the values to vary with the age and weight of the animal, but in the oldest animals studied (300 gram) the cord contained 10 per cent phosphatides, the medulla 8 per cent, the forebrain 4.5 per cent and the cerebellum 4.5 per cent. In 50 gram rats the cord, medulla, cerebellum and forebrain contained 8.3, 6.8, 4.0 and 4.0 per cent phosphatides, respectively, whereas in the one-week-old rat the cord contained about twice as much phosphatide as the cerebellum. This same progression in which the cord contains the highest and the medulla the second highest quantities of phosphatide was noted throughout the entire period of observation.

Phosphatides of the Nervous System

Palladin, Rashba and Helman (1935) found that the quantities of unsaturated phosphatides and the cholesterol decreased in the following order in the various portions of the nervous system of dogs: spinal cord (grey), nucleus caudatus, cerebral cortex and cortex cerebelli. The saturated phosphatides existed to a lesser extent in the spinal cord than in the other portions. These same workers found that the quantities of unsaturated phosphatides decreased in the vegetative nervous system of cows in the following order: ganglion *coeliacus*, ganglion of sympathetic trunk, and ganglion *nodosum nervus vagi*. For the saturated phosphatides, the order of the last two was reversed.

Mitolo (1933a) has described in detail a microprocedure for determining the individual phosphatides in the lipide fractions of components of the central nervous system. By this method, Mitolo (1933) determined that the cerebro-spinal axis of the frog contained 0.36 per cent lecithin combined with myelin tissue, 0.49 per cent cephalin fraction and 0.56 per cent sphingomyelin.

Alsterberg (1945) has reported on the lipide distribution in the various portions of the spinal cord of the cow.

From histochemical procedures, Richards (1943) has concluded that insect nerve cells and their processes are surrounded by sheaths composed of phosphatides with perhaps some cholesterol.

The carotid ganglion of the horse was found by deBoissezon and Valdiguié (1942) to contain 7.42 per cent total lipides of which 7 per cent was lecithin, 14 per cent was sphingomyelin and 78 per cent was galactolipides.

There have not been many studies of the phosphatide content of normal nerves. Randall (1938a) gives the following average values for human nerves in percentage of dry weight: femoral, 13.36 ± 2.23 (23 analyses); sciatic, 13.58 ± 3.56 (3 analyses); posterior tibial, 13.13 ± 4.00 (12 analyses).

Johnson, McNabb and Rossiter (1948) found that the quantities of total phosphatides, cerebrosides and cholesterol in the peripheral nerves of several animals and man are similar to the amounts present in white matter of brain. The nerves, however, contain more sphingomyelin and less cephalin fraction.

According to Knauer (1932) there is normally 1.0 milligram per cent of phosphatides in the spinal fluid.

Serine-containing Phosphatides

Modern investigators, unlike early workers, have realized that phosphatidylserine (see p. 28) is an important constituent of what was formerly termed "brain cephalin"; and have planned their analytical techniques accordingly. Chargaff and Ziff (1941) found phosphatidylserine in cattle brain, the serine having been isolated as the β-naphthalenesulfonyl derivative. Folch (1942) showed that phosphatidylserine from ox brain had an iodine number of 39.8 as compared to a value of 78 for phosphatidylaminoethyl alcohol.

Schuwirth (1941, 1943) showed that the amino nitrogen of the phosphatides of the human brain is equally divided between serine and aminoethyl alcohol.

Chargaff, Ziff and Rittenberg (1942) employed the technique of isotope dilution to show that the amino nitrogen of beef brain phosphatides comprised 75 per cent aminoethyl alcohol and 25 per cent amino acid which was undoubtedly choline. Of the nonamino nitrogen, 50 per cent was choline, whereas the remainder was unidentifiable.

Artom (1945) has studied the composition of rat brain phosphatides. The amino constituents in the hydrolysis products were estimated by periodate oxidation before and after removal of the aminoethyl alcohol by "Permutit". He has found that the choline-containing phosphatides comprise about 36.3 per cent of the total. In the remainder there is roughly twice as much phosphatidylaminoethyl alcohol as serine-containing phosphatides. The analyses are somewhat in error, however, because the noncholine-containing phosphatides determined by actual analysis exceed the quantity which would be expected from the difference between the choline-containing phosphatides and the total phosphatides. The author explains this as being due either to the presence of sphingosine which contains amino groups or to the presence of other impurities which might react to liberate ammonia with periodate. It should be noted, however, that Chargaff, Ziff and Rittenberg (1942, see above) could account for only 50 per cent of the nonamino nitrogen of beef brain phosphatides as choline.

Inositol-containing Phosphatides

The inositol-containing phosphatides have been discussed previously (see p. 35). They occur in what was classically termed "cephalin", and all references to the cephalin fraction are intended to include them.

The inositol-containing phosphatide mixture comprised about one-fourth of the cephalin fraction of ox brain (Folch and Woolley, 1942; Folch, 1942) and contained between 6 to 10 per cent of inositol. A great deal of work remains yet to be done on the occurrence of this interesting phosphatide in brain tissue.

Acetal Phosphatides

The acetal phosphatides discovered and studied by Feulgen and Bersin (1939, see p. 51) are also to be found in brain. According to Feulgen and Bersin (1939), the crude phosphatides of brain contain 8 to 10 per cent aldehydic materials which form an acetal with two of the hydroxyls of the glycerol portion of the phosphatide molecule. The base present in this phosphatide seems to be aminoethyl alcohol. The aldehydic constituents from the acetal phosphatides of brain are a complex mixture which, however, probably contain the aldehydes corresponding to palmitic and stearic acids.

Hydrolecithin

Thannhauser, Benotti and Boncoddo (1946) and Thannhauser and Boncoddo (1948) have found in the sphingomyelin fraction of beef brain a fully saturated phosphatide, dipalmityllecithin (see p. 54). It is readily overlooked and is isolated only with difficulty because its solubility characteristics are closely related to those of both sphingomyelin and the cerebrosides.

Free Bases

Müller (1940) was able to show the presence of free aminoethyl alcohol and free choline in the brain by precipitating them as the phosphotungstates. This salt of choline is soluble in 5 per cent sulfuric acid, whereas aminoethyl alcohol phosphotungstate is not. He found 3.5 milligrams of free aminoethyl alcohol and 68.4 milligrams of free choline per kilogram of brain tissue. There is, of course, a possibility that these bases were split from phosphatides at some time during the procedure.

Fatty Acids

The fatty acids of brain phosphatides, as indicated above, include high molecular weight compounds with multiple unsaturation. Various workers have offered contradictory evidence about the exact nature of these acids, and here again more careful work is necessary.

Among the earlier workers were MacArthur and Burton (1916), who isolated from the cephalin fraction of sheep brain, acids which on bromination yielded products containing 67.7 to 69.4 per cent bromine. These analytical data agree fairly well with those expected for octabromostearic acid, thus indicating the presence of clupanodonic acid, $C_{18}H_{28}O_2$. The authors, however, did not consider their evidence as absolute proof. By use of the standard lead soap procedure, they were able to show that stearic and oleic acids were the chief fatty acid constituents.

Levene and Rolf (1922a) in their extensive investigations found arachidonic acid, $C_{20}H_{32}O_2$, to be the most important high molecular weight acid in both the cephalin fraction and lecithin isolated from ox brain. They also noted the presence of oleic acid. Klenk (1929), on the other hand, found evidence for the presence of C_{24} acids. These, together with the presence of C_{18} acids, both of which are obviously multiples of six, as well as the 18-carbon chain of sphingosine and the 6-carbon chain of galactose which occurs generously in the brain, led him to postulate that the hexose sugars are the building blocks for these brain constituents. In a subsequent publication, however, Klenk (1930) reported in brain cephalin fraction, unsaturated acids which yielded behenic acid, $C_{22}H_{44}O_2$, on reduction. This, of course, could have resulted from β-oxidation of a C_{24} acid. These acids comprised approximately 25 per cent of the total acids and contained four or five double bonds. There was no trace in his experiments of the arachidonic acid mentioned by Levene and Rolf (1922a). In addition, he found stearic acid, a trace of palmitic acid, and certain unsaturated acids which yielded stearic acid on reduction. Later, Klenk and von Schoenbeck (1931) showed that the same unsaturated C_{22} acid also occurred in liver phosphatide.

In the total ether-soluble phosphatides of human brain, Klenk (1931) found that stearic and palmitic acids constituted about one-third of the total fatty acids, the former predominating. The remainder were unsaturated acids, and here again he found the C_{18} and C_{24} series to be the most important quantitatively. In addition, however, he obtained after reduction of the unsaturated fraction and careful distillation of the esters, palmitic and n-eicosanic acid, $C_{20}H_{40}O_2$. Since unsaturated C_{16} and C_{22} acids were also present, an uninterrupted chain of even-numbered fatty acids from C_{16} to C_{24} were isolated. Although Klenk (1930) did not find a C_{20} acid in the cephalin fraction of brain, he points out that his fractionation equipment in the previous experiments probably could not detect a C_{20} acid in the presence of large amounts of C_{18} and C_{22} acids. The amount of unsaturation was not determined, but the acids were believed to be highly unsaturated. In a later publication, Klenk (1932) pointed out that the C_{18} unsaturated fraction was chiefly oleic acid. The C_{20} fraction from the ether-soluble phosphatides of human brain yielded on careful examination two acids. One of these, $C_{20}H_{38}O_2$, seemed to correspond to gadoleinic acid which previously had been isolated from cod liver oil. The other, $C_{20}H_{32}O_2$, proved to be arachidonic acid in agreement with Levene and Rolf (1922a). The C_{22} fraction was not fully characterized, but as indicated above it probably contained an acid with four double bonds as well as one with five double bonds which may have been clupanodonic acid.

Brown and Ault (1930) offered evidence for the presence of a C_{24} penta-unsaturated acid in the total lipides of sheep and beef brains. Although they could not find arachidonic acid in these sources, they obtained some evidence from the bromides for the presence of arachidonic acid in hog brain. Later, however, Brown (1932) reinvestigated the fatty acids of the total lipides of beef brain and found the highly unsaturated fraction to consist chiefly of acids of the C_{22} series, predominately docosapentenoic acid with some docosatetrenoic acid. The presence of arachidonic acid could not be demonstrated, and there was some evidence for the presence of small amounts of tetracosapentenoic acid as was postulated in the earlier publication.

Rudy and Page (1932) and Page and Rudy (1931) prepared a sample of cephalin from human brain which they believed to be free of lecithin and practically free of cerebrosides. The only saturated acid which they found here was stearic acid which constituted about 30 per cent of the total. In the unsaturated series the C_{18} acids and the C_{22} acids each constituted about 22 per cent of the total. The latter on bromination yielded two octabromides, one of which was considerably more soluble in organic solvents than the other. Both of these on debromination and reduction yielded behenic acid. In accordance with Klenk (1931) and Brown (1932), these authors believe on the basis of iodine number that the C_{22} acids contain four or five unsaturated linkages, although they did not isolate a decabromide. The C_{18} unsaturated acids were not examined but there was some evidence for the presence of a C_{20} unsaturated acid.

Yokoyama and Suzuki (1932, 1932a) hydrolyzed lecithin from human brain and showed the presence of palmitic, oleic, linoleic and arachidonic acids.

Schuwirth (1943) has described a special apparatus for the fractionation of small quantities of fatty acid methyl esters under high vacuum. From the unsaturated acids of the brain he obtained what was probably palmitoleic acid and a small amount of an unsaturated non-acidic material which appeared to be an aldehyde and which brings to mind the acetal phosphatides of Feulgen and Bersin (1939).

Complex Formation

The phosphatides of the brain occur in part in complex formation with other substances. Thus, according to Gautrelet, Corteggiani and Carayon-Gentil (1941), at least a portion of the brain phosphatides are bound in a complex with acetylcholine. This may be proved by treating the material with cobra venom which has been heated at 100° C. for twenty minutes to destroy the proteinase activity of the venom but not the lecithinase activity. Accordingly, the enzyme present serves to liberate acetylcholine, lysolecithin and a fatty acid from the complex. The complex may also be decomposed by a concentrated solution of bile salts.

Variation of Phosphatide Content with Age

The phosphatide content of the brain and the nervous system has been found to vary with age and development. Gorodisska (1925) found that after an individual reaches fifty years of age the unsaturated phosphatides and the proteins diminish, whereas the cholesterol increases. The saturated phosphatides and the cerebrosides, on the other hand, do not change. These changes were most noticeable in the association centers.

Cattaneo (1932) found that the phosphatide content of human fetal brains increased with age but decreased in the infant. The phosphatide content was higher in the cerebrum than in the cerebellum in the fetus, but the reverse was true for the infant.

Lang (1937) found that the phosphatide content of the brain of rats increased from 17.3 per cent of the dry weight at one day to 25.1 per cent in the adult. The cholesterol during a similar period increased from 3.27 per cent to 7.62 per cent. McConnell and Sinclair (1937) likewise found that the phosphatide content of rat brain increases markedly with growth. May (1930) showed that in degeneration of a nerve the chief changes involved the degeneration of the phosphatide and the nucleoproteins.

According to Boldyreva (1937), the lipide phosphorus in the brain is greater in the male than in the female. Also, the lipide phosphorus content of the nerve centers of invertebrates is less than in the brains of vertebrates.

LIVER

General

The lipides, and particularly the phosphatides, of the liver have undergone extensive study because of the many-sided activities which the liver displays in metabolic and physiological processes (see p. 385). In analyzing for liver phosphatides, special attention must be given to the nutritive state of the organ, for it is known that absorbed fat is present in the liver during digestion. Likewise, the liver may serve as an emergency storage organ for lipides. Accordingly, only in the postabsorptive state can the analyses be considered representative of the normal liver.

The phosphatide content of the liver is approximately one-half that of the brain. Quantitatively the most important phosphatides are lecithin and the cephalin fraction which are present in almost equal quantities, whereas sphingomyelin is present only to a very small extent. The serine-containing phosphatides are included in the cephalin fraction. Acetal phosphatides have also been found in the liver. It is gratifying to note that many of the results in the literature are in close agreement. Of all the lipides of the liver, the phosphatides are the most abundant. According to Theis (1928), normal beef liver lipides are comprised of about 55 per cent phosphatides, whereas Bloor (1928) found 73 per cent phosphatides. The remainder is composed of glycerides, free fatty acids and small quantities of cholesterol, cholesterol esters and more obscure substances.

The acids of liver phosphatides, like those from the brain, are characterized by high molecular weight and a large degree of unsaturation.

Of interest is the work of Chantrenne (1947), who isolated five fractions of cytoplasmic granules of mouse liver by fractional centrifugation and observed a difference in the phosphatide content of these fractions.

Phosphatide Content

The isolation of liver phosphatides follows the pattern indicated for other organs and tissue. Many workers have used Bloor's (1929) oxidative procedure for the determination of total phosphatides, whereas the individual phosphatides are determined by analyzing for the hydrolysis products. The phosphatide content is affected markedly by diseases which cause degenerative processes in the liver, especially so-called fatty livers (see p. 355).

The most important of the early investigations on liver phosphatides was carried out by Levene (1916), who isolated and described the properties of sphingomyelin. Later Levene and Ingvaldsen (1920) studied the lecithin and cephalin fractions from liver, particularly with reference to the acids resulting from hydrolysis. In 1928 both Theis (1928) and Bloor (1928) studied the lipide content of beef liver. Their interesting results as compared by Bloor (1943, p. 210) are indicated in Table X.

TABLE X. THE LIPIDES OF NORMAL BEEF LIVER

	Theis (1928)	Bloor (1928)
Total lipide, weight %	4.6	4.2
Phosphatide { weight %	2.53	3.08
{ total lipide %	55.0	73.0
Acetone-soluble fat { weight %	2.07	1.12
{ total lipide %	45.0	27.0
Phosphatide fraction		
Iodine number of total phosphatide	100	82
Iodine number of mixed fatty acids	141	114
Iodine number of liquid fatty acids	246	170
Liquid acids, % of mixed acids	57.0	43.0
4-bond acids, % of liquid acids	36.0	20.0

Kaucher and co-workers (1943) analyzed two composite samples of beef liver. Their results, expressed as per cent of dry weight, are indicated below:

Sample	Total lipide	Total phosphatide	Cephalin fraction	Lecithin	Sphingomyelin
I	20.49	13.75	4.91	8.04	0.80
II	25.49	18.69	8.28	9.69	.72

Although the agreement is not particularly good, it is apparent that the sphingomyelin content is quite small.

Thannhauser and co-workers (1939) studied the phosphatide content of normal human liver according to the procedures developed by them (see p. 264) for the determination of individual phosphatides. In general agreement with other workers, they found sphingomyelin to be least important quantitatively, whereas lecithin and the cephalin fraction existed in almost equal amounts. As an average of three determinations, they found human liver on a dry basis to contain 9.8 per cent phosphatides. Lecithin comprised 4.8 per cent of the liver, cephalin, 4.6 per cent and sphingomyelin, 0.4 per cent.

A considerable amount of work has been done on rat and mouse liver, and Lang (1937) has shown that the phosphatide content of the rat liver from birth to the adult stage is approximately constant.

MacLachlan and co-workers (1942) found by the oxidative procedure that the moist liver of normal mice contains 3.8 per cent total phosphatides. This was an average of twenty determinations. The phosphatides comprised 62 per cent of the total lipides, and 58 per cent of the phosphatides consisted of lecithin. The remainder was chiefly cephalin fraction. The lecithin estimation was based on the total choline content, the sphingomyelin having been disregarded because it was present in such small amount.

The same school of workers previously reported (Hodge and co-workers, 1941) 4.3 per cent total phosphatides in the liver of a normal mouse. This likewise was an average of twenty samples and is in good agreement with the above results. The phosphatides in these determinations comprised 66 per cent of the total lipides.

Patterson and McHenry (1944), who were studying the effect of a choline-deficient diet on the liver of rats, obtained the results shown below for the total phosphatide content of the liver of normal rats on a wet basis. The oxidative procedure of Bloor (1929) was employed, and the results are averages of twenty animals. It is seen that these figures are somewhat low in comparison with the above results.

Experimental day	% Phosphatide based on moist liver	Ratio, total phosphatide to total lipide
0	2.6	0.76
7	2.4	.55
10	2.4	.63

Artom and Fishman (1943) analyzed for the phosphatides of the liver of rats which were raised to a 125 gram weight on a normal diet. The liver was minced under alcohol and the alcohol-dehydrated sample was extracted with alcohol and alcohol-ether, after which the solvents were removed to yield a residue which was dissolved in chloroform. This chloroform solution was used to determine lipide phosphorus, total choline and sphingomyelin. Thus, these workers determined the total phosphatide content of moist liver as 3.2 per cent. This was an average of ten determinations and is in agreement with other investigators cited above. The phosphatides comprised 70 per cent of the total lipides which is likewise in good agreement with other workers. The moist liver contained 1.9 per cent choline-containing phosphatides and 1.3 per cent noncholine-containing phosphatides. Thus the choline-containing phosphatides comprise about 60 per cent of the total phosphatides, and the noncholine-containing phosphatides comprise about 40 per cent. Sphingo-myelin comprised about 8 per cent of the total phosphatides but the determination was subject to considerable inaccuracy because of the low concentration.

Taurog and co-workers (1944) have devised a procedure for separating the choline-containing from the noncholine-containing phosphatides by adsorbing them on magnesium oxide and eluting the choline-containing phosphatides with methanol. In the course of this work they determined that 58 per cent of the phosphatides of the liver of the dog and the rat are choline-containing. This is in good accord with the values indicated above.

Okey, Gillum and Yokela (1934) found the moist liver of the male rat to contain 3.3 ± 0.05 (mean value) per cent phosphatides, whereas the liver of the female rat contained 3.1 ± 0.3 per cent. Thus, there was very little difference, and the phosphatide content was not affected appreciably by dietary cholesterol. Bloor's oxidative procedure (1929) was used for the determinations, and they are in close agreement with the results of the investigators cited above.

Likewise in agreement with these results, Cardini and Serantes (1942) found 2.04 per cent lecithin, 0.64 per cent cephalin fraction and 0.17 per cent sphingomyelin in the moist liver of an adult male albino rat.

Sperry, Brand and Copenhaver (1942), who determined the phosphatide content of dry rat liver from the amount of phosphorus in an alcohol-ether extract, found 11.2 to 12.7 per cent phosphatides in six samples.

The phosphatide content of the liver of chickens was investigated by Entenman, Lorenz and Chaikoff (1940), who found 1.6 to 2.5 per cent total phosphatides in the liver of the newly hatched chick. The liver of the sixteen-day-old fowl possessed 2.2 to 2.4 per cent total phosphatides, whereas that of the thirty-six-day old chick contained 2.7 to 2.8 per cent.

Lorenz, Chaikoff and Entenman (1938) and Entenman, Lorenz and Chaikoff (1940) found very little difference in the phosphatide content of the livers of mature or immature chickens or roosters. Nor did low or high fat diets effect great change. Thus in laying hens the ages of which varied from 199 to 299 days and which were on a low fat diet, the phosphatide content of the fresh liver varied from 1.8 to 3.4 per cent with no correlation between age and phosphatide content. Thirteen animals were used. On a high fat diet the values were somewhat more constant, varying from 2.2 per cent to 3.0 per cent.

The liver of the fish, *Polyprion oxygeneios*, commonly known as the New Zealand groper, was found by Shorland and Hilditch (1938) to contain varying amounts of phosphatides, depending on the season. In spring there was only a trace, whereas in early winter there was 2 per cent and in late winter 19 per cent.

Rubin, Present and Ralli (1937) found that the phosphatide content of dog liver did not change appreciably when the types of fat in the diet were varied or when phosphatides were added to the diet. Their results indicated an average value of 3.0 ± 0.4 per cent phosphatide in the wet liver of dogs, the individual values for various diets having ranged between 2.9 and 3.1 per cent.

Nature of the Phosphatides

Although sphingomyelin occurs to only a small extent in the liver, it has received some investigation. Thus Fränkel, Bielschowsky and Thannhauser (1933) found a sphingomyelin in liver which contained equal parts of lignoceric, palmitic and stearic acids and possessed a nitrogenphosphorus ratio of 2:1. This was incorrectly characterized as a "polysphingomyelin". Sphingosine and lignocerylsphingosine have likewise been shown to be present in liver (Fränkel and Löhr, 1933, Thannhauser and Fränkel, 1931).

Hunter (1942) has found in the liver of the cat 3.1 ± 0.4 per cent total phosphatides on a wet basis of which 7.5 ± 0.2 per cent was sphingomyelin. Artom (1945) has determined the phosphatide distribution in the liver of rats, and his results are indicated in Table XI. It will be seen that the serine-containing phosphatides are only a minor portion of the total phosphatides of the liver, comprising about 8 to 11 per cent. Each of the results is the average of several determinations.

TABLE XI. PHOSPHATIDES OF RAT LIVER (ARTOM, 1945)

(Values are in micromoles per gram)

Rat group	Total phosphatides	Choline-containing phosphatides	Noncholine-containing phosphatides (calculated values) (a − b)	Aminoethyl alcohol-containing	Serine containing	Aminoethyl alcohol serine-containing (d + e)	Difference from calculated values (f − c)
	(a)	(b)	(c)	(d)	(e)	(f)	(g)
A	39.8	22.4	17.4	10.9	4.5	15.4	−2.0
B	38.2	24.4	13.8	10.4	3.9	14.3	+0.5
C	39.2	23.5	15.7	12.6	2.9	15.5	−0.2

Feulgen and Bersin (1939) found that acetal phosphatides (see p. 51) occur in the liver only to the extent of 1 per cent.

Chargaff, Ziff and Rittenberg (1942) carried out a study of the bases of liver phosphatides by use of the isotope dilution method. These results indicated that all the nonamino nitrogen could be accounted for as choline. Of the amino nitrogen, however, 51.7 per cent was aminoethyl alcohol, 12.7 per cent was amino acid, probably serine, whereas the remainder was unaccounted for and could not be identified in this work.

Fatty Acids

One of the earliest reliable investigators of the fatty acids of liver lipides was Hartley (1909), who found in the fatty acids of pig liver, palmitic, stearic and linoleic acids. The neutral equivalent of the acids was found to be 308 to 312, which indicated the presence of higher molecular weight acids such as arachidonic acid. These were indeed found by later investigators. In addition, he postulated the presence of $\Delta^{12.13}$ octadecenoic acid which could not be found later by Channon, Irving and Smith (1934). However, Millican and Brown (1944) recently studied the C_{18} mono-unsaturated acid from many sources including pork liver lipides. They concluded in this latter case that the chief octdaecenoic acid was oleic acid, but that there was evidence for the presence of a small percentage of acids isomeric with ordinary oleic acid.

Levene and Simms (1921, 1922) found palmitic and stearic acids in liver lecithin together with two unsaturated acids which yielded stearic and arachidic acids on reduction. The more highly unsaturated material which they believed to be tetraenoic was shown by further work to be arachidonic acid. The C_{18} acid, on the other hand, was probably oleic acid. Brown (1928) later found arachidonic acid in the fatty acids of the total lipides of liver.

Snider and Bloor (1933) isolated lecithin from beef liver and found the saturated acids to consist of 71 per cent stearic and 29 per cent palmitic acid. In the corresponding glycerides, palmitic acid predominated. The unsaturated acids of liver lecithin consisted of 45 per cent linoleic, 31 per cent arachidonic and 21 per cent oleic acid. No triply unsaturated acids were found, and there was some evidence for acids higher than C_{20}.

A large amount of work on the fatty acids of liver lipides has been done by Klenk and associates. Klenk and von Schoenbeck (1931, 1932) investigated the fatty acids of the glycerides and ether-soluble phosphatides of ox liver. Their data are included in Table XII. They noted that the phosphatide fatty acids were somewhat similar to those of lecithin and the cephalin fraction in brain except that the latter contained more C_{22} acids than C_{20} acids, whereas in liver the reverse was true. Also, liver phosphatides contained more C_{18} unsaturated acids, especially linoleic acid which was present only in traces in brain. These workers likewise noted the tendency for acids of higher molecular weight and greater unsaturation to occur in the phosphatides rather than in the glycerides. The values given for highly unsaturated C_{20}

and C_{22} acids are usually low, since these tend to polymerize and cannot be distilled quantitatively. The C_{18} unsaturated acids described are oleic and linoleic, the C_{20} is arachidonic, and the C_{22} is clupanodonic acid.

TABLE XII. THE FATTY ACID CONTENT OF THE PHOSPHATIDES AND GLYCERIDES OF LIVERS OF VARIOUS ANIMALS

	Saturated acids				Unsaturated acids				
	C_{14}	C_{16}	C_{18}	C_{20}	C_{14}	C_{16}	C_{18}	C_{20}	C_{22}
Ox Liver:									
Glyceride[a]	1.6	32.5	5.0	—	1.5	11.7	40.3	7.4	(combined C_{20}, C_{22})
Glyceride[b]	—	25.0	20.0	—	—	9.0	37.0	8.0	1.0
Phosphatide[a]	1.5	29.7	17.0	0.2	0.6	1.6	27.7	21.7	(combined C_{20}, C_{22})
Phosphatide[b]	—	12.5	27.0	—	—	5.0	27.0	18.0	10.50
Cow Liver:									
Glyceride[a]	3.2	34.7	5.3	—	0.5	9.9	43.6	2.9	—
Phosphatide[a]	—	22.9	21.2	—	—	4.4	46.9	4.6	—
Pig Liver:									
Glyceride[a]	0.1	25.8	10.3	0.2	—	9.2	44.1	9.2	1.1
Phosphatide[a]	—	13.4	15.3	1.7	—	5.3	40.3	22.4	1.6
Sheep Liver:									
Glyceride[a]	0.3	24.2	12.5	—	—	5.3	44.1	10.5	3.2
Phosphatide[a]	—	13.9	21.7	0.7	—	9.9	28.0	21.9	3.9

[a] Hilditch and Shorland (1937); [b] Klenk and von Schoenbeck (1932)

Klenk (1933, 1933a, 1935) studied the fatty acids of the phosphatides and the oils of the liver of such animals as the shark, *Etmopterus spinax*, codfish, grass frog, steer and turtle. He found a striking similarity, the saturated acids consisting chiefly of C_{16} and C_{18} acids and the unsaturated ones of C_{18} and C_{22} acids. Likewise, the relative proportions of these acids were fairly uniform. In the total liver lipides, on the other hand, he found C_{16}, C_{18}, C_{20}, C_{22} and C_{24} acids. In the frog liver phosphatides he found a low content of stearic acid and a relatively large amount of the highly unsaturated C_{20} and C_{22} acids in contrast to the composition shown by higher vertebrate livers.

Hilditch and Shorland (1937) carried out rather extensive investigations of the fatty acid composition of the glycerides and phosphatides of livers of various New Zealand farm animals. They separated the lipide fraction into pure glycerides, pure phosphatides and a fraction consisting of a mixture of each. By suitable mathematical manipulation they were able to use the data for the mixed fraction to correct the other two fractions. They concluded that the liver phosphatides contain increased portions of stearic and higher molecular weight acids such as C_{20} and C_{22} unsaturated acids together with diminished portions of hexadecenoic acids, as compared with the corresponding glycerides. The tendency for the phosphatides to contain higher molecular weight acids than the glycerides seems to be typical of liver phosphatides. Their data, together with that of Klenk and von Schoenbeck (1932), are indicated in Table XII. The tendency for higher molecular weight acids to occur in the phosphatides is demonstrated in Table XIII.

TABLE XIII. THE MEAN MOLECULAR WEIGHTS OF THE PHOSPHATIDE AND GLYCERIDE FATTY ACIDS FROM LIVERS OF VARIOUS ANIMALS (HILDITCH AND SHORLAND, 1937)

	Mean mol. wt. of fatty acid
Ox Liver Glyceride	254.8
Ox Liver Phosphatide	262.3
Cow Liver Glyceride	253.9
Cow Liver Phosphatide	261.6
Pig Liver Glyceride	260.5
Pig Liver Phosphatide	268.7
Sheep Liver Glyceride	262.4
Sheep Liver Phosphatide	267.5

The degree of unsaturation of the fatty acids was also investigated by Hilditch and Shorland (1937). The C_{14} and the C_{16} acids contained one double bond; the C_{18} acids were mixtures of oleic and linoleic, with the latter predominating in many cases, whereas the C_{20} and C_{22} acids contained three to four double bonds. In the case of the C_{22} acid from the sheep liver phosphatide, an average of 5.3 double bonds was found.

Much of the fatty acid content described for liver lipides undoubtedly stems from dietary fat, for Sinclair (1930) has shown that the liver may absorb fatty acids from the intestine. However, the high molecular weight unsaturated acids as well as palmitoleic acid are not dietary constituents and are thus inherent in the liver lipides.

The iodine numbers of liver phosphatides and of their fatty acids have been the subject of various investigations. Thus Bloor (1928) found the average iodine number of beef liver cephalins to be 80, and of lecithin from the same source to be 83. Fatty acids comprised 48 per cent of the cephalins and had an iodine number of 119, whereas the lecithin consisted of 65 per cent fatty acids with an iodine number of 108. The fatty acids of the corresponding neutral fat had an iodine number of 87. Yasuda (1931/32) found rat liver phosphatides to possess an iodine number of 119. The corresponding fatty acids had an iodine number of 137, whereas the fatty acids of mouse liver phosphatides had an iodine number of 140. Terroine, Hatterer and Roehrig (1930) found the following iodine numbers for liver phosphatide fatty acids from various sources: frog, 148; rayfish, 170; and tortoise, 126.

LUNG

The phosphatides of lung tissue are of interest as a constant component of an important organ. Sammartino (1921) showed that phosphatides exist in beef lung tissue. Although the investigation of these phosphatides has not been extensive, sufficient work has been done to show that lecithin is probably present to a somewhat greater extent than the cephalin fraction, and that sphingomyelin is present in much larger quantity than it is in organs where the phosphatides are largely concerned with metabolic processes.

One of the earliest of the more competent examinations of lung lipides was carried out by Bloor (1928) on tissue obtained from beef. His work indicated that lecithin was present somewhat in excess of the cephalins. He did not analyze for sphingomyelin. The iodine number of his phosphatides ranged from approximately 70 to 80, whereas the average iodine number of the cephalin fraction fatty acids was 104 and of the lecithin fatty acids 93. In these fatty acids he was able to show the presence of almost 10 per cent of a tetraunsaturated acid which was probably arachidonic acid. The acetone soluble fat was less saturated than the phosphatides.

The iodine number of beef lung phosphatides prepared by Chargaff, Ziff and Rittenberg (1942) was 69.7. The iodine numbers of the fatty acids of lung phosphatides from various species were determined by Terroine, Hatterer and Roehrig (1930). They found the average values for beef, swine and sheep to be 109, 101 and 108, respectively. These values are in good agreement with those indicated by Bloor (1928).

Phosphatide Content

Thannhauser and co-workers (1939) applied the method developed by them (see p. 264) for the determination of the individual phosphatides of human lung tissue. Their average results on a dry basis indicate 1.5 per cent sphingomyelin, 2 per cent cephalin fraction and 3.9 per cent lecithin.

Cardini and Serantes (1942) found that moist lung tissue of the adult albino rat contained 1.8 per cent lecithin, 0.8 per cent cephalin fraction and 0.5 per cent sphingomyelin. The analytical procedure (Marenzi and Cardini, 1943) involved determination of total phosphatides from the lipide phosphorus content, determination of total choline, and determination of sphingomyelin from the phosphorus content of the reineckate. Suitable mathematical manipulation provided the quantities of all three phosphatides.

Kaucher and co-workers (1943) found the lung of the cow to contain an average of 14.4 per cent total lipides. The phosphatides averaged 9.8 per cent with 3.9 per cent cephalin fraction and 5.9 per cent choline-containing phosphatides. The latter was divided between 3.6 per cent lecithin and 2.3 per cent sphingomyelin. These results are per cent of dry weight.

The total phosphatides and the sphingomyelin content of cat lung were determined by Hunter (1942). The former was estimated from the lipide phosphorus content and the latter from the phosphorus content of the reineckate. The average results indicate 3.1 ± 0.4 per cent total phosphatides and $0.7 \pm .1$ per cent sphingomyelin based on the wet tissue. Thus the sphingomyelin comprises 33.2 ± 4.7 per cent of the total phosphatides. These results are of the same order as those of Cardini and Serantes (1942).

Nature of the Phosphatides

The presence of one or more amino acids as hydrolysis products of lung phosphatide was proved by Chargaff, Ziff and Rittenberg (1942), who used the method of isotope dilution with N^{15}. These workers found 15.7 per cent of the total nitrogen of beef lung to be in the form of amino acids. That this amino acid was serine was shown by Artom (1945), who in two sets of analyses found 7.8 per cent and 12.0 per cent of rat lung phosphatides to be serine-containing. The average values of his analyses made on two groups of rats raised to about 150 grams follow in micromoles per gram of moist tissue: total phosphatides, 23.2, 21.7; choline-containing phosphatides, 14.2, 12.9; aminoethyl alcohol-containing phosphatides, 8.9, 12.2; serine-containing phosphatides, 1.8, 2.6. It will be seen that the sum of the aminoethyl alcohol and serine-containing phosphatides is somewhat higher than the difference between the choline-containing and total phosphatides. This, Artom points out, could be attributed to incomplete removal of sphingosine or to the presence of other phosphatides or other amino-containing impurities. In this regard, the presence in the lung of lignocerylsphingosine has been reported by Tropp (1936).

Thannhauser, Benotti and Boncoddo (1946) have recently made the interesting observation that the sphingomyelin fraction of beef lung, isolated as such because of its ether insolubility, contains 20 to 40 per cent of dipalmityllecithin which is also ether-insoluble. The discovery resulted from the observation that hydrolysis of the sphingomyelin fraction with liver enzyme yielded palmitic acid, despite the fact that it had been demonstrated that the amide linkages of sphingomyelin were unaffected by this enzyme. The ability to prove qualitatively the presence of glycerol led to the identification of dipalmityllecithin. These workers believed that the quantity of hydrolecithin in lung is exceeded only by that in brain.

From their observation that the lung sphingomyelin fraction contained large quantities of dipalmityllecithin, Thannhauser, Benotti and Boncoddo (1946a) were prompted to reinvestigate the properties of pure sphingomyelin. They obtained the pure product by treating the crude material with 0.25 normal caustic at 37° C. for four days. Thus the glycerophosphatide was hydrolyzed. The pure sphingomyelin, on hydrolysis, yielded both palmitic and lignoceric acids in approximately equal quantities. Stearic acid, on the other hand, was not present.

KIDNEY

In the kidney phosphatides, lecithin probably predominates by a small margin. Although phosphatides from this source have not been extensively investigated, they seem to resemble the phosphatides of similar tissue in composition. Turner (1931) has shown the presence in cat kidney of oleic, linoleic, palmitic and stearic acids. These are undoubtedly present in both the glyceride and phosphatide fractions.

Bloor (1928) was among the more recent investigators to study beef kidney phosphatides. He found the cephalin fraction from this source to have an average iodine number of 88, whereas the corresponding value for the fatty acids was 109. The liquid fatty acids had an iodine number of 179, and there was present 11 per cent of what was probably arachidonic acid. The lecithin from this source had an average iodine number of 85, whereas the iodine number of the fatty acids was 110. The liquid fatty acids had an iodine number of 156, and arachidonic acid was likewise present. He was able to isolate an average of 16.2 grams of phosphatide per kilogram of kidney, and this was composed of somewhat more lecithin than cephalin fraction. No attempt was made to isolate sphingomyelin.

Sinclair (1935) studied the kidney phosphatides of the rat in some detail. The iodine number of the fatty acids varied from 100 to 142 in twelve samples. The solid acids comprised 22 ± 1.6 per cent of the total, whereas the liquid acids comprised 61.9 ± 3.8 per cent. The former had an iodine number of 4.7 ± 1.7 and the latter had iodine numbers varying from 135 to 197. Both the iodine numbers and the proportions of liquid and solid acids were determined by microprocedures which were not entirely quantitative.

Cardini and Serantes (1942) found in the moist kidney tissue of the albino rat 1.4 per cent lecithin, 1 per cent cephalin fraction and 0.3 per cent sphingomyelin.

Thannhauser and co-workers (1939), who investigated the phosphatide content of normal human organs, found an average of 8.0 per cent total phosphatides in kidney on a dry basis. Sphingomyelin was present to the extent of 0.7 per cent, cephalins to the extent of 3.3 per cent and lecithin to the extent of 5.1 per cent.

The work of Popják (1945) has shown that the cortex of the human kidney has a higher phosphatide content than the medulla, and that infant kidneys have a higher phosphatide content than adult kidneys. The following values are calculated from his data on the basis that the fatty acids comprise 69 per cent of the phosphatides. All the results are per cent of moist weight: adult kidney cortex, 1.5 per cent (mean of 18 cases); adult kidney medulla, 1.0 per cent (mean of 24 cases); infant kidney cortex, 2.1 per cent (mean of 7 cases); infant kidney medulla, 1.3 per cent (mean of 3 cases).

The following results were found by Kaucher and co-workers (1943) for beef kidneys, and are per cent of dry weight.

Total lipides	Total phosphatides	Cephalin fraction	Lecithin	Sphingomyelin
16.6	9.1	2.1	5.5	1.6
17.9	11.6	4.0	5.8	1.8

Patterson and McHenry (1944) studied the phosphatide content of rat kidneys in regard to choline-deficient diets. The kidney of the normal animal at weaning had a phosphatide content on a dry basis of 2.4 per cent. This was 83 per cent of the total lipide. At ten days the phosphatide content was 2.5 per cent, and this was 91 per cent of the total lipide. A choline deficiency caused a decrease in phosphatide content. Bloor's (1929) oxidative procedure was used for analyses.

The sphingomyelin content of cat kidney has been investigated by Hunter (1942), who estimated it from the phosphorus content of the reineckate. The total phosphatides comprised 2.7 ± 0.4 per cent of the kidney on a wet basis, and the sphingomyelin comprised 0.5 ± 0.1 per cent.

Artom (1945) has found serine-containing phosphatides in the kidneys of male albino rats. His average analyses in micromoles per gram of moist tissue are as follows: total phosphatides, 32.7; choline phosphatides, 17.4; aminoethyl alcohol phosphatides, 15.1; serine phosphatides, 8.0. Here, as with the analyses for lung, the sum of aminoethyl alcohol and serine phosphatides exceeds that expected from the difference in total and choline phosphatides, and the same explanation may be applied here as for lung tissue.

SPLEEN

The phosphatides of spleen are of interest because they increase markedly in lipidoses such as Niemann-Pick and Gaucher's diseases (see pp. 426, 428). The spleen is rich in lipides, containing, according to Morgulis and coworkers (1938), 27.0 per cent lipides on a dry basis. Lipide phosphorus was present to the extent of 0.35 per cent, which is roughly equivalent to 8 per cent phosphatides. Thus the phosphatides comprise about 30 per cent of the total lipides. Lecithin and the cephalin fraction occur in the spleen in approximately equal amounts, whereas sphingomyelin, normally at least, is a minor component. Teunissen and den Ouden (1938), however, are at variance, for according to their analyses normal spleen phosphatides consist primarily of lecithin. Thus, they report the presence of 4.1 per cent lecithin and 1 per cent sphingomyelin in normal spleen.

Most of the data in the literature, nevertheless, indicate that lecithin and the cephalin fraction are of approximately equal quantitative importance. Cardini and Serantes (1942) found the moist spleen of albino rats to contain 1.1 per cent lecithin, 1.2 per cent cephalin fraction and 0.2 per cent sphingomyelin. Thannhauser and co-workers (1939) have reported an average of 8.6 per cent total phosphatides in human spleen on a dry basis. Their values varied from 5.5 to 11.3 per cent. Cephalins comprised 1.6 to 6.9 per cent of the spleen, lecithin 3.1–4.0 per cent, and sphingomyelin 0.7–1.0 per cent. Artom (1945), who was interested in proving the presence of serine-containing phosphatides in the spleen, reported approximately equal quantities of choline and aminoethyl alcohol-containing phosphatides. His results for albino rats in micromoles per gram of moist tissue are as follows: total phosphatides, 16.3; choline phosphatides, 6.3; aminoethyl alcohol phosphatides, 7.1; serine phosphatides, 3.3.

The sphingomyelin of the spleen has received a fair amount of attention since it increases markedly in certain pathological conditions such as those mentioned above. Hunter (1942) has reported as an average of eleven determinations 0.3 ± 0.1 per cent sphingomyelin in the wet spleen of the cat. This was calculated from the phosphorus content of the reineckate.

Thannhauser and Benotti (1938) found the sphingomyelin of ox spleen to contain palmitic, stearic and lignoceric acids in a ratio of 1.6:1.6:1, whereas Klenk and Dittmer (1936) found evidence for the presence of a highly unsaturated C_{22} acid, in addition to arachidonic acid, in the total phosphatides of beef spleen.

Thannhauser, Benotti and Boncoddo (1946) have recently isolated dipalmityllecithin from beef spleen where it occurs in the sphingomyelin fraction.

GALL BLADDER AND BILE

Jones and Sherberg (1937) expressed doubt that either phosphatides or neutral fat exist in the bile of the ox, the hog or the dog inasmuch as they were unable to isolate glycerol from hydrolyzed ether-alcohol extracts of bile. Actually, the preponderance of literature indicates the presence of lipides, although this inability to isolate glycerol must not be overlooked. The first reports on the lipide constituents of bile were made by Strecker (1862), who isolated phosphatide material from hog bile. In addition, he found therein a new base to which he gave the name choline. Later, Hammarsten (1902, 1905) found phosphatides, choline and glycerophosphoric acid in polar bear bile.

The older work on the phosphatide content of bile is in poor agreement (Trifanowsky, 1874; Hammarsten, 1911, p. 413; Jacobson, 1873; von Zeynek, 1899; Bonanni, 1902).

Large amounts of choline were found in gall bladder bile of human cadavers by Müller (1936), who felt that it occurs in bile not only as a constituent of phosphatides, but also in the free state. These data were not substantiated by Worm (1939) nor by Johnston, Irvin and Walton (1939). They found when fresh material was used that only a small amount of free choline existed in hepatic and gall bladder bile of humans, dogs and hogs. This concentration, however, increased markedly on standing and on desiccation, indicating that it was a decomposition product, probably of phosphatides. This latter fact was likewise shown by Irvin and co-workers (1939), who also pointed out that the phosphatide content decreased as the choline content increased.

Johnston, Irvin and Walton (1939) extracted bile from various sources with ether-alcohol and isolated the phosphatides according to standard procedures. They found, in addition, that the total choline in bile was five to six times that which would be expected from the phosphatide content. Accordingly, either their extraction was incomplete or the excess choline exists in bile in forms other than lecithin or sphingomyelin. It was shown very early by Long and Gephart (1908) that the phosphatides of bile have a strong tendency to enter into complex formation with the bile salts, and it is entirely probable that to a large extent they occur this way naturally in the bile, making their complete extraction difficult.

The concentration of phosphatides, calculated as lecithin, which Johnston, Irvin and Walton (1939) found in various types of bile is indicated in Table XIV.

These same workers examined the phosphatides of hog bile and found what was probably sphingomyelin and lecithin. The presence of the former was not proved, although the actual lecithin isolated amounted to only

TABLE XIV. PHOSPHATIDE CONTENT OF BILE (JOHNSTON, IRVIN AND
WALTON, 1939)

Type of bile	Phosphatide mg./100 ml. bile
Hog bladder	282
	290
	271
Human bladder	194
	187
Human hepatic	61
	56
Dog bladder	250
	243
Dog hepatic	49
	57

one-third of the total phosphatides. The fatty acids of bile phosphatides
have not been studied.

Johnston, Irvin and Walton (1939) obtained human hepatic bile by
drainage of the bile ducts of individuals who had undergone choledo-
chostomy and cholecystectomy. The drainage in these cases is very large,
and these experimenters point out that on the basis of 1000 ml. per day
as much as 6 grams of phosphatide may be secreted.

The lipide phosphorus in the bile was observed by Leites (1928) to
increase when phosphatides were included in the diet and to decrease
after splenectomy.

BONE MARROW

The lipides of bone marrow are worthy of far more study than has
been given them since it has been shown (Krause, 1943) that marrow
contains a higher percentage of lipides than is normally found in any
other organ. In the cat, Krause (1943) found 5.2 grams of lipides per
10 grams of wet marrow. The lipide content of brain, which is next highest, is of the order of 13 per cent of the wet weight (Krause, 1943). In
marked contrast, Bernhard and Korrodi (1947) reported that bone marrow of adults contained practically no phosphatides. This again is an example of discrepant results which must eventually be rectified.

The presence of phosphatides in bone marrow was observed by Otoslki
(1907) and by Glikin (1907). The latter expressed the belief that the age
of the animal influenced the phosphatide content since it was high in
the young animal and lower in the adult. In some cases it disappeared
entirely. These findings were in agreement with those of Bolle (1910),
who likewise called attention to the great amount of individual variation
which was present. He pointed out that phosphatides were present in
bone marrow as soon as it appeared in the fetus.

Cheng (1931) likewise studied the effect of age on phosphatide content and showed that the marrow of calves was richer in phosphatides than the marrow of steers.

Krause (1943) has carried out the best analyses of the phosphatides of bone marrow. His data indicate that the red marrow of a normal cat contains 0.6 ± 0.2 per cent phosphatides expressed on the basis of wet weight. This is an average of 23 determinations. The choline-to-phosphorus ratio in the bone marrow lipides was 0.87, indicating a preponderance of choline-containing phosphatides over cephalins. Krause points out the interesting anomaly that the phosphatides of the red blood cells and the platelets are preponderantly cephalins. Since these are elaborated by the marrow, the small quantity of cephalins in that source seems anomalous. A possible explanation is that active hematopoiesis may increase the demand for cephalins to an extent such that it is kept at a low level in the marrow.

Krause (1943) has shown that in anemia the total bone marrow lipides decrease by approximately 50 per cent, whereas the phosphatides, together with the free fatty acids and cholesterol, increase by an almost equal amount. This, he points out, is another example of phosphatide content being increased when the tissue or organ increases its activity, for in anemia the marrow is called upon to increase its elaboration of blood cells.

The fatty acids of marrow phosphatides have not been investigated. Some work has been done, however, on the fatty acids of the total lipides. For the cat these have, according to Krause (1943), a mean molecular weight of 289 and an iodine number of 62. These figures, like those above, are the average of 23 determinations.

Cheng (1931) obtained marrow from the tibiae and femora of the beef and isolated the fatty acids from the total lipides. The gelatinous portion of the marrow was shown to contain more highly unsaturated acids than the yellow marrow. These consisted chiefly of oleic with some arachidonic acid. By distillation of the methyl esters a high boiling fraction was obtained whose molecular weight indicated the presence of an unknown acid above the C_{18} series. The saturated acids, as would be expected, were primarily palmitic and stearic.

Hilditch and Murti (1940) studied the fatty acid composition of the total lipides of the yellow marrow of ox bones. Their mixed fatty acids had a mean molecular weight of 275.9 and an iodine value of 47.9. They found a trace of lauric acid, a small amount of myristic acid and a preponderance of palmitic (34.1 per cent) over stearic acid (14.7 per cent). The chief unsaturated acid was oleic (41.5 per cent) with a small amount of doubly unsaturated C_{18} acids, and mono-unsaturated C_{16} and C_{14} acids.

These authors comment on the lack of C_{20-22} acids and point out that they may have had too little material to detect the higher molecular weight compounds.

REPRODUCTIVE SYSTEM

Phosphatides are fairly abundant in the reproductive organs, although a great deal of work remains to be done on the nature of the individual phosphatides present. Likewise, the fatty acids from phosphatides of this source have not been investigated with any degree of thoroughness. Several workers, as will be seen below, have carried on interesting studies on the effect of normal reproductive processes on the lipide content of the reproductive organs.

Distribution of Phosphatides

Phosphatides were observed many years ago in the testes and ovaries of the tunny fish by Dezani (1909). Lustig and Mandler (1933) compared the lipide contents of the corpora lutea, ovaries, testes and epididymis of cattle. The highest lipide content was found in the corpus luteum and consisted of one-third phosphatides. The ovaries possessed much less lipides, a similar portion of which was phosphatides. In the testes, one-half of the lipide present is phosphatides, whereas in the epididymis the values vary with the content of spermatozoa, the phosphatide content being higher when fewer spermatozoa were present.

Sorg (1924) found phosphatides in the seminal cells and the interstitial material of cattle testicles. In the former, the phosphatides were part of the cell itself, whereas in the latter they were deposition products. Benoit and Wenslow (1929) observed both cholesterol esters and phosphatides in the interstitial cells of the cock testicle.

Blumensaat (1929) has indicated that neutral fats and phosphatides are rare in the testes of the child from one to five years of age. Cholesterol esters are entirely absent. After the fifth year the lipide content increases slowly and after the twelfth year neutral fat, phosphatides and cholesterol esters are present.

Sinclair (1940) found that the liquid fatty acids from phosphatides of the rat testes had an iodine number of 200 to 224.

Artom (1945) has found small amounts of serine-containing phosphatides in the testes of albino rats. His analyses which follow are given in micromoles per gram of moist tissue: total phosphatides, 16.1; choline phosphatides, 8.4; aminoethyl alcohol phosphatides, 5.5; and serine phosphatides, 2.1.

Phosphatides are likewise present in the ovaries, and in one thousand analyses of swine ovaries Flössner (1929) found no nitrogenous bases except choline. This of course indicates the virtual absence of the cephalin fraction.

Sakaki (1914) reported the presence of two phosphatides in human placenta, one of which was ether-insoluble. The nitrogen-phosphorus ratio of both of these was approximately 1:1, which raises doubt as to the identity of the ether-insoluble product since sphingomyelin which has this solubility characteristic has a nitrogen-phosphorus ratio of 2:1.

Fenger (1917) found the maternal placenta of the cow at three to four months to contain 0.3 per cent phosphatides on a wet basis. At seven to nine months the value was 0.4 per cent. For the fetal placenta the corresponding values were 0.2 per cent and 0.1 per cent or roughly half as much.

Leone and Manzi (1948) found 242 ± 11 milligram per cent of lipide phosphorus in dry human placenta.

Watanabe (1923) estimated that about 30 per cent of the lipides of the human placenta are phosphatides, and these are chiefly lecithin with only a small amount of cephalin fraction. He also obtained an ether-insoluble product which probably was sphingomyelin.

Pratt and co-workers (1946) found that about 56 per cent of the total lipide content of human placenta was phosphatides. Lecithin comprised about one-half of the phosphatides and the cephalin fraction about one-third; and 14 per cent of sphingomyelin was found. The phosphatides accounted for 6.8 per cent of the dry weight of the placenta.

Variation in Phosphatide Content During Reproductive Processes

Boyd (1935a) has followed the phosphatide content of the ovary of the rabbit during pregnancy. The value increased during the first half of pregnancy from about 1000 milligram per cent to about 4000 milligram per cent on the sixteenth day. Thereafter, a decrease set in until the end of pregnancy on the thirty-second day when the average value was below 2000 milligram per cent. Values for pseudopregnant rabbits, i.e., animals mated with castrated bucks, were similar. It should be noted that these results were obtained on whole ovaries which included the corpora lutea.

Similarly, the lipides of the ovaries of the frog, *Rana pipiens*, increase 200 to 700 per cent during the production of ova, according to Boyd (1938a). Thus, the ovaries of six normal frogs contained 325 to 711 milligram per cent of phosphatides on a wet basis. In fifteen frogs who were in the process of ovulating, the phosphatide content of the ovaries varied from 888 to 3370 milligram per cent of the wet weight.

With guinea pigs, however, Boyd (1936) found that the phosphatide content of the ovaries did not increase during pregnancy. Although individual variation was great, the average was of the order of 1250 milligram per cent throughout pregnancy and this approximated the values maintained by controls. These results indicate that the ovaries of the rabbit are active during pregnancy, whereas those of the guinea pig are passive. This hypothesis is borne out by the fact that castration does not induce abortion in the pregnant guinea pig, whereas it does in the rabbit.

Boyd (1935, 1936a) has carried out interesting studies on the changes which take place in placental lipides during pregnancy of guinea pigs and rabbits. In the guinea pig the greatest changes occurred in the phosphatides since these increased from 820 milligram per cent on the fifteenth day of pregnancy to an average value of about 1600 milligram per cent on the fifty-fifth day. The rate of increase was greatest between the twentieth and thirtieth day and reached a plateau after the fortieth day. In the rabbit, however, the placental phosphatides fell from over 1500 milligram per cent at the start of pregnancy to about 1000 milligram per cent at the middle of the pregnancy. Thereafter they increased, reaching a plateau level equivalent to the original value. Similar data are advanced for the other lipides.

Corpus Luteum

The work of various early investigators has shown that the corpus luteum is a rich source of phosphatides. Fenger (1916) reported 2.1 per cent phosphatides on a wet basis in the corpus luteum of pregnant cows and noted that this was almost fifteen times the quantity present in muscle. Corner (1917) reported the high value of 0.63 milligram of P_2O_5 per gram of fresh tissue in the corpus luteum of pregnant sows. He noted that this decreased as pregnancy progressed. Kaufmann and Raeth (1927) likewise showed that phosphatides existed in large quantity in human corpora lutea. They showed further, contrary to earlier histochemical evidence, that at the height of function during pregnancy the lipides were not decreased and the phosphatides were actually increased. Hermstein (1925) also reported the presence of abundant quantities of phosphatides in human corpora lutea and noted that these increased as the organ attained its maximum function.

Bloor, Okey and Corner (1930) studied the lipide content of the corpus luteum of the sow in some detail. In the nonpregnant animal they found that the phosphatide content increased from the first to the tenth day after estrus and remained constant until the fourteenth day during which time the gland was functioning actively. Thereafter, however, a decline set in. The phosphatide content during this cycle varied from 1.4 per cent at two days after estrus to 4.5 per cent on the thirteenth day and 1.0 per cent on the twenty-fifth to the thirty-fifth day.

If, however, the animal became pregnant, a decline was not noted on the fourteenth day. Rather the value increased to 4.8 per cent on the eighteenth day which was the time of implantation. Thereafter it decreased slightly and remained fairly constant during pregnancy. It is thus seen that during periods of activity, the phosphatide content is two to three times as high as it is immediately after estrus.

Weinhouse and Brewer (1942) have studied rather extensively the lipides of human corpora lutea and have concluded that the phosphatides and the cholesterol esters undergo the greatest changes during the development of the organ. Table XV indicates their results for the various stages of development of the corpus luteum. The results are on the basis of moist tissue and the figures in parentheses indicate the individual variations. From these data it is seen that the lecithin content is approximately constant at 50 per cent of the total phosphatides, whereas the cephalin fraction comprises 40 per cent and the sphingomyelin 10 per cent.

Hart and Heyl (1926) have prepared pure lecithin from corpus luteum and have identified the fatty acids present. These include palmitic, oleic and arachidonic, together with an appreciable quantity of a triply unsaturated C_{20} acid. Linoleic, linolenic and possibly stearic acid were not present. They also examined the cephalin fraction but did not investigate the acids present.

GLANDS

Adrenal Glands

The lipides of the adrenal glands have been investigated more extensively than those of other glands because of their availability, and it is encouraging to note that the agreement here is much better than it is in most cases. The individual phosphatides of the adrenals have not been studied, although Coester (1933) identified lecithin and the cephalin fraction in adrenal glands and obtained some evidence for the presence of small amounts of sphingomyelin. Likewise, Ault and Brown (1934) obtained evidence which shows that lecithin and the cephalin fraction are the chief phosphatides of beef adrenal glands.

Whitehead (1931) found that lipides are more abundant in the adrenal cortex of female mice than of male mice. Similarly, Materna and Januschke (1927) found an average of 14 per cent lipides in the male guinea pig adrenal glands and 16 per cent in the glands of the female. These determinations are on a wet basis and were made by Soxhlet extraction. Oleson and Bloor (1941) have resolved the lipides of the guinea pig adrenal. As an average of twenty determinations they found on a wet basis that the adrenal gland of a guinea pig weighing 91.0 ± 6.39

Table XV. Phosphatides of the Human Corpus Luteum (Weinhouse and Brewer, 1942)

Stage of development	Age (days)	No. of specimens	Total lipides	Phosphatides	Lecithin	Cephalin fraction	Sphingomyelin
					(Per cent of total phosphatides)		
Young	1–3	6	2.92 (2.09–3.15)	1.32 (1.00–1.61)	52.0	38.2	9.8
Vascularization	5–8	6	2.99 (2.56–3.54)	1.66 (1.38–2.03)	48.2	33.1	18.7
Early Bloom	8–11	6	3.36 (2.78–4.25)	2.04 (1.78–2.82)	49.2	41.2	9.5
Late Bloom	11–13	6	3.82 (2.40–5.65)	1.96 (1.38–2.81)			
Regression	14–18	8	4.85 (2.70–7.00)	1.71 (0.83–2.30)	46.7	39.2	14.1
Pregnancy	2½–4½ months	5	3.63 (2.93–4.93)	2.64 (2.24–3.31)	49.2	41.3	9.5

(standard error) milligrams contained 3.7 ± 0.3 milligrams of phosphatides which is roughly 4 per cent. Fatty acids were present to the extent of 8.4 ± 0.52 milligrams, whereas cholesterol and its esters were present in considerably lesser quantities. The weight of the adrenals did not change on fasting, although the phosphatide content increased slightly.

Knouff and co-workers (1941) found the adrenal glands of the guinea pig to contain an average of 5.8 per cent phosphatides in one series of experiments and 6.1 per cent in another. Both figures are the averages of seven determinations and are on a wet basis. Muscular activity did not decrease the total lipide, although the cholesterol content was decreased. The corresponding increase in some other lipide which must necessarily have resulted was not detected.

Leulier and Revol (1931) found the medulla of the adrenal gland to contain three-fourths as much lipide phosphorus as the cortex, and this ratio was constant in goats, horses, mules and pigs. In agreement with this, Brown and co-workers (1937) found 3.1 per cent phosphatides in the cortex of the beef adrenal gland and 2.7 per cent in the medulla. They found 1.8 and 1.5 per cent total fatty acids, and 0.3 and 0.4 per cent total cholesterol, respectively. No neutral fat was found.

Baumann and Holly (1925) found in the normal adrenal glands of the guinea pig 1.8 per cent phosphatides, 3.7 per cent cholesterol and 7.7 per cent neutral fat. Rabbits showed a much greater individual variation, the average phosphatide content of the adrenals of twenty-six normal rabbits being 2.5 per cent.

The lipide content of the adrenal glands of rabbits was explored by MacLachlan, Hodge and Whitehead (1941). As an average of twenty analyses they found on a moist basis that an adrenal gland weighing 93 milligrams contained 11.5 milligrams total lipides of which 3 milligrams was phosphatides. Unlike the results of Oleson and Bloor (1941) for guinea pig adrenals, there was an equal quantity of neutral fat and a larger amount (5.4 milligrams) of total cholesterol.

Ault and Brown (1934) determined the fatty acid composition of the phosphatides of beef adrenal glands by distillation of the methyl esters. Their work showed the absence of linoleic acid and of all highly unsaturated acids except arachidonic, which was present to the extent of 22.2 per cent. Thus, this is probably the best natural source of this acid. What was probably myristic acid was present to the extent of 1.2 per cent. Likewise, there were present 23.8 per cent palmitic, 11.1 per cent stearic, 40.2 per cent oleic, and 2 per cent arachidic acids. Shinowara and Brown (1938) have evolved a procedure for the isolation of arachidonic acid from beef adrenals by the direct alcoholysis of the phosphatides. The isolation of methyl arachidonate and of a fraction believed to be methyl eicosapentenoate from adrenal phosphatides, by the use of chromatographic adsorption, has been reported by White and Brown (1948).

Klenk and Dittmer (1936) have shown the presence of highly unsaturated C_{22} acids in beef adrenal phosphatides and have expressed the belief that these always occur where C_{20} acids are found.

Pancreas

Bloor (1928) was able to isolate about 19 grams of phosphatides from a kilogram of beef pancreas. Lecithin was present to a somewhat greater extent than the cephalin fraction, and both had average iodine numbers of 68 to 69. The fatty acids of the cephalins had an iodine number of 98, whereas the lecithin fatty acids had an iodine number of 91. An acid with four unsaturated linkages was present in both and was probably arachidonic acid.

Jorpes (1928) has reported the presence of 0.13 per cent lipide phosphorus in fresh pancreas, and this is roughly equivalent to 2.9 per cent phosphatides.

Thymus

Kaucher and co-workers (1943) obtained the following results for beef thymus gland. The figures are per cent of dry weight.

Total lipides	Total phosphatides	Lecithin	Cephalin fraction	Sphingomyelin
10.47	6.72	4.09	1.96	0.67
30.36	6.70	2.48	3.48	.74

Miscellaneous Glands

Fenger (1916) determined the phosphatide content of various glands from cattle. His analyses, which are based on the somewhat doubtful values of the phosphorus content of petroleum ether extracts, are indicated in Table XVI.

TABLE XVI. PHOSPHATIDE CONTENT OF GLANDS (FENGER, 1916)

Gland	% Phosphatide in fresh tissue
Pituitary body, anterior lobe, calves	1.44
Pituitary body, anterior lobe, cattle	1.65
Pituitary body, posterior lobe, cattle	0.96
Pineal body, cattle	1.79
Thyroid, cattle	0.13
Thymus, calves	.43
Adrenals, cattle	2.37
Corpus luteum, pregnant cows	2.12

From these data it may be seen that with the exception of the thyroid the ductless glands have high phosphatide contents. The corpus luteum is discussed in greater detail under reproductive organs (see p. 302).

(see p. 302)

MUSCLE

General

The investigation of the phosphatide content of muscle and subsequent generalizations are complicated by the great amount of variation which exists in a given muscle, not only between species but also within a species. Muscles are a rich source of phosphorus compounds other than phosphatides, containing such materials as ortho-inorganic phosphate, adenylic pyrophosphate, phosphocreatine, free adenylic acid, and so-called Embden ester. All of these are related to muscular activity and their variation in given sets of conditions is the source of much interesting study.

In general, heart muscle contains the highest percentage of phosphatides, whereas the voluntary or skeletal muscles and the involuntary or smooth muscles contain roughly equal amounts of phosphatides. The cholesterol content, on the other hand, is highest in the heart and involuntary muscles and lowest in the voluntary muscles. The muscle phosphatides contain very little sphingomyelin and approximately equivalent amounts of lecithin and the cephalin fraction, although very often there is a slight excess of the former.

The relation of phosphatide content to muscle activity has been investigated extensively by Bloor and Snider (1934) and by Bloor (1927, 1936, 1937, 1940). Their work has shown that a marked difference occurs between the voluntary, smooth and heart muscles and that it also may occur in two muscles of the same type in the same animal, depending on use. In addition, differences exist in the same muscle in different species, likewise influenced by the amount of use to which the muscle is subjected. Data which substantiate this are discussed in some detail by Bloor (1943, pp. 199, 250) and will be mentioned only briefly here. As noted above, in a given animal, the heart muscle contains the highest percentage of phosphatide. An interesting comparison was made of the phosphatide content of the pectoralis major of three different winged animals. The domestic fowl, which seldom flies, had a phosphatide content of 1.4 per cent. In the pigeon the phosphatide content of this muscle was 4.7 per cent, whereas in the bat, which flies extremely well for long periods of time, the phosphatide content of the pectoralis muscle was 8.8 per cent. Bloor brings out a further interesting point in that the bat's pectoral muscles composed 6.4 per cent of its body weight, whereas the similar figure for the pigeon was 20 per cent. Thus the smaller size of the bat's muscles is compensated for by the higher phosphatide content.

In further work, Bloor (1940) called attention to the possibility that exercise through succeeding generations may increase the phosphatide content of the leg muscles of rats. Snider (1936) believes that the effect of activity of the muscle is not reflected in the unsaturation of the phosphatide fatty acids, which seems to remain constant.

Iosifova (1939, 1940) has shown that the phosphatide contents of frog and vertebrate muscles differ with the seasons, due possibly to the fact that the amount of activity varies from season to season.

Distribution of Phosphatides

Artom and Fishman (1943) carried out a careful study of the phosphatide content of the skeletal muscle of rats. The total phosphatide content was determined from the phosphorus content of an alcohol-ether extract. However, these workers unlike most others made the obvious assumption that nonlipide phosphorus was present in their extracts. Accordingly, they determined a correction factor by analyzing for phosphatides from fatty acid content and determining the ratio of phosphatide to phosphorus. Once this was established they could then use the simpler method of phosphorus analysis routinely. The choline-containing phosphatides were evaluated directly from choline content. The noncholine-containing materials were determined by difference, and the sphingomyelin from the phosphorus content of the reineckate. Their results, averages of determinations on ten rats raised to about a 125 gram weight, are expressed in milligrams per gram of lipide-free tissue: total lipides, 24.8 ± 6.1; total phosphatides, 11.0 ± 0.7; choline-containing phosphatides, 5.6 ± 0.5; sphingomyelins, 0.3 ± 0.3; noncholine-containing phosphatides, 5.4 ± 0.6. Thus it is seen from these data that lecithin and the cephalin fraction occur to about the same extent, whereas sphingomyelin is a very minor constituent.

Kaucher and co-workers (1943) have obtained the results indicated in Table XVII for voluntary or skeletal muscles from various sources. The values are per cent of dry weight.

Cardini and Serantes (1942) found 1.1 per cent total phosphatides in the leg muscle of the rat in excellent agreement with Artom and Fishman (1943). However, they found a preponderance of cephalins (0.8 per cent) as compared to lecithin (0.3 per cent). They, likewise, indicate the presence of a very small amount of sphingomyelin.

Buchwald and Cori (1931) found the rat gastrocnemius to contain 1.2 per cent phosphatides on a wet basis. The muscles of the hind leg of the frog contained 2.4 to 3.4 per cent phosphatides based on dry weight.

TABLE XVII. PHOSPHATIDE CONTENT OF MUSCLES (KAUCHER AND CO-WORKERS, 1943)

Muscle	Total lipide	Total phosphatide	Lecithin	Cephalin fraction	Sphingomyelin
Frog	10.88	7.14	2.79	4.16	0.19
Turtle	17.42	5.25	2.98	2.27	.00
Veal	11.84	5.04	2.70	2.15	.19
Lamb	11.19	4.74	2.55	1.90	.29
Salmon	18.30	4.39	2.53	1.86	.00
Chicken (dark)	12.67	4.36	1.70	2.39	.27
Codfish	9.47	4.28	3.31	0.49	.48
Shrimp	8.12	3.89	2.63	1.03	.23
Beef I	14.21	3.08	1.72	1.12	.24
Beef II	9.77	3.39	1.96	1.27	.16
Pork	22.40	3.06	1.69	1.25	.12
Chicken (light)	6.95	2.72	1.91	0.81	.00

They found that the lipide content, with the exception of fatty acids in one case, did not decrease during severe muscular work.

Morgulis and co-workers (1938) determined the lipide phosphorus content in various muscles of normal rabbits. The results are the average of nine determinations and are indicated in Table XVIII.

TABLE XVIII. PHOSPHATIDE CONTENT OF RABBIT MUSCLES (MORGULIS AND CO-WORKERS, 1938)

Muscle	Lipide phosphorus (% of dry substance)
Gastrocnemius	0.185
Biceps femoris	.171
Triceps	.197
Intercostal	.156
Abdominal	.123

Sorg (1929) analyzed for phosphatide content of various rabbit muscles by extracting with ether the residue resulting from the evaporation of the methanol extract of minced tissue. He found that the heart muscle of rabbit contained a maximum of 0.4 per cent phosphatide phosphoric acid, the semitendinosus a maximum of 0.4 per cent and the biceps femoris a maximum of 0.1 per cent. Sorg pointed out from this study that the phosphatide content paralleled the endurance capacity of the muscle.

Bloor (1936) studied the phosphatide-cholesterol ratio of various muscles of numerous animals. Table XIX shows his results for smooth muscle from various animals. The oxidative procedure developed by him was used for analysis.

The skeletal muscle of the cat was shown by Hunter (1942) to contain 0.8 ± 0.1 per cent total phosphatides on a wet basis. Sphingomyelin was present to the extent of 0.08 ± 0.01 per cent.

TABLE XIX. PHOSPHATIDE CONTENT OF SMOOTH MUSCLE (BLOOR, 1936)

Animal	Muscle	Phosphatide content (% of dry weight)
Wild rabbit	Stomach	2.50
Cat	Intestine	3.24
Hen	Gizzard	2.00
Pigeon	Gizzard	2.52
Owl	Gizzard	3.50
Sparrow	Gizzard	2.88
Human	Uterus	3.50
Laboratory rabbit	Uterus	4.40
Dog	Uterus	3.00

Cardiac Muscle

Cardiac muscle has also been investigated fairly extensively. Included herein are analyses performed on the entire heart since this organ is predominantly muscle.

Bloor (1936) has compared the phosphatide content of cardiac muscle with that of voluntary muscle from various sources. The results calculated from his data are indicated in Table XX.

The predominant phosphatide of heart seems to be lecithin. Thus the moist heart tissue of the adult albino rat, according to Cardini and Serantes (1942), consists of 1.8 per cent lecithin, 0.8 per cent cephalin fraction and 0.1 per cent sphingomyelin.

The phosphatides of the human heart have been investigated by Thannhauser and co-workers (1939). They report an average value of 6.9 per cent on a dry basis. Lecithin comprises 4.5 per cent, cephalin fraction 2.1 per cent and sphingomyelin 0.3 per cent.

Hunter (1942) has found 2.0 ± 0.3 per cent total phosphatides on a wet basis in the heart of the cat. The sphingomyelin comprised 0.15 ± 0.05 per cent which is equivalent to 7.8 ± 1.9 per cent of the total phosphatides.

Phosphatides occur in beef heart to the extent of 9.8 per cent, according to the investigations of Kaucher and co-workers (1943). Of this total 5.3 per cent is cephalin fraction, 4.0 per cent is lecithin, and 0.5 per cent is sphingomyelin.

Fatty Acids

The iodine numbers of the fatty acids of muscle phosphatides of various animals were determined by Terroine, Hatterer and Roehrig (1930). Their average results for cold-blooded animals follow: rayfish, 189; herring, 189; codfish, 173; tortoise, 136; frog, 162; snail, 83; shellfish, 188. For warm-blooded animals they obtained the following results: beef, 144; swine, 139; rabbit, 146; and pigeon, 144.

TABLE XX. PHOSPHATIDE CONTENT OF HEART AND VOLUNTARY MUSCLE
(BLOOR, 1936)

Animal	% Phosphatide in heart muscle (ventricle) (dry weight)	% Phosphatide in voluntary muscle (thigh) (dry weight)
Mammals		
Man	7.00	—
Sea lion	5.6	—
Kangaroo	6.72	2.38
Dog	8.54	8.00
Cat	5.72	2.47
Laboratory rabbit	9.12	1.70
Wild rabbit	7.65	3.75
Jack rabbit	7.22	8.75
Guinea pig	5.72	3.30
Gopher	9.60	7.50
Rat	7.95	3.50
Mouse	—	6.72
Birds		
Wild duck	7.80	3.78
Hen	7.56	3.75
Pigeon	7.28	4.51
Sparrow	8.55	4.40
Owl	6.16	3.64
Cold-blooded animals		
Turtle	6.40	3.50
Frog	4.20	3.80
Alligator	7.50	2.04
Grasshopper	—	5.40
Special		
Turtle auricle	5.25	—
Alligator auricle	7.20	—
Bat pectoralis	—	7.98
New-born wild rabbit thigh	—	6.75

Snider (1936) studied the iodine numbers of the phosphatide fatty acids of muscles from various sources. Her average values are listed in Table XXI.

Cuthbertson (1933) found the iodine numbers of the sartorius and the gastrocnemius muscle of the male human to be 111 in each case.

The iodine numbers of lecithin and the cephalin fraction of various voluntary muscles of beef were determined by Bloor (1927). Interestingly enough, Bloor and Snider (1934) found that the iodine number of phosphatide fatty acids showed no constant difference between muscles which were used extensively and those which were used only slightly.

The constitution of the fatty acids of muscle phosphatides has not been thoroughly investigated. Artom and Fishman (1943) found the mean molecular weight of the fatty acids of muscle phosphatides to be 265.3.

TABLE XXI. IODINE NUMBER OF MUSCLE PHOSPHATIDE FATTY ACIDS
(SNIDER, 1936)

Animal	Muscle	Average iodine number of phosphatide fatty acids
Wild rabbit	back	132
Laboratory rabbit	back	116
Exercised guinea pig	abdominal wall	125
Unexercised guinea pig	abdominal wall	131
Pigeon (fliers)	pectoralis major	136
Pigeon (fliers)	forearm	147
Pigeon (nonfliers)	pectoralis major	134
Pigeon (nonfliers)	forearm	128
Owl	pectoralis major	123
Hen	pectoralis major	126
Dog	diaphragm	133
Cat	jaw	116

This low value would indicate the presence of an appreciable quantity of relatively short-chain acids and possibly a considerable amount of unsaturation.

Snider (1936) found a rather remarkable constancy in the composition of muscle phosphatide fatty acids and concluded that an average of 73 per cent liquid acids and 27 per cent solid acids were present. The liquid fatty acids had an iodine number of about 173. Bloor (1927) observed that in beef heart muscle there were more unsaturated acids in the cephalin fraction than in the lecithin. The unsaturated acids of heart muscle included what was probably arachidonic acid, together with oleic and linoleic acids. No triply unsaturated acids were found.

Sinclair (1935) found the fatty acids of heart phosphatides of the rat to vary in iodine number from 115 to 157. The solid acids comprised 24.2 per cent with an iodine number of 3.5, whereas the liquid acids comprised 71.9 per cent and had an iodine number which varied from 159 to 214. Microtechniques were employed which were not subject to great accuracy.

Klenk and Ditt (1934) and Klenk and Dittmer (1936) have shown that the phosphatides of beef heart muscle contain about 15 per cent of C_{20} and C_{22} acids which have two, three or four double bonds. A considerable amount of work on fatty acids of muscle phosphatides remains yet to be accomplished.

Nature of the Phosphatides

Chargaff, Ziff and Rittenberg (1942) isolated 29.5 grams of phosphatides from 3831 grams of pig heart tissue. This product had a nitrogen-phosphorus ratio of 0.94:1 and an iodine number of 86.0. They studied this material by the method of isotope dilution. Of the nitrogen present, 52.5 per cent was amino nitrogen, 7.0 per cent was amino acid nitrogen and the remainder nonamino nitrogen. Whereas 86.8 per cent of the amino nitrogen could be identified as aminoethyl alcohol and amino acid, only 49.3 per cent of the nonamino acid could be identified as choline.

Urban (1937) had previously reported the presence of unidentified phosphatide nitrogen in heart tissue. Thus he reported 64 milligram per cent per 100 grams of fresh tissue of phosphatide nitrogen. Of this, 29 per cent was choline nitrogen, 49 per cent was amino nitrogen and the remainder was unidentified.

Artom (1945) has found small amounts of serine-containing phosphatides in the heart tissue of albino rats. His average results in micromoles per gram of moist tissue are as follows: total phosphatides, 20.6; choline phosphatides, 5.9; aminoethyl alcohol phosphatides, 10.3; serine phosphatides, 1.9. Here it will be noted that the figure for total phosphatides exceeds the sum of the constituent compounds. Artom suggests that this may be accounted for by unknown phosphatides or by phosphorus-containing contaminants.

Artom (1945) has also found serine-containing phosphatides in small amounts in the skeletal muscle of the rat. His data indicate about 12.6 micromoles of total phosphatides per gram of moist muscle. Choline-containing phosphatides account for about one-half of the total. Phosphatidylaminoethyl alcohol accounts for somewhat less than one-half, and the remainder (2.0, 1.5 and 0.7 micromoles per gram in three different determinations) is serine-containing material.

Muscle is a rich source of the acetal phosphatides described by Feulgen and Bersin (1939). According to them, muscle phosphatides contain 10 to 12 per cent of these. The aldehyde involved is chiefly palmitaldehyde, although in horse muscle and in beef muscle there is about 10 and 25 per cent of stearaldehyde, respectively.

SKIN AND MUCOSA

Skin

Nerking (1908), who made the first analysis of skin phosphatides, reported 0.2 per cent phosphatides in the fresh rabbit pelt and 0.4 per cent in the skin of the eagle.

The lipides of the cutaneous epithelium were investigated by Eckstein and Wile (1926), who used exfoliated scales of skin from patients suffering from various types of dermatitis. In four cases the total lipides varied from 6.9 to 8.2 per cent. Cholesterol was the lipide present in largest quantity. Phosphatides were definitely present, however, to the extent of about 0.2 per cent, which is approximately 2.7 per cent of the total lipides. These low values were believed by Koppenhoefer (1936) to be due to the keratinous nature of the material. It was also observed that the subcutaneous lipides contained, in marked contrast, less than 0.1 per cent phosphatides. The fatty acids of the epithelial lipides had an iodine number of 62 and possessed acids more unsaturated than oleic, since crystalline bromides could be prepared.

Matthews, Newton and Bloor (1935) in eight analyses found in the skin of the normal cat 0.8 ± 0.2 per cent phosphatides on a dry basis. In experimentally produced diabetes, the phosphatide content increased to an average value of 1.4 ± 0.4 per cent.

In an interesting study, Koppenhoefer (1936) separated the hide of a steer mechanically into six horizontal layers. The phosphatide content of each of these layers as per cent of dry weight is as follows: hair, 0; epidermal horn, 0.5; epidermal base, 2; transition layer, 0.2; corium major, 0.1; corium base, 0.1.

This work shows, in accord with the observations of Eckstein and Wile (1926), that the phosphatides occur preponderantly in the epidermal region. The phosphatides consisted of both lecithin and cephalins and, interestingly enough, were said to contain hydroxylated fatty acids. The cephalin fraction seemed to be somewhat more unsaturated than the lecithin and seemed to contain fatty acids of higher molecular weight.

It is interesting to note that Koppenhoefer (1936) reported the absence of phosphatides in beef hair, whereas Eckstein (1926) found that 0.8 per cent of the lipides of the hair of young adult albino rats (total lipides = 4.5 per cent) was in the form of phosphatides.

Rewald and Schweiger (1933) investigated the skin of several freshly slaughtered animals. The hair and fat were removed from the skin which was then cut in small pieces and extracted with alcohol-benzene. The

TABLE XXII. PHOSPHATIDE CONTENT OF SKIN (REWALD AND SCHWEIGER, 1933)

Animal	Phosphatide content (%)	
	Dry basis	Wet basis
Calf	1.18	0.40
Cow	0.73	.20
Pig	.71	.46
Sheep	1.05	.42

solvent was removed and the residue was taken up in ether. The phosphorus content of the ether extract was then determined and served as a measure of the phosphatide content of the skin. Their results are indicated in Table XXII.

The superficial lipides of the skin surface which arise probably from the sebaceous glands, the sweat glands and the epidermal cells have been studied by several investigators. In the lipides collected by washing the body with a fat solvent, Pachur (1931) found about 88 per cent neutral fat and a total of 4.2 per cent of phosphatides, cholesterol esters and soaps.

Engman and Kooyman (1934) found in two analyses 1.2 per cent and 1.1 per cent phosphatides in the lipides of the human skin surface. The material was obtained by washing the skin with fat-free cotton sponges moistened with alcohol and ether. Thereafter the sponges were extracted. The fatty acids of the total lipides were examined and were found to include oleic, linoleic, arachidonic and palmitic acids, together with a small amount of unidentified liquid saturated acids.

The phosphatide content of skin which is undergoing healing increases to a maximum and then declines, according to Taylor, Paul and Paul (1948).

Gums

Hodge (1933) has shown that the gums contain 2.2 ± 1.7 per cent total lipides and 1.0 ± 0.7 per cent phosphatides. These are the results of almost one hundred analyses. The values for infants are somewhat lower than those for adults.

Intestine and Intestinal Mucosa

The intestine of the beef contains 6.9 per cent phosphatides (dry weight), according to Kaucher and co-workers (1943). Lecithin predominates to the extent of 3.8 per cent. There is 1.9 per cent cephalin fraction and a rather large amount, 1.3 per cent, of sphingomyelin.

Sinclair (1929) has determined that phosphatides comprise 10.4 per cent of the dry mucosa of the small intestine. This is an average of eight determinations which varied from 5.4 per cent to 12.5 per cent. The average iodine number was 60, whereas the fatty acids comprised 53 per cent of the phosphatides and had an iodine number of 93 ± 1.2. His work showed that whereas the composition of the phosphatide fatty acids changed during fat absorption, their amount remained constant.

Reiser (1942), in accord with the results of Sinclair (1929), found that neither the cholesterol nor the phosphatide content of the duodenal mucosa changed during fat absorption. The results of twenty determinations were surprisingly constant, and indicated the presence of 10.2 per cent phosphatides in the dry duodenal mucosa.

Hunter (1942) has found as an average of eleven determinations 1.4 ± 0.2 per cent phosphatides in the intestinal mucosa of the cat. Sphingomyelin comprised 0.32 ± 0.06 per cent or 22.7 ± 6.0 per cent of the total phosphatides.

Youngburg (1937) found as an average of five determinations 43 milligram per cent of lipide phosphorus in the intestinal mucosa of rats. This is about 11.6 per cent of the total phosphorus present.

Gastric Mucosa

Uhnoo (1938) in an examination of the gastric mucosa found lecithin and the cephalin fraction as well as cerebrosides.

EYES

Goldschmidt (1922) showed that the lens of the human eye contained phosphatides. His analyses indicated that the maximum phosphatide content was reached between the ages of ten and twenty. A decline followed until the ages of sixty to seventy, whereupon an increase was noted.

The lipides of the sclera, cornea, choroid and iris have been investigated by Krause (1934). The lipides of the choroid and iris are chiefly phosphatides, whereas in the sclera and the *cornea substantia propria* the fat and phosphatide content are approximately equal. The total lipide content is small, reaching 2 per cent only in the cornea. Lecithin and the cephalin fraction seem to be the most predominant phosphatides, sphingomyelin being a minor constituent except in the cornea where it is present in fairly large amounts.

In the bovine retina, Krause (1935) has found the distribution of phosphatides indicated in Table XXIII.

TABLE XXIII. PHOSPHATIDES OF BOVINE RETINA (KRAUSE, 1935)

Lipide	% of wet tissue	% of dry tissue
Total lipides	2.26	19.7
Total phosphatides	1.57	13.7
Lecithin	0.81	7.02
Cepahlin fraction	.55	4.78
Sphingomyelin	.22	1.89

The retinal lipides of cattle were investigated by Leinfelder and Salit (1934), who found 3.4 per cent total lipides on a wet basis. This included 1.1 per cent phosphatides which was 32.4 per cent of the total lipides. Lecithin comprised 27.4 per cent of the total lipides, and the cephalin fraction comprised 11.2 per cent. The obvious discrepancy is due to the fact that the cephalin fraction was determined inaccurately by precipitating it with alcohol from ether solution.

Salit (1937) has shown interestingly enough that the lipide content of the crystalline lens of the human eye undergoes seasonal variation. The total lipides increased in summer and winter and decreased during the other two seasons. The phosphatide content, on the other hand, increased only during the summer, whereas the cholesterol increased only during the winter. When the data were plotted, the summation of the two latter curves was very similar to the curve obtained for the total lipides.

TOOTH PULP

Hodge (1936) analyzed normal human tooth pulp for lipides by Bloor's oxidative procedure (see p. 160). He found on the basis of moist weight 0.9 per cent total lipides and 0.7 per cent phosphatides. He also investigated cow teeth and found that fatty acids of the total lipides had an iodine number of 72.3.

THE ENTIRE ANIMAL ORGANISM

Vertebrates

Glikin (1908), who was one of the early investigators in the field of phosphatides, found about 5 per cent phosphatides in the entire body of the rabbit and the cat, and about 3.8 per cent phosphatides in the guinea pig.

The phosphatide content of several rodents was determined by Nerking (1908), who listed the following values for per cent lipide phosphorus on the basis of live weight: Belgian hare, 0.36; rabbit, 0.40, 0.38, 0.45; hedgehog, 0.82, 0.80. The results are per cent of live weight.

Boyd (1935) studied the change in phosphatide composition of the rabbit fetus. This work showed that the phosphatide as well as the free cholesterol increased rapidly until the middle of the gestation period. At this point the rate of increase lessened until the last week or ten days, when it again increased.

Sinclair (1930a) carried out an interesting study in which he analyzed for phosphatide fatty acids in the entire bodies of white rats during the period of the first four months of life. He concluded that the phosphatide content, when considered only on the basis of tissue solids, decreased rapidly after birth. Furthermore, he observed that the most rapid decline in phosphatide content coincided with the most rapid period of growth. However, on the basis of moist tissue, the phosphatide content of the animal actually increases after birth, reaching a maximum in about three weeks and declining thereafter. This is due to the fact that the water content of the tissues decreases rapidly in the first postnatal period. The phosphatide-cholesterol ratio in the entire body was found to be 7.0 and this remained constant during the three-month period of observation.

Marine Animals

The phosphatide content of various species of fish was found by Bähr and Wille (1931) to vary from 0.1 to 0.7 per cent on the basis of fresh weight, and 0.5 to 2.7 per cent on the basis of dry weight. Crab flesh contained 1.1 per cent phosphatides on a wet basis and 4.1 per cent on a dry basis. The values were found to vary with the species and the age of the fish, and even with the season. Thus codfish in spring had 0.2 per cent phosphatides, whereas in the fall they possessed 0.5 per cent.

The class of shellfish known as Pelecypoda contained about 0.7 per cent lipides on a wet basis of which 50 per cent were phosphatides with high iodine numbers, according to Tsujimoto and Koyanagi (1934). The class Gasteropoda contained about 1 per cent lipides, 40 to 60 per cent of which were phosphatides.

Rewald (1929) found in herring flesh a lipide fraction which contained 2.6 per cent phosphorus, indicating the presence of about 66 per cent phosphatides.

The phosphatide content of marine annelids has been studied by Wilber and Bayors (1947).

Cysticercus Fasciolaris

The lipides of the larval tapeworm *Cysticercus fasciolaris* were investigated by Salisbury and Anderson (1939). They found roughly 5 to 6 per cent lipides on a dry basis, and these consisted of about 30 per cent phosphatides, together with cholesterol, cerebrosides and a small amount of glycerides. The phosphatides were divided between lecithin and the cephalin fraction in the ratio of approximately 3:1 as indicated by the total nitrogen and amino nitrogen analyses. The phosphatide fatty acids were distributed equally between the saturated and unsaturated series. The former consisted of palmitic, stearic and arachidic acids together with an unidentified acid of higher molecular weight than arachidic. The unsaturated acids were probably chiefly oleic and palmitoleic acids, since the iodine number of the liquid acids was 66.1 and since stearic and palmitic acids were obtained on reduction. There was also obtained on reduction an appreciable quantity of acid of molecular weight higher than stearic.

In a later publication, Lesuk and Anderson (1941) describe the investigation of the ether-insoluble lipides of *Cysticercus fasciolaris*. These comprised about 34 per cent of the total lipides, and consisted of a mixture of cerebroside and phosphatide. The latter, after a somewhat tedious isolation, proved to be a dipalmityllecithin. This was the first observation of the occurrence of a hydrolecithin in nature. It was most unusual, and in this case was paralleled by the fact that the cerebroside, on hydrolysis, yielded dihydrosphingosine instead of the unsaturated sphingosine ordinarily found. The same dipalmityllecithin was later observed by Thannhauser, Benotti and Boncoddo (see p. 280) in beef brain, spleen and lung. The authors believe that these substances suggest the occurrence of peculiar metabolic processes in the parasite.

Miscellaneous

Silkworm pupae were shown to contain phosphatides by Yosida (1941), and the female pupa was said to contain more phosphatides than the male. The effect of metamorphosis of the silkworm on the phosphatide has been studied by Niemierko (1947).

Butterflies of the variety *Bombyx mori* were shown by Jona (1935) to contain 1.0 to 1.4 per cent phosphatides on a dry basis.

CHAPTER XIX

PHOSPHATIDES OF EGGS AND MILK

EGGS

A century ago, Gobley (1846, 1847) isolated phosphatides from eggs and learned that these remarkable substances are composed of glycerophosphoric acid, fatty acids and a nitrogenous substance in some sort of chemical combination. Subsequently eggs, which possess a relatively high phosphatide content, served as a commercial source of phosphatide until soybean technology made them an uneconomical source. The phosphatides of eggs are resident entirely in the yolk where at least a portion of them are in combination with proteins and carbohydrates. Their complete extraction, as is usual, may be effected with alcohol, either alone or in combination with other solvents (Grossfeld and Walter, 1934; Brooks and Hawthorne, 1944).

Phosphatide Content

The preparation from egg yolk of pure lecithin, which comprises the greater part of hen egg phosphatides, has been described by various investigators including MacLean (1915), Levene and Rolf (1921, 1927), Sueyoshi (1931) and Divinskiĭ and Rodzevich (1934). The total phosphatide content of egg yolk, which is undoubtedly variable within limits, is of the order of 9 to 10 per cent, whereas the total lipide content is 30 to 35 per cent. As Table XXIV indicates, there is fair agreement in the results of various investigators.

The predominance of the cephalin fraction over lecithin reported by Koch and Woods (1905/06) is in error in the light of subsequent work. The actual amount of cephalin fraction in hen eggs, however, is still questionable, the low value of 0.4 per cent isolated by Nishimoto (1934) having been substantiated by Riemenschneider, Ellis and Titus (1938) in opposition to the higher values reported by other workers. Sphingomyelin is obviously a minor constituent of egg phosphatides. Chargaff, Ziff and Rittenberg (1942) have shown by the method of isotope dilution that amino acids are absent in the hydrolysis products, which means that the cephalin fraction is almost entirely phosphatidylaminoethyl alcohol (see p. 85).

320

TABLE XXIV. THE PHOSPHATIDE CONTENT OF HEN EGG YOLKS (WET BASIS)

Phosphatide (%)	Lecithin (%)	Cephalin fraction(%)	Sphingomyelin (%)	Investigator
10.5–11.1	—	—	—	Lührig (1904)
9.9	3.0	6.9	—	Koch and Woods (1905/06)
9.41	—	—	—	Manasse (1906)
9.6–9.8	—	—	—	Cohn (1911)
8.6–9.3	—	—	—	van Meurs (1923)
6.8	—	—	—	Rewald (1928a)
9.3–11.1	—	—	—	Schremp (1932)
8.5–10.9	6.1–7.8	2.4–3.1	—	Nottbohm and Mayer (1933)
11.2	—	—	—	Grossfeld and Walter (1934)
8.24	—	—	—	Horrall (1935)
ca. 11.1	—	—	—	Erickson and co-workers (1938a)
13.73*	9.95*	3.44*	0.34*	Kaucher and co-workers (1943)

* Calculated on a dry weight basis.

Masuda and Hori (1937) found that lecithin was the predominant phosphatide in the eggs of chicken, duck, quail and peacock, although this was not the case for certain fish. Nottbohm and Mayer (1933) found that the yolk of duck eggs on a dry basis contained 8.0–9.8 per cent phosphatides. The yolk of turtle eggs according to Kaucher and co-workers (1943) contains 6.9 per cent phosphatides on a dry weight basis. This included 4.8 per cent lecithin, 1.9 per cent cephalin fraction and 0.3 per cent sphingomyelin. Halpern (1945) reported 6.2 per cent phosphatides with a phosphorus content of 2.9 to 3.4 per cent in the roe of sockeye salmon.

Fatty Acids

The fatty acids of egg yolk phosphatides were reported by Cousin (1903) to contain palmitic, stearic, oleic and linoleic acids. In addition to these, Levene and Rolf (1921, 1922) isolated from pure egg lecithin arachidonic acid. Unlike Cousin (1903), who found 24 per cent linoleic acid, they isolated very little of this dienoic acid. Hatakeyama (1930) likewise found arachidonic acid and a minor amount of oleic acid.

Clupanodonic acid was reported as an unsaturated constituent of egg lecithin by both Yokoyama (1934) and Sueyoshi and Furukobo (1931). The former investigator found in addition oleic and isopalmitic acids, whereas the latter investigators estimated from the bromine addition products that a large amount of oleic and a small amount of linoleic acids were present. Nishimoto (1934, 1935) isolated from egg yolk cephalin, palmitic, oleic and arachidonic acids.

More recently Riemenschneider, Ellis and Titus (1938) reinvestigated the fatty acids of pure egg lecithin by the method of ester fractionation. They found that palmitic acid predominates over stearic acid just as it does in the neutral fat of the yolk and that these are the only saturated fatty acids present. In the unsaturated series, they isolated oleic, linoleic, and clupanodonic acids rather than the arachidonic acid reported by Levene and Rolf (1922). Furthermore, they found that oleic acid was the chief unsaturated constituent. The palmitoleic acid which they found in the neutral fat was not found in the phosphatides. Their results are indicated in Table XXV and are compared with the composition of the glycerides.

TABLE XXV. FATTY ACID COMPOSITION OF EGG-YOLK LECITHIN AND
GLYCERIDES (RIEMENSCHNEIDER, ELLIS AND TITUS, 1938)

	Lecithin acids		Glyceride acids	
	Weight per cent	Mol per cent	Weight per cent	Mol per cent
Myristic			0.7	0.8
Palmitic	31.8	34.6	25.2	27.0
Stearic	4.1	4.0	7.5	7.3
Palmitoleic			3.3	3.6
Oleic	42.6	42.0	52.4	51.0
Linoleic	8.2	8.2	8.6	8.4
Clupanodonic	13.3	11.2	2.3	1.9
Total saturated	35.9	38.6	33.4	35.1
Total unsaturated	64.1	61.4	66.6	64.9

It is seen that the phosphatide acids are slightly more saturated than the glyceride acids, but that clupanodonic acid, nevertheless, is present to a considerably greater extent in the phosphatides.

Some of the discrepancies in the results of the above workers may be explained on the basis of variations in diet. Thus McCollum, Halpin and Drescher (1912) found that fat-free diets cause a marked decrease in iodine numbers of both the glyceride and the phosphatides of the egg yolk. Likewise Cruickshank (1934) in an extensive study has shown that diet may effect a wide variation in iodine number of the mixed fatty acids of egg yolks.

Complex Formation

The tendency of egg-yolk phosphatides to occur in complex formation has been investigated. Manasse (1906) was among the first to describe a phosphatide-protein complex. Halpern (1945) noted the presence of such a complex in salmon roe. Brooks and Hawthorne (1944) found that the lipides of fresh eggs were much less soluble in hydrocarbons than the lipides of dried eggs, although this observation sheds little light on the nature of the complex. The isolation of two phosphatide-protein complexes from eggs, lipovitellin and lipovitellenin, are described in detail by Fevold and Lausten (1946).

Sell, Olson and Kremer (1935) found that phosphatides in themselves are not good emulsifying agents for mayonnaise and concluded that the natural emulsifying agent is a lecithin-protein complex.

Rewald (1929a) found evidence for a phosphatide-carbohydrate complex in eggs, although the carbohydrate is present in very small amounts in the form of nonreducing di- or polysaccharides.

MILK AND DAIRY PRODUCTS

Although the phosphatide content of milk and its related products is comparatively low, it has nevertheless formed the basis for a fairly extensive literature. Most of this is concerned with analytical procedures for phosphatide determination and with data on the phosphatide content of milk and other dairy products from various sources and under various conditions. These data vary considerably, not only because the phosphatide content of natural products is undoubtedly variable, but also because the methods of analyses are not rigidly quantitative. From the relatively large amount of work that has been done one may assume that the phosphatide content of ordinary raw whole cow's milk is of the order of 0.035 per cent.

Phosphatide Content

Tables XXVI and XXVII indicate some of the representative lipide phosphorus values obtained by various investigators for milk and related dairy products. In certain cases literature values have been converted to milligrams of lipide phosphorus per 100 ml. of milk.

From the tables it is apparent that the phosphatide content of cream, butter and buttermilk is higher than that of milk, whereas the phosphatide content of skim milk is lower. Obviously, the phosphatide content of cream varies with the fat content, and this variation likewise affects the phosphatide content of butter and buttermilk. The wide variation noted in several instances is no doubt due to variation in fat content in the samples analyzed. Perlman (1935) showed that the phosphatide content of cream increases uniformly with the fat content until the latter reaches 55 to 58 per cent, after which a decrease is noted with further increase of fat content, due probably to reversion of the type of colloidal system present. For when the fat becomes the continuous phase, the phosphatide, which supposedly surrounds each fat globule in the form

TABLE XXVI. THE PHOSPHATIDE CONTENT OF RAW WHOLE COW'S MILK

Mg. phosphatide phosphorus per 100 ml. milk	No. of analyses	Investigator
1.6	Not stated	Schmidt-Muhlheim (1883)
3.6–4.5	Several	Stoklasa (1897)
2.2	4	Burow (1900)
1.6–2.4	Not stated	Bordas and de Raczkowski (1902)
3.1	3	Koch and Woods (1905/6)
1.5–4.7	17	Nerking and Haensel (1908)
2.1–4.7	3	Glikin (1909)
2.4	1	Dornic and Daire (1910, 1909/11)
2.4	Not stated	Laxa (1913)
1.0–1.5	11	Brodrick-Pittard (1914)
5.3–7.0	7	Hess and Helman (1925)
1.4–2.8	Not stated	Chapman (1928)
1.5	Not stated	Mohr, Brockman and Müller (1932)
1.2	Not stated	Lobstein and Flatter (1935)
0.52–1.2	18	Horrall (1935)
1.4	Not stated	Holm, Wright and Deysher (1936)
1.3	1	Rewald (1937)
1.4	8	Heinemann (1939)
6.8	10	Buruiana and Furtunesco (1941)

of a delicate membrane, is released in part and enters the aqueous phase. The fact that phosphatide remains in the fat phase is explained by the occlusion of globules of fat with intact phosphatide membranes. Heinemann (1939) found that the phosphatide content of cream increased uniformly with the fat content, in contrast to the results of Perlman (1935). The apparent discrepancy, however, is explainable on the basis of techniques employed. Heinemann obtained his creams of over 60 per cent fat content from 35 to 40 per cent cream, whereas it may be assumed that Perlman obtained all of his cream from whole milk.

The high phosphatide content of buttermilk is further evidence for the membrane theory (Dornic and Daire, 1910, 1909/11; Palmer and Samuelson, 1924), for as the fat globules coagulate to form butter, the membrane of phosphatide is in part released and is relegated to the plasma. Again, then, the phosphatide content of butter is due to occlusion rather than to actual solution or to any sort of attraction between the phosphatide and the fat. Indeed, melted, filtered butterfat contains no phosphatide.

Thus it may be assumed that the phosphatides of milk are associated with the fat (Horrall, 1935) by virtue of the fact that they are a part of a colloidal membrane which surrounds each globule. Within the membrane, however, they probably form a complex with milk protein (Lobstein and Flatter, 1935; Tayeau, 1940; Jack and Dahle, 1936, 1937;

TABLE XXVII. THE PHOSPHATIDE CONTENT OF DAIRY PRODUCTS

Mg. phosphatide phosphorus per 100 ml. substance	No. of analyses	Investigator
Cream		
3.6 (fat content = 15%)	2	Brodrick-Pittard (1914)
10.3 (fat content = 32%)	1	Hess and Helman (1925)
7.1 (fat content = 20%)	1	Hess and Helman (1925)
7.3–8.6 (fat content = 45.7%)	Not stated	Chapman (1928)
6.7 (fat content = 23%)	Not stated	Mohr, Brockman and Müller (1932)
4.8–9.2 (fat content = 34–50%)	10	Horrall (1935)
3.1 (fat content = 16.3%)	1	Perlman (1935)
5.7 (fat content = 34.9%)	1	Perlman (1935)
6.0 (fat content = 41.2%)	1	Perlman (1935)
5.6 (fat content = 47.3%)	1	Perlman (1935)
7.3 (fat content = 41.1%)	Not stated	Holm, Wright and Deysher (1936)
2.6 (fat content = 14.1%)	1	Heinemann (1939)
6.0 (fat content = 41.8%)	1	Heinemann (1939)
8.0 (fat content = 76.2%)	1	Heinemann (1939)
Skim Milk		
1.3	Not stated	Dornic and Daire (1910, 1909/11)
.06	1	Glikin (1909)
4.3	2	Hess and Helman (1925)
0.32–1.2	Not stated	Chapman (1928)
0.6	Not stated	Mohr, Brockman and Müller (1932)
0.5–1.4	11	Horrall (1935)
0.7	Not stated	Holm, Wright and Deysher (1936)
0.7	16	Heinemann (1939)
Butter		
5.9	3	Brodrick-Pittard (1914)
50–68	2	Rewald (1928a)
4.0–7.7	7	Smith (1930)
8.2	Not stated	Mohr, Brockman and Müller (1932)
6.0–9.6	12	Horrall (1935)
7.5	Not stated	Holm, Wright and Deysher (1936)
8.5	2	Heinemann (1939)
Buttermilk		
1.3	Not stated	Dornic and Daire (1910, 1909/11)
4.1–5.9	Not stated	Chapman (1928)
15.7–35.0*	4	Thurston and Petersen (1928)
4.5	Not stated	Mohr, Brockman and Müller (1932)
5.6–6.4	7	Horrall (1935)
7.3	Not stated	Holm, Wright and Deysher (1936)
4.9	3	Heinemann (1939)
Separation Slime		
10.8–28.8	4	Horrall (1935)
9.2	1	Heinemann (1939)

* Fat content of cream from which buttermilk resulted varied from 22–68%.

Bird, Breazeale and Bartle, 1937; North and Sommer, 1935; Osborne and Wakeman, 1916), which accounts in large part for the colloidal nature of milk. Because of this protein complex, it is necessary to use a dissociating solvent such as alcohol for phosphatide extraction.

The phosphatide content of human milk provided the subject of older researches. Glikin (1909) found an average phosphatide content of 0.13

per cent, whereas Hess and Helman (1925) reported values ranging from 0.04 to 0.10 per cent for samples obtained during the first two weeks following parturition and values of 0.05 to 0.07 per cent for samples obtained thereafter. Guillaumin and Vigne (1932) indicated the following average values for milk obtained at various times after childbirth: one to ten days, 0.12 per cent; eleven to twenty days, 0.12 per cent; twenty-one to thirty days, 0.9 per cent.

The average phosphatide content of whole buffalo milk was found to be 0.23 per cent by Buruiana and Furtunesco (1941), whereas skim buffalo milk contained 0.18 per cent. The determinations were made by a modification of Bloor's procedure (see p. 160).

Distribution of Phosphatides

One of the first quantitative procedures for the determination of phosphatide in milk was reported by Burow (1900). Since that time the Roese-Gottlieb procedure as modified by Mojonnier and Troy (1932, p. 93) has been recommended most frequently. Analytical procedures are discussed critically by Horrall (1935) and by other investigators (Chapman, 1928; Perlman, 1935; Wiese, Nair and Fleming, 1932; Petersen and Herreid, 1929; Wright and Holm, 1933; Holm, Wright and Deysher, 1933; Rewald, 1937).

The presence of lecithin and the cephalin fraction in milk products was demonstrated by Kurtz, Jamieson and Holm (1934), who showed that they existed in buttermilk powder in the ratio of 56:44. Koch and Woods (1905/06) had likewise previously proved the presence of the glycerophosphatides, and Bischoff (1928) had shown that there was approximately twice as much lecithin as cephalin fraction in milk phosphatides. Rewald (1937) on the basis of alcohol solubility found 58.3 per cent of milk phosphatides to be lecithin.

Crane and Horrall (1943) found 46 per cent lecithin in whole milk fat, 54 per cent in fat from cream, 48 per cent in butter lipides and 34 per cent in buttermilk lipides. These estimations were made on the basis of choline content.

Fatty Acids

Holm, Wright and Deysher (1936) showed oleic acid to be the chief component (70.6 per cent) of the fatty acids of the glycerophosphatides. They also isolated myristic, stearic, and arachidic acids, and postulated the presence of a docosatetraenoic acid. Strangly enough, no palmitic acid was found.

Hilditch and Maddison (1941) likewise reported oleic acid to be the chief component of the phosphatides of butter from various sources, although they found it in considerably smaller quantities (23.5 to 32.5 per cent). In addition, they showed the presence of myristic, palmitic and stearic acids and what may have been arachidic acid, together with a hexadecenoic acid, an octadecadienoic acid and some C_{20}–C_{22} unsaturated acids of undefined constitution. Unidentified higher saturated acids were also present. Neither of these workers found the lauric acid reported by Susaki and Hiratsuka (1931), and it is quite probable that the fatty acid composition may vary with the environment of the cattle from which the milk comes.

The fatty acid content of colostrum and milk from humans and cows has been investigated in detail by Baldwin and Longenecker (1944, 1944a).

Rancidity

The fishy flavor which sometimes develops during the storage of dairy products has been attributed to trimethylamine which may result from lecithin decomposition either by hydrolysis, which is most probable, or by bacterial or enzymatic cleavage (Rogers' associates, 1935, p. 94; Sommer and Smit, 1923; Thurston, Brown and Dustman, 1935; Supplee, 1919).

The interesting work of Swanson and Sommer (1940) showed that as the so-called oxidized flavor of milk developed, the iodine number of the phosphatide decreased, whereas the iodine number of the neutral fat remained constant.

BIBLIOGRAPHY—PART IV

Abderhalden, E., "Physiological Chemistry," trans. by W. T. Hall and G. Defren, New York, John Wiley and Sons, 1911.

Alsterberg, G., *Arkiv Zool.,* **36B**, No. 3, 1 (1945); *C. A.,* **42**, 659 (1948).

Artom, C., *Bull. soc. chim. biol.,* **14**, 1386 (1932); *C. A.,* **27**, 1023 (1933).

——, *J. Biol. Chem.,* **139**, 65 (1941).

——, *ibid.,* **157**, 585, 595 (1945).

——, and Fishman, W. H., *J. Biol. Chem.,* **148**, 405 (1943).

——, and Freeman, J. A., *J. Biol. Chem.,* **135**, 59 (1940).

Ault, W. C., and Brown, J. B., *J. Biol. Chem.,* **107**, 607 (1934).

Bähr, O., and Wille, O., *Fischwirtschaft,* **7**, 129 (1931); *C. A.,* **27**, 5827 (1933).

Baldwin, A. R., and Longenecker, H. E., *J. Biol. Chem.,* **154**, 255 (1944).

——, ——, *ibid.,* **155**, 407 (1944a).

Bang, I., *Biochem. Z.,* **91**, 86 (1918); *C. A.,* **13**, 2228 (1919).

Baumann, E. J., and Holly, O. M., *J. Biol. Chem.,* **63**, LXIII (1925).

Benoit, J., and Wenslaw, A., *Compt. rend. soc. biol.,* **102**, 45 (1929); *C. A.,* **25**, 5453 (1931).

Bensley, R. R., *Anat. Record,* **69**, 341 (1937); *C. A.,* **32**, 982 (1938).

Bensley, R. R., and Hoerr, N. L., *Anat. Record,* **60,** 449 (1934) ; *C. A.,* **29,** 6284 (1935).

Bernhard, K., and Korrodi, H., *Helv. Chim. Acta,* **30,** 1786 (1947) ; *C. A.,* **42,** 1345 (1948).

Bird, E. W., Breazeale, D. F., and Bartle, E. R., *Iowa Agr. Expt. Sta. Research Bull.,* **227,** 173 (1937) ; *C. A.,* **32,** 7588 (1938).

Bischoff, G., *Z., physiol. Chem.,* **173,** 227 (1928) ; *C. A.,* **22,** 1414 (1928).

Blix, G., *Biochem. Z.,* **305,** 129 (1940) ; *C. A.,* **35,** 471 (1941).

Bloor, W. R., *J. Biol. Chem.,* **17,** 377 (1914).

——, *ibid.,* **36,** 33 (1918).

——, *Bull. soc. chim. biol.,* **3,** 451 (1921).

——, *J. Biol. Chem.,* **56,** 711 (1923).

——, *ibid.,* **59,** 543 (1924).

——, *ibid.,* **63,** 1 (1925).

——, *ibid.,* **72,** 327 (1927).

——, *ibid.,* **80,** 443 (1928).

——, *ibid.,* **82,** 273 (1929).

——, *ibid.,* **114,** 639 (1936).

——, *ibid.,* **119,** 451 (1937).

——, *ibid.,* **132,** 77 (1940).

——, "Biochemistry of the Fatty Acids and Their Compounds, the Lipides," New York, Reinhold Publishing Corp., 1943.

——, and Snider, R. H., *J. Biol. Chem.;* **107,** 459 (1934).

——, Blake, A. G., and Bullen, S. S., *J. Allergy,* **9,** 227 (1938) ; *C. A.,* **32,** 9245 (1938).

——, Okey, R., and Corner, G. W., *J. Biol. Chem.,* **86,** 291 (1930).

Blumensaat, C., *Arch. path. Anat. Physiol. (Virchow's),* **271,** 639 (1929) ; *C. A.,* **23,** 3968 (1929).

Boldyreva, N. V., *Biokhimiya,* **2,** 216 (1937) ; *C. A.,* **31,** 5418 (1937).

Bolle, A., *Biochem. Z.,* **24,** 179 (1910) ; *C. A.,* **4,** 1500 (1910).

Bonanni, A., *Jahresber. Fortschr. Tierchem.,* **32,** 508 (1902).

Bordas, F., and de Raczkowski, Sig., *Compt. rend.,* **134,** 15 (1902) ; *Chem. Zentr.,* 488 (1902).

Boyd, E. M., *J. Biol. Chem.,* **91,** 1 (1931).

——, *ibid.,* **101,** 323, 623 (1933).

——, *Biochem. J., .* **29,** 985 (1935) ; *C. A.,* **29,** 5903 (1935).

——, *J. Biol. Chem.,* **108,** 607 (1935a).

——, *ibid.,* **112,** 591 (1936).

——, *Can. J. Research,* **14B,** 155 (1936a) ; *C. A.,* **31,** 3971 (1937).

——, *J. Biol. Chem.,* **115,** 37 (1936b).

——, *J. Lab. Clin. Med.,* **21,** 957 (1936c) ; *C. A.,* **30,** 7181 (1936).

——, *Am. J. Clin. Path., Tech. Suppl.,* **2,** 77 (1938) ; *C. A.,* **32,** 5864 (1938).

——, *J. Physiol.,* **91,** 394 (1938a) ; *C. A.,* **32,** 2632 (1938).

——, *J. Biol. Chem.,* **143,** 131 (1942).

——, *Can. J. Research,* **22E,** 39 (1944) ; *C. A.,* **38,** 3338 (1944).

——, and Stevenson, J. W., *J. Biol. Chem.,* **122,** 147 (1937).

Brante, G., *Biochem. Z.,* **305,** 136 (1940) ; *C. A.,* **35,** 498 (1941).

Brodrick-Pittard, N. A., *Biochem. Z.,* **67,** 382 (1914) ; *C. A.,* **9,** 639 (1915).

Brooks, J., and Hawthorne, J. R., *J. Soc. Chem. Ind.,* **63,** 310 (1944) ; *C. A.,* **39,** 1476 (1945).

Brown, J. B., *J. Biol. Chem.,* **80,** 455 (1928).

——, *ibid.,* **97,** 183 (1932).

Brown, J. B., and Ault, W. C., *J. Biol. Chem.*, **89**, 167 (1930).

——, and co-workers (Knouff, R. A., Conlin, M. M., and Schneider, B. M.), *Proc. Soc. Exptl. Biol. Med.*, **37**, 203 (1937); *C. A.*, **32**, 6703 (1938).

Buchwald, K. W., and Cori, C. F., *Proc. Soc. Exptl. Biol. Med.*, **28**, 737 (1931); *C. A.*, **25**, 4592 (1931).

Burow, R., *Z. physiol. Chem.*, **30**, 495 (1900).

Buruiana, L., and Furtunesco, A., *Lait*, **21**, 8 (1941); *C. A.*, **38**, 3029 (1944).

Carayon-Gentil, A., and Corteggiani, E., *Bull. soc. chim. biol.*, **24**, 89 (1942); *C. A.*, **38**, 6312 (1944).

Cardini, C. E., and Serantes, M.·E., *Anales farm. y. bioquím. (Buenos Aires)*, **13**, 102 (1942); *C. A.*, **37**, 4755 (1943).

Cattaneo, L., *Ann. ostet. ginec. No. 5*, (1932); *Arch. ital. biol.*, **88**, 39 (1932); *C. A.*, **27**, 1925 (1933).

Chaikoff, I. L., and Entenman, C. *J. Biol. Chem.*, **166**, 683 (1946).

Channon, H. J., and Collinson, G. A., *Biochem. J.*, **23**, 1212 (1929); *C. A.*, **24**, 2785 (1930).

——, Irving, E., and Smith, J. A. B., *Biochem. J.*, **28**, 840 (1934); *C. A.*, **28**, 6735 (1934).

Chantrenne, H., *Biochim. et Biophys. Acta*, **1**, 437 (1947); *C. A.*, **42**, 2336 (1948).

Chapman, O. W., *J. Dairy Sci.*, **11**, 429 (1928); *C. A.*, **23**, 1182 (1929).

Chargaff, E., *J. Biol. Chem.*, **142**, 491 (1942).

——, and Ziff, M., *J. Biol. Chem.*, **140**, 927 (1941).

——, ——, and Rittenberg, D., *J. Biol. Chem.*, **144**, 343 (1942).

Cheng, L. T., *Z. physiol. Chem.*, **201**, 209 (1931); *C. A.*, **26**, 761 (1932).

Coester, C., *Z. physiol. Chem.*, **215**, 207 (1933); *C. A.*, **27**, 2189 (1933).

Cohn, R., *Z. öffentl. Chem.*, **17**, 203 (1911); *C. A.*, **5**, 3598 (1911).

Corner, G. W., *J. Biol. Chem.*, **29**, 141 (1917).

Cousin, H., *Compt. rend. soc. biol.*, **55**, 913 (1903).

Crane, J. C., and Horall, B. E., *J. Dairy Sci.*, **26**, 935 (1943); *C. A.*, **38**, 3028 (1944).

Cruickshank, E. M., *Biochem. J.*, **28**, 965 (1934); *C. A.*, **28**, 6790 (1934).

Cusick, J. T., *Cornell Univ. Agr. Expt. Sta. Mem.*, **30**, 159 (1920); *C. A.*, **15**, 3343 (1921).

Cuthbertson, D. P., *Biochem. J.*, **27**, 1099 (1933); *C. A.*, **28**, 813 (1934).

deBoissezon, P., and Valdignié, P., *Compt. rend. soc. biol.*, **136**, 778 (1942); *C. A.*, **39**, 3051 (1945).

Delsal, J. L., *Bull. soc. chim. biol.*, **26**, 99 (1944); *C. A.*, **39**, 3560 (1945).

Dezani, S., *Acad. med. Torino* (1909); *C. A.*, **4**, 1992 (1910).

Divinskiĭ, A., and Rodzevich, V., *Khim. Farm. Prom. No. 3*, 18 (1934); *C. A.*, **29**, 1940 (1935).

Dornic, P., and Daire, P., *Ann. fals. et fraudes*, **3**, 533 (1910); *Rev. gen. lait*, **8**, 385 (1909/11); *C. A.*, **5**, 727, 1135 (1911).

Dziemian, A. J., *J. Cellular and Comp. Physiol.*, **14**, 103 (1939); *C. A.*, **33**, 8269 (1939).

Eckstein, H. C., *Proc. Soc. Exptl. Biol. Med.*, **23**, 581 (1926).

——, and Wile, U. J., *J. Biol. Chem.*, **69**, 181 (1926).

Engman, M. F., and Kooyman, D. J., *Arch. Dermatol. and Syphilol.*, **29**, 12 (1934); *C. A.*, **30**, 3038 (1936).

Entenman, C., Lorenz, F. W., and Chaikoff, I. L., *J. Biol. Chem.*, **133**, 231 (1940).

Erickson, B. N., and co-workers (Williams, H. H., Bernstein, S. S., Avrin, I., Jones, R. S., and Macy, I. G.), *J. Biol. Chem.*, **122**, 515 (1938).

Erickson, B. N., and co-workers (Williams, H. H., Avrin, I., and Lee, P.), J. Clin. Invest., 18, 81 (1939); C. A., 33, 5464 (1939).

——, and co-workers (Avrin, I., Teague, D. M., and Williams, H. H.), J. Biol. Chem., 135, 671 (1940).

Erickson, S. E., and co-workers (Boyden, R. E., Insko, W. M., Jr., and Martin, J. H.), Kentucky Agr. Expt. Sta. Bull., 378, 3 (1938a); C. A., 32, 7591 (1938).

Fawaz, G., Lieb, H., and Zacherl, M. K., Biochem. Z., 293, 121 (1937); C. A., 32, 607 (1938).

Fenger, F., J. Biol. Chem., 27, 303 (1916).

——, ibid., 29, 19 (1917).

Feulgen, R., and Bersin, Th., Z. physiol. Chem., 260, 217 (1939); C. A., 33, 8635 (1939).

Fevold, H. L., and Lausten, A., Arch. Biochem., 11, 1 (1946); C. A., 40, 7244 (1946).

Fiske, C. H., and Subbarow, Y., J. Biol. Chem., 66, 375 (1925).

Flössner, O., Arch. Gynäkol., 135, 474 (1929); C. A., 23, 2747 (1929).

Folch, J., J. Biol. Chem., 139, 973 (1941).

——, ibid., 146, 35 (1942).

Folch, J., and Schneider, H. A., J. Biol. Chem., 137, 51 (1941).

——, and Van Slyke, D. D., J. Biol. Chem., 129, 539 (1939).

——, ——, Proc. Soc. Exptl. Biol. Med., 41, 514 (1939a); C. A., 33, 8652 (1939).

——, and Woolley, D. W., J. Biol. Chem., 142, 963 (1942).

——, Schneider, H. A., and Van Slyke, D. D., J. Biol. Chem., 133, XXXIII (1940).

Fränkel, E., Bielschowsky, F., and Thannhauser, S. J., Z. physiol. Chem., 218, 1 (1933); C. A., 27, 3955 (1933).

——, and Löhr, G., Z. physiol. Chem., 218, 218 (1933); C. A., 28, 3427 (1934).

Fries, B. A., and co-workers (Entenman, C., Changus, G. W., and Chaikoff, I. L.), J. Biol. Chem., 137, 303 (1941).

Gautrelet, J., Corteggiani, E., and Mme. Carayon-Gentil, Compt. rend. soc. biol., 135, 832 (1941); C. A., 39, 4938 (1945).

Glikin, W., Biochem. Z., 4, 235 (1907); C. A., 1, 2264 (1907).

——, ibid., 7, 286 (1908); C. A., 2, 1576 (1908).

——, ibid., 21, 348 (1909); C. A., 5, 745 (1911).

Gobley, Compt. rend., 21, 766, 988 (1846); Pharm. Zentralhalle, 44 (1846).

——, J. pharm. chim. [3], 11, 409; 12, 1 (1847); Pharm. Zentralhalle, 584 (1847).

Goldschmidt, M., Biochem. Z., 127, 210 (1922); C. A., 16, 1611 (1922).

Gorodisska, H., Biochem. Z., 164, 446 (1925); C. A., 20, 925 (1926).

Grimmer, W., and Schwartz, G., Milchw. Forsch., 2, 163 (1925); C. A., 19, 2988 (1925).

Grossfeld, J., Chem. Ztg., 63, 381 (1939); C. A., 34, 2940 (1940).

——, Z. Untersuch. Lebensm., 79, 113 (1940); C. A., 34, 5190 (1940).

——, and Peter, J., Z. Untersuch. Lebensm., 69, 16 (1935); C. A., 29, 3059 (1935).

——, and Walter, G., Z. Untersuch. Lebensm., 67, 510 (1934); C. A., 28, 5546 (1934).

Guillaumin, C. O., and Vigne, H., Rev. path. comp. hyg. gén., 32, 1566 (1932); C. A., 27, 3746 (1933).

Hack, M. H., J. Biol. Chem., 169, 137 (1947).

Halpern, G. R., Nature, 155, 110 (1945); C. A., 39, 1932 (1945).

Hammarsten, O., Z. physiol. Chem., 36, 525 (1902).

——, Ergeb. Physiol., 4, 1 (1905).

——, "A Textbook of Physiological Chemistry," trans. by J. A. Mandel, 6th ed., New York, John Wiley & Sons, 1911.

Hart, M. C., and Heyl, F. W., J. Biol. Chem., 70, 663, 675 (1926).

Hartley, P., *J. Physiol.*, **38**, 353 (1909).

Hatakeyama, T., *Z. physiol. Chem.*, **187**, 120 (1930); *C. A.*, **24**, 1873 (1930).

Heinemann, B., *J. Dairy Sci.*, **22**, 707 (1939); *C. A.*, **33**, 8834 (1939).

Hermstein, A., *Arch. Gynäkol.*, **124**, 739 (1925); *C. A.*, **20**, 65 (1926).

Hertwig, R., *J. Assoc. Offic. Agr. Chemists*, **8**, 107 (1924); *C. A.*, **19**, 547 (1925).

Hess, A. F., and Helman, F. O., *J. Biol. Chem.*, **64**, 781 (1925).

Hilditch, T. P., and Maddison, L., *Biochem. J.*, **35**, 24 (1941); *C. A.*, **35**, 6679 (1941).

——, and Murti, K. S., *Biochem. J.*, **34**, 1299 (1940); *C. A.*, **35**, 2589 (1941).

——, and Shorland, F. B., *Biochem. J.*, **31**, 1499 (1937); *C. A.*, **32**, 1775 (1938).

Hodge, H. C., *J. Biol. Chem.*, **101**, 55 (1933).

——, *Proc. Soc. Exptl. Biol. Med.*, **35**, 53 (1936); *C. A.*, **31**, 438 (1937).

——, and co-workers (MacLachlan, P. L., Bloor, W. R., Stoneburg, C. A., Oleson, M. C., and Whitehead, R.), *J. Biol. Chem.*, **139**, 897 (1941).

Holm, G. E., Wright, P. A., and Deysher, E. F., *J. Dairy Sci.*, **16**, 445 (1933); *C. A.*, **27**, 5831 (1933).

——, ——, ——, *ibid.*, **19**, 631 (1936); *C. A.*, **31**, 164 (1937).

Horiuchi, Y., *J. Biol. Chem.*, **44**, 345 (1920).

Horrall, B. E., *Indiana (Purdue) Agr. Expt. Sta. Bull.*, **401**, 31 pp. (1935); *C. A.*, **30**, 1132 (1936).

Hunter, F. E., *J. Biol. Chem.*, **144**, 439 (1942).

Iosifova, M. A., *Biochem. J. (Ukraine)*, **13**, 495 (1939); *C. A.*, **34**, 4160 (1940).

——, *ibid.*, **14**, 367 (1940); *C. A.*, **34**, 7448 (1940).

Irvin, J. L., and co-workers (Merker, H., Anderson, C. E., and Johnston, C. G.), *J. Biol. Chem.*, **131**, 439 (1939).

Izzo, R. A., and Marenzi, A. D., *Pubs. centro invest. tisiol. (Buenos Aires)*, **8**, 163 (1944); *C. A.*, **39**, 4382 (1945).

Jack, E. L., and Dahle, C. D., *J. Dairy Sci.*, **19**, 476 (1936).

——, ——, *ibid.*, **20**, 637 (1937); *C. A.*, **32**, 251 (1938).

Jacobson, O., *Ber.*, **6**, 1026 (1873).

Johnson, A. C., McNabb, A. R., and Rossiter, R. J., *Biochem. J.*, **43**, 578 (1948); *C. A.*, **43**, 3912 (1949).

——, ——, ——, *ibid.*, **44**, 494 (1949); *C. A.*, **43**, 9207 (1949).

Johnston, C. G., Irvin, J. L., and Walton, C., *J. Biol. Chem.*, **131**, 425 (1939).

Jona, B., *Boll. uffic. regia staz. sper. seta*, **5**, 56 (1935); *C. A.*, **30**, 1873 (1936).

Jones, K. K., and Sherberg, R. O., *Proc. Soc. Exptl. Biol. Med.*, **35**, 535 (1937); *C. A.*, **31**, 3114 (1937).

Jorpes, E., *Veröffentl. Chem. Abt. Karolinischen Inst. Stockholm*, 253 (1928); *C. A.*, **23**, 5228 (1929).

Kaucher, M., and co-workers (Galbraith, H., Button, V., and Williams, H. H.), *Arch. Biochem.*, **3**, 203 (1943); *C. A.*, **38**, 1779 (1944).

Kaufmann, C., and Raeth, K., *Arch. Gynäkol.*, **130**, 128 (1927); *C. A.*, **21**, 3390 (1927).

Kirk, E., *J. Biol. Chem.*, **123**, 623, 637 (1938).

——, Page, I. H., and Van Slyke, D. D., *J. Biol. Chem.*, **106**, 203 (1934).

Klenk, E., *Z. physiol. Chem.*, **185**, 169 (1929); *C. A.*, **24**, 859 (1930).

——, *ibid.*, **192**, 217 (1930); *C. A.*, **25**, 120 (1931).

——, *ibid.*, **200**, 51 (1931); *C. A.*, **25**, 5439 (1931).

——, *ibid.*, **206**, 25 (1932); *C. A.*, **26**, 3523 (1932).

——, *ibid.*, **217**, 228 (1933); *C. A.*, **27**, 4311 (1933).

——, *ibid.*, **221**, 259, 264 (1933a); *C. A.*, **28**, 532 (1934).

Klenk, E., *Z. physiol. Chem.,* **232,** 47 (1935) ; *C. A.,* **29,** 2980 (1935).

——, and Ditt, F., *Z. physiol. Chem.,* **226,** 213 (1934) ; *C. A.,* **28,** 6729 (1934).

——, and Dittmer, J., *Z. physiol. Chem.,* **244,** 203 (1936) ; *C. A.,* **31,** 1051 (1937).

——, and von Schoenbeck, O., *Z. physiol. Chem.,* **194,** 191 (1931) ; *C. A.,* **25,** 1541 (1931).

——, ——, *ibid.,* **209,** 112 (1932) ; *C. A.,* **26,** 4614 (1932).

Knauer, *Monatsschr. Kinderheilk.,* **51,** 378 (1932) ; *C. A.,* **26,** 2784 (1932).

Knouff, R. A., Brown, J. B., and Schneider, B. M., *Anat. Rec.,* **79,** 17 (1941).

Koch, W., and Woods, H. S., *J. Biol. Chem.,* **1,** 203 (1905/06).

Koppenhoefer, R. M., *J. Biol. Chem.,* **116,** 321 (1936).

Krause, A. C., *Am. J. Physiol.,* **110,** 182 (1934) ; *C. A.,* **29,** 5173 (1935).

——, *Acta Ophthalmol.,* **12,** 372 (1935) ; *C. A.,* **30,** 7188 (1936).

Krause, R. F., *J. Biol. Chem.,* **149,** 395 (1943).

Kurtz, F. E., Jamieson, G. S., and Holm, G. E., *J. Biol. Chem.,* **106,** 717 (1934).

Lang, A., *Z. physiol. Chem.,* **246,** 219 (1937) ; *C. A.,* **31,** 4709 (1937).

Laxa, O., *Milchw. Zentr.,* **42,** 663, 691 (1913) ; *C. A.,* **8,** 1314 (1914).

LeBreton, E., *Bull. soc. chim. biol.,* **3,** 539 (1921) ; *C. A.,* **16,** 722 (1922).

Leinfelder, P. J., and Salit, P. W., *Am. J. Ophthalmol.,* **17,** 619 (1934) ; *C. A.,* **29,** 6287 (1935).

Leites, S., *Zhur. Eksp. Biol. Med.,* **9,** 181 (1928) ; *C. A.,* **23,** 883 (1929).

Leone, E., and Manzi, G., *Boll. soc. ital. biol. sper.,* **24,** 689 (1948) ; *C. A.,* **43,** 4314 (1949).

Lesuk, A., and Anderson, R. J., *J. Biol. Chem.,* **139,** 457 (1941).

Leulier, A., and Revol, L., *Compt. rend. soc. biol.,* **106,** 667 (1931) ; *C. A.,* **26,** 3556 (1932).

Levene, P. A., *J. Biol. Chem.,* **24,** 69 (1916).

——, and Ingvaldsen, T., *J. Biol. Chem.,* **43,** 359 (1920).

——, and Rolf, I. P., *J. Biol. Chem.,* **46,** 193, 353 (1921).

——, ——, *ibid.,* **51,** 507 (1922).

——, ——, *ibid.,* **54,** 91, 99 (1922a).

——, ——, *ibid.,* **72,** 587 (1927).

——, and Simms, H. S., *J. Biol. Chem.,* **48,** 185 (1921).

——, ——, *ibid.,* **51,** 285 (1922).

Lobstein, J. E., and Flatter, M., *Lait,* **15,** 946 (1935) ; *C. A.,* **30,** 1880 (1936).

Long, J. H., and Gephart, F., *J. Am. Chem. Soc.,* **30,** 1312 (1908) ; *C. A.,* **2,** 2702 (1908).

Lorenz, F. W., Chaikoff, I. L., and Entenman, C., *J. Biol. Chem.,* **123,** 577 (1938).

Lührig, H., *Z. Untersuch. Lebensm.,* **7,** 141 (1904) ; *Chem. Zentr.,* I, 838 (1904).

Lustig, B., and Mandler, E., *Biochem. Z.,* **261,** 132 (1933) ; *C. A.,* **27,** 4291 (1933).

MacArthur, C. G., *J. Am. Chem. Soc.,* **36,** 2397 (1914) ; *C. A.,* **8,** 3801 (1914).

——, and Burton, L. V., *J. Am. Chem. Soc.,* **38,** 1375 (1916) ; *C. A.,* **10,** 2222 (1916).

McCollum, E. V., Halpin, J. J., and Drescher, A. H., *J. Biol. Chem.,* **13,** 219 (1912).

McConnell, K. P., and Sinclair, R. G., *J. Biol. Chem.,* **118,** 131 (1937).

Macheboeuf, M. A., *Bull. soc. chim. biol.,* **11,** 268 (1929).

——, *Compt. rend.,* **188,** 109 (1929a) ; *C. A.,* **23,** 2743 (1929).

——, *Rev. gén. colloïdes,* **7,** 393 (1929b) ; *C. A.,* **24,** 2152 (1930).

——, *Bull. soc. chim.,* **45,** 662 (1929c) ; *C. A.,* **24,** 417 (1930).

——, and Sandor, G., *Bull. soc. chim. biol.,* **14,** 1168 (1932) ; *C. A.,* **27,** 327 (1933).

MacLachlan, P. L., and co-workers (Hodge, H. C., Bloor, W. R., Welch, E. A., Truax, F. L., and Taylor, J. D.), *J. Biol. Chem.,* **143,** 473 (1942).

MacLachlan, P. L., Hodge, H. C., and Whitehead, R., *J. Biol. Chem.*, **139**, 185 (1941).

MacLean, H., *Biochem. J.*, **9**, 351 (1915) ; *C. A.*, **10**, 345 (1916).

Macy, I. G., "Nutrition and Chemical Growth in Childhood," Springfield, Ill., Charles C. Thomas, 1942.

Manasse, A., *Biochem. Z.*, **1**, 246 (1906).

Marenzi, A. D., and Cardini, C. E., *J. Biol. Chem.*, **147**, 371 (1943).

Masuda, Y., and Hori, T., *J. Agr. Chem. Soc. Japan*, **13**, 200 (1937) ; *C. A.*, **31**, 7548 (1937).

Materna, A., and Januschke, E., *Virchow's Arch. path. Anat.*, **263**, 537 (1927).

Matthews, V. J., Newton, J. K., and Bloor, W. R., *J. Biol. Chem.*, **108**, 145 (1935).

May, R. M., *Bull. soc. chim. biol.*, **12**, 934 (1930).

Mayer, A., and Schaeffer, G., *J. physiol. path. gén.*, **15**, 984 (1913) ; *C. A.*, **9**, 647 (1915).

Merz, W., *Z. physiol. Chem.*, **196**, 10 (1931) ; *C. A.*, **25**, 3040 (1931).

Millican, R. C., and Brown, J. B., *J. Biol. Chem.*, **154**, 437 (1944).

Mitolo, M., *Arch. ital. biol.*, **89**, 172 (1933) ; *C. A.*, **28**, 1397 (1934).

——, *Boll. soc. ital. biol. sper.*, **8**, 69 (1933a) ; *C. A.*, **27**, 3963 (1933) ; *Arch. fisiol.* **32**, 451 (1933a) ; *C. A.*, **28**, 1733 (1934).

Mohr, W., Brockman, C., and Muller, W., *Molkerei-Ztg.*, **46**, 633 (1932) ; *C. A.*, **27**, 3991 (1933).

Mojonnier, T., and Troy, H. C., "The Technical Control of Dairy Products," Chicago, Mojonnier Bros. Co., 1932, Chap. 7, p. 93.

Morgulis, S., and co-workers (Wilder, M. W., Spencer, H. C., and Eppstein, S. H.), *J. Biol. Chem.*, **124**, 755 (1938).

Müller, E. F. W., *Z. physiol. Chem.*, **242**, 201 (1936) ; *C. A.*, **30**, 8331 (1936).

Müller, E., *Z. Biol.*, **100**, 249 (1940) ; *C. A.*, **36**, 5530 (1942).

Nerking, J., *Biochem. Z.*, **10**, 193 (1908) ; *C. A.*, **3**, 918 (1909).

——, and Haensel, E., *Biochem. Z.*, **13**, 348 (1908) ; *C. A.*, **3**, 1304 (1909).

Niemierko, W., *Acta Biol. Exptl. (Warsaw)*, **14**, 151 (1947) ; *C. A.*, **42**, 8980 (1948).

Nishimoto, U., *Proc. Imp. Acad. (Tokyo)*, **10**, 578 (1934) ; *C. A.*, **29**, 1830 (1935).

——, *J. Agr. Chem. Soc. Japan*, **11**, 157 (1935) ; *C. A.*, **29**, 5466 (1935).

——, and Suzuki, B., *Proc. Imp. Acad. (Tokyo)*, **8**, 424, 428 (1932) ; *C. A.*, **27**, 989 (1933).

North, G. C., and Sommer, H. H., *J. Dairy Sci.*, **18**, 21 (1935) ; *C. A.*, **29**, 2250 (1935).

Nottbohm, F. E., and Mayer, F., *Z. Untersuch Lebensm.*, **66**, 585 (1933) ; *C. A.*, **28**, 2803 (1934).

Okey, R., Gillum, H. L., and Yokela, E., *J. Biol. Chem.*, **107**, 207 (1934).

Oleson, M. C., and Bloor, W. R., *J. Biol. Chem.*, **141**, 349 (1941).

Osborne, T. B., and Wakeman, A. J., *J. Biol. Chem.*, **28**, 1 (1916).

Otoslki, S. W., *Biochem. Z.*, **4**, 124 (1907) ; *C. A.*, **1**, 2263 (1907).

Pachur, R., *Dermat. Z.*, **60**, 486 (1931).

Page, I. H., and Rudy, H., *Z. physiol. Chem.*, **205**, 115 (1932) ; *C. A.*, **26**, 3395 (1932).

——, Pasternack, L., and Burt, M. L., *Biochem. Z.*, **223**, 445 (1930) ; *C. A.*, **24**, 5363 (1930).

Palladin, A. V., Rashba, E. I., and Helman, R. M., *Ukraïn. Biokhem. Zhur.*, **8**, No. 1, 5, 27 (1935) ; *C. A.*, **30**, 5277 (1936).

Palmer, L. S., and Samuelson, E., *Proc. Soc. Exptl. Biol. Med.*, **21**, 537 (1924).

Pasternack, L., and Page, I. H., *Biochem. Z.*, **252**, 254 (1932) ; *C. A.*, **26**, 5663 (1932).

——, ——, *ibid.*, **274**, 122 (1934) ; *C. A.*, **29**, 1509 (1935).

Patterson, J. M., and McHenry, E. W., *J. Biol. Chem.*, **156**, 265 (1944).

Perlman, J. L., *J. Dairy Sci.*, **18**, 113 (1935); *C. A.*, **29**, 3054 (1935).

Peters, J. P., and Van Slyke, D. D., "Quantitative Clinical Chemistry," Vol. **I**, Baltimore, Williams & Wilkins Co., 1946.

Petersen, W. E., and Herreid, E. O., *Minn. Agr. Exp. Sta. Tech. Bull.*, **63**, 2 (1929); *C. A.*, **24**, 3838 (1930).

Popják, G., *J. Path. Bact.*, **57**, 87 (1945); *C. A.*, **39**, 2804 (1945).

Pratt, J. P., and co-workers (Kaucher, M., Richards, A. J., Williams, H. H., and Macy, I. G.), *Am. J. Obstet. Gynecol.*, **52**, 665 (1946); *C. A.*, **41**, 3191 (1947).

Pregl, F., "Quantitative Organic Microanalysis," Trans. by E. Fylemann, Philadelphia, P. Blakestons' Sons and Co., Inc., 1924.

Ramsay, W. N. M., and Stewart, C. P., *Biochem. J.*, **35**, 39 (1941); *C. A.*, **35**, 6645 (1941).

Randall, L. O., *J. Biol. Chem.*, **124**, 481 (1938).

——, *ibid.*, **125**, 723 (1938a).

Ranney, R. E., Entenman, C., and Chaikoff, L., *J. Biol. Chem.*, **180**, 307 (1949).

Reiser, R., *J. Biol. Chem.*, **143**, 109 (1942).

Rewald, B., *Biochem. Z.*, **198**, 103 (1928); *C. A.*, **22**, 4591 (1928).

——, *ibid.*, **202**, 391 (1928a); *C. A.*, **23**, 3239 (1929).

——, *ibid.*, **206**, 275 (1929); *C. A.*, **23**, 3275 (1929).

——, *ibid.*, **211**, 199 (1929a); *C. A.*, **23**, 5205 (1929).

——, *Allgem. Oel- u. Fett-Ztg.*, **27**, 363 (1930); *C. A.*, **25**, 2741 (1931).

——, *Lait*, **17**, 225 (1937); *C. A.*, **31**, 6354 (1937).

——, and Schweiger, A., *Biochem. Z.*, **259**, 180 (1933); *C. A.*, **27**, 2722 (1933).

Richards, Jr., A. G., *J. N.Y. Entomol. Soc.*, **51**, 55 (1943); *C. A.*, **37**, 3838 (1943).

Riemenschneider, R. W., Ellis, N. R., and Titus, H. W., *J. Biol. Chem.*, **126**, 255 (1938).

Roche, A., and Marquet, F., *Compt. rend. soc. biol.*, **119**, 1147 (1935); *C. A.*, **29**, 7427 (1935).

Rogers', L. A. associates, "Fundamentals of Dairy Science," New York, Reinhold Publishing Corp., 1935.

Root, H. F., and Bloor, W. R., *Am. Rev. Tuberc.*, **39**, 714 (1939); *C. A.*, **33**, 9417 (1939).

Rubin, S. H., Present, C. H., and Ralli, E. P., *J. Biol. Chem.*, **121**, 19 (1937).

Rudy, H., and Page, I. H., *Naturwissenschaften*, **19**, 774 (1931); *C. A.*, **26**, 325 (1932).

Rund, B., *Sborník Masarykovy Akad. Práce*, **11**, 86 (1937); *C. A.*, **33**, 5526 (1939).

Sakaki, C., *Biochem. Z.*, **54**, 1 (1914); *C. A.*, **8**, 142 (1914).

Salisbury, L. F., and Anderson, R. J., *J. Biol. Chem.*, **129**, 505 (1939).

Salit, P. W., *Arch. Ophthalmol. (Chicago)*, **18**, 403 (1937); *C. A.*, **32**, 2585 (1938).

Sammartino, U., *Biochem. Z.*, **124**, 234 (1921); *C. A.*, **16**, 723 (1922).

Schaible, P. J., *J. Biol. Chem.*, **95**, 79 (1932).

Schmidt, L. H., *J. Biol. Chem.*, **109**, 449 (1935).

Schmidt-Muhlheim, A., *Arch. ges. Physiol.* (Pflügers), **30**, 379 (1883); *Chem. Zentr.*, 558 (1883).

Schmitz, E., and Koch, F., *Biochem. Z.*, **223**, 257 (1930); *C. A.*, **24**, 5062 (1930).

Schremp, A., *Z. Volksernähr. u. Diätkost*, **7**, 6 (1932); *Chem. Zentr.*, **I**, 1963 (1932).

Schuwirth, K., *Z. physiol. Chem.*, **263**, 25 (1940); *C. A.*, **34**, 3336 (1940).

——, *ibid.*, **270**, I–III (1941); *C. A.*, **37**, 922 (1943).

——, *ibid.*, **277**, 87, 147 (1943); *C. A.*, **37**, 5471, 5285 (1943).

Sell, H. M., Olsen, A. G., and Kremers, R. E., *Ind. Eng. Chem.*, **27**, 1222 (1935); *C. A.*, **29**, 7515 (1935).

Shinowara, G. Y., and Brown, J. B., *Oil & Soap,* **15,** 151 (1938); *C. A.,* **32,** 5860 (1938).

Shorland, F. B., and Hilditch, T. P., *Biochem. J.,* **32,** 792 (1938); *C. A.,* **32,** 7294 (1938).

Sinclair, R. G., *J. Biol. Chem.,* **82,** 117 (1929)

——, *ibid.,* **86,** 579 (1930).

——, *ibid.,* **88,** 575 (1930a).

——, *ibid.,* **111,** 261 (1935).

——, *ibid.,* **115,** 211 (1936).

——, *ibid.,* **134,** 89 (1940).

——, *ibid.,* **174,** 343, 355 (1948).

——, and Dolan, M., *J. Biol. Chem.,* **142,** 659 (1942).

Smith, J. L., *J. Path. Bact.,* **17,** 418 (1912/13).

Smith, N. C., *J. Assoc. Offic. Agr. Chem.,* **13,** 272 (1930); *C. A.,* **24,** 4099 (1930).

Snider, R. H., *J. Biol. Chem.,* **116,** 503 (1936).

——, and Bloor, W. R., *J. Biol. Chem.,* **99,** 555 (1933).

Sommer, H. H., and Smit, B. J., *Wisconsin Agr. Expt. Sta., Research Bull.,* **57** (1923); *C. A.,* **18,** 718 (1924).

Sorg, K., *Z. Konstitutionslehre,* **10,** 67 (1924); *C. A.,* **18,** 3652 (1924).

——, *Z. physiol. Chem.,* **182,** 97 (1929); *C. A.,* **23,** 3961 (1929).

Sperry, W. M., Brand, F. C., and Copenhaver, W. M., *J. Biol. Chem.,* **144,** 297 (1942).

Stewart, C. P., and Hendry, E. B., *Biochem. J.,* **29,** 1683 (1935); *C. A.,* **29,** 7360 (1935).

Stoklasa, J., *Z., physiol. Chem.,* **23,** 343 (1897).

Strecker, A., *Ann.,* **123,** 353 (1862).

Sueyoshi, Y., *J. Biochem. (Japan),* **13,** 145 (1931); *C. A.,* **25,** 4295 (1931).

——, and Furukubo, T., *J. Biochem. (Japan),* **13,** 155, 177 (1931); *C. A.,* **25,** 4018 (1931).

Supplee, G. C., *Cornell Univ. Agr. Expt. Sta. Mem.,* **29,** 101 (1919); *C. A.,* **14,** 1166 (1920).

Susaki, R., and Hiratsuka, E., *Proc. Imp. Acad. (Tokyo),* **7,** 99 (1931); *C. A.,* **25,** 3406 (1931).

Swanson, A. M., and Sommer, H. H., *J. Diary Sci.,* **23,** 201 (1940); *C. A.,* **34,** 3383 (1940).

Taurog, A., and co-workers (Entenman, C., Fries, B. A., and Chaikoff, I. L.), *J. Biol. Chem.,* **155,** 19 (1944).

——, Entenman, C., and Chaikoff, I. L., *J. Biol. Chem.,* **156,** 385 (1944).

Tayeau, F., *Lait,* **20,** 129 (1940); *C. A.,* **34,** 4169 (1940).

Taylor, J. D., Paul, H. E., and Paul, M. F., *Arch. Biochem.,* **17,** 421 (1948); *C. A.,* **42,** 8312 (1948).

Terroine, E. F., Hatterer, C., and Roehrig, P., *Bull. soc. chim. biol.,* **12,** 657, 682 (1930); *C. A.,* **24,** 4946, 5357 (1930).

Teunissen, P. H., and den Ouden, A., *Nederland. Tijdschr. Geneesk.,* **82,** II, 2406 (1938); *C. A.,* **32,** 5483 (1938).

Thannhauser, S. J., and Benotti, J., *Z. physiol. Chem.,* **253,** 217 (1938); *C. A.,* **32,** 706 (1938).

——, and Boncoddo, N. F., *J. Biol. Chem.,* **172,** 135 (1948).

——, and co-workers (Benotti, J., Walcott, A., and Reinstein, H.), *J. Biol. Chem.,* **129,** 717 (1939).

——, and Fränkel, E., *Z. physiol. Chem.,* **203,** 183 (1931); *C. A.,* **26,** 1325 (1932).

——, and Setz, P., *J. Biol. Chem.,* **116,** 527, 533 (1936).

Thannhauser, S. J., Benotti, J., and Boncoddo, N. F., *J. Biol. Chem.*, **166**, 669 (1946).
——, ——, ——, *ibid.*, **166**, 677 (1946a).
——, ——, and Reinstein, H., *J. Biol. Chem.*, **129**, 709 (1939).
——, Setz, P., and Benotti, J., *J. Biol. Chem.*, **126**, 785 (1938).
Theis, E. R., *J. Biol. Chem.*, **76**, 107 (1928).
Thudichum, J. L. W., "Die Chemische Konstitution des Gehirns des Menschen und der Tiere," Tübingen, Franz Pietzcker, 1901.
Thurston, L. M., and Petersen, W. E., *J. Dairy Sci.*, **11**, 270 (1928); *C. A.*, **22**, 3238 (1928).
——, Brown, W. C., and Dustman, R. B., *J. Dairy Sci.*, **18**, 301 (1935); *C. A.*, **29**, 4843 (1935).
Trifanowsky, D., *Arch. ges. Physiol. (Pflügers)* **9**, 492 (1874).
Tropp, C., *Verk. physik-med. ges. Würzburg (N. F.)*, **59**, 74 (1936); *C. A.*, **32**, 9223 (1938).
Tsujimoto, M., and Koyanagi, H., *J. Soc. Chem. Ind. Japan*, **37**, Suppl. binding 81, 85 (1934); *C. A.*, **28**, 3257 (1934).
Turner, K., *Biochem. J.*, **25**, 49 (1931); *C. A.*, **25**, 4032 (1931).
Turner, M. E., and Gibson, R. B., *J. Clin. Invest.*, **11**, 735 (1932); *C. A.*, **27**, 124 (1933).
Uhnoo, B., *Z. physiol. Chem.*, **256**, 104 (1938); *C. A.*, **33**, 1378 (1939).
Urban, F. F., *Biochem. Z.*, **293**, 274 (1937); *C. A.*, **32**, 636 (1938).
Van Meurs, G. J., *Rec. trav. chim.*, **42**, 800 (1923); *Chem. Zentr.*, I, 1286 (1924).
Van Slyke, D. D., and co-workers (Page, I. H., Kirk, E., and Farr, L. E.), *Proc. Soc. Exptl. Biol. Med.*, **32**, 837 (1934/35).
Vauquelin, *Ann. chim.*, **81**, 37 (1812).
von Zeynek, R., *Wien. klin. Woch.*, **12**, 568 (1899).
Watanabe, H., *J. Biochem. (Japan)*, **2**, 369 (1923); *C. A.*, **17**, 2738 (1923).
Weinhouse, S., and Brewer, J. I., *J. Biol. Chem.*, **143**, 617 (1942).
White, M. F., and Brown, J. B., *J. Am. Chem. Soc.*, **70**, 4269 (1948); *C. A.*, **43**, 2260 (1949).
Whitehead, R., *Brit. J. Exptl. Path.*, **12**, 305 (1931); *C. A.*, **26**, 762 (1932).
Wiese, H. F., Nair, J. H., and Fleming, R. S., *Ind. Eng. Chem., Anal. Ed.*, **4**, 362 (1932); *C. A.*, **26**, 6029 (1932).
Wilber, C. G., and Bayors, W. M., *Biol. Bull.*, **93**, 99 (1947); *C. A.*, **42**, 2026 (1948).
Williams, H. H., and co-workers (Erickson, B. N., Avrin, I., Bernstein, S. S., and Macy, I. G.), *J. Biol. Chem.*, **123**, 111 (1938).
——, and co-workers (Erickson, B. N., Beach, E. F., and Macy, I. G.), *J. Lab. Clin. Med.*, **26**, 996 (1941); *C. A.*, **35**, 3317 (1941).
Wilson, W. R., and Hansen, A. E., *J. Biol. Chem.*, **112**, 457 (1936).
Woolley, D. W., *J. Biol. Chem.*, **147**, 581 (1943).
Worm, M., *Z. physiol. Chem.*, **257**, 140 (1939); *C. A.*, **33**, 2961 (1939).
Wright, P. A., and Holm, G. E., *J. Dairy Sci.*, **16**, 455 (1933); *C. A.*, **27**, 5831 (1933).
Yasuda, M., *J. Biol. Chem.*, **94**, 401 (1931/32).
——, *J. Biochem. (Japan)*, **26**, 203 (1937); *C. A.*, **32**, 1772 (1938).
Yokoyama, Y., *Proc. Imp. Acad. (Tokyo)*, **10**, 582 (1934); *C. A.*, **29**, 1830 (1935).
——, and Suzuki, B., *Proc. Imp. Acad. (Tokyo)*, **8**, 183 (1932); *C. A.*, **26**, 4834 (1932).
——, ——, *ibid.*, **8**, 358, 361 (1932a); *C. A.*, **27**, 1374 (1933).
Yosida, T., *Bull. Imp. Sericult. Expt. Sta. Japan*, **10**, 145 (1941); *C. A.*, **38**, 1800 (1944).
Youngburg, G. E., *Proc. Soc. Exptl. Biol. Med.*, **36**, 230 (1937); *C. A.*, **31**, 8635 (1937).

PART V

THE BIOCHEMISTRY AND PHYSIOLOGY OF THE PHOSPHATIDES

CHAPTER XX

INTRODUCTION TO BIOCHEMISTRY OF THE PHOSPHATIDES

Biochemically and physiologically, the phosphatides appear to be involved in a multiplicity of functions of the greatest importance, about which knowledge is scanty. This section presents the available knowledge, meager though certain aspects of it may be, of the role of the phosphatides in organic functions. The difficulties which beset this work are legion. For example, practically nothing is known of the roles of the individual phosphatides in metabolic activity, because until recently analytical techniques have not been sufficiently refined to permit such investigations. Similarly, pure phosphatides have not been available and comparison of published results is often difficult because the choices of animals and of techniques of investigation have varied. All this, coupled with the usual difficulties which accompany feeding experiments and the tracing of the course of a compound or an element within the body, has made the accumulation of knowledge of lipide metabolism a slow process.

PROPOSED FUNCTIONS OF THE PHOSPHATIDES

It has long been thought that phosphatides are structural components of the cell. This view was reinforced by the observation of the French workers (see p. 341) that in many organs relatively constant amounts of phosphatides are maintained despite serious nutritional deficiencies. The concept of a structural function of the phosphatides is acceptable only when it is understood that a phosphatide molecule—or one of its constituent parts—which has a structural function at one moment may have a metabolic function the next. Thus an over-all constancy of amount should not be interpreted as an indication that the phosphatide molecules are static entities. This phase of phosphatide activity will be discussed first in this chapter.

The obvious chemical relationship of the glycerophosphatides to the triglycerides, and the ability of the former to yield colloidal solutions, led Loew to postulate in 1891 that the phosphatides possess certain metabolic functions. Metabolism embraces absorption of substances in the body and their subsequent mobilization and use; it also involves the contributions of the various organs to these processes and in turn the contributions of the compounds to the functioning of the organs. There is little doubt that phosphatides are intermediary metabolites, although the complete course they follow cannot yet be defined.

Metabolically the phosphatides are concerned with a variety of biochemical and physiological processes, many of which are at the moment seemingly without correlation. The enzymes associated with the degradation of the phosphatides have already been discussed. The role of enzymes in phosphatide catabolism and anabolism remains to be elucidated, for the precise relationships that have been discovered for carbohydrate metabolism are lacking in the field of lipides.

The phosphatides, however, participate in all phases of lipide metabolism, although some of the classical functions attributed to the phosphatides are now questionable. Thus, it was until recently a popular belief that lipides may be carried through the epithelial cells in a phosphorylated form and that these participate in the resynthesis of triglycerides. Actually, Pihl and Bloch (1950) have shown that this is not so, since acetate labeled with C_{14} was incorporated into the triglyceride fatty acids of rat liver at a faster rate than into phosphatide fatty acids. Similarly the phosphatides were earlier believed to possess vehicular function, providing a means for transporting the lipides to their ultimate destination. This too appears now to have been postulated on insufficient evidence (see p. 384). The phosphatides are, however, active metabolic components of many organs and tissues, particularly the gastrointestinal tract, the liver and the blood. There is, for example, little doubt that the liver converts to phosphatides the neutral fat brought to it either by mobilization from the depots or as a result of fat absorption from the intestine. Thus the greater part of this chapter is devoted to the relationships existing in these and other tissues. Phosphatide metabolism is upset during the course of a variety of pathological conditions, which are also discussed.

Of great interest is the possible role which phosphatides play in the blood-clotting mechanism, although again definitive proof of their actual participation remains to be provided.

The participation of the phosphatides in the oxidation systems of the organism is a distinct, although obscure, possibility. The early workers (Leathes, 1909) postulated—on the basis that phosphatide fatty acids are often more unsaturated than glyceride fatty acids—that the phosphatides take on acids which have been desaturated as a primary step in their ultimate combustion. More logically the unsaturation provides a means for alternately absorbing and releasing oxygen for normal cellular functions.

Other possible metabolic functions of the phosphatides have been postulated. Thus, because they are colloidal in character, it has been suggested (Loeb and Beuttner, 1914) that the permeability of the cell to certain materials is a function of the phosphatide content of the cell. The phosphatides may provide a source of phosphorus for bone formation (Kugler, 1936) and a source of phosphate buffer for regulation of the pH of the blood by the kidney (Weissberger, 1940).

The component entities which combine to form phosphatides—although the method and location of the combining process in the body are not known—also possess metabolic character. Thus the effect of choline on the preservation of the normal metabolic functions of the liver is now well established, and these relationships, too, will be examined at some length.

Certainly these functions which have been mentioned are not mutually exclusive, nor are they necessarily the only ones in which the phosphatides may participate. It may well be that the individual phosphatides show a preference for some given function, although, for the most part, experimental proof must yet be found for such a statement. Recent workers have contributed much to this complex subject, and it is hoped that such research will continue.

THE PHOSPHATIDES AS STRUCTURAL ELEMENTS

The concept has long been held that body lipides are divided into "depot" or "storage" fat and "tissue" fat. The latter, largely by implication, is considered structural whereas the former is believed to provide a source of reserve fuel for body needs. Mayer and Schaeffer (1914) investigated the nature of the lipides in fattened animals and in animals permitted to die of inanition. Their work was expanded by Terroine (1920) and his school (e.g., Terroine and Belin, 1927; Terroine, Hatterer and Roehrig, 1930, 1930a). From these studies it appeared that the concentrations and iodine numbers of the lipides from comparable organs and tissues of starved animals were quite similar, but differed markedly from the lipides of similar parts of fattened animals. Mayer and Schaeffer (1913) had already found that the lipide phosphorus content of most organs did not change markedly either in inanition or overfeeding; and Terroine and Weill (1913) had confirmed the observation of Mayer and Schaeffer (1913) that there is considerable constancy in the cholesterol content of various tissues. The interpretation followed that there is, within limits, an irreducible minimum of lipides which are such an integral part of the protoplasm that they cannot be released even in starvation. To these substances was given the name *élément constant* as opposed to the more labile *élément variable* or depot fat.

The *élément constant* was related to cholesterol by analysis and to the glycerophosphatides (Mayer and Schaeffer, 1914; Terroine and Belin, 1927) not by actual chemical isolation but by virtue of a proper ratio of fatty acids to lipide phosphorus content. On this basis, then, the structural role of the phosphatides was postulated. The liver and other organs intimately concerned with metabolic functions were soon shown to be exceptional in containing both phosphatides and glycerides whose quantities fluctuated markedly with the condition of the organism.

The historical development of the structural role of the phosphatides has been well outlined by Bloor (1943, p. 244).

Later work has provided cause for doubting the existence of an *élément constant* from both a quantitative and a qualitative point of view. Thus Bloor (1927, 1936) and Bloor and Snider (1934) found that the phosphatide and cholesterol content of muscle varied quantitatively with the type of muscle and with the extent to which the muscle was used, for which reason the phosphatide content of a given type of muscle could vary not only within a species but within an animal. Analogously, the phosphatide content of the corpus luteum and the mammary gland (Bloor, Okey and Corner, 1930) was found to increase as the activity of the organ increased. The cholesterol content is apparently more constant in these organs. In malignant tumors, however, both the phosphatide and cholesterol contents are considerably higher than in benign tumors (Yasuda and Bloor, 1932; Bierich and Lang, 1933). Boyd (1934, 1934a, 1935) noted similar differences and is of the opinion that variation in phosphatide content is an index of the physiological activity of a tissue or of an entire organism. Thus he found that the phosphatide content of the white corpuscles increases as much as 200 per cent after an operation, if recovery is imminent. If post-operative complications follow, a decrease is noted. Immediately after parturition in the rabbit the phosphatide content of the white corpuscles increases, returning to normal after three weeks. Similarly, the phosphatide content of the rabbit ovary starts to increase with pregnancy, reaching a value 300 per cent greater than normal after fourteen to sixteen days. After birth the value returns to normal.

Qualitatively, even greater differences have been demonstrated. Sinclair (1932) has shown that fatty acid composition of phosphatides may be influenced by diet. Thus, when cod-liver oil was fed to rats which previously had been on a fat-poor diet, the turnover in liver phosphatide, as measured by iodine value, was 100 per cent complete in three days. In carcass phosphatide it was 50 per cent complete in a similar length of time. Measurement of iodine number does not, of course, indicate the fate of the saturated acids. Very slow replacement was observed in the muscles. Furthermore, the tissue phosphatides demonstrated a marked tendency both to attain and maintain as high a degree of unsaturation as the diet allowed. Thus the iodine number of the liver phosphatide fatty acids of a group of rats was raised to 160 by a diet of cod-liver oil. Upon interruption of the diet, Sinclair (1935a) observed that this value persisted for 39 days. The reverse situation did not obtain, for the feeding of olive oil of iodine number 86 or of coconut oil which was practically saturated did not lower the iodine number readily (Sinclair, 1932).

These experiments will be discussed in greater detail in their relation to metabolic functions. At this point it should be indicated that they served the very important purpose of proving that the assignment of an exclusively static condition to the phosphatides was untenable—a concept which was greatly strengthened by the work of Stetten and Schoenheimer (1940). Thus the phosphatides must be regarded as dynamic components of tissue which maintain a fairly constant pattern through delicately balanced cycles of closely related reactions. This constant pattern, nevertheless, can change its course as the functional aspects of the tissue or organ change.

The Phosphatides as Components of Particulate Portions of Cells

The problem of cellular organization and the isolation of particulate portions of cells is an intriguing one which has not yet attracted many workers. Bensley and Hoerr (1934) demonstrated initially that mitochondria could be prepared from cytoplasmic extract of guinea pig liver by centrifugal techniques. Subsequently Claude (1941, 1946) has used similar methods to fractionate cytoplasmic particulates from various tissues. These procedures have made possible the accumulation of sufficient quantities of particulates for chemical analysis. The work, however, has not proceeded beyond the analytical stage, for which reason virtually no conclusions can be reached about the relationship of the location of the phosphatides within a cell to their function, to enzymatic syntheses and to other metabolic activities. It is hoped that more work will be done in this field in the next decade.

Of the available particulates, the mitochondria have been investigated most carefully. These have been shown to consist largely of lipoprotein by Bensley (1937) and others. Bensley found 4.2 per cent phosphatides in the lipide fraction, although he himself questioned his analytical techniques. Chargaff (1942a), however, found only 4 per cent phosphatides in the mitochondria of rabbit liver on a dry basis, but he obtained in addition a large fraction which was high in both cerebroside and phosphorus content. These facts, he believes, can be reconciled by assuming the presence of about 4.3 per cent lysophosphatides. This receives further substantiation from the observation of Bensley and Hoerr (1934) that a similar fraction obtained by them possessed hemolytic activity.

Schneider (1948) has shown that the enzymes responsible for the oxidation of fatty acids are resident in the mitochondria of the liver.

The incorporation of P^{32} into the phosphatides, pentose nucleic acid and an unidentified acid-insoluble "phosphoprotein" residue of particulate material of rat liver has been demonstrated by Friedkin and Lehninger (1949). The material consisted largely of nuclei and mitochondria and the incorporation was effected during the oxidation of l-malate by way of the Krebs tricarboxylic acid cycle in the presence of labeled inorganic phosphate, adenine nucleotide and magnesium ions. Oxidation and the phosphorylation of the adenylic acid system were prerequisite for the incorporation.

Three particulate fractions of mouse liver cell cytoplasm were investigated by Barnum and Huseby (1948), who isolated these fractions essentially in the manner proposed by Claude (1946). The microsome fraction contained about 35 per cent lipides of which 63 per cent was phosphatides. The large granule fraction was also rich in lipides (27 per cent) and over half of these was phosphatides. The fraction which was sedimented last was relatively poor in lipides. Subsequent work (Huseby and Barnum, 1950) showed that most of the cytoplasmic phosphatide is associated with the particulate fraction of the liver, whereas the neutral fat is present in the nonparticulate portion of the cytoplasm. The phosphatides in the microsome fraction and the fraction sedimented last appear to be present as lipoproteins which combine in complex formation with the nucleoproteins to provide the structural basis for these fractions.

The composition of mouse liver cell nuclei was investigated by Barnum and co-workers (1950), who found 3.4 per cent phosphatides in the isolated cells. More extensive work of this nature had previously been carried out by Williams and co-workers (1945a), who found 12 to 14 per cent "essential" lipide in liver cell nuclei, 90 per cent of which was phosphatides. Of the phosphatide fraction, 70 per cent was lecithin and 5 per cent was sphingomyelin. Nuclei isolated from tumorous liver cells contained much less phosphatide and an increased quantity of cholesterol ester. Barnum and co-workers (1950) feel that the lower phosphatide content observed by them may be due to the prolonged washing to which they subjected their samples since this could remove cytoplasmic contamination.

Chantrenne (1947) has also analyzed particulate portions of liver, using in his work five fractions of cytoplasmic granules obtained by fractional centrifugation.

CHAPTER XXI

GENERAL ASPECTS OF LIPIDE METABOLISM

INTRODUCTION

This review will not purport to discuss in great detail all the facets of lipide metabolism, for this is more properly accomplished in biochemistry texts (see, e.g., Peters and Van Slyke, 1946, pp. 373–589). Lipide metabolism is discussed here so that the contributions made by phosphatides may be better understood.

The transformations whereby lipides are reduced to simpler materials are controlled largely by enzymes such as lipases and lecithinases. The latter have already been described, although these are undoubtedly responsible for only a part of the transformations. In carbohydrate metabolism considerable insight has been gained into the nature of enzyme activity. In lipide metabolism, on the other hand, enzyme relationships are quite obscure, the present state of knowledge having been well reviewed by Stadie (1945).

The early work on the role of fat in the body's economy was carried out by Munk (1880, 1884) and by Munk and Friedenthal (1901), who established the fundamentals which made possible much of the subsequent work.

LIPIDE METABOLISM

Digestion of Lipides

Lipides are not affected by the stomach lipases (Inouye, 1924), but are supposedly hydrolyzed in the intestines to glycerol and fatty acids by pancreatic and intestinal lipases. Frazer (see p. 346) is of the opinion that only partial hydrolysis, if any, is required prior to absorption. It was early established (Fejer, 1913) that fat must be liquid at body temperatures in order to be digested. Furthermore, emulsification was believed to be prerequisite.

In the literature there are many references to the action of natural emulsifying agents such as soaps, glycocholic and taurocholic acids (Klumpp, 1941) and phosphatides (Augur, Rollman and Deuel, 1947; Frazer, 1949). Emulsifying agents added to the fat prior to ingestion are

345

also said to facilitate digestion and absorption; and Tidwell (1950) has shown that fat absorption is increased in the presence of either lecithin or choline. The problem of lipide emulsification has been studied extensively by Elkes and co-workers (1944) and by Frazer, Schulman and Stewart (1944).

The bile also contributes to digestion since occlusion of the bile duct leads to the recovery of large quantities of undigested fat in the feces (Moggi, 1934).

Although most of the above discussion has been directed to glycerides, phosphatides are perhaps digested similarly, as shown by the work of Ackermann (1936), except that lecithinases replace the lipases. The liberated fatty acids lose their identity in subsequent treatment, save that the more highly unsaturated ones appear to be favored in the resynthesis of phosphatides. Sinclair (1934), however, has pointed out that even partial hydrolysis is probably not as important a prerequisite for phosphatide absorption as it is for glyceride absorption.

The glycerol liberated during digestion appears to be absorbed directly and to pass into the portal blood for transportation to the liver where, like carbohydrates, it is converted to glycogen. The possibility must not be overlooked, however, that the glycerol may be routed to sites where it can be used in the resynthesis of phosphatides.

Absorption of Lipides

Undoubtedly nature has provided several pathways for the absorption of lipides. Frazer (1938, 1946, 1948) has provided important although not entirely conclusive evidence that a portion of the fat enters the systemic blood stream via the lymphatics unchanged. He observed, under dark field illumination, that unhydrolyzed particles of fat increased rapidly in systemic blood but not in portal blood after oral administration of olive oil. The reverse was true when glycerol and oleic acids were given. In addition, ingestion of fat stained with Sudan III caused the fat depots to become stained, whereas ingestion of glycerol, oleic acid and Sudan III caused the liver to become stained. Frazer concluded, accordingly, that the portion of fat which is unhydrolyzed is taken directly to the depots by the systemic blood, whereas the hydrolyzed fat goes via the portal blood to the liver.

Evidence has been obtained by Artom and Swanson (1948, see p. 391) that phosphatides, too, may be absorbed intact.

The three classical means proposed for removing fatty acids from the intestines are as phosphatides, as cholesterol esters and as complexes with bile acids. Other possibilities may involve the lipoproteins, mono-, di- and triglycerides and soaps.

It has been generally assumed that fatty acids are converted to phosphatides in the intestinal mucosa since the phosphatide content of the intestinal lymph increases after ingestion of fat (Süllmann and Wilbrandt, 1934) and since "labels" are so readily incorporated into intestinal phosphatides (Fries and co-workers, 1938; Sinclair and Smith, 1937). That this may not be the case follows from the work of Zilversmit, Chaikoff and Entenman (1948), who fed various fats and radioactive phosphorus to animals and found no increase in amount or turnover of the phosphatides in the mucosa or the villi of the small intestines. These observations will be discussed in greater detail later (see p. 390). At present it is doubtful that phosphatides serve as transport media for fatty acids.

That cholesterol provides a means for removing fatty acids from the intestine has been assumed from the work of Müller (1915, 1916), who found an increase in cholesterol ester content in thoracic duct lymph after feeding cholesterol to dogs with thoracic duct fistulae. Esterification and absorption were inhibited, as might be expected, when bile and pancreatic juices were diverted from the intestine, since both are necessary for fat digestion. The experiments of Frölicher and Süllmann (1934), who found that both free and esterified cholesterol increase in the intestinal lymph of rabbits during cholesterol absorption, tend to show that the ester formation takes place in the intestinal wall. More recently, Favarger (1942) observed that ingested elaidic acid serves to esterify cholesterol in the intestine, thus lending support to the concept that fatty acids are absorbed partly as cholesterol esters.

The role of bile acids in fat absorption is yet to be entirely clarified. Verzar and Laszt (1934) as well as Riegel, Elsom and Ravdin (1935) observed that oleic acid was not absorbed *in vitro* in the intestines of dogs until taurocholic acid was added. This caused them to ascribe to the bile acids a hydrotropic action which served to transport the fatty acids to a location for further synthesis. It thus may be that transport under the influence of bile acids precedes the phosphatide or cholesterol ester formation described above. However, similar experiments performed by Doubilet and Reiner (1937) indicate that bile acids are not necessary for the absorption of fat from the iliac loop of man. Jeker (1936) observed histochemically that the fatty acids of the intestinal mucosa changed to glycerides as absorption continued. He inferred that the fatty acids were brought into the mucosa as bile acid complexes.

That fatty acids may reach the intestinal mucosa as complexes with soaps, despite the fact (McClendon, 1915) that the contents of the intestinal tract are not alkaline, follows from the work of Schmidt-Nielsen

(1946). He has shown that fatty acids can exist as soaps in the neutral or acid pH of the gastrointestinal tract.

From these studies it is obvious that much remains to be learned about the process of absorption of fat from the intestines.

Transportation and Disposition of Absorbed Lipides

The fate of the absorbed lipides beyond the intestine or intestinal mucosa is again somewhat uncertain. They have a choice of entering the venous or systemic blood stream via the lymph channels or thoracic duct. Or they may enter the portal blood for transportation to the liver (Joannovics and Pick, 1910). As Best (1946) has pointed out, there are some very old and rather dubious data (Munk, 1880; Munk and Rosenstein, 1891) which indicate that 60 per cent of the fat enters the thoracic duct. Although the idea has been held that virtually all the digested fat enters the systemic blood system, it would be logical to assume that at least some of it goes directly to the liver since this organ is the chief site of fat metabolism. As Best (1946) has proposed, however, it is possible that most of the absorbed fat enters the lymph or thoracic duct rather than the blood stream because a gradual presentation of the lipides to the liver is desired.

There is nevertheless evidence which favors the concept that some of the lipides enter the portal blood directly. Little and Robinson (1941) collected left thoracic lymph in dogs after injecting cream into the duodenum. They found that only 4 to 17 per cent of the absorbed fat was recoverable in the thoracic lymph. Hughes and Wimmer (1935), having fed butter fat or tributyrin to animals could detect no butyric acid in thoracic duct lymph. Frazer (1938), on the other hand, detected visible fat particles in the systemic blood but not in the portal blood. Thus it is possible that the most soluble materials such as butyric acid, and possibly even phosphatides, may enter the blood stream directly for transportation to the liver, whereas the less soluble substance such as neutral fat must go first to the lymph ducts. Winter and Crandall (1941), however, were unable to demonstrate the direct portal absorption of fatty acids in dogs.

An interesting study by Peretti and Tore (1933) showed that the percentage increase in liver fat and blood fat after feeding depended on the type of fat ingested. Thus iodized fat yielded a maximum increase in liver fat of 281.2 per cent and in blood fat of 234 per cent. Linseed oil, on the other hand, increased the liver fat only 6.2 per cent but increased the blood fat 282 per cent.

Several experiments, including those of Sulze (1933), have demonstrated that fat absorption continues when the lymph ducts are ligated.

The alternative route is probably the portal blood. Clarke, Ivy and Goodman (1948), in this same regard, have shown that interruption of the mesenteric lymph drainage did not alter fat absorption since it did not affect the fecal lipides.

The route of the phosphatides might logically be expected to involve the portal blood since there appears to be a marked interdependency between them and the liver. This may be inferred from studies such as those of Artom and co-workers (1937) and Cavanagh and Raper (1939). The former workers fed fats and radioactive phosphate to animals, and recovered most of the labeled atom in the liver. The latter worker carried out similar experiments with deuterium as a label and likewise recovered most of the deuterium in the liver phosphatides. Nevertheless, the systemic blood also receives its share of the phosphatides, for Süllman and Wilbrandt (1934) have shown that both neutral fat and phosphatides increase in thoracic duct lymph after the feeding of olive oil. Reinhardt, Fishler and Chaikoff (1944) found that over 20 per cent of labeled phosphatides could be recovered in thoracic duct lymph subsequent to injection into the blood stream. An actual rise in phosphatides in the systemic blood after ingestion of fat has been shown to take place by Tajima (1935) and by Artom and Freeman (1940). The latter workers showed that the lecithin content in particular increased, for which reason they postulate that lecithin is the phosphatide responsible for fatty acid transport. Other work, however (see p. 384), casts considerable doubt on the role of phosphatides as vehicular agents for fatty acids.

Cholesterol and its esters appear largely to enter the lymph rather than the portal blood. This conclusion, which depends largely on the work of Müller (1915, 1916) and Frölicher and Süllmann (1934), is in accord with the hypothesis that the less soluble materials enter the lymph. Nevertheless, some entry of free or esterified cholesterol into the portal blood cannot be excluded.

Bile acids are apparently liberated from their complexes with fatty acids and enter the portal blood stream in the free state for transportation to the liver (Josephson and Rydin, 1936).

From this discussion it appears, then, that absorbed lipides are directed largely to the lymphatic ducts, although some go directly to the liver through the portal blood. The fat which enters the lymph goes into the systemic blood stream and reaches the liver only after it has come in contact with all the other tissues and organs of the body. It would seem that some of it is deposited in the fat depots without ever reaching the liver at all. Thus Ellis, Rothwell and Pool (1931) showed that cottonseed oil, which could be identified by its fatty acids, was deposited in fat depots in a relatively short period of time. Kohl (1938) using elaidic acid and Longenecker (1939a) using coconut oil were able to show essentially the same rapid uptake of ingested fatty acids by the fat depots. Nevertheless, the disposition of the fat, whether it goes through the liver or not, appears to be markedly influenced by the liver. In addition, as will be seen later, other organs and tissues aside from the fat depots and the liver are concerned with the circulating lipides.

The Storage of Lipides

In classical biochemistry, it was assumed that part of the ingested fat was consumed immediately to satisfy energy requirements, whereas the remainder was relegated to the fat depots from whence it might be mobilized in time of need. Thus it was assumed that the composition of the storage fat remained uniform in adult animals of constant weight. That the composition of depot fat could be influenced by diet was indicated by the experiments described above, as well as by many similar ones. The true dynamic state of the stored lipides was convincingly demonstrated by Stetten and Schoenheimer (1940), who fed rats ethyl palmitate labeled with deuterium in the fatty acid residue. At the end of eight days 44 per cent of the labeled fat was found in the depots. Of importance is the evidence that it occurred there not only as palmitic acid, but also as stearic, myristic, lauric and palmitoleic acids. Since the body weight remained constant, it followed that a corresponding quantity of depot fat had been removed for metabolic purposes. Obviously, the demonstration of this state of flux within depot fats which are relatively stable from an over-all qualitative and quantitative point of view could not have been demonstrated without the use of isotopes.

Although depot fat is characteristic of a given species, it must not be concluded that the fat depots are not selective in the fatty acids they remove from dietary fat. Thus Sinclair (1932a) fed rats highly unsaturated acids and found that, whereas the iodine numbers of the phosphatides were rapidly increased, those of the depot fats were hardly affected. Nor have fatty acids with less than ten carbon atoms been found in the depot fats; for these, presumably, are called upon first for oxidative purposes. Ricinoleic acid from castor oil, on the other hand, was found, after ingestion, in the depot fats of the rat, but not in the phosphatides (Stewart and Sinclair, 1945).

Selectivity was also demonstrated by Bernhard and Schoenheimer (1940) and by Schoenheimer and Rittenberg (1936, 1936a), who fed deuterium-labeled lipides to mice on a carbohydrate diet. In mice one-half of the saturated acids in the carcass were replaced in 24 hours. After six days one-third of the hydrogen atoms in the saturated acids were replaced by deuterium, whereas only one-ninth of the hydrogen atoms in the unsaturated acids were replaced. This is further evidence of the desire of the fat depots for saturated fatty acids. It was also demonstrated in this work that carbon chains may be lengthened (up to 18 carbon atoms) or shortened, and that both saturation and desaturation to monoenoic acids may take place.

The selectivity of the depot fats is secondary to the selectivity of the phosphatides which occur in the parenchymatous tissue cells. Furthermore the phosphatides demonstrate an over-all preference—even during starvation—for the more highly unsaturated fatty acids. Thus during inanition saturated acids disappear in preference to oleic acid (Longenecker, 1939a), whereas oleic acid is consumed in preference to linoleic and linolenic acids (Hilditch and Pedelty, 1940). Longenecker (1939) showed, in addition, that after a period of starvation the dietary lipides have a great effect on the depot fat but very little effect on the phosphatides. The latter, having maintained their status quo during starvation, can afford to demonstrate preference when fats are once again introduced into the diet. The depot fat, on the other hand, having been consumed during starvation must rebuild itself with whatever is offered, despite the fact that in more normal situations there would be demonstrated a preference for saturated fatty acids. The same conclusions may be derived from the work of Sinclair (1935, 1935a).

The selective utilization of lipides during starvation has been denied by MacLachlan (1944), who reported that the iodine number of blood lipides did not decrease in the fasting mouse. On the contrary, Miller and Hansen (1944) found that dogs on low fat diets could maintain a normal lipide level in blood cells and plasma but could not synthesize sufficient unsaturated acids to maintain the normal degree of unsaturation.

Of interest is the recent work of Campbell, Olley and Blewett (1949), who found that the feeding of large amounts of a saturated acid such as palmitic acid to rats on alipotropic diets was accompanied by the release of large amounts of depot fat and the coincident accumulation of liver fat. When oleic acid was fed, these phenomena were not observed. Furthermore, dietary palmitic acid appeared to reduce the phosphatide content of the liver when this was measured in relationship to body weight. There was no correlation, on the other hand, between feeding of oleic or palmitic acids and the phosphatide turnover rates in the liver, as measured by radioactive inorganic phosphorus.

The Synthesis of Lipides from Carbohydrate and Protein

The inability of the rat to synthesize fatty acids more unsaturated than oleic was demonstrated by Burr and Burr (1930). The ability of the organism to control the chain length of fatty acids, which in a sense is synthesis, was demonstrated by Stetten and Schoenheimer (1940). These workers fed palmitic acid labeled with deuterium to rats. They were later able to detect the deuterium not only in palmitic acid but also in stearic, myristic, lauric, palmitoleic and oleic acids. The deuterium content of the linoleic acid was within the range of experimental error, thus confirming the above experiments of Burr and Burr (1930). The presence of deuterium in the mono-unsaturated acids indicated that the body may saturate or desaturate fatty acids to the extent of one double bond. This was also shown by experiments with deuterium by Schoenheimer and Rittenberg (1936). Hilditch, Lea and Pedelty (1939) examined the depot fats of pigs reared on controlled diets, and concluded that there was synthesized only palmitic, stearic and oleic acids with minor amounts of myristic and palmitoleic acids. Recent evidence provided by Rieckehoff, Holman and Burr (1949) shows that arachidonic acid (four double bonds) is deposited in appreciable quantities when a fat-deficient diet is supplemented by corn oil. Since the corn oil contains linoleic acid, it would follow that the arachidonic acid is synthesized from the di-unsaturated acid, which itself cannot be synthesized in the body.

It has long been known, largely from empirical observation, that carbohydrate is converted by the body to lipides. More recent confirmation of this fact has been provided by work of the type carried out by Feyder (1935). The intermediary products involved in the conversion of carbohydrates to fat are still subjects for conjecture. Since 6 is a multiple of 18, it was early theorized that the C_{18} fatty acids could form by condensation of three hexose units. Thereafter the shorter fatty acids could form by β-oxidation. Actually there is little evidence to support such a theory.

Of great interest is the observation of Rittenberg and Bloch (1944) that dietary acetic acid containing both isotopic carbon and deuterium could be detected after ingestion in the fatty acids of the rat. Ponticorvo, Rittenberg and Bloch (1949) determined recently that when sodium deuteroacetate was fed to rats on a lipide-free diet, isotope concentrations showed that 20 per cent of the fatty acid carbon atoms and 45 per cent of the cholesterol carbon atoms were derived from the acetate. If the fatty acids are built up from C_2 units such as acetic acid, the proper number of multiples must be condensed without leaving the synthetic site and without the formation of intermediates. This follows from the evidence provided by Rittenberg, Schoenheimer and Evans (1937) that short-chain fatty acids, which would necessarily be intermediates in the stepwise condensation of C_2 units, are not incorporated into fatty acids, but are oxidized to carbon dioxide and water.

Of importance is the recent study of Masoro, Chaikoff and Dauben (1949), who fed C^{14}-labeled glucose to mice and rats under various conditions. In the normal mouse on a high carbohydrate, fat-free diet, it was possible to account for all of the ingested label on the basis of fatty acid and carbon dioxide production. Furthermore, the very high specific activity of the fatty acids of the liver made feasible the hypothesis that the conversion of glucose to fatty acid takes place primarily in that organ. That nature has provided other sites for this activity, however, was demonstrated by the observation that C^{14}-labeled palmitic acid could be isolated subsequent to feeding of labeled glucose from rats deprived of their livers and gastrointestinal tracts.

Kaufmann (1948) has carried out preliminary studies which indicate that phosphatides may be involved in the conversion of carbohydrates to fats.

The conversion of proteins to fats may be inferred from work carried out by Brown and co-workers (1938). It is quite likely, although further investigation is certainly necessary, that the proteins do not go directly to lipides, but that an indirect route is followed through the carbohydrates which are known to form from proteins.

Of great interest in this phase of fat metabolism are the observations of Stetten and Boxer (1944), who used deuterium to show that carbohydrate conversion to lipides is a continuous process and not one which takes place only when carbohydrate is in relative excess. The amount of carbohydrate to be converted to fat depends, of course, on the nutritional state of the animal; but the continuous nature of the process is necessary if the full nutritional advantage of the carbohydrate is to be gained. This follows from the fact that the body can store only a limited amount of glycogen, whereas its facility for fat storage is much greater. Thus the carbohydrate is saved through the medium of fat and is used as needed.

Such observations necessarily presuppose an interrelationship of fat and carbohydrate catabolism; for the types of fragments formed by the oxidation of these two foods may well be entirely independent of their progenitors. Thus the fragments may be free to engage in whatever cycle the body deems necessary at the moment. Witzemann (1942, p. 265) has attempted to present a basis for the correlation of fat and carbohydrate metabolism based largely on the concept of "recapture synthesis". According to this theory, fragments of fat catabolism such as acetoacetic acid or acetic acid condense with fragments of carbohydrate catabolism such as pyruvic acid to provide new intermediates which are active metabolites. Obviously this theory is but a point of departure in this complex problem. Breusch (1943) and Wieland and Rosenthal (1943) have published significant work indicating that ketone compounds may condense with oxaloacetic acid to yield intermediates with metabolic activity. Weinhouse, Medes and Floyd (1944) were actually able to isolate C^{13}-labeled citric acid from a system containing rat kidney homogenate, C^{13} carboxyl and carbonyl-labeled acetoacetate and oxaloacetate. Dickens (1945) has reviewed much of the work in this field.

Deuel and Morehouse (1946, p. 120) have presented a review of the present state of knowledge in this difficult field; and Bloch (1947) also has reviewed much of the evidence concerned with both the synthesis and degradation of fatty acids, particularly from the point of view of the two carbon fragments which may form from β-oxidation.

The reverse situation of conversion of lipides to carbohydrates has never been observed to occur. Although experimental data on this question are difficult to obtain, Page and Young (1932) contributed evidence when they found that glucose excretion and the glucose-nitrogen ratio in the urine of phlorhizinized dogs did not increase after injection of brain phosphatides. The same conclusion was reached by Yriart (1931). The subject has been reviewed in detail by Soskin (1941).

The Role of the Liver in Fat Transportation and Disposition

The close relationship of the liver to fat metabolism is suggested by the composition of the liver lipides. In addition to phosphatides and cholesterol there are present glycerides and cholesterol esters, and these as well as the phosphatides are characterized by highly unsaturated fatty acids (Bloor, 1943, p. 208). This high degree of unsaturation was responsible for the early idea that the liver desaturates the fatty acids in preparation for their subsequent conversion to energy by oxidation. That extensive desaturation could not be a function of the liver was demonstrated by Burr and Burr (1930), who showed that synthesis of di- and tri-unsaturated acids within the body of the rat is not possible. This must not be interpreted to mean that the liver is totally incapable of removing hydrogen from fatty acids; for Rittenberg and Schoenheimer (1937) have shown, just as with depot fat, that palmitic and stearic acids of the liver may be desaturated to palmitoleic and oleic acids, and that these in turn may be saturated to the parent compounds. Indeed, this appears to be a rather general means for controlling the consistency of the body fat under ideal conditions.

In addition to the above observation, there are many others which must necessarily arise from an intimate relationship between the liver and lipide metabolism. The most important of these is that the liver is prone, in certain abnormal situations, to become "fatty"—i.e., to be characterized by an abnormal accumulation of lipide deposits.

Fatty livers are observed in several physiological or pathological conditions which serve to interfere, for a variety of reasons, with the necessary mobilization of fatty acids in the body. The route of fatty acid transport within the body undoubtedly involves the liver for a high percentage of the lipides. When abnormal conditions interfere with the transportation, the fatty acids accumulate in the liver in the form of neutral fat, phosphatides or cholesterol esters. Why the fatty acids must be routed through the liver, especially since, as indicated previously, most of them do not go directly to the portal blood, is a problem of great interest. The work of Fishler and co-workers (1943) provides important evidence, for they have shown that radioactive phosphorus could be detected in liver phosphatides (as well as in kidney and small intestine phosphatides) shortly after injection. After a lapse of time the phosphatides of the blood plasma and the organs and tissues other than the liver assumed the labeled atom at the expense of the liver phosphatides. Removal of the liver led to a decrease of the radioactive phosphorus in the blood plasma but not in the muscles, intestines and kidneys. This work shows that at least one of the functions of the liver is to convert the proper fatty acids from dietary and depot fat into phosphatides which then become available via the blood to the tissues and organs of the body.

Thus in the normal liver it may be assumed from the above data that the fatty acids stream through and are converted, in whatever quantities are necessary, to phosphatides which in turn are delivered to the extrahepatic tissues. When, as already mentioned above, certain abnormal conditions prevail which interfere with phosphatide formation in the liver, fatty livers result. This rather simple explanation which assumes that phosphorylation is obligatory in fat transport is hardly in accord with the observations of Bollman and Flock (1946). These workers calculated that the liver formed phosphatides equivalent only to 3 per cent of the fatty acids involved in metabolism. Whatever part the liver plays, it is nevertheless well established that fatty livers develop when the liver is not allowed to carry out its customary role.

Dietary Fatty Livers. By far the best studied of these conditions is alipotropism—the development of fatty livers due to the absence of lipotropic factors in the diet. The intricacies of lipotropism will be detailed later (see p. 413). Lipotropic substances have been shown to include choline, betaine, methionine and inositol (Raymond and Treadwell, 1949). The sodium salt of nucleic acid has also been reported to exert lipotropic activity by Leites and Rossinskaya (1948).

An important dietary condition which may be remedied by dietary choline is the fatty liver observed in the pancreatized animal which is being maintained on insulin. This condition, according to Ralli and

Rubin (1942), may also be remedied by methionine-containing protein, provided that the protein is in a finely divided form so that it may be readily absorbed. It appears, therefore, that the fatty liver in this instance is due to the inability of the pancreatized animal to absorb lipotropic factors as readily as does a normal animal.

The fatty liver of the depancreatized dog has been shown to respond to factors other than the lipotropic ones, although this situation, as summarized by Best (1946), requires considerable clarification. One of these antifatty infiltration factors has been named "lipocaic" by its discoverers, Dragstedt, Prohaska and Harms (1936), who isolated it from pancreas and showed that it conferred complete protection upon the liver of the pancreatized dog. Montgomery, Entenman and Chaikoff (1939) showed that similar results could be obtained with pancreatic juice, an observation which was denied by Allen and co-workers (1943), who could not repeat it. It is Best's (1946) opinion that the presence of factors other than the usual lipotropic agents in lipocaic remains yet to be established.

In the meanwhile, Entenman, Chaikoff and Montgomery (1944) have isolated a fraction from pancreas whose content of choline and other lipotropic agents appears to be very low. This material, which differs from lipocaic, likewise prevents fatty livers from developing in depancreatized dogs. This antifatty liver substance may be enzymatic in nature, and Best (1946) has provided evidence to this effect. This pancreatic material has been discussed in detail by Chaikoff and Entenman (1948, p. 172).

Excess cystine (Tucker and Eckstein, 1938), as well as excess thiamine and riboflavin (McHenry, 1937; Gavin and McHenry, 1940), has been shown to produce fatty livers which may be remedied by methyl donors. The effect of these substances appears to be due to general stimulation of appetite with subsequent increase in the conversion of carbohydrates and proteins to fatty acids. The increased amount of fat apparently demands more choline for its mobilization through the liver (Stetten and Salcedo, 1944).

The lipotropic action of inositol is not yet clearly understood (Blewett, Campbell and Olley, 1949). It appears to be of value in treating fatty livers resulting from excess biotin, as was demonstrated by Gavin, Patterson and McHenry (1943). The effect of biotin on inositol is yet to be determined, but it may well be that inositol performs its lipotropic duties by incorporating fatty acids into the inositol-containing phosphatides just as choline may convert them into lecithin. A prolonged absence of pyridoxine in the diet has the same effect as excess biotin, for Engel (1942) has shown that it produces a fatty liver which yields to inositol.

Excessive cholesterol in the diet provides a fatty liver which is characterized by large amounts of cholesterol esters (Cook, 1936). A possible explanation for this phenomenon is that fatty acids are not removed readily from the liver in the form of cholesterol esters which form preferentially when excess cholesterol is present in the diet.

Aminoethyl alcohol and serine, like choline, are constituents of phosphatides. Nevertheless their absence from the diet does not manifest itself in alipotropic symptoms since they are apparently readily synthesized in the body. An excess of d-serine, however, has been shown by Artom, Fishman and Morehead (1945) to create a pathological condition which does not exist when the diet contains only the naturally occurring l-serine. Yet to be explained is the observation of Scudi and Hamlin (1942) that a deficiency of pantothenic acid in the dog resulted in fatty livers.

Still another means for producing fatty livers in experimental animals depends on the ingestion of certain fractions obtained from the anterior lobe of the pituitary gland. This phenomenon, which is best demonstrated in fasting rats or mice, has been discussed by Best (1946) and by Stetten and Salcedo (1944). The anterior pituitary substance appears to cause excessive mobilization of depot fat which migrates to the liver. The condition is greatly improved by resumption of normal food intake.

Finally a dietary condition unrelated to alipotropism has been found to produce fatty livers. This is the absence of the essential fatty acids first described by Burr and Burr (1930). Engel (1942) has observed that their continued absence leads to fatty infiltration of the liver. The condition, as might be expected, was remedied by addition of unsaturated acids to the diet.

Fatty Livers Produced by Factors Other Than Dietary. Fatty livers from causes other than dietary ones also relate the liver closely to lipide metabolism. When a normal amount of fat is present in the diet the liver lipides readily reflect the ingested fatty acids, as has been demonstrated by Sinclair (1935b) and by Best and Ridout (1938). When the dietary fat is below the minimum required for normal functions, the liver assumes the task of synthesizing fatty acids, as has been shown by Bernhard and Schoenheimer (1940) and by Stetten and Grail (1943). These workers used deuterium and were able to show that the synthesized fats appeared readily in the liver, whereas as much as a week was required for their appearance in the fat depots.

In these two conditions, then, the quantity of fat in the liver remains normal. In starvation, however, it is possible to demonstrate in some animals the occurrence of fatty livers. Thus Hynd and Rotter (1930) observed the presence of fatty livers in rats on a carbohydrate-free diet. The dog or cat, according to these workers, is less prone to display fatty livers in starvation. In either case, however, the liver is mobilizing fat from the depots, and Barrett, Best and Ridout (1938) have shown, with the aid of deuterium, that the depots are virtually the sole source of liver lipides during starvation. Thus further evidence is provided for the postulation that the liver serves to prepare the lipides for their end use in the body.

Lipides also accumulate in the liver under the influence of certain toxic agents which injure it and cause hepatic disfunction. In some instances it is possible to approach normal liver function by administering factors which influence dietary fatty livers. Thus Barrett and co-workers (1939) were able to remedy to a large extent with choline a fatty liver caused by carbon tetrachloride poisoning. Similarly Goodell, Hanson and Hawkins (1944) found that the administration of methionine to a dog prevented subsequent poisoning with mepharsen.

Degradation of Fatty Acids by the Liver. Thus far, lipides in the body have been represented as arising from two sources: the dietary fat and synthesis within the body. From some of the observations described above it follows that there probably exists between the fat depots and the liver a cycle wherein the fatty acids are circulated continuously, for which reason it is probably of little consequence at what point the fatty acids are introduced. As already indicated, when this cycle suffers interference either for physiological or pathological reasons, fat accumulates in the liver.

In normal conditions where the flow of fatty acids between the fat depots and the liver proceeds smoothly, certain fatty acids must be removed, probably continuously, to provide energy for the functioning of the body. As these are removed they are replaced by fatty acids from the two sources indicated above. The location in the body for the removal of some of the fatty acids and their preparation for use as energy appears to be the liver. The mechanism by which this is accomplished has provided inspiration for much research and discussion.

As is well known, the first clues to the fate of fatty acids on oxidation were provided by Knoop (1904, 1931). His work has been so well detailed in numerous texts that it requires little elaboration here. Briefly, he observed that when animals are fed phenyl-substituted fatty acids, products are isolated in the feces which could arise only by the removal of the aliphatic carbon atoms in pairs. These experiments were based on the well-known observation that the body does not utilize ingested benzoic or phenylacetic acids, but excretes them as hippuric and phenylaceturic acids, respectively. Knoop observed that β-phenylpropionic acid was excreted in part as hippuric acid, whereas γ-phenylbutyric acid was excreted as phenylaceturic acid and δ-phenylvaleric acid as hippuric acid. Thus the carbon atoms had been removed in units of two, for which reason Knoop postulated that oxidative attack occurred first of all on the carbon atom β to the carboxyl group to yield a β-hydroxy acid which was further oxidized to a β-keto acid and subsequently cleaved. Other workers have supported the concept of β-oxidation and have offered al-

$$R-CH_2-CH_2-COOH \longrightarrow R-\underset{\underset{OH}{|}}{CH}-CH_2-COOH \longrightarrow R-\underset{\underset{O}{\|}}{C}-CH_2-COOH \longrightarrow RCOOH$$

ternative mechanisms for its occurrence (e.g., Witzemann, 1932, 1942, p. 276; Raper and Wayne, 1928; Dakin, 1909, 1921; Stetten and Schoenheimer, 1940; Bernhard and Vischer, 1946; Jowett and Quastel, 1935; Deuel and co-workers, 1936; Hurtley, 1916; McKay and co-workers, 1940; Stadie, Zapp and Lukens, 1941; Weinhouse, Medes and Floyd, 1944; Leloir, 1948).

Still another type of degradation, ω-oxidation, has been observed. Verkade (1938) found that the triglyceryl ester of undecylenic acid (C_{11}) is excreted as undecanedioic acid, $HOOC - (CH_2)_9 - COOH$; azelaic acid, $HOOC - (CH_2)_7 - COOH$; and pimelic acid, $HOOC - (CH_2)_5 - COOH$. Obviously, in the production of the two latter acids both β- and ω-oxidation have occurred. Stadie (1945) has pointed out that oxidation may take place at both ends of a fatty acid at the same time. ω-Oxidation appears to be limited to fatty acids of twelve or fewer carbon atoms, although further investigation is necessary before its application to higher fatty acids can be excluded completely.

Formation and Role of Ketone Bodies. The ketone bodies, β-hydroxybutyric acid, acetoacetic acid and acetone are produced solely by the liver (Stadie, 1945; Quastel and Wheatley, 1933) which supplies them to the blood. Muscles and other tissues serve, according to Himwich, Goldfarb and Weller (1931), to remove them from the blood stream.

Thus, despite early evidence to the contrary (Shaffer, 1924), ketone bodies are produced normally and are removed from the blood by other tissues. The condition in which excess quantities of ketone bodies may be detected in the blood or the more advanced stage where they are excreted via the urine arises when the rate of production of ketone bodies by the liver exceeds their rate of consumption by the other tissues. Alternatively there is a possibility that ketone bodies form from two carbon fragments when conditions necessary for the oxidation of these are not available. Such conditions exist in starvation, in diabetes and after pancreatectomy where it appears that ketone-body production is accelerated to compensate, in some way, for the inability of the tissues to utilize carbohydrate. The corresponding consumption of ketone bodies, however, is not accelerated, for which reason the excess ketones are readily observed in blood or urine by qualitative procedures. Some of the experimental work which relates excess ketone-body formation to lack of utilization of carbohydrates and to the subsequent necessary conversion of proteins to glycogen has been well summarized by Peters and Van Slyke (1946, p. 451). However, it is still undetermined whether ketosis or ketonuria occurs because the metabolism of fat and carbohydrate must occur simultaneously, or whether the presence of carbohydrate prevents fat degradation by subjecting itself to preferential oxidation.

The ketogenic properties of the higher fatty acids appear to be shared to some extent by other compounds. Butts and co-workers (1935) and Deuel and co-workers (1936) showed that the lower even-carbon acids through C_8 produced as high a concentration of ketone bodies in the urine as did equivalent amounts of acetoacetic and β-hydroxybutyric acids. Thus these experiments disclose the fate of these acids in the body, for Rittenberg, Schoenheimer and Evans (1937) showed that the even-carbon acids through C_{10} cannot be converted into fat, and Deuel and co-workers (1935) demonstrated that they are not converted to carbohydrates.

Some of the odd-carbon acids are also degraded by the organism to ketone bodies, although this is of little practical importance since odd-carbon acids occur in nature only very rarely. Thus McKay, Wick and Barnum (1940) showed that the odd-carbon acids from C_5 through C_{11} were all able to produce slight amounts of ketone bodies. All the acids including propionic were simultaneously converted to glycogen, unlike the even-carbon acids which are not convertible to carbohydrates. Certain amino acids, such as leucine, tyrosine and phenylalanine, appear also to be ketogenic (Shaffer, 1927; Cohen, 1937).

The role of ketone bodies in fat metabolism has been discussed in detail by Stadie (1945).

The Complete Oxidation of Fatty Acids

Actually only a small number of fatty acids are converted to carbon dioxide and water via the ketone bodies. The remainder of the fatty acids are oxidized to these end products directly in the tissues.

The mechanism of the combustion of the fatty acids or of the ketone bodies is obscure. Since the latter contain the functional groups of carbohydrates, they may be treated like intermediary products of carbohydrate metabolism (Crandall, 1941). Borek and Rittenberg (1949) have shown that rat liver slices metabolize acetone since deuteriocholesterol forms from deuterioacetone. Acetic acid, which may be a component of fatty acids, also may form from acetone.

The ketone bodies are probably not intermediates in the direct combustion of fatty acids since there is no evidence to show that tissues other than the liver can produce ketone bodies. Still smaller fragments such as acetic acid may be involved, in which case the ultimate disposition may be indistinguishable from the disposition of carbohydrates. Graffln and Green (1948) have shown that the enzyme system prepared from kidney and liver and designated as the "cyclophorase system" is capable of oxidizing lower normal fatty acids with an even number of carbon atoms completely to carbon dioxide and water. They reviewed the prior work of Leloir and Munoz (1944), who had established the requirements for activity in this system. Knox, Noyce and Auerbach (1948) showed that the initial step in the oxidation of fatty acids by the cyclophorase system is a "sparking effect" by compounds of the citric acid cycle. That β-oxidation is operative under these conditions was demonstrated by Atchley (1948), who actually isolated by countercurrent distribution techniques propionic and isobutyric acids, respectively, from the oxidation of valeric and isocaproic acids. He showed further that butyric acid was not an intermediate in the oxidation of valeric acid. However, propionic acid was found as an unexpected oxidation product of isobutyric acid, and a mechanism involving methylmalonic semialdehyde as an intermediate was advanced to explain this observation.

Schneider (1948) has separated rat liver homogenates into nuclear, mitochondrial, submicroscopic particles and supernatant fractions. Thereafter he was able to show that the enzymes associated with the mitochondrial fraction were responsible for the oxidation of fatty acids.

Requiring still more elucidation is the procedure whereby the fatty acids are prepared for oxidation. The direct combustion process undoubtedly takes place in the cells where the fatty acids are present not as glycerides but as phosphatides. The series of reactions by which the phosphatides transfer the fatty acids across the cell membrane, release them for oxidation, and then take on new fatty acids remains to be elucidated. Nor is there evidence which allows one to determine when a fatty acid, as it travels between the liver and the fat depots, is ready for removal and direct oxidation. The metabolic character of the phosphatides must, however, in some way be related to their ability to preserve most of the di-, tri- and poly-unsaturated acids from oxidation (see p. 343) while at the same time allowing the combustion of the saturated or mono-unsaturated acids.

The Role of Extrahepatic Tissues and Organs in Fat Metabolism

Thus far, the liver, as the organ most vitally concerned in lipide metabolism, has been discussed in detail. The role of the fat cells which send fatty acids to the liver and receive them from that source has also been explained. The role of the intestine wherein initial absorption of lipides occurs has been discussed, as has the role of the blood by means of which the fatty acids are transported to the sites where metabolic activity occurs. Other tissues have been mentioned collectively as removing ketone bodies from the blood and as providing sites for the direct oxidation of fatty acids. Some of these tissues perform additional tasks which are worthy of discussion.

Pancreas. The role of the pancreas in lipide metabolism is largely an indirect one, arising from the ability of the pancreas to influence the proper utilization of carbohydrate. The appearance of excess ketone bodies in the blood and the urine coincident with the inability of the organism to utilize carbohydrate has already been noted (see p. 359). In pancreatectomy, the utilization of carbohydrates is greatly decreased, and accordingly an attempt is made by the body to rectify this deficiency by mobilizing great quantities of fatty acids from the depots to the liver. This is reflected by the presence of increased quantities of lipides in the blood, as shown by the work of Bloor, Gillette and James (1927) and Gibbs and Chaikoff (1941). Fat combustion increases, as does the production of ketone bodies which, accordingly, are detected in the blood and subsequently in the urine.

The hyperlipemia as well as the excess production of ketone bodies may be relieved in the pancreatized animal by the administration of insulin. This does not, however, prevent fat infiltration in the liver (see p. 355).

The pancreas, in addition, is the source of a lipase which aids in the digestion of lipides. Lipides are partially absorbed after pancreatectomy (Pratt, 1942) however, indicating either that other lipases are operative or else, as Frazer (see p. 346) contends, that hydrolysis is not obligate for fat absorption. (See also Lombroso, 1940).

Kidneys. It is known (see p. 418) that one of the symptoms of alipotropism may be the occurrence of kidney lesions. This suggests a relationship between the kidneys and the liver in metabolic activity. Thus it is possible that the kidneys participate in phosphatide synthesis, as shown by the experiments of Perlman, Ruben and Chaikoff (1937), who fed radioactive phosphorus to rats and noted the rate of appearance of labeled phosphatide in various tissues. Their experiments, however, do not exclude the possibility that the kidneys concentrate the phosphatides after they have been synthesized by the liver, rather than providing a site for synthesis. A similar rapid appearance of labeled phosphatides in the kidneys after ingestion of radioactive phosphorus was noted by Chargaff, Olson and Partington (1940). Sinclair (1940), however, found that the uptake of elaidic acid by the kidney phosphatides did not at all parallel the rapid uptake of radioactive phosphorus, although he indicates that his conditions were quite different from those used in the above work. Nevertheless, if rapid incorporation of elaidic acid is an indication of metabolic activity, and if elaidic acid actually behaves as do the more common dietary acids in the body, then Sinclair's results do not check those obtained with radioactive phosphorus. Hence further experimentation is indicated.

There do not appear to be data which show that the kidneys may take over the functions of the liver in animals with hepatic disfunction.

Adrenal Glands. The retardation of lipide absorption in adrenalectomized rats was first reported by Verzár and Laszt (1934a, 1935) who also showed (Laszt and Verzár, 1936) that normal absorption was restored by administration of the adrenal cortex hormone. In their opinion the adrenals exert an influence on phosphatide formation which appears to be necessary in the intestine for normal fat absorption. Issekutz, Laszt and Verzár (1938) and Laszt and Verzár (1938) observed further the presence of excessive quantities of fat in the feces of adrenalectomized cats on a high fat diet which was well tolerated by a normal cat. These results were in the main corroborated by Bavetta and Deuel (1942), who observed, however, that tributyrin absorption as well as tricaproin and tricaprylin absorption (Bavetta, 1943) were not affected by adrenalectomy.

Contradictory evidence was supplied by Barnes, Rusoff and Burr (1942), who reported that the rate of absorption of corn oil, olive oil, "Crisco" and mutton tallow was not affected by adrenalectomy. The absorption of hydrogenated vegetable oil fed as an emulsion with skim milk did decrease appreciably. In all instances, however, free fatty acids were observed in the intestines.

Of great interest is the report of Stillman and co-workers (1942), who showed by use of radioactive phosphorus that phosphatide formation in the liver and the small intestine is not interrupted in adrenalectomized rats, regardless of whether the animals were suffering from untreated cortical insufficiency or were maintained by administration of salt. Similarly Barnes, Miller and Burr (1941) showed that adrenalectomy did not inhibit the rate of incorporation of deuterium-containing fatty acids into phosphatides.

Adrenalectomy appears to increase the production of ketone bodies, as shown by MacKay and Barnes (1937) in their report that removing the adrenals neutralized the effect of extracting the anterior lobe of the hypophysis, which ordinarily causes excess production of ketone bodies as well as fatty livers.

Other Tissues. That the testes do not appear to be concerned with lipide metabolism is indicated by the experiments of Sinclair (1940a), who found that ingested elaidic acid did not appear in the phosphatides of the rat testes.

The brain, likewise, does not seem to participate in lipide metabolism since the rate of incorporation of labels into brain phosphatides is very slow, as shown, for example, by the experiments of Changus, Chaikoff and Ruben (1938) in which radioactive phosphorus was used.

Excretion of Lipides

Thus far the role of the lipides within the body has been described. There have been discussed the means by which they gain entrance into the metabolic pathways of the body; the important role of the liver in their proper disposition; the dynamic relationship of the lipides as they travel between the fat depots, the liver and other tissues; and the ultimate utilization of fatty acids for the production of energy which is, of course, their main metabolic function.

Finally, a certain quantity of lipides is normally excreted in the feces, and it is of interest to explore the source of these. Mention has already been made of the excessive amount of lipides found in the feces due to steatorrhea occasioned by pancreatectomy, adrenalectomy or other causes. These are probably unabsorbed dietary lipides, whereas those normally found in feces are believed to be true excretions, as was concluded many years ago by Müller (1884), who observed that fecal lipides persist even during starvation. More recently, Shapiro and co-workers (1936) were able to show with the aid of deuterium that the increase in fecal lipides in patients with bile fistula was due to increased secretion into the lumen of the intestine.

The contention that the composition of the lipides in the feces is to a large extent independent of diet is well supported experimentally. Thus Holmes and Kerr (1923) found no significant differences in the fecal lipides of individuals fed different easily digested fats. Güntherberg (1930) observed lipides in the feces of birds maintained on a fat-free diet. Hill and Bloor (1922) and Sperry and Bloor (1924) studied rather extensively the origin of fecal lipides; and Sperry (1926) concluded that the normal lipides excreted were those found in the feces originating from a fat-free diet. On the other hand, Wollaeger, Comfort and Osterberg (1947) have shown that the amount of fecal fat is influenced by the quantity of lipides ingested. They suggest, accordingly, that unabsorbed dietary fat accounts for a portion of the lipides excreted.

It is also possible, despite the opinion of Sperry and Angevine (1932) to the contrary, that the fecal lipides result from the ability of the intestinal flora to saturate some of the unsaturated dietary acids and also actually to synthesize fatty acids from carbohydrates.

The lipides of the feces comprise about 18 per cent of the solid material present (Fowweather, 1926) and were found by Sperry (1926) to consist of 35 to 40 per cent unsaponifiables, largely sterols, about 6 per cent glycerides, and 55 to 60 per cent fatty acids. The fatty acids were the usual dietary ones with the possible exception of a small amount of arachidonic acid. Di- and tri-unsaturated acids were absent, the liquid constituent consisting largely of oleic acid. Volatile acids were also excreted, acetic acid being the chief one and butyric and caproic acids the lesser components.

CHAPTER XXII

THE PHOSPHATIDES AS METABOLIC ELEMENTS

The Role of the Phosphatides in Metabolism

Introduction

In the above general discussion of lipide metabolism, reference was frequently made to studies of the active metabolic nature of phosphatides. In this section these studies will be examined in greater detail in an attempt to determine what role the phosphatides in the body play in the utilization and disposition of ingested lipides. Most fruitful has been the employment of easily identified "labels" from which much of the behavior of the phosphatides in the body tissues may be determined. Sinclair (1935b) used elaidic acid in some of the first work of this nature. Iodinated fatty acids were used as labels by Artom (1933), whereas Miller and Burr (1937) conceived of the idea of using fatty acids which could be identified by their characteristic absorption spectra. Needless to say, labels of this nature, in order to be effective, must be absent from the ordinary diet, but must nevertheless elicit no reactions in the body which are not characteristic of dietary fats. In addition, they must be readily identifiable at any desired stage in the experiment.

Powerful tools for so-called turnover or incorporation experiments are radioactive isotopes such as P^{32}. The use of this element in phosphatide turnover studies has been described in some detail by Hevesy (1948, p. 274) who has also discussed some of the attendant problems.

All this work is directed at gaining insight into how, where, at what rate and under what conditions phosphatides are broken into their components and how these components in turn are utilized in the body's metabolic activities. Much of the work up to the present time has necessarily been concerned with the determination of the scope of tools such as "labels". Furthermore, a given label provides information about only one constituent of the phosphatide molecule, and thus a great variety of studies of the correlation of activity of labels in several parts of the molecule under identical conditions is indicated.

366

Labeling Techniques

Elaidic Acid in the Study of Phosphatide Metabolism. Elaidic acid (*trans*-9-octadecenoic acid) is virtually absent in ordinary animal fat; and, because it is a solid it is readily isolable by the lead salt technique where it appears with the saturated acids, but is detected by its unsaturation. It nevertheless appears to be metabolized like its *cis* isomer, oleic acid. Accordingly, Sinclair (1935b) conceived of the idea that it might serve as a valuable tracer in phosphatide metabolism studies. Its applicability is, however, somewhat inhibited by its inability to replace entirely all of the fatty acids in a given tissue. Obviously, no single fatty acid could ever do this. Thus Sinclair (1940, 1940a) and Sinclair and Smith (1937) have shown that one-half of the fatty acids in the phosphatides of the intestinal mucosa may be replaced by elaidic acid. Twenty-six per cent of the phosphatide fatty acids of liver and only 7 per cent of those of brain may be replaced. The applicability of elaidic acid is further limited by lack of information as to the saturation and desaturation processes to which the body may subject it. Furthermore, its degree of permeability to the cell membrane, as compared to that of the more usual fatty acids, is a source of conjecture. Nevertheless, the work is important because it disclosed the wide applicability of tracer studies and served as an indicative introduction to the somewhat more definitive experiments carried out with radioactive tracers.

Very early work (Joannovics and Pick, 1910a) had shown that highly unsaturated dietary fat served to increase the unsaturation of liver phosphatides. Sinclair (1929) and Sinclair and Bloor (1929) extended this observation to the phosphatides of the intestinal mucosa and blood plasma. Sinclair (1935, 1935a) showed further that this was not simple replacement, since it was not reversible, the phosphatides clinging tenaciously to their newly acquired unsaturated acids. In an attempt to gain further insight into this situation, Sinclair (1935b) conceived of the idea of determining the rate of uptake of elaidic acid by various tissue phosphatides.

His work showed first of all (Sinclair, 1941) that after continued feeding, elaidic acid appeared in appreciable quantity in the intestinal mucosa, liver, skeletal muscle, kidney, heart, blood plasma, red blood cells and lungs. Most of the elaidic acid appeared to have replaced saturated acids. As indicated above, maximum replacement in the brain was 7 per cent, whereas only half that replacement was possible in the testes. In additional experiments, McConnell and Sinclair (1937) fed elaidic acid to female rats during the gestation and nursing period and then fed it to the young rats until they had reached maturity. Even under these strenuous conditions the brain phosphatides contained only one-fourth as much elaidic acid as was present in the liver and the muscle phosphatides of the same animals. Waelsch, Sperry and Stoyanoff (1940), in essential agreement with these observations, found that deuterium-containing fatty acids could not be detected in the brain of rats into which was injected heavy water.

Sinclair (1941) concluded that the maximum elaidic acid content of the intestines was reached after one day's feeding. As would be expected the liver was provided with its maximum amount of elaidic acid shortly afterwards, 84 per cent of the maximum having been achieved in one day. The kidneys and muscle exhibited considerably slower replacement, for one-half of the maximum uptake was observed in these organs after one and one-half days and three days, respectively. Rapid replacement of the fatty acids of plasma phosphatides was shown (Sinclair, 1936) by the observation that 30 per cent turnover occurred a few hours after ingestion of elaidic acid. The phosphatides of the red blood cells, on the other hand, contained no elaidic acid. Likewise, the skeletal muscles, like the brain and the testes, took up elaidic acid very slowly (Sinclair, 1935b). This phosphatide turnover rate as measured by fatty acid replacement is in essential agreement, as Sinclair (1941) points out, with the results obtained by radioactive phosphorus studies.

In a further study, Sinclair (1940a) determined the uptake of elaidic acid by the lecithin and cephalin fractions of the rat liver. The work must be considered in the light of the obvious complexity of the cephalin fraction and the practical limitations involved in obtaining pure phosphatides, especially in small-scale experiments. His results, observed over a period of 12 hours to 8 weeks, showed that the uptake by lecithin was slightly higher than by the cephalin fraction, although the actual similarity was very marked. Chargaff, Olson and Partington (1940) observed with the aid of radioactive phosphorus that lecithin formed in rat livers more rapidly than did the cephalin fraction. A similar study by Hevesy and Hahn (1940) and Hahn and Tyrén (1945) using radioactive phosphorus showed that in rat and rabbit livers the turnover rate was considerably greater in the cephalin fraction up to the twelfth hour. Thereafter the rate for lecithin and the cephalin fraction became identical and remained so. These workers also investigated other organs and showed, for example, for the brain that the turnover rate in the cephalin fraction was greater than that for lecithin even after several days. On this basis they postulated the presence of at least two components in the cephalin fraction. The sphingomyelin fraction, likewise, was observed to exhibit a rather rapid turnover rate, especially in the muscles, which is perhaps explainable on the basis that tissue components, regardless of their metabolic activity, exist in a dynamic state.

Haven (1937) has shown that elaidic acid enters the phosphatides of Carcinoma 256 at a rate intermediate between its entry into liver and muscle phosphatide. This, too, is in accord with observations made with radioactive phosphorus.

Sinclair (1935b) concluded from his early work that the more unsaturated phosphatides function as essential elements of cell composition, whereas the less unsaturated ones are intermediary products in fatty acid metabolism. Such a clear-cut division, however, no longer appears tenable in view of the complex relationships outlined in the above general discussion of lipide metabolism. Insight into the speed with which tissue constituents are replaced or regenerated makes it impossible to visualize a static structural element.

Sinclair concluded also that the tissues in which the rate of elaidic acid uptake is greatest are the ones most vitally concerned with lipide metabolism, an observation which has been borne out by other investigations.

Miscellaneous Fatty Acid Labels in the Study of Phosphatide Metabolism. Labels other than elaidic acid have been used in attempts to determine the role of ingested fatty acids in phosphatide metabolism. Highly unsaturated acids have been used (Sinclair, 1934), but the value of this work is limited by the apparent ability of phosphatides to extract from the diet highly unsaturated fatty acids in preference to all other acids. Accordingly, one cannot be sure that a normal course is being followed. Iodine-containing fatty acids have been shown by Artom (1933) and Artom and Peretti (1932, 1933, 1935, 1936) to enter the phosphatides of liver, blood corpuscles and plasma, intestinal mucosa and milk. Interpretation of such work is limited by the instability of iodinated fats and the opportunity present for the exchange of iodine between fatty acids. Furthermore, iodinated fatty acids are chemically different from ordinary ones, for which reason the body may metabolize them differently.

Conjugated Acids. Conjugated fatty acids are of interest as labels since they are readily detected by their characteristic absorption spectra. Nevertheless, the body may alter the conjugated structure of the acids, making it necessary to perform experiments of short duration. In addition, the limitations mentioned above for other fatty acid labels apply here. Conjugated fatty acids which have been used as labels include eleostearic acid from tung oil (Miller and Burr, 1937) and corn oil acids conjugated by treatment with alkali (Miller and co-workers, 1939). These acids fed orally were shown by Barnes, Miller and Burr (1941) to enter into the glyceride and phosphatide fractions of intestinal mucosa. The neutral fat exhibited a greater affinity for these acids, maximum replacement (50 per cent) resulting in one hour. The phosphatides, on the other hand, exhibited 15 per cent replacement after eight hours.

Fatty Acids Labeled with Radioactive Atoms. Perhaps the most satisfactory type of fatty acid label, although one which has not enjoyed wide usage, is a fatty acid which contains isotopic carbon or hydrogen atoms. Cavanagh and Raper (1939) treated linseed oil with deuterium to obtain a glyceryl ester containing 4.87 per cent deuterium. These fatty acids after ingestion by rats were readily incorporated into the phosphatides of the liver, kidney, brain, blood corpuscles and blood plasma. Deuterium concentration was measured after 6, 10 and 24 hours, and at all times the concentration in the liver was highest. The kidney phosphatides contained about one-third as much deuterium as the liver phosphatides, whereas very low incorporation was demonstrated by brain phosphatides, as was the case with elaidic acid. Since the plasma phosphatides contained less deuterium at the end of six hours than did the liver phosphatides, it was suggested that the liver was the site of incorporation of deuterium-containing acids. Experiments with isotopic phosphorus (see p. 383) led to like conclusions.

Barrett, Best and Ridout (1938) conducted similar experiments and observed the incorporation of deuterium-containing acids into both the phosphatides and neutral fat of the liver, the liver phosphatides containing nearly three times as much deuterium as the body phosphatides.

Results of a similar nature are also recorded by Sperry, Waelsch and Stoyanoff (1940), who showed that ingestion of deuterium-treated linseed oil led to the appearance of large quantities of the labeled acids in the liver and the small intestine, and only minute quantities in the brain.

More recently, palmitic acid containing C^{14} in the sixth carbon atom has been used in feeding experiments as a labeled fatty acid (Lerner and co-workers, 1949, 1949a). The acid was synthesized by Dauben (1948) and converted to a triglyceride and emulsified. The emulsion was administered parenterally to rats. The experiment served to show that the fat introduced into the blood stream directly was available for caloric purposes since expired carbon dioxide contained isotopic carbon. In addition, 50 per cent of the labeled fatty acids were recovered in the liver after 24 hours, thus serving to corroborate the experiments described above. The labeled acids were also found in the phosphatides of the small intestine.

Choline and Aminoethyl Alcohol Labels in the Study of Phosphatide Metabolism. Experiments employing, as labels, choline containing isotopic nitrogen or choline in which the nitrogen atom has been replaced by arsenic are chiefly of interest in studies concerned with lipotropism (see p. 418). They are mentioned here in order to provide a complete account of labeling techniques. Stetten (1942) fed choline containing N^{15} to rats and observed after three days that 21 per cent of the choline in the phosphatides of the entire animal had been replaced. Similarly, with aminoethyl alcohol containing N^{15}, 28 per cent or more replacement was observed. As would be expected, the phosphatides of the liver demonstrated the greatest activity. Somewhat less was shown by the phosphatides of the gastrointestinal tract, whereas brain phosphatides, in accord with previously described results, underwent a very slow rate of reversal.

Channon and co-workers (1937) fed an ethyl analogue of choline, triethyl-β-hydroxyethylammonium hydroxide, to rats with fatty livers. Although the material exerted lipotropic action, it could not be detected in the liver phosphatides. Too much weight, however, cannot be based on experiments with choline analogues since the body might well subject these unnatural substances to a metabolic route difference from that experienced by choline.

Radioactive Phosphorus in the Study of Phosphatide Metabolism. The availability of radioactive phosphorus as a tracer element has relegated to positions of lesser importance the labels discussed above, although the fact must not be overlooked that the correlation of the activity of labels in various fragments of the phosphatide molecule will prove fruitful. Especially is this true when one considers that a phosphatide molecule is probably not formed from its components simultaneously. Probably the molecule is assembled more or less in random fashion, for which reason the turnover of any given label measures only the rate at which the labeled component is introduced into the molecule.

The virtue of a tracer isotope such as P^{32} depends on its ability to impart to a compound a unique means for identification without altering in any way the chemical properties or physiological reactions of the compound. Most of the fatty acid tracers discussed above cannot fulfill entirely this prerequisite, for which reason newer metabolism studies requiring tracers with a wide range of applicability have employed isotopic elements to the virtual exclusion of other labels. The application of this technique is not simple but requires careful analytical control and wise judgment in the interpretation of data. In addition, the specific use of isotopic elements in studies of phosphatide metabolism makes necessary the isolation of microquantities of phosphatides in pure form (see p. 153). Hevesy (1948) and Chaikoff (1942) have discussed in detail the techniques involved in the application of isotopic tracers to the solution of chemical and biological problems.

Most of the experiments using P[32] have involved the administration of radioactive inorganic phosphate to an animal followed by the measurement of the rate at which the isotopic element is incorporated into the phosphatides of the various tissues. As will be seen below, some workers (Zilversmit and co-workers, 1943) have generated phosphatides containing P[32] in blood plasma of dogs by administering radioactive inorganic phosphate to them. They have then used this plasma as a source of labeled phosphatide for administration to other test animals. Phosphatides labeled with P[32] have been isolated from the organs of animals which have ingested inorganic radioactive phosphate (Haven and Bale, 1939; Artom and Swanson, 1948). The use of these in tracer studies has been successful, although hydrolysis appears to be a limiting factor.

The terminology involved in the use of labels in the study of metabolic activity has been outlined by Chaikoff (1942). *Phosphatide turnover* is the process of phosphatide renewal or replacement in tissue and may include the processes of uptake, synthesis, decomposition and outgo. Phosphatide renewal, however, applies only to the replacement of that component of the phosphatide which contains the label being studied. *Phosphatide turnover rate* is the percentage of phosphatide renewed per unit of time. It must take into account the breakdown not only of the unlabeled phosphatide but also of the phosphatide formed during the experiment at the expense of the labeling agent. *Complete phosphatide turnover time* is the time required for the synthesis or accumulation of labeled phosphatide equal in quantity to that present in the organ in the steady state.

The use of radioactive inorganic phosphorus as a label obviously offers no information as to whether a phosphatide molecule in the organism found to contain P[32] is formed by the exchange of a phosphoric group in a preformed molecule or whether a new union of structural elements has occurred. In other words, the path of conversion of inorganic phosphate to phosphatide remains yet to be determined. In an interesting experiment, Chargaff and Keston (1940) injected subcutaneously into rats disodium aminoethyl phosphate labeled with P[32]. Since the label appeared largely in lecithin rather than the cephalin fraction, it may be concluded that the organic compound was hydrolyzed and the P[32] was utilized as inorganic phosphate. On the other hand, Chaikoff (1942) describes work of Taurog which showed that glycerophosphate and aminoethylphosphate labeled with P[32] were incorporated into the phosphatides of liver and kidney, both *in vivo* and *in vitro*, thus providing no clue as to the probability of initial breakdown and resynthesis.

The initial results of experiments with P[32] parallel rather well the results obtained with elaidic acid even though these labels measure turnover of different parts of the molecule. When isotopic inorganic phosphate is administered to test animals it may be readily detected in the phosphatides of the organism within a few hours. One of the early studies which proved this was carried out by Perlman, Ruben and Chaikoff (1937). These workers fed radioactive phosphate and cod liver oil to rats which previously had been starved for 30 to 40 hours. The animals were then sacrificed at intervals and the phosphatides were isolated from the various tissues and analyzed for P^{32} content. In the total phosphatides of the animal the radioactive phosphorus content rose sharply in the first 15 hours, after which a gradual leveling occurred. At the end of 50 hours, 80 per cent of the maximum amount of labeled phosphatide formed was present and this quantity remained constant throughout the duration of the experiment (100 hours). This of course does not preclude utilization of the synthesized phosphatide by the various tissues.

Labeled phosphatide accumulated very rapidly in the liver and the gastrointestinal tract, the maximum quantity appearing in about five hours in the former tissue and in about ten hours in the latter. In both tissues, rapid decline followed the accumulation of the maximum quantity. This decline continued in the liver throughout the duration of the experiment (100 hours), whereas in the gastrointestinal tract, a "steady state" was reached after the fiftieth hour. The kidney demonstrated a somewhat slower accumulation of labeled phosphatide, the maximum appearing after 15 hours. Here, also, gradual decline was noted throughout the term of the experiment.

The brain demonstrated the slowest and smallest response to labeled phosphatide formation. The maximum was not reached until 60 hours after feeding and the concentration of P^{32} soon declined to the extent that accurate measurement was precluded. The animal, less the tissues mentioned above, was termed the "carcass", and the rate of phosphatide formation was studied here also. The labeled phosphatides in the carcass increased continually and had not yet reached a steady state after 102 hours. Since the carcass was largely muscle, it must be concluded either that the rate of formation of phosphatides in the muscle is very low, or else that the phosphatides, once formed, find it difficult to penetrate into the muscle cell.

Thus it appears from this study that when cod-liver oil is available in the diet, phosphatides form most rapidly in the liver and gastrointestinal tract and more slowly in the kidney, brain and carcass, the latter being largely muscle tissue. The question of which of these tissues actually synthesize phosphatides and which merely accumulate them is not entirely settled, although the work of Fishler and co-workers (1943) proves that synthesis takes place in the liver, intestines and kidneys. The rate of disappearance of the phosphatides was greatest in the liver, somewhat less in the intestine and least in the kidney.

In experiments concurrent with those described above, Perlman, Ruben and Chaikoff (1937) administered radioactive phosphate to rats in the absence of cod-liver oil feeding. Thus phosphatide formation was truly endogenous except possibly in the intestine where traces of fat may have been present despite the period of fasting. It was thus demonstrated that the rate of phosphatide formation in the liver, kidney and carcass is barely affected by the presence of ingested fat. In the gastrointestinal tract, however, considerably less phosphatide formed in the absence of cod-liver oil feeding.

That radioactive phosphorus may be detected in the phosphatides of the blood after ingestion was shown by Hevesy and Lundsgaard (1937). Thus these early investigations left little doubt that radioactive phosphorus is an effective labeling agent, and in initial experiments, results paralleled fairly well those obtained with elaidic acid.

Artom and co-workers (1937, 1937a) and Perrier and co-workers (1937) who worked only with single rats injected parenterally radioactive inorganic phosphorus in a rat on a non-fat diet and also included it in the diet of a rat receiving large amounts of lipide. In the first instance P^{32} was detected quickly and in large quantities in the liver, intestine and kidney. The parenchymous organs, which include pancreas, adrenals, testes and lungs, demonstrated medium activity in both rate and amount of uptake, whereas a very sluggish response to the labeling agent was shown by muscle, brain and medulla.

When fat was included in the diet, P^{32} uptake was very high—i.e., more phosphatides were formed in the liver and the intestine. Sufficient labeled material was available from the liver to allow a crude fractionation into a lecithin fraction and a cephalin fraction. The former predominated in a ratio of 4:1. The uptake of labeled atom by the kidney phosphatides was less when the diet contained lipides than when it did not. Likewise, uptake by the parenchymous organs and muscle was very sluggish although the experiment involving the high lipide diet lasted only nine hours. In a later publication (Artom and co-workers, 1937b) it was reported that lipides in the diet did not affect the activity of P^{32} in the parenchymous organs. It was pointed out in these papers that these experiments left little doubt that complete phosphatide synthesis was possible in the body. This work was in essential agreement with that of Perlman, Ruben and Chaikoff (1937), although the latter workers used more rats and allowed the experiments to proceed for much longer periods of time, thus allowing them to determine when maximum activity was reached. From all these observations it may be concluded that the highest percentage of labeled phosphatides, subsequent to the administration of radioactive inorganic phosphorus, is found in the liver and intestinal tract. The kidneys are somewhat less active, and these are followed by the eviscerated carcass and the brain.

The work described above proved that uptake of labeled phosphorus by the phosphatides of the gastrointestinal tract was rapid. Since this region consists of several tissues differing both structurally and functionally, Fries and co-workers (1938) examined the rates of phosphatide turnover in the stomach, small intestine and large intestine of rats. They found that the major portion of the phosphatide turnover exhibited by the gastrointestinal tract took place in the small intestine, the phosphatides of the stomach and the large intestine absorbing slowly small quantities of the labeled atom. This proved to be the case in both the absence and presence of fats.

These workers also studied the turnover of radioactive phosphorus in the liver phosphatides of rats in which both the kidney and the gastrointestinal tracts were excised. The activity under these circumstances was very similar to normal activity despite the fact that two of the three tissues most active in phosphatide turnover had been removed. This makes it possible to attribute to the liver the ability to synthesize as well as to accumulate phosphatides.

Entenman and co-workers (1938) studied the uptake of radioactive phosphorus by the various tissues of laying and nonlaying birds. The label was administered by subcutaneous injection of inorganic phosphate marked with P^{32} into Leghorns. The tissues were examined after 6- and 12-hour intervals. As in previous experiments, the phosphatides of the liver, kidney and small intestine showed the greatest uptake in the shortest period of time. Likewise, the small intestine exhibited much greater activity than did the other portions of the gastrointestinal tract. The authors point out that although phosphatide activity in blood, muscle and bone was low, their amount is such that 2 per cent of the administered labeled phosphorus was found therein as compared to 5 per cent for the phosphatides of the entire organism. The phosphatides of cardiac muscle demonstrated greater activity than did those of skeletal muscle.

In laying birds, increased phosphatide activity was observed in the blood, ovary and oviduct. The latter organ increased 12- to 16-fold in size and this increase was associated with a marked increase in its ability to deposit labeled phosphatide .Other workers (see p. 307) have correlated increased phosphatide content with increased tissue function. The labeled atom was detected in egg yolk phosphatides as early as six hours after injection. This observation was also made by Hevesy and Hahn (1938).

Dols and co-workers (1938, 1939) injected radioactive sodium phosphate into normal and rachitic rats and measured the uptake of the label by the entire animal. Rachitic rats were found to contain more labeled phosphatide but less total P^{32} than normal rats. The lipide phosphorus content of normal rats weighing 35 to 40 grams was approximately 11 per cent of the total phosphorus content.

Several studies have been directed at determining the rate of P^{32} uptake by specific phosphatides. As indicated previously, Artom and co-workers (1937) found four times as much labeled lecithin as cephalin fraction in the liver of a rat fed radioactive phosphate. In a more careful study, Chargaff (1939) found that the rates of lecithin and cephalin fraction formation in the entire rat, subsequent to ingestion of radioactive phosphorus, were approximately equal. In the various tissues, however, vast differences were noted. The intestinal tract was found to contain almost twice as much labeled lecithin as cephalin fraction, 24 hours after the time of feeding. Similarly, in agreement with Artom and co-workers (1937) and with Perlman, Ruben and Chaikoff (1937), the liver was found to contain significantly larger amounts of labeled lecithin. In the brain and the eviscerated carcass the quantities of the two phosphatide fractions in this study were approximately equal. Since these comprise the bulk of the phosphatides, the differences exhibited by the gastrointestinal tract and the liver were not apparent in the analysis of the phosphatides of the total rat. In a later study, Chargaff, Olson and Partington (1940) found in the brain that the cephalin fraction formed to a greater extent than did lecithin.

Different results were reported by Hevesy and Hahn (1940), who injected labeled inorganic phosphate intravenously into rabbits, chickens, rats and frogs. They found that the cephalin fraction of the liver had a higher rate of turnover than did lecithin. After 12 hours, however, both fractions demonstrated the same activity. In muscle and brain, several days were required before the rate of turnover of the phosphorus of both fractions reached equal activity. Sphingomyelin phosphorus exhibited a lower turnover rate in the liver and a faster turnover rate in the muscles than did the other phosphatides.

In a later publication, Hahn and Tyrén (1945) reported that 20.4 per cent of the lecithin phosphorus and 18.6 per cent of the cephalin fraction phosphorus of rat liver was renewed after four hours. In rabbit liver the percentages were 6.3 and 6.0, respectively.

Hunter (1941), who studied the effect of oral administration of P^{32} on sphingomyelin, found the largest amount of incorporation in the sphingomyelin of the liver, lungs and intestinal mucosa. In most tissues maximum replacement occurred in about two days. It was observed in the liver that the sphingomyelin renewal rate was much lower than the corresponding rate for the total phosphatide fraction. In the kidney, however, the same rate of renewal was found for all the phosphatide fractions (Hunter and Levy, 1942).

Metabolic Activity of Phosphatides of Various Organs and Tissues

Metabolic Activity of Blood Phosphatides. The importance of blood lipides in biochemical processes is attested to by the vast amount of literature in this field. The lipides of the blood have already been considered in some detail in Part IV. Peters and Van Slyke (1946, p. 467 ff.) and Bloor (1943, p. 115 ff.) have also discussed this subject extensively.

Phosphatides, as pointed out by Frazer (1946), are important in maintaining the physical state of blood since they provide stabilizing films for the other lipide particles, thus preventing their flocculation in the presence of plasma protein.

Effect of Dietary Factors on Blood Phosphatides. The lipides of normal plasma are characterized by high percentages of phosphatides and cholesterol esters and small amounts of triglyceryl esters. About one-half of the phosphatide fraction of plasma appears to be lecithin (see p. 259), one-fifth appears to be phosphatidylaminoethyl alcohol, and the remainder is divided between phosphatidylserine and sphingomyelin (Artom, 1945). The lipide composition of the red blood cells is less well defined (see p. 262), although there is little doubt that the phosphatides are present in even greater quantity than in the plasma. Erickson and co-workers (1937) have published the analyses of lipides of plasma and red blood cells of children.

After ingestion of large quantities of fat, the fatty acids of blood plasma and corpuscles exhibit a sharp rise. Bloor (1915, 1922, 1933) is responsible for the initial observation of this phenomenon. According to Man and Gildea (1932), neutral fat accounts for most of this increase, although a small but definite increase was noted for the phosphatide fraction. Wendt (1932) noted a sharp increase in phosphatide and cholesterol content of the plasma of normal men four hours after massive doses of olive oil had been administered. No increase at all was noted in the lipides of the red blood cells. Artom and Peretti (1932), on the other hand, found that iodized fat taken orally or intravenously increased the iodized glycerides and iodized phosphatides in the corpuscles to a greater extent than in the plasma. Artom and Freeman (1940) have reported that the increase in phosphatides in blood plasma of rabbits noted during olive oil diets is due entirely to an increase in lecithin content. They found that the cephalin fraction may actually decrease, whereas sphingomyelin behavior was inconsistent. On the other hand, Artom (1941) found that the slight increase in phosphatide content of human plasma after ingestion of milk and cream was due to the cephalin fraction rather than the choline-containing phosphatides. Brante (1940) is of the opinion that the plasma lecithin and cephalin fraction increase equally during alimentary lipemia. In general, marked increases in blood lipides are noted only when large quantities of fat are administered. With lesser quantities of fat the effect is less marked, and is presumably of shorter duration, although there is insufficient evidence for this in the literature.

Several workers (Eichhaltz, 1924; Pasternak and Page, 1932; Sueyoshi and Okonogi, 1934) have reported a slight increase in the phosphatide content of blood plasma after the feeding or injection of phosphatides. Adlersberg and Sobotka (1943), on the other hand, found in cases of sprue that the lipides of plasma were greatly increased after the addition of lecithin to a fatty meal containing Vitamin A. Similarly, Flock, Corwin and Bollman (1938) had observed that addition of crude phosphatides from adrenal glands to a fatty diet increased the neutral fat of blood serum two to three times. The cholesterol and phosphatides increased to a lesser degree. The diet without the phosphatides did not affect the blood lipides.

When dogs were subjected to continued over-nutrition, it was observed by Entenman and Chaikoff (1942) that total fatty acids and phosphatides of the blood serum increased slightly, whereas some question existed regarding the behavior of the cholesterol.

Malnutrition due either to inadequate diet or to wasting diseases causes a decrease in the cholesterol and phosphatide content of blood plasma, according to Man and Gildea (1936) and Entenman and co-workers (1940). The cholesterol appears to undergo the greatest decrease. In extensive starvation in the rat, Sure, Kik and Church (1933) reported that the fatty acids and phosphatides of blood plasma declined appreciably, whereas the cholesterol remained constant. Lipide content of plasma during acute starvation of dogs remained relatively constant, according to Entenman and co-workers (1940). In chronic malnutrition, however, the phosphatide, cholesterol and fatty acid levels of the blood fell considerably. Izzo and Marenzi (1943) noted that acute fasting had no constant effect on the lipides of dog plasma. On the other hand, Hodge and co-workers (1947) have observed a moderate lipemia in the fasting mouse until the fifth day, after which a decrease in plasma lipide was noted. The blood phosphatide content increased accordingly until the fourth day and fell on the fifth. This confirms previous work of Mac-Lachlan (1944). The data of Kartin and co-workers (1944) are of interest. These workers found, as in some of the above work, that after two days of starvation, cholesterol and lipide phosphorus of human serum increased considerably. Neutral fat changes were inconsistent. There seemed to be a correlation, although not a direct one, between increase in lipide content and production of ketone bodies in serum.

It would be expected that starvation, initially, would produce the same effect on the blood lipides as a high fat diet, for in starvation the fat depots are called upon to mobilize large quantities of lipides since these are the sole means of energy production. As starvation proceeds to the extent that the fat depots are depleted, the blood lipide content and distribution should resemble that found in severe malnutrition. Definitive experimentation on these points remains yet to be accomplished.

Effect of Drugs and Biological Substances on Blood Phosphatides. Flock and Bollman (1942) observed that administration to cocks of the synthetic estrogen, diethylstilbestrol, increased appreciably the phosphatide content of blood plasma after one week. When the drug was removed from the diet, normal values resulted. The ratio of choline-containing phosphatides to cephalin fraction was not altered appreciably during the period of increased production, yet the cephalin fraction decreased somewhat more rapidly upon cessation of administration of the estrogen. The increase may be due either to stimulation of synthesis or to an inhibition of phosphatide destruction. Investigation of the problem with the aid of P^{32} by Flock and Bollman (1944) led to the conclusion that diethylstilbestrol caused an increase in both synthesis and utilization of plasma phosphatides. Ranney, Entenman and Chaikoff (1949) have observed a similar effect in chicks. They found that the lecithin and cephalin fractions of the plasma of the domestic fowl increased sixfold after administration of diethylstilbestrol, thus indicating metabolic activity for both of these phosphatides. The sphingomyelin content, on the other hand, showed relatively little change. A different effect was observed in female rats by Cardini and Serantes (1943), who reported that the over-all phosphatide content decreased after injection of stilbestrol, but that the phosphatide content of the blood plasma did not change.

The natural female sex hormones have likewise been found to influence blood lipide levels. Loeb (1942) found that large doses of estradiol benzoate increased the lipide content of the serum of rats whose diet included saturated but not unsaturated fatty acids. With ordinary diets, the effect was not observed. According to Bogdanovitch and Man (1938), estrone and antuitrin-S cause the fatty acids of guinea pig blood and liver to increase but do not affect the cholesterol and phosphatides. The male sex hormones, conversely, do not appear to exert any effect on blood lipide levels, as shown by Looney and Romanoff (1940).

Insulin does not affect the total blood lipide concentrations in the normal individual, according to Rony and Ching (1930), although it inhibits lipemia due to fat ingestion. Conversely, Page, Pasternak and Burt (1931) reported that the phosphatides of serum decreased 30 per cent after administration of insulin.

Munoz (1933) found that repeated injections of crude extract of the anterior lobe of the hypophysis increased the fatty acid, cholesterol and phosphatide content of the blood of normal and thyroidectomized dogs. Foglia and Mazzoco (1938), likewise, reported hyperlipemia as a consequence of injection of this material, although in their work the effect was due largely to increase in neutral fat. An increase in liver and muscle lipides was also noted. Raab (1934) claimed the isolation of a substance from both the anterior and posterior lobes of the hypophysis which lowers the lipide content of blood. This, however, has never been confirmed.

Bloor (1914, 1916a) observed a rise in blood lipides following ether anesthesia. All the constituent lipides increased proportionately. Since Mahler (1926) observed that the hyperlipemia was alleviated by insulin, it follows that the ether probably serves to inhibit carbohydrate metabolism.

Lehnherr (1935) reported that phosphorus and carbon tetrachloride, because they promote hepatic disfunction, cause hyperlipemia followed by hypolipemia if the damage is sufficiently severe. In both conditions, however, the phosphatide content is reduced and is low compared to the triglyceride and cholesterol content. Lehnherr (1935) has reported that hypolipemia results from chloroform poisoning. Oral administration of bile salts for 14 days was observed by Tashiro and Schmidt (1931) to cause a decrease in blood lipide phosphorus.

Kellner, Correll and Ladd (1949) and Ladd, Kellner and Correll (1949) have observed a sustained elevation of blood cholesterol and phosphatide in rabbits subsequent to the intravenous injection of detergents. These injections appeared to be valuable in atherosclerosis therapy.

Chanutin and Gjessling (1949) subjected rats to partial hepatectomy, laparotomy, scalding, and the action of tris(β-chloroethyl)-amine. They found that the total lipide, phosphatide and cholesterol concentrations in the plasma were elevated slightly under these conditions, and that the elevation was most marked during periods of liver regeneration.

Effect of Pregnancy and Menstruation on Blood Phosphatides. The lecithin content of the blood of pregnant women was observed to be higher than normal by Chatterjee and Ghosh (1940). Baumann and Holly (1926) had previously observed that in rabbits, unlike in human beings, pregnancy causes the blood phosphatides and cholesterol to diminish. They believed that the decrease is occasioned by a corresponding increase in the mammary gland. In the dog they found that blood lipides were not affected by pregnancy.

Okey (1925) and Kaufmann and Mühlbock (1929) have observed that the phosphatide content of blood is not altered by menstruation, although the cholesterol content decreases. Davanzo (1936) found that the lecithin content of blood is not affected by the menstrual cycle.

Turnover of Blood Phosphatides. As already mentioned (see p. 374), Hevesy and Lundsgaard (1937) detected radioactive phosphorus in the blood phosphatides after administration of P^{32}. Previously, Sinclair (1936) had fed elaidin to cats and had detected elaidic acid in the blood plasma phosphatides within a few hours. After continued feeding for several days, he found that 37 per cent of the phosphatide fatty acids had been replaced by elaidic acid. He concluded from these experiments that plasma phosphatides serve as a mechanism for the transport of fatty acids to the tissues for utilization. The phosphatides of the red blood cells contained only minute amounts of elaidic acid after extensive feeding of elaidin, thus indicating that they possess low metabolic activity.

Several other experimenters have confirmed and extended these results. Hevesy and Hahn (1940) observed also that labeled inorganic phosphorus was readily incorporated into the plasma phosphatides. Fishler and co-workers (1943) determined that 0.1 to 0.5 per cent of injected radioactive phosphorus was incorporated per gram into plasma phosphatides 6 to 98 hours after administration.

As would be expected from Sinclair's (1936) work, the phosphatides of the corpuscles incorporate P^{32} at a much slower rate than do the phosphatides of the plasma. This was observed by Hevesy and Hahn (1940) and by Hevesy and Aten (1939). The latter workers showed by means of radioactive phosphorus that the laying bird in 28 hours renews only one-third as much of its corpuscle phosphatides as of its plasma phosphatides. Similarly, in man, eight days are required before the specific activity of the lipide phosphorus of the corpuscles is one-half that of the plasma.

Since plasma phosphatide is formed in the liver (see p. 383), its formation in the blood directly would probably not be expected. Accordingly, Hahn and Hevesy (1938) found, after shaking dog's blood with radioactive inorganic phosphorus for 4.5 hours, that only about 0.3 milligram per cent radioactive phosphatide formed. This is very small in comparison with the notable quantities which appear after administration of radioactive phosphorus to an animal.

The exchange of phosphatides between plasma and corpuscles has been shown to be slight by Hahn and Hevesy (1939). Thus plasma from rabbits into which had been injected inorganic P^{32} was shaken with rabbit blood cells. Only 5 per cent of the red blood cell phosphatides was exchanged in 4.5 hours. Thus it was concluded that the red blood cell phosphatides are incorporated at the time of formation of the cells and are not totally replaced during the lifetime of the cells.

Hevesy and Hahn (1938) were also concerned with the role of blood plasma in phosphatide transport. Because of the above observation it may be concluded that the cells are not actively engaged in transporting phosphatides. Accordingly, the burden rests with the plasma, whose significance in this regard was established by showing that in the laying hen the plasma must transport to the eggs 1500 milligrams of phosphatide per day. This is particularly striking since the total phosphatide content of the plasma of the hen is only 500 milligrams.

The rate of disappearance from rabbit plasma of labeled phosphatides introduced intravenously has been studied by Hahn and Hevesy (1939a). The labeled phosphatide was obtained from the blood of animals to which had previously been administered inorganic P^{32}. These workers found that the plasma gave up its phosphatide quickly, one-half of the labeled material having disappeared in one and one-half hours. Analysis of various tissues showed that the liver was most active in the removal of the phosphatide. Lesser activity was exhibited by the lungs, kidneys, spleen, heart, small intestine, brain and muscles. Essentially similar results were obtained by Zilversmit and co-workers (1943), who worked with dogs. In their experiments, 40 to 50 per cent of the injected labeled phosphatides disappeared from the plasma in five hours, and approximately one-third of this was found in the liver. They found further that 76 to 83 per cent of the injected labeled phosphatides could be found in the seven tissues which they analyzed. This suggests that phosphatide decomposition in the animal tissue is not a very rapid process.

Haven and Bale (1939) carried out work of a similar nature using labeled phosphatides isolated from the liver of rats into which had been injected radioactive inorganic phosphorus. They noted considerable hydrolysis of their phosphatides, but were still able to determine that the liver and spleen, and to a lesser degree the lungs, were active in removal of the labeled phosphatide from the blood. Of significance is similar work of Entenman, Chaikoff and Zilversmit (1946). These workers showed by measuring the rate of disappearance of labeled phosphatides that 6 to 10 hours were required for complete turnover of phosphatides in the plasma of normal dogs weighing 7 to 18 kilograms. Thereafter they excluded the liver from the route of blood circulation and found that the complete turnover time was prolonged to 33 to 160 hours. They had previously shown that the phosphatide content of plasma is not appreciably decreased when blood was made to by-pass the liver. Thus it follows, unequivocally, that the liver is the chief tissue in the body concerned with removal of plasma phosphatides. It is also (see below) the principal source of plasma lipide.

The actual turnover time of plasma lecithin and sphingomyelin of the dog has been determined by Zilversmit, Entenman and Chaikoff (1948). Their results varied from 6 to 11 hours for lecithin and 10 to 13 hours for sphingomyelin and were based on a procedure which determined the rate at which phosphatides are delivered to the plasma by the liver. Subsequently they (Zilversmit, Entenman and Chaikoff 1948a) determined turnover time by measuring the rate of disappearance of labeled phosphatide from the plasma of the dog. By this method the turnover time for lecithin was found to be 10 to 13 hours and for sphingomyelin 10 to 27 hours. Six determinations were made. In addition, turnover rates for these two plasma phosphatides were calculated. In six determinations the turnover rate for lecithin varied from 4.0 to 5.6 milligrams of phosphorus per hour. The corresponding range for sphingomyelin was 0.4 to 1.0. Thus it is seen that the rate of turnover of plasma lecithin is more than five times as great as that for sphingomyelin.

The fate of the phosphatides removed from the blood by various tissues has been investigated by Reinhardt, Fishler and Chaikoff (1944). They injected labeled phosphatides into the blood stream of dogs and showed that 9 to 20 per cent of this material could be recovered after 3 to 6 hours in thoracic duct lymph. Thus it follows that a measurable portion of the phosphatides which are removed from the blood pass through one or more tissues on their way to the lymph channels, from whence they are returned to the blood. Prerequisite to this conclusion is the important observation that phosphatide molecules can pass a capillary membrane such as that provided by the thoracic duct.

Origin of Blood Phosphatides. The experiments of several investigators (Hevesy and Aten, 1939; Hevesy and Hahn, 1940; Fishler and co-workers, 1943) have shown that the specific activity of the phosphatide phosphorus of the plasma is greatly exceeded by that of the liver. Furthermore, the specific activity of the phosphatide phosphorus of the liver exceeded that of any other tissue. These observations were compatible with the theory that plasma phosphatides originated in the liver, although they were not absolute proof thereof. The observation of Nedswedsky and Alexandry (1928) that the venous blood leaving the liver contained more phosphatide than the portal blood entering it was not in accord with the work of Leites (1927).

Accordingly, to obtain more nearly absolute proof, Fishler and co-workers (1943) studied the phosphatide turnover in the hepatectomized dog which had been fed radioactive inorganic phosphorus. The recovery of labeled phosphatide from the kidney and small intestine proved that phosphatide was synthesized in these tissues as well as in the liver, at least under the conditions of the experiment. The recovery of only negligible amounts of labeled phosphatide from blood plasma, however, left little doubt that the liver was the primary source of plasma phosphatides.

In further experiments, Friedlander, Chaikoff and Entenman (1945) fed choline to dogs on a high-fat, low-protein diet and thereafter determined lipide phosphorus activity in various tissues by following the course of injected radioactive phosphorus. Their results indicated that phosphatide turnover was accelerated in the plasma after choline feeding, and the authors attributed this directly to the increased activity which was first observed under these conditions in the liver. In further work, Entenman, Chaikoff and Friedlander (1946) determined the effect of choline feeding on the specific activities of the choline-containing and noncholine-containing phosphatides of the liver of the dog. Their results showed that the specific activity of the former was accelerated, whereas that of the latter was depressed. Since it had already been shown that choline feeding increases the specific activity of plasma phosphatides, and since these workers believe that plasma phosphatides are largely choline-containing, further evidence was provided to support the conclusion that the liver is the source of the plasma phosphatides in the dog.

In a subsequent paper, Zilversmit, Entenman and Chaikoff (1948) point out that the increase in specific activity that was observed in the choline-containing lipide phosphorus of plasma could result from increased phosphatide turnover or could reflect an increase in the specific activity of the phosphatide precursors. The latter situation would not require an actual increase in the turnover of the phosphatides. Accordingly, they measured the actual turnover rates and found that there was no increase after administration of choline in plasma choline or sphingomyelin. On the other hand, choline was found to stimulate lecithin turnover in the liver. These observations which correlate actual lecithin turnover in the plasma with lecithin turnover in the liver are very important in view of the fact that plasma phosphatides originate in the liver. Ordinarily one might expect increased turnover in the liver to be reflected in the plasma. Since this is not so, it would appear that the lipotropic action of choline (see p. 413) depends not on the ability of the choline to increase fat transport of phosphatides from the liver to the plasma, but rather on the ability of the choline to stimulate the utilization of lipides by the liver itself.

Phosphatides as Transport Agents for Fatty Acids. The suggestion (see p. 340) has frequently been made that phosphatides function as transport agents for fatty acids throughout the body. Experimentation, however, has cast doubt on this suggestion just as it has on the concept that phosphatides are agents for the transport of fatty acids across the intestinal wall (see p. 347). The older work has been discussed by Page (1937, p. 86), and for the most part is of slight value.

It is perhaps significant that fatty acids in normal blood, at least during fasting, are present largely as phosphatides and cholesterol esters. Of the phosphatides present, lecithin and the cephalin fraction appear to predominate. Thus, on the basis of such observations, it has been suggested (e.g., Thannhauser, Benotti and Reinstein, 1939) that the glycerophosphatides are responsible for the transport of fatty acids. Yet Bollman and Flock (1946) have shown that one-fourth of the total amount of phosphatide formed in the liver is transferred to the plasma, and this accounts for only about 3 per cent of the fat undergoing transport for caloric purposes in the course of metabolism.

Further evidence has been reviewed by Chaikoff, Zilversmit and Entenman (1948). These workers showed with the aid of radioactive inorganic phosphorus that the fat which accumulates in the liver of diabetic dogs does not arrive there via phosphatides. This follows from the assumption that the fat originates in the depots, yet the turnover of plasma phosphatide during the accumulation of the fat in the liver is no greater than normal.

As has already been indicated (see p. 383), the liver appears to be the sole source and the sole agent of utilization of plasma phosphatides. If this is actually the case, then there is little reason to believe that fatty acids are transported between liver and other organs by means of phosphatides.

Finally, it has been shown (Zilversmit, Entenman and Chaikoff, 1948, see p. 388) that choline stimulates the turnover rate of liver lecithin, but not of plasma phosphatides. This again would indicate that the phenomenon of lipotropism, although influenced by choline, is not based on increased transport of fatty acids to points outside the liver via phosphatides.

Metabolic Activity of Liver Phosphatides. Much of the activity of the liver in relation to lipide metabolism has been described in other discussions. The lipides present in the liver (see p. 284), the formation of fatty livers and the lipotropic action of various substances (see p. 355), the general role of the liver in lipide metabolism (see p. 284), and the liver as a source and means of removal of plasma phosphatides (see p. 383)—all these topics have been detailed elsewhere. In addition, some of the turnover studies involving the use of elaidic acid (see p. 368) and P^{32} (see p. 373) have been described. This section will discuss further studies which contribute to the elucidation of the metabolic role of liver phosphatides.

As far as is known, phosphatides comprise the largest portion of the lipides of the normal liver in the postabsorptive state. Neutral fat is present to a lesser extent and unsaponifiable lipides are also to be found. Rubin, Present and Ralli (1937) found that the lipide content of dog liver was not affected by the feeding of various types of fats or of lecithin. Artom (1933a) fed large quantities of neutral fat to dogs and concluded that the hepatic phosphatide content was raised. In later work Fishman and Artom (1946) found that rats receiving a diet containing zero to 40 per cent fat possessed livers with large amounts of triglycerides and low levels of phosphatides. Addition of choline to these diets did not affect the phosphatide level until the fat content of the diet reached 20 per cent. Thereafter the levels of the choline-containing phosphatides reached the levels found in the livers of animals on a stock diet. It is interesting that the increase in choline-containing lipides was accompanied by a decrease in noncholine-containing lipides. The authors conclude that under the conditions of their experiments the lecithin level of the liver is dependent upon the supplies of both choline and fat.

Hodge and co-workers (1941) have shown that the neutral fat increases markedly in the liver of the fasting mouse, due to mobilization of the available stored fat for metabolic purposes. The total liver phosphatides, on the other hand, remain constant in percentage, since the weights of both the phosphatides and the liver decrease by half during the first four days of fasting (MacLachlan and co-workers, 1942). Furthermore, the ratio of lecithin to cephalin fraction is not altered appreciably. Certain changes were found in the α- and β-lecithin and cephalin fractions as starvation progressed. Inadequate methods of analysis for these fractions, however, make the value of these data questionable.

The effect of maturity on lipide composition has been studied by several workers. Williams and co-workers (1945) found that the phosphatide content of the various tissues of the rat increased as the animal grew from 15 to 70 days old. The increase was largely attributed to the cephalin fraction. Lang (1937), who worked with rats from the age of one day to maturity, reported a constant hepatic phosphatide level, but an increase in cholesterol up to the fifteenth day, followed by a decrease. In laying hens, Lorenz, Chaikoff and Entenman (1938a) found that the triglyceride content of the liver increased over that of the male or immature female bird. No change was observed in the phosphatide or cholesterol ester content of the liver. In the blood, on the other hand, neutral fat, phosphatide and cholesterol esters were all increased during ovulation.

The effect of hormones on hepatic lipide levels has also occupied the attention of several workers. The lipides of the liver increase during the latter stages of pregnancy when hormonal activity is high, according to Coope and Mottram (1914). This may be correlated with the observation of Coope and Chamberlain (1925) that injected pituitrin doubled the hepatic lipide content. The stimulation lasted only 30 hours. Similarly, Anselmino, Hoffman and Rhoden (1936) observed that anterior pituitary extracts increased the fat content of rat livers by 50 per cent. Correspondingly, Artom and Marziani (1924) reported that removal of the ovaries of rabbits with the corresponding hormones they produce causes a decrease in hepatic phosphatide levels. Thyroidectomy and depancreatization produce similar results (Artom, 1923; Artom and Marziani, 1924). In these instances the glycerides maintain or slightly increase their levels. Schmidt (1935) found that injected thyroxin caused the phosphatide content of the liver to decrease and the fatty acids from other lipides to increase. The reverse was true for skeletal muscle, whereas in blood both increased. Pollack (1939) found that subcutaneous injection of one milligram per kilogram of adrenalin into rabbits caused a large increase in liver lipides soon thereafter.

The effect of the synthetic estrogen, diethylstilbestrol, on hepatic phosphatide levels *in vitro* has been observed by Taurog and co-workers (1944). They found that radioactive, inorganic phosphorus was incorporated into the phosphatides of liver slices of immature male white Leghorns at an increased rate as early as six hours after administration of the hormone. The increase in phosphatide content of the blood, which was also observed, was probably a reflection of the increased activity in the liver. Ranney, Entenman and Chaikoff (1949) found by actual analysis that the amount and distribution of liver phosphatides of the chick were not affected by injections of diethylstilbestrol. Alvarez (1945) reported that diethylstilbestrol decreased the phosphatides in all the tissues of intact and castrated female rats. In the liver the lecithin content was constant, whereas the cephalin fraction decreased.

As has already been indicated (see p. 368), labels such as elaidic acid, deuterium (Cavanagh and Raper, 1939) and radioactive phosphorus are incorporated more rapidly into liver phosphatides than into the phosphatides of any other tissue. Thus Perlman, Ruben and Chaikoff (1937) reported that the maximum quantity of P^{32} appeared in the phosphatide of rat liver in about five hours after administration. Later Jones, Chaikoff and Lawrence (1939) found that approximately eight hours after injection are necessary for its appearance. The incorporation of P^{32} into liver phosphatides is increased during fasting, according to Hodge and co-workers (1948), although half of the total liver phosphatide was lost by mice on a five-day fast. The effect of high fat diets on the incorporation of P^{32} into liver phosphatides has been investigated by Artom and co-workers (1937b) and by Artom, Sarzana and Segré (1938). They found that both the total radioactivity and the specific activity—i.e., the quantity and the amount of turnover—of the lipide phosphorus were increased in the liver of rats on a high fat diet. The work of Chargaff (1939) and of Chargaff, Olson and Partington (1940) indicates that P^{32} is incorporated more rapidly into the lecithin fraction of liver than into the cephalin fraction. Hunter and Levy (1942) have shown that sphingomyelin is synthesized in the liver at an even slower rate.

The ability of the liver to synthesize phosphatides was inferred from the work of Sinclair (1934). More precise evidence in support of this was provided by Fries and co-workers (1938), who showed that labeled phosphatides accumulated in the liver of the rat subsequent to injection of inorganic P^{32} even when the animal was deprived of its kidneys and gastrointestinal tract. The importance of the liver as a source of phosphatide synthesis in the body is apparent from the experiments of Entenman and co-workers (1938) on laying hens. These produce daily about 60 milligrams of phosphatide phosphorus in the yolks, and it was shown that 50 per cent of radioactive phosphorus could be detected in the liver six hours after administration to these animals. Abbott (1933, 1934) had previously reported that eggs from hens on a diet devoid of Vitamin A and lipides contained as much phosphatides as those from normal hens.

The precursors of liver phosphatides have not been determined with certainty, thus making difficult the exact determination of turnover rates. According to Hevesy and Hahn (1940), about 19 per cent of the phosphatides of the liver is renewed in four hours, if it is assumed that the phosphatides are formed at the expense of the intracellular inorganic phosphorus. Zilversmit, Entenman and Chaikoff (1948) have established that an acid-soluble alkali-stable fraction of liver, rich in glycerophosphate, meets the requirements previously proposed by Zilversmit, Entenman and Fishler (1943) for a lecithin precursor. From specific activity-time relationships, they were able to calculate that the turnover time—i.e., the time required for the turnover of an amount of liver phosphatide equal to that present in the liver—varied in three dogs from 3.6 to 6.1 hours. Choline feeding increased the turnover of liver lecithin markedly. Since, however, the total lecithin remained normal, it follows that the choline also stimulated the rate of synthesis of lecithin in the liver. Previously, Entenman, Chaikoff and Friedlander (1946) had shown that the curves obtained by plotting specific activity versus time were very similar for choline-containing and noncholine-containing hepatic lipide phosphorus. Ingestion of choline, however, increased the specific activity of the former and decreased that of the latter.

Bollman, Flock and Berkson (1948) calculated phosphatide turnover rate in the liver of the rat on the assumption that the specific activity of the hepatic inorganic phosphate is not materially different from the specific activity of the phosphatide precursor. Their results showed that the phosphatide phosphorus in the liver of the rat was turned over at the rate of 5 per cent per hour. This is equivalent to about 6 milligrams of phosphorus per hour per 100 grams of fresh liver or 0.2 milligrams of phosphorus per 100 grams of body weight.

Campbell and Kosterlitz (1948) have made the interesting observation that the total turnover of liver phosphatides is, within limits, independent of their concentration. Thus, they showed that whereas protein-free diets cause a decrease in phosphatide content in the liver, the turnover of the phosphatides is not affected appreciably. Their experiments extended only over a period of seven days, and the authors mention unpublished work that indicates that prolonged protein deficiency may affect hepatic phosphatide turnover.

As indicated above, choline has been shown to increase the specific activity and the turnover rate of liver lecithin. Perlman, Stillman and Chaikoff (1940) have shown with the aid of P^{32} that three sulfur-containing amino acids, methionine, cystine, and cysteine also stimulate phosphatide turnover in the liver. Perlman and Chaikoff (1939a) showed that betaine behaves similarly. Cholesterol (Perlman and Chaikoff, 1939) was shown to decrease hepatic lipide phosphorus turnover as early as 30 hours after feeding was initiated, whereas combined feeding of choline and cholesterol promoted the formation of new phosphatide molecules in the liver. Cholesterol in quantity, of course, is known to produce fatty livers (Best and Ridout, 1933).

Metabolic Activity of the Phosphatides of the Gastrointestinal Tract. As has already been mentioned (see p. 345), the phosphatides probably contribute to the emulsification of lipides in the gastrointestinal tract. The ready incorporation of labels into the phosphatides of the gastrointestinal tract has been explored by several workers. Sinclair and Smith (1937) reported that the phosphatides of the intestinal mucosa of rats contained elaidic acid eight hours after elaidin was added to the diet. On this basis it was postulated that fatty acids are removed from the intestines via phosphatides. Numerous workers (e.g., Hevesy and Hahn, 1940; Artom, Sarzana and Segré, 1938; Perlman, Ruben and Chaikoff, 1937; Fries and co-workers, 1938; Chargaff, 1939) have observed that injected radioactive, inorganic phosphorus is readily incorporated into the phosphatides of the intestinal tract, although the activity of various portions differs. Thus Fries and co-workers (1938) found greater activity in the small intestine than in the stomach or the large intestine. Perlman, Ruben and Chaikoff (1937) also found that the quantity of labeled phosphatide per gram formed in the stomach and the large intestine was much smaller than that formed in the small intestine. The activity appears to be influenced somewhat by the mode of administration, since Fries and co-workers (1938) reported that oral administration of P^{32} causes more active incorporation of the label in the small intestine than does subcutaneous injection.

Hevesy and Hahn (1940) found that P^{32} is incorporated more rapidly in the cephalin fraction of the intestinal mucosa during the first four hours after administration. According to Chargaff (1939), however, the situation is reversed at later intervals.

The effect of choline on phosphatide synthesis in the small intestine has been studied with the aid of P^{32} by Artom and Cornatzer (1946). It was shown that a single large dose of choline, administered with fat, serves to increase both the amount of intestinal phosphatides and their activity. Obviously, then, choline facilitates phosphatide synthesis in the small intestine. These workers showed further that the administration of fat to choline-deficient rats had no effect on either total radioactivity or specific activity. However, if these factors are not affected by dietary fat under normal conditions, as the discussion below indicates, then little can be concluded from the observation on rats on a choline-deficient diet.

That phosphatide synthesis in the small intestine is independent of the liver was proved by Fishler and co-workers (1943), who demonstrated that P^{32} was incorporated into the intestinal phosphatides of hepatectomized dogs.

In much of the above work it was demonstrated that phosphatide formation in the intestine, as shown by incorporation of P^{32}, is not limited to animals ingesting fat, although several workers (Reiser, 1942; Schmidt-Nielsen, 1946; Fries and co-workers, 1938; Artom, Sarzana and Segré, 1938) provided evidence that activity was greatest during fat absorption. This latter observation, however, has been refuted by Zilversmit, Chaikoff and Entenman (1948), who showed that the phosphatides of the intestinal mucosa and villi increase neither in amount nor turnover when various dietary fats are administered together with inorganic radioactive phosphorus.

The original observations that labeled fats such as elaidin are incorporated into phosphatide molecules during their absorption led to the assumption (Sinclair, 1929) that phosphorylation is an obligate stage in fat absorption (see p. 347)—i.e., that phosphatides are intermediary products in the resynthesis of absorbed fatty acids and glycerol, and that this process takes place in the intestinal walls. Although this assumption was weakened by the fact that P^{32} is rapidly incorporated into intestinal phosphatides in the fasting stage as well as during fat absorption, it received support from other sources. Much of this support was provided by Verzár and his co-workers (e.g., Verzár and McDougall, 1936), who showed that techniques ordinarily used to interfere with phosphorylation such as administration of iodoacetic acid or phlorhizin or adrenalectomy also interfere with fat absorption in the intestine. The use of the above-named drugs, however, leads to pathological intestinal disfunction (Klinghoffer, 1938), whereas adrenalectomy has been shown by Stillman and co-workers (1942) not to interfere with the process of phosphorylation in the small intestine. Weissberger (1941) has shown that the administration of phlorhizin to the intact animal does not inhibit incorporation of P^{32} into tissues such as the intestine, liver and kidney.

The theory of obligate phosphorylation in fat absorption, however, is supported by the frequently confirmed observation (Flock and co-workers, 1947) that the phosphatide content of intestinal or thoracic duct lymph is increased during fat absorption. Although the triglyceride content is increased to a considerably greater extent than the phosphatide content, it has been pointed out by Zilversmit, Chaikoff and Entenman (1948) that the phosphatides which might form during fat absorption could go to the portal blood or else be retained in the intestinal wall. Neither of these possibilities has yet been investigated. The final support for the theory comes, as already indicated, from the observations which stated that lipide phosphorus activity in the intestine is increased during fat absorption. The more definitive investigation of Zilversmit, Chaikoff and Entenman (1948), however, shows that this situation does not obtain. This evidence, coupled with the conclusive refutation of results of experiments based on interference with phosphorylation, casts serious doubt on the concept that phosphatides are necessary intermediates in the transport of fats across the intestinal walls.

Artom and Swanson (1948) have concerned themselves with the mechanism of absorption of ingested phosphatides. Very little work has been done on this phase of fat metabolism since most workers have concerned themselves chiefly with the fate of the triglycerides. Obviously, the phosphatides could be hydrolyzed in the gastrointestinal tract by various lecithinases. On the other hand, absorption of the intact phosphatide molecule might be considered an even greater possibility than absorption of intact triglyceride because of its hydrophilic nature. In order to investigate this possibility, Artom and Swanson (1948) fed to rats labeled phosphatides obtained from plasma of other rats which had ingested P^{32}. As controls, inorganic radioactive phosphorus was fed to rats receiving nonlabeled phosphatides in their diet. Thereafter a study was made of the isotopic distribution of P^{32} in the lipides and other phosphorus-containing fractions of the liver and plasma. It was found that the specific activity of the plasma lipides in the animals fed labeled phosphatides was much higher than that of the controls and also much higher than that of the liver lipides in the same animal. Since it has been shown (see p. 383) that the liver is ordinarily the source of plasma phosphatides, and since the phosphatide activity in these animals was higher in the plasma than in the tissue which was the precursor of the plasma phosphatides, it follows that at least some of the phosphatides in the plasma must have arrived there by direct absorption. The techniques of experimentation, as pointed out by the authors, did not preclude from consideration as plasma phosphatides, molecules from which one fatty acid or the nitrogenous base had been hydrolyzed, since such products would still be soluble in alcohol-ether but insoluble in trichloracetic acid.

Further work in which the acid-soluble phosphorus-containing fractions were explored showed that a part of the phosphatide is hydrolyzed in the gastrointestinal tract, as might be expected; and that absorption was possible at various stages of hydrolysis.

Metabolic Activity of Kidney Phosphatides. Labeling experiments with P^{32} have given some insight into the metabolic activity of the kidney phosphatides. Although the activity of the kidney phosphatides is much more limited in scope than that of the liver phosphatides, a resemblance can be noted. Several workers (Artom and co-workers, 1937; Cavanagh and Raper, 1939; Chargaff, Olson and Partington, 1940; Perlman, Ruben and Chaikoff, 1937) have administered either deuterium or radioactive inorganic phosphorus to test animals on various diets and have observed the rate of deposition and the disappearance of labeled kidney phosphatide. The results indicate that phosphatide formation in the kidney is slightly slower than in the liver or in the small intestine and, correspondingly, the disappearance of labeled phosphatide is slower.

The work of Chargaff (1939) and of Chargaff, Olson and Partington (1940) indicates that the turnover rates of lecithin and the cephalin fraction in the kidney are equal. Likewise, Hunter and Levy (1942) have shown that the turnover rate for kidney sphingomyelin is the same as that for the total phosphatides, indicating that all three types of phosphatides are synthesized in the kidney at the same rate.

The specific activity of the lipide phosphorus of the kidney has been calculated by Artom and co-workers (1937, 1937a), who found it to be lower than that of the liver and small intestine shortly after administration of labeled inorganic phosphorus. Chaikoff (1942) quotes evidence, however, which shows that the specific activity in these three tissues is the same 98 hours after intraperitoneal injection of P^{32}. Hevesy and Hahn (1940) have measured the specific activity of both lipide and inorganic phosphorus in the kidney and have calculated turnover rates.

Fishler and co-workers (1943) have shown that the kidney is a site of phosphatide synthesis, since they were able to recover labeled phosphatides from the kidney of a hepatectomized dog to which had been administered P^{32}. Furthermore, the quantity of labeled phosphatide did not differ markedly from that found in control animals. However, the plasma of the hepatectomized dog contained no labeled phosphatides, indicating that, although the kidney resembles the liver in that it can synthesize phosphatides, it differs from it in that it cannot supply these phosphatides to the plasma.

The turnover rate of kidney phosphatides was shown by Weissberger (1941) to be unaffected by the administration of phlorhizin. This same worker (Weissberger, 1940) observed that when ammonium chloride was fed to rats which had received radioactive inorganic phosphate, less labeled phosphatide than normal was recovered from the kidney phosphatides. Since ammonium chloride accelerates urinary excretion of inorganic phosphate, it is possible that there exists a relationship between kidney phosphatides and urinary phosphate, particularly in regard to regulation of blood and body pH.

Patterson and McHenry (1942) have found that both the liver and the kidneys of choline-deficient rats contain a subnormal quantity of phosphatides (see p. 414).

The work of Jowett and Quastel (1935) shows that the kidneys demonstrate ketogenic activity, although to a lesser extent than the liver. Here, as in phosphatide synthesis, however, the kidneys seem to engage in this activity only for reasons of their own, since they seem to be incapable of providing for the blood stream, either acetoacetic acid or phosphatides.

Metabolic Activity of Muscle Phosphatides. The phosphatides of the muscles have been subjected to a fair amount of study, particularly in regard to the effect of muscle activity on phosphatide content (Sinclair, 1938, see p. 307).

The lipide content of normal muscles has already been discussed (see p. 307), and it has been pointed out that heart muscle has a higher phosphatide content than other muscles. The work of Sinclair (1932) indicates that phosphatides of muscle, like those of other tissues, have the ability to extract preferentially and to retain highly unsaturated fatty acids from the diet. Sinclair (1935) has also shown that neither the diet nor the extent of unsaturation of the fatty acids of muscle phosphatides affects in any way the ratio of saturated to unsaturated acids therein.

The effect of growth on the phosphatide and other lipide components of the various muscles has been studied by Williams and co-workers (1945). They found, in general, that the cephalin fraction increased with growth, whereas the sphingomyelin content of skeletal and cardiac muscle decreased.

Thyroid extract was reported by Pasternak and Page (1935) to increase greatly the phosphatide content of rat muscles. That phosphatide could still be utilized under these circumstances was demonstrated by the fact that injected phosphatide was completely metabolized. Thus, the increase is probably due to the increased metabolic rate produced by the thyroid extract. Thyroxin was found by Schmidt (1935) to increase muscle phosphatide content and decrease liver phosphatide content. Morgulis and co-workers (1938) found in nutritional muscle dystrophy of rabbits that the phosphatide content of the affected skeletal muscle was higher than it is in the muscles of the normal animals.

Radioactive inorganic phosphorus is incorporated into skeletal muscle phosphatides much more slowly than into the phosphatides of the liver, plasma or gastrointestinal tract, as has been shown by Chargaff, Olson and Partington (1940) and by Entenman and co-workers (1938). This observation has been correlated by Hevesy and Hahn (1940) and by Manery and Bale (1941) with the slow rate of entry of the labeled phosphatides into muscle cells. Friedlander, Perlman and Chaikoff (1941) have shown that 5.3 per cent of P^{32} is found in the muscles of adult rats 48 hours after administration. Cardiac muscle phosphatides, as shown by Entenman and co-workers (1938), incorporate a greater amount of P^{32} than do those of skeletal muscle and accordingly demonstrate a greater specific activity. These results do not indicate whether the muscle may synthesize phosphatides, although it is unlikely that they do. Indirect evidence on this score arises from experiments in which plasma containing labeled phosphatide was injected into test animals. Under these circumstances the musculature removed appreciable quantities of the labeled compound since Hevesy and Hahn (1940) found that rabbit muscles contained 2.5 per cent of labeled phosphatides four hours after injection and Zilversmit and co-workers (1943) found that dog muscles contained 4.5 per cent of labeled phosphatides five hours after injection.

Artom (1941a) and Friedlander, Perlman and Chaikoff (1941) have shown that denervation of muscle in rats and cats by scission of the femoral and sciatic nerves leads to an increase as great as 200 per cent in uptake of P^{32} by the muscle phosphatides. In addition, the total phosphatide content increases slightly. This increase, which started before atrophy of the muscle set in, was still apparent 19 days after the start of the experiment.

Hevesy and Smedley-MacLean (1940) have found that a fat-deficient diet increases the turnover rate of muscle phosphatides in the rat. This was not the experience of Artom, Sarzana and Segré (1938), and, accordingly, the problem is worthy of further investigation.

Metabolic Activity of the Phosphatides of the Brain and Central Nervous System. The quantity and composition of the phosphatides of the brain have already been discussed (see p. 274). It was seen that the brain is a rich source of many types of lipides. Nevertheless, the brain oxidizes only carbohydrate and does not metabolize lipides. Thus McConnell and Sinclair (1937) fed rats large amounts of elaidic acid throughout their entire prenatal and postnatal periods. The resulting elaidic acid content of the cephalin fraction and lecithin of the brain was only about one-fourth that of the liver and the muscles, indicating that the brain phosphatides demonstrate a high degree of selectivity. These observations correlate with those of Cavanagh and Raper (1939) and Sperry, Waelsch and Stoyanoff (1940), who employed deuterium-containing fatty acids as labels.

Radioactive inorganic phosphorus, on the other hand, is readily incorporated into brain phosphatides, as shown by the experiments of Hahn and Hevesy (1937), who found P^{32} in the brains of adult rats, mice and rabbits one hour after subcutaneous injection. However, despite the rapid appearance of the label, the maximum amount of P^{32}, as shown by Fries, Changus and Chaikoff (1940) and Changus, Chaikoff and Ruben (1938), is not deposited in the brain phosphatides until 200 to 300 hours after administration. Similarly, the brain is loath to release the label, over 70 per cent of the maximum amount being present as long as four weeks after administration. Other workers (Artom, Sarzana and Segré, 1938; Fries and Chaikoff, 1941) also have attested to the lack of facility with which the brain phosphatides incorporate radioactive inorganic phosphorus.

Hevesy and Hahn (1940) and Chargaff, Olson and Partington (1940) have shown that sphingomyelin and the cephalin fraction of brain are renewed more rapidly than is brain lecithin. The above workers, as well as Perlman, Ruben and Chaikoff (1937) have shown that total phosphatide turnover in the brain is much smaller than that found in other organs. Changus, Chaikoff and Ruben (1938) and Fries and Chaikoff (1941) have demonstrated, however, that it is approximately twice as great in young animals as in mature ones. Fries, Changus and Chaikoff (1940) and Fries and co-workers (1941) have carried out interesting studies in which the degree of incorporation of P^{32} into the various portions of the rat brain is compared with the age of the animal. The P^{32} was administered to the parents prior to the birth of the rat. The activity in the spinal cord of rats was at least twice as great as in the fore-brain from the time of birth until the animals weighed 50 grams. The second largest amount of P^{32} incorporation was observed during this period in the medulla, whereas the activity in the cerebellum was inter-mediate between that of the medulla and the forebrain. In rats whose growth had reached a stage where they weighed more than 50 grams, the order of P^{32} activity was reversed, the greatest activity having been observed in the cerebellum. The activities of the medulla and the fore-brain were intermediate, and the activity of the spinal cord was least. Not only was there a reversal in order with maturity, but also the activity declined to the point that the active phosphatide content in the spinal cord was only 5 per cent of what it was in the newborn rat. This decline in active phosphatide content is due to degradation of the phosphatide molecules followed by resynthesis with the incorporation of less active inorganic phosphorus. Thus the rapid decline in activity indicates a fast rate of phosphatide renewal.

The work of Fries, Schachner and Chaikoff (1942) on phosphorylation *in vitro* by surviving brain slices (see p. 408) indicates that the brain is capable of synthesizing phosphatides in its own right. This type of experimentation obviously does not preclude the possibility that some or all of the brain phosphatides are provided by the plasma. Waelsch, Sperry and Stoyanoff (1940a) have also provided evidence that the brain is capable of synthesizing lipides at certain periods.

Foá, Weinstein and Kleppel (1948) have shown that a choline-deficient diet does not affect the total lipide, phosphatide or cholesterol content of the rat brain.

Metabolic Activity of the Phosphatides of the Reproductive System. The phosphatide content of the various reproductive organs has been discussed previously (see p. 300). Likewise, the interesting varia-tions in lipide content of the ovaries, placenta and corpus luteum during reproductive processes have been described (see p. 301). The present state of knowledge makes possible very little elaboration on the metabolic activity of the phosphatides of the reproductive organs.

Metabolically the lipides of the testes appear to be even more inactive than those of the brain, since Sinclair (1940a) found that dietary elaidic acid, which was incorporated into most tissues with a fair degree of ease, was rigidly excluded from the phosphatides of the testes. Castration of dogs, according to Kochakian, MacLachlan and McEwen (1938), does not affect the level of plasma phosphatides. Likewise, no change in phosphatide concentration was observed after testosterone or androstenedione injections.

McConnell and Sinclair (1937a) carried out experiments to show that the placenta of rats is permeable to fatty acids. Mother rats were fed elaidin, and the livers and entire bodies of the new-born young were analyzed for elaidic acid. It was found that elaidic acid, under these circumstances, comprised 16 per cent of the liver phosphatide fatty acids and 11 per cent of the fatty acids of the entire body. If the young were allowed to suckle, the elaidic acid content of the liver and of the entire body increased several fold. From these results, then, it appears that fatty acids may pass through the placenta and into the milk of rats.

The mechanism of transfer of the fatty acids across the placenta is obscure, since Nielson (1942) has shown that transfer of the entire phosphatide molecule is a very slow process. He injected radioactive inorganic phosphorus into pregnant rats eight days prior to parturition and found the P^{32} content of the fetus during this time to be very low. If placental transfer were facile, a high P^{32} concentration in the fetus would be expected.

The fetus at birth, according to Boyd and Wilson (1935), absorbs both phosphatide and cholesterol from the umbilical blood. Their conclusions were based on an analysis of the lipides of the blood from the umbilical artery and vein in the human fetus. It was estimated that over 40 grams of lipide, 75 per cent of which is phosphatide, is absorbed at birth by an average fetus. A preference seems to be exerted for saturated phosphatides. The phosphatides are hydrolyzed by the fetus and the phosphorus is retained. The fatty acids may be used to form depot fat or else may be returned as glycerides to the umbilical blood.

Phosphatides influence the motility of bull spermatozoa, as shown by Lardy and Phillips (1941, 1941a). These workers found that phosphatides maintained the motility of bull spermatozoa in a sugar-free medium under aerobic conditions. They showed further that when glucose was absent from the medium, the phosphatide content decreased about 40 per cent in ten hours at room temperature. In the presence of glucose, no decrease was apparent. Thus it appears that the energy for sperm motility may be obtained either from glycolysis, if sugar is present, or from intracellular oxidation of phosphatides if sugar is not present. If sugar is the preferred source of energy, this observation explains the inhibition by glucose of "endogenous" respiration.

Metabolic Activity of the Phosphatides of the Egg and the Developing Embryo. Closely associated with the functions of the reproductive organs is the production in the female of milk and eggs. The nature of egg phosphatides has already been discussed (see p. 320). Their metabolic activity is of great interest, although more investigation is still necessary.

The egg is, of course, the source of nourishment for virtually all embryonic animals except mammals where the function is assumed by the mother's blood (Boyd and Wilson, 1935). Once the animal is born, his maintenance, where necessary, is provided by mother's milk. The high percentage of phosphatides and cholesterol in eggs as contrasted with the very low percentage in milk makes it obvious that the growing embryo must be provided with these essential lipides until such time that its development makes possible phosphatide and cholesterol anabolism.

Several studies have concerned themselves with phosphatide behavior during the development or incubation of the egg. Öhman (1942) found that the phosphatide content of sea urchin eggs decreased about 17 per cent and the cholesterol content about 25 per cent shortly after fertilization. Subsequently, an increase was noted. Previously, Robertson and Wasteneys (1914) had reported that the phosphatide of sea urchin eggs decreased considerably during development. Jost and Sorg (1932) reported that the ratio of total fat to the phosphatide content of the hen's egg remains constant during development. The total phosphatide content of the hen's egg was shown by Cahn and Bonot (1928) to decrease 50 per cent during formation of the embryo. Similarly, Serono, Montezomolo and Balboni (1936) reported a gradual diminution of phosphatide content in the yolk and a corresponding increase of phosphatide content in the embryo during incubation of hen's eggs.

Kugler (1936) found that phosphatide metabolism reaches its maximum in the chick embryo between the fifteenth and seventeenth days of incubation since at this time the size of the yolk decreases the most and the phosphatide content of the embryo shows its greatest increase. During this time, also, ossification is most pronounced, which suggests that phosphatides provide phosphorus for bone formation. This period, in addition, marks the greatest conversion of lipide phosphorus into other forms; and in a later study, Kugler (1944) has shown that acid-soluble phosphorus does not appear in the embryo until half of the incubation period is completed. The ratio of lecithin to cephalin fraction is maintained, according to this worker, at 3:1 throughout the entire development in both the yolk where a decrease in phosphatide content is observed, and in the embryo where an increase is noted. Needham (1931, p. 1165) also states that fat metabolism in the developing chick embryo increases markedly at about the fourteenth day of incubation.

The change in lipide phosphorus during development of the chick embryo has likewise been studied by Cahn (1931, pp. 1169, 1170). He found that although the embryo phosphatide content increased throughout the entire period of incubation, the neutral fat did not increase until the fourteenth day of incubation. This corresponds to the decrease of yolk phosphatide noted below, for it is possible that yolk phosphatide could be transformed to neutral fat in the embryo. This is especially so since studies with radioactive phosphorus detailed below show that the embryo prefers to synthesize phosphatides rather than to use them unchanged after absorption from the yolk.

The work on the developing embryo described above parallels work on the egg yolk reported by Plimmer and Scott (1909) and Masai and Fukutomi (1923). They found that the phosphatide content of the egg yolk starts to diminish markedly on the twelfth to fourteenth day of incubation due probably to its consumption by the embryo (Riddle, 1916) and its conversion to other forms of phosphorus. Thus, it was observed that the inorganic phosphorus content of the yolk increased at this time.

Eaves (1910) observed that the iodine number of the fatty acids of the chick embryo increased during development, apparently at the expense of the yolk whose fatty acids demonstrated a decrease in iodine number.

Once the chick is hatched, according to Cahn (1931, p. 1169), its phosphatide content increases markedly. The large quantities of liver, blood and yolk sac lipides of the newly hatched chick were investigated by Entenman, Lorenz and Chaikoff (1940). The liver contained an average of 7.3 per cent cholesterol, 90 per cent of which was esterified. This comprised about one-half of the total lipides of the liver. The esterified cholesterol content decreased markedly from the third to the thirtieth day of life. Between the second and seventh day there was a temporary rise in neutral fat coincident with the decrease in cholesterol esters. The phosphatide fatty acids remained constant throughout. Thus it appears that cholesterol was largely responsible for the fatty liver in the newborn chick. Corresponding to the fatty liver was a lipemia, indicated by the presence of 1 gram of fat per 100 ml. of blood. This likewise started to diminish after the third day of life and by the fifteenth day 0.45 per cent lipides remained in the blood. The yolk sac, which in the hatched chick represents an extension of the small intestine, contained at birth 12 per cent fatty acids, 1.6 per cent phosphatides and 1.3 per cent total cholesterol. The absorption of these lipides was virtually complete by the fifth day of life, the glycerides having been absorbed most rapidly. These workers point out the resemblance between the fatty liver of the new-born chick and the fatty liver produced by feeding egg yolk or cholesterol to rats. They further propose that the high lipide content of the blood of the new-born chick may be due to the known presence of estrogens in the yolk of the egg, since Lorenz, Chaikoff and Entenman (1938) had previously shown that administration of estrogenic hormones to immature birds produces a lipemia similar to that found in laying birds.

The Origin and Behavior of Yolk and Embryo Phosphatides. Extensive work on the origin of the phosphatides of egg yolk was carried out by Hahn and Hevesy (1937a) and by Hevesy and Hahn (1938). These workers pointed out that a hen laying daily may incorporate as much as 1.5 grams of phosphatide into the egg yolk. Furthermore, as much as 0.5 gram of phosphorus may be present in the combined phosphorus-containing compounds of a single egg. Obviously, this large amount of phosphatide is not present in the diet of the hen. Accordingly, it must be assumed that the phosphatide of the egg yolk is synthesized by the hen, probably in the liver. As a matter of fact, McCollum, Halpin and Drescher (1912/13) showed many years ago that virtual absence of phosphatides from the diet did not affect markedly the phosphatide content of the hen's egg. To determine where in the body of the hen the synthesis occurred, Hevesy and Hahn (1938) administered P^{32} to laying hens and determined the specific activity of the lipide phosphorus of the egg yolks and of various tissues five hours later. The liver demonstrated a relative specific activity of 100 per cent. The value for the plasma was 79 per cent, whereas the ovary, yolk and intestine had values of 7.2, 9.2 and 18 per cent, respectively. On the basis of these results they postulated that the phosphatides are synthesized by the liver and delivered by the plasma to the ovaries whose task it is to remove the phosphatides from the blood and incorporate them into the yolk. The blood is undoubtedly aided in its role as transport medium by the lipemia mentioned above. Nevertheless, during the five-hour duration of the experiment the phosphatide content of the plasma (about 15 milligrams) was almost entirely renewed, since the laying bird incorporates about four times this much into the egg yolk. It can further be shown that about one-fourth of the liver phosphatides was renewed during the five-hour period in order to supply the requisite amount. The low activity of the yolk is accounted for by the large dilution to which the active phosphatides, incorporated during the five-hour period, were subjected. The egg itself, unlike the embryo which will later form from it, appears to be incapable of synthesizing phosphatide, as shown by the fact that P^{32} injected into the egg once it leaves the ovary is not incorporated into the yolk phosphatides.

Entenman and co-workers (1938) showed that egg-laying increases the rate of incorporation of P^{32} into the phosphatides of the blood, oviduct and ovary. Lorenz, Perlman and Chaikoff (1943) demonstrated that the amount of P^{32} deposited in the egg yolk is a function of yolk growth and availability of the labeled atom during the corresponding period of new formation. Their work shows that once the phosphatides are incorporated into the egg yolk they do not undergo any sort of breakdown which releases them to the plasma. They also showed that the phosphoproteins of the albumen are formed during the early stages of yolk formation, and are ready for deposition around the yolk when the yolk is fully grown. Thus, egg which entered the magnum (where albumen is supplied) when the plasma P^{32} was at its maximum had only a small amount of P^{32} in the albumen, since this had been formed previously. The eggs laid later, on the other hand, had higher quantities of P^{32} in their albumen since this albumen was being formed when the P^{32} was available to it. Similarly, eggs which were in the uterus (where the shell is formed) when the P^{32} was administered had shells with high P^{32} contents. Those which entered the uterus some hours later contained much smaller amounts of P^{32} in their shells.

Chargaff (1942) investigated with the aid of radioactive inorganic phosphorus the rate of formation of the cephalin fraction and lecithin of egg yolk as compared to the rate of formation of the phosphatide-containing complex protein, lipovitellin. His results showed that all three were formed at the same rate, although the vitellin phosphorus exhibited a higher specific activity in the first six hours of the experiment. All fractions exhibited their maximum specific activities after six days.

The question of the origin of the phosphatides of the chick embryo has been studied by Hevesy, Levi and Rebbe (1938), who introduced radioactive inorganic phosphorus into the white of fertilized hens' eggs prior to incubation. Thereupon the P^{32} distribution was examined in the egg yolk and the embryo after 6, 11, 16 and 18 days of incubation. They found that P^{32} had been incorporated in the phosphatides of the embryo, whereas virtually none was present in the yolk phosphatides. This indicates that the embryo synthesized its own phosphatide molecules in preference to absorbing them intact from the egg yolk. Since only small quantities of the inorganic phosphorus are present in the egg yolk, it follows that the requisite phosphorus for skeleton formation and for other organs of the chick must be supplied by the hydrolysis of the yolk phosphatides.

Popják (1947) has shown with the aid of P^{32} that phosphatides of a fetus may be synthesized independently of those of the mother.

Metabolic Activity of Milk Phosphatides. The production of milk, like that of eggs, is closely associated with the functioning of the reproductive system. The occurrence of phosphatides in milk has already been discussed (see p. 323).

It has been shown by numerous observers that the nature of the fat of milk may be altered by varying the character of the diet. These researches have been well reviewed by Bloor (1943, pp. 355–357).

Considerable effort has been expended in order to determine the source of the lipides in milk. The first report on this subject, published by Meigs, Blatherwick and Cary (1919), contended that phosphatides were removed from the blood by the mammary glands. These were converted, presumably, to neutral fat, and the inorganic phosphorus was returned to the blood. The glycerides of the blood, according to this work, were not involved. These results were based on comparisons of analyses of blood in general circulation and blood leaving the mammary glands of milk-producing cows.

This observation, however, has not proved capable of corroboration. Thus Blackwood (1934) found no differences in the lipide, cholesterol or lipide phosphorus contents of blood prior to and after contact with mammary gland tissue. Trautmann and Kirchhoff (1932), Lintzel (1934) and McCay and Maynard (1931) all carried out experiments which indicated that blood phosphatides were not the progenitors of milk lipides. Indications were obtained, however, that the non-phosphatide fatty acids of blood provided a source for milk lipides. Further confirmation of this results from the work of Graham, Jones and Kay (1936) and Voris, Ellis and Maynard (1940), who found a lesser glyceride content in the venous blood leaving the mammary gland than in the arterial blood entering it.

One of the first labeling experiments intended to shed light on the source of milk lipides was carried out by Aylward, Blackwood and Smith (1937), who fed iodinated fats to cows and observed that the glyceride fatty acids of the blood contained more iodine than the phosphatide fatty acids. The same proportionate difference was observed in the milk lipides. On this basis it was assumed that blood lipides contribute to milk fat. More definitive evidence was provided by Aten and Hevesy (1938) and by Aten (1939), who injected subcutaneously radioactive inorganic phosphate into goats. Subsequently, the phosphatides of the milk were found to possess a higher specific activity than those of the blood. It was obvious, then, that blood phosphatides could not be a precursor of milk phosphatides which must have been anabolized in the mammary gland. As would be expected, the specific activity of the phosphorus of the phosphatides extracted from the mammary gland itself was higher than the corresponding value for the lipide phosphorus of either blood or milk. In this regard, milk phosphatides differ from yolk phosphatides which are derived from plasma. The formation of phosphatides in the mammary glands appears to be a slow process, since over two days were required for the entry of P^{32} into milk phosphatides. Entry into milk casein and phosphate was much more rapid.

The respiratory quotient of mammary glands of lactating goats was estimated as slightly more than 1.0 by Reineke, Stonecipher and Turner (1941). It could thus be inferred that mammary glands convert carbohydrate to fat, an observation for which evidence had previously been obtained by Sheehy (1921) and Bürger and Rückert (1931).

The short-chain fatty acids which characterized milk lipides have been the source of considerable speculation. Since the mono-unsaturated lower fatty acids possess C_9–C_{10} double bonds, it is likely, as Bloor (1944) has observed, that the mammary glands possess the ability to shorten the acid chains from the methyl rather than the carboxyl end by ω-oxidation.

Metabolic Activity of Miscellaneous Tissues. Experiments with P^{32} have indicated that certain tissues are not prone to incorporate the labeled atom into their phosphatides. Reference has already been made to the limited activity demonstrated by the brain and the lack of activity characteristic of the testes. Perrier and co-workers (1937) observed that administration of olive oil and radioactive inorganic phosphorus to rats did not lead to the incorporation of the labeled atom into the phosphatides of heart and spleen. Artom and co-workers (1937) and Entenman and co-workers (1938) have likewise found a very low degree of phosphatide activity in the lung, spleen, pancreas, muscle, blood and bones of the rat and the bird. However, the latter workers point out that the quantity of the blood, muscle and bones makes them significant; for although their activity is low they incorporated 2 per cent of the total labeled phosphorus administered, whereas the entire body incorporated only 5 per cent.

Williams and co-workers (1945) have reported an extensive study of the effect of growth on the lipide composition of rat tissues including spleen, thymus, lung, heart, testes, skeletal muscle and brain in addition to the liver and kidney. In all the tissues the phosphatide content increased during growth from the fifteenth to the seventieth day. An increase was noted especially in the cephalin fraction, except in lung tissue. In the kidney, lung and spleen the sphingomyelin content increased, whereas in skeletal and cardiac muscle it decreased. In the thymus gland the phosphatide increase was greater on the forty-fifth day than on the seventieth day, due possibly to retrogression of the organ.

Alvarez (1945) reported that stilbestrol caused the total phosphatide content of the organs of intact and castrated rats to decrease. Lecithin increased in the intact rats in the brain and kidneys, decreased in the heart and lungs and was unchanged in the spleen and liver. The cephalin fraction decreased markedly in all organs except the heart, and the sphingomyelin content decreased markedly without exception.

In the white blood cells (Boyd, 1934, 1935b) the phosphatide content has been shown to increase sharply in humans recovering after surgical operation or during the course of an infection. This resembles closely the increase in phosphatide content of muscles under the stress of increased function.

Metabolic Activity of Plant Phosphatides

Very little is known about the course of phosphatide metabolism in plants, primarily because of the difficulty of the work involved and because phosphatides are, for the most part, rather minor constituents of the members of the plant kingdom, despite the fact that plants provide their commercial source.

The distribution and characteristics of plant phosphatides are discussed in Part III. The mode of occurrence of plant phosphatides as complexes has also been discussed previously (see p. 192). In general, it may be said that phosphatides are prone to occur in plants as complexes with carbohydrates, and such combinations have been observed in numerous instances. Recent work, in addition, has shown that complexes with proteins, similar to those found in animal tissue, likewise exist, although very little is known about them.

Experiments with labeling agents intended to elucidate phosphatide metabolism in plants have not been carried out. Phosphorus metabolism in general, however, has been studied in plants with the aid of P^{32} by Hevesy, Linderstrøm-Lang and Olsen (1936, 1937). They found that phosphorus atoms migrate freely within maize and sunflower plants which were grown in nutrient solutions until a few leaves had sprouted. Thereafter, the plants were placed in culture solutions containing labeled phosphorus. New leaves formed, and after nine days these, as well as the leaves formed in the inactive medium, were found to contain appreciable quantities of P^{32}. Thus, phosphorus exchange must take place between the phosphorus-containing compounds present in the leaves and those in the circulation stream.

Cut sunflower leaves were also capable of absorbing a few per cent of P^{32} from a nutrient solution. When maize seeds containing short rootlets were placed in a culture solution containing P^{32}, it was found that the germ incorporated appreciable quantities of the labeled atom, whereas the endosperm took on none at all. This distinction did not occur with pea seeds. Other experiments of this nature have been carried out by Biddulph (1939) and Gustafson and Darken (1937).

Several studies have described the change in phosphatide content which occurs in the various parts of plants during growth. An early study by McClenahan (1913) showed that the lipides of the ovule of the black walnut are predominantly phosphatides at first. As the fruit matures, however, the phosphatides become quantitatively less important, eventually disappearing entirely. Zlataroff (1916), on the other hand, found that the phosphatide content of the seeds of the chickpea, *Cicer arietinum,* did not decrease nearly as much during germination as did the protein content.

Rewald and Riede (1933) studied the phosphatide content of the various parts of the soybean plant in three stages of maturation. It was observed that the phosphatide content of the roots, stem, leaves and pods decreased as the plant ripened, whereas that of the beans remained constant, despite the increase in the weight of the beans and the decrease in the weight of the other parts. Halden and Hinrichs (1942) studied the phosphatide content of germinating soybeans and found that it increased from the second to the thirteenth day of germination and decreased thereafter. The total lipides, on the other hand, decreased throughout.

Ulrich (1939) found that the phosphatide content of the berry of the ivy plant increased until the fruit attained a weight of 22 milligrams. Thereafter it decreased steadily until maturity when the berry attained a weight of 365 milligrams.

Hée and Bayle (1932) found that the phosphatide content of the seeds of *Lupinus albus* decreased during the first 15 days of germination. Variation in phosphatide content during growth of various parts of the runner bean, *Phaseolus multiflorus,* was studied by Jordan and Chibnall (1933). Magnesium phosphatidate is present in the growing portions, and on germination this increases until the prophylls start to expand. Thereafter the magnesium is slowly replaced with calcium, and calcium phosphatidate becomes the chief phosphatide of the mature prophylls and pinnate leaves. On germination the phosphatides of the cotyledons were observed to decrease more rapidly than the phosphatides of the growing parts increased. Thus the seed phosphatides are believed to provide a source of reserve food.

A suggested relationship between phosphatide formation and the production of chlorophyll in plants may be derived from the work of Smith (1947); however, much more definitive work is necessary.

The effect of plant nutrition on phosphatide content has been studied. Pfützer and Roth (1942) found that higher percentages of nitrogen, phosphorus and potassium in the soil provided spinach, rapeseed and barley with higher phosphatide contents. Hanne (1931) reported that soluble phosphate-containing fertilizers stimulate phosphatide synthesis in plants. Sherbakov (1935) has found that the efficiency of utilization of phosphate by plants is greatly enhanced by microquantities of elements such as boron, fluorine, iodine, manganese, zinc, aluminum and copper. Lüdecke, Sammet and Lesch (1941) found that increased quantities of nutrient phosphorus increased the protein content and to some extent the phosphatide content of soybeans. However, the variations due to variety seemed greater than those due to added nutrients.

The work of Stephenson and Whetham (1922) is of interest in regard to the effect of nutrients on the lipide content of bacteria. They grew the timothy bacillus on a synthetic medium containing potassium hydrogen phosphate, ammonium diphosphate, magnesium sulfate, a trace of sodium chloride and a source of carbon no more complex than glucose. Calcium carbonate served to maintain a slightly alkaline medium. When 1 per cent each of glucose and sodium acetate provided the source of carbon, the organism utilized these completely to synthesize proteins and lipides. Thereafter the bacillus decreased in size as it utilized its own lipides. As might be expected, the glyceride fraction disappeared more rapidly than the phosphatide fraction until an equilibrium was established in which the phosphatide content was the higher. The maintenance provided the organism by sodium lactate was similar to that provided by glucose. Sodium acetate, however, was not assimilated unless glucose or sodium lactate was also present. Propionic acid and n-butyric acid proved capable of conversion to protein and lipides without the aid of auxiliary substances. Bretin, Manceau and Cochet (1931) found that a medium containing tartaric acid, ammonium nitrate, sulfate and phosphate and the carbonates of potassium, magnesium, manganese and zinc retards the utilization of sucrose as well as the formation of lecithin in *Penicillium glaucum.*

Phosphatides have been reported as nutrients for various plants. Thus Bialosuknia (1924) reported that lecithin in the presence of sugars provided a source of nitrogen for mustard and cabbage seedlings. Similarly, Tanaka (1931) found that lecithin was more readily assimilated than phytin as a source of nitrogen for various plants. Obviously, phosphatides do not compare with inorganic nitrates as sources of nitrogen. In contrast to the work of Tanaka (1931), Rogers, Pearson and Pierre (1940) found that whereas corn and tomato plants absorb both phytin and lecithin from nutrient solutions, the former is absorbed much more rapidly. Neither compound is hydrolyzed by the root enzymes. Bertramson and Stephenson (1942), in contrast to this work, found that lecithin is a somewhat better source of phosphorus for the tomato plants than phytin, although both were inferior to calcium ethyl phosphate and nucleic acid. There was no indication that any of these organic fertilizers increased the organic phosphorus content of the plant.

Various fractions of the *Bacterium tumefaciens,* and especially the phosphatide fraction, were found to produce great cell proliferation of injured plants (Levine and Chargaff, 1937). This is reminiscent of the action of the phosphatide fraction of the tubercle bacillus on animal tissue (see p. 194).

The ability of plants to convert lipides to carbohydrates has been suggested by Murlin (1933), who found that the respiratory quotients of single castor beans vary from 0.30 to 0.58.

The Synthesis of Phosphatides by Isolated Tissues

The incorporation of radioactive inorganic phosphorus into the phosphatides of isolated tissues maintained under physiological conditions should provide a measure of the ability of that tissue to synthesize phosphatides. This technique has formed the basis of several studies, although it has been criticized by Peters and Van Slyke (1946, p. 411) on the basis that there is no means of distinguishing between true synthesis and exchange of lipide phosphorus with inorganic phosphorus. This is, of course, a danger which pervades all work with radioactive indicators, although in the present instance Chaikoff (1942) does not believe that the experimental facts support the possibility of simple exchange, since available evidence indicates that energy other than activation energy is involved.

A study of isolated tissue activity was carried out by Robinson and co-workers (1938), who reported that surviving slices of liver, intestine and kidney of rats could incorporate P^{32} into their phosphatides. They suggested further that the process might be stimulated by glucose, an observation later shown to be true (see below). Similarly, Bulliard, Grundland and Moussa (1938) found that P^{32} could be incorporated into the phosphatides of surviving sections of suprarenal gland but not into nucleoproteins. Fishler and co-workers (1941) were able to show that P^{32} could be incorporated into liver slices as early as one hour after they were suspended in a Ringer-bicarbonate buffer solution containing radioactive Na_2HPO_4. The quantity of P^{32} incorporated increased during the first four hours of the experiment, at the end of which time 6 per cent of the inorganic labeled atom had entered the phosphatide molecule. The incorporation of P^{32} increased despite the fact that there is, under these conditions, a net decrease in total phosphatide content with time due to autolysis. This decomposition may liberate inorganic phosphorus which would serve to dilute the labeled phosphorus and thus decrease the percentage of it incorporated into the phosphatide molecule.

In this work, cellular organization appeared necessary, since incorporation of P^{32} took place only in tissue slices, and not in homogenates. In subsequent work by Fries, Schachner and Chaikoff (1942), it appeared that incorporation of P^{32} was possible in both brain homogenates and brain slices, although the process occurred to a lesser extent in the former case. These workers also showed that the surviving sciatic nerve of the dog was capable of incorporating inorganic radioactive phosphorus into its phosphatides.

These experiments, as well as those carried out with kidney and liver slices by Taurog, Chaikoff and Perlman (1942), have shown that P^{32} incorporation takes place only under oxidative conditions. This is to be expected from thermodynamic considerations, as pointed out by Chaikoff (1942). Schachner, Fries and Chaikoff (1942) observed that the conversion of P^{32} into lipide phosphorus by surviving brain slices is accelerated as much as fivefold by the addition of hexoses such as glucose, galactose, mannose or fructose to the physiological solution in which the experiment is conducted. The presence of these sugars may influence the oxygen balance of the system in such a way as to provide more oxidative energy for phosphatide formation. The presence of hexoses was ineffectual both when oxygen was excluded from the system and when the tissue was homogenized. The pentoses did not behave similarly to the hexoses. According to Kaplan, Memelsdorff and Dodge (1945) the presence of fluoride serves to increase the quantity of P^{32} incorporated into the phosphatides of surviving rat, kidney and liver slices due to increased phosphorylation.

The presence of respiratory inhibitors such as cyanide, azide and hydrogen sulfide was shown by Taurog, Chaikoff and Perlman (1942) to inhibit the incorporation of P^{32} into the phosphatides of surviving liver and kidney slices. Carbon monoxide similarly exerted an inhibitory effect which was greater in the dark than in the light.

The experiments described above have shown that the phosphatides of surviving brain, nerve, kidney and liver tissue are capable of incorporating P^{32}. Chernick, Srere and Chaikoff (1949) have shown that surviving arterial tissue of the rat, as well as liver slices, can convert acetic acid in which both carbon atoms are labeled with C^{14} into fatty acids. Furthermore, the incorporation of P^{32} into the phosphatide molecule is also readily accomplished by the rat artery. This work is discussed further elsewhere (see p. 433) because of its relationship to atherosclerosis.

The Mechanism of Formation of Phosphatides

The numerous observations which prove that inorganic phosphorus, fatty acids and nitrogenous bases may be incorporated *in vivo* into phosphatides leaves no doubt whatsoever of the ability of the organism to synthesize phosphatides. On the other hand, the elucidation of the mechanism of the synthesis of phosphatides by the body would provide a welcome contribution to biochemistry, for the present state of knowledge does not allow one to pass beyond the conjectural stage. Nor is it possible to decide at the moment whether or not several mechanisms are mutually operable within the organism, although one might predict that there may be alternative routes.

The complicated structure of lecithin or its aminoethyl alcohol and serine analogues makes possible the postulation of numerous intermediates such as mono-, di- and triglycerides; glycerophosphoric acid; phosphatidic acids; aminoethyl phosphate; phosphorylcholine and phosphorylserine. In addition, the structural relationship of the various lipides makes possible postulations (see, e.g., Sobotka, 1930) such as the interaction of cholesterol ester and lecithin to yield a triglyceride with the subsequent release of cholesterol and phosphorylcholine. Either of these could then be incorporated once again into fatty acid-containing structures, or else the phosphorylcholine could contribute to the formation of sphingomyelin.

The double esterification of the phosphoric acid portion may occur simultaneously or stepwise, although it is not likely that the phosphatide molecule is assembled at one place and at one time, in an orderly fashion. Thus there is evidence from work with tumor phosphatides, for example (see p. 437), that P^{32} and labeled fatty acids may be incorporated into phosphatides at different rates. This may be an example either of a total synthesis in which each of the bonds is formed at a different rate, or of a partial synthesis in which one portion of the molecule is involved to a greater extent than another portion. Fishler and co-workers (1941) point out that the "synthesis" or "formation" of phosphatides containing P^{32} means only that in the over-all situation the labeled atom is incorporated into a phosphatide molecule, irrespective of the route involved. They do not believe it possible that all of the bonds between the five parts of lecithin or phosphatidylaminoethyl alcohol can form at one time. Rather there is the possibility that they may form in a given orderly fashion or else that each bond may demonstrate a distinct equilibrium for formation and hydrolysis. In the former case the rate of incorporation of any one label would represent the rate of formation of the molecule. In the latter case, which may be exemplified by the study of formation of tumor phosphatides cited above, the labels would be incorporated at different rates, depending on which portion of the molecule they represented. Nor would the rate of incorporation of labeled fatty acids, nitrogen or phosphorus necessarily be the same in different tissues.

As a matter of fact, the site of the synthesis need not necessarily be limited to one tissue (Fishler and co-workers, 1943), for present methods of analyses do not allow the ready detection of the phosphatide intermediates. Thus it is conceivable, although experimental evidence is lacking, that a reaction such as esterification of the phosphatide skeleton with fatty acids could take place at a different time and place than incorporation of the phosphorus-containing portion.

Chargaff (1939) has described several routes which could possibly lead to phosphatide formation. The first likely possibility is that a diglyceride unites with phosphoric acid to form a phosphatidic acid which then undergoes esterification with the appropriate aminoalcohol.

Alternatively, the phosphatidic acid could result from the acylation with fatty acids of glycerophosphoric acid. The second possibility involves the interaction of a diglyceride with a phosphorylated aminoalcohol. Circumstantial evidence in support of this postulation is found in the report of Outhouse (1937) that aminoethylphosphate may be isolated from tumors. Similarly, Inukai and Nakahara (1935) isolated phosphorylcholine from normal beef liver. The presence of such esters may be due, however, to isolation procedures rather than to metabolic processes. Furthermore, Chaikoff (1942) reports some unpublished work of A. Taurog in which two possible phosphatide intermediates, glycerophosphoric acid and phosphorylcholine, were synthesized so as to contain P^{32}. When these compounds were employed either *in vitro* with isolated kidney and liver tissue or *in vivo* with rats, the phosphatides of both liver and kidney contained P^{32}. These experiments provide some support for both of the routes of phosphatide synthesis proposed above, although again the evidence is circumstantial since there is no way of determining whether the labeled compounds were hydrolyzed prior to the incorporation of the P^{32} into the phosphatide molecule. However, Chaikoff (1942) mentions evidence in the literature which shows that both glycerophosphate and phosphorylcholine are not hydrolyzed under physiological conditions. Yet Riley (1944), who investigated the metabolic activity of labeled phosphorylcholine extensively, found that it hydrolyzed readily *in vivo* and could produce no evidence to show that it was utilized as a unit in phosphatide synthesis. Similarly, Chargaff and Keston (1940) found that both the lecithin and cephalin fractions of rats contained less P^{32} when labeled aminoethyl phosphate was fed than when labeled inorganic phosphate was administered. It would appear, then, that the second of the mechanisms outlined above is not a favored one.

A third synthetic route for consideration depends on the interchangeability of lecithin and phosphatidylaminoethyl alcohol. Chargaff's (1939) experiments showed that the former possessed a higher activity than the latter in the intestinal tract, liver, kidneys, eviscerated carcass and brain of rats. This would indicate that phosphatidylaminoethyl alcohol is not a precursor of lecithin—i.e., that methylation is not a feasible process, but rather that the reverse process of demethylation is possible. This is corroborated on a simpler scale by the observation that the body is incapable of converting aminoethyl alcohol to choline in order to remedy fatty livers (Best and Huntsman, 1932). On the other hand, the excellent work of Stetten (1941, 1942) shows that ingestion of labeled aminoethyl alcohol leads to the formation of labeled choline in the body, whereas the administration of labeled choline does not give rise to labeled aminoethyl alcohol. Thus it would appear that the physiological methylation of aminoethyl alcohol is impossible. Although clarification is desirable, it must be stressed that observations on the methylation or demethylation of complex compounds like phosphatides are not comparable to similar observations made on simpler compounds such as aminoethyl alcohol and choline.

Chargaff (1942) has observed that the vitellin fraction of egg yolk of hens, to which was administered P^{32}, had higher radioactivity in the earlier stages of development than did the phosphatide fraction. Although such an observation is far from definitive, it made possible the postulation that a metabolic link exists between the phosphoproteins and the phosphatides. It is possible that the protein could be phosphorylated at the serine hydroxyl group. This could be followed by esterification with diglycerides and cleavage of the peptide linkages to release phosphatidylserine. Obviously, decarboxylation would provide phosphatidylaminoethyl alcohol. Such statements at this time, however, are highly conjectural.

The Effect of Radiant Energy on Phosphatides

The effect of radiant energy on phosphatides has received some study. Schwarz and Zehner (1912) and Roffo and Correa (1936) had indicated, on the one hand, that radiation from "Thorium X" or ultraviolet light served to decompose lecithin into its constituent parts. Likewise, Kögl (1938) found that lecithin was decomposed by x-rays. Neuberg and Karczag (1913) and Fernau and Pauli (1922), on the other hand, found that radiation from either "Thorium X" or radium had very little effect on lecithin. Accordingly, it is difficult to conclude which situation obtains until more definitive work is reported.

The exposure of the spleen of the dog to ultraviolet radiation effects an increase in the lipide phosphorus content of the blood, according to Kan (1941) and Yosida (1940). The latter worker states that the effect, which is more pronounced with Röntgen rays, applies particularly to the cephalin fraction of the blood. The effect was not observed in splenectomized animals.

Wile, Cameron and Eckstein (1935) found that the total lipide, phosphatide and cholesterol content of epidermis removed from cadavers immediately after death decreased after irradiation with Röntgen rays.

Ultraviolet irradiation does not alter the lipide phosphorus content of blood, although the inorganic phosphorus content is increased, according to Stiemans and Heringa (1933). Levin and Piffault (1934) found that lecithin delayed the lysis of blood *in vitro* which occurs ordinarily under the influence of x-radiation.

The reaction of neoplastic and normal tissue to Röntgen radiation, as measured by phosphatide turnover, has been studied by Hevesy (1946). Rats suffering with sarcoma were subjected to irradiation as were control animals. Thereafter they were dosed with labeled phosphate and after two hours were killed. The specific activities of the lipide phosphorus of both the tissue and the nuceli of the sarcoma and of the liver were determined. It was found in every case that the rate of phosphatide turnover was depressed by irradiation. The greatest diminution was observed in the liver nuclei and the least was found in the liver tissue.

CHAPTER XXIII

THE ROLE OF PHOSPHATIDE HYDROLYSIS PRODUCTS IN METABOLISM

Certain of the hydrolysis products of the phosphatides demonstrate definite physiological and metabolic functions. These will be discussed in this chapter. The activities of choline in this sphere are by far the best defined.

CHOLINE

Choline is considered by some investigators to be a vitamin (György and Goldblatt, 1940). Rosenberg (1942) refers to it as a "vitagen" and Lucas and Best (1943, p. 1) in their excellent review content themselves with the term "dietary factor". However one may define it, choline has been proved in recent years to be of great importance in human nutrition. The story of its metabolic activities is a fascinating one and is reviewed here, although briefly, because of the intimate relationship between choline and lecithin.

Lipotropism

The importance of choline in the diet evolved from a series of observations in regard to fatty livers in animals. In certain instances large, yellow or pink livers were noted in animals due to a pathological increase in the fat and cholesterol ester content. Allen and co-workers (1924) and Fisher (1924) noted the occurrence of such conditions in depancreatized dogs which were being maintained with insulin. It was logical to assume that some dietary deficiency was to blame, especially in view of the observation that a diet including raw beef pancreas improved the condition. Of great importance was the observation of Hershey (1930) and Hershey and Soskin (1931) that egg yolk phosphatides also remedied the fatty livers found in depancreatized dogs. And this led to the conclusive experiments of Best, Hershey and Huntsman (1932) and Best and Huntsman (1932) which proved that the presence of choline, one of the components of phosphatides, in the diet not only prevented the occurrence of fatty livers in animals but also cured them once they developed. Thus it became apparent that choline served in some way or another to prevent

413

the accumulation of fat in the liver. Subsequent work (see p. 355) showed that compounds such as betaine, methionine and inositol accomplished the same effect, and these substances which are essential for the normal metabolism of fats came to be known as lipotropic factors.

Manifestations of Alipotropism

A variety of pathological conditions in addition to fatty livers have been observed when the diet is deficient in choline or other lipotropic factors.

The hemorrhagic degeneration of the kidneys was first noted in rats by Griffith and Wade (1939), and Engel and Salmon (1941) showed that a diet free of lipotropic factors may induce hemorrhages of adrenals, lungs, myocardium and eye as well as of the kidney. All these changes are prevented by the addition to the diet of as little as one or two milligrams of choline daily. Griffith (1941) has attempted to correlate the effect of choline deficiency on the kidneys and the liver by pointing out that in both instances the difficulties may arise from inability of glycerides to form phosphatides. In the case of the kidneys, however, the problem may not be one of fat transfer but rather of nutrition of the kidney cells. That kidney damage is consequent to an inadequate supply of phosphatide may be further concluded from the work of Patterson, Keevil and McHenry (1944) and Patterson and McHenry (1944).

A diffuse nodular hepatic cirrhosis has been observed in numerous animals as a result of choline deficiency (see, e.g., Rich and Hamilton, 1940, and György and Goldblatt, 1942). This, as pointed out by Chaikoff and Connor (1940) and György and Goldblatt (1942), seems to be the second stage in liver degeneration due to alipotropism, and like fatty livers may be cured by the administration of choline.

Choline deficiency has been observed by Christensen (1940) and Engel and Salmon (1941) to cause involution of the thymus gland, enlargement of the spleen and a transformation of the lymph nodes to hemolymph nodes. Sharpless (1940) has found choline in combination with the Vitamin B complex to be essential in the maintenance of a normal gastric epithelium and the prevention of hyperplasia in rats. In this instance it is significant, although unexplainable, that choline by itself is an aggravating factor, thus showing an interdependency among the protective factors.

Sure (1940) has described experiments showing the necessity of choline for normal growth and lactation of rats, and it is also necessary (Abbott and DeMasters, 1940) for normal egg production in chicks. In turkeys and chicks, as a result of choline deficiency, perosis, a shortening and thickening of the bones, has been observed (Jukes, 1941) together with inhibition of growth.

A relationship between choline and tumors has been suggested by Jacobi and Baumann (1942) on the basis of the high phosphatide turnover in tumors and particularly on the basis of the very high lecithin turnover.

Choline may exert a protective (Andrews and Brown, 1940) action against cholesterol-induced atherosclerosis although the situation is very obscure and not too probable.

The report by Davis (1944, 1946) that choline induces anemia in dogs, which incidentally was not observed in humans (Moosnick, Schleicher and Peterson, 1945), has been refuted by Clarkson and Best (1947).

Horowitz and Beadle (1943) and Horowitz (1946) reported that choline was necessary for the growth of two mutants of *Neurospora crassa* (Nos. 34486 and 47904) in a medium of sugar, salts and biotin.

Obviously the significance of some of these observations is still obscure, but there is little doubt that choline and its lipotropic companions are essential for the normal functioning of the animal organism.

Transmethylation

Insight into the role which choline plays in metabolic activity has been provided by the elucidation of the process of transmethylation which has been reviewed by du Vigneaud (1942/43). As has been indicated previously, methionine and betaine were shown to be lipotropic factors, the former by Tucker and Eckstein (1937) and the latter by Best

$$
\begin{array}{ll}
\begin{array}{l}
CH_3 \\
| \\
S \\
| \\
CH_2 \\
| \\
CH_2 \\
| \\
CH-NH_2 \\
| \\
COOH
\end{array}
&
(CH_3)_3-N-CH_2-C=O \\
\qquad\qquad\qquad\quad |\quad\;\;\; | \\
\qquad\qquad\qquad\quad O\_\_\_\_\_|
\end{array}
$$

Methionine   *Betaine*

and Huntsman (1932). The idea soon occurred to several workers that lipotropism was in some way associated with the ability of a compound to yield methyl groups in metabolic reactions. du Vigneaud and co-workers (1939) subsequently observed that the essential amino acid, methionine, could be replaced in the diet of rats by homocysteine if choline or betaine were fed at the same time. They suggested that this phenomenon was due to the fact that in the organism homocysteine was

$$HS—(CH_2)_2—CH—COOH$$
$$|$$
$$NH_2$$

Homocysteine

converted to methionine by methyl groups from the lipotropic factors in the diet. If this were so, then the organism should also be able to synthesize choline when fed a diet deficient in choline, but rich in the methyl-donating methionine. That this was the case was shown by the work of du Vigneaud and co-workers (1940) in which the fate of methionine was traced by "labeling" the methyl group attached to the sulfur with deuterium. This deuteromethionine was fed to rats on a choline-deficient diet. After several weeks the animals were killed and choline was isolated from them. The choline contained deuterium, and what is more, all of this deuterium was present in the methyl groups as shown by an experiment (du Vigneaud and co-workers, 1941) in which the choline was degraded to trimethylamine by use of potassium permanganate. In subsequent work, Keller, Rachelle and du Vigneaud (1949) labeled the methyl group of methionine with both deuterium and C^{14} and fed this compound to rats. After four days the rats were killed and choline and creatine were isolated from their bodies. The labels were found in the methyl groups of these compounds in the same ratio as they existed in the methyl groups of the methionine. These conclusive experiments established as fact the hypothesis that certain compounds have the ability to yield methyl groups for the *in vivo* synthesis of physiologically necessary compounds. Among these are choline and methionine.

It is interesting to note that fatty livers are caused by the ingestion of methyl usurpers such as guanidinoacetic acid which on N-methylation yields creatine (Stetten, 1942; Stetten and Grail, 1942) and nicotinic acid amide which on methylation yields trigonelline (Handler and Dann, 1942).

The ability to act as a methyl donor is apparently limited to very few substances. The search for other lipotropic factors, however, soon made it apparent that all lipotropic substances—that is, factors which prevent fatty livers, do not necessarily support growth or act as methyl donors. Thus the methyl diethyl homologue of choline prevented perosis in chicks, but did not support growth (Jukes, 1941). The dimethyl ethyl homologue of choline, on the other hand, not only proved to be lipotropic, but also supported growth according to Moyer and du Vigneaud (1942), who have tabulated the compounds which up to 1942 have been found to be lipotropic and to prevent some of the other conditions for which alipotropic diets are responsible.

The methyl-donating capacity of methionine has already been mentioned. Chaikoff, Entenman and Montgomery (1945) have shown that in certain protein-containing substances an enzyme may exist which releases methionine from the protein with the over-all effect that the protein appears to be lipotropic. This is apparently the case with raw pancreas whose lipotropic action was originally attributed to the presence of lecithin or choline (see p. 356).

A possible mechanism for the formation of choline in the organism by the transmethylation which was shown to have taken place by du Vigneaud and co-workers (1940) has evolved from the work of Stetten (1941), who fed successively to rats aminoethyl alcohol, choline, glycine, betaine and ammonia, all labeled with N^{15}. He found that the dietary choline and aminoethyl alcohol replaced a large precentage of these components of the total phosphatides. The phosphatide choline isolated after aminoethyl alcohol feeding was very rich in isotopic nitrogen, whereas the phosphatide aminoethyl alcohol was poor in this element. The glycine of the proteins contained very little N^{15} after labeled aminoethyl alcohol was fed. But when isotopic glycine was fed, the aminoethyl alcohol of the phosphatides contained a great deal of N^{15}. Isotopic betaine increased the N^{15} content of both the glycine and the aminoethyl alcohol.

These observations led to the conclusion that betaine is readily demethylated to glycine which in turn is changed to aminoethyl alcohol. This latter compound is in turn converted to choline possibly by the methyl groups provided by the betaine. This is represented schematically as follows:

$$(CH_3)_3\text{—}N\text{—}CH_2\text{—}C\text{=}O \xrightarrow[-3CH_3]{} H_2N\text{—}CH_2\text{—}COOH \longrightarrow H_2N\text{—}CH_2\text{—}CH_2OH$$

Betaine	*Glycine*	*Aminoethyl alcohol*

$$\xrightarrow{+3CH_3} [(CH_3)_3\text{—}\overset{+}{N}\text{—}CH_2\text{—}CH_2OH]OH^-$$
$$\textit{Choline}$$

Serine is a possible intermediate between glycine and aminoethyl alcohol, a fact which assumes significance in view of the wide occurrence of phosphatidylserine.

This cycle has been elaborated in a review by Jukes (1947). who has presented evidence from the literature to show that choline may be degraded by physiological means to betaine aldehyde which in turn may be oxidized to the methyl-donating betaine. The conversion of this compound to glycine, which in turn may be reduced to aminoethyl alcohol, follows Stetten's representation. From here on, however, the methylation of the aminoethyl alcohol to choline is shown to proceed stepwise through methylaminoethyl alcohol and dimethylaminoethyl alcohol, the methyl groups having been provided by the betaine as well as by dietary methionine. The evidence for the stepwise methylation of aminoethyl alcohol has been provided by du Vigneaud and co-workers (1946) by experiments employing methylaminoethyl alcohol and dimethylaminoethyl alcohol labeled with deuterium. Similar evidence for the stepwise formation of choline is found in the work of Horowitz (1946). This worker produced by gene mutations two strains of *Neurospora crassa* which no longer were able to synthesize choline. From one of these strains (No. 47904) he was actually able to isolate methylaminoethyl alcohol which is undoubtedly a precursor of choline. Furthermore this substance supported the growth of the other mutant (No. 34486), indicating that the block in choline formation preceded this intermediate in strain 34486 and followed it in strain 47904.

The Mechanism of Lipotropism

Closely related to the process of transmethylation is the mechanism by means of which lipotropic factors function. Although a great deal remains to be elucidated on this score, it is fairly well established that lipotropism is closely related to phosphatide formation. Best, Channon and Ridout (1934) proposed that choline prevented fatty livers by the formation of phosphatides. Direct evidence for this hypothesis, despite the fact that the phosphatide content of the liver did not obviously increase, was obtained by Welch (1936) and Welch and Landau (1942). These investigators fed arsenocholine, which was known to be lipotropic, to rats. In the phosphatides from these animals they found large quantities of arsenocholine, indicating that this lipotropic analogue of choline had been utilized in the synthesis of the phosphatides. Arsenocholine, however, is not a methyl donor, indicating that it, and probably choline as well, is utilized intact in the *in vivo* synthesis of phosphatides. Thus the prevention of fatty livers may be explained on the basis that choline provides a means for fat transfer. Further evidence that the lipotropic action of choline is associated with the intact molecule and that the methyl groups do not take part has been provided recently by the work of McArthur, Lucas and Best (1947). These workers fed the ethyl analogue of choline, triethyl-β-hydroxyethylammonium hydroxide, to rats and proved chemically that the unnatural base was incorporated directly into the phosphatides isolated from the liver.

This explanation, however, would not necessarily be expected to apply to other pathological conditions caused by alipotropic diets such as renal hemorrhage which may result because there is insufficient phosphatide present for a healthy cell structure. That the various manifestations of lipotropism demand separate mechanisms is shown by the observation of Jukes (1940) that betaine prevents fatty livers in rats but does not prevent perosis in fowl. Similarly lacking in explanation is the observation of György, Rose and Shipley (1947) that the female hormone, estrone, demonstrates a small but definite lipotropic effect by itself and greatly augments the lipotropic action of methionine.

Evidence similar to that of Welch (1936) has been obtained by other investigators who carried out tracer studies with choline containing isotopic elements. Perlman and Chaikoff (1939b) and Perlman, Stillman and Chaikoff (1940a) used choline containing isotopic phosphorus, whereas Stetten (1941) used choline with isotopic nitrogen. Both sets of experiments showed convincingly that choline accelerated the rate of phosphatide formation, particularly in the liver, which proved to be the most active center since the liver phosphatides contained the greatest amount of isotopic element. Platt and Porter (1947) found with the aid of radioactive inorganic phosphorus not only that choline accelerated lecithin formation in the liver, but also that aminoethyl alcohol, which is not lipotropic, accelerated the formation of the cephalin fraction. According to Artom, Cornatzer and Crowder (1949), a single large dose of either aminoethyl alcohol or diethanolamine causes an increase in both the choline and noncholine-containing phosphatides of the liver. The administration of choline, on the other hand (Artom and Cornatzer, 1948), accelerated only the formation of the choline-containing lipides.

Other Functions of Choline

From the above discussion it is obvious that choline is important in the regulation of lipide metabolism and serves the important function of preventing a variety of pathological conditions resulting from alipotropic diets. It serves further as a structural unit of tissue since it is a component of both lecithin and sphingomyelin, the former being present in every living cell. Dietary choline, as mentioned previously, is incorporated directly into tissue phosphatides. This is confirmed by the work of Boxer and Stetten (1944). These investigators fed choline containing isotopic nitrogen to rats and found that this labeled substance was readily incorporated into the tissue phosphatides.

Choline has still another function which is not yet too clearly understood. This involves the acetylation of choline in the organism to yield acetylcholine. The first demonstration that the acetylation of choline yields a material of greatly enhanced physiological activity resulted from the work of Hunt and Taveau (1906). Since that time it has been shown to be an agent which lowers blood pressure and which stimulates peristaltic activity. The acetylation and the deacetylation of choline seem to proceed at will in the organism, depending apparently on whether the blood pressure level is in need of lowering. Dale (1914) showed that acetylcholine stimulates the parasympathetic nerves as well as the sympathetic ganglia and probably the autonomic ganglia. It seems to be the chemical agent involved in the transmission of nerve impulses to muscles. Some of the ramifications of the physiological action of acetylcholine are discussed by Page (1937, pp. 70–73).

The possibility that acetylcholine formation is related to lipotropism has been investigated by Solandt and Best (1939), but more conclusive experimentation is necessary.

AMINOETHYL ALCOHOL, SERINE AND SPHINGOSINE

Physiologically, aminoethyl alcohol is practically inert except for its basic properties. This is indeed an interesting observation in view of the widespread occurrence of this substance in plant and animal tissue and in view of its role as a precursor of choline (see p. 417). The minimum lethal dose of aminoethyl alcohol has been determined for rats as 860 to 900 milligrams per kilogram (Chen, 1932). Page and Allen (1930) noted that the neutralized base had no observable physiological effect on rabbits or cats when injected intravenously. The soaps formed with fatty acids, on the other hand, effected a marked lowering of blood pressure. These soaps also tended to stop the coagulation of fibrinogen, although the parent aminoethyl alcohol actually accelerates the coagulation (Kuwashima, 1923).

Outhouse (1936) isolated from tumors the phosphoric acid ester of aminoethyl alcohol.

Trier (1912a) proposed many years ago that aminoethyl alcohol may be synthesized in the body by the amination of ethylene glycol. A similar amination of glycollic acid would provide glycine. Both the glycol and glycollic acid, according to his postulations, would arise from a Cannizzaro type of reaction on glycollic aldehyde which in turn would be formed from two moles of formaldehyde. Actually, the work of Stetten (1941), see p. 417) has shown that glycine is a precursor of aminoethyl alcohol and that the glycine arises from the demethylation of the lipotropic substance, betaine. The possibility that aminoethyl alcohol might arise from the decarboxylation of serine was pointed out by Nord (1919), who found that certain bacteria could effect such a reaction.

Serine is considered to be nonessential in human nutrition although it serves, in the rat but not in the chick, as a precursor of glycine (Sahyun, 1948, p. 225). According to Schmidt (1938, p. 224), it is metabolized to glucose in an animal in which diabetes has been produced by phlorhizin, whereas in the normal animal its breakdown products are water and carbon dioxide. The first step in the metabolic process is deamination to yield $CH_2OHCOCHO$ which is reduced to glyceric aldehyde. This compound, in turn, produces the end products indicated above.

Very little is known about the biochemistry of sphingosine, save that in Niemann-Pick's disease (see p. 426) the sphingomyelin content of the liver and the spleen increases greatly at the expense of the brain cerebrosides. Thus it appears that sphingomyelin plays a role in lipide metabolism.

Drury and co-workers (1936) found that sphingosine is bactericidal, that it hemolyzes red blood cells, and that it gives characteristic precipitations with serum.

GLYCEROPHOSPHORIC ACID

The physiological implications of glycerophosphoric acid are manifold, although a detailed discussion is again beyond the scope of the present work. It appears to play a part in the catabolism of carbohydrates, and glycerophosphate dehydrogenase is active in nerve tissue, since Thunberg (1923) found that glycerophosphate accelerated the rate of decolorization of methylene blue by guinea pig nerve. Goda (1938) observed that the oxidation-reduction reaction between glycerophosphate and pyruvic acid yields lactic acid in fresh muscle extract and produces three times more product with α-glycerophosphate than with the β-isomer.

INOSITOL-CONTAINING PHOSPHATIDES

Certain properties of physiological interest have been attributed to the inositol-containing phosphatides. Hesselbach and Burk (1944) found that the inositol phosphatides from soybeans, as well as inositol itself, effected malignant tumor regression in mice.

Rhymer and co-workers (1947) have observed that inositol-containing phosphatides exert an inhibiting action on the antibacterial effect of streptomycin, 0.0002 milligram of phosphatide suppressing the effect of 0.06 milligram of streptomycin.

LYSOPHOSPHATIDES

As already indicated, Kyes (1903, 1907, see p. 99) observed and recorded the marked hemolytic properties of the lysophosphatides. A considerable amount of work in the literature describes the hemolytic action of the lysophosphatides, although a great deal remains to be done, especially in regard to normal and abnormal body processes.

The poisonous nature of the lysophosphatides was recognized early and their role in snake poisoning has already been discussed (see p. 99). Belfanti (1925) found that lysolecithin from brain or egg yolk was strongly toxic, dissolving leucocytes and red blood cells and injuring the brain by the production of edema and hemorrhage. Lysolecithins from other tissues such as pancreas and salivary glands were less active, and Belfanti pointed out that they were probably held in check in the body by antagonistic substances such as cholesterol. Guerrini (1925) likewise observed that lysolecithin was a strong capillary poison, causing extensive hemorrhage wherever injected. Its hemolytic properties were also studied by Gronchi (1932a).

Magistris (1929) observed that lysolecithin maintained its hemolytic powers in dilutions of 1:26,400. Gorter and Hermans (1943) studied the hemolyzing action of lysophosphatides and concluded that the amount necessary to hemolyze one cell was sufficient to cover this cell with a unimolecular layer. On this basis, one milligram of lysophosphatide prepared from egg yolk hemolyzed 5.5×10^9 human red blood cells, $7.7 \pm 0.4 \times 10^9$ rabbit cells and $15 \pm 2 \times 10^9$ sheep cells.

Iwata (1934) observed that the lysolecithin from polished rice behaved similarly to that obtained by the action of snake venom on egg yolk. The lethal dose for the rabbit was estimated to be one milligram per kilogram of body weight.

Rousseau and Pascal (1938) found that lysophosphatides dissolved certain portions of the streptococcus cell, leaving other fragments unaffected. Hassegawa and Nakamoto (1939) observed that lysolecithin dissolves living but not dead pneumococci.

The relationship of lysophosphatides to adrenalin production has been studied by Feldberg (1940). Ajazzi-Mancini and Donatelli (1941) have reported other pharmacological studies which compare the action of lysophosphatides with the action of toxin of *Bothrop jararacussu* which contains lecithinase.

It has long been known that the hemolyzing and toxic action of the lysophosphatides is inhibited by cholesterol. This was first observed by Kyes (1903, 1907) and was confirmed by Delezenne and Ledebt (1911, 1912) and Delezenne and Fourneau (1914), who showed that the cholesterol united molecularly with the lysolecithin to form a new compound devoid of hemolytic activity. The hemolytic activity of the saponins is likewise inhibited by cholesterol. Although according to Wilbur and Collier (1943) the mechanisms of hemolysis by the two materials are different, Gronchi (1932) observed that repeated injections of lysolecithin or the injection of a relatively large dose of the substance into rabbits caused the cholesterol content of the serum to increase.

The hemolytic activity of pure lysolecithin and of a pure lysocephalin was compared by Noguchi (quoted by Belfanti, Contardi and Ercoli, 1936, p. 220, footnote 1), who used samples prepared by Levene, Rolf and Simms (1924). He found both of them to be active, although lysolecithin was three times as powerful a hemolytic agent as the lysocephalin. Magistris (1929) believed that the lysocephalins have no hemolytic activity whatsoever. The work of Dunn (1934), on the other hand, would indicate that the lysocephalins are hemolytic. The question will stand reinvestigation with highly purified materials.

Chargaff and Cohen (1939) reported that neither lysolecithin nor the lysocephalins possess any activity in blood clotting. Rousseau and Pascal (1938a) found that lysolecithin has a stronger oxidative action on methylene blue than does glutathione. This is of interest since Grassman, Dyckerhoff and Schoenbeck (1930) showed that reduced glutathione is a natural activator of certain enzymes.

CHAPTER XXIV

THE ROLE OF THE PHOSPHATIDES IN PATHOLOGICAL CONDITIONS

A disturbed lipide metabolism which may be reflected in lipide analyses of blood serum (e.g., Ciaccio, 1917) may be either the cause or the result of various pathological conditions. Thannhauser (1947a) has presented a summary of the lipide analyses of serum in various diseases. Bloor (1943, p. 158 ff.) has also discussed this subject in detail. For the most part, the role of the phosphatides has been but little explored, and much work remains to be done. The lipide chemistry of various diseases exclusive of alipotropism (see p. 355) will be summarized briefly in this section. Undoubtedly, phosphatide distribution is affected in practically all pathological conditions. The diseases discussed here are those for which data are available.

Lipidoses

General obesity, or the accumulation of fat in the body, is ordinarily not considered pathological so long as the structure of the lipides, as well as the composition and distribution of the lipide deposits, is normal, and so long as a disturbed lipide metabolism is not indicated. Dietary fatty livers, on the other hand, provide an example of a localized, abnormal accumulation of lipides due to disturbed lipide metabolism. The quirks of lipide metabolism which are manifested by infiltration of fat into the liver are now well understood. Considerably more obscure are the metabolic disturbances which give rise to a variety of less common diseases, all of which are characterized by the abnormal accumulation of lipide masses in various tissues and organs. These pathological conditions have been classified by Thannhauser (1940) and Thannhauser and Magendantz (1938) as lipidoses, and are distinguished one from the other by the site chosen for lipide accumulation, the composition of the accumulated lipides and the reflection of the condition in the lipide composition of the blood. Lipidoses include xanthomatoses, Niemann-Pick's disease, Tay-Sachs' disease and Gaucher's disease, each of which will be discussed in turn. Thannhauser's (1940) book should be consulted for a complete treatment of these diseases from a medical point of view.

424

Xanthomatoses

Xanthomatosis is a rather general category for a group of disturbances characterized by lipide deposits high in cholesterol content. Phosphatides, however, are not lacking, whereas glycerides are only very minor constituents of the deposits. Hypercholesterolemia may be demonstrated, although it is not prerequisite. The site of lipide deposition varies in the several types of xanthomatoses.

Schüller-Christian disease or Hand (1891/93) syndrome is a type of xanthomatosis free of hypercholesterolemia (Pick, 1933; Thannhauser, 1940) which is characterized by defects in the membranous bones of the skull with the resulting syndromes of exophthalmos and diabetes insipidus (Rowland, 1928). Less commonly, according to Thannhauser (1940, p. 136 ff.), the defects may be found in the mastoid and sinuses, and in reticular bone tissue. The peculiar yellow deposits were shown by Epstein and Lorenz (1930) to contain when dried 3.2 per cent cholesterol, 15.4 per cent cholesterol esters and 1.6 per cent phosphatides. When the skin is involved, the disease is termed *xanthoma disseminata*. According to Sosman (1932), therapy must involve x-ray treatment, since dietary control is without effect.

The type of xanthomatosis termed primary by Thannhauser (1940, p. 44 ff.) differs from Schüller-Christian disease in that hypercholesterolemia is invariably demonstrated (Thannhauser and Magendantz, 1938). The phosphatide and total lipide content of the blood is likewise high. Extensive analyses of the blood of individuals suffering from this form of the disease have been reported by Kornerup (1942). The disease is characterized by involvement of cutaneous or subcutaneous tissue or tendons, and the fat accumulations are large, spongy and tumorous in nature. The lipides of such a tumor were found by Eckstein and Wile (1930) to contain 48.8 per cent cholesterol and 8.1 per cent phosphatides. Dreyfuss and Fishberg (1943) reported a case of primary xanthomatosis accompanied by anemia and splenomegaly in which lecithin, cephalin fraction and total cholesterol of the spleen were increased. The blood picture is ordinarily not normalized by dietary control, according to Sperry and Schick (1936), although Schoenheimer (1933) has described a case which responded to a cholesterol-free diet. Adlersberg and Sobotka (1934a) have reported on five cases of xanthomatosis in which the hypercholesterolemia was alleviated by prolonged feeding of phosphatides. The interruption of this therapy caused the lipemia to return. The disease tends to be hereditary.

The secondary xanthomatosis of Thannhauser (1940, p. 179 ff.) is characterized by an extremely high degree of lipemia which is caused not by the xanthomatosis but by a disease such as diabetes, chronic pancreatitis, Von Gierke's disease or by some undefinable cause. The latter situation has been termed an essential lipemia by Bernstein and co-workers (1939). The lipemia which characterizes secondary xanthomatosis thus becomes a possible but not an obligate source of the scattered lipide deposits found in the skin. These deposits are smaller than those which distinguish primary xanthomatosis; and the lipemia, which arises largely from glycerides, although phosphatides and cholesterol are not absent (Chapman and Kinney, 1941), responds to dietary control, according to Bernstein and co-workers (1939). In advanced cases, the liver may become involved, as indicated by the development of jaundice or hepatic cirrhosis. Likewise, the liver and spleen may become enlarged.

Thannhauser (1940, p. 152 ff.) also recognizes the presence of xanthomatoses whose symptoms place them in categories intermediate to those described above.

The cause of xanthomatosis is little understood. According to Chanutin and Ludewig (1937) and Holt, Aylward and Timbres (1939), the disease does not respond to lipotropic agents or thyroid materials. Whereas lipide metabolism is definitely disturbed in instances where hyperlipemia is typical, a similar conclusion cannot be reached in the case of Schüller-Christian disease where the blood picture is normal. Secondary xanthomatosis may be a direct result of the initial hyperlipemia, although this sheds no light on the fact that all hyperlipemias are not accompanied by xanthomatosis.

Niemann-Pick's Disease

Niemann-Pick's disease is characterized by its familial nature, by normal quantities of blood lipids (Thannhauser, 1940, p. 323 ff.; Sperry, 1942) and by accumulations of lipides in any of the organs of the body, but primarily in the spleen, liver, lymph nodes, bone marrow and central nervous system. Characteristically, these fat accumulations contain large amounts of sphingomyelin. The glycerophosphatides increase to a lesser degree, and cholesterol and its esters are also present (Lignac and Teunissen, 1938). Thus in its familial nature it resembles primary xanthomatosis, whereas its characteristic blood picture is reminiscent of Schüller-Christian disease, although it must be noted that Pick (1933) has described cases involving hypercholesterolemia.

Epstein and Lorenz (1930a, 1932) were among the first to analyze the lipides in organs affected by Niemann-Pick's disease. On the basis of these analyses they were able to differentiate between the various types of lipidoses. Klenk (1934, 1935) and Baumann, Klenk and Scheidegger (1936) studied in detail the lipide accumulations which accompany

Niemann-Pick's disease. They readily determined the typical high concentration of sphingomyelin which, however, is also accompanied by lesser amounts of glycerophosphatides and, according to Sperry (1942), by some cholesterol. Menten and Welton (1946) found a large increase in the glycerophosphatides and sphingomyelin content of the liver and spleen of a victim of this disease.

Since the blood demonstrates no increase whatsoever in sphingomyelin content, it is probable that this phosphatide is produced by the spleen rather than deposited in it. The sphingomyelin obtained by Klenk (1934) from the fatty spleen of a child victim of Niemann-Pick's disease demonstrated a normal fatty acid content in that lignoceric acid was present together with what was believed to be palmitic, stearic and nervonic acids. The sphingomyelin content of the brain and the liver (Klenk, 1935) was also high, especially in the latter organ, where it existed in excess of the glycerophosphatides. In neither of these organs, however, had fat accumulated to the extent that it had in the spleen. The sphingomyelin from the liver yielded the same fatty acids as that from the spleen, whereas the brain sphingomyelin was unique in containing only stearic acid. The total lipides of the brain, unlike those of the liver, were further distinguished by the absence of the highly unsaturated C_{20} and C_{22} acids normally present. Normal cerebrosides also were lacking in the brain, although a galactoside, usually found in small amounts, was present in large quantities. This galactoside was later shown (Klenk, 1941) to contain, in addition to galactose, certain impurities and a nitrogen-containing acid of unknown composition termed neuraminic acid.

Tropp and Eckardt (1936, 1937), like Klenk, isolated the sphingomyelin from the brain, liver and spleen of victims of Niemann-Pick's disease. Unlike Klenk, they found in the sphingomyelin of the brain palmitic and lignoceric as well as stearic acids, although the latter acid was quantitatively the most important.

Chargaff (1939a) has also reported the analysis of the lipides of the spleen in Niemann-Pick's disease. He found the sphingomyelin to yield largely lignoceric acid on hydrolysis together with a mixture of palmitic and stearic acids. No evidence whatsoever was obtained for the presence of nervonic or other unsaturated acids. The quantity of glycerophosphatides present was less than half that of the sphingomyelin and about 70 per cent of them consisted of cephalin fraction.

Although Sjövall (1935) found that parenteral administration of lecithin did not produce sustained lipidosis, Ferraro and Jervis (1940) reported that large doses of sphingomyelin produced in rabbits and monkeys symptoms resembling those of Niemann-Pick's disease. Tompkins (1942, 1943, 1943a) carried out very interesting studies following the injection of various brain lipide fractions into test animals. In this way she has partially reproduced some of the pathology of lipidoses. When a mixture of sphingolipides was used with rabbits an infiltration into the reticulo-endothelial system of macrophages was observed in addition to hyperplasia of the bone marrow, splenomegaly and diffuse pulmonary infiltrations.

Tay-Sachs' Disease

Tay-Sachs' disease, which is closely associated with amaurotic familial idiocy (Spielmeyer, 1929), resembles Niemann-Pick's disease very closely in its familial nature and in the fact that here, too, the blood picture is normal. The lipide accumulations are prone to occur in the brain (Davison and Jacobson, 1936) as well as in the spleen, and it is their composition which differentiates this disorder from Niemann-Pick's disease. Thus the lipide accumulations in Tay-Sachs' disease contain a decreased rather than an increased amount of sphingomyelin, as has been shown by Klenk (1939) and by Sperry (1942). Another important difference lies in the presence of large quantities of the neuraminic acid-containing galactoside (Klenk, 1941; Klenk and Schumann, 1940) which occurs to a much lesser extent in Niemann-Pick's disease and which is present in minute quantities in normal brain.

Gaucher's Disease

Gaucher's disease resembles Niemann-Pick's and Tay-Sachs' diseases only in that it is familial. The sites of accumulation are chiefly the spleen, liver and lymph nodes. The brain does not appear to be involved. The chief difference, however, is that the lipide accumulation, as noted by Epstein (1924), is primarily composed of cerebrosides. Thus this disease does not actually involve phosphatides in any unique way and is included primarily to make the discussion of lipidoses complete.

According to Emanuel (1941), phosphatides and cholesterol are also present in the lipide accumulations.

GENERAL DISEASES

Diseases of the Liver and Bile Ducts

Although pathological conditions in the liver are reflected by various lipemias, as would be expected because of the important role of the liver in lipide metabolism, there are many conflicting reports in the literature on this subject. Very little attention has been given to the variation in phosphatide content, and it is to be hoped that this will be rectified in the future. Man and co-workers (1945) have studied definitively the course of serum lipides in various hepatic disfunctions. Because of the variation which appears normal in these cases, generalizations are made only with difficulty. However, it may be concluded that the ratio of free to total cholesterol in the blood increases in diseases such as cholelithiasis and the development of calculi, tumors or inflammation which effect biliary obstruction and subsequent destruction of tissue. This is also the case in acute, chronic, infectious or toxic hepatitis where destruction of the parenchymatous cells results (Thannhauser, 1947). It follows then, since there is ordinarily a dearth of free cholesterol in the blood, that the quantity of this material must increase, and this appears to be the case even when the total amount of cholesterol is subnormal. The phosphatide concentration increases along with the cholesterol content (Chanutin and Ludewig, 1936) to the point where the ratio of lipide phosphorus to cholesterol is above normal. This increase in phosphatide content, noted by Davanzo (1936), was found by Weil and Russell (1942) to occur in both blood plasma and blood cells, although the increase in the former was greater. Tayeau (1943) observed that the total phosphatide and cholesterol content of the blood of patients with obstructive jaundice could be extracted with ether, indicating that the protein complexes normally present were in some way dissociated.

Normal or low phosphatide and total cholesterol contents are not unusual in cases involving destruction of the liver cells. Thus a lesser degree of lipemia accompanies hepatitis than conditions involving obstruction of the bile ducts. In the latter situation a moderate increase in the neutral fat content of the blood is common along with hypercholesterolemia and hyperlecithinemia. Elimination of the obstruction leads to the return of normal blood lipide values, the neutral fat and phosphatide concentrations falling more rapidly than the cholesterol content.

Destruction of the liver by various chemical poisons brings about a distribution similar to that observed in hepatitis where subnormal quantities of cholesterol and lipide phosphorus are present (Man and co-workers, 1945; Lehnherr, 1935).

Wachstein (1937) has determined the iodine numbers of blood fatty acids present in hepatic disfunctions. He has concluded that unusually large quantities of unsaturated fatty acids are present in jaundice due to parenchymatous destruction of the liver.

Cirrhosis appears to be the ultimate stage of hepatic disfunction due either to destruction of the parenchyma or to dietary fatty liver. The administration of lipotropic agents does not ordinarily aid cirrhosis, especially if it is due to the former cause (Man and co-workers, 1945);

but Goldstein and Rosahn (1945) have reported that a combination of choline and inositol was effective in relief of cirrhosis which did not respond to choline alone.

The lipide content of the liver itself may deviate from normal in certain pathological conditions, and some of these variations have been studied by Theis (1928, 1929). Weil and Russell (1942) found that jaundice due to ligated bile ducts did not affect the lipide content of the liver of rats. Contrariwise, partial hepatectomy was observed by Ludewig, Minor and Hortenstine (1939) to cause an increase in neutral fat, phosphatide and total cholesterol content of the liver, together with an increase in unsaturation of the phosphatide fatty acids.

Diseases of the Kidneys

Diseases of the kidneys, like those of the liver, are usually associated with lipemias. The severity of the lipemia is indicated in a report by Thomas (1943) on a case in which plasma lipides, due to the nephrotic syndrome, reached a level of 6.6 grams per 100 ml. In the early stages of the disease the increase was accounted for largely by cholesterol, although the ratio of cholesterol ester to total cholesterol remained constant (cf. Page, Kirk and Van Slyke, 1936), unlike the situation in hepatic disfunctions. As the disease progressed, the neutral fat content increased until, after five months, it accounted for nearly one-half of the total lipides. The phosphatide content maintained a constant and normal relationship to the total lipide content, and accordingly must necessarily have increased. The lipemia was accentuated when the disease was most severe.

Other workers (Peters and Man, 1943; King and Bruger, 1935; Lichtenstein and Epstein, 1931) have studied the nephrotic syndrome and have concluded that the associated lipemia is characteristic of the syndrome regardless of its origin. It was further obvious to Peters and Man (1943) that the intensity of the edema, which is the most important symptomatic expression of the syndrome, may not be directly correlated with the intensity of the lipemia. Nevertheless, in the general situation, the lipemia is most severe when the edema is largest and when the serum albumin (Peters and Man, 1943) is lowest and the albumen of the urine (Campbell, 1925) is highest in concentration. As a matter of fact, nephritis unaccompanied by edema is not characterized by lipemia, according to Page, Kirk and Van Slyke (1936).

The lipide values of blood of partially nephrectomized rats have been investigated by Ludewig and Chanutin (1938), who found, as would be expected from results with nephritis, that the cholesterol content increased and that the phosphatide content varied correspondingly.

A possible relationship between diet and the lipemia of nephritis has been observed by Hiller and co-workers (1924).

The situation in which the kidney, by means of double nephrectomy or ligation of both ureters, is prevented entirely from functioning has been explored by Winkler and co-workers (1943). They observed in dogs and monkeys a marked lipemia in which phosphatides and neutral fat increased as well as cholesterol. Since the lipide content of the liver increased at the same time, it was assumed that the source of the lipemia was the fat depots. The authors believe that this lipemia is basically different from that of the nephrotic syndrome, since in the latter condition the lipemia tends to disappear when the kidneys become entirely incapable of functioning. In similar work, Heymann (1942) has demonstrated in nephrectomized or mercuric chloride-poisoned dogs a distinct lipemia in which the cholesterol content increases steadily until death.

The hypercholesterolemia of nephritis is accompanied, as indicated by Govaerts and Cordier (1929) and Hahn and Wolff (1921), by the excretion of cholesterol in the urine. Page (1936) has detected only very small quantities of phosphatides in this type of urine.

Narat (1938) has reported some success in the treatment of pyelitis by intravenous injection of lecithin and olive oil emulsions.

Diseases of the Pancreas and the Gastrointestinal Tract

One of the most common manifestations of diseases which prevent the production of enzymes in the pancreas and the gastrointestinal tract is *steatorrhea*—the presence of lipides in the feces.

The blood lipide picture which accompanies steatorrhea is one of hypolipemia, both the cholesterol and the phosphatide concentrations being reduced (Snell, 1939). So dominant is the hypolipemia that the hyperlipemia which normally follows the ingestion of food is eliminated (Snell, 1939). This blood picture, then, appears to be a reflection of the decreased absorption of fat which accompanies steatorrhea. Hypolipemia is also the end result of gastrointestinal obstruction, according to Peters and Van Slyke (1946, p. 518), who quote unpublished work of E. B. Man. In this investigation it was shown that the initial hyperlipemia changed to the opposite condition as the disease progressed and nutritional deficiencies resulted.

Complete depancreatization, with the elimination of all external and internal secretory processes, has been observed many times to produce diabetes in experimental animals (e.g., Hershey and Soskin, 1931). Steatorrhea, for the reasons indicated above, is to be expected; and, as shown by White and co-workers (1938), fatty livers are common, especially in children. That these livers are of the dietary type may be surmised from the work of Hershey and Soskin (1931), who found that depancreatized dogs could be maintained on insulin, sugar and protein, together with egg yolk lecithin which contains, of course, the lipotropic agent, choline. The fatty liver usually disappears when the diabetes is properly controlled.

Diseases of the Blood

As was pointed out many years ago by Bloor and MacPherson (1917), the long-recognized disturbed picture of blood lipides encountered in various types of anemia is not a causative factor, but rather is the result of loss of blood cells and hemoglobin which characterizes the disease. These workers were among the first to show that in anemia the phosphatides and cholesterol of the plasma decrease, whereas the glyceride content, as measured by per cent fatty acid, increases. Furthermore, the change as observed by these workers is much more marked in the plasma than in the blood cells, indicating that the difficulty may be a nutritional one. This is not a hard and fast generalization, however, since Erickson and co-workers (1937a) reported that the triglyceride and esterified cholesterol content of the blood cells increased markedly in the childhood anemias, and especially in erythroblastic anemia. This same group of investigators (Williams and co-workers, 1937) found that the cholesterol esters increased considerably and the phosphatides decreased slightly in the cells during pernicious anemia, whereas (Williams and co-workers, 1940) in the plasma lecithin, sphingomyelin and the cephalin fraction were far below normal. In anemia of dogs produced by propyl disulfide (Williams and co-workers, 1941), cholesterol esters and phosphatides of the plasma were decreased, whereas neutral fat was increased, according to the usual pattern. In the red blood cells the most striking change was a marked decrease in cephalin fraction content. In the brain of the anemic dog an increase in cerebroside content and a decrease in triglyceride content was observed.

Hodges, Sperry and Andersen (1943) noted that although the total cholesterol content of the serum was markedly reduced in anemia, there was no alteration in the ratio of combined to free cholesterol.

Bloor and MacPherson (1917) observed that the changes in lipide concentrations in the plasma usually appear only after the red blood cell count has fallen to one-half its normal value. Thereafter a decrease in red blood cells bears no direct relationship to the lipide distribution. As the anemia improves, the blood picture returns to normal (Muller and Heath, 1933). After treatment of pernicious anemia, Kirk (1938) observed a marked increase in the concentration of ether-insoluble phosphatides of blood plasma.

According to Heki (1930), Johansen (1930) and Chamberlain and Corlett (1932), the blood lipides of the rabbit respond quite differently to anemia produced by bleeding or by other means, since the blood phosphatides and cholesterol increase markedly rather than decrease. In fowls with erythroblastosis, according to Caselli and Cutinelli (1941), lipide phosphorus decreases. A similar effect was noted in severe human leukemia.

Cassafousth, Brage and Rivas (1948) observed that the phosphatides and free and esterified cholesterol of the spinal fluid increased during pernicious anemia.

Diseases of the Blood Vessels

Several groups of workers (Schoenheimer, 1928; Rosenthal, 1934; McArthur, 1942; Leary, 1941) have pointed out that the portions of the blood vessels affected in arteriosclerosis are characterized by abnormal quantities of lipides. The term *atherosclerosis* is often used to designate the condition in which the lipide accumulation is largely cholesterol. Hirsh and Weinhouse (1943) have pointed out that atheromatous patches in advanced stages of arteriosclerosis are composed entirely of lipides and minerals. As a matter of fact, the lipide content of the artery increases with aging even in the absence of definite pathology.

Since hyperlipemia may accompany arteriosclerosis in test animals, various workers have suggested a relationship between the two. Thus, cholesterol feeding (Dauber, 1944) or stilbestrol injections (Chaikoff and co-workers, 1948) induce a hyperlipemia in birds which eventually produces atherosclerosis. Similar results are obtained after feeding of cholesterol to rabbits (Rosenthal, 1934). Shreder (1935) and Chaikoff and co-workers (1948) have reported an increase in the phosphatide as well as the cholesterol content of the blood. Of interest is the recent work of Chernick, Srere and Chaikoff (1949), who have shown by *in vitro* studies that arterial tissue is capable of synthesizing fatty acids from labeled sodium acetate and of incorporating labeled inorganic phosphate into phosphatides. This suggests the possibility that the blood vessels themselves may be responsible for the lipide deposits which characterize atheromatous lesions, especially in instances where infiltration from the plasma is not possible.

Downs (1935), and Kesten and Silbowitz (1942) have reported that the ingestion of phosphatides diminishes both the hypercholesterolemia and the arteriosclerosis which results from the feeding of cholesterol to rabbits.

Hypertension is, of course, frequently the most readily discerned symptom of arteriosclerosis. It may, however, result from other causes and does not appear to be characterized by any consistent lipide blood picture. Hoesch (1931) was of the opinion that the phosphatide content of blood remained normal in essential hypertension. Fahrig and Wacker (1932) found that hypercholesterolemia as well as an increase in neutral fat and phosphatide content of the blood is common in patients with hypertension. Peters and Man (1943), on the other hand, are of the opinion that the lipide blood picture is not disturbed by hypertension unless associated causes for hyperlipemia, such as nephritis, exist. Harris and co-workers (1949) have found that all the lipides of the serum, including the phosphatides, increase with hypertension. Of extreme interest is the recent work of Gofman and co-workers (1950) which is actively progressing. These investigators have shown that a relationship may exist between the incidence of atherosclerosis and the presence of the so-called $S_f 10$–20 fraction of blood which may be isolated by ultracentrifugation. This fraction is high in cholesterol content and its concentration is influenced by exogenous cholesterol.

It is interesting to note that Geyer and co-workers (1949) have isolated from commercial soybean phosphatides a fraction which demonstrates appreciable vasodepressor activity for man and the cat but very little for the dog and none for the rat or the rabbit. The active material appeared to develop only after the phosphatides had been allowed to stand in air, but did not appear to comprise any of the obvious hydrolysis products.

Diseases of the Central Nervous System

The relationship of lipide metabolism to diseases of the brain and spinal cord has not been well established. Although obesity may stem from hypothalamic injury, the cause appears to depend on a stimulation of appetite rather than on a disturbed lipide metabolism (Brobeck, Tepperman and Long, 1943).

In various psychoses the blood lipides may or may not be disturbed. Any departure from normal, however, does not appear to follow a definite pattern (Jokivartio, 1939; Slight and Long, 1933). Difficulty in diagnosing the type of psychosis may contribute to this situation. Yasuda (1937) found that the lipide composition of the brain does not change with various mental conditions. Roeder (1940) reported that the phosphatide content of the cerebrospinal fluid is decreased in patients with schizophrenia.

Epilepsy has very little effect on blood lipides, as shown by McQuarrie and co-workers (1933) who analyzed the plasma lipides of epileptic and non-epileptic children. There appeared to be a slight increase in cholesterol content and a slight decrease in phosphatide content. The changes are probably not great enough to be significant. Ox brain lipides have been reported to be successful therapeutic agents for chorea (Hollander, 1940).

Diabetes

Diabetes is characterized not only by hyperglycemia but also very frequently by lipemia. On the other hand, the reverse situation of hypoglycemia, such as may be induced by insulin, does not affect the blood picture (Kaplan, Entenman and Chaikoff, 1943). According to Joslin, Bloor and Gray (1917), the lipemia of diabetes is usually associated with the incidence of ketosis and acidosis. Williams and co-workers (1940) found that the phosphatides of the blood in diabetic lipemia increased severalfold, lecithin accounting for much of the elevation. Sphingomyelin content also increased slightly, whereas the cephalin fraction appeared to be lacking entirely. The red blood cells were not affected, presenting a normal phosphatide content and distribution. The other lipides of the blood, in addition to the phosphatides, increase also, as earlier work has shown (Bürger and Beumer, 1913; Imrie, 1915; Klemperer and Umber, 1907). Once the carbohydrate utilization is normalized by the therapeutic measures now available for diabetes, the lipemia disappears, as shown by Chaikoff, Smyth and Gibbs (1936).

Man and Peters (1934) have studied the lipides of the blood in the hyperlipemia occasioned by diabetic acidosis. The neutral fat demonstrated the greatest increase, whereas the phosphatides and cholesterol content increased at a lesser rate, the latter increasing the least. On recovery, the greatest decreases were observed in the components which initially were at the highest levels, although these initial ratios of concentrations tended to be reflected in the normal distribution which accompanied recovery.

Various other diseases are frequently associated with diabetes. Among these is atherosclerosis which may, in some way, be related to the hypercholesterolemia often encountered in diabetic individuals, although Gofman and co-workers (1950) point out that hypercholesterolemia alone cannot account for the marked susceptibility of diabetics to atherosclerosis. Steatorrhea and enlargement of the liver is not uncommon in diabetic patients. The latter condition, which is probably due to fatty infiltration, is improved once carbohydrate utilization is normalized. The cirrhosis of the liver which may coincide with diabetes has been attributed by Connor (1938) to the effects of continued fatty infiltration.

Cutaneous xanthomatosis may likewise accompany diabetes, and although it is most intense when the hyperlipemia is at its worst, there does not appear to be a direct correlation between the two. McGavack and Shepardson (1933) have shown that the xanthomatosis subsides when the diabetes, and thus the hyperlipemia, is controlled. A condition known as *lipemia retinalis* (McKee and Rabinowitch, 1931) in which excess lipides are found in the retina appears to be associated almost solely with diabetics. Like xanthomatosis it is correlated with the incidence but not with the intensity of hyperlipemia.

Matthews, Newton and Bloor (1935) induced experimental diabetes in cats and observed that the phosphatide and cholesterol content of the skin increased. The neutral fat content of both the skin and the muscles decreased and were probably mobilized to the liver as a result of undernutrition accompanying incomplete utilization of carbohydrate.

The phosphatide, cholesterol and cerebroside contents of the peripheral nerves decrease in diabetics, according to Randall (1938). This is probably due to degenerating processes in the nerves. The fatty acids which are liberated in the decomposition of the phosphatides reappear in an increased neutral fat fraction.

Engelhardt and Derbes (1944) found that subcutaneous fat of diabetics had a slightly higher content of phosphatides and unsaponifiable matter than did similar fat of nondiabetics.

Tumors and Neoplasms

Bullock and Cramer (1914) reported that actively growing tumors in mice contained a higher lipide content than tumors whose rate of growth was small. Furthermore, 39 per cent of the total lipides in sarcoma were phosphatides as compared to 7 to 10 per cent in carcinoma. Bierich, Detzel and Lang (1931), Yasuda and Bloor (1932) and Muntoni (1947) found that malignant tumors have higher phosphatide and cholesterol contents than benign tumors. According to Costello and co-workers (1947), this increase takes place, in part at least, at the expense of the epidermal lipides.

The lipide content of various portions of Carcinosarcoma 256 in rats was examined by Haven (1937a). She found that the growing tissue of the periphery had approximately twice as great a phosphatide content as the nongrowing center tissue. The cholesterol, cholesterol ester, glyceride and water content, on the other hand, was much lower in the peripheral tissue. Possibly the phosphatides undergo transformation to other lipides once growing ceases. Haven and Levy (1942) found that the phosphatide content of the nuclei of Carcinosarcoma 256 was 9.7 per cent on a dry basis. This same value was obtained for the entire tumor, but choline analysis indicated the presence of more lecithin in the whole cells than in the nuclei. Sphingomyelin was not found in the nuclei.

A phosphatide-ribonucleoprotein complex was found in chicken tumor

I tissue as well as in normal tissue by Claude (1941), who separated and analyzed particulate components of cytoplasm from various sources. A positive test for aldehydes in the lipide fraction indicated the presence of acetal phosphatides.

Analyses by Sueyoshi and Miura (1939) indicated that the phosphatides from rabbit sarcoma are less highly saturated than those from normal tissue such as muscle. Contrariwise, D'Alessandro and Greco (1938) found in Jensen sarcoma a high content of lecithin more unsaturated than that of normal tissue.

Haven (1937) studied the rate of incorporation of elaidic acid into Carcinosarcoma 256 of rats. The label was found to enter the tumor to the extent of one-fifth of the phosphatides present. The rate of turnover of tumor phosphatides as measured by elaidic acid uptake was slow as compared to those of liver and intestinal mucosa.

Several workers have studied the metabolism of tumor phosphatides with the aid of P^{32}. Jones, Chaikoff and Lawrence (1939, 1940, 1940a) administered radioactive inorganic phosphorus to rats into which had been implanted mammary carcinoma, lymphoma, lymphosarcoma and Sarcoma 180. These tumors demonstrated different cell sizes, rates of growth and ability to produce metastases in distant parts. It was found that each tumor possessed a characteristic rate of phosphatide turnover which was independent of the host since measurements were made on tumors growing side by side in the same animal. Thus, phosphatide turnover in lymphoma was about one-third that in mammary carcinoma or lymphosarcoma. Despite the individual differences, however, the activity displayed by tumors in converting inorganic P^{32} into phosphatides is relatively high as compared to that of liver, kidney and intestine. Unlike the case in other tissues, maximum deposition of P^{32} in tumors may not be achieved until 10 to 50 hours.

It appears, accordingly, that results obtained with P^{32} differ from those obtained with elaidic acid. This suggests that partial rather than total synthesis of phosphatides takes place in tumors and that the phosphoric acid component is more rapidly replaced than the fatty acids.

In a study carried out by Hevesy (1939) it was shown that the rate of labeled phosphatide formation was the same in spontaneous as in transplanted tumors. In the particular tumors studied, the rate of formation was intermediate between that of liver and muscle.

Haven (1940) measured the turnover rate of lecithin, the cephalin fraction and sphingomyelin in Carcinosarcoma 256. The turnover of lecithin was most rapid. Haven and Levy (1942) observed that the specific activity of sphingomyelin, like that of the cephalin fraction, reaches its maximum 42 hours after introduction of P^{32} by stomach tube. With subcutaneous administration no such maximum is observed.

Weil-Malherbe and Dickens (1944) reported that the incidence of local tumors produced by subcutaneous implantation of benzopyrene was markedly less when the carcinogenic drug was dissolved in purified lecithin or cephalin fraction than when it was dissolved in glyceride oils. The administration of the cephalin fraction, however, had no retarding effect whatsoever on the growth of rat Sarcoma 39 or spontaneous breast tumors in mice, according to Selle, Paquin and Brindley (1940).

The effect of x-rays on phosphatide turnover in Jensen sarcoma was studied by Hevesy (1947).

Tuberculosis

Of great interest is the work of Sabin, Doan and Forkner (1930) and Sabin (1932), which showed that phthioic acid, isolated by Anderson from the phosphatides of the tubercle bacillus (see p. 210), as well as the phosphatides themselves which contain this acid, produces typical tubercles when injected into animals. The reaction is specific for the dextrorotatory isomer of the acid. It was believed to result from the stimulation of monocytes from connective tissue with the formation of epithelioid cells which are phagocytic for phosphatides and fatty acids of the tubercle bacilli. Thus, phagocytic cells were believed to attack injected phosphatide with the subsequent release of fatty acids which produce the characteristic reaction.

The plasma phosphatides and cholesterol in tuberculous individuals are reduced, according to Izzo and Marenzi (1944), although individual variation was very great. A decrease of over 50 per cent was observed in the lecithin content, whereas the cephalin fraction decreased considerably less and the sphingomyelin hardly at all. Contrariwise, Sprinsky (1944) found the lipide phosphorus content of the blood of tuberculous individuals to be normal, whereas Koch and Westphal (1938) observed a slight increase in serum lecithin content. Obviously this situation is in need of clarification.

The cholesterol ester content of tuberculous blood was found by Sweany (1924) to increase in healing fibroid cases and to decrease in unfavorable and terminal cases. Similarly, King and Bruger (1935) found that a consistent low level of blood cholesterol indicated early death.

Gerstl and Tennant (1943) have found that the typical tuberculous lesions do not form when the sodium salt of the cinnamoyl ester of glycerophosphoric acid is injected into test animals at the same time that the tubercle bacillus is injected. In similar work, Tompkins (1936) found that egg yolk lecithin, injected before or after intravenous inoculation of rabbits with bovine tubercle bacillus, caused more rapid and extensive healing of the pulmonary lesions than was evident in the control animals. This may be related to an activating effect exerted by the phosphatides on the enzymes which break down the tubercle bacillus.

Diseases of the Heart

According to Ide (1940), the phosphatide and cholesterol contents of heart muscle decrease markedly in functional cardiac disturbances. Ludewig and Chanutin (1936) determined the phosphatide content of hypertrophied heart and kidneys of nephrectomized rats on meat extract diets. The phosphatide content per unit of surface remained the same, indicating that the phosphatides increased proportionally to cell hypertrophy.

The plasma lipides are generally increased in coronary sclerosis, as shown by Willius (1939), who found that the total lipides were higher in 71 per cent of 107 cases examined. In 56, 57 and 61 per cent of the cases, the lecithin, cholesterol esters and cholesterol contents, respectively, were increased. Davis, Stern and Lesnick (1937) found blood cholesterol, fatty acid and phosphatide contents to be high in individuals suffering from angina pectoris. In rheumatic heart disease with cardiac failure the serum cholesterol may decrease, according to the observations of Poindexter and Bruger (1938), although the results are not considered statistically significant.

Diseases of the Skin

From the data of Strickler and Adams (1932) and Rosen and Krasnow (1931, 1932) it may be assumed that blood lipides do not undergo excessive alteration in skin diseases, except where the disorders are due to lipidoses. According to Hansen (1939), the phosphatide fatty acids and the total fatty acids in eczematous infants demonstrate iodine numbers that are lower than normal. The phosphatide fatty acids, however, are more unsaturated than the total fatty acids.

The use of phosphatides as therapeutic agents for psoriasis is of interest (Smith, Goldman and Fox, 1942). Prokopchuk and Kerson (1936) found that the cholesterol content of blood serum may increase three to ten times in patients with psoriasis.

Avitaminoses

The effects of choline deficiency are discussed elsewhere in detail (see p. 355). The relationship of the absence of other nutritional factors or vitamins to lipide metabolism has received very little study.

Javillier (1935) found in mice deprived of Vitamin A that the total lipide content of the entire animal, particularly the fatty acids, decreased. The cholesterol content remained unchanged, however, whereas the lecithin content actually increased. Adlersberg and Sobotka (1943) found that ingestion of soybean lecithin during Vitamin A therapy led to Vitamin A levels in excess of those demonstrated by the controls in the blood of man; whereas Slanetz and Scharf (1945) have provided evidence to show that commercial soybean phosphatides contain a factor which influences the storage, utilization and blood levels of Vitamin A in the rat. Esh and co-workers (1948) have shown that soybean phosphatides enhance the absorption of Vitamin A in the cow and also increase the transmission of colostral Vitamin A to the calf.

From the data of Boldyreva (1940) it may be concluded that the phosphatides of the pigeon brain are little affected by B-avitaminoses. This is not in agreement with the data of Schmitz and Hiraoka (1928). Palladin and Kudrajawzewa (1924) reported that rabbits deficient in Vitamin B demonstrated diminished contents of blood neutral fat and cholesterol and increased amounts of blood phosphatides, cholesterol esters and fatty acids. This is worthy of further investigation.

Pantothenic acid deficiency, according to György (1948), causes hemorrhagic syndromes which may be related to a general blood dyscrasia caused by a disturbance of the synthesis and utilization of phosphatides.

The tissues of the guinea pig maintained on a Vitamin C-deficient diet contain, in general, more lecithin and free cholesterol than the corresponding tissues of normal animals, according to Hongo (1934). Sueyoshi and Mitimoto (1939) found that scorbutic guinea pigs have lesser amounts than normal of highly unsaturated cephalin fractions in their tissue. Because of the coagulant effect of the cephalin fraction, this observation may be related to the capillary bleeding observed in the scorbutic condition.

Dols and co-workers (1938a) and Dols (1938) observed that normal and Vitamin D-deficient rats converted injected radioactive inorganic phosphorus into phosphatides at the same rate. Similarly, no difference was found in the phosphatide content of the entire bodies of normal and rachitic rats (Dols and co-workers, 1938a). Vitamin D, however, facilitates the conversion of inorganic phosphorus to phosphatides, according to Branson, Banks and Dodson (1947).

Krieger and co-workers (1941) found that the phosphorus of soybean phosphatides, as well as that from yeast nucleic acid, is as available as inorganic phosphorus for the calcification of bone. The phosphorus from phytic acid, on the other hand, was utilized to a much lesser extent.

The liver lipides of chicks on a Vitamin K-free diet were not appreciably different in quantity from those of control chicks, even though the former exhibited the hypoprothrombinemia typical of Vitamin K deficiencies (Field and Dam, 1945).

Diseases of the Thyroid Gland

Hyperthyroidism, as shown by Boyd and Connell (1936), Gildea, Man and Peters (1939), Man, Gildea and Peters (1940) and Peters and Man (1943), is characterized by a deficiency of lipides in the serum, whereas hypothyroidism is reflected in the increased lipide content of the serum. Boyd and Connell (1936) reported that the neutral fat content of serum was decreased the most and the phosphatide content the least in hyperthyroidism. Contrariwise, Man, Gildea and Peters (1940) found that neutral fat was the least affected, whereas serum cholesterol and phosphatides decreased appreciably, the cholesterol falling somewhat faster. In the lipemia of hypothyroidism, on the other hand, the phosphatide content increases faster than the cholesterol does.

The blood cell lipide values were found to be relatively constant in both hyper- and hypothyroidism by Foldes and Murphy (1946).

The relief of either hyper- or hypothyroidism causes the blood picture to return to normal, as shown by Gildea, Man and Peters (1939), Man, Gildea and Peters (1940) and Hurxthal (1934).

Miscellaneous Diseases

Pneumonia, according to Stoesser and McQuarrie (1935) and Stoesser (1941), is characterized by decreased quantities of blood phosphatides and fatty acids, the latter being depressed the least. Relief of the disease and its accompanying temperature, either chemotherapeutically or with specific sera, occasions a rapid rise in total fatty acid content and a less rapid return to normal of the phosphatide content. From the work of Denis (1917) and Stoesser and McQuarrie (1935) it appears that serum lipides decrease during the course of diseases which are fever-producing. The latter workers, however, could not produce a hypolipemia in patients to whom artificial fever had been imparted by various means. They did show that the hypolipemia in pneumonia patients was not nutritional, since it was observed even in normal nutritional states.

The early stages of syphilis, according to Rosen, Krasnow and Lyons (1933) and Feraru and Offenkrantz (1937) is accompanied by a slight decrease in serum cholesterol. The phosphatide content tends to remain normal.

According to Harris and co-workers (1934), the resolution of syphilitic lesions, produced experimentally in the rabbit, was hastened by injection of lecithin. This phenomenon was attributed to stimulation by the lecithin of the phagocytic mononuclear cells.

Human malaria, according to Kehar (1937), is characterized by hyper-cholesterolemia in the rigor stage and hypocholesterolemia in the afebrile stages before and after the paroxysm as well as in chronic infections. In monkeys the serum cholesterol and phosphatide content increased sharply if death due to hemoglobinuria occurred. If recovery took place, the serum lipide content decreased gradually. Ball and co-workers (1948) found that monkey red blood cells infected with the malarial parasite, *Plasmodium knowlesi*, contained two to four times as much phosphatide as was normal.

In diphtheria, Koch and Westphal (1938) found that blood lipide levels were practically normal, unlike Peritz (1921) who had previously reported that lecithinemia is characteristic.

The serum lipides of individuals suffering from allergies are not essentially different from those of normal persons, according to Bloor, Blake and Bullen (1938). Plasma phosphatide fatty acids increased in allergic individuals who were fed soybean oil for one month and decreased in normal individuals who were treated similarly, according to Wheeler and Goetzl (1947).

In progressive paralysis there is a loss of phosphatides in the brain as shown by the work of Carbone and Pighini (1912) and Singer (1928). These observations are worthy of reinvestigation.

The use of lecithin as a therapeutic measure for drug addiction has been reported by Chopra and Chopra (1940) and by Ma (1933).

The serum lipides in patients with active arthritis are practically normal, according to Bayles and Riddell (1944) and Hartung and Bruger (1935).

The successful treatment, in 80 per cent of 130 cases, of multiple sclerosis with lecithin has been reported by Miner (1939). Weil (1948) has found that the phosphatide content of the white and the grey matter of brain is markedly decreased in patients afflicted with multiple sclerosis.

CHAPTER XXV

SEROLOGICAL AND OXIDATIVE FUNCTIONS OF THE PHOSPHATIDES

Blood Coagulation

Introduction

One of the most interesting physiological functions in which there is evidence of phosphatide participation is the clotting of blood. The classical mechanism which has been advanced for the coagulation of blood postulates the production at the time of injury and loss of blood of an active enzymatic clotting agent, thrombin. Under the influence of this agent, the fibrinogen of the blood is converted to the insoluble fibrin which is the basis of the clot. The precursor of thrombin is supposedly present in the blood at all times, and is termed "prothrombin" or "thrombogen". Its conversion to thrombin is accomplished by the combined influence of calcium ions (Drinker and Zinsser, 1943; Ferguson, 1936) and an activator (Mills, 1927), the latter having been designated in the literature as "thromboplastin", "thrombokinase", "thrombozyme", or "cytozyme". This representation is a highly simplified one which, in the literature, has been subjected to innumerable variations. The present state of knowledge of the coagulation of blood has been well reviewed by Chargaff (1945) and by Astrup (1950, p. 1).

The isolation from blood of thrombin and prothrombin has been described by Seegers (1940), who postulates that they are carbohydrate-containing proteins. It has long been realized that phosphatides have a marked accelerating effect on the coagulation of blood; and, following an early observation of Howell (1912), it has generally been believed that the classical cephalin fraction demonstrates activity in this regard, whereas lecithin and sphingomyelin do not. Thus the inference follows that the cephalin fraction is an integral part of thromboplastin, which accordingly is a lipoprotein (see p. 82). In this regard the work of Leathes and Mellanby (1939) must be mentioned. They found, unlike previous workers, that lecithin was thromboplastic, whereas the cephalin fraction was actually a slight anticoagulant. The work was carried out with thromboplastins supposedly free of lipides which were isolated from

443

brain tissue and from *daboia* venom. These were activated by brain and egg lecithin, the latter being somewhat more effective. Furthermore, the thromboplastin from the *daboia* venom could be activated tenfold by the lecithin, whereas the thromboplastin from the brain was capable of much less activation, indicating that it possessed to a greater degree than the *daboia* venom whatever factor was responsible for the activation. The activating effect of lecithin on *daboia* venom was also observed by Trevan and Macfarlane (1936/37).

The discrepancy between this work and the preponderance of older data which attribute the activating effect to the cephalin fraction is not easily resolved until one realizes that much of the data in the literature are of little value because of the difficulties involved in isolating and identifying pure phosphatides. And, as will be seen later, there is not yet sufficient evidence to allow the positive identification of the active material with any of the known phosphatides.

The Thromboplastic Factor

Thromboplastin, as the phosphatide-containing component in the blood-coagulating system, is the material of greatest interest here. The general existence of thromboplastin in protoplasm was postulated many years ago by Morawitz (1905), and its identity as a lipoprotein had been postulated even earlier by Wooldridge (1886). The thromboplastic factor is extractable from tissue with both water and organic solvents, although the same product does not result in both instances since the water-soluble material is by far the more active (Mills, 1921). Nor are the thromboplastic factors extracted from different tissues or from different species necessarily identical. Fischer (1935) studied the thromboplastic activity of aqueous extracts of the various tissues of the hen and found the activity of the extracts to decrease in the following order: lung, striated muscle, heart, kidney, spleen, brain and liver.

Chargaff and his colleagues have examined in detail the thromboplastic substances isolable from lung and from other tissues by water extraction. Thus, Cohen and Chargaff (1940) investigated the thromboplastic lipoprotein obtained from beef lungs by fractional salt precipitation of saline extracts. The product contained 18 per cent firmly bound lipides, and was shown by electrophoresis experiments to be 90 to 95 per cent homogeneous (Cohen and Chargaff, 1941a). Examination in the ultra-centrifuge, however, indicated that lack of homogeneity existed with respect to particle size. This inhomogeneity was not exhibited, on the other hand, when the thromboplastic factor was isolated by centrifugation techniques (Chargaff, Bendich and Cohen, 1944). These preparations from beef lung were very stable towards heat, possessed high molecular weights and contained in the protein fraction pentose nucleic acid (Chargaff, 1945, 1945a). When this lipoprotein was treated with heparin (Chargaff, Ziff, and Cohen, 1940), the lipide constituents were displaced with the subsequent formation of a strongly anticoagulant heparin-protein complex.

Removal of the lipide fraction of the lipoprotein brought about a loss of thromboplastic activity (Cohen and Chargaff, 1940). Immunologically, however, the lipide-free protein still exhibited the precipitation reaction with rabbit antibodies engendered by the intact lipoprotein. Thus it appears that the phosphatides are necessary for thromboplastic activity, but not for reaction with antibodies. It was observed that the product produced by the reaction of the antibodies with the thromboplastic protein possessed thromboplastic activity.

Cohen and Chargaff (1941) examined the lipide constituent of the thromboplastic lipoprotein isolated from beef lung by precipitation methods. The mixture was very complex, consisting of both alcohol-soluble and alcohol-insoluble phosphatides, which is to say that both lecithin and the cephalin fraction were present. Both of these demonstrated clotting activity of approximately equal intensity, indicating as pointed out previously that the identity of the specific phosphatide responsible for the thromboplastic activity remains yet to be determined. Among the hydrolysis products were found palmitic, stearic and unsaturated acids, chief of which appeared to be oleic acid in addition to choline, aminoethyl alcohol and glycerophosphoric acid.

The lipide fraction of the thromboplastic lipoprotein isolated from beef lung by differential centrifugation has been investigated by Chargaff, Bendich and Cohen (1944). About half of this product was soluble in alcohol-ether and 40 to 45 per cent of it was recoverable as purified lipides. These were distributed (per cent total lipides) as follows: cholesterol, 19; neutral fat, 18; lecithin fraction, 26; cephalin fraction, 25; sphingomyelin fraction, 12; acetal phosphatides, 1.5.

In subsequent work, Chargaff (1945b) isolated the thromboplastic proteins from human lung and placenta. These appeared to be similar to material from beef lung, although identity, as pointed out by the investigator, was by no means established.

The Lipide Constituent of the Thromboplastic Factor

Some of the characteristics of the lipides present in the thromboplastic lipoprotein have already been described. As indicated above, a water extract of tissue provides a potent thromboplastic material, whereas an alcohol or ether extract provides a product with very much less activity. Since this latter substance is essentially lipide, most of the work directed at identification of the active lipide has been carried out on material isolated by extraction with organic solvents.

The supposed identity of this material with the classical cephalin fraction (Howell, 1912; McLean, 1917) has already been noted, and its presence even in plants and microorganisms was pointed out by Chargaff, Bancroft and Stanley-Brown (1936). Numerous other workers isolated the thromboplastic lipide and most were in accord with the concept that it was probably "cephalin" (see, e.g., Wadsworth, Maltaner and Maltaner, 1930, 1931, 1936; Maltaner and Maltaner, 1943; Ferguson and Erickson, 1939; Erickson and Ferguson, 1940; Widenbauer and Reichel, 1941; Kurosawa, 1938; Gratia and Levene, 1922; Waksman, 1918; and McLeod, 1916).

Of great interest was the observation of Zunz and LaBarre (1921) that the active material could be extracted from the cephalin fraction with alcohol. This was confirmed by Chargaff, Bancroft and Stanley-Brown (1936) and by Cohen and Chargaff (1941), who obtained comparatively active material by the alcohol fractionation of phosphatides from horse blood platelets and beef lungs.

In an extensive study, Chargaff (1944) has attempted to determine the exact nature of the lipide which contributes to thromboplastic activity. Numerous phosphatide fractions obtained from pig heart and from heart and brain of beef were examined. The fractions which exhibited the most activity, especially those from pig heart, were very soluble in ethyl alcohol. Nevertheless, phosphatidylserine from beef brain was entirely inactive, whereas the phosphatidylaminoethyl alcohol fraction from beef brain demonstrated only very slight activity. In addition, the most active specimens, which were obtained from pig heart, did not resemble cephalin at all. Chargaff (1944) concludes that the present state of knowledge does not allow the identification of the thromboplastic lipide with any of the known phosphatides. He points out that the difference in the level of activity of the aqueous extract of tissue and the material extractable with organic solvents is so great (as much as one thousandfold) that it is hardly justifiable to assert definitely that a lipide is involved. This work makes obvious the present state of uncertainty in this important field, and emphasizes the need for a large body of careful investigation.

Lipide Inhibitors of Thromboplastic Activity

Chargaff (1937, 1937a) has obtained evidence that certain lipide fractions exist which inhibit the coagulation of blood. These fractions were found in the brain of sheep and pigs, in the spinal cord of cattle and in the blood cells of sheep. Material of similar activity was found in the spleen of a victim of Niemann-Pick's disease (Chargaff, 1938). The material was found in the ether-insoluble sphingomyelin fraction, although alone it is slightly soluble in ether. This solubility characteristic distinguishes it from the lipide fraction mentioned in some of the older literature which was believed to be lecithin and which was said to inhibit the coagulation of blood. Chargaff does not believe that his inhibitors contain heparin. There is present a small amount of sulfur which may be an impurity, but which nevertheless calls to mind the synthetic cerebroside sulfuric acids prepared by Chargaff (1937a) since these were shown to have anticoagulant activity.

Tocantins (1944) has described an anti-clotting agent in blood which may be removed by various adsorbents. De Sütö-Nagy (1944) has carried out experiments which suggest that sphingomyelin normally present in blood may be an anticoagulant. A recent report by Overman and Wright (1948) indicates that an anticoagulant isolated by them from beef brain and rabbit lung thromboplastins and from soybean phosphatides and human plasma is an inositol-containing phosphatide.

ANTIGENIC REACTIONS

A vast literature, much of which was accumulated prior to the last ten years, exists which describes the participation of phosphatides in immunological reactions. Much of this must be discounted since it was carried out with impure or improperly characterized substances which make the resulting data an unsuitable basis for generalization. In addition, much of the work is controversial and is better appraised in discussions where the primary interest is centered about the mechanisms of antigenic and immunological reactions. There is very little unanimity of view as to the nature of these important reactions, and for the various theories proposed the reader is referred to works by Landsteiner (1945), Marrack (1938), Heidelberger (1939) and Pauling (1940, and many subsequent papers). The concern here is largely with the evidence which shows that phosphatides and related lipides, either alone or combined with proteins, may under certain conditions behave as antigens or as haptens.

Lipide Antigens or Haptens

There are numerous reports in the literature (e.g., Pinner, 1928) that phosphatides by themselves possess antigenic activity. Thus Aoki (1938) reported that both lecithin and cholesterol form antibodies which may be detected serologically. It was, on the other hand, the opinion of Plaut and Rudy (1932) that the antigenic activity reported for commercial lecithin (see, e.g., Guggenheim, 1929) was due to extraneous antigenic material which was present. Kimizura (1935) could detect no antigenic activity with purified egg lecithin and Fujimura (1937) also is of the opinion that the antigenic activity of crude phosphatides may be attributed to protein impurities.

Wadsworth, Maltaner and Maltaner (1934, 1935) and Maltaner and Maltaner (1934) have found that purified lecithin or cephalin fraction reacted neither as antigens nor as haptens in the quantitative complement-fixation method devised by them. They also found that the union of the cephalin fraction with serum proteins to provide water-soluble complexes did not change the specificity of the proteins or convert the cephalin fraction to a hapten.

Wadsworth and Crowe (1936), on the other hand, have found that lecithin and cephalin fractions exhibit absorption spectra similar to that of beef-heart antigens. The region investigated was from 6800 to 2150 Å, and one of the absorption bands was typical of the range in which proteins are known to absorb.

Two haptens have been found by Sachs and Schwab (1935) and by Schwab (1936) in fractions of brain tissue rich in phosphatides and cerebrosides. According to Roeder (1942), this material is transported, along with brain lipides, to the blood where it may be detected serologically.

The Forssman (1911) antigen, which is widely distributed in animal tissue, has long been believed to contain phosphatides (Taniguchi, 1920; Landsteiner and Simms, 1923). This antigen was studied by Brunius (1936), who found it to yield hexosamine and fatty acids on hydrolysis. The Forssman antigen was studied in the ultracentrifuge by Furth and Kabat (1940), who showed that it was sedimentable at 27,000 rpm for one hour.

The lipide antigens of the tapeworm, *Taenia saginata*, which had previously been described by Meyer (1928), were studied by Etcheverry (1940), who found that the acetone-insoluble portion contains the material which demonstrates antigenic activity in echinococcus serous fluid but does not demonstrate anticomplementary action. The acetone-soluble fraction shows reverse activity.

The ability of diphtheria anatoxin coupled with lecithin to behave as an antigen has been described by Pico and Modern (1934). The ability of both lecithin and cholesterol to neutralize diphtheria toxin is discussed by Malesani (1937).

The findings of Horsfall and Goodner (1936) and Horsfall (1938) are of interest in regard to the possible role of lipides in antigenic reactions. When Type I antipneumococcus sera are extracted with lipide solvents, they lose to a very large extent their flocculating capacity.

When, however, a small amount of lecithin was added to horse serum or a small quantity of cephalin fraction to rabbit serum, the ability to participate in the flocculation reaction was regained. Wertheimer and co-workers (1938), on the other hand, have found that guinea pig complement is inactivated by the addition of phosphatides. According to Hazato (1936), both cholesterol and lecithin increase the hapten reactivity of alcoholic extracts of tissue. The phenomenon was observed for both complement fixation and flocculation reactions and its intensity appears to depend on the degree of dispersion of the extracts. Brain extracts, already rich in lipides, did not behave like the other extracts since lecithin caused a decrease in activity.

Bacterial Lipide Antigens

Much of the work carried out on lipide antigens has centered about the products isolated from the tubercle bacillus. This has already been referred to under the discussion of tuberculosis (see p. 438). The complexity of the products present in these bacilli is equaled by the complexity of the immunological reactions they produce. The bacilli themselves, according to Schaefer (1940), produce several antibodies which are engendered by the lipides, the polysaccharides and the proteins present. Much work of this nature has been carried out by Sabin and her associates (see, e.g., Smithburn and Sabin, 1932). The local tubercular tissue produced specifically by phthioic acid has already been described (see p. 438). Sandor (1936) is of the opinion that a lipide hapten is bound to tuberculin, although the extensive work of Seibert (1944, 1949) has not shown this to be the case. The nature of the lipide-containing antigens of the tubercle bacillus has been explored in work of which the following is representative: Macheboeuf and Faure (1939), Doan, Sabin and Forkner (1930), Bloch (1936), Yamasaki (1935), and Heidelberger and Menzel (1934).

The antigenic activity of the Bacillus Calmette-Guerin was investigated by Chargaff and Schaefer (1935), who were of the opinion that all of this activity resides in the phosphatide fractions.

Hettche (1934) found that the bactericidal and hemolytic action exhibited by the lipides of *B. pyocyaneum* was occasioned by the liquid fatty acids present. A similar conclusion was reached by Dennis (1940), who studied the serological activity of the lipides of the typhoid bacillus.

An antigen containing a phosphatide-carbohydrate complex was isolated from the gram-negative *B. aertrycke* by Boivin and Mesrobeanu (1934) and by Raistrick and Topley (1934). Subsequently, similarly constituted antigens were found in dysentery bacilli by Morgan (1937,

1941) and by Goebel, Binkley and Perlman (1945); in various species of *Pasturella* by Pirosky (1938); in *B. pyocyaneus* by Boivin and Mesrobeanu (1937); in *B. anthracis* by Ionesco-Mihaiesti, Soru and Wissner (1937); in many types of *Salmonella* by Boivin, Delaunay and Sarciron (1940); in *Eberthella typhosa* by Topley and co-workers (1937); and in *V. cholerae* by White (1937).

Miles and Pirie (1939) isolated a phosphatide-containing antigen from *Brucella meletensis,* and Freeman, Challinor and Wilson (1940) and Freeman and Anderson (1941) obtained a similar material from *B. typhosum.* Freeman (1943) prepared an antigenic complex from *Salmonella typhimurium* and has found it to consist of 69 per cent specific polysaccharide containing d-glucose, d-mannose and d-galactose; 16 per cent of a conjugated protein; 3 to 4 per cent of lipide and 8 per cent of an alcohol-soluble acetylated polysaccharide.

Morgan and Partridge (1940, 1941) are of the opinion that the antigen which they isolated from *Shigella dysenteriae* is a homogeneous substance composed of a phosphatide, a polysaccharide and a "polypeptide-like" substance. Although the first two components alone or combined are not antigenic, the last two components—that is, the complex minus the phosphatide—is antigenic.

An antigen from pneumococcus which contains both lipide and carbohydrate has been studied by Goebel and co-workers (1943) and Goebel and Adams (1943).

A hemorrhage-producing fraction has been isolated from *S. marcescens* by Shear and co-workers (1943) and by Hartwell, Shear and Adams (1943). This fraction contains a lipide-polysaccharide complex and an unidentified nitrogen-containing fraction. This material may well be an antigen similar to the other lipide-carbohydrate-containing materials described in this section.

Lipide-containing Antigens in the Detection of Disease

Syphilis. The antigens used for the detection of syphilis by either the Wassermann or ·the Kahn methods are believed to consist largely of mixtures of varying proportions of phosphatides and cholesterol. The literature concerned with the Wassermann and related antigens has been reviewed by Weil (1941).

Lipide beef heart antigen is most commonly used in the serological diagnosis of syphilis. It has been studied by Oe. Fischer (1937) and Oe. Fischer and Steinert (1936), and by O. Fischer and Günsberger (1936); and its preparation is described by Letonoff (1948). Sakakibara (1936) attributed the antigenic activity in the Wassermann reaction to a fraction which he characterized incorrectly as β-lecithin.

The Wassermann antigen from both normal and neoplastic tissue was shown by Furth and Kabat (1941) to be sedimentable in the ultra-centrifuge at 27,000 rpm for one hour.

An antigen which may be used for the diagnosis of syphilis was isolated by Ravich-Shcherbo, Marchenko and Nartsisov (1936) from human heart, suprarenal glands, brain, kidneys, egg yolk and from the primary lesion of a syphilitic rabbit. The antigens possessing the greatest amount of activity were those with a minimum amount of neutral fat, a large amount of phosphatide and an intermediate amount of cholesterol.

A mixture of pure lecithin and cholesterol was found to be an artificial antigen specific for the Wassermann test, according to Ravich-Shcherbo and Bass (1940). Pure lecithin alone or improperly balanced mixtures of phosphatides and cholesterol produced hemolysis.

Cardiolipin (see p. 50), the phosphatide isolated from heart tissue, is reported by Pangborn (1942, 1944, 1945) to possess the property of fixing complement with syphilitic sera, if lecithin or cholesterol is present (Brown, 1943). Maltaner and Maltaner (1945) have standardized suspensions of cardiolipin, lecithin and cholesterol for complement fixation tests for syphilis. Kahn and McDermott (1948) also have described a mixture of cardiolipin, purified lecithin and cholesterol which is an antigen suitable for use in the standard Kahn test. A mixture of cardiolipin and dipalmityllecithin (Rosenberg, 1949) has also been found to be an effective antigen for the detection of syphilis.

The floccules resulting in the Kahn test were found by Brown and Kolmer (1941) to contain what appeared to be lecithin and cephalin fraction. An unidentified phosphorus and nitrogen-containing substance was also present which may have been the active material.

The factors effecting the inhibition of the Kahn flocculation reaction have been discussed by Volkin and co-workers (1945).

Liver Disorders. Hanger (1938, 1939) was the first to observe that saline emulsions of the cephalin fraction or of cholesterol were flocculated by serum of individuals suffering from degenerative or destructive diseases of the liver. The test results because of an alteration of the serum proteins rather than a disturbance of the lipide pattern; and, as shown by Kabat and co-workers (1943), the degree of flocculation may be correlated with the concentration of γ-globulin in the serum. The test has found its widest application as an index of the extent and severity of injury to the liver parenchyma in hepatitis and other diffuse liver diseases and in cirrhosis (Hanger and Patek, 1941). Simple obstructive jaundice, on the other hand, does not lead to flocculation, as shown by Gutman and Hanger (1941). The virtues of the test have been discussed by Wachstein (1943) and Rosenberg and Soskin (1941).

Oxidative Functions of the Phosphatides

The ease with which the glycerophosphatides oxidize even after slight exposure to the air is well known to every researcher in the field. Quantitative measurements of this oxidation and its relationship to metabolic reactions within the body have been but little studied. It was suggested long ago by Koch (1903) and by Fränkel and Dimitz (1909) that unsaturated fatty acids, especially those contained in phosphatide molecules, may provide a means for oxygen transport within the tissue cells. As yet the evidence for this still remains to be defined (Sinclair, 1934).

The complete oxidation of fatty acids within the body has already been discussed (see p. 360). Since very little, if any, neutral fat is present within the cells, it follows that the fatty acids whose fate it is to be oxidized are present largely in the form of phosphatides. For the most part these acids are saturated or mono-unsaturated with chain lengths of 16 or 18 carbon atoms. The more highly unsaturated acids, as has already been noted (see p. 343), are carefully preserved in the fat depots even under the stress of starvation. The intermediary processes involved in the presentation for oxidation of the fatty acids by the phosphatides are quite obscure. Here the available data will be presented which relate the phosphatides to oxidative reactions.

The Oxidation of Phosphatides

Tait and King (1936) provided evidence to show that the ready oxidizability of lecithin is not due entirely to the fatty acids present, since the oxidative activity of the latter is in some way enhanced by the structural make-up of the molecule. Thus they showed that the rate of uptake of oxygen by lecithin in either acid or basic medium in the presence of glutathione was much greater than the rate of oxygen uptake by the fatty acids derived from the lecithin by hydrolysis. Furthermore, the oxygen uptake rate was very much greater for the intact lecithin molecule than for a mixture of the hydrolyzed constituents of lecithin. Oxidations of this type which are accelerated by thiol groups were shown by Meyerhof (1923a) to be inhibited by hydrocyanic acid.

The work of Tait and King (1936) would indicate that lecithin is more readily oxidized than the cephalin fraction. In view of the complexity of this material and the impurities associated with it, there is little of value to be gained from such observations. Page and Bülow (1935), who probably had a pure sample of phosphatidylaminoethyl alcohol, found that the autoöxidation of their substance proceeded slowly. The addition of iron as a catalyst, however, caused the absorption of oxygen to proceed at a faster rate and to a much greater extent than was noted for lecithin under similar conditions. Copper, cobalt and manganese exhibited only very weak activity.

The catalytic effect of iron had first been noted by Thunberg (1911) and was later studied by Warburg and Meyerhof (1913). Rusch and Kline (1941) have described the catalytic influence not only of glutathione which was used by Tait and King (1936), but also of cysteine, ascorbic acid, thiamin, riboflavin, pyridoxin and methylene blue on the oxidation of crude phosphatide preparations from egg yolk and rat liver. Numerous substances including carcinogenic compounds (Deutsch, Kline and Rusch, 1941; Mueller, Miller and Rusch, 1945) inhibited the oxidation. All this work was done with phosphatide fractions which were not characterized. Diphtheria toxin was reported by Peters and Cunningham (1941) to enhance the oxidation of lecithin in the presence of glutathione.

A system comprising a vanadium salt and a rat or guinea pig liver suspension was found by Bernheim and Bernheim (1939) to oxidize phosphatides rapidly, whereas vanadium salts alone had no effect and the suspension alone had only a slight effect. This oxidation is inhibited by manganese and cobalt (Bernheim and Bernheim, 1939a).

Elliott and Libet (1944) have described an iron-protein complex obtained from the heated liver of various animals which together with ascorbic acid catalyzes the oxidation of phosphatides.

Simon, Horwitt and Gerard (1944) have reported that hemoglobin increases the oxidation of phosphatides mildly. This had previously been observed by Bernheim and Bernheim (1939). Ferrous-o-phenanthroline is a much more active catalyst for the same reaction. A combination of the two serves to decrease somewhat the effect of the more active catalyst. Accordingly, the authors postulate that hemins may serve to preserve the phosphatides from rapid destruction by active catalysts, merely by replacing these active materials in situations where the phosphatides are possibly called upon to provide intracellular reserve energy.

Lembke (1942) studied the oxidative action of fluorescent bacteria on various substances, and found that lecithin was oxidized by *B. pyocyaneus*, *B. fluorescens* and *B. syncyaneum*.

The action of dehydrogenating enzymes on phosphatides has received some study. Annau (1941) and Annau, Eperjessy and Felszeghy (1942) have found that the dehydrogenase of surviving beef liver desaturates lecithin, as demonstrated by a resulting increase in iodine number. The enzyme was studied in a system including methylene blue as a hydrogen acceptor and xanthine or hypoxanthine as activators.

At least two reports in the literature (Gutstein, 1929; Magat, 1934) attribute to phosphatides the ability to exert a catalytic effect on oxidation processes. The ability of oxidized phosphatides to restore the color to reduced methylene blue under physiological conditions was demonstrated by Bloor and Snider (1937). Under similar conditions, however, glucose proved incapable of oxidation (Bloor, 1943, p. 311). The initial observation may be taken as circumstantial evidence of the ability of phosphatides to reserve the process of oxidation, so that they may actually serve as oxygen transport mechanisms within the body.

Very little can be said about the chemistry of phosphatide oxidation. Although there are no doubt many analogies between phosphatide and neutral fat oxidation, the former have been subjected to much less study than the latter. Meyerhof (1923) observed the marked catalytic effect of the —SH group on the oxidation of lecithin and reported that the unsaturated acids, particularly the linoleic acid, formed peroxides. Szent-György (1924), on the other hand, was of the opinion that an oxido linkage was formed. Peroxides would be expected by analogy to the oxidation of oils.

Bülow and Page (1932) showed that the oxidation of the cephalin fraction resulted in the production of both hydroxy and keto acids, the former predominating. O'Connell and Stotz (1949) oxidized beef brain phosphatide and beef lung hydrolecithin by rat liver homogenates containing adenosine triphosphate. The oxidation products were not identified, although free fatty acids under similar conditions produced acetoacetic acid.

The Phosphatides as Antioxidants

The literature contains a great variety of conflicting data concerning the antioxidant effect of the phosphatides. Much of this work is discussed under the commercial uses of phosphatides (see p. 507). For the most part, crude fractions have been used which make it impossible to determine whether the antioxidant activity is due to the phosphatides which themselves are so readily oxidized or to accompanying substances. Thus, very little of theoretical significance can be offered until more definitive experimental data are available.

Bollmann (1926) was perhaps the first to observe that commercial soybean phosphatides in small quantities served to retard oxidative rancidity in refined vegetable oils. Kochendorfer and Smith (1932) observed that commercial soybean phosphatides possessed weak antioxidant activity. Attempted purification by precipitation with acetone provided a material with variable activity. Evans (1935) found that vegetable phosphatides were excellent antioxidants for cottonseed oil whose oxidation was accelerated by the peroxide of cobalt oleate. The validity of his testing procedure is open to question. Lecithin was, however, ineffective as an antioxidant for carotene (Hove and Hove, 1944).

Olcott and Mattill (1936) found that commercial phosphatides had slight antioxygenic action on refined cottonseed oil. With lard the effect was very slight and with lard-cod liver oil mixtures it was absent. In an attempt to discover the active constituent, they prepared a purified sample of lecithin and found it to be inactive. On the other hand, a cephalin fraction prepared by repeated precipitation of an alcohol-insoluble phosphatide fraction possessed activity. Accordingly, these workers are of the opinion that the cephalin phosphatides are the active antioxidants. They obtained additional evidence which might indicate that the free hydroxyl group of the phosphoric acid residue (which in lecithin is largely involved in zwitterionic combination) may be responsible for the activity.

Hilditch and Paul (1939) also found that a purified lecithin prepared from soybean phosphatides did not retard the oxidation of distilled esters of olive oil fatty acids.

Diemair, Strohecker and Reuland (1940) studied the antioxidant activity of some of the hydrolysis products of phosphatides including glycerol, oleic and linoleic acids, glycerophosphoric acid, aminoethyl alcohol and choline. The latter substance was the only one found to have antioxidant activity. The concentrations necessary, however, were very high.

Dutton and co-workers (1949) are of the opinion that phosphatides are effective antioxidants because they provide a fat-soluble form of phosphoric acid which functions as a "scavenger" for metals such as iron which exert prooxidant effects on oils. This is in essential agreement with the finding of Olcott and Mattill (see above) that the phosphoric acid residue is responsible for the antioxygenic activity of the cephalin fraction.

Olcott (1944) isolated from cottonseed what may possibly be an inositol-containing phosphatide and found this material to be an antioxidant for the ethyl esters of cottonseed oil fatty acids.

Phosphatides, choline and amino acids were postulated by Altman (1947) as the agents responsible for the natural retardation of oxidation in *Hevea* latex.

BIBLIOGRAPHY—PART V

Abbott, O. D., *Fla. Agr. Expt. Sta., Ann. Rept.,* 84 (1933); *C. A.,* 30, 3472 (1936).
——, *ibid.,* 57 (1934); *C. A.,* 30, 3472 (1936).
——, and DeMasters, C. U., *J. Nutrition,* 19, 47 (1940); *C. A.,* 34, 2037 (1940).
Ackermann, J., *Bull. intern. acad. polon. sci., Classe sci. math. nat.,* II, 177 (1936); *C. A.,* 31, 1475 (1937).

Adlersberg, D., and Sobotka, H., *J. Nutrition,* **25,** 255 (1943); *C. A.,* **37,** 2789 (1943).

——, ——, *J. Mt. Sinai Hosp., N. Y.,* **9,** 955 (1943a); *C. A.,* **37,** 5137 (1943).

Ajazzi-Mancini, M., and Donatelli, L., *Boll. ist. sieroterap milan.,* **20,** 307 (1941); *C. A.,* **38,** 2391 (1944).

Allen, F. N., and co-workers (Bowie, D. J., Macleod, J. J. R., and Robinson, W.), *Brit. J. Exptl. Path.,* **5,** 75 (1924).

Allen, J. G., and co-workers (Vermeulen, C., Owens, F. M., Jr., and Dragstedt, L. R.), *Am. J. Physiol.,* **138,** 352 (1943); *C. A.,* **37,** 1760 (1943).

Altman, R. F. A., *Trans. Inst. Rubber Ind.,* **23,** 179 (1947); *C. A.,* **42,** 4779 (1948).

Alvarez, M. D. A. de, *Arch. farm. y bioquím. Tucumán,* **1,** 323 (1945); *C. A.,* **39,** 3822 (1945).

Andrews, K. R., and Brown, G. O., *J. Clin. Invest.,* **19,** 786 (1940).

Annau, E., *Enzymologia,* **9,** 150 (1941); *C. A.,* **36,** 789 (1942).

——, Eperjessy, A., and Felszeghy, Ö., *Z. physiol. Chem.,* **277,** 58 (1942); *C. A.,* **37,** 5426 (1943).

Anselmino, K. J., Hoffman, F., and Rhoden, E., *Arch. ges. Physiol. (Pflügers),* **237,** 515 (1936); *C. A.,* **30,** 7176 (1936).

Aoki, M., *Mitt. med. Ges. Okayama,* **50,** 2015, 2055 (1938); *C. A.,* **34,** 7397 (1940).

Artom, C., *Arch. sci. biol.,* **5,** 22 (1923); *C. A.,* **18,** 2553 (1924).

——, *Arch. intern. physiol.,* **36,** 101 (1933); *C. A.,* **27,** 5821 (1933).

——, *Arch. fisiol.,* **32,** 57 (1933a); *C. A.,* **27,** 2484 (1933).

——, *J. Biol. Chem.,* **139,** 65 (1941).

——, *ibid.,* **139,** 953 (1941a).

——, *ibid.,* **157,** 595 (1945).

——, and Cornatzer, W. E., *J. Biol. Chem.,* **165,** 393 (1946).

——, ——, *ibid.,* **176,** 949 (1948).

——, and co-workers (Sarzana, G., Perrier, C., Santangelo, M., and Segré, E.), *Arch. intern. physiol.,* **45,** 32 (1937); *C. A.,* **32,** 3003 (1938).

——, and co-workers (Sarzana, G., Perrier, C., Santangelo, M., and Segré, E.), *Nature,* **139,** 836 (1937a); *C. A.,* **31,** 5397 (1937).

——, and co-workers (Perrier, C., Santangelo, M., Sarzana, G., and Segré, E.), *Boll. soc. ital. biol. sper.,* **12,** 708 (1937b); *C. A.,* **32,** 977 (1938).

——, and Freeman, J. A., *J. Biol. Chem.,* **135,** 59 (1940).

——, and Marziani, R., *Bull. soc. chim. biol.,* **6,** 713 (1924); *C. A.,* **19,** 850 (1925).

——, and Peretti, G., *Boll. soc. ital. biol. sper.,* **7,** 980 (1932); *C. A.,* **27,** 342 (1933).

——, ——, *Arch. intern. physiol.,* **36,** 351 (1933); *C. A.,* **27,** 5821 (1933).

——, ——, *ibid.,* **42,** 61 (1935); *C. A.,* **30,** 4204 (1936).

——, ——, *Boll. soc. ital. biol. sper.,* **10,** 867 (1936); *C. A.,* **30,** 2624 (1936).

——, and Swanson, M. A., *J. Biol. Chem.,* **175,** 871 (1948).

——, Cornatzer, W. E., and Crowder, M., *J. Biol. Chem.,* **180,** 495 (1949).

——, Fishman, W. H., and Morehead, R. P., *Federation Proc.,* **4,** 81 (1945).

——, Sarzana, G., and Segré, E., *Arch. intern. physiol.,* **47,** 245 (1938); *C. A.,* **32,** 9202 (1938).

Astrup, T., in "Advances in Enzymology," Vol. 10, New York, Interscience Publishers, Inc., 1950.

Atchley, W., *J. Biol. Chem.,* **176,** 123 (1948).

Aten, A. H. W., Jr., "Isotopes and Formation of Milk and Eggs," Dissertation, Utrecht, 1939.

——, and Hevesy, G., *Nature,* **142,** 111 (1938); *C. A.,* **32,** 7553 (1938).

Augur, V., Rollman, H. S., and Deuel, H. J., Jr., *J. Nutrition,* **33,** 177 (1947); *C. A.,* **41,** 2470 (1947).

Aylward, F. X., Blackwood, J. H., and Smith, J. A. B., *Biochem. J.*, **31**, 130 (1937) ; *C. A.*, **31**, 4375 (1937).

Ball, E. G., and co-workers (McKee, R. W., Anfinsen, C. B., Cruz, W. O., and Geiman, Q. M.), *J. Biol. Chem.*, **175**, 547 (1949).

Barbour, A. D., *J. Biol. Chem.*, **106**, 281 (1934).

Barnes, R. H., Miller, E. S., and Burr, G. O., *Proc. Soc. Exptl. Biol. Med.*, **42**, 45 (1939) ; *C. A.*, **34**, 455 (1940).

——, ——, ——, *J. Biol. Chem.*, **140**, 233, 241, 247 (1941).

——, Rusoff, I. I., and Burr, G. O., *Proc. Soc. Exptl. Biol. Med.*, **49**, 84 (1942) ; *C. A.*, **36**, 2302 (1942).

Barnum, C. P., and co-workers (Nash, C. W., Jennings, E., Nygaard, O., and Vermund, H.), *Arch. Biochem.*, **25**, 376 (1950).

——, and Huseby, R. A., *Arch. Biochem.*, **19**, 17 (1948) ; *C. A.*, **43**, 4315 (1949).

Barrett, H. M., and co-workers (Best, C. H., MacLean, D. L., and Ridout, J. H.), *J. Physiol.*, **97**, 103 (1939) ; *C. A.*, **34**, 1082 (1940).

——, Best, C. H., and Ridout, J. H., *J. Physiol.*, **93**, 367 (1938) ; *C. A.*, **32**, 9234 (1938).

Baumann, E. J., and Holly, O. M., *Am. J. Physiol.*, **75**, 618, 633 (1926) ; *C. A.*, **20**, 1835, 1839 (1926).

Baumann, T., Klenk, E., and Scheidegger, S., *Ergeb. allg. Path. u. path. Anat.*, **30**, 183 (1936).

Bavetta, L. A., *Am. J. Physiol.*, **140**, 44 (1943) ; *C. A.*, **38**, 151 (1944).

——, and Deuel, H. J., Jr., *Am. J. Physiol.*, **136**, 712 (1942) ; *C. A.*, **36**, 5232 (1942).

Bayles, T. B., and Riddell, C. B., *Am. J. Med. Sci.*, **208**, 343 (1944) ; *C. A.*, **39**, 747 (1945).

Belfanti, S., *Z. Immunitätsforsch.*, **44**, 347 (1925) ; *C. A.*, **20**, 1268 (1926).

——, Contardi, A., and Ercoli, A., "Ergebnisse der Enzymforschung," Vol. 5, Leipzig, R. Weidenhagen, Akademische Verlagsgesellschaft M.B.H., 1936.

Bensley, R. R., *Anat. Record*, **69**, 341 (1937) ; *C. A.*, **32**, 982 (1938).

——, and Hoerr, N. L., *Anat. Record*, **60**, 449 (1934) ; *C. A.*, **29**, 6284 (1935).

Bernhard, K., and Schoenheimer, R., *J. Biol. Chem.*, **133**, 713 (1940).

——, and Vischer, E., *Helv. Chim. Acta*, **29**, 929 (1946) ; *C. A.*, **40**, 5816 (1946).

Bernheim, F., and Bernheim, M. L. C., *J. Biol. Chem.*, **127**, 353 (1939).

——, ——, *ibid.*, **128**, 79 (1939a).

Bernstein, S. S., and co-workers (Williams, H. H., Hummel, F. C., Shepherd, M. L., and Erickson, B. N.), *J. Pediat.*, **14**, 570 (1939) ; *C. A.*, **34**, 5494 (1940).

Bertramson, B. R., and Stephenson, R. E., *Soil Sci.*, **53**, 215 (1942) ; *C. A.*, **36**, 4258 (1942).

Best, C. H., *Am. J. Digestive Diseases*, **13**, 155 (1946) ; *C. A.*, **40**, 6142 (1946).

——, and Huntsman, M. E., *J. Physiol.*, **75**, 405 (1932) ; *C. A.*, **26**, 5620 (1932).

——, and Ridout, J. H., *J. Physiol.*, **78**, 415 (1933) ; *C. A.*, **27**, 5790 (1933).

——, ——, *ibid.*, **94**, 47 (1938) ; *C. A.*, **33**, 1024 (1939).

——, Channon, H. J., and Ridout, J. H., *J. Physiol.*, **81**, 409 (1934) ; *C. A.*, **29**, 4413 (1935).

——, Hershey, J. M., and Huntsman, M. E., *Am. J. Physiol.*, **101**, 7 (1932).

Bialosuknia, V., *Bull. Intern. acad. polon. B*, **7**, 15 (1924) ; *C. A.*, **20**, 1646 (1926).

Biddulph, O., *Science*, **89**, 393 (1939) ; *C. A.*, **33**, 6391 (1939).

Bierich, R., and Lang, A., *Z. physiol. Chem.*, **216**, 217 (1933) ; *C. A.*, **27**, 3515 (1933).

——, Detzel, A., and Lang, A., *Z. physiol. Chem.*, **201**, 157 (1931) ; *C. A.*, **26**, 511 (1932).

Blackwood, J. H., *Biochem. J.*, **28**, 1346 (1934) ; *C. A.*, **29**, 1471 (1935).

Blewett, M., Campbell, I. G., and Olley, J., *Nature*, **164**, 621 (1949).

Bloch, K., *Biochem. Z.*, **285**, 372 (1936); *C. A.*, **30**, 8291 (1936).

——, *Physiol. Rev.*, **27**, 574 (1947).

Bloor, W. R., *J. Biol. Chem.*, **19**, 1 (1914).

——, *ibid.*, **23**, 317 (1915).

——, *ibid.*, **24**, 447 (1916).

——, *ibid.*, **25**, 577 (1916a).

——, *Physiol. Rev.*, **2**, 92 (1922).

——, *J. Biol. Chem.*, **72**, 327 (1927).

——, *ibid.*, **80**, 443 (1928).

——, *ibid.*, **103**, 699 (1933).

——, *ibid.*, **114**, 639 (1936).

——, *ibid.*, **119**, 451 (1937).

——, *ibid.*, **132**, 77 (1940).

——, "Biochemistry of the Fatty Acids and Their Compounds, the Lipids," New York, Reinhold Publishing Corp., 1943.

——, *Nutrition Reviews*, **2**, 289 (1944).

——, and MacPherson, D. J., *J. Biol. Chem.*, **31**, 79 (1917).

——, and Snider, R. H., *J. Biol. Chem.*, **107**, 459 (1934).

——, ——, *Proc. Soc. Exptl. Biol. Med.*, **36**, 215 (1937).

——, Blake, A. G., and Bullen, S. S., *J. Allergy*, **9**, 227 (1938); *C. A.*, **32**, 9245 (1938).

——, Gillette, E. M., and James, M. S., *J. Biol. Chem.*, **75**, 61 (1927).

——, Okey, R., and Corner, G. W., *J. Biol. Chem.*, **86**, 291 (1930).

Bogdanovitch, S. B., and Man, E. B., *Am. J. Physiol.*, **122**, 73 (1938); *C. A.*, **32**, 4225 (1938).

Boivin, A., and Mesrobeanu, L., *Compt. rend.*, **198**, 2211 (1934); *C. A.*, **28**, 5880 (1934).

——, ——, *Compt. rend. soc. biol.*, **125**, 273 (1937); *C. A.*, **31**, 6278 (1937).

——, Delaunay, A., and Sarciron, R., *Compt. rend. soc. biol*, **134**, 357 (1940); *C. A.*, **36**, 1056 (1942).

Boldyreva, N. V., *J. Physiol. U.S.S.R.*, **29**, 582 (1940); *C. A.*, **36**, 6215 (1942).

Bollman, J. L., and Flock, E. V., *J. Lab. Clin. Med.*, **31**, 478 (1946).

——, ——, and Berkson, J., *Proc. Soc. Exptl. Biol. Med.*, **67**, 308 (1948); *C. A.*, **42**, 5530 (1948).

Bollmann, H., U. S. Pat. 1,575,529 Mar. 2 (1926); *C. A.*, **20**, 1531 (1926).

Borek, E., and Rittenberg, D., *J. Biol. Chem.*, **179**, 843 (1949).

Boxer, G. E., and Stetten, D., Jr., *J. Biol. Chem.*, **153**, 617 (1944).

Boyd, E. M., *Can. Med. Assoc. J.*, **31**, 626 (1934).

——, *Surg. Gynecol. Obstet.*, **59**, 744 (1934a).

——, *J. Clin. Invest.*, **13**, 347 (1934b); *C. A.*, **28**, 3114 (1934).

——, *J. Biol. Chem.*, **108**, 607 (1935).

——, *Am. J. Obstet. Gynecol.*, **29**, 797 (1935a).

——, *Surg. Gynecol. Obstet.*, **60**, 205 (1935b).

——, and Connell, W. F., *Quart. J. Med.*, **5**, 455 (1936); *C. A.*, **31**, 1876 (1937).

——, and Wilson, K. M., *J. Clin. Invest.*, **14**, 7 (1935); *C. A.*, **29**, 1468 (1935).

Branson, H., Banks, H. W., Jr., and Dodson, L. B., *Science*, **106**, 637 (1947); *C. A.*, **42**, 1997 (1948).

Brante, G., *Biochem. Z.*, **305**, 136 (1940); *C. A.*, **35**, 498 (1941).

Bretin, Manceau, and Cochet, *Compt. rend. soc. biol.*, **106**, 195 (1931); *C. A.*, **26**, 3817 (1932).

Breusch, F. L., *Science*, 97, 490 (1943); *C. A.*, 37, 4454 (1943).

Brobeck, J. R., Tepperman, J., and Long, C. N. H., *Yale J. Biol. Med.*, 15, 831, 893 (1943).

Brown, H., and Kolmer, J. A., *J. Biol. Chem.*, 137, 525 (1941).

Brown, R., *N. Y. State Dept. Health, Ann. Rept. Div. Labs. and Research*, 16 (1943); *C. A.*, 38, 5938 (1944).

Brown, W. R., and co-workers (Hansen, A. E., Burr, G. O., and McQuarrie, I.), *J. Nutrition*, 16, 511 (1938); *C. A.*, 33, 1787 (1939).

Brunius, E., *Arkiv Kemi, Mineral. Geol.*, 12B, No. 18 (1936); *C. A.*, 30, 6057 (1936).

Bulliard, H., Grundland, I., and Moussa, A., *Compt. rend.*, 207, 745 (1938); *C. A.*, 33, 1349 (1939).

Bullock, W. E., and Cramer, W., *Proc. Roy. Soc. (London)*, 87B, 236 (1914); *C. A.*, 8, 960 (1914).

Bülow, M., and Page, I. H., *Z. physiol. Chem.*, 205, 25 (1932); *C. A.*, 26, 3551 (1932).

Bürger, M., and Beumer, *Berlin. klin. Wochschr.*, 50, 112 (1913); *C. A.*, 7, 2962 (1913).

——, and Rückert, W., *Z. physiol. Chem.*, 196, 169 (1931); *C. A.*, 25, 3702 (1931).

Burr, G. O., and Burr, M. M., *J. Biol. Chem.*, 86, 587 (1930).

Butts, J. S., and co-workers (Cutler, C. H., Hallman, L. F., and Deuel, H. J., Jr., *J. Biol. Chem.*, 109, 597 (1935).

Cahn, T., quoted by Needham, J., "Chemical Embryology," Cambridge, University Press, 1931.

——, and Bonot, A., *Ann. physiol. physicochim. biol.*, 4, 399 (1928); *C. A.*, 24, 3046 (1930).

Campbell, I. G., Olley, J., and Blewett, M., *Biochem. J.*, 45, 105 (1949).

Campbell, J. M. H., *Quart. J. Med.*, 18, 393 (1925); *C. A.*, 20, 238 (1926).

Campbell, R. M., and Kosterlitz, H. W., *J. Biol. Chem.*, 175, 989 (1948).

Carbone, D., and Pighini, G., *Biochem. Z.*, 46, 450 (1912); *C. A.*, 7, 824 (1913).

Cardini, C. E., and Serantes, M. E., *Rev. soc. argentina biol.*, 19, 59 (1943); *C. A.*, 38, 1012 (1944).

Caselli, P., and Cutinelli, C., *Tumori*, 15, 118 (1941); *C. A.*, 39, 2126 (1945).

Cassafouth, C. F. C., Brage, D., and Rivas, L., *Semana Méd. (Buenos Aires)*, I, 403 (1948); *C. A.*, 42, 6923 (1948).

Cavanagh, B., and Raper, H. S., *Biochem. J.*, 33, 17 (1939); *C. A.*, 33, 4648 (1939).

Chaikoff, I. L., *Physiol. Rev.*, 22, 291 (1942); *C. A.*, 37, 1758 (1943).

——, and Connor, C. L., *Proc. Soc. Exptl. Biol. Med.*, 43, 638 (1940); *C. A.*, 34, 4423 (1940).

——, and co-workers (Lindsay, S., Lorenz, F. W., and Entenman, C.), *J. Exptl. Med.*, 88, 373 (1948); *C. A.*, 42, 8945 (1948).

——, and Entenman, C., in "Advances in Enzymology," Vol. 8, New York, Interscience Publishers, Inc., 1948.

——, ——, and Montgomery, M. L., *J. Biol. Chem.*, 160, 489 (1945).

——, ——, and Zilversmit, D., "Absorption of Fat in Various Nutritional and Environmental States," Chicago, U. S. Army Quartermaster Corps, 1947.

——, Smyth, F. S., and Gibbs, G. E., *J. Clin. Invest.*, 15, 627 (1936); *C. A.*, 31, 1089 (1937).

——, Zilversmit, D. B., and Entenman, C., *Proc. Soc. Exptl. Biol. Med.*, 68, 6 (1948); *C. A.*, 42, 6445 (1948).

Chamberlain, E. N., and Corlett, R. L., *Brit. J. Exptl. Path.*, 13, 299 (1932); *C. A.*, 26, 5643 (1932).

Changus, G. W., Chaikoff, I. L., and Ruben, S., *J. Biol. Chem.,* **126,** 493 (1938).

Channon, H. J., and co-workers (Platt, A. P., Loach, J. V., and Smith, J. A. B.), *Biochem. J.,* **31,** 2181 (1937); *C. A.,* **32,** 2627 (1938).

Chantrenne, H., *Biochim. et Biophys. Acta,* **1,** 437 (1947); *C. A.,* **42,** 2236 (1948).

Chanutin, A., and Gjessling, E. C., *J. Biol. Chem.,* **178,** 1 (1949).

——, and Ludewig, S., *J. Biol. Chem.,* **115,** 1 (1936).

——, ——, *J. Lab. Clin. Med.,* **22,** 903 (1937); *C. A.,* **31,** 7108 (1937).

Chapman, F. D., and Kinney, T. D., *Am. J. Diseases Children,* **62,** 1014 (1941); *C. A.,* **36,** 2007 (1942).

Chargaff, E., *Science,* **85,** 548 (1937); *C. A.,* **31,** 5425 (1937).

——, *J. Biol. Chem.,* **121,** 175, 187 (1937a).

——, *ibid.,* **125,** 677 (1938).

——, *ibid.,* **128,** 587 (1939).

——, *ibid.,* **130,** 503 (1939a).

——, *ibid.,* **142,** 505 (1942).

——, *ibid.,* **142,** 491 (1942a).

——, *ibid.,* **155,** 387 (1944).

——, in Nord, F. F., and Werkman, C. H., "Advances in Enzymology," Vol. **5,** p. 31, New York, Interscience Publishers, Inc. (1945).

——, *J. Biol. Chem.,* **160,** 351 (1945a).

——, *ibid.,* **161,** 389 (1945b).

——, and Cohen, S. S., *J. Biol. Chem.,* **129,** 619 (1939).

——, and Keston, A. S., *J. Biol. Chem.,* **134,** 515 (1940).

——, and Schaefer, W., *Ann. Inst. Pasteur,* **54,** 708 (1935); *C. A.,* **30,** 3494 (1936).

——, Bancroft, F. W., and Stanley-Brown, M., *J. Biol. Chem.,* **116,** 237 (1936).

——, Bendich, A., and Cohen, S. S., *J. Biol. Chem.,* **156,** 161 (1944).

——, Olson, K. B., and Partington, P. F., *J. Biol. Chem.,* **134,** 505 (1940).

——, Ziff, M., and Cohen, S. S., *J. Biol. Chem.,* **136,** 257 (1940).

Chatterjee, H. N., and Ghosh, S. M., *J. Indian Chem. Soc.,* **17,** 356 (1940); *C. A.,* **35,** 1481 (1941).

Chen, A. L., *J. Pharmakol.,* **45,** 1 (1932); *C. A.,* **26,** 3620 (1932).

Chernik, S., Srere, P. A., and Chaikoff, I. L., *J. Biol. Chem.,* **179,** 113 (1949).

Chopra, R. N., and Chopra, G. S., *Indian Med. Gaz.,* **75,** 388 (1940); *C. A.,* **34,** 8064 (1940).

Christensen, K., *J. Biol. Med.,* **133,** Proc. XX (1940).

Ciaccio, C., *Arch. farm. sper.,* **24,** 231 (1917); *C. A.,* **12,** 1302 (1918).

Clarke, B. G., Ivy, A. C., and Goodman, D., *Am. J. Physiol.,* **153,** 264 (1948); *C. A.,* **42,** 8309 (1948).

Clarkson, M. F., and Best, C. H., *Science,* **105,** 622 (1947); *C. A.,* **41,** 5596 (1947).

Claude, A., *Cold Spring Harbor Symposia Quant. Biol.,* **9,** 263 (1941); *C. A.,* **38,** 988 (1944).

——, *J. Exp. Med.,* **84,** 51, 61 (1946); *C. A.,* **40,** 5483 (1946).

Cohen, P. P., *J. Biol. Chem.,* **119,** 333 (1937).

Cohen, S. S., and Chargaff, E., *J. Biol. Chem.,* **136,** 243 (1940).

——, ——, *ibid.,* **139,** 741 (1941).

——, ——, *ibid.,* **140,** 689 (1941a).

Connor, C. L., *Am. J. Path.,* **14,** 347 (1938).

Cook, R. P., *Biochem. J.,* **30,** 1630 (1936); *C. A.,* **31,** 1077 (1937).

Coope, R., and Chamberlain, E. N., *J. Physiol.,* **60,** 69 (1925); *C. A.,* **19,** 3319 (1925).

——, and Mottram, V. H., *J. Physiol.,* **49,** 23 (1914); *C. A.,* **9,** 1073 (1915).

Costello, C. J., and co-workers (Caruthers, C., Kainen, M. D., and Simoes, R. L.), *Cancer Research*, **7**, 642 (1947).

Crandall, L. A., Jr., *J. Biol. Chem.*, **138**, 123 (1941).

Dakin, H. D., *J. Biol. Chem.*, **6**, 221 (1909).

——, *Physiol. Rev.*, **1**, 394 (1921); *C. A.*, **17**, 1036 (1923).

Dale, H. H., *J. Pharmacol.*, **6**, 147 (1914); *C. A.*, **9**, 104 (1915).

D'Alessandro, G., and Greco, A., *Z. Immunitätsforsch.*, **94**, 147 (1938); *C. A.*, **33**, 221 (1939).

Danielson, I. S., Hall, C. H., and Everett, M. R., *Proc. Soc. Exptl. Biol. Med.*, **49**, 569 (1942); *C. A.*, **36**, 3840 (1942).

Dauben, W. G., *J. Am. Chem. Soc.*, **70**, 1376 (1948); *C. A.*, **42**, 6746 (1948).

Dauber, D. V., *Arch. Path.*, **38**, 46 (1944).

Davanzo, I. G., *Deut. Z. Chir.*, **247**, 622 (1936); *C. A.*, **32**, 3463 (1938).

Davis, D., Stern, B., and Lesnick, G., *Ann. Internal Med.*, **11**, 354 (1937); *C. A.*, **31**, 7999 (1937).

Davis, J. E., *Am. J. Physiol.*, **142**, 65 (1944); *C. A.*, **38**, 5976 (1944).

——, *ibid.*, **147**, 404 (1946).

Davison, C., and Jacobson, S. A., *Am. J. Diseases Children*, **52**, 345 (1936).

Delezenne, C., and Fourneau, E., *Bull. soc. chim.* [4], **15**, 421 (1914); *C. A.*, **8**, 3591 (1914).

——, and Ledebt, E., *Compt. rend.*, **153**, 81 (1911); *C. A.*, **5**, 3093 (1911).

——, ——, *ibid.*, **155**, 1101 (1912); *C. A.*, **7**, 1752 (1913).

Denis, W., *J. Biol. Chem.*, **29**, 93 (1917).

Dennis, E. W., *Am. J. Hyg.*, **32B**, 1 (1940).

De Sütö-Nagy, G. I., *Am. J. Physiol.*, **141**, 338 (1944); *C. A.*, **38**, 4023 (1944).

Deuel, H. J., Jr., and co-workers (Butts, J. S., Hallman, L. F., and Cutler, C. H.), *J. Biol. Chem.*, **112**, 15 (1935).

——, and co-workers (Hallman, L. F., Butts, J. S., and Murray, S.), *J. Biol. Chem.*, **116**, 621 (1936).

——, and Morehouse, M. G., in "Advances in Carbohydrate Chemistry," Vol. **II**, New York, Academic Press, Inc., 1946.

Deutsch, H. F., Kline, B. E., and Rusch, H. P., *J. Biol. Chem.*, **141**, 529 (1941).

Dickens, F., *Ann. Repts. on Progress of Chem.*, **42**, 197 (1945).

Diemair, W., Strohecker, R., and Reuland, K., *Z. Untersuch. Lebensm.*, **79**, 23 (1940); *C. A.*, **34**, 2474 (1940).

Doan, C. A., Sabin, F. R., and Forkner, C. E., *J. Exptl. Med.*, **52**, Suppl. 3, 73 (1930); *C. A.*, **25**, 541 (1931).

Dols, M. J. L., *Nederland. Tijdschr. Geneesk.*, **82**, 2645 (1938); *C. A.*, **32**, 8489 (1938).

——, and co-workers (Jansen, B. C. P., Sizoo, G. J., and Barendregt, F.), *Proc. Acad. Sci. Amsterdam*, **41**, 997 (1938); *C. A.*, **33**, 1795 (1939).

——, and co-workers (Jansen, B. C. P., Sizoo, G. J., and Barendregt, F.), *Nature*, **141**, 77 (1938a); *C. A.*, **32**, 2583 (1938).

——, and co-workers (Jansen, B. C. P., Sizoo, G. J., and van der Maas, G. J.), *Proc. Acad. Sci. Amsterdam*, **42**, 499 (1939); *C. A.*, **33**, 8249 (1939).

Doubilet, H., and Reiner, M., *Arch. Internal Med.*, **59**, 857 (1937); *C. A.*, **31**, 5417 (1937).

Downs, W. G., Jr., *Am. Med.*, **41**, 460 (1935); *C. A.*, **30**, 160 (1936).

Dragstedt, L. R., Prohaska, J. V., and Harms, H. P., *Am. J. Physiol.*, **117**, 175 (1936); *C. A.*, **30**, 8347 (1936).

Dreyfuss, M. L., and Fishberg, E. H., *Am. J. Med. Sci.*, **206**, 458 (1943); *C. A.*, **38**, 151 (1944).

Drinker, N., and Zinsser, H. H., *J. Biol. Chem.*, **148**, 187 (1943).

Drury, A. N., and co-workers (Miles, J. A. R., Platt, A. E., Plaut, G., Weil, H., and Hughes, A. R.), *Path. Bact.*, **42**, 363 (1936); *C. A.*, **30**, 4931 (1936).

Dunn, E. E., *J. Pharmacol.*, **50**, 393 (1934); *C. A.*, **28**, 5540 (1934).

Dutton, H. J., and co-workers (Schwab, A. W., Moser, H. A., and Cowan, J. C.), *J. Am. Oil Chem. Soc.*, **26**, 441 (1949).

du Vigneaud, V., *Harvey Lectures*, **38**, 39 (1942/43).

——, and co-workers (Chandler, J. P., Moyer, A. W., and Keppel, D. M.), *J. Biol. Chem.*, **131**, 57 (1939).

——, and co-workers (Chandler, J. P., Cohn, M., and Brown, G. B.), *J. Biol. Chem.*, **134**, 787 (1940).

——, and co-workers (Cohn, M., Chandler, J. P., Schenk, J. R., and Simmonds, S.), *J. Biol. Chem.*, **140**, 625 (1941).

——, and co-workers (Chandler, J. P., Simmonds, S., Moyer, A. W., and Cohn, M., *J. Biol. Chem.*, **164**, 603 (1946).

Eaves, E. C., *J. Physiol.*, **40**, 451 (1910); *C. A.*, **4**, 2840 (1910).

Eckstein, H. C., and Wile, U. J., *J. Biol. Chem.*, **87**, 311 (1930).

Eichhaltz, F., *Biochem. Z.*, **144**, 66 (1924); *C. A.*, **18**, 2742 (1924).

Elkes, J. J., and co-workers (Frazer, A. C., Schulman, J. H., and Stewart, H. C.), *J. Physiol.*, **103**, 6P (1944); *C. A.*, **39**, 337 (1945).

Elliott, K. A. C., and Libet, B., *J. Biol. Chem.*, **152**, 617 (1944).

Ellis, N. R., Rothwell, C. S., and Pool, W. O., *J. Biol. Chem.*, **92**, 385 (1931).

Emanuel, E., *Edinburgh Med. J.*, **48**, 843 (1941).

Engel, R. W., *J. Nutrition*, **24**, 175 (1942); *C. A.*, **36**, 5861 (1942).

——, and Salmon, W. D., *J. Nutrition*, **22**, 109 (1941); *C. A.*, **35**, 8029 (1941).

Engelhardt, H. T., and Derbes, V. J., *Am. J. Med. Sci.*, **207**, 776 (1944); *C. A.*, **38**, 5937 (1944).

Entenman, C., and Chaikoff, I. L., *J. Biol. Chem.*, **142**, 129 (1942).

——, and co-workers (Ruben, S., Perlman, I., Lorenz, F. W., and Chaikoff, I. L.), *J. Biol. Chem.*, **124**, 795 (1938).

——, and co-workers (Changus, G. W., Gibbs, G. E., and Chaikoff, I. L.), *J. Biol. Chem.*, **134**, 59 (1940).

——, Chaikoff, I. L., and Friedlander, H. D., *J. Biol. Chem.*, **162**, 111 (1946).

——, ——, and Montgomery, M. L., *J. Biol. Chem.*, **155**, 573 (1944).

——, ——, and Zilversmit, D. B., *J. Biol. Chem.*, **166**, 15 (1946).

——, Lorenz, F. W., and Chaikoff, I. L., *J. Biol. Chem.*, **133**, 231 (1940).

Epstein, E., *Biochem. Z.*, **145**, 398 (1924); *C. A.*, **19**, 342 (1925).

——, and Lorenz, K., *Z. physiol. Chem.*, **190**, 44 (1930); *C. A.*, **24**, 5060 (1930).

——, ——, *ibid.*, **192**, 145 (1930a); *C. A.*, **25**, 135 (1931).

——, ——, *ibid.*, **211**, 217 (1932); *C. A.*, **27**, 130 (1933).

Erickson, B. N., and co-workers (Williams, H. H., Hummel, F. C., and Macy, I. G.), *J. Biol. Chem.*, **118**, 15 (1937).

——, and co-workers (Williams, H. H., Hummel, F. C., Lee, P., and Macy, I. G.), *J. Biol. Chem.*, **118**, 569 (1937a).

——, and Ferguson, J. H., *Proc. Soc. Exptl. Biol. Med.*, **45**, 579 (1940); *C. A.*, **35**, 785 (1941).

Esh, G. C., and co-workers (Sutton, T. S., Hibbs, J. W., and Krauss, W. E.), *J. Dairy Sci.*, **31**, 461 (1948); *C. A.*, **42**, 739 (1948).

Etcheverry, M. A., *Rev. méd. quir. patol. femenina* (*Buenos Aires*), **16**, No. 1, 1 (1940); *C. A.*, **34**, 7403 (1940).

Evans, E. I., *Ind. Eng. Chem.*, **27**, 329 (1935); *C. A.*, **29**, 3060 (1935).

Fahrig, C., and Wacker, L., *Klin. Wochschr.*, **11**, 886 (1932); *C. A.*, **26**, 4847 (1932).

Favarger, P., *Arch. intern. pharmacodynamie*, **68**, 409 (1942); *C. A.*, **38**, 5911 (1944).

Fejer, A. von, *Biochem. Z.*, **53**, 168 (1913); *C. A.*, **8**, 1811 (1914).

Feldberg, W., *J. Physiol.*, **99**, 104 (1940); *C. A.*, **35**, 4497 (1941).

Feraru, F., and Offenkrantz, F. M., *Am. J. Syphilis, Gonorrhea, Venereal Diseases*, **21**, 267 (1937); *C. A.*, **31**, 5035 (1937).

Ferguson, J. H., *Physiol. Revs.*, **16**, 640 (1936); *C. A.*, **31**, 141 (1937).

——, and Erickson, B. N., *Am. J. Physiol.*, **126**, 661 (1939); *C. A.*, **33**, 6937 (1939).

Fernau, A., and Pauli, W., *Kolloid Z.*, **30**, 6 (1922); *C. A.*, **16**, 2069 (1922).

Ferraro, A., and Jervis, G. A., *Arch. Path.*, **30**, 731 (1940); *C. A.*, **35**, 2604 (1941).

Feyder, S., *J. Nutrition*, **9**, 457 (1935); *C. A.*, **29**, 4411 (1935).

Field, J. B., and Dam, H., *Proc. Soc. Exptl. Biol. Med.*, **60**, 146 (1945); *C. A.*, **40**, 627 (1946).

Fischer, A., *Biochem. Z.*, **278**, 334 (1935); *C. A.*, **29**, 8090 (1935).

Fischer, O., and Günsberger, O. D., *Z. Immunitätsforsch.*, **87**, 400 (1936); *C. A.*, **30**, 6056 (1936).

Fischer, Oe., *Z. Immunitätsforsch.*, **90**, 348 (1937).

——, and Steinert, J., *Klin. Wochschr.*, **15**, 1322 (1936).

Fisher, N. F., *Am. J. Physiol.*, **67**, 634 (1924); *C. A.*, **18**, 1695 (1924).

Fishler, M. C., and co-workers (Taurog, A., Perlman, I., and Chaikoff, I. L.), *J. Biol. Chem.*, **141**, 809 (1941).

——, and co-workers (Entenman, C., Montgomery, M. L., and Chaikoff, I. L.), *J. Biol. Chem.*, **150**, 47 (1943).

Fishman, W. H., and Artom, C., *J. Biol. Chem.*, **164**, 307 (1946).

Flock, E. V., and Bollman, J. L., *J. Biol. Chem.*, **144**, 571 (1942).

——, ——, *ibid.*, **156**, 151 (1944).

——, and co-workers (Cain, J. C., Grindlay, J. H., and Bollman, J. L.), *Federation Proc.*, **6**, 252 (1947).

——, Corwin, W. C., and Bollman, J. L., *Am. J. Physiol.*, **123**, 558 (1938); *C. A.*, **32**, 8500 (1938).

Foá, P. P., Weinstein, H. R., and Kleppel, B., *Arch. Biochem.*, **19**, 209 (1948); *C. A.*, **43**, 1842 (1949).

Foglia, V. G., and Mazzocco, P., *Compt. rend. soc. biol.*, **127**, 150 (1938); *C. A.*, **32**, 2998 (1938).

Foldes, F. F., and Murphy, A. J., *Proc. Soc. Exptl. Biol. Med.*, **62**, 218 (1946); *C. A.*, **40**, 5828 (1946).

Forssman, J., *Biochem. Z.*, **37**, 78 (1911); *C. A.*, **6**, 394 (1912).

Fowweather, F. S., *Brit. J. Exptl. Path.*, **7**, 7, 15 (1926); *C. A.*, **20**, 1825 (1926).

Fränkel, S., and Dimitz, L., *Wien klin. Wochschr.*, **22**, 1777 (1909).

Frazer, A. C., *Analyst*, **63**, 308 (1938); *C. A.*, **32**, 5468 (1938).

——, *Physiol. Rev.*, **26**, 103 (1946); *C. A.*, **40**, 2514 (1946).

——, *J. Roy. Soc. Arts*, **96**, 582 (1948).

——, *Research* (*London*), *Suppl., Surface Chemistry*, **241** (1949); *C. A.*, **44**, 2618 (1950).

——, and Stewart, H. C., *J. Physiol.*, **95**, 21P (1939); *C. A.*, **33**, 5020 (1939).

——, Schulman, J. H., and Stewart, H. C., *J. Physiol.*, **103**, 306 (1944); *C. A.*, **39**, 972 (1945).

Freeman, G. G., *Biochem. J.*, 37, 601 (1943); *C. A.*, 38, 2385 (1944).

——, and Anderson, T. H., *Biochem. J.*, 35, 564 (1941); *C. A.*, 35, 7024 (1941).

——, Challinor, S. W., and Wilson, J., *Biochem. J.*, 34, 307 (1940); *C. A.*, 34, 4413 (1940).

Friedkin, M., and Lehninger, A. L., *J. Biol. Chem.*, 177, 775 (1949).

Friedlander, H. D., Chaikoff, I. L., and Entenman, C., *J. Biol. Chem.*, 158, 231 (1945).

——, Perlman, I., and Chaikoff, I. L., *Am. J. Physiol.*, 132, 24 (1941); *C. A.*, 35, 2201 (1941).

Friedmann, E., and Türk, W., *Biochem. Z.*, 55, 436 (1913); *C. A.*, 8, 1169 (1914).

Fries, B. A., and Chaikoff, I. L., *J. Biol. Chem.*, 141, 479 (1941).

——, and co-workers (Ruben, S., Perlman, I., and Chaikoff, I. L.), *J. Biol. Chem.*, 123, 587 (1938).

——, and co-workers (Entenman, C., Changus, G. W., and Chaikoff, I. L.), *J. Biol. Chem.*, 137, 303 (1941).

——, Changus, G. W., and Chaikoff, I. L., *J. Biol. Chem.*, 132, 23 (1940).

——, Schachner, H., and Chaikoff, I. L., *J. Biol. Chem.*, 144, 59 (1942).

Frölicher, E., and Süllmann, H., *Biochem. Z.*, 274, 21 (1934); *C. A.*, 29, 836 (1935).

Fujimura, S., *J. Biochem. (Japan)*, 25, 595 (1937); *C. A.*, 31, 8671 (1937).

Furth, J., and Kabat, E. A., *Science*, 91, 483 (1940); *C. A.*, 34, 5162 (1940).

——, ——, *ibid.*, 94, 46 (1941).

Gavin, G., and McHenry, E. W., *J. Biol. Chem.*, 132, 41 (1940).

——, Patterson, J. M., and McHenry, E. W., *J. Biol. Chem.*, 148, 275 (1943).

Gerstl, B., and Tennant, R., *Proc. Soc. Exptl. Biol. Med.*, 52, 154 (1943); *C. A.*, 37, 2814 (1943).

Geyer, R. P., and co-workers (Watkin, D. M., Matthews, L. W., and Stare, F. J.), *J. Lab. Clin. Med.* 34, 688 (1949).

Gibbs, G. E., and Chaikoff, I. L., *Endocrinology*, 29, 877 (1941); *C. A.*, 36, 1083 (1942).

Gildea, E. F., Man, E. B., and Peters, J. P., *J. Clin. Investigation*, 18, 739 (1939); *C. A.*, 34, 5150 (1940).

Goda, T., *Biochem. Z.*, 297, 347 (1938); *C. A.*, 32, 9114 (1938).

Goebel, W. F., and Adams, M. H., *J. Exptl. Med.*, 77, 435 (1943); *C. A.*, 37, 3822 (1943).

——, and co-workers (Shedlovsky, T., Lavin, G. I., and Adams, M. H.), *J. Biol. Chem.*, 148, 1 (1943).

——, Binkley, F., and Perlman, E., *J. Exptl. Med.*, 81, 315 (1945); *C. A.*, 39, 2536 (1945).

Gofman, J. W., and co-workers (Lindgren, F., Elliott, H., Mantz, W., Hewitt, J., Strisower, B., and Herring, V.), *Science*, 111, 166 (1950).

Goldstein, M. R., and Rosahn, P. D., *Connecticut State Med. J.*, 9, 351 (1945).

Goodell, J. P. B., Hanson, P. C., and Hawkins, W. B., *J. Exptl. Med.*, 79, 625 (1944); *C. A.*, 38, 3731 (1944).

Gorter, E., and Hermans, J. J., *Rec. trav. chim.*, 62, 681 (1943); *C. A.*, 38, 4690 (1944).

Govaerts, P., and Cordier, R., *Bull. acad. roy. med. Belg.*, [5], 8, 510 (1929); *C. A.*, 23, 5498 (1929).

Grafflin, A. L., and Green, D. E., *J. Biol. Chem.*, 176, 95 (1948).

Graham, W. R., Jr., Jones, T. S. G., and Kay, H. D., *Proc. Roy. Soc. (London)*, 120B, 330 (1936); *C. A.*, 30, 5315 (1936).

Grassman, W., Dyckerhoff, H., and Schoenbeck, O. v., *Z. physiol. Chem.*, 186, 183 (1930); *C. A.*, 24, 1871 (1930).

Gratia, A., and Levene, P. A., *J. Biol. Chem.,* **50**, 455 (1922).

Griffith, W. H., *Biol. Symposia,* **5**, 193 (1941); *C. A.,* **36**, 2299 (1942).

——, and Wade, N. J., *J. Biol. Chem.,* **131**, 567 (1939).

Gronchi, V., *Boll. soc. ital. biol. sper.,* **7**, 1019 (1932); *C. A.,* **27**, 342 (1933).

——, *ibid.,* **7**, 1297 (1932a); *C. A.,* **27**, 1404 (1933).

Guerrini, G., *Z. Immunitätsforsch.,* **45**, 249 (1925); *C. A.,* **20**, 1268 (1926).

Guggenheim, A., *Z. Immunitätsforsch.,* **61**, 361 (1929); *C. A.,* **24**, 422 (1930).

Güntherberg, K., *Wiss. Arch. Landw., Abt. B,* **3**, 339 (1930); *C. A.,* **25**, 5451 (1931).

Gustafson, F. G., and Darken, M., *Science,* **85**, 482 (1937); *C. A.,* **31**, 5407 (1937).

Gutman, A. B., and Hanger, F. M., *Med. Clinics N. Amer., N. Y. number,* **25**, 837 (1941).

Gutstein, M., *Biochem. Z.,* **207**, 177 (1929); *C. A.,* **23**, 3241 (1929).

György, P., *N. Y. Acad. Sci.,* **49**, 525 (1948); *C. A.,* **42**, 8892 (1948).

——, and Goldblatt, H., *J. Exptl. Med.,* **72**, 1 (1940); *C. A.,* **34**, 5901 (1940).

——, ——, *ibid.,* **75**, 355 (1942); *C. A.,* **36**, 3533 (1942).

——, Rose, C. S., and Shipley, R. A., *Arch. Biochem.,* **12**, 125 (1947); *C. A.,* **41**, 2479 (1947).

Hahn, A., and Wolff, E., *Z. Klin. Med.,* **92**, 393 (1921); *C. A.,* **17**, 1835 (1923).

Hahn, L., and Hevesy, G., *Skand. Arch. Physiol.,* **77**, 148 (1937); *C. A.,* **32**, 640 (1938).

——, ——, *Nature,* **140**, 1059 (1937a); *C. A.,* **32**, 2200 (1938).

——, ——, *Compt. rend. trav. lab. Carlsberg, Sér. chim.,* **22**, 188 (1938); *C. A.,* **32**, 6315 (1938).

——, ——, *Nature,* **144**, 72 (1939); *C. A.,* **33**, 7370 (1939).

——, ——, *ibid.,* **144**, 204 (1939a); *C. A.,* **33**, 8277 (1939).

——, and Tyrén, H., *Arkiv. Kemi, Mineral. Geol.,* **21a**, No. 11, 1 (1945); *C. A.,* **40**, 6599 (1946).

Halden, W., and Hinrichs, H., *Fette u. Seifen,* **49**, 697 (1942); *C. A.,* **37**, 6003 (1943).

Halliday, N., and co-workers (Deuel, H. J., Jr., Tragerman, L. J., and Ward, W. E.), *J. Biol. Chem.,* **132**, 171 (1940).

Hand, A., *Proc. Philadelphia Path. Soc.,* **16**, 281 (1891/93).

Handler, P., and Dann, W. J., *J. Biol Chem.,* **146**, 357 (1942).

Hanger, F. M., *Trans. Assoc. Am. Physicians,* **53**, 148 (1938).

——, *J. Clin. Invest.,* **18**, 261 (1939).

——, and Patek, Jr., A. J., *Am. J. Med. Sci.,* **202**, 48 (1941).

Hanne, R., *Superphosphat,* **7**, 199 (1931); *C. A.,* **25**, 5949 (1931).

Hansen, A. E., *Proc. Soc. Exptl. Biol. Med.,* **41**, 205 (1939); *C. A.,* **33**, 8769 (1939).

Harris, I., and co-workers (Vernon, C. E., Jacob, N., and Harris, M. E.), *Lancet,* **257**, 283 (1949); *C. A.,* **43**, 8522 (1949).

Harris, S., and co-workers (Thompkins, E. H., Morgan, H. J., and Cunningham, R. S.), *Am. J. Syphilis Neurol.,* **18**, 333 (1934); *C. A.,* **28**, 7354 (1934).

Hartung, E. F., and Bruger, M., *J. Lab. Clin. Med.,* **20**, 675 (1935); *C. A.,* **29**, 4078 (1935).

Hartwell, J. L., Shear, M. J., and Adams, J. R., Jr., *J. Natl. Cancer Inst.,* **4**, 107 (1943); *C. A.,* **38**, 2991 (1944).

Hassegawa, S., and Nakamoto, T., *Japan J. Exptl. Med.,* **17**, 139 (1939); *C. A.,* **33**, 5435 (1939).

Haven, F. L., *J. Biol. Chem.,* **118**, 111 (1937).

——, *Am. J. Cancer,* **29**, 57 (1937a); *C. A.,* **31**, 3139 (1937).

——, *J. Natl. Cancer Inst.,* **1**, 205 (1940); *C. A.,* **35**, 2969 (1941).

Haven, F. L., *J. Biol. Chem.*, **141**, 417 (1941).

——, and Bale, W. F., *J. Biol. Chem.*, **129**, 23 (1939).

——, and Levy, S. R., *J. Biol. Chem.*, **141**, 417 (1941).

——, ——, *Cancer Research*, **2**, 797 (1942); *C. A.*, **37**, 1766 (1943).

Hazato, H., *Z. Immunitätsforsch.*, **89**, 1 (1936); *C. A.*, **31**, 449 (1937).

Hée, A., and Bayle, L., *Bull. soc. chim. biol.*, **14**, 758 (1932); *C. A.*, **26**, 5122 (1932).

Heidelberger, M., *Chem. Rev.*, **24**, 323 (1939); *C. A.*, **33**, 5909 (1939).

——, and Menzel, A. E. O., *J. Biol. Chem.*, **104**, 655 (1934).

Heki, M., *J. Biochem. (Japan)*, **11**, 369 (1930); *C. A.*, **24**, 3557 (1930).

Hershey, J. M., *Am. J. Physiol.*, **93**, 657P (1930).

——, and Soskin, S., *Am. J. Physiol.*, **98**, 74 (1931); *C. A.*, **25**, 5919 (1931).

Hesselbach, M. L., and Burk, D., *Record Chem. Progress*, **5**, 37 (1944); *C. A.*, **39**, 1930 (1945).

Hettche, H. O., *Z. Immunitätsforsch.*, **83**, 499 (1934); *C. A.*, **29**, 7379 (1935).

Hevesy, G., *Acta Unio Intern. contra Cancrum*, **4**, 175 (1939).

——, *Nature*, **158**, 268 (1946); *C. A.*, **40**, 7381 (1946).

——, *Arkiv. Kemi, Mineral. Geol.*, **24A**, No. 26 (1947); *C. A.*, **42**, 6871 (1948).

——, "Radioactive Indicators," New York, Interscience Publishers, Inc., 1948.

——, and Aten, A. H. W., Jr., *Kgl. Danske Videnskab. Selskab., Biol. Medd.*, **14**, No. 5 (1939); *C. A.*, **33**, 5046 (1939).

——, and Hahn, L., *Kgl. Danske Videnskab. Selskab., Biol. Medd.*, **14**, No. 2 (1938); *C. A.*, **32**, 5478 (1938).

——, ——, *ibid.*, **15**, No. 5, 6 (1940); *C. A.*, **36**, 138 (1942).

——, and Lundsgaard, E., *Nature*, **140**, 275 (1937); *C. A.*, **31**, 7953 (1937).

——, and Smedley-MacLean, I., *Biochem. J.*, **34**, 903 (1940); *C. A.*, **34**, 8008 (1940).

——, Levi, H. B., and Rebbe, O. H., *Biochem. J.*, **32**, 2147 (1938); *C. A.*, **33**, 3441 (1939).

——, Linderstrøm-Lang, K., and Olsen, C., *Nature*, **137**, 66 (1936); *C. A.*, **30**, 2605 (1936).

——, ——, ——, *ibid.*, **139**, 149 (1937); *C. A.*, **31**, 4698 (1937).

Heymann, W., *Science*, **96**, 163 (1942); *C. A.*, **37**, 941 (1943).

Hilditch, T. P., and Paul, S., *J. Soc. Chem. Ind.*, **58**, 21 (1939); *C. A.*, **33**, 2745 (1939).

——, and Pedelty, W. H., *Biochem. J.*, **34**, 40 (1940); *C. A.*, **34**, 4431 (1940).

——, Lea, C. H., and Pedelty, W. H., *Biochem. J.*, **33**, 493 (1939); *C. A.*, **33**, 8726 (1939).

Hill, E., and Bloor, W. R., *J. Biol. Chem.*, **53**, 171 (1922).

Hiller, A., and co-workers (Linder, G C., Lundsgaard, C., and Van Slyke, D. D.), *J. Exptl. Med.*, **39**, 931 (1924); *C. A.*, **18**, 2193 (1924).

Himwich, H. E., and Nahum, L. H., *Am. J. Physiol.*, **101**, 446 (1932); *C. A.*, **26**, 5632 (1932).

——, Goldfarb, W., and Weller, A., *J. Biol. Chem.*, **93**, 337 (1931).

Hirsh, E. F., and Weinhouse, S., *Physiol. Rev.*, **23**, 185 (1943); *C. A.*, **37**, 6030 (1943).

Hodge, H. C., and co-workers (MacLachlan, P. L., Bloor, W. R., Stoneburg, C. A., Oleson, M. C., and Whitehead, R.), *J. Biol. Chem.*, **139**, 897 (1941).

——, and co-workers (MacLachlan, P. L., Bloor, W. R., Welch, E. A., Kornberg, S. L., and Falkenheim, M.), *J. Biol. Chem.*, **169**, 707 (1947).

——, and co-workers (MacLachlan, P. L., Bloor, W. R., Welch, E., Kornberg, S. L., and Falkenheim, M.), *Proc. Soc. Exptl. Biol. Med.*, **68**, 332 (1948); *C. A.*, **42**, 7846 (1948).

Hodges, R. G., Sperry, W. M., and Andersen, D. H., *Am. J. Diseases Children,* **65,** 858 (1943); *C. A.,* **37,** 6735 (1943).

Hoesch, K., *Klin. Wochschr.,* **10,** 881 (1931); *C. A.,* **26,** 196 (1932).

Hollander, E., *Med. Record,* **152,** 300 (1940); *C. A.,* **35,** 203 (1941).

Holmes, A. D., and Kerr, R. H., *J. Biol. Chem.,* **58,** 377 (1923).

Holt, L. E., Jr., Aylward, F. X., and Timbres, H. G., *Bull. Johns Hopkins Hosp.,* **64,** 279 (1939).

Hongo, S., *Sei-i-kwai Med. J.,* **53,** No. 5, 1 (1934); *C. A.,* **29,** 3381 (1935).

Horowitz, N. H., *J. Biol. Chem.,* **162,** 413 (1946).

——, and Beadle, G. W., *J. Biol. Chem.,* **150,** 325 (1943).

Horsfall, F. L., Jr., *J. Bact.,* **35,** 207 (1938); *C. A.,* **32,** 3814 (1938).

——, and Goodner, K., *J. Immunol.,* **31,** 135 (1936); *C. A.,* **30,** 8354 (1936).

Hove, E. L., and Hove, Z., *J. Biol. Chem.,* **156,** 611 (1944).

Howell, W. H., *Am. J. Physiol.,* **31,** 1 (1912); *C. A.,* **7,** 617 (1913).

Hughes, R. H., and Wimmer, J. E., *J. Biol. Chem.,* **108,** 141 (1935).

Hunt, R., and Taveau, R., *Brit. Med. J.,* **2,** 1788 (1906).

Hunter, F. E., *Proc. Soc. Exptl. Biol. Med.,* **46,** 281 (1941); *C. A.,* **35,** 2977 (1941).

——, and Levy, S. R., *J. Biol. Chem.,* **146,** 577 (1942).

Hurtley, W. H., *Quart. J. Med.,* **9,** 301 (1916).

Hurxthal, L. M., *Arch. Internal Med.,* **53,** 762 (1934); *C. A.,* **28,** 4465 (1934).

Huseby, R. A., and Barnum, C. P., *Arch. Biochem.,* **26,** 187 (1950).

Hynd, A., and Rotter, D. L., *Biochem. J.,* **24,** 1390 (1930); *C. A.,* **25,** 726 (1931).

Ide, S., *Hukuoka Acta Med.,* **33,** 35 (1940); *C. A.,* **36,** 820 (1942).

Imrie, C. G., *J. Biol. Chem.,* **20,** 87 (1915).

Inouye, T., *Am. J. Physiol.,* **69,** 116 (1924); *C. A.,* **18,** 2746 (1924).

Inukai, F., and Nakahara, W., *Proc. Imp. Acad. (Tokyo),* **11,** 260 (1935); *C. A.,* **30,** 125 (1936).

Ionesco-Mihaiesti, C., Soru, E., and Wissner, B., *Compt. rend. soc. biol.,* **125,** 765 (1937); *C. A.,* **31,** 8600 (1937).

Issekutz, B. V., Jr., Laszt, L. D., and Verzár, F., *Arch. ges. Physiol. (Pflügers),* **240,** 612 (1938); *C. A.,* **33,** 1799 (1939).

Iwata, M., *Sci. Papers Inst. Phys. Chem. Research (Tokyo),* **24,** 174 (1934); *C. A.,* **28,** 6844 (1934).

Izzo, R. A., and Marenzi, A. D., *Rev. soc. argentina biol.,* **19,** 557 (1943); *C. A.,* **38,** 4025 (1944).

——, ——, *Pubs. centro invest. tisiol. (Buenos Aires),* **8,** 163 (1944); *C. A.,* **39,** 4382 (1945).

Jacobi, H. P., and Baumann, C. A., *Cancer Research,* **2,** 175 (1942); *C. A.,* **36,** 3251 (1942).

Javillier, M., *Congr. pharm. (Liége 1934),* 109 (1935); *C. A.,* **30,** 5273 (1936).

Jeker, L., *Arch. ges. Physiol. (Pflügers),* **237,** 1 (1936); *C. A.,* **30,** 7216 (1936).

Joannovics, G., and Pick, E. P., *Verhandl. deut. path. Ges.,* **14,** 268 (1910); *C. A.,* **5,** 318 (1911).

——, ——, *Wien, klin. Wochschr.,* **23,** 281 (1910a).

Johansen, A. H., *J. Biol. Chem.,* **88,** 669 (1930).

Jokivartio, E., *Acta Psychiat. Neurol., Suppl. No. 21,* 98 pp. (1939); *C. A.,* **34,** 2451 (1940).

Jones, C. M., and co-workers (Culver, P. J., Drummey, G. D., and Ryan, A. E.), *Ann. Internal Med.,* **29,** 1 (1948).

Jones, H. B., Chaikoff, I. L., and Lawrence, J. H., *J. Biol. Chem.,* **128,** 631 (1939).

Jones, H. B., Chaikoff, I. L., and Lawrence, J. H., *ibid.,* **133**, 319 (1940).

——, ——, ——, *Am. J. Cancer,* **40**, 235 (1940a); *C. A.,* **35**, 5994 (1941).

Jordan, R. C., and Chibnall, A. C., *Ann. Botany,* **47**, 163 (1933); *C. A.,* **27**, 4269 (1933).

Josephson, B., and Rydin, A., *Biochem. J.,* **30**, 2224 (1936); *C. A.,* **31**, 3549 (1937).

Joslin, E. P., Bloor, W. R., and Gray, H., *J. Am. Med. Assoc.,* **69**, 375 (1917); *C. A.,* **11**, 2695 (1917).

Jost, H., and Sorg, K., *Arch. ges. Physiol.* (*Pflügers*), **231**, 143 (1932); *C. A.,* **27**, 1038 (1933).

Jowett, M., and Quastel, J. H., *Biochem. J.,* **29**, 2159, 2181 (1935); *C. A.,* **30**, 1428 (1936).

Jukes, T. H., *J. Nutrition,* **20**, 445 (1940); *C. A.,* **35**, 2936 (1941).

——, *Proc. Soc. Exptl. Biol. Med.,* **46**, 155 (1941); *C. A.,* **35**, 2183 (1941).

——, *Ann. Rev. Biochem.,* **16**, 193 (1947); *C. A.,* **41**, 6961 (1947).

Kabat, E. A., and co-workers (Hangar, F. M., Moore, D. H., and Landow, H.), *J. Clin. Invest.,* **22**, 563 (1943); *C. A.,* **37**, 6732 (1943).

Kahn, R. L., and McDermott, E. B., *Am. J. Clin. Path.,* **18**, 364 (1948); *C. A.,* **42**, 5107 (1948).

Kan, S., *Japan J. Med. Sci. II Biochem.,* **4**, 291 (1941); *C. A.,* **36**, 106 (1942).

Kaplan, A., Entenman, C., and Chaikoff, I. L., *Endocrinology,* **32**, 247 (1943); *C. A.,* **37**, 2463 (1943).

Kaplan, N. O., Memelsdorff, I., and Dodge, E., *J. Biol. Chem.,* **160**, 631 (1945).

Kartin, B. L., and co-workers (Man, E. B., Winkler, A. W., and Peters, J. P.), *J. Clin. Invest.,* **23**, 824 (1944); *C. A.,* **39**, 1904 (1945).

Kaufmann, C., and Mühlbock, O., *Arch. Gynäkol.,* **139**, 254 (1929); *C. A.,* **24**, 3545 (1930).

Kaufmann, H. P., *Chem. Ber.,* **81**, 159 (1948); *C. A.,* **43**, 136 (1949).

Kehar, N. D., *Records Malaria Survey India,* **7**, 117 (1937); *C. A.,* **32**, 3482 (1938).

Keller, E. B., Rachelle, J. R., and du Vigneaud, V., *J. Biol. Chem.,* **177**, 733 (1949).

Kellner, A., Correll, J. W., and Ladd, A. T., *Federation Proc.,* **8**, 359 (1949).

Kesten, H. D., and Silbowitz, R., *Proc. Soc. Exptl. Biol. Med.,* **49**, 71 (1942); *C. A.,* **36**, 2005 (1942).

Kimizura, K., *J. Biochem.* (*Japan*), **21**, 141 (1935); *C. A.,* **29**, 2595 (1935).

King, S. E., and Bruger, M., *Ann. Internal Med.,* **8**, 1427 (1935).

Kirk, E., *Am. J. Med. Sci.,* **196**, 648 (1938); *C. A.,* **33**, 8764 (1939).

Klemperer, G., and Umber, H., *Z. klin. Med.,* **61**, 145 (1907).

Klenk, E., *Z. physiol. Chem.,* **229**, 151 (1934); *C. A.,* **29**, 482 (1935).

——, *ibid.,* **235**, 24 (1935); *C. A.,* **29**, 6942 (1935).

——, *ibid.,* **262**, 128 (1939); *C. A.,* **34**, 2060 (1940).

——, *ibid.,* **268**, 50 (1941); *C. A.,* **36**, 3204 (1942).

——, and Schumann, E., *Z. physiol. Chem.,* **267**, 128, 130 (1940); *C. A.,* **35**, 3314 (1941).

Klinghoffer, K. A., *J. Biol. Chem.,* **126**, 201 (1938).

Klumpp, T. G., *J. Am. Med. Assoc.,* **117**, 361 (1941).

Knoop, F., *Beitr. chem. Physiol. Path.,* **6**, 150 (1904).

——, "Oxydationen im Tierkörper: Ein Bild von den Hauptwegen physiologischer Verbrennung," Stuttgart, F. Enke, 1931.

Knox, W. E., Noyce, B. N., and Auerbach, V. H., *J. Biol. Chem.,* **176**, 117 (1948).

Koch, K., and Westphal, K., *Deut. Arch. klin. Med.,* **181**, 413 (1938); *C. A.,* **33**, 1385 (1939).

Koch, W., *Z. physiol. Chem.*, **37**, 181 (1903).

Kochakian, C. D., MacLachlan, P. L., and McEwen, H. D., *J. Biol. Chem.*, **122**, 433 (1938).

Kochendorfer, E. W., and Smith, H. G., *Proc. Iowa Acad. Sci.*, **39**, 169 (1932); *C. A.*, **28**, 6583 (1934).

Kögl, G., *Z. Krebsforsch.*, **47**, 169 (1938); *C. A.*, **32**, 7062 (1938).

Kohl, M. F. F., *J. Biol. Chem.*, **126**, 709 (1938).

Kornerup, V., *Nord. Med.*, **16**, 3300 (1942); *C. A.*, **40**, 6622 (1946).

Krieger, C. H., and co-workers (Bunkfeldt, R., Thompson, C. R., and Steenbock, H.), *J. Nutrition*, **21**, 213 (1941); *C. A.*, **35**, 4420 (1941).

Kugler, O. E., *Am. J. Physiol.*, **115**, 287 (1936); *C. A.*, **30**, 4556 (1936).

——, *J. Cellular Comp. Physiol.*, **23**, 69 (1944); *C. A.*, **38**, 4987 (1944).

Kurosawa, T., *J. Biochem. (Japan)*, **28**, 297, (1938); *C. A.*, **33**, 712 (1939).

Kuwashima, K., *J. Biochem. (Japan)*, **3**, 91 (1923); *C. A.*, **18**, 110 (1924).

Kyes, P., *Berlin. klin. Wochschr.*, **40**, 956, 982 (1903).

——, *Biochem. Z.*, **4**, 99 (1907); *C. A.*, **1**, 2263 (1907).

Ladd, A. T., Kellner, A., and Correll, J. W., *Federation Proc.*, **8**, 360 (1949).

Landé, K. E., and Sperry, W. M., *Arch. Path.*, **22**, 301 (1936); *C. A.*, **30**, 8362 (1936).

Landsteiner, K., "The Specificity of Serological Reactions," Cambridge, Mass., Harvard University Press, 1945.

——, and Simms, S., *J. Exptl. Med.*, **38**, 127 (1923); *C. A.*, **17**, 3209 (1923).

Lang, A., *Z. physiol. Chem.*, **246**, 219 (1937); *C. A.*, **31**, 4709 (1937).

Lardy, H. A., and Phillips, P. H., *Am. J. Physiol.*, **133**, 602 (1941); *C. A.*, **35**, 6301 (1941).

——, ——, *ibid.*, **134**, 542 (1941a); *C. A.*, **35**, 8067 (1941).

Laszt, L., and Verzár, F., *Biochem. Z.*, **288**, 351 (1936); *C. A.*, **31**, 1480 (1937).

——, ——, *Verhandl. Ver. schweiz. Physiol.*, **13**, 21 (1938); *C. A.*, **33**, 6410 (1939).

Leary, T., *Arch. Path.*, **32**, 507 (1941); *C. A.*, **36**, 552 (1942).

Leathes, J. B., *Lancet*, **176**, 593 (1909); *C. A.*, **3**, 1295 (1909).

——, and Mellanby, J., *J. Physiol.*, **96**, 39P (1939); *C. A.*, **33**, 8647 (1939).

——, and Raper, H. S., "The Fats," 2nd ed., London, Longmans, Green and Co., 1925.

Lehnherr, E. R., *Arch. Internal Med.*, **56**, 98 (1935); *C. A.*, **29**, 6648 (1935).

Leites, S., *Biochem. Z.*, **184**, 273 (1927); *C. A.*, **21**, 2296 (1927).

Leites, S. M., and Rossinskaya, I. M., *Biokhimiya*, **13**, 152 (1948); *C. A.*, **42**, 8285 (1948).

Leloir, L. F., *Enzymologia*, **12**, 263 (1948).

——, and Munoz, J. M., *J. Biol. Chem.*, **153**, 53 (1944).

Lembke, A., *Vorratspflege u. Lebensmittelforsch.*, **5**, 265 (1942); *C. A.*, **38**, 5872 (1944).

Lerner, S. R., and co-workers (Chaikoff, I. L., Entenman, C., and Dauben, W. G.), *Science*, **109**, 13 (1949).

——, and co-workers (Chaikoff, I. L., Entenman, C., and Dauben, W. G.), *Proc. Soc. Exptl. Biol. Med.*, **70**, 384 (1949a).

Letonoff, T. V., *Am. J. Clin. Path.*, **18**, 625 (1948); *C. A.*, **42**, 8856 (1948).

Levene, P. A., Rolf, I. P., and Simms, H. S., *J. Biol. Chem.*, **58**, 859 (1924).

Levin, B. S., and Piffault, C., *Compt. rend*, **199**, 466 (1934); *C. A.*, **28**, 6745 (1934).

Levine, M., and Chargaff, E., *Am. J. Botany*, **24**, 461 (1937); *C. A.*, **31**, 7936 (1937).

Lichtenstein, L., and Epstein, E. Z., *Arch. Internal Med.*, **47**, 122 (1931); *C. A.*, **25**, 1892 (1931).

Lignac, G. O. E., and Teunissen, P. H., *Beitr. path. Anat. u. allgem. Path.*, **101**, 139 (1938); *C. A.*, **33**, 1387 (1939).

Lintzel, W., *Z. Zücht., Reihe B. Z. Tierzücht. Züchtungsbiol.*, **29**, 219 (1934); *C. A.*, **28**, 5511 (1934).

Little, J. M., and Robinson, C. S., *Am. J. Physiol.*, **134**, 773 (1941).

Loeb, H. G., *Proc. Soc. Exptl. Biol. Med.*, **49**, 340 (1942); *C. A.*, **36**, 3530 (1942).

Loeb, J., and Buetner, R., *Biochem. Z.*, **59**, 195 (1914); *C. A.*, **8**, 1795 (1914).

Loew, O., *Biol. Zentr.*, **11**, 269 (1891).

Lombroso, U., *Ann. physiol. physiochim. biol.*, **16**, 298 (1940); *C. A.*, **35**, 6294 (1941).

Longenecker, H. E., *J. Biol. Chem.*, **129**, 13 (1939).

——, *ibid.*, **130**, 167 (1939a).

Looney, J. M., and Romanoff, E. B., *J. Biol. Chem.*, **136**, 479 (1940).

Lorenz, F. W., Chaikoff, I. L., and Entenman, C., *J. Biol. Chem.*, **126**, 763 (1938).

——, ——, ——, *ibid.*, **123**, 577 (1938a).

——, Entenman, C., and Chaikoff, I. L., *J. Biol. Chem.*, **122**, 619 (1938).

——, Perlman, I., and Chaikoff, I. L., *Am. J. Physiol.*, **138**, 318 (1943); *C. A.*, **37**, 1760 (1943).

Lucas, C. C., and Best, C. H., in "Vitamins and Hormones," New York, Academic Press, Inc., 1943.

Lüdecke, H., Sammet, K., and Lesch, W., *Bodenkunde u. Pflanzenernähr.*, **25**, 1 (1941); *C. A.*, **38**, 6466 (1944).

Ludewig, S., and Chanutin, A., *J. Biol. Chem.*, **115**, 327 (1936).

——, ——, *Arch. Internal Med.*, **61**, 854 (1938); *C. A.*, **32**, 7080 (1938).

——, Minor, G. R., and Hortenstine, J. C., *Proc. Soc. Exptl. Biol. Med.*, **42**, 158 (1939); *C. A.*, **34**, 491 (1940).

Ma, Wen-Chao, *Chinese J. Physiol.*, **7**, 287 (1933); *C. A.*, **28**, 3794 (1934).

McArthur, C. S., *Biochem. J.*, **36**, 559 (1942).

——, Lucas, C. C., and Best, C. H., *Biochem. J.*, **41**, 612 (1947).

McCay, C. M., and Maynard, L. A., *J. Biol. Chem.*, **92**, 273 (1931).

McClenahan, F. M., *J. Am. Chem. Soc.*, **35**, 485 (1913); *C. A.*, **7**, 3144 (1913).

McClendon, J. F., *J. Am. Med. Assoc.*, **65**, 12 (1915); *C. A.*, **9**, 2264 (1915); *Am. J. Physiol.*, **38**, 191 (1915); *C. A.*, **9**, 2937 (1915).

McCollum, E. V., Halpin, J. J., and Drescher, A. H., *J. Biol. Chem.*, **13**, 219 (1912/13).

McConnell, K. P., and Sinclair, R. G., *J. Biol. Chem.*, **118**, 131 (1937).

——, ——, *ibid.*, **118**, 123 (1937a).

McGavack, T. H., and Shepardson, H. C., *Ann. Internal Med.*, **7**, 582 (1933); *C. A.*, **28**, 1765 (1934).

Macheboeuf, M. A., and Faure, M., *Compt. rend.*, **209**, 700 (1939); *C. A.*, **34**, 2407 (1940).

McHenry, E. W., *J. Physiol.*, **89**, 287 (1937); *C. A.*, **31**, 4377 (1937).

McKay, E. M., and Barnes, R. H., *Am. J. Physiol.*, **118**, 525 (1937); *C. A.*, **31**, 3130 (1937).

——, and co-workers (Barnes, R. H., Carne, H. O., and Wick, A. N.), *J. Biol. Chem.*, **135**, 157 (1940).

——, Wick, A. N., and Barnum, C. P., *J. Biol. Chem.*, **136**, 503 (1940).

McKee, S. H., and Rabinowitch, I. M., *Can. Med. Assoc. J.*, **25**, 530 (1931).

MacLachlan, P. L., *J. Biol. Chem.*, **152**, 391 (1944).

——, and co-workers (Hodge, H. C., Bloor, W. R., Welch, E. A., Truax, F. L., and Taylor, J. D.), *J. Biol. Chem.*, **143**, 473 (1942).

McLean, J., *Am. J. Physiol.*, **43**, 586 (1917); *C. A.*, **11**, 2583 (1917).

McLeod, J., *Am. J. Physiol.*, **41**, 250 (1916); *C. A.*, **10**, 2586 (1916).

McQuarrie, I., and co-workers (Bloor, W. R., Husted, C., and Patterson, H. A.), *J. Clin. Invest.*, **12**, 247, 255 (1933); *C. A.*, **27**, 2487 (1933).

Magat, J., *Compt. rend. soc. biol.*, **116**, 1367 (1934); *C. A.*, **28**, 7272 (1934).

Magistris, H., *Biochem. Z.*, **210**, 85 (1929); *C. A.*, **23**, 4956 (1929).

Mahler, A., *J. Biol. Chem.*, **69**, 653 (1926).

Malesani, S., *Atti soc. med. chir. Padova*, **15**, 66 (1937); *C. A.*, **32**, 5901 (1938).

Maltaner, E., and Maltaner, F., *J. Immunol.*, **26**, 332 (1934); *C. A.*, **30**, 8352 (1936).

——, ——, *ibid.*, **51**, 195 (1945).

Maltaner, F., and Maltaner, E., *Arch. Biochem.*, **2**, 37 (1943); *C. A.*, **37**, 3805 (1943).

Man, E. B., and co-workers (Kartin, B. L., Durlacher, S. H., and Peters, J. P.), *J. Clin. Invest.*, **24**, 623 (1945); *C. A.*, **40**, 1582 (1946).

——, and Gildea, E. F., *J. Biol. Chem.*, **99**, 61 (1932).

——, ——, *J. Clin. Invest.*, **15**, 203 (1936); *C. A.*, **30**, 2608 (1936).

——, and Peters, J. P., *J. Clin. Invest.*, **13**, 237 (1934); *C. A.*, **28**, 3122 (1934).

——, Gildea, E. F., and Peters, J. P., *J. Clin. Invest.*, **19**, 43 (1940); *C. A.*, **34**, 5151 (1940).

Manery, J. F., and Bale, W. F., *Am. J. Physiol.*, **132**, 215 (1941); *C. A.*, **35**, 2202 (1941).

Marrack, J. R., "The Chemistry of Antigens and Antibodies," 2nd ed., London, H. M. Stationery Office, 1938.

Masai, Y., and Fukutomi, T., *J. Biochem. (Japan)*, **2**, 271 (1923); *C. A.*, **17**, 1845 (1923).

Masoro, E. J., Chaikoff, I. L., and Dauben, W. G., *J. Biol. Chem.*, **179**, 1117 (1949).

Matthews, V. J., Newton, J. K., and Bloor, W. R., *J. Biol Chem.*, **108**, 145 (1935).

Mayer, A., and Schaeffer, G., *J. physiol. et path. gén.*, **15**, 510, 534, 773 (1913); *C. A.*, **9**, 647 (1915).

——, ——, *ibid.*, **16**, 203 (1914); *C. A.*, **9**, 645 (1915).

Meigs, E. B., Blatherwick, N. R., and Cary, C. A., *J. Biol. Chem.*, **37**, 1 (1919).

Menten, M. L., and Welton, J. P., *Am. J. Diseases Children*, **72**, 720 (1946); *C. A.*, **41**, 4222 (1947).

Meyer, K., *Z. Immunitätsforsch.*, **57**, 42 (1928); *C. A.*, **22**, 4628 (1928).

Meyerhof, O., *Arch. ges. Physiol. (Pflügers)*, **199**, 531 (1923); *C. A.*, **18**, 2349 (1924).

——, *ibid.*, **200**, 1 (1923a); *C. A.*, **18**, 91 (1924).

Miles, A. A., and Pirie, H. W., *Brit. J. Exptl. Path.*, **20**, 83, 109, 278 (1939); *C. A.*, **33**, 5435, 8670 (1939).

Miller, E. S., and Burr, G. O., *Proc. Soc. Exptl. Biol. Med.*, **36**, 726 (1937).

——, and co-workers (Barnes, R. H., Kass, J. P., and Burr, G. O.), *Proc. Soc. Exptl. Biol. Med.*, **41**, 485 (1939); *C. A.*, **33**, 8652 (1939).

Miller, E. v. O., and Hansen, A. E., *Proc. Soc. Exptl. Biol. Med.*, **56**, 244 (1944); *C. A.*, **38**, 5266 (1944).

Mills, C. A., *J. Biol. Chem.*, **46**, 135 (1921).

——, *Chinese J. Physiol.*, **1**, 435 (1927); *C. A.*, **22**, 2594 (1928).

Miner, I., *Münch. med. Wochschr.*, **86**, 1038 (1939); *C. A.*, **34**, 1747 (1940).

Moggi, D., *Riv. clin. pediatr.*, **32**, 257 (1934).

Montgomery, M. L., Entenman, C., and Chaikoff, I. L., *J. Biol. Chem.*, **128**, 387 (1939).

Moosnick, F. B., Schleicher, E. M., and Petersen, W. E., *J. Clin. Invest.*, **24**, 278 (1945).

Morawitz, P., *Ergeb. Physiol.*, **4**, 369 (1905).

Morgan, W. T. J., *Biochem. J.*, **31**, 2003 (1937); *C. A.*, **32**, 2169 (1938).

——, *Chemistry and Industry*, **60**, 722 (1941).

——, and Partridge, S. M., *Biochem. J.*, **34**, 169 (1940); *C. A.*, **34**, 4143 (1940).

——, ——, *ibid.*, **35**, 1140 (1941); *C. A.*, **36**, 6640 (1942).

Morgulis, S., and co-workers (Wilder, V. M., Spencer, H. C., and Eppstein, S. H.), *J. Biol. Chem.*, **124**, 755 (1938).

Moyer, A. W., and du Vigneaud, V., *J. Biol. Chem.*, **143**, 373 (1942).

Mueller, G. C., Miller, J. A., and Rusch, H. P., *Cancer Research,* **5**, 401 (1945); *C. A.*, **39**, 4140 (1945).

Mulder, A. G., and Crandall, L. A., Jr., *Am. J. Physiol.*, **137**, 436 (1942); *C. A.*, **36**, 7091 (1942).

Müller, F., *Z. Biol.*, **20**, 327 (1884).

Muller, G. L., and Heath, C. W., *Arch. Internal Med.*, **52**, 288 (1933); *C. A.*, **27**, 5106 (1933).

Müller, J. H., *J. Biol. Chem.*, **22**, 1 (1915).

——, *ibid.*, **27**, 463 (1916).

Munk, I., *Arch. path. Anat. Physiol.*, **80**, 10 (1880).

——, *ibid.*, **95**, 401 (1884).

——, and Friedenthal, H., *Centr. Physiol.*, **15**, 297 (1901).

——, and Rosenstein, A., *Arch. path. Anat. Physiol.*, **123**, 230, 484 (1891).

Munoz, J. M., *Compt. rend. soc. biol.*, **112**, 502 (1933); *C. A.*, **27**, 1925 (1933).

Muntoni, E., *Sperimentale,* **98**, 612 (1947); *C. A.*, **42**, 5549 (1948).

Murlin, J. R., *J. Gen. Physiol.*, **17**, 283 (1933); *C. A.*, **28**, 2392 (1934).

Narat, J. K., *J. Urol.*, **39**, 75 (1938); *C. A.*, **32**, 7084 (1938).

Nedswedsky, S. W., and Alexandry, A. K., *Arch. ges. Physiol. (Pflügers)*, **219**, 619 (1928); *C. A.*, **22**, 4161 (1928).

Needham, J., "Chemical Embryology," Cambridge, University Press, 1931.

Neuberg, C., and Karczag, L., *Zentr. Biochem. u. Biophys.*, **14**, 819 (1913); *C. A.*, **7**, 2627 (1913).

Nielson, P. E., *Am. J. Physiol.*, **135**, 670 (1942); *C. A.*, **36**, 2000 (1942).

Nikitin, V. N., *Compt. rend. acad. sci. U.S.S.R.*, **2**, 434 (1935); *C A.*, **29**, 6639 (1935).

Nord, F. F., *Biochem. Z.*, **95**, 281 (1919); *C. A.*, **14**, 932 (1920).

O'Connell, P. W., and Stotz, W., *Proc. Soc. Exptl. Biol. Med.*, **70**, 675 (1949); *C. A.*, **43**, 5472 (1949).

Öhman, L. O., *Naturwissenschaften,* **30**, 240 (1942); *C. A.*, **37**, 6348 (1943).

Okey, R., *J. Biol. Chem.*, **63**, xxxiii–xxxv (1925); *C. A.*, **19**, 3525 (1925).

Olcott, H. S., *Science,* **100**, 226 (1944); *C. A.*, **38**, 6334 (1944).

——, and Mattill, H. A., *Oil & Soap,* **13**, 98 (1936); *C. A.*, **30**, 3669 (1936).

Outhouse, E. L., *Biochem. J.*, **30**, 197 (1936); *C. A.*, **30**, 3510 (1936).

——, *ibid.*, **31**, 1459 (1937); *C. A.*, **32**, 1782 (1938).

Overman, R. S., and Wright, I. S., *J. Biol. Chem.*, **174**, 759 (1948).

Page, I. H., *Am. J. Med. Sci.*, **192**, 217 (1936).

——, "Chemistry of the Brain," Springfield, Ill., Charles C. Thomas, 1937.

——, and Allen, E. V., *Arch. exptl. Path. Pharmakol.*, **152**, 1 (1930); *C. A.*, **25**, 1905 (1931).

——, and Bülow, M., *Z. physiol. Chem.*, **231**, 10 (1935); *C. A.*, **29**, 1836 (1935).

——, and Young, F. G., *Biochem. J.*, **26**, 1528 (1932).

——, Kirk, E., and Van Slyke, D. D., *J. Clin. Invest.*, **15**, 101 (1936); *C. A.*, **30**, 1861 (1936).

Page, I. H., Pasternak, L., and Burt, M. L., *Biochem. Z.*, 231, 113 (1931); *C. A.*, 25, 2485 (1931).

Palladin, A., and Kudrajawzewa, A., *Biochem. Z.*, 154, 104 (1924); *C. A.*, 19, 2364 (1925).

Pangborn, M. C., *J. Biol. Chem.*, 143, 247 (1942).

——, *ibid.*, 153, 343 (1944).

——, *ibid.*, 161, 71 (1945).

Pasternak, L., and Page, I. H., *Biochem. Z.*, 252, 254 (1932); *C. A.*, 26, 5663 (1932).

——, ——, *ibid.*, 282, 282 (1935); *C. A.*, 30, 1870 (1936).

Patterson, J. M., and McHenry, E. W., *J. Biol. Chem.*, 145, 207 (1942).

——, ——, *ibid.*, 156, 265 (1944).

——, Keevil, N. B., and McHenry, E. W., *J. Biol. Chem.*, 153, 489 (1944).

Pauling, L., *J. Am. Chem. Soc.*, 62, 2643 (1940); *C. A.*, 34, 8047 (1940).

Peretti, G., and Tore, D., *Boll. soc. ital. biol. sper.*, 8, 1429 (1933); *C. A.*, 28, 3110 (1934).

Peritz, G., *Deut. med. Wochschr.*, 47, 859 (1921); *C. A.*, 17, 2604 (1923).

Perlman, I., and Chaikoff, I. L., *J. Biol. Chem.*, 128, 735 (1939).

——, ——, *ibid.*, 130, 593 (1939a).

——, ——, *ibid.*, 127, 211 (1939b).

——, Ruben, S., and Chaikoff, I. L., *J. Biol. Chem.*, 122, 169 (1937).

——, Stillman, N., and Chaikoff, I. L., *J. Biol. Chem.*, 135, 359 (1940).

——, ——, ——, *ibid.*, 133, 651 (1940a).

Perrier, C., and co-workers (Artom, C., Santangelo, M., Sarzana, G., and Segré, E.), *Nature*, 139, 1105 (1937); *C. A.*, 31, 6314 (1937).

Peters, B. A., and Cunningham, R. N., *Biochem. J.*, 35, 219 (1941); *C. A.*, 35, 7031 (1941).

Peters, J. P., and Man, E. B., *J. Clin. Invest.*, 22, 715, 721 (1943); *C. A.*, 37, 6733 (1943).

——, and Van Slyke, D. D., "Quantitative Clinical Chemistry," I, Baltimore, Williams & Wilkins Co., 1946.

Pfützer, G., and Roth, H., *Die Chemie*, 55, 289 (1942); *C. A.*, 38, 2360 (1944).

Pick, L., *Am. J. Med. Sci.*, 185, 453, 601 (1933).

Pico, C. E., and Modern, F., *Anales asoc. quím. argentina*, 22, 11 (1934); *C. A.*, 29, 222 (1935).

Pihl, A., and Bloch, K., *J. Biol. Chem.*, 183, 431 (1950).

Pinner, M., *Am. Rev. Tuberc.*, 18, 497 (1928); *C. A.*, 23, 431 (1929).

Pirosky, I., *Compt. rend. soc. biol.*, 127, 966 (1938); *C. A.*, 32, 5484 (1938).

Platt, A. P., and Porter, R. R., *Nature*, 160, 905 (1947); *C. A.*, 42, 2356 (1948).

Plaut, F., and Rudy, H., *Z. Immunitätsforsch.*, 73, 385 (1932); *C. A.*, 26, 5147 (1932).

Plimmer, R. H. A., and Scott, F. H., *J. Physiol.*, 38, 247 (1909); *C. A.*, 4, 2512 (1910).

Poindexter, C. A., and Bruger, M., *Arch. Internal Med.*, 61, 714 (1938); *C. A.*, 32, 7106 (1938).

Pollack, A., *Compt. rend. soc. biol.*, 130, 149 (1939); *C. A.*, 33, 3460 (1939).

Ponticorvo, L., Rittenberg, D., and Bloch, K., *J. Biol. Chem.*, 179, 839 (1949).

Popják, G., *Nature*, 160, 841 (1947).

Pratt, J. H., *J. Am. Med. Assoc.*, 120, 175 (1942).

Prokopchuk, A., and Kerson, M., *Arch. Dermatol. u. Syphilis*, 174, 90 (1936); *C. A.*, 30, 7666 (1936).

Quastel, J. H., and Wheatley, A. H. M., *Biochem. J.*, 27, 1753 (1933); *C. A.*, 28, 3115 (1934).

Raab, W., *Klin. Wochschr.*, **13**, 281 (1934); *C. A.*, **28**, 3776 (1934).

Raistrick, H., and Topley, W. W. C., *Brit. J. Exptl. Path.*, **15**, 113 (1934); *C. A.*, **28**, 4467 (1934).

Ralli, E. P., and Rubin, S. H., *Am. J. Physiol.*, **138**, 42 (1942); *C. A.*, **37**, 1505 (1943).

Randall, L. O., *J. Biol. Chem.*, **125**, 723 (1938).

Ranney, R. E., Entenman, C., and Chaikoff, I. L., *J. Biol. Chem.*, **180**, 307 (1949).

Raper, H. S., and Wayne, E. T., *Biochem. J.*, **22**, 188 (1928); *C. A.*, **22**, 2598 (1928).

Ravich-Shcherbo, M. I., and Bass, R. M., *Z. Microbiol. Epidemiol. Immunitäts-forsch. (U.S.S.R.)* No. 11, 29 (1940); *C. A.*, **36**, 2909 (1942).

——, Marchenko, V. F., and Nartsisov, N. V., *Z. Microbiol. Epidemiol. Immunitäts-forsch. (U.S.S.R.)*, **17**, 131 (1936); *C. A.*, **30**, 8367 (1936).

Raymond, M. J., and Treadwell, C. R., *Proc. Soc. Exptl. Biol. Med.*, **70**, 43 (1949).

Reineke, E. P., Stonecipher, W. D., and Turner, C. W., *Am. J. Physiol.*, **132**, 535 (1941); *C. A.*, **35**, 2959 (1941).

Reinhardt, W. O., Fishler, M. C., and Chaikoff, I. L., *J. Biol. Chem.*, **152**, 79 (1944).

Reiser, R., *J. Biol. Chem.*, **143**, 109 (1942).

Rewald, B., and Riede, W., *Biochem. Z.*, **260**, 147 (1933); *C. A.*, **27**, 3500 (1933).

Rhymer, I., and co-workers (Wallace, G. I., Byers, L. W., and Carter, H. E.), *J. Biol. Chem.*, **169**, 457 (1947).

Rich, A. R., and Hamilton, J. D., *Bull. Johns Hopkins Hosp.*, **66**, 185 (1940); *C. A.*, **34**, 6679 (1940).

Riddle, O., *Am. J. Physiol.*, **41**, 409 (1916); *C. A.*, **10**, 2923 (1916).

Rieckehoff, I. G., Holman, R. T., and Burr, G. O., *Arch. Biochem.*, **20**, 331 (1949).

Riegel, C., Elsom, K. O., and Ravdin, I. S., *Am. J. Physiol.*, **112**, 669 (1935); *C. A.*, **29**, 8100 (1935).

Riley, R. F., *J. Biol. Chem.*, **153**, 535 (1944).

Rittenberg, D., and Bloch, K., *J. Biol. Chem.*, **154**, 311 (1944).

——, and Schoenheimer, R., *J. Biol. Chem.*, **117**, 485 (1937).

——, ——, and Evans, E. A., Jr., *J. Biol. Chem.*, **120**, 503 (1937).

Robertson, T. B., and Wasteneys, H., *Arch. Entwicklungsmech. Organ.*, **37**, 485 (1914); *C. A.*, **8**, 183 (1914).

Robinson, A., and co-workers (Perlman, I., Ruben, S., and Chaikoff, I. L.), *Nature*, **141**, 119 (1938); *C. A.*, **32**, 2965 (1938).

Roeder, F., *Z. ges. Neurol. Psychiat.*, **168**, 519 (1940); *C. A.*, **34**, 8036 (1940).

——, *Klin. Wochschr.*, **21**, 1093 (1942); *C. A.*, **38**, 2722 (1944).

Roffo, A., and Correa, L., *Bol. inst. med. exptl. estud. cáncer (Buenos Aires)*, No. 42 (1936); *C. A.*, **32**, 201 (1938).

Rogers, H. T., Pearson, R. W., and Pierre, W. H., *Soil Sci. Soc. Am. Proc.*, **5**, 285 (1940); *C. A.*, **36**, 3607 (1942).

Rony, H. R., and Ching, T. T., *Endocrinology*, **14**, 355 (1930); *C. A.*, **26**, 3558 (1932).

Rosen, I., and Krasnow, F., *Arch. Dermatol. and Syphilol.*, **23**, 132 (1931); *C. A.*, **25**, 3384 (1931).

——, ——, *ibid.*, **26**, 48 (1932); *C. A.*, **27**, 2993 (1933).

——, ——, and Lyons, M. A., *Arch. Dermatol. and Syphilol.*, **27**, 383 (1933).

Rosenberg, A. A., *J. Venereal Disease Inform.*, **30**, 194 (1949); *C. A.*, **43**, 7575 (1949).

Rosenberg, D. H., and Soskin, S., *Am. J. Digestive Diseases*, **8**, 421 (1941); *C. A.*, **36**, 822 (1942).

Rosenberg, H. R., "Chemistry and Physiology of the Vitamins," New York, Inter-science Publishers, Inc., 1942.

Rosenthal, S. R., *Arch. Path.*, **18**, 473, 600, 827 (1934); *C. A.*, **29**, 505, 3036 (1935).

Rousseau, E., and Pascal, J., *Compt. rend. soc. biol.*, **128**, 63 (1938); *C. A.*, **32**, 7501 (1938).

——, ——, *ibid.*, **128**, 514 (1938a); *C. A.*, **38**, 5511 (1944).

Rowland, R. S., *Arch. Internal Med.*, **42**, 611 (1928).

Rubin, S. H., Present, C. H., and Ralli, E. P., *J. Biol. Chem.*, **121**, 19 (1937).

Rusch, H. P., and Kline, B. E., *Cancer Research*, **1**, 465 (1941); *C. A.*, **35**, 8080 (1941).

Sabin, F. R., *Physiol. Rev.*, **12**, 141 (1932); *C. A.*, **26**, 4836 (1932).

——, Doan, C. A., and Forkner, C. E., *J. Exptl. Med.*, **52**, Suppl. No. 3, 3 (1930); *C. A.*, **25**, 541 (1931).

Sachs, H., and Schwab, E., *Schweiz. med. Wochschr.*, **65**, 547 (1935).

Sahyun, M., "Proteins and Amino Acids in Nutrition," New York, Reinhold Publishing Corp., 1948.

Sakakibara, I., *J. Biochem. (Japan)*, **24**, 31 (1936); *C. A.*, **30**, 8372 (1936).

Sandor, G., *Ann. inst. Pasteur*, **57**, 565 (1936); *C. A.*, **31**, 6688 (1937).

Schachner, H., Fries, B. A., and Chaikoff, I. L., *J. Biol. Chem.*, **146**, 95 (1942).

Schaefer, W., *Ann. inst. Pasteur*, **64**, 301 (1940); *C. A.*, **34**, 7000 (1940).

Schaible, P. J., *J. Biol. Chem.*, **95**, 79 (1932).

Schmidt, C. L. A., "The Chemistry of the Amino Acids and the Proteins," Springfield, Ill., C. C. Thomas, 1938.

Schmidt, L. H., *Am. J. Physiol.*, **111**, 138 (1935); *C. A.*, **29**, 6311 (1935).

Schmidt-Nielsen, K., *Acta Physiol. Scand.*, **12**, Suppl. 37, 83 pp. (1946); *C. A.*, **40**, 7348 (1946).

Schmitz, E., and Hiraoka, T., *Biochem. Z.*, **193**, 1 (1928); *C. A.*, **22**, 2772 (1928).

Schneider, W. C., *J. Biol. Chem.*, **176**, 259 (1948).

Schoenheimer, R. J., *Z. physiol. Chem.*, **177**, 143 (1928).

——, *Z. klin. Med.*, **123**, 749 (1933).

——, and Rittenberg, D., *J. Biol. Chem.*, **113**, 505 (1936).

——, ——, *ibid.*, **114**, 381 (1936a).

Schwab, E., *Z. Immunitätsforsch.*, **87**, 426 (1936); *C. A.*, **30**, 6057 (1936).

Schwarz, G., and Zehner, L., *Deut. med. Wochschr.*, **38**, 1776 (1912); *C. A.*, **6**, 3426 (1912).

Scudi, J. V., and Hamlin, M., *J. Nutrition*, **24**, 273 (1942); *C. A.*, **36**, 7080 (1942).

Seegers, W. H., *J. Biol. Chem.*, **136**, 103 (1940).

Seibert, F. B., *Chem. Revs.*, **34**, 107 (1944); *C. A.*, **38**, 4025 (1944).

——, "Abstracts of Papers, 116th Meeting Am. Chem. Soc.," p. 10c, Sept. 1949.

Selle, W. A., Paquin, F., and Brindley, P., *Am. J. Cancer*, **38**, 86 (1940); *C. A.*, **34**, 5539 (1940).

Serono, C., Montezemolo, R., and Balboni, G., *Rass. clin. terap. e sci. affini*, **35**, 241 (1936); *C. A.*, **31**, 1478 (1937).

Shaffer, P. A., *Ann. Clin. Med.*, **3**, 93 (1924); *C. A.*, **18**, 3640 (1924).

——, *J. Biol. Chem.*, **47**, 449 (1927).

Shapiro, A., and co-workers (Koster, H., Rittenberg, D., and Schoenheimer, R.), *Am. J. Physiol.*, **117**, 525 (1936); *C. A.*, **31**, 151 (1937).

Sharpless, G. R., *Proc. Soc. Exptl. Biol. Med.*, **45**, 487 (1940); *C. A.*, **35**, 784 (1941).

Shear, M. J., and co-workers (Turner, F. C., Perrault, A., and Shovelton, T.), *J. Natl. Cancer Inst.*, **4**, 81 (1943); *C. A.*, **38**, 2990 (1944).

Sheehy, E. J., *Biochem. J.*, **15**, 703 (1921); *C. A.*, **16**, 1456 (1922).

Sherbakov, A. P., *Z. Pflanzenernähr. Düngung u. Bodenk.*, **39**, 129 (1935); *C. A.*, **29**, 6924 (1935).

Shreder, V. N., *Biol. Zhur.*, **4**, 507 (1935); *C. A.*, **32**, 7561 (1938).

Simon, F. P., Horwitt, M. K., and Gerard, R. W., *J. Biol. Chem.,* **154,** 421 (1944).

Sinclair, R. G., *J. Biol. Chem.,* **82,** 117 (1929).

——, *ibid.,* **95,** 393 (1932).

——, *ibid.,* **96,** 103 (1932a).

——, *Physiol. Rev.,* **14,** 351 (1934) ; *C. A.,* **28,** 5863 (1934).

——, *J. Biol. Chem.,* **111,** 261 (1935).

——, *ibid.,* **111,** 275 (1935a).

——, *ibid.,* **111,** 515 (1935b).

——, *ibid.,* **115,** 211 (1936).

——, *ibid.,* **118,** 131 (1937).

——, *Oil & Soap,* **15,** 70 (1938) ; *C. A.,* **32,** 3472 (1938).

——, *J. Biol. Chem.,* **134,** 71 (1940).

——, *ibid.,* **134,** 83, 89 (1940a).

——, *Biol. Symposia,* **5,** 82 (1941) ; *C. A.,* **36,** 2314 (1942).

——, and Bloor, W. R., *Am. J. Physiol.,* **90,** 516 (1929).

——, and Smith, C., *J. Biol. Chem.,* **121,** 361 (1937).

Singer, K., *Biochem. Z.,* **198,** 340 (1928) ; *C. A.,* **23,** 192 (1929).

Sjövall, A., *Acta Path. Microbiol. Scand.,* **12,** 307 (1935) ; *C. A.,* **29,** 8118 (1935).

Slanetz, C. A., and Scharf, A., *J. Nutrition,* **30,** 239 (1945) ; *C. A.,* **40,** 925 (1946).

Slight, D., and Long, C. N. H., *Am. J. Psychiatry,* **13,** 141 (1933).

Smith, C. C., Goldman, L., and Fox, H. H., *J. Investigative Dermatol.,* **5,** 321 (1942) ; *C. A.,* **37,** 3816 (1943).

Smith, J. H. C., *J. Am. Chem. Soc.,* **69,** 1492 (1947) ; *C. A.,* **41,** 5924 (1947).

Smithburn, K. C., and Sabin, F. R., *J. Exptl. Med.,* **56,** 867 (1932) ; *C. A.,* **27,** 323 (1933).

Snell, A. M., *Ann. Internal Med.,* **12,** 1632 (1939).

Snider, R. H., *J. Biol. Chem.,* **116,** 503 (1936).

Sobotka, H., *Naturwissenschaften,* **18,** 619 (1930) ; *C. A.,* **24,** 5357 (1930).

——, "Physiological Chemistry of the Bile," Baltimore, William & Wilkins Co., 1937.

Solandt, D. Y., and Best, C. H., *Nature,* **144,** 376 (1939) ; *C. A.,* **33,** 8729 (1939).

Soskin, S., *Physiol. Rev.,* **21,** 140 (1941).

Sosman, M. C., *J. Am. Med. Assoc.,* **98,** 110 (1932).

Sperry, W. M., *J. Biol. Chem.,* **68,** 357 (1926).

——, *ibid.,* **71,** 351 (1927).

——, *ibid.,* **96,** 759 (1932).

——, *J. Mt. Sinai Hosp., N. Y.,* **9,** 799 (1942) ; *C. A.,* **37,** 443 (1943).

——, and Angevine, A. W., *J. Biol. Chem.,* **96,** 769 (1932).

——, and Bloor, W. R., *J. Biol. Chem.,* **60,** 261 (1924).

——, and Schick, B., *Am. J. Diseases Children,* **51,** 1372 (1936).

——, Waelsch, H., and Stoyanoff, V. A., *J. Biol. Chem.,* **135,** 281 (1940).

Spielmeyer, W., *J. Psychol. Neurol.,* **38,** 120 (1929).

Sprinsky, P., *Pubs. centro invest. tisiol. (Buenos Aires),* **8,** 7 (1944) ; *C. A.,* **39,** 4382 (1945).

Stadie, W. C., *Physiol. Rev.,* **25,** 395 (1945) ; *C. A.,* **40,** 122 (1946).

——, Zapp, J. A., Jr., and Lukens, F. D. W., *J. Biol. Chem.,* **137,** 75 (1941).

Stephenson, M., and Whetham, M. D., *Proc. Roy. Soc. (London),* **93B,** 262 (1922) ; *C. A.,* **16,** 3923 (1922).

Stetten, D., Jr., *J. Biol. Chem.,* **138,** 437, and **140,** 143 (1941).

——, *ibid.,* **142,** 629 (1942).

Stetten, D., Jr., *ibid.*, 147, 327 (1943).
——, and Boxer, G. E., *J. Biol. Chem.*, 155, 231, 237 (1944).
——, and Grail, G. F., *J. Biol. Chem.*, 144, 175 (1942).
——, ——, *ibid.*, 148, 509 (1943).
——, and Salcedo, J., Jr., *J. Biol. Chem.*, 156, 27 (1944).
——, and Schoenheimer, R., *J. Biol. Chem.*, 133, 329, 347 (1940).
Stewart, W. C., and Sinclair, R. G., *Arch. Biochem.*, 8, 7 (1945); *C. A.*, 41, 2136 (1947).
Stiemans, H., and Heringa, G. C., *Nederland. Tijdschr. Geneesk.*, 77, II, 1635 (1933); *C. A.*, 28, 2732 (1934).
Stillman, N., and co-workers (Entenman, C., Anderson, E., and Chaikoff, I. L.), *Endocrinology*, 31, 481 (1942); *C. A.*, 37, 924 (1943).
Stoesser, A. V., *Proc. Soc. Exptl. Biol. Med.*, 46, 83 (1941); *C. A.*, 35, 2216 (1941).
——, and McQuarrie, I., *Am. J. Diseases Children*, 49, 658 (1935); *C. A.*, 29, 4078 (1935).
Strickler, A., and Adams, P. D., *Arch. Dermatol. and Syphilol.*, 26, 11 (1932); *C. A.*, 27, 2200 (1933).
Sueyoshi, Y., and Mitimoto, H., *J. Biochem. (Japan)*, 30, 155 (1939); *C. A.*, 33, 9384 (1939).
——, and Miura, K., *J. Biochem. (Japan)*, 29, 481 (1939); *C. A.*, 33, 9430 (1939).
——, and Okonogi, T., *J. Biochem. (Japan)*, 19, 489 (1934); *C. A.*, 28, 5116 (1934).
Süllmann, H., and Wilbrandt, W., *Biochem. Z.*, 270, 52 (1934); *C. A.*, 28, 5114 (1934).
Sulze, W., *Ber. Verhandl. sächs Akad. Wiss. Leipzig Math. phys. Klasse*, 85, 150 (1933); quoted in *Ann. Rev. Biochem.*, 4, 203 (1935).
Sure, B., *J. Nutrition*, 19, 71 (1940).
——, Kik, M. C., and Church, A. E., *J. Biol. Chem.*, 103, 417 (1933).
Sweany, H. C., *Am. Rev. Tuberc.*, 10, 329 (1924); *C. A.*, 19, 3533 (1925).
Szent-György, A. v., *Biochem. Z.*, 146, 245 (1924); *C. A.*, 19, 307 (1925).
Tait, H., and King, E. J., *Biochem. J.*, 30, 285 (1936); *C. A.*, 30, 3845 (1936).
Tajima, K., *Biochem. Z.*, 276, 343 (1935); *C. A.*, 29, 4415 (1935).
Tanaka, I., *Japan J. Botany*, 5, 323, 350 (1931); *C. A.*, 28, 2388 (1934).
Taniguchi, T., *J. Path. Bact.*, 23, 364 (1920); *C. A.*, 14, 3458 (1920).
Tashiro, S., and Schmidt, L. H., *Med. Bull. Univ. Cincinnati*, 6, 151 (1931); *C. A.*, 26, 1306 (1932).
Taurog, A., and co-workers (Lorenz, F. W., Entenman, C., and Chaikoff, I. L.), *Endocrinology*, 35, 483 (1944); *C. A.*, 39, 985 (1945).
——, Chaikoff, I. L., and Perlman, I., *J. Biol. Chem.*, 145, 281 (1942).
Tayeau, F., *Compt. rend. soc. biol.*, 137, 240 (1943); *C. A.*, 38, 2723 (1944).
Terroine, E. F., *Ann. sci. nat. Zool.* [10], 4, 5 (1920).
——, and Belin, P., *Bull. soc. chim. biol.*, 9, 12 (1927); *C. A.*, 21, 1484 (1927).
——, and Weill, J., *J. physiol. path. gén.*, 15, 549 (1913); *C. A.*, 9, 647 (1915).
——, Hatterer, C., and Roehrig, P., *Bull. soc. chim. biol.*, 12, 657 (1930); *C. A.*, 24, 5357 (1930).
——, ——, ——, *ibid.*, 12, 682 (1930a); *C. A.*, 24, 4946 (1930).
Thannhauser, S. J., "Lipidoses: Diseases of the Cellular Lipid Metabolism," London and New York, Oxford University Press, 1940.
——, *New England J. Med.*, 237, 515 (1947); *C. A.*, 42, 272 (1948).
——, *ibid.*, 237, 546 (1947a); *C. A.*, 42, 272 (1948).
——, and Magendantz, H., *Ann. Internal Med.*, 11, 1662 (1938); *C. A.*, 32, 3814 (1938).

Thannhauser, S. J., Benotti, J., and Reinstein, H., *J. Biol. Chem.*, **129**, 709 (1939).

Theis, E. R., *J. Biol. Chem.*, **76**, 107 (1928).

——, *ibid.*, **82**, 327 (1929).

Thomas, E. M., *Am. J. Diseases Children*, **65**, 770 (1943); *C. A.*, **37**, 6328 (1943).

Thunberg, T., *Skand. Arch. Physiol.*, **24**, 90 (1911); *C. A.*, **5**, 1934 (1911).

——, *ibid.*, **43**, 275 (1923); *C. A.*, **18**, 110 (1924).

Tidwell, H. C., *J. Biol. Chem.*, **182**, 405 (1950).

Tocantins, L. M., *Am. J. Med. Sci.*, **207**, 814 (1944); *C. A.*, **38**, 5912 (1944).

Tompkins, E. H., *Am. Rev. Tuberc.*, **33**, 625 (1936); *C. A.*, **30**, 7684 (1936).

——, *Bull. Johns Hopkins Hosp.*, **70**, 55 (1942); *C. A.*, **36**, 2331 (1942).

——, *Arch. Path.*, **35**, 695 (1943); *C. A.*, **37**, 6321 (1943).

——, *ibid.*, **35**, 787 (1943a); *C. A.*, **38**, 574 (1944).

Topley, W. W. C., and co-workers (Raistrick, H., Wilson, J., Stacey, M., Challinor, S. W., and Clark, R. O. J.), *Lancet*, I, 252 (1937); *C. A.*, **31**, 6279 (1937).

Trautmann, A., and Kirchhof, H., *Biochem. Z.*, **247**, 275 (1932); *C. A.*, **26**, 3826 (1932).

Trevan, J. W., and Macfarlane, R. G., *Ann. Report Med. Res. Council*, 143 (1936/37).

Trier, G., *Z. physiol. Chem.*, **80**, 409 (1912a); *C. A.*, **7**, 800 (1913).

Tropp, C., and Baserga, A., *Z. Immunitätsforsch.*, **83**, 234 (1934); *C. A.*, **29**, 7456 (1935).

——, and Eckardt, B., *Z. physiol. Chem.*, **243**, 38 (1936); *C. A.*, **31**, 156 (1937).

——, ——, *ibid.*, **245**, 163 (1937); *C. A.*, **31**, 4390 (1937).

Tucker, H. F., and Eckstein, H. C., *J. Biol. Chem.*, **121**, 479 (1937).

——, ——, *ibid.*, **126**, 117 (1938).

Ulrich, R., *Compt. rend.*, **208**, 664 (1939); *C. A.*, **33**, 4293 (1939).

Verkade, P. E., *Chemistry & Industry*, 704 (1938); *C. A.*, **32**, 7487 (1938).

Verzár, F., and Laszt, L., *Biochem. Z.*, **270**, 24 (1934); *C. A.*, **28**, 5114 (1934).

——, ——, *Schweiz. med. Wochschr.*, **64**, 1178 (1934a).

——, ——, *Biochem. Z.*, **276**, 11 (1935); **278**, 396 (1935); *C. A.*, **29**, 3015, 8091 (1935).

——, and McDougall, E. J., "Absorption from the Intestine," London, Longmans, Green & Co., 1936.

Volkin, E., and co-workers (Erickson, J. O., Craig, H. W., and Neurath, H.), *J. Am. Chem. Soc.*, **67**, 2210 (1945); *C. A.*, **40**, 1225 (1946).

Voris, L., Ellis, G., and Maynard, L. A., *J. Biol. Chem.*, **133**, 491 (1940).

Wachstein, M., *Z. klin. Med.*, **131**, 625 (1937); *C. A.*, **31**, 3137 (1937).

——, *J. Lab. Clin. Med.*, **28**, 1462 (1943); *C. A.*, **38**, 6310 (1944).

Wadsworth, A., and Crowe, M. O., *J. Phys. Chem.*, **40**, 739 (1936); *C. A.*, **30**, 7037 (1936).

——, Maltaner, F., and Maltaner, E., *Am. J. Physiol.*, **91**, 423 (1930); *C. A.*, **24**, 4818 (1930).

——, ——, ——, *ibid.*, **97**, 74 (1931); *C. A.*, **25**, 4306 (1931).

——, ——, ——, *J. Immunol.*, **30**, 417 (1936); *C. A.*, **30**, 8354 (1936).

——, Maltaner, E., and Maltaner, F., *J. Immunol.*, **26**, 25 (1934); *C. A.*, **30**, 8352 (1936).

——, ——, ——, *ibid.*, **28**, 183 (1935); *C. A.*, **29**, 7461 (1935).

Waelsch, H., Sperry, W. M., and Stoyanoff, V. A., *J. Biol. Chem.*, **135**, 291 (1940).

——, ——, ——, *ibid.*, **135**, 297 (1940a).

——, ——, ——, *ibid.*, **140**, 885 (1941).

Waksman, S. A., *Am. J. Physiol.*, **46**, 375 (1918); *C. A.*, **12**, 2357 (1918).

Warburg, O., and Meyerhof, O., *Z physiol. Chem.*, **85**, 412 (1913); *C. A.*, **8**, 136 (1914).

Weil, A. J., *Bact. Revs.*, **5**, 293 (1941).

——, *J. Neuropathol. Exptl. Neurol.*, **7**, 453 (1948); *C. A.*, **43**, 3924 (1949).

Weil, L., and Russell, M. A., *J. Biol. Chem.*, **144**, 307 (1942).

Weil-Malherbe, H., and Dickens, F., *Cancer Research*, **4**, 425 (1944); *C. A.*, **38**, 6369 (1944).

Weinhouse, S., Medes, G., and Floyd, N. F., *J. Biol. Chem.*, **153**, 689 (1944); **155**, 143 (1944).

Weissberger, L. H., *J. Biol. Chem.*, **132**, 219 (1940).

——, *ibid.*, **139**, 543 (1941).

Welch, A. D., *Proc. Soc. Exptl. Biol. Med.*, **35**, 107 (1936).

——, and Landau, A. L., *J. Biol. Chem.*, **144**, 581 (1942).

Wendt, H., *Biochem. Z.*, **250**, 212 (1932); *C. A.*, **26**, 5139 (1932).

Wertheimer, D., and co-workers (Pillemer, L., Lawson, J., and Ecker, E. E.), *Proc. Soc. Exptl. Biol. Med.*, **39**, 393 (1938); *C. A.*, **33**, 8279 (1939).

Wheeler, P., and Goetzl, F. R., *Permanente Foundation Med. Bull.*, **5**, 63 (1947); *C. A.*, **43**, 5107 (1949).

White, P., and co-workers (Marble, A., Bogan, I. K., and Smith, R. M.), *Arch. Internal Med.*, **62**, 751 (1938).

White, P. B., *J. Path. Bact.*, **44**, 706 (1937).

Widenbauer, F., and Reichel, C., *Biochem. Z.*, **309**, 415 (1941); *C. A.*, **37**, 3180 (1943).

Wieland, H., and Rosenthal, C., *Ann.*, **554**, 241 (1943); *C. A.*, **37**, 6731 (1943).

Wilbur, K. M., and Collier, H. B., *J. Cellular Comp. Physiol.*, **22**, 233 (1943); *C. A.*, **38**, 3358 (1944).

Wile, U. J., Cameron, O. J., and Eckstein, H. C., *Arch. Dermatol. and Syphilol.*, **32**, 69 (1935); *C. A.*, **30**, 496 (1936).

Williams, H. H., and co-workers (Erickson, B. N., Bernstein, S., Hummel, F. C., and Macy, I. G.), *J. Biol. Chem.*, **118**, 599 (1937).

——, and co-workers (Erickson, B. N., Bernstein, S. S., and Macy, I. G.), *Proc. Soc. Exptl. Biol. Med.*, **45**, 151 (1940); *C. A.*, **35**, 507 (1941).

——, and co-workers (Erickson, B. N., Beach, E. F., Macy, I. G., Avrin, I., Shepherd, M., Souders, H., Teague, D. M., and Hoffman, O.), *J. Lab. Clin. Med.*, **26**, 996 (1941); *C. A.*, **35**, 3317 (1941).

——, and co-workers (Galbraith, H., Kaucher, M., Moyer, E. Z., Richards, A. J., and Macy, I. G.), *J. Biol. Chem.*, **161**, 475 (1945).

——, and co-workers (Kaucher, M., Richards, A. J., and Moyer, E. Z.), *J. Biol. Chem.*, **160**, 227 (1945a).

Willius, F. A., *Proc. Staff Meetings Mayo Clinic*, **14**, 751 (1939); *C. A.*, **35**, 4457 (1941).

Winkler, A. W., and co-workers (Durlacher, S., Hoff, H. E., and Man, E. B.), *J. Exptl. Med.*, **77**, 473 (1943); *C. A.*, **37**, 3815 (1943).

Winter, I. C., and Crandall, L. A., Jr., *J. Biol. Chem.*, **140**, 97 (1941).

Witzemann, E. J., *J. Phys. Chem.*, **25**, 55 (1921); *C. A.*, **15**, 1146 (1921).

——, *J. Biol. Chem.*, **95**, 219, 247 (1932).

——, in Nord, F. F., and Werkman, C. H., "Advances in Enzymology," Vol. II, New York, Interscience Publishers, Inc., 1942.

Wollaeger, E. E., Comfort, M. W., and Osterberg, A. E., *Gastroenterology*, **9**, 272 (1947).

Wooldridge, L. C., *Arch. Anat. u. Physiol., Physiol. Abt.*, 397 (1886).

Yamasaki, M., *Juzenkaizasshi*, **40**, No. 7 (1935); *C. A.*, **32**, 3808 (1938).

Yasuda, M., and Bloor, W. R., *J. Clin. Invest.*, **11**, 677 (1932); *C. A.*, **26**, 5142 (1932).

Yasuda, M., *J. Biochem. (Japan)*, **26**, 203 (1937); *C. A.*, **32**, 1772 (1938).

Yosida, N., *J. Biochem. (Japan)*, **32**, 1 (1940); *C. A.*, **35**, 762 (1941).

Yriart, M., *Compt. rend. soc. biol.*, **108**, 136 (1931); *C. A.*, **27**, 3978 (1933).

Zilversmit, D. B., and co-workers (Entenman, C., Fishler, M. C., and Chaikoff, I. L.), *J. Gen. Physiol.*, **26**, 333 (1943); *C. A.*, **37**, 1758 (1943).

——, Chaikoff, I. L., and Entenman, C., *J. Biol. Chem.*, **172**, 637 (1948).

——, Entenman, C., and Chaikoff, I. L., *J. Biol. Chem.*, **176**, 193 (1948).

——, ——, ——, *ibid.*, **176**, 209 (1948a).

——, ——, and Fishler, M. C., *J. Gen. Physiol.*, **26**, 325 (1943); *C. A.*, **37**, 1733 (1943).

Zlataroff, S., *Biochem. Z.*, **75**, 200 (1916); *C. A.*, **10**, 3093 (1916).

Zunz, E., and LaBarre, J., *Arch. intern. physiol.*, **18**, 116 (1921); *C. A.*, **16**, 952 (1922).

PART VI
THE INDUSTRIAL ASPECTS OF THE PHOSPHATIDES

CHAPTER XXVI

THE MANUFACTURE OF PHOSPHATIDES

INTRODUCTION

The phosphatides used industrially are obtained, for the most part, from soybeans and may be considered as by-products resulting from the production and refining of crude soybean oil. Although a variety of procedures employing solvents have been patented, the so-called Bollmann process, which is used almost universally (see below), makes it possible to obtain the phosphatides from the oil without solvent extraction.

The early patent literature describes the extraction of phosphatides from material of animal origin such as egg yolk, brain tissue or spinal cord (e.g., Fischer, Habermann and Ehrenfeld, 1907; Riedel Akt.-Ges., 1910).

Such sources provided only small quantities of phosphatides, most of which were used pharmaceutically. The development of solvent extraction procedures for the isolation of soybean oil made available phosphatides in large quantities, and uses for these were readily found.

It is generally held that the commercial phosphatides from soybeans are superior to those from other sources. The phosphatide content of soybean oil varies from 0.4 to 2.5 per cent (Anonymous, 1944; Markley and Goss, 1944, p. 101), and the yield, in commercial processing, is greater than from other oil seeds as indicated in Table I (Goss, 1947, p. 39).

TABLE I. YIELD OF PHOSPHATIDES FROM COMMERCIAL OIL SEEDS (GOSS, 1947)

Seed	Per cent phosphatides
Soybean	0.45–0.50
Rapeseed	.35
Linseed	.25
Peanut	.20
Sunflower (with hulls)	.15
Palm kernel	.10

Commercial phosphatides are categorically termed "lecithin" and contain, in addition to phosphatides, 35 to 40 per cent oil which is believed to exert a stabilizing influence on these moisture- and oxygen-sensitive products. The article of commerce is ordinarily a waxy, sticky, dark yellow or orange-brown solid. Minor proportions of carbohydrates, which may be in the form of glycosides, as well as inositol, sterols, pigments and incompletely characterized substances are also present. Commercial phosphatides from soybeans are reminiscent in taste and odor of the parent oil. The chemistry of these commercial phosphatides has already been discussed (see p. 3 ff., 220).

Whereas the exact extent of phosphatide production in the world is not known with certainty, estimates are of the order of 15 to 20 million pounds per year of the product containing 35 to 40 per cent oil. Although phosphatides once sold for as much as $1.00 per pound, their price now parallels closely that of soybean oil.

Prior to 1934, commercial lecithin used in this country was imported largely from Germany and Denmark. The principal German manufacturer, Hanseatische Mühlenwerke A. G. (Hansa-Mühle), marketed its lecithin products in the United States through the American Lecithin Corporation. The principal Danish manufacturer, Aarhus Oliefabrik, A/S (Aarhus), marketed its lecithin products in the United States through Ross & Rowe, Inc.

In 1934 the first commercial lecithin plant in America was built in Chicago by the Archer-Daniels-Midland Company, and in 1935 the Glidden Company built a similar plant in Chicago.

All the above foreign and domestic corporations either owned or controlled process and use patents or operated under license agreements from one another. In order to promote the widespread distribution and use of lecithin in the United States and because of the very confusing and complicated patent situation in 1935, the above concerns entered into an agreement to pool their patent interests. Under this agreement all the companies except Ross & Rowe, Inc. received stock in a new patent holding and licensing company—The American Lecithin Company, Inc. This new company granted exclusive manufacturing licenses to Archer-Daniels-Midland Company and the Glidden Company and a sales license to Ross & Rowe, Inc. The American Lecithin Company also, for a time, continued to sell lecithin in competition with its licensee, Ross & Rowe, Inc. For the most part no royalties were imposed on lecithin consumers.

Under this arrangement the volume of lecithin production expanded, and at times large quantities of lecithin accumulated at the plants in excess of demand. As the quantity of domestic lecithin increased, the price continued to decline to provide a broader market.

Certain trade practices of the American Lecithin Company were modified by Federal Trade Commission action in 1941, and the patent pool arrangement was terminated by Consent Decree in 1946.

There are now about a dozen known producers of commercial lecithin in the United States, most of whom are operating under license from

TABLE II. COMMERCIAL LECITHIN SPECIFICATIONS

Type	Acetone-insoluble (%)	Phospho-rous (%)	Acid num-ber (max.)	Color (Lovibond)* Yellow	Red	Consistency (penetrometer)	Viscosity (Poises at 80° C.)
Plastic (Non-pourable)							
Minimum Bleach							
Product 1	67	2.2	26	35	2.5	8–12 mm	—
Product 2	65	—	30	30	2.5	8–12 mm	—
Product 3	65–68	2.1–2.9	—	35	10.0**	—	—
Product 4	67	2.25	26	30	2.0	10 mm	—
Product 5	64–68.5	—	—	25	3.0	10 mm	—
Single Bleach							
Product 6	67	2.2	26	35	1.2	8–12 mm	—
Product 7	67	2.3	26	15	0.7	10 mm	—
Product 8	64–68.5	—	—	10	1.0	10 mm	—
Double Bleach							
Product 9	67	2.2	27	3.5	0.8	—	—
Soft (Pourable)							
Minimum Bleach							
Product 10	65	2.1	32	35	2.5	30–40 mm	—
Product 11	62	2.1	32	35	2.5	30–40 mm	—
Product 12	63	2.1	30	30	2.5	—	—
Product 13	61–64	2.0–1.8	—	35	10.0**	—	100–300
Product 14	65	2.1	32	30	2.0	36 mm	—
Product 15	64–68.5	—	—	25	3.0	—	—
Single Bleach							
Product 16	65	2.1	32	30	1.2	30–40 mm	—
Product 17	62–65	1.9–2.1	—	35	7.5**	—	100–300
Product 18	63	—	30	—	1.0	32–40 mm	—
Product 19	65	2.1	32	15	0.7	36 mm	—
Product 20	64–68.5	—	—	10	1.0	—	—
Double Bleach							
Product 21	65	2.2	32	3.5	0.8	30–40 mm	—
Product 22	62–65	1.9–2.1	—	35.0	2.5**	—	100–300
Product 23	62–65	1.9–2.1	—	35.0	2.5**	—	—
Product 24	65	2.1	32	3.5	0.8	36 mm	—
Fluid (Readily Pourable)							
Product 25	59–61	1.9	36	35	2.5	—	—
Product 26	54–57	1.7–1.9	—	35	7.5**	—	30–70

* One per cent solution dissolved in white mineral oil, except where indicated.
** Five per cent solution.

the American Lecithin Company. The specifications of typical products which they produce are shown in Table II.

In this chapter will be described the means by which phosphatides are obtained and refined commercially and the modification to which they may be subjected.

THE ISOLATION OF PHOSPHATIDES

The Bollmann Process

Phosphatide production on a large scale was pioneered for the most part in Germany, for it was there that the processing of Manchurian soybeans which had started at the turn of the century assumed importance shortly after World War I. Soybean oil in order to be acceptable for many uses must be a so-called "non-break" oil—i.e., it must not become cloudy when heated, either alone or in the presence of a few drops of hydrochloric acid, due to the presence of phosphatides and accompanying substances such as mucilaginous materials, phytins, carbohydrates, glycosides, etc. These materials separate in the form of a sludge if the unrefined oil is allowed to stand, since the oil takes on moisture from the air. This sludge proved to be a by-product which was readily subject to decomposition and which was of practically no utility to the early refiners. The Bollmann (1923, 1930) patents, assigned to the Hanseatische Mühlenwerke Akt.-Ges., described a relatively simple means for obtaining these substances during the refining of the oils in a form sufficiently "pure" and stable to make them industrially useful materials.

Phosphatides are isolated largely from oil obtained by solvent extraction rather than by expelling or hydraulic pressing. The high temperatures employed in the two latter processes tend to decompose the phosphatides. Thus, solvent extraction is particularly favorable since operating temperatures do not exceed 100° C.

The essential step in the original process for the isolation of phosphatides from solvent-extracted oil involves treatment of the oil with hot water or with slightly superheated steam (103° C.) in order to effect precipitation of the phosphatides and associated material in the form of an emulsion with the water and some of the oil. This process is termed "degumming". It should be noted that Ayres and Clark (1929) patented a degumming process for cottonseed oil which employed a dispersion of starch in water. The effect of free fatty acids in the oil on this precipitation reaction has been discussed by Molines and Desnuelle (1950). The precipitated mass which includes 30 to 40 per cent oil is isolated in modern practice by centrifugation, after which the water is removed by vacuum drying to obtain the brownish-yellow article of commerce.

In some German mills, such as the Hamburg plant of Hanseatische Mühlenwerke A.-G., it was customary, according to Grün (1936, p. 506), to employ hydrocarbon-alcohol mixtures for the extraction of the soybeans. Thus benzene, petroleum ether or a mixture of these with as much as 40 per cent of ethanol could be used (Bollmann, 1923; Rewald, 1933).

In this way, virtually all of the phosphatides were extracted, due no doubt to the dissociating influence of the alcohol on the phosphatide complexes. As a matter of fact, an early patent issued to Bollmann and Rewald (1927) suggested that soybeans be treated with methanol or ethanol, prior to extraction. It was shown by Sorenson and Beal (1935), however, that the alcohol also caused bitter substances to be extracted. If alcohol is used it is necessary to subject the phosphatide fraction to vacuum-steam deodorization at 60° C. until all odor and bad flavors are removed.

In most American soybean processing plants, soybeans are extracted with a single hydrocarbon solvent such as the hexane fraction of petroleum distillation. The absence of alcohol causes phosphatide extraction to be less complete, but the product obtained is more readily purified. The correspondingly higher phosphatide content of the meal increases its nutritional value. Bull and Hopper (1941) have described the effect of the boiling point of the hydrocarbon solvent on the material extracted. An attempt is usually made to maintain in the flaked soybeans a moisture content no greater than 11 per cent. This effects a less complete extraction of the phosphatides since as much as one per cent may be left in the extracted meal. The bitter constituents, however, are not extracted, making the subsequent processing of the phosphatides easier. Instead of the high temperature originally prescribed for precipitation of the phosphatides with water, temperatures of 70 to 80° C. may be used with agitation. The time of precipitation may vary from 15 minutes to one hour; and the resulting precipitated emulsion, as indicated above, is obtained by centrifugation and is subjected to drying *in vacuo*.

This process is also employed in England, and a detailed description of its use by J. Bibby & Sons, Ltd. is available (Anonymous, 1948).

A patent issued to Kruse (1942) describes a variation in the process and equipment so that the phosphatides obtained by centrifuging contain very little moisture and need not be dried *in vacuo* prior to use.

Some newer American mills are using trichloroethylene as an extraction solvent, since this material is nonexplosive.

Goss (1947, pp. 19, 47) has described the procedures employed by various German mills as observed by him in 1945. Thus, at the Moorstrasse plant of Noblee and Thörl, G.m.b.H., oil obtained both by pressing and extraction was stirred vigorously and heated while two per cent of hot water was added by spraying. The resulting emulsion was separated in Westphalia centrifuges and the oil was again treated as above to obtain another emulsion. This second sludge is not used to obtain lecithin, but may be separated by use of salt into sediment and oil. The sediment is added to the meal from the extractor, to the initial feed, or to the mixer where the oil will be treated with water to precipitate lecithin. The oil, of course, is recovered and added to the crude oil. This second sludge is removed primarily to refine the oil more highly and particularly to enhance its properties organoleptically. The first sludge is dried *in vacuo* in a drier equipped with a rotating, ball-shaped coil through which sufficient warm water is circulated to maintain a temperature of 60 to 70° C. Hydrogen peroxide (see p. 495) is employed as a bleaching agent during the drying process.

The process employed at F. Thörl Akt.-Ges. was quite similar, save that the oil was allowed to flow continuously through a steam-jacketed tank where it was stirred vigorously and treated with 5 to 10 per cent water at 95 to 100° C. The resulting emulsion was centrifuged as in the previous process and was dried in stainless steel kettles. This product contained only 20 to 22 per cent oil as contrasted to the more usual figure of 30 to 40 per cent. In this process, too, the oil was subjected to a second desludging operation.

The above procedures were employed for both soybean and rapeseed oil, although the latter material provided an inferior product. The facilities of the Hanseatische Mühlenwerke Akt.-Ges. in 1945 were used entirely for the production of rapeseed lecithin, according to Goss (1947, p. 29). The process was very similar to those described above. The kettle employed for mixing the oil and water was in the form of a vertical cylinder with heating coils at the bottom and a vertical shaft with stirring arms. Radial pipes were arranged at the top with perforations through which hot water was sprayed on the surface of the oil. A temperature of 60 to 70° C. was used for mixing the oil with 2 to 3 per cent water.

Other Extraction Processes

Although numerous other extraction procedures for obtaining phosphatides have been patented, virtually none of them is in use. Exemplary of these older patents is one granted to Fischer (1906) which describes a process for isolating phosphatides from natural substances by extracting extraneous material first of all with acetone. Then the residue is treated with methanol to dissociate any complexes with proteins, and subsequently to dissolve the phosphatides. Many of the older methods, most of which are similar to this one, are discussed by Grün (1936, p. 501 ff.).

Isolation of Phosphatides from Oil Residues. Of historical interest are the patents issued to Riedel Akt.-Ges. (1922) and Riedel and de Haën A.-G. (1923). These patents described the isolation and purification of the phosphatides from the sludges or "foots" which collected in unrefined soybean oil by means of solvents such as alcohol and benzene. The subsequent introduction of the centrifuge to obtain the sludge immediately was an important advance in phosphatide technology.

A more recent patent (Noblee and Thörl G.m.b.H., 1937) describes the use of acetone or glacial acetic acid for precipitating phosphatides from a soybean oil suspension. The mixture is cooled and centrifuged simultaneously.

A process for obtaining phosphatides from "foots" such as those which accumulate in oil obtained by the expeller process has been described in a patent issued to Julian and Engstrom (1941). In this process the sludge is dissolved in lecithin-free soybean oil and the solution is treated with water containing a bleaching agent to obtain the phosphatides in the form of an emulsion. This emulsion may be processed similarly to the one obtained when solvent-extracted oil is refined.

According to Ginn (1936), phosphatides may also be obtained from the sludge which accumulates in expressed oil. The sludge may be deodorized by blowing with air, after which it is centrifuged, preferably at 55 to 70° C., to separate the adhering oil from the phosphatides. The oil may then be recombined with a refined oil.

Another means for obtaining phosphatides from expressed oil, which at the same time is converted from a "break" to a "non-break" oil, has been described by Kraybill (1937). This process involves treating the oil with water or hot alcohol. The water, as would be expected, emulsified the phosphatides and these, together with some oil, are removed by centrifugation. If, on the other hand, hot alcohol is used, there results, on cooling, an oil layer and an alcohol layer in which the phosphatides are dissolved.

A patent issued to Sifferd (1945) describes the removal of phosphatides from oil "foots" or sludge by treatment of these residues with ethylene dichloride. If at least 10 per cent water is present, the phosphatides are insoluble and comprise the main portion of the extracted aqueous residue. The process may also be applied to the emulsion obtained in the refining of oil by the Bollmann process and to an emulsion obtained during the extraction of phosphatides from eggs.

Gehrke (1935) proposed that the sludge which collected in unrefined soybean oil be converted to an edible phosphatide product by treating it, while fresh, with glycerol at about 60° C. On cooling, an aqueous glycerol layer separates and is removed to leave a phosphatide-oil layer suitable for use in foods. Sugar may be employed together with the glycerol. Supposedly the use of these dehydrating agents precludes the necessity for vacuum distillation of volatile material. Similar processes employing glycerol or concentrated aqueous sugar solutions as dehydrating media have been described in patents by Noblee and Thörl G.m.b.H. (1934, 1934a).

The use of acetone for the precipitation of phosphatides from soybean oil "foots" has been described by Salmoiraghi (1937). A recent patent (Singer and Deobald, 1950) describes the mechanical separation of phosphatides from emulsified soybean oil "foots". The composition of soybean oil "foots" has been explored by Okano, Ohara and Kato (1936) and by Mori (1938).

Isolation of Phosphatides from Soapstock. The phosphatides present in the soapstock accumulating from the alkali-refining of cottonseed oil may be obtained by treating the entire mixture with acetone or methyl acetate, according to Thurman (1937). By this means a residue rich in phosphatides is obtained. Purification is effected by washing with dilute acid or sodium chloride solution. The product may be mixed with refined oils, or with commercial phosphatides obtained from other sources. A method for obtaining the soapstock for this purpose is described in another patent (Thurman, 1943).

A patent to Thurman (1939) describes the use of a variety of solvents such as petroleum ether, ethyl ether, benzene, chlorinated solvents or acetone in order to dissolve either the phosphatides or the soap and oil as a means of separating the phosphatides from soapstock.

A similar process employing acetone has been applied by Thurman (1947) to the solid material obtained when oils are "degummed" by the addition of water or weak electrolytes. In this instance the acetone-insoluble residue may be further extracted with hexane.

The Extraction of Phosphatides with Alcohol. The early patent literature (e.g., Buer, 1910, 1912; Berczeller, 1930) indicates that alcohol was used extensively for isolating phosphatides from natural sources. As indicated previously, soybeans are extracted now primarily with hydrocarbon solvents or with these in the presence of a small amount of alcohol. Mashino (1933) described procedures employing warm azeotropic mixtures of hydrocarbons and alcohols. The resulting solutions, on cooling, stratified in such a way that the oil was contained in the upper hydrocarbon layer, whereas the phosphatides and associated impurities were present in the lower alcohol layer. The phosphatides could be isolated by removal of the solvent or by precipitation from the solution with acetone or solutions of inorganic salts.

The use of alcohol alone has also been suggested (Chemische Fabrik Promonta G.m.b.H, 1926), and according to Schofield (1945) and Horvath (1937), there was in use at one time in northern Manchuria a process which employed only warm alcohol for the extraction of soybeans. On cooling, the solution separated into a layer of oil and a layer of phosphatides dissolved, together with other substances, in the alcohol. The refining of phosphatides obtained in this way is described by Sato and co-workers (1940). According to Belter, Beckel and Smith (1944) a superior soybean protein is obtained when the bean is extracted with alcohol.

The use of mixtures of ethyl alcohol (70 to 80 per cent) and isopropyl alcohol (30 to 20 per cent) for the extraction of oil from seeds is described in a patent issued to Singer and Deobald (1945). Beckel and Belter (1949) have patented a continuous process for the extraction of soybeans with alcohol. In this process, too, the phosphatides are readily isolated.

The Use of Adsorbents for Isolating Phosphatides. The use of inorganic adsorbents for obtaining phosphatides has been described by several workers. A patent issued to I. G. Farbenind. A.-G. (1933) described a process in which a solution of phosphatides in an organic solvent, obtained by extraction, was treated with an inorganic oxide sol in order to precipitate the phosphatides. Examples of the latter were ethanol sols of the oxides of silicon, aluminum and iron. A similar process was described by Klein and Tauboeck (1935), who obtained the phosphatides from the adsorption complex by extraction with solvents such as ethanol or carbon tetrachloride.

The use of tricalcium phosphate is advocated by Beck and Klein (1940) as an adsorbent for the phosphatides present in oils. The adsorbed material may be removed by treatment of the complex with acetone to dissolve the oil and then with benzene-alcohol mixtures to dissolve the phosphatides. The adsorbent is prepared for use by washing with methanolic caustic and finally with methanol.

The use of adsorbents to refine vegetable oils and, at the same time, to make possible the recovery of phosphatides, has been discussed by Thornton and Kraybill (1942). They employed an aluminum silicate adsorbent whose preparation from aqueous sodium silicate and an acidic aluminum salt is described by Kraybill, Brewer and Thornton (1939). This serves to adsorb not only phosphatides but also any sterols, glycosides, free fatty acids, pigments and mucilages which may be present. Since drastic conditions are avoided, it is the belief of these workers that the phosphatides are recovered virtually as they exist in the oil. In a subsequent patent (Kraybill, Brewer and Thornton, 1944), a variety of other adsorbents which may be used are listed. For obtaining the phosphatides adhering to the adsorbent, the successive use of acetone, ether, absolute ethanol and 50 per cent ethanol was found effective. Other solvents are listed by Kraybill, Brewer and Thornton (1944). The acetone-soluble fraction is largely oil, sterols and sterol glycosides.

The other solvents serve to extract phosphatide fractions of different compositions (Kraybill, Brewer and Thornton, 1942), one of which is a good emulsifying agent and another of which has marked foaming properties. When the adsorption was carried out in a column, no fractionation of the adsorbed material was observed.

. **Miscellaneous Modifications for Precipitating Phosphatides.** The use of dilute acids, sodium chloride and other electrolyte solutions for precipitating phosphatides from oils, together with various modifications of apparatus and methods for refining the phosphatides, is described in several patents by Bollmann (1925), Thurman (1934, 1939a, 1940, 1941a), Clayton (1932), Clayton and Thurman (1940), Hansa-Mühle A.-G. (1937), Gensecke (1933, 1934) and Metallgesellschaft A.-G. (1929).

Thurman (1941) has also described a procedure for obtaining phosphatides, particularly from expressed oils, in which the oil is first treated with dilute solutions of alum or tannic acid buffered to a neutral pH. This serves to precipitate protein material and, supposedly, impurities other than phosphatides. Thereafter the phosphatides are precipitated with a slightly acidic aqueous solution.

The use of hyposulfite in addition to water for precipitating phosphatides from oil is described in a patent issued to the Dansk Sojakagefabrik Akt. (1937). This is said to cause such complete separation that an aqueous, phosphatide-containing layer may readily be removed from the bottom of the vessel. Steam distillation to remove impurities may be employed prior to the separation. The phosphatides are precipitated from the aqueous layer with sodium chloride.

Rewald (1934) isolated phosphatides by washing with alcohol the emulsion obtained by the addition of water to soybean oil. The alcohol served to remove most of the water and some impurities.

The Role of the Phosphatides During Oil Refining. The refining of oils is largely a process of removing the phosphatides, free fatty acids, proteins, pigments, mucilaginous bodies and the like which are probably present in colloidal suspension. As previous discussion has indicated, when the phosphatides are desired as commercial by-products, the most widely used refining process requires that the oil be "degummed" by addition of water or possibly dilute solutions of various electrolytes (see p. 486). The emulsion thus obtained is then processed to provide commercial phosphatides, whereas the oil may be further refined by treatment with alkali to remove, in particular, free fatty acids.

In certain mills it is impractical to "degum" oil, for which reason other refining processes are used. These remove the phosphatides and associated impurities, but do not, for the most part, make it possible to recover the phosphatides. The most common procedure is to stir the oil with alkali while applying heat to obtain an emulsion which separates on heating and agitation into oil and by-products. The effect of the phosphatides of various oils on the conditions necessary for alkali-refining of this sort has been discussed by Fash (1947). The use of sodium carbonate as a refining reagent (Clayton, 1942) has been described by Mattikow (1948).

Sulfuric acid likewise serves as a reagent for removing the "break" from oils as does alum, tannic acid, phosphoric acid and a variety of other reagents, some of which are discussed in greater detail by Schönfeld (1937, p. 17 ff.). Heating at critical temperatures also serves to coagulate the impurities in oils such as linseed and rapeseed oil (Sullivan, 1948), whereas the use of adsorbents has already been discussed (see p. 491).

Phosphatides are obtained in the first step of the oil-refining procedure patented by Tischer (1938). Here soybean oil is treated with alcoholic magnesium chloride solution and acetone to dissolve the oil and precipitate the phosphatides. The oil is refined, after removal of the acetone, by high vacuum distillation.

Recent technology has provided several refining processes which not only remove the constituents generally considered undesirable in a refined oil, but which also separate the oil into fractions of high and low iodine number. One of these methods depends on liquid-liquid extraction with a variety of polar solvents, the most important of which is furfural. The application of this process, particularly for the removal of phosphatides and free fatty acids, is described in a patent issued to Freeman (1945).

Still another refining process makes use of liquid propane (Ewing, 1942). Passino (1949, 1950) has described the techniques involved in some detail, the initial step being the removal of various oils from their sources by means of countercurrent extraction with liquid propane. The solubility relations here are unique in that the various oil components become less soluble as the temperature of the liquid propane is raised. Thus in the refining of soybean oil, for example, the first fraction which settles out after extraction is a dark-colored material amounting to about two per cent of the oil. This fraction contains the phosphatides as well as pigments and associated materials (Mattikow, 1950; Anonymous, 1946). As the temperature of the solution is increased, fractions of oil with low and high iodine numbers precipitate. There does not appear to be any information on specific means for refining the phosphatide fraction obtained in this way.

Phosphatides from Miscellaneous Sources. As already indicated, soybeans are the most important source of commercial phosphatides.

The isolation of phosphatides from linseed oil in Germany during World War II is described in an official report by Wornum and co-workers (1946). The oil itself was extracted from the seeds with benzene, after which it was treated with water and centrifuged to obtain a mixture of oil and phosphatides which was dried *in vacuo*. The phosphatide content, however, was said to be too low and the impurity content too high for the product to be of practical value.

A process similar to the Bollmann procedure was shown to be applicable for the recovery of phosphatides from peanut oil (Helme and Desnuelle, 1948). Peanut oil has been used most widely as a source of phosphatides in England, and the product is believed to be superior to the one obtained from cottonseed oil.

The isolation of phosphatides from rapeseed oil in Germany during World War II has already been discussed (see p. 488).

Phosphatides from cottonseed oil have been produced commercially on a small scale, but their dark color and strong odor have proved to be deterrents to their use. Phosphatides from corn oil are also produced on a small scale.

Recently, patents have appeared describing the isolation of phosphatides from animal sources. Thornley and Jones (1944) have described a method for obtaining phosphatides from animal glands by solvent extraction. Similarly, Rosenbusch and Reverey (1936) have patented a process employing solvents for the extraction of phosphatides from brain tissue.

The removal of phosphatides by the addition of water to oil expressed from land or marine animal tissue is described in a patent issued to Aktieselskapet Flesland Fabrikker (1940).

The lipoprotein, lipovitellenin, present in egg yolk may be obtained according to a procedure patented by Fevold and Dimick (1948).

THE REFINING OF PHOSPHATIDES

Improvement of Odor and Taste

It is obvious that phosphatides intended for edible use should be as free as possible of unpleasant odor and taste. As indicated previously (see p. 487), the use of a hydrocarbon solvent alone for the extraction of soybeans provides phosphatides relatively free of bitter taste, whereas the presence of alcohol during the extraction appears to cause bitter substances to concentrate in the phosphatide fraction.

The purification of commercial phosphatides by chemical means such as the formation of complexes with inorganic salts (see, e.g., Soc. anon. pour l'ind. chim, à Bâle, 1926) has been advocated but has never been used. The most important means for the removal of odor and taste from phosphatides is by use of steam. A patent issued to Bollmann (1925a) described the removal of impurities from phosphatides by vacuum steam deodorization of the product resulting from the drying of the emulsion obtained by centrifuging the "degummed" oil. A patent issued to Hall (1925) also advocated the removal of odor and taste-imparting impurities from phosphatides by distillation with steam. Inert gases could be used in addition to the steam, if desired. Steam distillation, in commercial practice, has proved to be an inexpensive and effective means for removing most of the offensive impurities from phosphatides.

A unique and simple process for the refining of phosphatides, said to be used commercially in Denmark, is described in a patent issued to Christiansen (1944). In this method, oil-containing phosphatide mixtures which may also contain water are combined with 10 to 20 per cent of a solvent such as methyl or ethyl alcohol or acetone which is somewhat compatible with oil as well as water. The mixture is heated to 60 to 70° C. to cause fluidity, whereupon addition of water causes a stratification, the lower layer consisting almost wholly of phosphatides, water and alcohol and the upper layer consisting of oil and impurities which impart odor, bad taste and color. Separation of the lower layer, possibly with the aid of a centrifuge, and removal of the solvent provides a purified phosphatide which may be further purified by repetition of the above process. It may also be used as such or may be mixed with various oil carriers. Even without the presence of large amounts of oil, the phosphatides prepared by this means appear to be very stable. The proportions of reagents used in this process are apparently critical. A related procedure is described by Sato and co-workers (1940).

Bollmann (1928) has described a procedure for purifying commercial phosphatides which depends on subjecting alcohol solutions to successively lower temperatures in order to precipitate the impurities.

A microbiological procedure for the purification of phosphatides and other organic materials is described in a patent issued to Ekhard (1936). The material to be purified is mixed with a fermentable sugar and with organisms capable of producing lactic acid and alcohol. When the fermentation, which apparently destroys the impurities, is complete, the liquids produced by fermentation are removed to obtain a pure material.

Improvement of Color

The bleaching of phosphatides is common practice in modern technology. Whereas the color of the phosphatides varies with the type of soybeans used, some degree of uniformity can be attained by the use of bleaching materials. The action of hydrogen peroxide, the decolorizing agent most commonly used, is described in a patent issued to Bollmann (1929). The peroxide solution, according to this patent, is added to the phosphatide emulsion prior to drying. In modern practice a maximum of 2 per cent of 30 to 35 per cent aqueous peroxide is used, based on the phosphatides. The concentration used is influenced by the source of the phosphatides and the processing conditions. Color variation with different types of soybeans is often noted. The use of hydrogen peroxide is described also in patents issued to Bollmann (1929a) and to Bollmann and Schwieger (1933). Claim is made that bleaching with peroxide increases the capacity of the phosphatides for emulsification. The ease with which any excess hydrogen peroxide decomposes to harmless products makes its use desirable.

The use of benzoyl peroxide as a bleaching agent has also been suggested (Hanseatische Mühlenwerke, A.-G., 1932, 1934; Schwieger, 1932). Among the advantages claimed is a softer consistency for the final product.

The use of sodium chlorite as a bleaching agent for phosphatides is described by Greenfield (1944). Epstein (1942) has suggested the use of fatty peroxides such as lauroyl peroxide.

The use of clays and earths for the adsorption of color from phosphatides is described by Markman and Vuishnepolskaya (1932). In a recent patent, Marmor and Moyer (1949) propose to improve the color and odor of phosphatides by the use of acid-activated bleaching clays such as those normally used for glyceride oils. These are added, for a period of one hour, to the miscella or solution of oil and phosphatides in organic solvent, obtained in the first step of oil extraction from vegetable material. Julian and Iveson (1946) have patented a procedure in which the miscella from soybeans is treated first with an acid clay and then with an alkaline clay. The phosphatides, however, are precipitated prior to the addition of the alkaline material.

The use of hydrogen peroxide as a "degumming" agent for oils leads to the recovery of light-colored phosphatides, according to Thurman (1940a).

Replacement of the Oil

The soybean oil ordinarily present to the extent of 30 to 40 per cent in commercial phosphatides is a semidrying oil. Accordingly, it is subject, because of its unsaturation, to oxidative degradation and the formation of fragments imparting a bitter taste and a bad odor to the phosphatides. Interestingly enough, the oil nonetheless appears to exert a stabilizing effect on the phosphatides, probably because it prevents exposure of the phosphatides to the atmosphere. A patent issued to Bollmann (1926) suggested that the oil be replaced by repeated washings with refined oil. In modern practice the soybean oil is often replaced by more highly saturated oils in order to provide a refined product particularly suited for edible purposes. The process used is essentially the one described in a patent issued to Rewald (1933a). Thus the dried phosphatide-oil mixture is agitated with four to five volumes of acetone in which only the oil is soluble. The supernatant oil solution is then removed from the insoluble phosphatides, and the oil and acetone are separated by distillation and recovered. It may be necessary to repeat the extraction several times. The phosphatides, which contain some acetone, are stirred with refined, edible oils such as cocoa butter, peanut oil, coconut oil or hydrogenated oils. This step is facilitated by the presence of a small amount of residual acetone. The resulting mixture is then heated *in vacuo*, often with steam, to remove the last traces of solvent.

A description of this technique as practiced by Bibby and Sons has been published (Anonymous, 1948). Essentially the same process is described by Pollak (1934). Schweiger (1936) has described a process in which the oil, removed from the phosphatides as above, is replaced by carriers such as sugar or sugar syrups, cocoa powder, starch or starch degradation products. Other patents of a similar nature are described later.

For certain uses the oil is undesirable in phosphatides and is not replaced. A product of this type is described in a patent issued to Buer (1914), who recommended preliminary washings with aqueous acetone containing sodium bicarbonate and a final washing with pure acetone. Products of this nature are usually quite unstable and must be stored carefully and used as soon as possible.

THE MODIFICATION OF COMMERCIAL PHOSPHATIDES

Numerous patents have been granted which describe the physical or chemical modification of commercial phosphatides. Usually improvement in stability, ease of emulsifiability, or greater adaptability for a specific use is claimed. Only a few of these products are in use.

The Admixture of Phosphatides with Organic Carriers

Mixtures with Sugars and Related Substances. Carbohydrates, when used as carriers for phosphatides, appear to exert a stabilizing influence just as oils do (Martin, 1913; 1918). According to Kunzer (1933), carbohydrates such as invert cane sugar may even impart stability to phosphatides dispersed in water when the sugar is present in high concentration in relation to the water content.

The stability of phosphatide mixtures with oil, such as the "foots" or residues of soybean oil, is enhanced by the addition of glycerol or concentrated solutions of sugar or molasses, or a solution of sugar in glycerol (Noblee and Thörl G.m.b.H., 1934b). The substitution of carbohydrates for the oil normally present in commercial phosphatides is described in a patent issued to Hanseatische Mühlenwerke A.-G. (1935).

For use in foods, Rewald (1936) has patented a composition prepared by adding sugar, and possibly cocoa powder, to a phosphatide emulsion and subsequently removing the water. Likewise for use in foods, Fitzpatrick and Wagner (1944) mix commercial phosphatides with sugar or salt and grind the mass to distribute the phosphatides uniformly over the particles. In this way a dry, granular product is prepared. The conversion of phosphatides to granular material is accomplished by Bigelow (1947) by mixing them with oil and water and then adding sugar.

The admixture of phosphatides with glycerol to obtain readily emulsifiable solutions is described by Bergell (1910, 1928). According to Rosenbusch (1939) the addition of a maximum of 15 per cent glycerol to oil-free phosphatides reduces their adhesiveness.

Mixtures with Lactates. The addition of lactic acid to phosphatide emulsions in order to stabilize the aqueous dispersion has been described by Rewald (1937). If excess acid is added, two phases result, one of which is the emulsion with the maximum amount of lactic acid in it. The other is an aqueous solution of the acid. Thus, a means is provided for effecting concentration of the phosphatide emulsion. The lactic acid may be neutralized, if desired. Christlieb (1941) has used concentrated lactic acid as a solvent for commercial phosphatides in order to facilitate the formation of an emulsion with water. This product is said to be of value in the baking industry where difficulty is often encountered in emulsifying ordinary commercial phosphatides.

Esters of lactic acid such as ethyl lactate also facilitate the dispersion of oil-free phosphatides in water and stabilize the resulting emulsions, according to a patent issued to Jordan (1940). About 40 per cent of ethyl lactate, based on the weight of the phosphatides present, should be used. Propylene glycol may also be used, but is not acceptable in food products. A later patent (Jordan, 1942) describes solutions of oil-free lecithin in solvents such as the alkyl ethers of condensed ethylene glycols.

Thurman (1942) has described compositions prepared from oil-free corn phosphatides and aqueous sodium lactate solutions.

Mixtures with Miscellaneous Materials. A patent issued to Datz (1934) describes the stabilization of phosphatide-containing soybean oil sludge by the addition of a variety of carriers such as casein, gelatin, vegetable albumin, glucose, gelatinized starch, blood serum or flour. The mixtures which contained at least 25 per cent phosphatides were spray-dried. Schweiger (1936) has stabilized soybean "foots" with carriers such as albumin, starch or vegetable meals. A method for mixing phosphatides with carriers such as flour and cocoa has been described by Bollmann (1928a).

Martin (1928) proposed the use of a mixture of dried milk and cocoa butter as a carrier for egg lecithin. The use of grain germ such as barley malt germ as a carrier is described by Rosenbusch and Reverey (1935). The product is a dry powder.

A patent issued to Allingham (1948) describes a dry lecithin preparation consisting of a mixture of commercial phosphatides and dry Irish moss gel in the ratio of one to two. The product mixes easily with flour, and may be used in baking. It is also dispersed readily in water or in oil.

A composition comprising a mixture of phosphatides, cholesterol and bile has been described in a patent issued to Chemische Fabrik Promonta G.m.b.H. (1943).

Epstein and Harris (1936) have described mixtures of commercial phosphatides and diglycerides. These are said to disperse more readily in water than the conventional product. Epstein (1942) has patented compositions consisting of mixtures of phosphatides and monoglycerides which have been heated with small quantities of fatty acid peroxides. If monostearin is used, a composition results with the consistency of beeswax.

The emulsifiability of phosphatides is improved, according to Feibelmann (1940), by mixing with urea.

A patent issued to Buer and Buer (1927) states that the stability of phosphatides may be increased by dissolving them in peppermint oil. According to Sauer, Ltd. (1906), lecithin may be stabilized by mixing it in solution with quinine and removing the solvent. Stable solutions of lecithin for injection can be prepared, according to Mossini and Caliumi (1940), by dissolving lecithin in benzyl alcohol and adding ethylene glycol to the solution. The use of benzyl alcohol in order to solubilize phosphatides in oil has been patented by Chemische-Pharmazeutische A.-G. (1926). Benzyl alcohol is also known to facilitate the preparation of emulsions from oil-containing phosphatides.

The Admixture of Phosphatides with Salts, Acids and Bases

Mixtures with Salts. Thurman (1942a, 1942b) has treated phosphatides, such as those from corn oil, with aqueous solutions of various sodium phosphates. The mixture was heated at 49° C. for two hours, after which the water was removed to yield a product dispersible in water and soluble in petroleum ether. The inventor believes that an actual chemical reaction takes place. Other alkali metal salts of inorganic acids may be used. Mattikow (1942) has heated glycerol with phosphatides in the presence of sodium phosphate. Temperatures of the order of 149° C. for a period of one hour were employed. The products are said to be more effective than the unmodified phosphatides in various food uses.

A patent granted to Fitzpatrick (1948) describes a mixture of sodium chloride and phosphatides in which the salt comprises the bulk (96 per cent) of the composition. This mixture when properly processed is a free flowing powder which is stabilized by the addition of a small quantity of magnesium oxide or carbonate or calcium carbonate, phosphate or citrate.

Therapeutic value has been attributed to an addition product of phosphatides and calcium bromide (Soc. anon. pour l'ind. chim. à Bâle, 1926a).

Mixtures with Acids. Mixtures of phosphatides with hydroxylated organic acids such as lactic acid have already been discussed. The treatment of phosphatides with inorganic acids containing phosphorus or sulfur, in order to obtain water-soluble or water-dispersible products, is described by Dziengel (1942). Julian and Meyer (1945) propose to make phosphatides more soluble in glyceride oils by the addition of up to 7 per cent of oil-dispersible sulfonic acids such as benzenesulfonic acid. This also tends to destroy the emulsifying properties of the phosphatides, which for some purposes are undesirable. Phosphoric acid or glycerophosphoric acid is said to accomplish a similar purpose (Julian and Meyer, 1944), and in a subsequent patent (Julian and Meyer, 1945a) hydrochloric and sulfuric acids are claimed for a similar purpose. The use of acid-liberating compounds such as stearoyl chloride, stearoyl pyridinium chloride, and toluenesulfonyl chloride is also possible (Julian and Meyer, 1946).

Mixtures with Bases. Schweiger (1935) has proposed that phosphatides can be made more stable and more readily emulsifiable by trituration with solid alkali. The phosphatides may be free of oil or, like the usual commercial product, they may contain as much as 40 per cent oil. Up to 50 per cent water may also be present, in which case the mixture must be dried after it has been pulverized. The alkali used comprises 10 to 20 per cent of the mixture. A similar treatment is described in a patent issued to Hanseatische Mühlenwerke A.–G. (1935a).

The addition of organic bases such as pyridine or quinoline to phosphatides is said to enhance their ability to stabilize lubricating oils (Loane, 1942). The use of sodium silicate to stabilize either solid phosphatides or aqueous phosphatide emulsions is described in a patent issued to Noblee and Thörl G.m.b.H. (1935). The stabilization of phosphatide emulsions by the addition of alkali or alkaline earth peroxides has been described by Engelmann (1934).

Fluidization of Phosphatides

Commercial phosphatides frequently demonstrate a wax-like consistency. This makes difficult the uniform dispersion of small quantities in mixtures with which they are to be used. Since the consistency of the phosphatides varies with their source and with other practically uncontrollable factors, it is important that a means of standardizing fluidity be available. Although the addition of rather large amounts of oil makes phosphatides more fluid, it also decreases the concentration of the desired ingredient. Most widely used is the process described by Wiesehahn (1940) which involves the addition to the commercial phosphatide mixture of 2 to 20 per cent of higher fatty acids such as stearic acid. The obvious disadvantage of this method is that the acid number of the phosphatides is increased appreciably. This is overcome by the observation (Wittcoff, 1949) that the addition of 5 to 10 per cent of fatty acid esters such as methyl oleate accomplishes the same purpose. When the oil carrier present is replaced by a lower aliphatic monohydric alcohol ester of higher fatty acids, a marked increase in fluidity is also observed.

A patent issued to Markley (1950) describes specifically the fluidizing effect on phosphatides of small quantities of oleic or sorbic acid. The addition of strong acids such as those described in the patents issued to Julian and Meyer (see p. 500) also serve to fluidize phosphatides.

The specific use of castor oil acids, either alone or in the presence of small quantities of polyaminoethyl alcohols, has been described by Braun and Rosenbusch (1939) as a means of fluidizing phosphatides.

According to a patent issued to Riedel and de Haën A.–G. (1923), the substitution of palm kernel oil for the usual oil carriers serves to fluidize phosphatides because this fat is composed predominantly of fatty acids with fewer than 16 carbon atoms.

Chemical Modifications of Phosphatides

Sulfonation. The sulfonation or sulfation of phosphatides (see p. 61) serves to make them more water-soluble and supposedly to enhance their emulsifying and wetting properties. Typical sulfonation techniques are those described by Strauch (1937, 1938), who suggests as sulfonating agents concentrated or 70 per cent sulfuric acid, sulfuric acid monohydrate, sulfur trioxide, oleum, chlorosulphonic acid or mixtures of these. The sulfonations are ordinarily carried out in the presence of solvents at temperatures below 10° C. Dehydrating agents such as acetic anhydride may be included. At least 60 per cent of sulfonating agent based on the weight of the phosphatide is used. Similar procedures are described in patents issued to Chemische Fabrik Stockhausen and Cie (1936, 1938).

Dziengel (1942a) has increased the water solubility of phosphatides by heating them in acid or alkaline medium with neutral or acid sulfites in the presence of a solvent. In a subsequent patent (Dziengel, 1943), the sulfonation of these adducts is described.

Several patents (Rosenthal, 1939; Kimbara and Rosenthal, 1940; Chemische Fabrik Stockhausen and Cie, 1940) describe the sulfonation of phosphatides in the presence of aldehydes such as acrolein or croton-aldehyde which apparently enter into the reaction. The alternative use of ketones, alcohols, carboxylic acids and even aromatic hydrocarbons is mentioned.

Halogenation. The addition of halogen or halogen-containing acids to the double bonds of phosphatide fatty acids has already been discussed (see p. 61). This type of reaction also forms the basis for several older patents. The direct bromination of phosphatides in the presence of a solvent such as chloroform is described in patents issued to Aktiengesell-schaft für Anilin Fabrikation (1904) and to Bergell (1905, 1918). The reaction of phosphatides with hydrogen iodide in carbon tetrachloride solution has been described by Richter (1908). The reaction of ferric bromide or iodide with phosphatides in alcohol solution has been patented by Chemische Fabrik Gedeon Richter (1910).

Hydrogenation. The hydrogenation (see p. 60) of the unsaturated fatty acid residues in the phosphatide molecule takes place in warm alcoholic solution in the presence of platinum or palladium catalysts (Riedel Akt.-Ges., 1911). The hydrogenation of phosphatides in the presence of triglycerides and other naturally associated impurities has been described by Baumann and Grossfeld (1919). The hydrogenated material is more readily purified than the natural product.

Shinozaki and Sato (1934) have used nickel catalysts at pressures above 80 atmospheres for the hydrogenation of lecithin. The hydrogen-ated product is said to enhance the emulsifying power of cocoa butter more than the normal product.

Arveson (1942) has found that a mixture of hydrogenated phospha-tides and organic amines is effective in preventing sludge formation in lubricating oils.

Hydration. The formation of stable hydrates of phosphatides has been described by Lund (1937) and by Voss, Fromm and Man (1937). The hydration procedure involves the stratification of 15 to 25 per cent oil-containing phosphatides in aqueous alcohol, the bulk of which is water. The pH is maintained at 4.0 to 6.0 by using materials such as phosphoric acid, sodium acetate or sodium lactate. Three layers form, the lowest of which contains the bulk of the phosphatides in the form of a hydrate. Most of the oil is in the middle layer. The syrupy hydrate is said to be very stable and to form emulsions readily with water. It is also soluble in oils.

Metallic Complexes. The phosphatides as components of complex systems have already been discussed (see p. 94). Various metallic complexes have been described in the patent literature, usually for therapeutic purposes. Linden, Meissen and Strauss (1913) have prepared copper complexes which are said to be tuberculostatic.

Liebrecht (1930) has reacted high molecular weight bismuth salts such as bismuth quinine iodide, bismuth cholate, bismuth 2-phenylquinoline-4-carboxylate and bismuth trichlorobutyl malonate with phosphatides. The products were proposed as therapeutic agents for syphilis. For a similar purpose a phosphatide-arsenic complex has been prepared by the use of arsenic acid (Hoffmann-LaRoche & Co., 1914). Complexes made with ferric chloride and iodine have been described by Kruft (1913).

Levis (1949) has reacted phosphatides, with or without an oil carrier, with the copper, iron, calcium or manganese salts of phytic acid. These substances also are said to have therapeutic value.

Miscellaneous. The interaction of phosphatides and epoxides such as ethylene oxide, propylene oxide or glycidol has been described by De Groote and Keiser (1943). The products are resinous in nature with improved solubility in water. Trueger and Sprague (1947) have patented a reaction product prepared by interacting phosphatides containing the cephalin fraction with 2-nitrobutan-1-ol. The product is acetone-soluble and is said to be valuable as an additive to oils.

The mercuration of the double bonds of phosphatides has been carried out by Schoeller and Schrauth (1911).

The hydroxylation of the unsaturated fatty acid residues of commercial phosphatides has been described by Wittcoff (1948). Hydrogen peroxide in acidic medium is a suitable hydroxylating reagent, and the product is stable even in the absence of the usual oleaginous carriers.

CHAPTER XXVII

THE INDUSTRIAL USES OF PHOSPHATIDES

INTRODUCTION

The ability of phosphatides to function as protective colloids in both aqueous and fatty media, as wetting and emulsifying agents, as moisture absorbents, and as antioxidants contributes to the wide variety of industrial uses discussed below. In food manufacture, phosphatides are used in chocolate preparation, in bread, pastries and other baked goods, in oleomargarine manufacture, in candy formulation, in shortenings and in a variety of other products. Thus the largest quantities of phosphatides are consumed in the manufacture of edible products. Phosphatides may also be incorporated into products of the petroleum industry as well as into rubber, leather, protective coatings and printing inks. Their use in textile and plastic fabrication has been described, as has their incorporation into soaps and a variety of other products. The antioxidant activity of phosphatides is the subject of numerous studies, and the ability of the phosphatides to act as emulsifying agents has made them useful in a variety of pharmaceutical and industrial products.

The industrial uses of phosphatides have been reviewed by Stanley (1946, p. 263), Markley and Goss (1944, p. 110), Hilty (1948), Eichberg (1939), Wiesehahn (1937), Working (1936) and Rewald (1933b).

FOOD USES

Chocolate

Phosphatides are used extensively in the United States as additives to chocolate, primarily because they act as viscosity-reducing agents. As would be expected, the cocoa butter does not wet the sugar of chocolate unless aided by an external emulsifying or wetting agent. The phosphatides facilitate the wetting action and, in general, assure more complete mixing of the other ingredients which may include shortening, butter and water. As a result, when approximately 0.3 per cent phosphatide is used, a viscosity reduction as great as 50 per cent may result. This has been demonstrated graphically by Cook (1949). At the same time, as pointed out by Working (1930), it is possible to lower the cocoa butter content from 35 to 30 per cent. Similar results were reported by Rewald and Höfling (1932) and by Lefèvre-Lebeau (1934), all of whom agree that in the presence of phosphatides, less cocoa butter is required in order to attain the fluidity which modern high-speed equipment demands. The phosphatides are also said to protect the chocolate from imbibition of moisture (Langwill, 1939), which is undesirable since moisture increases the viscosity of the chocolate. For this purpose, 0.5 per cent is normally used. However, Erb and Collins (1939) have pointed out that a small amount of moisture is necessary in order for the phosphatides to exert their maximum effect.

The viscosity relationships were studied by Avent and Morgan (1932), who pointed out the importance of the phosphatides in reducing surface tension. The maximum reduction of interfacial tension between cocoa butter and water was effected by 1 per cent of phosphatides, whereas 0.5 per cent caused the maximum decrease in viscosity.

Phosphatides are said also to improve the keeping qualities of chocolate (Langwill, 1939) and to prevent the disappearance of gloss (Bollmann and Rewald, 1929). Working (1930) claimed that the addition of 0.1 to 1.0 per cent phosphatides prevented "greying" or "blooming" of chocolate, which ordinarily is attributed to the crystallization of the fat at the surface. Clayton and co-workers (1937), on the other hand, are of the opinion that only a slight beneficial effect results. The effect of a variety of materials on the crystallization of cocoa butter in chocolate has been studied by Karpov (1941).

According to Julian, Meyer and Iveson (1945a), the product obtained by them by the methylation of the cephalin fraction is valuable for reducing the viscosity of chocolate. Jordan (1941) has found that a condensation product of lanolin and phosphorus pentoxide behaves similarly, whereas Voroshilova and Pisarev (1941) have shown that triethanolamine lowers the viscosity of chocolate, although not as effectively as do phosphatides.

Margarine

Commercial margarine may be considered as an emulsion of cultured or ripened skim milk in edible fat. Numerous fats may be used, although cottonseed and soybean oils are the most important vegetable oils in this country, and lard is the most important animal fat. Coconut oil, hydrogenated whale oil and palm oil are popular in Europe. In order to improve the emulsifying properties of the margarine and to cause it to resemble butter more closely—which, incidentally, does contain phosphatides (Ritter and Nussbaumer, 1937)—it was originally common practice, especially in Europe, to add egg yolk (Reynolds and Epstein, 1931). This was eventually replaced by commercial phosphatides, the use of which was proposed a number of years ago in several patents (Bollmann, 1925a; Riedel and de Haën, A.–G., 1926; Rewald, 1933a). The largest outlet for phosphatides in Europe at the present time is in margarine manufacture.

The addition of phosphatides is said to impart a more uniform, butterlike texture and better spreading consistency and shortening value to the margarine. The dispersion or intermixing of fats of different melting points is probably improved, and it is claimed that the retention of salt is facilitated. The phosphatides may also exert antioxidant properties. The effect on digestibility has not been adequately studied. Most important is the fact that the phosphatides prevent spattering during the frying process (Rosenbusch and Reverey, 1927), facilitate browning and prevent the milk solids from sticking to the pan during frying. When the margarine is heated, water is lost, causing the milk solids to precipitate. When phosphatides are present at the fat-water interface, they impede the coalescence of the water to the extent that water evolution is gradual—i.e., the product does not foam badly—and thus there are no big droplets to spatter. At the same time, the phosphatides lower the surface tension of the fat, allowing it to coat the milk solids so that they do not stick to the pan. The affinity of the phosphatides for water prevents syneresis or "bleeding" on storage. Modern processing techniques also help to eliminate this latter condition.

The phosphatides may be added at any stage, although it is convenient to incorporate them in the churn. The quantity added, based on the fat content, is usually 0.1 to 0.5 per cent.

According to Conway and May (1934), a portion of the phosphatides is lost during the churning process, and this may be corrected if the phosphatides are added in the presence of condensed or dried milk. Mixtures of cholesterol and phosphatides for incorporation into margarine have also formed the basis for patents (Aktiengesellschaft für medizinische Produkte, 1935, 1936).

Rewald (1933c) has described a phosphatide-oil emulsion prepared with the aid of benzyl alcohol which is said to be well-suited for margarine manufacture.

The use of mono- and diglycerides as emulsifying agents for margarine is common, especially in the United States. These, however, have no antispattering action, although the sodium sulfoacetate derivative of these (Harris, 1933) is said to be an effective antispattering agent. Patents issued to Epstein and Harris (1936, 1937) and to Stanley (1946a) propose that a mixture of phosphatides and partial esters of glycerol be used.

A patent issued to Hanseatische Mühlenwerke A.–G. (1932a) claims that the color and other properties of natural butter may be improved by the addition of phosphatides.

Shortening

Although the use of phosphatides in shortenings has been advocated rather extensively, their use in such materials, other than as an antioxidant, appears to be rather limited. They appear to be effective in lowering the interfacial tension of shortening (Bailey, 1945, p. 245) but do not appear to be as effective as other materials in making the shortening sufficiently "strong" so that a higher than ordinary ratio of sugar to flour may be used. Nevertheless, there are patents advocating the use of phosphatides or modified phosphatides for this purpose (Morris, 1938; Thurman, 1940b; Thurman, 1942a, 1942c).

Phosphatides in concentrations of 0.5 to 2.0 per cent are also said to increase the homogeneity of compound fats, to cause more uniform distribution of the shortening in the dough, and to improve air retention, lubricating properties and shortening value (Working, 1931; Jordan, 1933).

Shortenings said to increase the quality of baked goods are described in patents issued to Chapin (1946) and to North, Alton and Little (1946). These shortenings consist of particles of fat encased in buttermilk, soybean milk or skim milk solids. Phosphatides and alginates are present in the coatings to facilitate their water dispersibility and their uniform distribution through the dough. The products are granular, nongreasy and siftable.

A recent patent issued to Markley (1950) describes a shortening containing 2 to 5 per cent phosphatides and 0.1 to 0.2 per cent oleic acid. This material is said to be fluid and to yield bread with a softer, silkier crumb.

Antioxidants

The antioxidant activity of the phosphatides has already been discussed in general (see p. 454). Although unequivocal evidence for such activity remains yet to be established, the literature contains numerous references to the effectiveness of commercial phosphatide mixtures as antioxidants. A review article on this subject has been written by Bibby (1945) and a general review on fat stabilization has been published by Lundberg (1947).

Procedures for evaluating antioxidants and their limitations have been discussed by Riemenschneider and co-workers (1945) and by Piskur (1946).

Several workers are of the opinion that phosphatides are active in preventing the rancidity of lard (Thurman, 1940b; Bollmann, 1923; Nagy, Vibrans and Kraybill, 1944; Douglass, 1937). The antioxygenic effect of phosphatides on lard is greater when supported synergistically by other antioxidants such as propyl gallate (Hall, 1949).

Phosphatides are believed by Täufel and Köchling (1939) to be effective antioxidants for olive, peanut and poppyseed oils as well as for lard. This activity is not destroyed when the oil is heated. Nakamura and Tomita (1940), on the other hand, found that soybean phosphatides exerted very little protective action for soybean oil. Similarly, Royce (1931) found that phosphatides were only weak antioxidants for cottonseed oil and hydrogenated shortening.

Diemair, Ludwig and Weiss (1943) studied the antioxidant effect of various substances on ethyl oleate and methyl linoleate and concluded that oatmeal phosphatides and lecithin were good antioxidants. Phosphatides in proportions of 0.1 per cent appear to be effective antioxidants for plastic oleo oil (Bailey, 1945, p. 230). Dhar and Aggarwal (1949) found that whereas soybean phosphatides were antioxidants for ghee and hydrogenated vegetable oil, egg phosphatides were effective for vegetable oil but not for ghee. Evans (1935) found that phosphatides are effective stabilizers for cottonseed oil.

Commercial phosphatides were found by Bailey and Feuge (1944) to be effective antioxidants for partially hydrogenated peanut oil in quantities of 0.1 per cent. Phosphoric acid in smaller quantities was equally effective. These could be added either before or after steam deodorization. If the antioxidants are to be used on a partially oxidized oil, however, it was found that addition prior to deodorization was more effective. The oils used in this study contain tocopherols, for which reason a synergistic effect was probably observed.

Scharf (1947) has patented a procedure for stabilizing cottonseed oil which involves heating the oil to about 204° C., cooling it to 149° C. and adding up to 1 per cent phosphatides.

The enhancement of the antioxidant effect of phosphatides by the phenomenon of synergism has been explored extensively. Swift, Rose and Jamieson (1942) showed that such an effect occurred between tocopherols and the cephalin fraction of crude phosphatides since the antioxygenic effect of the combined substances was greater than the sum of the individual effects. They used distilled methyl esters of cottonseed oil as a subtrate. Tocopherols and soybean phosphatides were shown by Riemenschneider and co-workers (1944) to be an active antioxidant combination for lard.

A patent to Mitchell (1938) claims that oleo oils and shortenings may be stabilized by addition of phosphatides and hydrogenated soybean oil. Since the latter material contains tocopherols, a synergistic effect is probably being exercised here, too. Phosphatide preparations themselves may contain tocopherols although these are removed if acetone washing is employed during processing.

Other types of synergistic activity have also been described. Musher (1940) has patented mixtures of carbohydrates and phosphatides as antioxidants for lard and similar compounds. Hall and Gershbein (1949) have patented a ternary combination comprising phosphatides, tocopherols and low molecular weight esters of gallic acid. Stirton, Turer and Riemenschneider (1945) found that a mixture of α-tocopherol, soybean phosphatides and d-isoascorbyl palmitate was antioxygenic for methyl linoleate, methyl oleate and distilled methyl esters of lard. This is described in detail in a patent issued to Riemenschneider and Turer (1945). These same workers (Riemenschneider and Turer, 1945a) have patented antioxygenic compositions containing soybean phosphatides, sodium carbonate, sodium stearate and d-isoascorbyl palmitate. A more recent patent (Riemenschneider and Turer, 1948) describes antioxidant compositions containing phosphatides, fatty monoesters of ascorbic acid and a saturated aliphatic monobasic acid of 12 to 18 carbon atoms.

Of interest is the work of El-Rafey, Richardson and Henderson (1944), who showed that butter oil is more resistant to oxidation when prepared by a process employing a temperature of 110° C. than when a lower temperature is used. It was thus postulated that the higher temperature caused a denaturation of the protein of the phosphatide-protein complex in the fat globule membrane. This permitted the phosphatides to be incorporated into the oil phase. These acted as antioxidants alone and also, possibly, in synergistic combination with reducing substances which may be present. It is possible also that the heat destroyed any prooxidants present.

The use of phosphatides as antioxidants for Vitamin A or carotene-containing oils has received considerable study (Holmes, 1936). The marked synergistic effect of phosphatides and hydroquinone in Vitamin A stabilization has been discussed by Holmes, Corbet and Hartzler (1936). The oxidation of carotene in soybean and hemp seed oil was inhibited by lecithin, as shown by Süllmann (1941). The stabilizing effect of phosphatides alone and combined with other antioxidants for carotene dissolved in cottonseed oil and in mineral oil was studied by Williams, Bickoff and Lowrimore (1944).

Buxton (1947) found that 1.0 per cent phosphatides enhance the effectiveness of natural and synthetic α-tocopherols as inhibitors of Vitamin A destruction. Kern, Antoshkiw and Maiese (1949) found that 4 per cent phosphatides offered protection for Vitamin A diluted with cottonseed oil. A combination of 4 per cent phosphatides and 2 per cent tocopherols gave even greater protection. Feigenbaum (1946) has found that soybean phosphatides were effective antioxidants for Vitamin A-fortified margarine.

A British patent (National Oil Products Co., 1947) claims that the antioxidant activity of phosphatides for Vitamin A may be enhanced by refluxing the phosphatides with acetone and ammonia. In this same vein, Buxton and Dryden (1950) have found that the treatment of phosphatides with ammonia greatly enhances their antioxidant effect on fatty materials.

Taub and Simone (1947) have patented mixtures of phosphatides and nicotinic acid or its derivatives as antioxidants for Vitamins A or D.

Synthetic materials related to phosphatides have also been postulated to be antioxidants. Royce (1938) patented synthetic lysophosphatides as superior antioxidants. Eckey (1935) and Richardson (1938) claimed that phosphoric acid and related substances are antioxidants for oils.

Suggestions are fairly frequent in the literature that phosphatides or their decomposition products are responsible for flavor reversion in products such as soybean oil (Golumbic and Daubert, 1947; Goss, 1946), milk (Brown and Thurston, 1940; Dahle and Josephson, 1943), butter (Hartmann, 1947; Van der Waarden, 1947) and eggs (Edwards and Dutton, 1945; Fevold and co-workers, 1946). Storgårds and Hietaranta (1949) are of the opinion that linoleic acid and not lecithin is responsible for the fishy flavor which develops in butter. Obviously there is much here which remains to be defined, especially in relation to the antioxidant activity of the phosphatides.

Bakery Goods

The use of phosphatides in bakery goods appears to be increasing. Originally, phosphatides were used only in icings and coatings where they appear to promote better flow, higher gloss and greater volume, probably because the wetting of the sugar by the shortening is facilitated.

When quantities up to 2 per cent are used in bread dough or cake batters, the shortening effect is said to be improved, as indicated above, probably by promoting better mixing and dispersion. In addition

(Working, 1931; Jordan, 1935; Kühl, 1935; Rewald, 1936a; Schweiger, 1938), the products are more tender and have a more uniform structure. Improvement in flavor retention is claimed. Thiele (1932) is of the opinion that phosphatides nourish the yeast and increase the dilatability of the gluten. Yeast-raised doughs (Jordan, 1933) are said in the presence of phosphatides to provide products of improved structure and crumb and greater shelf-life. A trace of phosphatides may also promote browning and thus improve color. The doughs may be machined more easily and the webs and dies are said to be left cleaner.

Many of the phosphatide modifications previously described, especially those with carriers such as sugar, salt and lactic acid, are said to provide improved compositions for baking. Gmünder (1947) has described a baking aid comprising malt and phosphatides which accelerates fermentation, increases lightness of the dough and improves keeping qualities.

One of the earliest studies of the action of phosphatides on bread dough was made by Working (1928), who concluded that phosphatides serve to reduce the tensile strength of the gluten strands by aiding the absorption of water. In addition, the ductility of the dough is increased because the phosphatides lubricate the gluten strands.

Several articles describe the technical aspects of employing phosphatides in bread baking (Pratt, 1946; Anonymous, 1947). The use of phosphatides in bakery goods in general is discussed by Cook (1947, 1945).

Macaroni and Noodles

The use of phosphatides in the manufacture of alimentary pastes such as noodles and macaroni is of long standing, especially in Europe (Hanseatische Mühlenwerke A.-G., 1925; Jesser, 1934; Niescher, 1940). They are said to prevent disintegration and to preserve the shape, on cooking, of noodles or macaroni made from "soft" or low-protein wheat flour. Ziegelmayer (1930) explains this on the basis that a protein-lipide adsorption complex is formed which prevents the imbibition of water by the swelling colloids, which otherwise would form sols. This observation is not important in the United States where high protein flour is available. The phosphatides also prevent syneresis of the dough (Nottbohm and Mayer, 1933).

According to Winston and Jacobs (1947), phosphatides inhibit the oxidation of pigments in macaroni, thus causing greater retention of the yellow color. The general quality of the cooked product is also improved since increases in weight and volume take place. A means for detecting phosphatides in alimentary pastes, based on their ability to fluoresce under ultraviolet light, has been described by Winston and Jacobs (1945).

Candy

Jordan (1932) has described the beneficial action exerted by phosphatides during the manufacture of fat-containing candy such as caramels, brittles, nougats and taffies. The sugar and the oil ordinarily mix only with great difficulty, and demonstrate a tendency to separate on cooling. The phosphatides serve as an emulsifying agent which causes these phases, together with water, to intermix rapidly and distribute evenly. Thus greasiness, graining and streaking is prevented (Langwill, 1939; Cook, 1945a). Since the fat does not come to the surface, the freshness of the candy is maintained.

The use of hydroxylated phosphatides (see p. 503) as components which improve starch molding compositions for candy has been patented by Glabe (1950).

Ice Cream

According to Stanley (1942, 1946, p. 265), the addition of 0.5 per cent phosphatides to ice cream increases the smoothness of the product and prevents "sandiness" on storage even when the solids content is high. It also is said to stabilize the fat and reduce the quantity of egg yolk needed. The advantages of using phosphatides in chocolate ice cream manufacture have been outlined by Masurovsky (1945). The use of a small quantity of phosphatides in ice-cream mixes, powdered milk or powdered cream has been described by North and Alton (1946) and by Snyder (1949). Bigelow (1947) has patented the use of a mixture of phosphatides and sugar as a stabilizer for ice cream.

Miscellaneous Food Uses

Bollmann (1928b) has described the use of phosphatides as a protective colloid for "solubilizing" cocoa powder to the extent that the solid particles and the fat droplets do not separate in the dispersing medium. The determination of phosphatides in cocoa products may be carried out according to a procedure described by Bornmann (1942). Phosphatides also function as protective colloids in dried soups and sauces (Hanseatische Mühlenwerke, A.–G., 1934b).

The use of phosphatides in winterized cottonseed oil in order to inhibit crystallization has been patented by Grettie (1936). On the other hand, Brown (1946) discloses the use of 0.1–2.0 per cent phosphatides as an additive to oil prior to winterization in order to obtain harder, more easily separated crystals, on cooling. A patent of a similar nature has been issued to Gooding and Rich (1948). Wolff and Guellerin (1937) are of the opinion that phosphatides should be added to olive oil after they have been removed by refining processes.

Phosphatides increase the smoothness and decrease the tackiness and cohesiveness of chewing gum, according to Conner (1940). Cohoe (1949) also recommends the use of phosphatides in chewing gum.

Schmidt (1944) is of the opinion that small quantities of phosphatides may replace egg yolks in baking. Rewald (1930) has obtained a patent on a phosphatide composition to be used as an egg yolk substitute. It is not possible, however, to use phosphatides as an egg yolk substitute for mayonnaise (Sell, Olsen and Kremers, 1935).

Phosphatides are said to increase cohesion and prevent crumbliness when incorporated into cheese (Hanseatische Mühlenwerke A.–G., 1934a).

According to Jordan (1935), a small amount of phosphatide aids in the distribution and fixation of volatile flavoring agents. A patent issued to Thurman (1940c) claims that phosphatides impart beneficial properties to a large variety of foods including peanut butter, sandwich spreads, soups, sauces, catsup, prepared milk products, gelatin desserts, corn starch, chocolate puddings and beverages.

Pässler (1940) describes the use of phosphatides in the homogenization of milk which subsequently is converted by lactic acid bacillus to cheese which contains phosphatides. The phosphatides serve to fix the flavor of the cheese.

Schultz and Frey (1939) have employed phosphatides to reduce the tendency of yeast to crumble and to improve its color.

A patent granted to Allingham (1949) describes the use of a hydrous mixture of phosphatides and Irish moss gel as a protective coating for meat.

The use of phosphatides as a stabilizer for frozen desserts has been discussed by Masurovsky (1942). They have also been proposed as stabilizers for artificial cream (Sandelin, 1939). Schantz and co-workers (1940) studied the nutritive effect of adding 0.25 to 0.5 per cent egg lecithin to corn oil or coconut oil which later was homogenized with skim milk. Although the nutritive value of the oil was improved by addition of phosphatides, it was not equal to that of butterfat.

Phosphatides have been used as stabilizers for synthetic spices based on cinnamaldehyde (Rapaport, 1948).

Phosphatides function as emulsifying agents in the preparation of fat emulsions for parenteral nutrition, as shown by Geyer, Mann and Stare (1948). A patent issued to Klein and Grosse (1936) describes the use of phosphatides as emulsifiers for a variety of pharmaceuticals in order to prepare emulsions suitable for injection.

A patent to Bollmann (1927) describes an emulsion of coconut oil and water prepared with the aid of phosphatides.

Other miscellaneous uses are discussed by Cook (1945a, 1945b).

Petroleum Derivatives

Phosphatides are used at present as additives to hydrocarbon lubricants in order to inhibit gum formation (Jacobs and Othmer, 1943). An early patent describing this use was issued to Sollmann (1932), who claimed that 0.5 per cent soybean phosphatides served to extend the life of lubricating oil. The phosphatide serves not only as an antioxidant but also as a detergent which counteracts varnish and sludge formation. An increase in viscosity and acid formation in the lubricant is also said to be prevented by the phosphatides. According to Hendrey (1940), Oosterhout and Quimby (1940), and Benning (1939), 0.1–1.0 per cent phosphatides when added to lubricating oils reduces bearing corrosion and ring sticking in automotive engines. Similar activity is claimed by Musher (1940a) for an additive comprising a mixture of soybean phosphatides and an aromatic polyfunctional compound. Other patents (Ashburn and Alsop, 1940; Hall and Towne, 1941; Jacobs, 1946) likewise describe the advantages of adding phosphatides to lubricating oils in order to inhibit corrosion of bearings and the formation of sludge and varnish. A patent issued to Proell (1948) indicates that phosphatides prevent clogging of fine passages of fuel oil burners and diesel engines.

According to Ashburn and Alsop (1940), phosphatides may be used in lubricating oils as corrosion inhibitors in conjunction with alkali metal naphthenates which prevent formation of emulsions. A patent issued to Adams, Brunstrum and Weitkamp (1942) describes the use of phosphatides to solubilize calcium stearate in lubricating oils.

The tendency of phosphatides to cause foam formation in lubricants may be inhibited, according to Julian and Meyer (1945b), by the coincident use of acidic substances such as mineral, sulfonic or fatty acids. A pH of about 2 appears to be optimum.

The combined use of phosphatides and sulfur-containing compounds such as thiodiphenylamine or phenyl sulfide has been patented by Musher (1946) as a means of preventing sludge formation in lubricating oils. Trueger (1947) has reacted phosphatides with thiocyanogen in order to obtain sulfur-containing lipides which are said to function effectively for inhibiting deterioration of lubricating oils.

A patent issued to Loane (1942) describes the interaction of phosphatides with aromatic amines such as pyridine or quinoline in order to obtain additives for lubricating oils. A patent granted to Arveson (1942) is similar, save that the use of hydrogenated phosphatides is specified.

The use of phosphatides as stabilizers for gasoline has also undergone considerable investigation. Eichberg (1941) has pointed out that 1 to

10 pounds of phosphatide per 1000 barrels of gasoline stabilizes lead tetraethyl-containing gasolines against cloud formation, color change and aluminum and other metal corrosion. Rees, Quimby and Oosterhout (1940) have also described work leading to similar conclusions. A possible explanation for the effectiveness of phosphatides as stabilizers for gasoline has been advanced by Allen (1945). He proposes either that the phosphatides form an inert layer which retards the diffusion of oxygen into the gasoline or else that the phosphatides are preferentially attacked by oxygen. He points out further that the source of the oxygen may be the water over which the gasoline is stored. A patent issued to Rathbun (1940) claims that soybean phosphatides together with anthracene help to maintain the octane value of leaded fuels and to prevent corrosion and clogging of fuel tanks and lines. Oosterhout (1939) has also patented the use of phosphatides as stabilizers for leaded gasoline, whereas Rees and Oosterhout (1939) have proposed the use of phosphatides in the presence of an aromatic amine or phenol. According to Bell (1944), phosphatides are effective as stabilizers for gasoline containing metal carbonyl compounds. A solidified motor fuel in which phosphated, oxidized, or sulfated phosphatides have been used as the agent for gelation has been described by Wiczer (1945).

Textiles

The possibility of using phosphatides in the textile industry was recognized early in the commercial development of this product, especially in Europe, and there are numerous patents which describe the advantages to be gained. Most of these advantages are resident in the emulsifying and unusual softening properties of the phosphatides. Much of this work has been reviewed by Mecheels (1931), by Tatu (1934), and by Schwarz (1940, 1940a), who point out that neutral or alkaline emulsions of the phosphatide are preferable since they are not suitable for acid baths. These emulsions, among other things, provide lubrication for cotton during spinning (Detwiler and co-workers, 1935) as well as for wool, and perhaps most important serve as softening and finishing agents for rayon and other fabrics whose "hand feel" they improve (Rewald, 1935). They are also effective as additives in kier-boiling.

Ohl (1931, 1934) points out that textile and rayon oils containing phosphatides penetrate the fibers more deeply and spread more uniformly in thin films. Phosphatides also serve as stabilizing agents in the bleaching of rayon and other synthetic yarns. Lederer (1933) states that phosphatides used in wet doubling solutions serve to "load" the yarn and to impart a luster which remains after mercerization. In the mercerizing bath it serves as a wetting-out agent. Mixtures of phosphatides and cation-active substances are useful for treating both textiles and leather since they impart to these substances a soft feel and good draping qualities (Roth, 1945).

Phosphatides have also been proposed as stabilizers for synthetic fibers spun from soybean proteins (Kazita and Inoue, 1940).

Phosphatides are of value in the dyeing of textiles, as pointed out in patents issued to Bollmann and Rewald (1930) and to the Hanseatische Mühlenwerke, A.–G. (1932b). They are said to cause more even and thorough dyeing and to enhance the brilliancy of the colors. They may be used with cotton, wool, silk and rayon where they cause better penetration of the dyes. They also facilitate removal of the oil from the fabric prior to dyeing. Another patent issued to Hanseatische Mühlenwerke, A.–G. (1934c) describes the use of phosphatides as thickening agents in the dyeing of rayon and as color intensifiers in calico printing pastes. Rewald (1935a) also describes the use of phosphatides in printing fabrics where they may be used with starch as a thickening agent, replacing some or all of the expensive gums ordinarily used. According to Bolen (1936), phosphatides prevent the premature oxidation of the leuco form of vat dyes.

Various modified phosphatides have been proposed for use in textiles. These include hydrated phosphatides (Lund, 1937) and sulfonated phosphatides (Bollmann and Rewald, 1927f). The use of urea to facilitate the emulsification of phosphatides for use in textile processing has been proposed by Feibelmann (1940). According to Schweiger (1935), phosphatides, free of oil, may be mixed with 10 per cent by weight of sodium hydroxide to obtain a readily emulsifiable material for use in the textile industry.

Other patents, in addition to those cited above, which describe the use of phosphatides in the textile industry have been granted to Bollmann and Rewald (1930a); I. G. Farbenind., A.–G. (1933a); Rewald (1934a); Frey and Jozsa (1940); Dreyfus and Whitehead (1932) and Freund (1935).

Leather

Phosphatides were originally proposed in the leather trade as substitutes for the more costly egg yolk which was widely used in tanning processes (Rewald, 1928; Oranienburger Chemische Fabrik, A.–G., 1928; Bollmann and Rewald, 1927e; Rewald, 1930a; Thiele and Sisley, 1949). A 10 per cent emulsion has been found practical.

When phosphatides are incorporated into fat liquors (Bollmann and Rewald, 1928; Auerbach, 1929; Anonymous, 1929), they impart softness to the leather without impairing tensile strength, and for this application approximately 1 per cent is used. According to Rewald (1928a), the phosphatides cause the oil to penetrate into the hide more readily, thus providing a pliable finished product with a minimum amount of "working". A composition consisting of phosphatides and lactic acid has been proposed as an additive to the fat liquor by Rewald (1937a).

The use of phosphatides in leather dressings and greases has also been proposed (Bollmann and Rewald, 1927a, 1927b, 1927c, 1927d). Rewald (1932) points out that phosphatides have a greater affinity for leather than sulfonated oils and describes (Rewald, 1930a) dressings consisting of phosphatides in aqueous emulsions or mixed with oils. Dressings may also be prepared with phosphatides and water-miscible solvents (Oranienburger Chemische Fabrik A.–G., 1928).

Rewald (1935b) has proposed for use in the leather and textile industries a mixture of phosphatides from which the oil has been removed and an emulsifying agent such as sulfonated castor oil has been added. Mixtures of phosphatides, bleached with hydrogen peroxide and water glass, have been described as useful for the fabrication of leather, textiles and soap in a patent issued to Noblee and Thörl G.m.b.H. (1935).

Protective Coatings

The use of phosphatides in the protective coating industry is comparatively recent, although Merz and Wagner (1932) pointed out some years ago that phosphatides may impart valuable properties to paint. They serve as wetting and dispersing agents since they are effective in producing pigment stability. They also prevent the settling of pigments and make possible maximum color strength. This is also true in water paints where the phosphatides serve in addition to stabilize the emulsion (Anonymous, 1948a; Stieg, 1945). Phosphatides, furthermore, are believed to aid in the grinding of pigments which are wet with difficulty (New York Paint Varnish & Production Club, 1935, 1936; Figaret, 1947). Their use to facilitate the pigmentation of varnishes and lacquers has been described by Schlack (1934). Saunders and Downs (1938) have incorporated phosphatides into "pulped" pigments such as those containing lithopone. When these, in turn, are incorporated into vehicles such as linseed oil, a less grainy, more free-flowing suspension results and the pigment is said to have better texture, greater softness, and a high degree of whiteness and opacity. Ordinarily about 1 per cent phosphatides is used on a pigment basis.

Phosphatides also help to control the "sagging" often exhibited by architectural enamels formulated from alkyd resins. They are said to improve the brushing power of these compositions without affecting gloss or drying properties. The presence of phosphatides helps to correct "flooding" especially with chrome pigments. The covering power of such enamels is also improved by the presence of phosphatides (Anonymous, 1948a).

Bollmann and Rewald (1929a) have described a procedure for using phosphatides to emulsify casein which has been solubilized with alkali. This material was proposed as a binder for paints, which were said to have greater durability and resistance to rub-off because of the presence of the phosphatides. Fincke (1930) has pointed out that paints containing phosphatides may properly be made with less oil than usual.

Rubbers and Resins

Since phosphatides are present in natural rubber latex (see p. 239) the effect of adding them during rubber processing has been studied. Thus Rewald (1934b) has observed that phosphatides incorporated into rubber compositions prior to vulcanization serve as accelerators and as softening agents in addition to facilitating the mixing process. The acceleration of vulcanization by phosphatides was also observed by Minatoya and Kurahashi (1934, 1934a), who were of the opinion that they should be used only with hard rubber. The accelerating action of phosphatides on the vulcanization of rubber has also been pointed out by Esch (1934) and by Behre (1938), who found further that phosphatides in solution increased the swelling properties of latex, whereas without the solvent the opposite effect was produced.

Phosphatides are useful in the reclaiming of rubber, according to Behre (1938a), who accomplished this by heating, in the presence of steam, a mixture of oil, phosphatides and vulcanized rubber. Kirby and Steinle (1947) have found that phosphatides added prior to digestion are valuable in the process for reclaiming neoprene scrap.

Phosphatides also facilitate the incorporation and dispersion of fillers in rubber (Behre, 1938). According to Talalay (1936, 1936a), phosphatides may be heated with higher fatty acids or fatty acid soaps to give compositions useful in the manufacture of articles from vulcanized rubber. In particular, rubber treated with such compositions either before or after vulcanization does not develop undesirable tackiness.

In the fabrication of plastics and resins, phosphatides have been used as mold lubricants. They are generally milled into the molding stock and during application of pressure the phosphatides serve as efficient lubricants between the resin and the surface of the mold. As a result, the molded articles separate readily from the mold and demonstrate a smooth surface. Usually about 0.5 per cent phosphatides are used for this purpose. It is desirable to use phosphatides from which the oil has been removed by acetone extraction since the oil may impart an odor to the molded articles. The use of phosphatides which preferably are oil-free in the molding of recordings is described in two patents (Hanseatische Mühlenwerke A.-G. and Polyphonwerke A.-G., 1933; Frank, 1934) which point out that the phosphatides serve as homogenizing agents for the resinous mixtures as well as facilitating mold release. Phosphatides have also been proposed as mold release agents in the fabrication of plastic sheeting.

The use of phosphatides to prevent the flocculation of insoluble pigment particles in polymethyl methacrylate which is polymerized in the presence of the pigment is described by Gordon and Heckert (1937).

According to Auxier and Weltman (1945), phosphatides, as well as other nitrogen-containing organic compounds, function as polymerization inhibitors, stabilizing drying-oil modified phenolaldehyde resins in the "B" stage against rapid aging. Quantities of the order of 0.1 to 2.0 per cent are used.

The use of phosphatides as components of baked coating compositions based on vinyl copolymers has been patented by du Pont de Nemours & Co. (1944).

Bernstein (1946) has described a coating material prepared from a mixture of phosphatide and oil (30 to 40 per cent phosphatide) together with aluminum hydroxide and starch which, when applied to a container surface, prevents the adherence of synthetic elastomers such as butyl rubber.

Phosphatides have also been proposed as constituents of putty (Esch, 1934) and, in linoleum cement, as materials which enhance the action of the softening agents (Lehmann and Voss G.m.b.H., 1931).

Soaps

The use of phosphatides in soap fabrication is especially common in Europe primarily because of their ability to act as emulsifiers and to reduce surface and interfacial tensions (Génin, 1934). The phosphatides improve the keeping characteristics of the soap, especially if the oil present is replaced by stable fatty substances such as glyceryl monostearate, lanolin, wool wax or petroleum jelly (Anonymous, 1949). Since phosphatides are split by alkali, they must be added to the soap subsequent to the saponification step. A study by Inaba, Kitagawa and Sato (1934) showed that phosphatides, when added to soap solutions, lowered the surface tension. The drop number against kerosene was lowered if the concentration was above 0.25 per cent. The stability of the foam was enhanced, although its volume was decreased. Finally, the gold number was increased, indicating that the phosphatides inhibited the ability of the soap to act as a protective colloid.

According to Lederer (1933), the enhancement of emulsifying and lathering properties of soap by the phosphatides leads to greater cleaning efficiency. The phosphatides also inhibit hydrolysis of the soap, thus depressing the alkalinity and preventing skin irritation (Lesser, 1946). Because of this property, phosphatides may be used in soap as super-fatting agents. Trusler (1931) has found in this regard that phosphatides inhibit the rate of catalytic splitting of fats.

A German patent (Hanseatische Mühlenwerke A.–G., 1933) describes the use of phosphatides as emulsifying agents for soaps containing organic solvents such as carbon tetrachloride.

Phosphatides fluidized by the addition of castor oil fatty acids and triethanolamine have been proposed by Braun and Rosenbusch (1939) for use in soap. A mixture of bleached phosphatides and water glass has also been patented for use in soap (Noblee and Thörl G.m.b.H., 1935). Aoyama (1939) has proposed, as an additive to soap, a product prepared by treating a phosphatide solution with alkali carbonate and trihydroxy-naphthalene. The solvent is then removed and the residue treated with dilute mineral acid.

Phosphatides are also said to be of value in shaving creams (Kritchev-sky, 1939; Kröper and Thomae, 1940).

Pharmaceuticals and Proprietary Articles

The cosmetic and pharmaceutical industry has found that up to 5 per cent of phosphatides are valuable as emulsifiers and stabilizers in oint-ments, salves, creams, lotions, shampoos, bath salts, perfumes, and numer-ous other preparations. The phosphatides serve to improve the stability and penetration of compositions containing petroleum jelly, mineral oil, paraffin, and beeswax; and, in general, help to make formulation easier. They have been proposed as components of vehicles for dispersing drugs and medicinals including vitamin preparations and liver extracts. Re-views on the use of phosphatides in cosmetics and pharmaceuticals have been published by Rapp (1930), Matagrin (1936), Redgrove (1938), Belcot (1938), Augustin (1935, 1938), Schwarz (1936, 1938, 1940b), Sonol (1929), Grün (1936) and I. G. Farbenind. A.–G. (1939).

Epstein and Harris (1936) have proposed that a mixture of phospha-tides and diglycerides be used in the formulation of lipstick since the dye is dispersed readily in the presence of this combination. Schwarzkopf (1941) has included phosphatides in hair tonic and Higuti (1939) has combined phosphatides with zinc oxide and starch to obtain a product for use in skin ailments.

The use of phosphatides in an ozone-containing disinfectant has been described by Salis (1942).

Miscellaneous Non-food Uses

Many miscellaneous uses of phosphatides depend on their ability to function as emulsifiers and as agents for lowering surface tension, just as many of the uses already cited have depended on these properties. The preparation of emulsions containing phosphatides, water and oil have formed the basis of several patents. Rewald (1933c) has found that a small quantity of benzyl alcohol facilitates the formation of such emulsions. Bollmann (1934) and Engelmann (1934) have both treated phosphatides with alkaline substances in order to obtain more stable emulsions.

A patent issued to Sturgis and Baum (1947) describes the use of phosphatides in the preparation of stable dispersions of secondary amines in water. Phosphatides may be used to disperse silica in xylene, according to Damerell, Gayer and Laudenslager (1945). Koppenhoefer (1945) has patented an aqueous emulsion of petroleum oil which depends for its stability on the presence of phosphatides and a partial fatty acid ester of mannitan. Moberly (1950) has described the use of phosphatides as stabilizing agents, particularly at low temperatures for concentrated solutions of 2,2,-bis-(p-chlorophenyl)-1,1,1-trichloroethane (DDT).

The use of phosphatides as emulsifying agents for asphalt and tar has been described in patents issued to Schweiger (1935) and to Hanseatische Mühlenwerke A.–G. (1932c, 1934d).

Phosphatides have been shown (White and Vaughan, 1936; Hanseatische Mühlenwerke A.–G., 1934e) to facilitate the penetration into wood of preservatives such as creosote and mineral oil. Approximately 0.25 to 2.0 per cent phosphatides is needed.

Several patents (e.g., Bousquet, 1935) concern themselves with the use of phosphatides in insecticidal and fungicidal sprays, especially when it is necessary to disperse polar substances in oily solvents. Although Woodman (1932) is of the opinion that phosphatides are not effective emulsifiers for polyphase systems such as those found in insecticide emulsions, Bollmann and Rewald (1927g) have reported that phosphatides cause better dispersion of solid poisons such as arsenicals and improve the adhesion of these to plants. Rewald (1933d) has proposed the use of the copper salts of phosphatides in insecticide compositions.

Thurman (1946) has patented the use of cottonseed phosphatides as dispersants in aqueous insecticides containing nicotine sulfate and calcium arsenate. Steiner, Arnold and Fahey (1943) have described formulas for lead arsenate and nicotine bentonite-containing insecticides which include phosphatides for the purpose of increasing the spray deposit. An insecticidal spray containing moderately refined petroleum oil and phosphatides as oxidation inhibitors has been patented by Burkhard (1949). It is claimed that without the phosphatides more highly refined oils are necessary.

Dry disinfectants for seeds consisting of mixtures of phosphatides and salts of mercury or copper have been described by Wolff (1938).

Numerous other miscellaneous uses have formed the bases for patents. Weetman (1945) has added phosphatides to bituminous coating compositions so that better wetting of the aggregate will result. A steam cylinder lubricant based largely on mineral oil is said to be improved by the presence of small quantities of phosphatides (Adams and MacLaren, 1945).

A patent issued to Hansa-Mühle A.-G. (1936) describes a mixture of rubber and de-oiled phosphatides useful as an electrical insulator or as a linoleum cement.

Wolter (1933) has described a mixture of phosphatides, an organic salt of iron, and nitrocellulose as a sensitive layer for producing tanned photographic prints.

Phosphatides have been proposed as defoaming agents in the manufacture of paper by Fromm (1937).

Alkanolamine salts of sulfonated phosphatides may serve as demulsifying agents for petroleum emulsions, according to De Groote (1937).

The presence of phosphatides in cold swelling starch inhibits lumping, according to Möller (1939).

Adhesives of the type necessary for decalcomania transfers may be made from glue, phosphatides, glycerol and a plasticizer, according to Heberer (1939).

The possible use of phosphatides in the flotation of oxide minerals has been discussed by Sato, Nagai and Tamamushi (1946).

Both hardening and loss of absorbency of paper towels fabricated from rosin and alum-sized cellulose fibers are prevented by the presence of phosphatides (Rowland, 1940).

Musher (1943) has patented a process for making paper board free of odors which involves the use of phosphatides.

Eichberg (1944) has found that phosphatides improve the clarity and prevent the formation of turbidity in turpentine.

Hilty (1945) has reviewed the possible uses of phosphatides in ink.

The addition of 0.01 per cent phosphatides in electroplating baths has been shown to make possible the deposition of finer, denser, more uniform and more adherent coatings (Jorre and Stalmann, 1934).

The use of phosphatides as a coating for spinnerets to prevent the adherence of collagen films has been patented by Cresswell (1949).

BIBLIOGRAPHY—PART VI

Adams, E. W., and MacLaren, F. H., U. S. Pat. 2,373,733, Apr. 17 (1945); *C. A.,* **39,** 3424 (1945).

——, Brunstrum, L. C., and Weitkamp, A. W., U. S. Pat. 2,270,241, Jan. 20 (1942); *C. A.,* **36,** 3955 (1942).

Aktiengesellschaft für Anilin Fabrikation, Ger. Pat. 349,985, June 13 (1904); *C. A.,* **1,** 377 (1907).

Aktiengesellschaft für medizinische Produkte, Ger. Pat. 615,027, June 25 (1935); *C. A.,* **29,** 6322 (1935).

——, Ger. Pat. 628,250, Mar. 3 (1936); *C. A.,* **30,** 4584 (1936).

Aktieselskapet Flesland Fabrikker, Norwegian Pat. 62,726, Dec. 2 (1940); *C. A.,* **40,** 750 (1946).

Allen, F. H., *J. Inst. Petroleum,* **31,** 9 (1945); *C. A.,* **39,** 2864 (1945).

Allingham, W. J., U. S. Pat. 2,447,726, Aug. 24 (1948); *C. A.,* **42,** 8997 (1948).

——, U. S. Pat. 2,470,281, May 17 (1949); *C. A.,* **43,** 5881 (1949).

Anonymous, *Ledertech. Rundschau,* **21,** 105 (1929); *C. A.,* **23,** 4843 (1929).

——, U. S. Dept. Agr. Northern Regional Research Lab. AIC–45, 8 pp. (1944); *C. A.,* **38,** 6581 (1944).

——, *Chemical Industries,* **59,** 1016 (1946).

——, *Bakers' Weekly,* **133,** [12], 61 (1947).

——, *Food,* **17,** 41 (1948).

——, *Lacke- u. Farben-Chem.,* **2,** 35 (1948a).

——, *Soap and Sanit. Chemicals,* **25,** [10], 81 (1949).

Aoyama, K., Japanese Pat. 130,557, June 15 (1939); *C. A.,* **35,** 2024 (1941).

Arveson, M. H., U. S. Pat. 2,295,192, Sept. 8 (1942); *C. A.,* **37,** 1595 (1943).

Ashburn, H. V., and Alsop, W. G., U. S. Pat. 2,221,162, Nov. 12 (1940); *C. A.,* **35,** 1984 (1941).

——, ——, U. S. Pat. 2,244,416, June 3 (1941); *C. A.,* **35,** 6105 (1941).

Auerbach, M., *Gerber,* **55,** 209, 217 (1929); *C. A.,* **24,** 1246 (1930).

Augustin, J., *Seifensieder-Ztg.,* **62,** 174 (1935); *C. A.,* **29,** 3465 (1935).

——, *ibid.,* **65,** 633 (1938); *C. A.,* **32,** 8699 (1938).

Auxier, R. W., and Weltman, W. C., U. S. Pat. 2,383,283, Aug. 21 (1945); *C. A.,* **40,** 1060 (1946).

Avent, A. G., and Morgan, R. H., *J. Soc. Chem. Ind.,* **51,** 169 (1932); *C. A.,* **26,** 4109 (1932).

Ayres, E. E., Jr., and Clark, L. H., U. S. Pat. 1,737,402, Nov. 26 (1929); *C. A.,* **24,** 744 (1930).

Bailey, A. E., "Industrial Oil & Fat Products," New York, Interscience Publishers, Inc., 1945.

——, and Feuge, R. O., *Oil & Soap,* **21,** 286 (1944); *C. A.,* **39,** 429 (1945).

Baumann, C., and Grossfeld, J., Brit. Pat. 144,895, July 11 (1919); *C. A.,* **14,** 3127 (1920).

Beck, T. M., and Klein, G. I., U. S. Pat. 2,214,520, Sept. 10 (1940); *C. A.,* **35,** 926 (1941).

Beckel, A. C., and Belter, P. A., U. S. Pat. 2,469,147, May 3 (1949); *C. A.,* **43,** 5613 (1949).

Behre, J., U. S. Pat. 2,112,802, Mar. 29 (1938); *C. A.,* **32,** 4008 (1938).

——, U. S. Pat. 2,112,803, Mar. 29 (1938a); *C. A.,* **32,** 4010 (1938).

Belcot, E., *Curierul Farm.*, **8**, No. 2, 18; No. 3, 1 (1938); *C. A.*, **34**, 6017 (1940).

Bell, R. T., U. S. Pat. 2,365,377, Dec. 19 (1944); *C. A.*, **39**, 4750 (1945).

Belter, P. A., Beckel, A. C., and Smith, A. K., *Ind. Eng. Chem.*, **36**, 799 (1944); *C. A.*, **38**, 5616 (1944).

Benning, A. F., U. S. Pat. 2,167,867, Aug. 1 (1939); *C. A.*, **33**, 8985 (1939).

Berczeller, L., French Pat. 700,999, Aug. 23 (1930); *C. A.*, **25**, 3777 (1931).

Bergell, P., U. S. Pat. 803,541, Nov. 7 (1905).

——, Ger. Pat. 231,233, June 10 (1910); *C. A.*, **5**, 2700 (1911).

——, Ger. Pat. 307,490, (1918); *C. A.*, **13**, 1127 (1919).

——, Ger. Pat. 520,742, Jan. 22 (1928); *C. A.*, **25**, 3440 (1931).

Bernstein, I. M., U. S. Pat. 2,396,633, Mar. 19 (1946); *C. A.*, **40**, 3275 (1946).

Bibby, C. L., *Food Manuf.*, **20**, 441 (1945); *C. A.*, **40**, 907 (1946).

Bigelow, F. E., U. S. Pat. 2,430,553, Nov. 11 (1947); *C. A.*, **42**, 698 (1948).

Bolen, P., U. S. Pat. 2,020,496, Nov. 12 (1935); *C. A.*, **30**, 625 (1936).

Bollmann, H., U. S. Pat. 1,464,557, Aug. 14 (1923); *C. A.*, **17**, 3234 (1923).

——, Brit. Pat. 243,643, Dec. 3 (1925); *C. A.*, **20**, 3830 (1926).

——, Brit. Pat. 259,166, Oct. 6 (1925a); *C. A.*, **21**, 3401 (1927).

——, Ger. Pat. 485,676, Sept. 1 (1926); *C. A.*, **24**, 1184 (1930).

——, Ger. Pat. 474,879, Jan. 14 (1927); *C. A.*, **23**, 3118 (1929).

——, U. S. Pat. 1,667,767, May 1 (1928); *C. A.*, **22**, 2285 (1928).

——, Ger. Pat. 508,353, July 6 (1928a); *C. A.*, **25**, 750 (1931).

——, U. S. Pat. 1,660,541, Feb. 28 (1928b); *C. A.*, **22**, 1416 (1928).

——, Ger. Pat. 511,851, Oct. 22 (1929); *C. A.*, **25**, 1336 (1931).

——, Brit. Pat. 356,384, Oct. 21 (1929a); *C. A.*, **26**, 4418 (1932).

——, U. S. Pat. 1,776,720, Sept. 23 (1930); *C. A.*, **24**, 5437 (1930).

——, Ger. Pat. 581,763, Sept. 13 (1934); *C. A.*, **29**, 950 (1935).

——, and Rewald, B., Ger. Pat. 505,354, Dec. 22 (1927); *C. A.*, **24**, 6048 (1930).

——, ——, Ger. Pat. 514,399, July 17 (1927a); *C. A.*, **25**, 1704 (1931).

——, ——, Ger. Pat. 516,187, Sept. 7, (1927b); *C. A.*, **25**, 2019 (1931).

——, ——, Ger. Pat. 516,188, Oct. 25 (1927c); *C. A.*, **25**, 2019 (1931).

——, ——, Ger. Pat. 516,189, Dec. 25 (1927d); *C. A.*, **25**, 2019 (1931).

——, ——, Ger. Pat. 517,353, Dec. 8 (1927e); *C. A.*, **25**, 2327 (1931).

——, ——, Ger. Pat. 480,157, Dec. 25 (1927f); *C. A.*, **23**, 4982 (1929).

——, ——, Ger. Pat. 476,293, Dec. 8 (1927g); *C. A.*, **23**, 3770 (1929).

——, ——, French Pat. 647,456, Jan. 18 (1928); *C. A.*, **23**, 2598 (1929).

——, ——, Brit. Pat. 330,450, July 8 (1929); *C. A.* **24**, 5894 (1930).

——, ——, Ger. Pat. 505,033, Dec. 28 (1929a); *C. A.*, **24**, 6039 (1930).

——, ——, Brit. Pat. 353,873, Jan. 11 (1930); *C. A.*, **26**, 5434 (1932).

——, ——, Brit. Pat. 369,990, May 24 (1930a); *C. A.*, **27**, 2772 (1933).

——, and Schwieger, A., U. S. Pat. 1,893,393, Jan. 3 (1933); *C. A.*, **27**, 2225 (1933).

Bornmann, J. H., *J. Assoc. Offic. Agr. Chemists*, **25**, 717 (1942); *C. A.*, **36**, 6691 (1942).

Bousquet, E. W., U. S. Pat. 2,006,227, June 25 (1935); *C. A.*, **29**, 5589 (1935).

Braun, K., and Rosenbusch, R., U. S. Pat. 2,168,468, Aug. 8 (1939); *C. A.*, **33**, 9698 (1939).

Brown, L. C., U. S. Pat. 2,393,744, Jan. 29 (1946); *C. A.*, **40**, 2327 (1946).

Brown, W. C., and Thurston, L. M., *J. Dairy Sci.*, **23**, 629 (1940); *C. A.*, **34**, 7023 (1940).

Buer, H., Ger. Pat. 236,605, Sept. 17 (1910); *C. A.*, **5**, 3881 (1911).

——, U. S. Pat. 1,019,945, Mar. 12 (1912); *C. A.*, **6**, 1343 (1912).

——, Ger. Pat. 291,494, June 10 (1914); *C. A.*, **11**, 1522 (1917).

Buer, H., and Buer, C., Ger. Pat. 548,437, June 15, (1927); *C. A.,* **26,** 3623 (1932).

Bull, W. C., and Hopper, T. H., *Oil & Soap,* **18,** 219 (1941); *C. A.,* **36,** 674 (1942).

Burkhard, M. J., U. S. Pat. 2,465,335, Mar. 29 (1949); *C. A.,* **43,** 4420 (1949).

Buxton, L. O., *Ind. Eng. Chem.,* **39,** 225 (1947); *C. A.,* **41,** 2208 (1947).

——, and Dryden, C. E., U. S. Pats. 2,511,427–8, June 13 (1950).

Chapin, E. K., U. S. Pat. 2,392,833, Jan. 15 (1946); *C. A.,* **40,** 2558 (1946).

Chemische Fabrik Gedeon Richter, Ger. Pat. 237,394, Sept. 16 (1910); *C. A.,* **6,** 1501 (1912).

Chemische Fabrik Promonta G.m.b.H., Ger. Pat. 479,353, Aug. 8 (1926); *C. A.,* **23,** 4841 (1929).

——, Ger. Pat. 734,403, Mar. 18 (1943); *C. A.,* **38,** 1326 (1944).

Chemische Fabrik Stockhausen and Cie, Brit. Pat. 449,132, June 22 (1936); *C. A.,* **30,** 7727 (1936).

——, Ger. Pat. 667,085, Nov. 7 (1938); *C. A.,* **33,** 4380 (1939).

——, Ger. Pat. 691,486, Apr. 30 (1940); *C. A.,* **35,** 4159 (1941).

Chemische-Pharmazeutische A.-G., Ger. Pat. 501,502, Dec. 12 (1926); *C. A.,* **24,** 4900 (1930).

Christiansen, A., U. S. Pat. 2,356,382, Aug. 22 (1944); *C. A.,* **39,** 208 (1945).

Christlieb, H., Ger. Pat. 708,805, June 19 (1941); *C. A.,* **37,** 3198 (1943).

Clayton, B., Brit. Pat. 413,923, Nov. 23 (1932).

——, U. S. Pat. re-issue 21,992, Jan. 6 (1942); *C. A.,* **36,** 3060 (1942).

——, and Thurman, B. H., U. S. Pat. 2,205,971, June 25 (1940); *C. A.,* **34,** 7639 (1940).

Clayton, W., and co-workers (Back, S., Johnson, R. I., and Morse, J. F.), *J. Soc. Chem. Ind.,* **56,** 196 (1937); *C. A.,* **31,** 6365 (1937).

Cohoe, W. P., U. S. Pat. 2,469,861, May 10 (1949); *C. A.,* **43,** 6004 (1949).

Conner, H. W., U. S. Pats. 2,197,718–9, Apr. 16 (1940); *C. A.,* **34,** 5575 (1940).

Conway, J. W., and May, A., U. S. Pat. 1,965,490, July 3 (1934); *C. A.,* **28,** 5552 (1934).

Cook, L. R., *Baker, Miller, and Pastrycook,* **9,** 26 (1945).

——, *Food Inds.,* **17,** 740 (1945a); *C. A.,* **39,** 4699 (1945).

——, *ibid.,* **17,** 900 (1945b); *C. A.,* **39,** 4699 (1945).

——, *Bakers' Helper,* **87,** 1093, 56 (1947).

——, *Food Inds.,* **21,** 449 (1949).

Cresswell, A., U. S. Pat. 2,475,129, July 5 (1949); *C. A.,* **43,** 7248 (1949).

Dahle, C. V., and Josephson, D. V., *Southern Dairy Products J.,* **34,** No. 4, 12 (1943); *C. A.,* **38,** 800 (1944).

Damerell, V. R., Gayer, K., and Laudenslager, H., *J. Phys. Chem.,* **49,** 436 (1945); *C. A.,* **40,** 2374 (1946).

Dansk Sojakagefabrik Akt., Danish Pat. 52,614, Jan. 25 (1937); *C. A.,* **31,** 2752 (1937).

Datz, A., British Pat. 417,552, Oct. 8 (1934); *C. A.,* **29,** 1212 (1935).

De Groote, M., U. S. Pat. 2,086,215, July 6 (1937); *C. A.,* **31,** 5990 (1937).

——, and Keiser, B., U. S. Pat. 2,310,679, Feb. 9 (1943); *C. A.,* **37,** 4164 (1943).

Detwiler, J. G., and co-workers (Heisig, T. C., Rosnell, J. E., and Hall, F. W.), U. S. Pat. 2,002,885, May 28 (1935); *C. A.,* **29,** 4954 (1935).

Dhar, D. C., and Aggarwal, J. S., *J. Sci. Ind. Research (India),* **8B,** No. 1, 1 (1949); *C. A.,* **43,** 5127 (1949).

Diemair, W., Ludwig, H., and Weiss, K., *Fette u. Seifen,* **50,** 349 (1943); *C. A.,* **38,** 3497 (1944).

Douglass, W. F., U. S. Pat. 2,071,457, Feb. 23 (1937); *C. A.,* **31,** 2846 (1937).

Dreyfus, C., and Whitehead, W., U. S. Pat. 1,872,913, Aug. 23 (1932); *C. A.*, **26**, 6159 (1932).

du Pont de Nemours & Co., I. E., Brit. Pat. 566,048, Dec. 11 (1944); *C. A.*, **40**, 5580 (1946).

Dziengel, K., Ger. Pat. 729,796, Nov. 26 (1942); *C. A.*, **38**, 504 (1944).

——, Ger. Pat. 721,002, Apr. 23 (1942a); *C. A.*, **37**, 2604 (1943).

——, Ger. Pat. 732,744, Feb. 11 (1943); *C. A.*, **38**, 754 (1944).

Eckey, E. W., U. S. Pat. 1,993,152, Mar. 5 (1935); *C. A.*, **29**, 2770 (1935).

Edwards, B. G., and Dutton, H. J., *Ind. Eng. Chem.*, **37**, 1121 (1945); *C. A.*, **40**, 646 (1946).

Eichberg, J., *Oil & Soap*, **16**, 51 (1939); *C. A.*, **33**, 3617 (1939).

——, *News Ed.* (*Am. Chem. Soc.*), **19**, 575 (1941); *C. A.*, **35**, 5682 (1941).

——, U. S. Pat. 2,355,061, Aug. 8 (1944); *C. A.*, **38**, 6440 (1944).

Ekhard, W., Brit. Pat. 452,682, Aug. 7 (1936); *C. A.*, **31**, 1155 (1937).

El-Rafey, M. S., Richardson, G. A., and Henderson, J. L., *J. Dairy Sci.*, **27**, 807 (1944); *C. A.*, **39**, 359 (1945).

Engelmann, F. W., U. S. Pat. 1,972,764, Sept. 4 (1934); *C. A.*, **28**, 6947 (1934).

Epstein, A. K., U. S. Pat. 2,299,743, Oct. 27 (1942); *C. A.*, **37**, 1800 (1943).

——, and Harris, B. R., U. S. Pat. 2,062,782, Dec. 1 (1936); *C. A.*, **31**, 787 (1937).

——, ——, U. S. Pat. 2,089,470, Aug. 10 (1937); *C. A.*, **31**, 7141 (1937).

Erb, J. H., and Collins, H., *Dairy Inds.*, **4**, 52 (1939); *C. A.*, **33**, 3909 (1939).

Esch, W., *Gelatine, Leim, Klebstoffe*, **2**, 209 (1934); *C. A.*, **28**, 7437 (1934).

Evans, E. I., *Ind. Eng. Chem.*, **27**, 329 (1935); *C. A.*, **29**, 3060 (1935).

Ewing, F. J., U. S. Pat. 2,288,411, June 30 (1942); *C. A.*, **37**, 277 (1943).

Fash, R. H., *J. Am. Oil Chemists' Soc.*, **24**, 397 (1947); *C. A.*, **42**, 1074 (1948).

Feibelmann, R., U. S. Pat. 2,203,295, June 4 (1940); *C. A.*, **34**, 6846 (1940).

Feigenbaum, J., *Nature*, **157**, 770 (1946); *C. A.*, **40**, 5503 (1946).

Fevold, H. L., and co-workers (Edwards, B. G., Dimick, A. N., and Boggs, M. M.), *Ind. Eng. Chem.*, **38**, 1079 (1946); *C. A.*, **40**, 7433 (1946).

——, and Dimick, A. N., U. S. Pat. 2,454,915, Nov. 30 (1948).

Figaret, J., *Farbe u. Lack*, **55**, 234 (1947); *C. A.*, **43**, 8698 (1949).

Fincke, H., Ger. Pat. 524,118, Aug. 6 (1930); *C. A.*, **25**, 3854 (1931).

Fischer, French Pat. 371,391, Nov. 13 (1906); *C. A.*, **2**, 2429 (1908).

Fischer, C. A., Habermann, J., and Ehrenfeld, S., Ger. Pat. 223,593, May 29 (1907); *C. A.*, **4**, 3121 (1910).

Fitzpatrick, W. J., U. S. Pat. 2,444,984, July 13 (1948); *C. A.*, **42**, 6961 (1948).

——, and Wagner, H. H., U. S. Pat. 2,334,401, Nov. 16 (1944); *C. A.*, **38**, 2762 (1944).

Frank, F., U. S. Pat. 1,977,940, Oct. 23 (1934); *C. A.*, **29**, 256 (1935).

Freeman, S. E., U. S. Pat. 2,390,528, Dec. 11 (1945); *C. A.*, **40**, 3283 (1946).

Freund, H. H., U. S. Pat. 2,017,242, Oct. 15 (1935); *C. A.*, **29**, 8359 (1935).

Frey, C. N., and Jozsa, S., U. S. Pat. 2,194,932, Mar. 26 (1940); *C. A.*, **34**, 5299 (1940).

Fromm, R., U. S. Pat. 2,097,121, Oct. 26 (1937); *C. A.*, **32**, 356 (1938).

Gehrke, A., U. S. Pat. 2,018,781, Oct. 29 (1935); *C. A.*, **30**, 318 (1936).

Génin, G., *Parfumerie moderne*, **28**, 75, 77 (1934); *C. A.*, **28**, 6584 (1934).

Gensecke, W., U. S. Pat. 1,928,531, Sept. 26 (1933); *C. A.*, **27**, 6000 (1933).

——, U. S. Pat. 1,968,252, July 31 (1934); *C.A.*, **28**, 6009 (1934).

Geyer, R. P., Mann, G. V., and Stare, F. J., *J. Lab. Clin. Med.*, **33**, 175 (1948).

Ginn, W. W., U. S. Pat. 2,029,261, Jan. 28 (1936); *C. A.*, **30**, 1907 (1936).

Glabe, E. F., U. S. Pat. 2,513,638, July 4 (1950).

Gmünder, E. M., Swiss Pat. 245,056, June 16 (1947); *C. A.*, **43**, 6757 (1949).

Golumbic, C., and Daubert, B. F., *Food Inds.,* **19,** 1074, 1075 (1947); *C. A.,* **41,** 7554 (1947).

Gooding, C. M., and Rich, J. R., U. S. Pat. 2,435,626, Feb. 10 (1948); *C. A.,* **42,** 2790 (1948).

Gordon, W. E., and Heckert, W. W., U. S. Pat. 2,067,234, Jan. 12 (1937); *C. A.,* **31,** 1527 (1937).

Goss, W. H., *Oil & Soap,* **23,** 241 (1946); *C. A.,* **40,** 6273 (1946).

——, "The German Oilseed Industry," Washington, Hobart Publishing Co., 1947.

Greenfield, R. E., U. S. Pat. 2,339,164, Jan. 11 (1944); *C. A.,* **38,** 3866 (1944).

Grettie, D. P., U. S. Pat. 2,050,528, Aug. 11 (1936); *C. A.,* **30,** 6844 (1936).

Grün, A., in Schönfeld, H., and Hefter, G., "Chemie und Technologie der Fette und Fettprodukte," Vol. **I,** Vienna, Julius Springer, 1936.

Hall, F. W., and Towne, C. C., U. S. Pat. 2,257,601, Sept. 30 (1941); *C. A.,* **36,** 650 (1942).

Hall, H., Ger. Pat. 487,335, Nov. 17 (1925); *C. A.,* **24,** 2258 (1930).

Hall, L. A., U. S. Pat. 2,464,928, Mar. 22 (1949); *C. A.,* **43,** 6333 (1949).

——, and Gershbein, L. L., U. S. Pat. 2,464,927, Mar. 22 (1949); *C. A.,* **43,** 6333 (1949).

Hansa-Mühle, A.-G., Ger. Pat. 627,580, Mar. 18 (1936); *C. A.,* **30,** 6094 (1936).

——, Ger. Pat. 647,649, July 9 (1937); *C. A.,* **31,** 8123 (1937).

Hanseatische Mühlenwerke, A.-G., Ger. Pat. 528,238, Dec. 1 (1925); *C. A.,* **25,** 4634 (1931).

——, Brit. Pat. 372,232, May 5 (1932); *C. A.,* **27,** 3560 (1933).

——, French Pat. 741,520, Aug. 25 (1932a); *C. A.,* **27,** 2738 (1933).

——, Ger. Pat. 566,149, Jan. 12 (1932b); *C. A.,* **27,** 1204 (1933).

——, Brit. Pat. 382,432, Oct. 27 (1932c); *C. A.,* **27,** 4391 (1933).

——, Ger. Pat. 578,126, June 15 (1933); *C. A.,* **27,** 4434 (1933).

——, Ger. Pat. 602,933, Oct. 10 (1934); *C. A.,* **29,** 950 (1935).

——, Brit. Pat. 407,461, Mar. 22 (1934a); *C. A.,* **28,** 4802 (1934).

——, Brit. Pat. 409,687, Apr. 30 (1934b); *C. A.,* **28,** 6214 (1934).

——, Ger. Pat. 596,385, Apr. 30 (1934c); *C. A.,* **28,** 4607 (1934).

——, French Pat. 771,284, Oct. 4 (1934d); *C. A.,* **29,** 859 (1935).

——, Ger. Pat. 597,183, June 11 (1934e); *C. A.,* **28,** 5626 (1934).

——, French Pat. 779,402, Apr. 4 (1935); *C. A.,* **29,** 5540 (1935).

——, Brit. Pat. 436,859, Oct. 9 (1935a); *C. A.,* **30,** 2291 (1936).

——, and Polyphonwerke A.-G., Brit. Pat. 388,297, Feb. 23 (1933); *C. A.,* **27,** 5908 (1933).

Harris, B. R., U. S. Pats. 1,917,249–60, July 11 (1933); *C. A.,* **27,** 4600 (1933).

Hartmann, S., XIth Intern. Congr. Pure Appl. Chem., Author's Summary 261 (1947).

Heberer, A. J., U. S. Pat. 2,181,129, Nov. 28 (1939); *C. A.,* **34,** 2102 (1940).

Helme, J. P., and Desnuelle, P., *Oléagineux,* **3,** 121 (1948); *C. A.,* **42,** 6140 (1948).

Hendrey, W. B., U. S. Pats. 2,212,020–1, Aug. 20 (1940); *C. A.,* **35,** 615 (1941).

Higuti, T., Japanese Pat. 129,206, Mar. 15 (1939); C. A., **34,** 8183 (1940).

Hilty, W. K., *Am. Ink Maker,* **23,** No. 7, 29, 31, 45 (1945); *C. A.,* **39,** 4237 (1945).

——, *J. Am. Oil Chemists' Soc.,* **25,** 186 (1948); *C. A.,* **42,** 4694 (1948).

Hoffmann-LaRoche and Co., Ger. Pat. 282,611, Mar. 6 (1914); *C. A.,* **9,** 2568 (1915).

Holmes, H. N., U. S. Pat. 2,051,257, Aug. 18 (1936); *C. A.,* **30,** 6897 (1936).

——, Corbet, R. E., and Hartzler, E. R., *Ind. Eng. Chem.,* **28,** 133 (1936); *C. A.,* **30,** 1178 (1936).

Horvath, A. A., *J. Chem. Education,* **14,** 424 (1937); *C. A.,* **31,** 8970 (1937).

I. G. Farbenind. A.—G., French Pat. 756,952, Dec. 18 (1933); *C. A.*, **28**, 2380 (1934).

——, Ger. Pat. 579,936, July 3 (1933a); *C. A.*, **28**, 911 (1934).

——, Brit. Pat. 505,983, May 17 (1939); *C. A.*, **33**, 9494 (1939).

Inaba, T., Kitagawa, K., and Sato, M., *J. Soc. Chem. Ind. Japan*, **37**, Suppl. binding 595 (1934); *C. A.*, **29**, 1273 (1935).

Jacobs, J. J., Jr., U. S. Pat. 2,403,284, July 2 (1946); *C. A.*, **40**, 5914 (1946).

——, and Othmer, D. F., *Ind. Eng. Chem.*, **35**, 883 (1943); *C. A.*, **37**, 5851 (1943).

Jesser, H., *Chem. Ztg.*, **58**, 632 (1934); *C. A.*, **28**, 6873 (1934).

Jordan, S., U. S. Pat. 1,859,240, May 17 (1932); *C. A.*, **26**, 3857 (1932).

——, U. S. Pat. 1,936,718, Nov. 28 (1933); *C. A.*, **28**, 1116 (1934).

——, U. S. Pat. 2,019,494, Nov. 5 (1935); *C. A.*, **30**, 531 (1936).

——, U. S. Pat. 2,193,873, Mar. 19 (1940); *C. A.*, **34**, 4864 (1940).

——, U. S. Pat. 2,237,441, Apr. 8 (1941); *C. A.*, **35**, 4514 (1941).

——, U. S. Pat. 2,296,933, Sept. 29 (1942); *C. A.*, **37**, 1558 (1943).

Jorre, F., and Stalmann, G., Ger. Pat. 601,036, Aug. 7 (1934); *C. A.*, **28**, 7177 (1934).

Julian, P. L., and Engstrom, A. G., U. S. Pat. 2,249,002, July 15 (1941); *C. A.*, **35**, 6825 (1941).

——, and Iveson, H. T., U. S. Pat. 2,392,390, Jan. 8 (1946); *C. A.*, **40**, 2326 (1946).

——, and Meyer, E. W., U. S. Pat. 2,355,081, Aug. 8 (1944); *C. A.*, **38**, 6585 (1944).

——, ——, U. S. Pat. 2,374,681, May 1 (1945); *C. A.*, **39**, 3379 (1945).

——, ——, U. S. Pat. 2,391,462, Dec. 25 (1945a); *C. A.*, **40**, 3283 (1946).

——, ——, U. S. Pat. 2,374,682, May 1 (1945b); *C. A.*, **39**, 3660 (1945).

——, ——, U. S. Pat. 2,400,120, May 14 (1946); *C. A.*, **40**, 5938 (1946).

——, ——, and Iveson, H. T., U. S. Pat. 2,373,686, Apr. 17 (1945); *C. A.*, **39**, 3093 (1945).

——, ——, ——, U. S. Pat. 2,373,687, Apr. 17 (1945a); *C. A.*, **39**, 3093 (1945).

Karpov, M. F., *Trudy Vsesoyuz. Nauch. Issledovatel'. Inst. Konditerskoĭ Prom. No. 4*, 52 (1941); *C. A.*, **37**, 5798 (1943).

Kazita, T., and Inoue, R., U. S. Pat. 2,192,194, Mar. 5 (1940); *C. A.*, **34**, 4589 (1940).

Kern, C. J., Antoshkiw, T., and Maiese, M. R., *Ind. Eng. Chem.*, **41**, 2849 (1949).

Kimbara, R., and Rosenthal, W., Brit. Pat. 518, 194, Feb. 20 (1940); *C. A.*, **35**, 8214 (1941).

Kirby, W. G., and Steinle, L. E., U. S. Pat. 2,414,428, Jan. 14 (1947); *C. A.*, **41**, 4952 (1947).

Klein, G., and Grosse, A., U. S. Pat. 2,055,083, Sept. 22 (1936); *C. A.*, **30**, 7786 (1936).

——, and Tauboeck, K., U. S. Pat. 2,013,804, Sept. 10 (1935); *C. A.*, **29**, 7021 (1935).

Koppenhoefer, R. M., U. S. Pat. 2,387,157, Oct. 16 (1945); *C. A.*, **40**, 729 (1946).

Kraybill, H. R., U. S. Pat. 2,069,187, Jan. 26 (1937); *C. A.*, **31**, 2038 (1937).

——, Brewer, P. H., and Thornton, M. H., U. S. Pat. 2,174,177, Sept. 26 (1939); *C. A.*, **34**, 656 (1940).

——, ——, ——, U. S. Pats. 2,276,316–7, Mar. 17 (1942); *C. A.*, **36**, 4636 (1942).

——, ——, ——, U. S. Pat. 2,353,571, July 11 (1944); *C. A.*, **38**, 6121 (1944).

Kritchevsky, W., U. S. Pat. 2,164,717, July 4 (1939); *C. A.*, **33**, 8364 (1939).

Kröper, H., and Thomae, E., U. S. Pat. 2,185,255, Jan. 2 (1940); *C. A.*, **34**, 3026 (1940).

Kruft, H., Ger. Pat. 292,961, Sept. 4 (1913); *C. A.*, **11**, 1884 (1917).

Kruse, N. F., U. S. Pat. 2,269,772, Jan. 13 (1942); *C. A.*, **36**, 3060 (1942).

Kühl, H., *Mühle*, **72**, 177 (1935); *C. A.*, **29**, 6960 (1935).

Kunzer, H., Brit. Pat. 388,382, Feb. 21 (1933); *C. A.*, **27**, 4630 (1933).

Langwill, K. E., *Mfg. Confectioner*, **19**, [5], 37 (1939); *C. A.*, **33**, 5083 (1939).

Lederer, E. L., *Seifensieder-Ztg.*, **60**, 919 (1933); *C. A.*, **28**, 2209 (1934).

——, *ibid.*, **62**, 180 (1935).

Lefèvre-Lebeau, Y., *Bull. offic. office intern, cacao chocolat,* **4**, 333 (1934); *C. A.*, **30**, 2658 (1936).

Lehmann and Voss G.m.b.H., Ger. Pat. 549,760, July 11 (1931); *C. A.*, **26**, 4925 (1932).

Lesser, M. A., *Soap Sanit. Chemicals,* **22**, No. 5, 37, 143 (1946); *C. A.*, **40**, 3915 (1946).

Levis, I. B., U. S. Pat. 2,465,733, Mar. 29 (1949); *C. A.*, **43**, 5155 (1949).

Liebrecht, A., U. S. Pat. 1,777,173, Sept. 30 (1930); *C. A.*, **24**, 5939 (1930).

Linden, G. M. von, Meissen, E., and Strauss, A., U. S. Pat. 1,072,745, Sept. 9 (1913); *C. A.*, **7**, 3640 (1913).

Loane, C. M., U. S. Pat. 2,295,179, Sept. 8 (1942); *C. A.*, **37**, 1595 (1943).

Lund, A. A., U. S. Pat. 2,090,537, Aug. 17 (1937); *C. A.*, **31**, 7151 (1937).

Lundberg, W. O., *Hormel Inst. Univ. Minn. Pub. No. 20* (1947); *C. A.*, **42**, 773 (1948).

Markley, K. S., and Goss, W. H., "Soybean Chemistry & Technology," Brooklyn, Chemical Publishing Co., Inc., 1944.

Markley, M. C., U. S. Pat. 2,494,771, Jan. 17 (1950).

Markman, A., and Vuishnepolskaya, F., *Masloboĭno-Zhirovoe Delo No. 4–5,* 45 (1932); *C. A.*, **27**, 2594 (1933).

Marmor, R. A., and Moyer, W. W., U. S. Pats. 2,461,750–1, Feb. 15 (1949); *C. A.*, **43**, 3948 (1949).

Martin, H., Ger. Pat. 286,907, Nov. 11 (1913); *C. A.*, **10**, 1695 (1916).

——, Dutch Pat. 2,583, Sept. 5 (1918); *C. A.*, **13**, 248 (1919).

——, Austrian Pat. 110,850, May 15 (1928); *C. A.*, **23**, 1216 (1929).

Mashino, M., *J. Soc. Chem. Ind., Japan,* **36**, Suppl. binding, 309 (1933); *C. A.*, **27**, 4704 (1933).

Masurovsky, B. I., *Food Inds.*, **14**, No. 12, 66 (1942); *C. A.*, **37**, 1523 (1943).

——, *Ice Cream Trade J.*, **41**, No. 10, 84 (1945).

Matagrin, A., *Rev. chim. ind. (Paris)*, **45**, 72, 104, 126, 158 (1936); *C. A.*, **30**, 6227 (1936).

Mattikow, M., U. S. Pat. 2,271,127, Jan. 27 (1942); *C. A.*, **36**, 3577 (1942).

——, *J. Am. Oil Chemists' Soc.*, **25**, 200 (1948); *C. A.*, **42**, 5691 (1948).

——, *ibid.*, **27**, 11 (1950).

Mecheels, O., *Melliand Textilber.*, **12**, 123 (1931); *C. A.*, **26**, 3673 (1932).

Merz, O., and Wagner, F., *Farbe u. Lack*, 535 (1932); *C. A.*, **27**, 197 (1933).

Metallgesellschaft A.-G., Brit. Pat. 366,996, Dec. 5 (1929); *C. A.*, **27**, 2056 (1933).

Minatoya, S., and Kurahashi, K., *J. Soc. Chem. Ind. Japan*, **37**, Suppl. binding, 207 (1934); *C. A.*, **28**, 6024 (1934).

——, ——, *J. Soc. Rubber Ind. Japan*, **7**, 272 (1934a); *C. A.*, **28**, 6591 (1934).

Mitchell, H. S., U. S. Pat. 2,113,216, Apr. 5 (1938); *C. A.*, **32**, 4372 (1938).

Moberly, C. W., U. S. Pat. 2,516,477, July 25 (1950).

Molines, J., and Desnuelle, P., *Oléagineux*, **5**, 17 (1950).

Möller, F. A., U. S. Pat. 2,147,104, Feb. 14 (1939); *C. A.*, **33**, 4074 (1939).

Mori, S., *J. Agr. Chem. Soc. Japan*, **14**, 1404 (1938); *C. A.*, **33**, 9025 (1939).

Morris, C. E., U. S. Pat. 2,125,849, Aug. 2 (1938); *C. A.*, **32**, 7601 (1938).

Mossini, A., and Caliumi, V., *Boll. chim. farm.*, **79**, 177 (1940); *C. A.*, **34**, 7529 (1940).

Musher, S., U. S. Pats. 2,198,213–4, Apr. 23 (1940); *C. A.*, **34**, 5690 (1940).

——, U. S. Pat. 2,216,711, Oct. 1 (1940a); *C. A.*, **35**, 1218 (1941).

——, U. S. Pat. 2,324,529, July 20 (1943); *C. A.*, **38**, 256 (1944).

——, U. S. Pat. 2,408,090, Sept. 24 (1946); *C. A.*, **41**, 1098 (1947).

Nagy, J. J., Vibrans, F. C., and Kraybill, H. R., *Oil & Soap,* **21,** 349 (1944); *C. A.,* **39,** 826 (1945).

Nakamura, M., and Tomita, S., *J. Soc. Chem. Ind. Japan,* **43,** Suppl. binding, 245, 271 (1940); *C. A.,* **35,** 1256 (1941).

National Oil Products Co., British Pat. 589,273, June 16 (1947); *C. A.,* **41,** 6740 (1947).

New York Paint & Varnish Production Club, *Paint, Oil, Chem. Rev.,* **97,** [23], 81 (1935).

——, *ibid.,* **98,** [24], 90, 94 (1936); *C. A.,* **31,** 4513 (1937).

Niescher, M. F., Brit. Pat. 518,103, Feb. 16 (1940); *C. A.,* **35,** 7055 (1941).

——, Ger. Pat. 719,268, Mar. 5 (1942); *C. A.,* **37,** 1799 (1943).

Noblee and Thörl G.m.b.H., Ger. Pats. 602,934–5, Sept. 19 (1934); *C. A.,* **29,** 950 (1935).

——, Brit. Pat. 410,357, May 17 (1934a); *C. A.,* **28,** 6250 (1934).

——, French Pat. 759,007, Jan. 27 (1934b); *C. A.,* **28,** 3187 (1934).

——, French Pat. 788,632, Oct. 14 (1935); *C. A.,* **30,** 1600 (1936).

——, Ger. Pat. 653,878, Dec. 17 (1937); *C. A.,* **32,** 3180 (1938).

North, G. C., and Alton, A. J., U. S. Pat. 2,399,565, Apr. 30 (1946); *C. A.,* **41,** 234 (1947).

——, ——, and Little, L., U. S. Pats. 2,392,994–5, Jan. 15 (1946); *C. A.,* **40,** 2558 (1946).

Nottbohm, F. E., and Mayer, F., *Z. Untersuch. Lebensm.,* **66,** 21 (1933); *C. A.,* **27,** 5829 (1933).

Ohl, F., *Melliand. Textilber.,* **12,** 123 (1931).

——, *ibid.,* **15,** 555 (1934).

Okano, K., Ohara, I., and Kato, J., *J. Agr. Chem. Soc. Japan,* **12,** 714 (1936); *C. A.,* **31,** 1238 (1937).

Oosterhout, J. C. D., U. S. Pat. 2,155,678, Apr. 25 (1939); *C. A.,* **33,** 6039 (1939).

——, and Quimby, W. S., U. S. Pat. 2,222,487, Nov. 19 (1940); *C. A.,* **35,** 2316 (1941).

Oranienburger Chemische Fabrik A.-G., Brit. Pat. 317,730, Aug. 20 (1928); *C. A.,* **24,** 2259 (1930).

Passino, H. J., *Ind. Eng. Chem.,* **41,** 280 (1949).

——, U. S. Pat. 2,523,630, Sept. 26 (1950).

Pässler, J., Ger. Pat. 697,440, Sept. 19 (1940); *C. A.,* **35,** 6688 (1941).

Piskur, M. M., *Oil & Soap,* **23,** 151 (1946); *C. A.,* **40,** 4231 (1946).

Pollak, J. E., Brit. Pat. 412,224, June 19 (1934); *C. A.,* **28,** 6878 (1934).

Pratt, D. B., Jr., *Food Inds.,* **18,** 16, 160 (1946); *C. A.,* **40,** 1947 (1946).

Proell, W. A., U. S. Pat. 2,437,041, Mar. 2 (1948); *C. A.,* **42,** 3555 (1948).

Rapaport, G. H., U. S. Pat. 2,449,411, Sept. 14 (1948); *C. A.,* **43,** 787 (1949).

Rapp, *Pharm. Ztg.,* **75,** 303 (1930); *C. A.,* **24,** 2237 (1930).

Rathbun, R. B., U. S. Pat. 2,208,105, July 16 (1940); *C. A.,* **34,** 8255 (1940).

Redgrove, H. S., *Mfg. Perfumer,* **3,** 5, 18 (1938); *C. A.,* **33,** 1102 (1939.)

Rees, H. V., and Oosterhout, J. C. D., U. S. Pat. 2,165, 651, July 11 (1939); *C. A.,* **33,** 8395 (1939).

——, Quimby, W. S., and Oosterhout, J. C., *Refiner Natural Gasoline Mfr.,* **19,** 414 (1940); *C. A.,* **35,** 1611 (1941).

Rewald, B., Brit. Pat. 306,672, Jan. 23 (1928); *C. A.,* **23,** 5349 (1929).

——, *Ledertech. Rundschau,* **20,** 268 (1928a); *C. A.,* **23,** 1769 (1929).

——, U. S. Pat. 1,762,077, June 3 (1930); *C. A.,* **24,** 3577 (1930).

——, U. S. Pat. 1,779,012, Oct. 21 (1930a); *C. A.,* **25,** 231 (1931).

——, *Collegium,* 929 (1932); *C. A.,* **27,** 3849 (1933).

Rewald, B., U. S. Pat. 1,917,734, July 11 (1933); *C. A.*, **27**, 4706 (1933).

——, U. S. Pat. 1,895,424, Jan. 24 (1933a); *C. A.*, **27** 2505 (1933).

——, *Chem. Ztg.*, **57**, 595 (1933b); *C. A.*, **27**, 4852 (1933).

——, U. S. Pat. 1,934,005, Nov. 7 (1933c); *C. A.*, **28**, 579 (1934).

——, U. S. Pat. 1,938,864, Dec. 12 (1933d); *C. A.*, **28**, 1459 (1934).

——, Ger. Pat. 602,637, Sept. 13 (1934); *C. A.*, **29**, 950 (1935).

——, U. S. Pat. 1,946,332, Feb. 6 (1934a); *C. A.*, **28**, 2921 (1934).

——, U. S. Pat. 1,946,333, Feb. 6 (1934b); *C. A.*, **28**, 2571 (1934).

——, U. S. Pat. 2,020,517, Nov. 12 (1935); *C. A.*, **30**, 627 (1936).

——, U. S. Pat. 1,986,360, Jan. 1 (1935a); *C. A.*, **29**, 1265 (1935).

——, Ger. Pat. 619,235, Sept. 25 (1935b); *C. A.*, **30**, 630 (1936).

——, U. S. Pat. 2,039,739, May 5 (1936); *C. A.*, **30**, 4234 (1936).

——, *Chemistry & Industry*, 1002 (1936a); *C. A.*, **31**, 1504 (1937).

——, Brit. Pat. 464,100, Apr. 8 (1937); *C. A.*, **31**, 6774 (1937).

——, Brit. Pat. 464,100, Apr. 8 (1937a); *C. A.*, **31**, 6774 (1937).

——, and Höfling, W., *Bull. offic. office intern. cacao chocolat*, **2**, 69 (1932); *C. A.*, **27**, 3758 (1933).

Reynolds, M. C., and Epstein, A. K., U. S. Pat. 1,815,739, July 21 (1931); *C. A.*, **25**, 5477 (1931).

Richardson, A. S., U. S. Pat. 2,104,242, Jan. 4 (1938); *C. A.*, **32**, 1970 (1938).

Richter, G., Ger. Pat. 223,594, June 4 (1908); *C. A.*, **4**, 3121 (1910).

Riedel Akt.-Ges., J. D., Ger. Pat. 260,886, Oct. 12 (1910); *C. A.*, **7**, 3199 (1913).

——, Ger. Pat. 256,998, Nov. 18 (1911); *C. A.*, **7**, 2454 (1913).

——, Ger. Pat. 464,554, Feb. 11 (1922).

——, and Haën Akt.-Ges., E. de, Ger. Pat. 474,543, Aug. 29 (1923); *C. A.*, **23**, 5054 (1929).

Riedel and de Haën A.-G., Ger. Pat. 474,269, July 21 (1923); *C. A.*, **23**, 3052 (1929).

——, Ger. Pat. 516,119, July 28 (1926); *C. A.*, **25**, 1922 (1931).

Riemenschneider, R. W., and co-workers (Herb, S. F., Hammaker, E. M., and Luddy, F. E.), *Oil & Soap*, **21**, 307 (1944); *C. A.*, **39**, 1232 (1945).

——, and co-workers (Luddy, F. E., Herb, S. F., and Turer, J.), *Oil & Soap*, **22**, 174 (1945); *C. A.*, **39**, 3947 (1945).

——, and Turer, J., U. S. Pat. 2,383,815, Aug. 28 (1945); *C. A.*, **39**, 5517 (1945).

——, ——, U. S. Pat. 2,383,816, Aug. 28 (1945a); *C. A.*, **39**, 5517 (1945).

——, ——, U. S. Pat. 2,440,383, Apr. 27 (1948); *C. A.*, **42**, 5694 (1948).

Ritter, W., and Nussbaumer, T., *Schweiz. Milchztg.*, *No. 7–11*, 31 pp. (1937); *C. A.*, **33**, 4334 (1939).

Rosenbusch, R., Ger. Pat. 676,077, May 25 (1939); *C. A.* **33**, 6532 (1939).

——, and Reverey, G., *Margarine-Industrie, No. 17* (1927); *C. A.*, **22**, 4669 (1928).

——, ——, U. S. Pat. 1,988,050, Jan. 15 (1935); *C. A.*, **29**, 1586 (1935).

——, ——, Ger. Pat. 635,325, Sept. 15 (1936); *C. A.*, **31**, 216 (1937).

Rosenthal, W., French Pat. 842,621, June 15 (1939); *C. A.*, **34**, 5971 (1940).

Roth, M. H., U. S. Pat. 2,372,985, Apr. 3 (1945); *C. A.*, **39**, 4252 (1945).

Rowland, B. W., U. S. Pat. 2,186,709, Jan. 9 (1940); *C. A.*, **34**, 3494 (1940).

Royce, H. D., *Soap*, **7**, No. 9, 25, 38 (1931); *C. A.*, **26**, 1145 (1932).

——, U. S. Pat. 2,123,863, July 12 (1938); *C. A.*, **32**, 7159 (1938).

Salis, T. v., Swiss Pat. 223,432, Sept. 15 (1942); *C. A.*, **43**, 1532 (1949).

Salmoiraghi, E., *Ann. chim. applicata*, **27**, 332 (1937); *C. A.*, **32**, 378 (1938).

Sandelin, A. E., *Maataloustieteellinen Aikakauskirja*, **11**, 230 (1939); *C. A.*, **35**, 4107 (1941).

Sato, K., Nagai, M., and Tamamushi, B., *J. Chem. Soc. Japan,* **67,** 24 (1946); *C. A.,* **41,** 2670 (1947).

Sato, M., and co-workers (Ishida, Y., Umemoto, T., and Yokoty, M), Brit. Pat. 529,114, Nov. 14 (1940); *C. A.,* **35,** 8334 (1941).

Sauer, Ltd., F. G., Ger. Pat. 189,110, Mar. 16 (1906); *C. A.,* **2,** 735 (1908).

Saunders, H. F., and Downs, C. D., U. S. Pat. 2,117,366, May 17 (1938); *C. A.,* **32,** 5237 (1938).

Schantz, E. J., and co-workers (Boutwell, R. K., Elvehjem, C. A., and Hart, E. B.), *J. Diary Sci.,* **23,** 1201 (1940); *C. A.,* **35,** 2233 (1941).

Scharf, A., U. S. Pat. 2,431,347, Nov. 25 (1947); *C. A.,* **42,** 3199 (1948).

Schlack, P., U. S. Pat. 1,953,438, Apr. 3 (1934); *C. A.,* **28,** 3921 (1934).

Schmidt, W., *Mehl u. Brot,* **44,** 98 (1944); *C. A.,* **40,** 6710 (1946).

Schoeller, W., and Schrauth, W., U. S. Pat. 1,012,923, Dec. 26 (1911); *C. A.,* **6,** 535 (1912).

Schofield, M., *Paint Manuf.,* **15,** 45 (1945); *C. A.,* **39,** 1999 (1945).

Schönfeld, H., in Schönfeld, H., and Hefter, G., "Chemie und Technologie der Fette und Fettprodukte," Vol. **II,** Vienna, Julius Springer, 1937.

Schultz, A. S., and Frey, C. N., U. S. Pat. 2,136,399, Nov. 15 (1939); *C. A.,* **33,** 1440 (1939).

Schwarz, E. W. K., *Am. Dyestuff Reptr.,* **29,** 220, 234 (1940); *C. A.,* **34,** 4180 (1940).

——, *Textile Mfr.,* **61,** 289 (1940a); *C. A.,* **34,** 7114 (1940).

Schwarz, H., *Seifensieder-Ztg.,* **63,** 170 (1936); *C. A.,* **30,** 3165 (1936).

——, *ibid.,* **65,** 438 (1938); *C. A.,* **32,** 8698 (1938).

——, *ibid.,* **67,** No. 15, 146; No. 16, 156 (1940b); *C. A.,* **35,** 3388 (1941).

Schwarzkopf, H., Ger. Pat. 715,803, Dec. 4 (1941); *C. A.,* **38,** 2168 (1944).

Schwieger, A., U. S. Pat. 1,892,588, Dec. 27 (1932); *C. A.,* **27,** 2225 (1933).

——, U. S. Pat. 2,020,662, Nov. 12 (1935); *C. A.,* **30,** 609 (1936).

——, U. S. Pat. 2,057,695, Oct. 20 (1936); *C. A.,* **31,** 188 (1937).

——, U. S. Pat. 2,115,008, Apr. 26 (1938); *C. A.,* **32,** 4684 (1938).

Sell, H. M., Olsen, A. G., and Kremers, R. E., *Ind. Eng. Chem.,* **27,** 1222 (1935); *C. A.,* **29,** 7515 (1935).

Shinozaki, Y., and Sato, M., *J. Soc. Chem. Ind. Japan,* **37,** Suppl. binding, 432 (1934); *C. A.,* **28,** 7566 (1934).

Sifferd, R. H., U. S. Pat. 2,371,476, Mar. 13 (1945); *C. A.,* **39,** 3376 (1945).

Singer, P. A., and Deobald, H. J., U. S. Pat. 2,377,975, June 12 (1945); *C. A.,* **39,** 4505 (1945).

——,——, U. S. Pat. 2,508,624, May 23 (1950).

Snyder, W. E., *Milk Plant Monthly,* **38,** No. 6, 30, 43 (1949); *C. A.,* **43,** 9281 (1949).

Soc. anon. pour l'ind. chim. à Bâle, Swiss Pat. 127,256, Dec. 23 (1926); *C. A.,* **23,** 1216 (1929).

——, Swiss Pat. 136,239, Dec. 23 (1926a); *C. A.,* **24,** 4358 (1340).

Sollmann, E. I., U. S. Pat. 1,884,899, Oct. 25 (1932); *C. A.,* **27,** 1160 (1933).

Sonol, J., *Rev. facultad cienc. quím. (Univ. nacl. La Plata),* **5,** 83 (1929); *C. A.,* **23,** 3306 (1929).

Sorensen, S. O., and Beal, G. F., U. S. Pat. 2,024,398, Dec. 17 (1935); *C. A.,* **30,** 1143 (1936).

Stanley, J., *Food Inds.,* **14,** No. 7, 69 (1942); *C. A.,* **36,** 4923 (1942).

——, in Alexander, J., "Colloid Chemistry," Vol. **VI,** New York, Reinhold Publishing Corp., 1946.

——, U. S. Pat. 2,402,690, June 25 (1946a); *C. A.,* **40,** 7450 (1946).

Steiner, L. F., Arnold, C. H., and Fahey, J. E., *J. Econ. Entomol.*, **36**, 70 (1943) ; *C. A.*, **37**, 4195 (1943).

Stieg, F. B., *Paint, Oil, Chem. Rev.*, **108**, No. 13, 9 (1945) ; *C. A.*, **39**, 4236 (1945).

Stirton, A. J., Turer, J., and Riemenschneider, R. W., *Oil & Soap*, **22**, 81 (1945) ; *C. A.*, **39**, 2417 (1945).

Storgårds, T., and Hietaranta, M., *Proc. 12th Intern. Dairy Congr. (Stockholm)*, **2**, 389 (1949) ; *C. A.*, **44**, 2664 (1950).

Strauch, G., U. S. Pat. 2,079,973, May 11 (1937) ; *C. A.*, **31**, 4747 (1937).

——, Ger. Pat. 660,736, June 1 (1938) ; *C. A.*, **32**, 6809 (1938).

Sturgis, B. M., and Baum, A. A., U. S. Pat. 2,432,381, Dec. 16 (1947) ; *C. A.*, **42**, 2468 (1948).

Sullivan, F. M., U. S. Pat. 2,441,923, May 18 (1948) ; *C. A.*, **42**, 5586 (1948).

Süllmann, H., *Helv. Chim. Acta*, **24**, 465 (1941) ; *C. A.*, **35**, 7423 (1941).

Swift, C. E., Rose, W. G., and Jamieson, G. S., *Oil & Soap*, **19**, 176 (1942) ; *C. A.*, **37**, 276 (1943).

Talalay, J. A., Brit. Pat. 445,534, Apr. 14 (1936) ; *C. A.*, **30**, 6984 (1936).

——, Brit. Pat. 447,256, May 11 (1936a) ; *C. A.*, **30**, 6984 (1936).

Tatu, H., *Tiba*, **12**, 427 (1934) ; *C. A.*, **28**, 5246 (1934).

Taub, A., and Simone, R. M., U. S. Pat. 2,432,698, Dec. 16 (1947) ; *C. A.*, **42**, 2130 (1948).

Täufel, K., and Köchling, J., *Fette u. Seifen*, **46**, 554 (1939) ; *C. A.*, **35**, 2350 (1941).

Thiele, F. W., U. S. Pat. 1,843,051, Jan. 26 (1932) ; *C. A.*, **26**, 1677 (1932).

Thiele, M., and Sisley, J. P., *Bull. mens. ITERG (Inst. tech. études et recherches corps gras)*, **3**, 77 (1949) ; *C. A.*, **43**, 5520 (1949).

Thornley, B. D., and Jones, N. W. V., Brit. Pat. 561,334, May 16 (1944) ; *C. A.*, **39**, 5412 (1945).

Thornton, M. H., and Kraybill, H. R., *Ind. Eng. Chem.*, **34**, 625 (1942) ; *C. A.*, **36**, 3379 (1942).

Thurman, B. H., Brit. Pat. 413,923, July 26 (1934) ; *C. A.*, **29**, 370 (1935).

——, U. S. Pat. 2,078,428, Apr. 27 (1937) ; *C. A.*, **31**, 4410 (1937).

——, U. S. Pat. 2,182,767, Dec. 5 (1939) ; *C. A.*, **34**, 2200 (1940).

——, U. S. Pat. 2,150,732, Mar. 14 (1939a) ; *C. A.*, **33**, 4808 (1939).

——, U. S. Pat. 2,206,210, July 2 (1940) ; *C. A.*, **34**, 7639 (1940).

——, U. S. Pat. 2,204,109, June 11 (1940a) ; *C. A.*, **34**, 7130 (1940).

——, U. S. Pat. 2,201,063, May 14 (1940b) ; *C. A.*, **34**, 6470 (1940).

——, U. S. Pat. 2,201,064, May 14 (1940c) ; *C. A.*, **34**, 6470 (1940).

——, U. S. Pat. 2,245,537, June 10 (1941) ; *C. A.*, **35**, 6138 (1941).

——, U. S. Pat. 2,242,188, May 13 (1941a) ; *C. A.*, **35**, 5336 (1941).

——, U. S. Pat. 2,271,410, Jan. 27 (1942) ; *C. A.*, **36**, 3577 (1942).

——, U. S. Pat. 2,272,616, Feb. 10 (1942a) ; *C. A.*, **36**, 3577 (1942).

——, U. S. Pat. 2,271,409, Jan. 27 (1942b) ; *C. A.*, **36**, 3577 (1942).

——, U. S. Pat. 2,280,427, Apr. 21 (1942c) ; *C. A.*, **36**, 5578 (1942).

——, U. S. Pat. 2,327,569, Aug. 24 (1943) ; *C. A.*, **38**, 885 (1944).

——, U. S. Pat. 2,407,041, Sept. 3 (1946) ; *C. A.*, **41**, 1381 (1947).

——, U. S. Pat. 2,415,313, Feb. 4 (1947) ; *C. A.*, **41**, 2595 (1947).

Tischer, A. O., U. S. Pat. 2,117,776, May 17 (1938) ; *C. A.*, **32**, 5242 (1938).

Trueger, E., U. S. Pat. 2,431,652, Nov. 25 (1947) ; *C. A.*, **42**, 1417 (1948).

——, and Sprague, B. S., U. S. Pat. 2,422,321, June 17 (1947) ; *C. A.*, **41**, 5712 (1947).

Trusler, R. B., *Oil & Fat Inds.*, **8**, 141 (1931) ; *C. A.*, **25**, 2867 (1931).

Van der Waarden, *Research in Holland*, 155 (1947).

Voroshilova, L. A., and Pisarev, N. S., *Trudy Vsesoyuz. Nauch. Issledovatel'. Inst. Konditerskoĭ Prom. No. 4,* 78 (1941); *C. A.,* **37,** 5798 (1943).

Voss, H., Fromm, R., and Man, J., Brit. Pat. 465,153, Apr. 28 (1937); *C. A.,* **31,** 7151 (1937).

Weetman, B., U. S. Pat. 2,383,097, Aug. 21 (1945); *C. A.,* **39,** 5067 (1945).

White, R. H., Jr., and Vaughan, J. A., U. S. Pats. 2,054,399 and 2,054,400, Sept. 15 (1936); *C. A.,* **30,** 7814 (1936).

Wiczer, S. B., U. S. Pat. 2,388,719, Nov. 13 (1945); *C. A.,* **40,** 1023 (1946).

Wiesehahn, G. A., *Oil & Soap,* **14,** 119 (1937); *C. A.,* **31,** 4520 (1937).

——, U. S. Pat. 2,194,842, Mar. 26 (1940); *C. A.,* **34,** 5209 (1940).

Williams, K. T., Bickoff, E., and Lowrimore, B., *Oil & Soap,* **21,** 161 (1944); *C. A.,* **38,** 4462 (1944).

Winston, J. J., and Jacobs, B. R., *J. Assoc. Offic. Agr. Chemists,* **28,** 607 (1945); *C. A.,* **40,** 646 (1946).

——, ——, *Food Inds.,* **19,** 166, 327 (1947); *C. A.,* **41,** 7547 (1947).

Wittcoff, H., U. S. Pat. 2,445,948, July 27 (1948); *C. A.,* **42,** 8372 (1948).

——, U. S. Pat. 2,483,748, Oct. 4 (1949).

Wolff, F., U. S. Pat. 2,109,143, Feb. 22 (1938); *C. A.,* **32,** 3080 (1938).

Wolff, G., and Guellerin, H., *Compt. rend. 17me. congr. chim. ind. Paris,* Sept.–Oct. 919 (1937); *C. A.,* **32,** 6893 (1938).

Wolter, E., Ger. Pat. 584,562, Sept. 21 (1933); *C. A.,* **28,** 983 (1934).

Woodman, R. M., *J. Soc. Chem. Ind.,* **51,** 95 (1932); *C. A.,* **26,** 3164 (1932).

Working, E. B., *Cereal Chem.,* **5,** 223 (1928); *C. A.,* **22,** 2796 (1928).

——, U. S. Pat. 1,781,672, Nov. 11 (1930); *C. A.,* **25,** 154 (1931).

——, U. S. Pat. 1,831,728, Nov. 10 (1931); *C. A.,* **26,** 784 (1932).

——, *Oil & Soap,* **13,** 261 (1936); *C. A.,* **31,** 175 (1937).

Wornum, W. E., and co-workers (Annand, D. L., Jolly, V. G., Plowman, E. W., and Holbeow, G. L.) in "Investigation of the German Paint Industry," B.I.O.S. Final Report #628, Item #22, p. 3. Quoted in U. S. Office of Technical Services, Report #66,130 (1946).

Ziegelmayer, W., *Kolloid-Z.,* **53,** 224 (1930); *C. A.,* **25,** 544 (1931).

Author Index

Abbott, O. D., 388, 414
Abderhalden, E., 270
Åborg, C. G., 70
Ackermann, J., 346
Adair, G. S., 87
Adair, M. E., 87
Adam, N. K., 69
Adams, E. W., 514, 522
Adams, J. R., 450
Adams, M. H., 450
Adams, P. D., 439
Adler, R., 86
Adlersberg, D., 378, 425, 440
Affonskiĭ, S. I., 78
Aggarwal, J. S., 508
Agid, R., 178
Agulhon, H., 202
Ajazzi-Mancini, M., 422
Akamatsu, S., 105, 110
Alexander, A. E., 70
Alexandry, A. K., 383
Allen, D. M., 149
Allen, E. V., 420
Allen, F. H., 515
Allen, F. N., 413
Allen, J. G., 356
Allilaire, E., 196
Allingham, W. J., 499, 513
Alpers, E., 229, 232
Alsop, W. G., 514
Alsterberg, G., 183, 278
Altman, R. F. A., 239, 240, 455
Alton, A. J., 507, 512
Alvarez, M. D. A. de, 387, 403
Anchel, M., 173
Andersen, D. H., 432
Anderson, R. J., 6, 15, 16, 35, 36,
42, 53, 54, 59, 63, 88, 155, 193,
194, 196, 198, 199, 201, 202, 203,
204, 205, 206, 207, 208, 210, 211,
212, 213, 214, 215, 216, 229, 235,
257, 258, 318
Anderson, T. H., 450
Andrews, J. S., 156, 225
Andrews, K. R., 415
Angevine, A. W., 364
Annau, E., 453
Anselmino, K. J., 387
Antener, I., 89, 226, 227
Antoshkiw, T., 510
Aoki, M., 447
Aoyama, K., 521
Arbenz, E., 157, 238, 239, 241
Arnaudi, C., 106, 107, 108
Arney, S. E., 233
Arnold, C. H., 521
Arnold, H., 90, 121, 123, 125, 126
Aronson, H., 202
Artom, C., 31, 110, 151, 152, 153,
161, 162, 167, 169, 170, 171, 176,
177, 256, 257, 258, 260, 261, 264,

267, 268, 279, 286, 288, 293, 295,
296, 300, 308, 311, 313, 346, 349,
357, 366, 369, 372, 374, 376, 377,
386, 387, 388, 389, 390, 391, 392,
394, 395, 403, 419
Arveson, M. H., 502, 504
Ashburn, H. V., 514
Aso, K., 216
Astrup, T., 443
Atchley, W., 361
Aten, A. H. W., Jr., 381, 383, 402
Auclair, J., 202
Auerbach, M., 516
Auerbach, V. H., 361
Augur, V., 345
Augustin, J., 520
Ault, W. C., 22, 282, 303, 305
Austin, W. C., 194, 214
Auxier, R. W., 519
Avent, A. G., 505
Awny, A. J., 106
Aylward, F. X., 402, 426
Ayres, E. E., Jr., 486

Babo, L., 23
Baer, E., 10, 15, 16, 17, 19, 20, 95,
116, 119, 120, 122, 123, 125, 126
Baeyer, A., 23
Bähr, O., 317
Bailey, A. E., 507, 508
Bailey, C. H., 156, 225, 226
Bailly, O., 16, 17, 18
Baker, Z., 89
Balboni, G., 398
Baldwin, A. R., 327
Bale, W. F., 372, 382, 394
Ball, E. G., 442
Bamberger, P., 77
Bancroft, F. W., 446
Bang, I., 160
Banks, H. W., Jr., 440
Barbieri, N. A., 9
Barnes, R. H., 363, 369
Barnum, C. P., 344, 360
Barrett, H. M., 358, 370
Bartle, E. R., 325
Barton-Wright, E. C., 227
Baskoff, A., 25, 26
Bass, R. M., 451
Baudran, G., 202
Baughman, W. F., 230
Baum, A. A., 521
Baumann, A., 26
Baumann, C., 502
Baumann, C. A., 174, 415
Baumann, E. J., 305, 380
Baumann, T., 426
Bavetta, L. A., 363
Bayle, L., 405
Bayles, T. B., 442
Bayors, W. M., 318

Beadle, G. W., 176, 415
Beal, G. F., 487
Beattie, F. J. R., 174
Bechhold, H., 72
Beck, G. E., 97
Beck, T. M., 491
Beck, W., 77
Beckel, A. C., 491
Becker, H. C., 78
Behre, J., 518
Behrens, M., 51
Belcot, E., 520
Belfanti, S., 101, 103, 104, 105,
106, 107, 108, 109, 421, 422
Belgrave, W. N. C., 239
Belin, P., 341, 342
Bell, R. D., 180
Bell, R. T., 515
Belozerskiĭ, A. N., 220, 222
Belter, P. A., 491
Bendich, A., 86, 92, 444, 445
Bengis, R. O., 235
Benning, A. F., 514
Benoit, J., 300
Benotti, J., 16, 21, 44, 46, 53, 54,
165, 167, 171, 172, 173, 174, 257,
264, 265, 274, 280, 293, 296, 318,
385
Bensley, R. R., 86, 343, 344
Benz, P., 19
Berczeller, L., 96, 490
Bergell, P., 23, 61, 95, 110, 498, 502
Berkson, J., 389
Bernardini, L., 224
Bernhard, K., 298, 350, 357, 359
Bernheim, F., 453
Bernheim, M. C. L., 453
Bernstein, I. M., 519
Bernstein, S. S., 426
Bernton, A., 236
Berry, W. B., 69
Bersin, Th., 52, 53, 124, 257, 280,
283, 288, 313
Berthier, P., 72
Bertramson, B. R., 406
Best, C. H., 174, 176, 348, 356, 357,
358, 370, 389, 411, 413, 415, 418,
420
Beumée-Nieuwland, N., 239
Beumer, H., 55, 435
Beuttner, R., 341
Beveridge, J. M. R., 180
Bialosuknia, V., 406
Bibby, C. L., 507
Bickoff, E., 510
Biddulph, O., 404
Bielschowsky, F., 43, 288
Bierich, R., 342, 436
Bigelow, F. E., 498, 512
Billon, F., 99
Bing, H. J., 93, 96, 97

Binkley, F., 450
Birch, A. J., 211
Bird, E. W., 325
Bischoff, C., 174
Bischoff, G., 326
Bishop, R. O., 239, 240
Bitte, B., 224
Blackwood, J. H., 84, 402
Blake, A. G., 273, 442
Blanquet, P., 71
Blatherwick, N. R., 402
Blewett, M., 351, 356
Bleyer, B., 55, 225, 226, 227, 231, 233, 234, 236
Blix, G., 29, 87, 88, 177, 178, 266
Bloch, K., 194, 204, 207, 340, 352, 354, 449
Bloor, W. R., 3, 6, 21, 148, 149, 150, 151, 154, 158, 159, 160, 161, 164, 181, 197, 261, 271, 273, 277, 284, 285, 286, 287, 289, 291, 292, 294, 295, 302, 303, 305, 306, 307, 308, 309, 310, 311, 312, 314, 342, 354, 362, 364, 367, 377, 380, 402, 403, 424, 432, 436, 442, 454
Blumensaat, C., 300
Boas, E., 97
Bode, J., 23
Bogdanovitch, S. B., 379
Bohart, G. S., 158
Boivin, A., 213, 449, 450
Bókay, A., 99, 110
Bolaffio, C., 54
Boldyreva, N. V., 284, 440
Bolen, P., 516
Bolle, A., 298
Bollman, J. L., 355, 378, 379, 385, 389
Bollmann, H., 454, 486, 492, 495, 496, 497, 499, 505, 506, 508, 512, 513, 516, 517, 518, 521
Bonanni, A., 297
Boncoddo, N. F., 16, 21, 42, 44, 45, 46, 53, 54, 65, 67, 173, 257, 280, 293, 294, 296, 318
Bonot, A., 398
Booth, F. J., 47
Borek, E., 360
Bornmann, J. H., 512
Bouquet, P., 107
Bousquet, E. W., 521
Boutaric, A., 72
Boxer, G. E., 353, 419
Boyd, E. M., 149, 150, 160, 182, 262, 267, 270, 271, 272, 301, 302, 317, 342, 397, 398, 404, 441
Boyd, J. I., 180
Bracaloni, L., 59
Brage, D., 433
Brain, R. T., 20
Brand, E., 31
Brand, F. C., 287
Branson, H., 440
Brante, G., 267, 378
Braun, K., 501, 520
Breazeale, D. F., 325
Bredemann, G., 221
Bretin, 406
Breuer, J., 97
Breusch, F. L., 73, 353
Brewer, J. I., 303
Brewer, P. H., 230, 491, 492

Brewster, L. E., 113
Briggs, D. R., 229
Brindley, P., 438
Brobeck, J. R., 434
Brodrick-Pittard, N. A., 158
Brooks, J., 320, 322
Brown, G. O., 415
Brown, H., 451
Brown, J. B., 22, 37, 60, 282, 283, 289, 303, 305, 306
Brown, L. C., 512
Brown, R., 451
Brown, W. C., 327, 510
Brown, W. R., 353
Bruger, M., 430, 438, 439, 442
Brunius, E., 100, 448
Brunstrum, L. C., 514
Bryndówna, W., 13
Buchwald, K. W., 308
Buer, C., 499
Buer, H., 490, 497, 499
Bull, H. B., 6, 14, 33, 76, 78
Bull, W. C., 487
Bullen, S. S., 273, 442
Bulliard, H., 407
Bullock, W. E., 436
Bülow, M., 452, 454
Bungenberg de Jong, see Jong
Bürger, M., 202, 403, 435
Burgevin, H., 233
Burk, D., 421
Burkhard, M. J., 522
Burmaster, C. F., 17, 170
Burow, R., 326
Burr, G. O., 351, 352, 354, 357, 363, 366, 369
Burr, M. M., 351, 352, 354, 357
Burt, M. L., 208, 273, 380
Burton, L. V., 37, 281
Buruiana, L., 158, 326
Butts, J. S., 360
Buu-Hoi, N. P., 211
Buxton, L. O., 510

Cagniant, P., 211
Cahn, T., 178, 398, 399
Calabék, J., 77
Caliumi, V., 499
Cameron, O. J., 412
Campbell, G. F., 82, 84
Campbell, I. G., 351, 356
Campbell, J. M. H., 430
Campbell, R. M., 389
Capizzi, I., 181
Carayon-Gentil, A., 176, 276, 283
Carbone, D., 442
Cardini, C. E., 167, 171, 172, 175, 264, 272, 277, 287, 292, 293, 294, 296, 308, 310, 379
Carré, P., 18
Carter, H. E., 7, 31, 38, 40, 41, 42, 46, 64, 116
Cary, C. A., 402
Casanova, C., 182
Caselli, P., 433
Cason, J., 35, 209, 211
Cassafouth, C. F. C., 433
Cattaneo, L., 283
Cavanagh, B., 349, 370, 387, 392, 395
Césari, E., 107

Chaikoff, I. L., 20, 49, 65, 66, 104, 110, 111, 148, 156, 175, 236, 266, 268, 272, 273, 287, 347, 349, 353, 356, 362, 364, 371, 372, 373, 374, 376, 378, 379, 382, 383, 384, 385, 386, 387, 388, 389, 390, 391, 392, 393, 394, 395, 396, 399, 400, 401, 407, 408, 410, 414, 416, 419, 433, 435, 437
Chain, E., 13, 14, 33, 45
Challinor, S. W., 450
Chamberlain, E. N., 387, 433
Chang, L. H., 205
Changus, G. W., 364, 395
Channon, H. J., 6, 16, 48, 49, 65, 194, 195, 204, 207, 227, 238, 240, 273, 289, 371, 418
Chantrenne, H., 284, 344
Chanutin, A., 380, 426, 429, 430, 439
Chapin, E. K., 507
Chapman, F. D., 426
Chapman, O. W., 326
Chargaff, E., 34, 82, 83, 85, 86, 89, 90, 91, 92, 98, 102, 103, 104, 165, 168, 169, 170, 176, 177, 196, 197, 198, 199, 200, 201, 208, 210, 211, 212, 256, 279, 280, 288, 292, 293, 312, 320, 343, 362, 368, 372, 376, 388, 389, 390, 392, 394, 395, 401, 407, 410, 411, 423, 427, 443, 444, 445, 446, 447, 449
Chatterjee, H. N., 380
Cheesman, D. F., 70
Chen, A. L., 420
Cheng, L. T., 299
Chernik, S., 408, 433
Chiarulli, G., 224
Chibnall, A. C., 6, 16, 48, 49, 65, 194, 195, 204, 207, 237, 238, 240, 242, 405
Chick, H., 86, 90
Ching, T. T., 379
Chopra, G. S., 442
Chopra, R. N., 180, 442
Christensen, H. N., 29, 45, 96, 152, 169
Christensen, K., 414
Christiansen, A., 495
Christlieb, H., 235, 498
Church, A. E., 378
Ciaccio, C., 183, 424
Clark, L. H., 486
Clarke, B. G., 349
Clarkson, M. F., 415
Claude, A., 86, 343, 344, 437
Claus, A., 23
Clayton, B., 492, 493
Clayton, W., 505
Clementi, A., 100, 110
Clogne, R., 110
Clowes, G. H. A., 96
Coca, A. F., 99
Cochet, 406
Coester, C., 303
Coghill, R. D., 31
Cohen, H. R., 180
Cohen, P. P., 360
Cohen, S. S., 86, 92, 102, 103, 423, 444, 445, 446
Cohoe, W. P., 513
Collier, H. B., 422

Collins, H., 505
Collinson, G. A., 273
Colmer, A. R., 106
Comfort, M. W., 364
Connell, W. F., 441
Conner, H. W., 513
Connor, C. L., 414, 435
Contardi, A., 21, 95, 101, 103, 105, 107, 108, 109, 110, 112, 122, 422
Conway, J. W., 506
Cook, L. R., 504, 511, 512, 513
Cook, R. P., 356
Coope, R., 387
Copenhaver, W. M., 287
Corbet, R. E., 509
Cordier, R., 431
Cori, C. F., 308
Corlett, R. L., 433
Cornatzer, W. E., 390, 419
Corner, G. W., 302, 342
Corran, J. W., 78
Correa, L., 411
Correll, J. W., 380
Corteggiani, E., 176, 276, 283
Corwin, W. C., 378
Costello, C. J., 436
Couerbe, 9
Cousin, H., 25, 37, 95, 321
Cramer, E., 31, 196
Cramer, W., 436
Crandall L. A., Jr., 348, 360
Crane, E. J., 4
Crane, J. C., 159, 175, 326
Creighton, M. M., 204, 205, 212, 213
Cresswell, A., 522
Crowder, J. A., 199, 205, 213
Crowder, M., 419
Crowe, M. O., 448
Cruickshank, E. M., 322
Cruickshank, J., 97, 98
Cunningham, R. N., 453
Cushing, I. B., 126
Cuthbertson, D. P., 311
Cutinelli, C., 433
Czapek, Fr., 195

Da Cruz, A., 105
Daft, F. S., 31
Dahle, C. D., 78, 324
Dahle, C. V., 510
Daire, P., 324
Dakin, H. D., 359
Dale, H. H., 419
D'Alessandro, G., 437
Dam, H., 441
Damerell, V. R., 77, 521
Dann, W. J., 416
Darken, M., 404
Darrah, J. E., 15, 29
Datz, A., 498
Dauben, W. G., 353, 370
Dauber, D. V., 433
Daubert, B. F., 510
Daubney, C. G., 214
Davanzo, I. G., 381, 429
Davis, D., 439
Davis, J. E., 415
Davis, W. W., 96
Davison, C., 428
Dawson, A. I., 196
deBoissezon, P., 279

De Groote, M., 503, 522
Delage, B., 92
Delaunay, A., 450
Delezenne, C., 100, 101, 103, 107, 422
Delfini, D., 104
Delsal, J. L., 91, 153, 261
De Masters, C. U., 414
Denis, W., 441
Dennis, E. W., 449
den Ouden, A., 296
Deobald, H. J., 490, 491
Derbes, V. J., 436
Dervichian, D., 71, 97
Desnuelle, P., 69, 180, 486, 494
de Sütö-Nagy, G. I., 36, 204, 447
Detwiler, J. G., 515
Detzel, A., 436
Deuel, H. J., Jr., 345, 354, 359, 360, 363
Deutsch, H. F., 453
Deutsch, W., 74, 75, 76
Deysher, E. F., 158, 326
Dezani, S., 300
Dhar, D. C., 508
Diakanow, C., 10, 21
Dickens, F., 354, 438
Diebold, W., 40, 47
Diemair, W., 55, 179, 182, 215, 225, 226, 227, 231, 233, 234, 236, 238, 455, 508
Dimick, A. N., 494
Dimitz, L., 16, 37, 452
Dirr, K., 215
Ditt, F., 312
Dittmer, J., 258, 296, 306, 312
Divinskiĭ, A., 320
Doan, C. A., 208, 210, 438, 449
Dodge, E., 408
Dodson, L. B., 440
Doisy, E. A., 180
Dolan, M., 112, 165, 262, 263, 264
Dols, M. J. L., 376, 440
Donatelli, L., 422
Dornic, P., 324
Doubilet, H., 347
Douglass, W. F., 508
Dounce, A. L., 85
Downs, C. D., 517
Downs, W. G., Jr., 433
Dragstedt, L. R., 356
Drescher, A. H., 322, 400
Dreyfuss, C., 516
Dreyfuss, M. L., 425
Drinker, N., 443
Drury, A. N., 421
Dryden, C. E., 510
Duboss, R. J., 89
Duftschmid, H., 223
Duhamel, J., 71
Dungern, E., 99
Dunn, E. E., 101, 103, 423
Dustman, R. B., 327
Dutton, H. J., 181, 230, 455, 510
du Vigneaud, V., 31, 415, 416, 417, 418
Dykerhoff, H., 423
Dziemian, A. J., 85, 272
Dziengel, K., 500, 502

Earle, F. R., 156, 175, 181, 220
Eaves, E. C., 399

Echevin, R., 243
Eckey, E. W., 510
Eckardt, B., 64, 427
Eckstein, H. C., 196, 313, 314, 356, 412, 415, 425
Edsall, J. T., 87, 92
Edwards, B. G., 510
Egsgaard, J., 153
Ehrenfeld, R., 96
Ehrenfeld, S., 483
Ehrlich, G., 173
Eichberg, J., 77, 504, 514, 522
Eichgorn, G., 156
Eichhaltz, F., 378
Eiler, J. J., 18
Eisler, M., 55
Ékhard, W., 495
Ekkert, L., 182
Elkes, J. J., 346
Elliott, H., 88
Elliott, K. A. C., 453
Ellis, G., 152, 179, 402
Ellis, N. R., 320, 322, 349
El-Rafey, M. S., 509
Elsom, K. O., 347
Emanuel, E., 428
Engel, I. A., 232
Engel, R. W., 356, 357, 414
Engelhardt, H. T., 436
Engelmann, F. W., 500, 521
Engman, M. F., 315
Engstrom, A., 489
Entenman, C., 148, 175, 266, 268, 272, 273, 287, 347, 356, 375, 378, 379, 382, 383, 384, 385, 386, 387, 388, 390, 391, 394, 399, 400, 403, 416, 435
Eperjessy, A., 453
Eppler, J., 26, 95
Epshteĭn, Ya. A., 162, 163, 168
Epstein, A. K., 499, 506, 520
Epstein, E., 425, 426, 428, 430
Erb, J. H., 505
Ercoli, A., 101, 103, 105, 107, 108, 109, 110, 112, 422
Erickson, B. N., 151, 164, 166, 169, 171, 174, 176, 265, 266, 267, 273, 276, 377, 432, 446
Erlandsen, A., 25, 26, 95
Erlenmeyer, E., 31
Esch, W., 518, 519
Escher, H. H., 58
Esh, G. C., 440
Etcheverry, M. A., 448
Evans, E. A., Jr., 352, 360
Evans, E. I., 454, 508
Evans, J. W., 229
Ewan, M. A., 58, 223
Ewing, F. J., 493

Fabisch, W., 12, 33
Fahey, J. E., 521
Fahrig, C., 434
Fairbairn, D., 109
Falk, F., 25
Fash, R. H., 493
Faure, M., 13, 207, 449
Favarger, P., 347
Fawaz, G., 153, 275
Feibelmann, R., 499, 516
Feigenbaum, J., 510
Feinschmidt, J., 14, 74

Fejer, A. von, 345
Feldberg, W., 422
Felsenfeld, O., 110
Felszeghy, Ö., 453
Fenaroli, A., 121, 123
Fenger, F., 301, 302, 306
Feraru, F., 441
Ferguson, J. H., 443, 446
Fernández, O., 182
Fernau, A., 411
Ferraro, A., 427
Feuge, R. O., 508
Feulgen, R., 51, 52, 53, 173, 183, 257, 280, 283, 288, 313
Fevold, H. L., 84, 85, 323, 494, 510
Feyder, S., 352
Fiandaca, S., 181
Field, J. B., 441
Fiessinger, N., 110
Figaret, J., 517
Fincke, H., 518
Fischer, 488
Fischer, A., 444
Fischer, C. A., 483
Fischer, E., 18, 19, 31
Fischer, H. O. L., 17, 19, 20, 116, 126
Fischer, O., 450
Fischer, Oe., 450
Fischgold, H., 13, 14, 33, 45
Fishberg, E. H., 425
Fisher, N. F., 413
Fishler, M. C., 349, 355, 373, 383, 388, 390, 393, 407, 409, 410
Fishman, W. H., 31, 151, 162, 167, 171, 176, 286, 308, 311, 357, 386
Fiske, C. H., 180, 261
Fitelson, J., 179
Fitzpatrick, W. J., 498, 500
Flatter, M., 324
Fleming, R. S., 159, 326
Fletcher, J. P., 176
Fleury, P., 17, 175
Flexner, S., 99, 106
Flock, E. V., 355, 378, 379, 385, 389, 391
Flössner, O., 300
Floyd, N. F., 354, 359
Foá, P. P., 396
Foglia, V. G., 380
Folch, J., 5, 16, 17, 28, 29, 30, 31, 32, 34, 35, 36, 62, 152, 164, 166, 168, 169, 256, 257, 261, 267, 279, 280
Folch, R., 182
Foldes, F. F., 441
Folley, S. S., 113
Fomin, S., 169, 176
Forkner, C. E., 210, 438, 449
Forssman, J., 448
Foster, C. A. M., 227, 240
Foster, M. L., 18
Fourcroy, A., 9
Fourneau, E., 16, 34, 100, 101, 103, 107, 148, 422
Fowweather, F. S., 365
Fox, H. H., 439
Fraenkel-Conrat, H. L., 108
Frampton, V. L., 14, 33
Francioli, M., 104, 106, 108, 110, 214

Frank, F., 519
Fränkel, E., 43, 288
Fränkel, S., 16, 37, 54, 452
Frankfurt, E., 224
Frazer, A. C., 345, 346, 348, 362, 377
Freeman, G. G., 450
Freeman, J. A., 177, 268, 349, 377
Freeman, S. E., 493
Frémy, E., 9
Freund, H. H., 516
Frey, C. N., 513, 516
Frey-Wissling, A., 89
Friedemann, U., 100
Friedenthal, H., 345
Friedkin, M., 344
Friedlander, H. D., 384, 388, 394
Fries, B. A., 151, 278, 347, 375, 388, 389, 390, 395, 396, 408
Friese, H., 225, 232
Fritsch, R., 242
Frölicher, E., 347, 349
Fromm, R., 502, 522
Frouin, A., 202
Fujimura, S., 60, 448
Fujii, N., 14, 90
Fukutomi, T., 399
Fürth, O., 97
Furth, R., 13
Furtunesco, A., 158, 326
Furukobo, T., 321

Gainsborough, H., 86
Galeotti, G., 82, 90
Gardner, J. A., 86
Gaumé, J., 17
Gautrelet, J., 283
Gavin, G., 356
Gayer, K., 521
Gehrke, A., 489
Geiger, W., 31
Geiger, W. B., Jr., 198
Génin, G., 519
Gensecke, W., 492
Geoffroy, R., 224, 225
Gephart, F., 72, 74, 297
Gerard, R. W., 453
Gershbein, L. L., 509
Gerstl, B., 115, 438
Geyer, R. P., 434, 513
Ghosh, B. N., 106, 108
Ghosh, S. M., 380
Giampalmo, G., 82, 90
Gibbs, G. E., 362, 435
Gibson, B. B., 87, 182, 274
Gigli, G., 155
Gildea, E. F., 149, 377, 378, 441
Gillette, E. M., 362
Gillum, M. L., 287
Gilson, E., 10, 121, 122
Ginger, L. G., 211
Ginn, W. W., 489
Gjessling, E. C., 380
Glabe, E. F., 512
Glick, D., 175, 183, 224
Glikin, W., 298, 317, 325
Gmünder, E. M., 511
Gobley, M., 9, 18, 255, 275, 320
Goda, T., 421
Goebel, W. F., 450

Goetzl, F. R., 442
Gofman, J. W., 88, 434, 435
Goldblatt, H., 413, 414
Goldfarb, W., 359
Goldman, L., 439
Goldovskiĭ, A. M., 228
Goldschmidt, M., 316
Goldstein, M. R., 430
Golumbic, C., 510
Gonzalez, A., 34
Goodell, J. P. B., 358
Gooding, C. M., 512
Goodman, D., 349
Goodner, K., 448
Gorbach, G., 157
Gordon, W. E., 519
Goreczky, L., 87
Goris, A., 202
Gorodisska, H., 277, 283
Gorter, E., 422
Goss, W. H., 221, 483, 487, 488, 504, 510
Gough, G. A. C., 212
Govaerts, P., 431
Grafe, V., 55, 217, 221, 236, 237, 238, 241
Graff, L. H., 97
Grafflen, A. L., 361
Graham, W. R., Jr., 402
Grail, G. F., 357, 416
Grant, J., 181
Grassman, W., 423
Gratia, A., 446
Gray, E. L., 27, 31, 62, 63, 118, 122
Gray, H., 435
Greco, A., 437
Green, C., 177
Green, D. E., 361
Greenfield, R. E., 496
Greenwood, F. L., 41
Grettie, D. P., 512
Griess, P., 23
Griffith, W. H., 414
Griffiths, W. J., 54
Grigaut, A., 91
Grimbert, L., 16
Gronchi, V., 99, 106, 108, 422
Gros, F., 97
Grosse, A., 513
Grossfeld, J., 158, 320, 502
Grün, A., 12, 13, 59, 108, 112, 122, 486, 488, 520
Grünberg, H., 173
Grundland, I., 407
Guastalla, L., 97
Guellerin, H., 512
Guerrant, N. B., 156, 225, 228, 229, 232, 233, 234, 237, 243
Guerrini, G., 422
Guggenheim, A., 447
Guillaumin, C. O., 326
Guitard, H., 175
Gulaesy, Z. V., 55
Gulland, J. M., 18
Günsberger, O. D., 450
Güntherberg, K., 364
Gupta, A. C., 235
Gurd, F. R. N., 88
Gustafson, F. G., 404
Gutman, A. B., 451
Gutstein, M., 55, 453

Guyon, G., 233
György, P., 413, 414, 419, 440

Haas, E., 180
Habermann, J., 483
Hack, M. H., 15, 167, 172, 173, 175, 180, 266, 268
Hahn, A., 376, 431
Hahn, L., 165, 368, 375, 381, 382, 383, 388, 389, 390, 393, 394, 395, 400
Halász, P., 237
Halden, W., 179, 223, 225, 405
Hall, F. W., 514
Hall, H., 495
Hall, L. A., 508, 509
Halpern, G. R., 321, 322
Halpin, J. J., 322, 400
Hamilton, J. D., 414
Hamlin, M., 357
Hammarsten, O., 54, 55, 96, 97, 297
Hammerschlag, A., 202
Hanahan, D. J., 20, 49, 65, 66, 104, 110, 111, 156, 236
Hand, A., 425
Handler, P., 416
Handovsky, H., 90
Hanger, F. M., 451
Hanke, U., 224, 233
Hann, A. C. O., 18, 19
Hanne, R., 405
Hansen, A. E., 273, 351, 439
Hanson, P. C., 358
Hansteen-Cranner, B., 55, 98
Hardy, W. B., 86
Harms, H. P., 356
Harris, B. R., 499, 506, 520
Harris, I., 434
Harris, S., 441
Harrow, G., 23
Hart, M. C., 303
Hartkamp, J. L. L. F., 85
Hartley, P., 289
Hartmann, S., 510
Hartung, E. F., 442
Hartwell, J. L., 450
Hartzler, E. R., 509
Hassegawa, S., 422
Hastings, A. B., 29, 45, 96
Hatakeyama, T., 59, 161, 321
Hatterer, C., 291, 292, 310, 341
Hattori, K., 72
Hauser, C. R., 217, 218
Hausser, I., 13, 45
Haven, F. L., 369, 372, 382, 436, 437
Hawkins, W. B., 358
Hawthorne, J. R., 320, 322
Hazato, H., 449
Heath, C. W., 432
Heberer, A. J., 522
Hecht, E., 202
Heckel, E., 191
Heckert, W. W., 519
Hée, A., 405
Heffels, J., 73
Heidelberger, M., 94, 447, 449
Heiduschka, A., 230
Heinemann, B., 324
Heki, M., 433
Helman, F. D., 158, 326

Helman, R. M., 278
Helme, J. P., 494
Henderson, J. L., 509
Hendry, E. B., 149, 161, 180, 261
Hendrey, W. B., 514
Henny, G. C., 73
Hensing, J. T., 9
Heringa, G. C., 412
Hermans, J. J., 422
Hermstein, A., 302
Herreid, E. O., 326
Herrmann, H., 97
Hershey, J. M., 413, 431, 432
Hershman, B., 16, 109
Hess, A. F., 158, 326
Hesselbach, M. L., 421
Hettche, H. O., 449
Hevesy, G., 153, 165, 366, 368, 371, 374, 375, 376, 381, 382, 383, 388, 389, 390, 393, 394, 395, 400, 401, 402, 404, 412, 437, 438
Heyl, F. W., 303
Heymann, W., 431
Hiestand, O., 93, 193, 221
Hietaranta, M., 510
Higuti, T., 520
Hilditch, T. P., 22, 178, 194, 222, 227, 228, 231, 232, 234, 287, 290, 291, 299, 326, 351, 352, 455
Hill, E., 364
Hiller, A., 431
Hilty, W. K., 504, 522
Himwich, H. E., 359
Hinrichs, H., 223, 405
Hirao, S., 104, 227
Hiraoka, T., 440
Hiratsuka, E., 327
Hirschbrunn, M., 23
Hirsh, E. F., 433
Hoagland, C. L., 213
Hobday, G. F., 18
Höber, R., 74
Hodge, H. C., 286, 305, 315, 317, 378, 386, 387
Hodges, R. G., 432
Hodson, A. Z., 177
Hoerr, N. L., 343, 344
Hoesch, K., 434
Hofer, E., 90
Hoffman, F., 387
Höfling, W., 505
Hofmann, A. W., 23
Hogg, B. M., 91
Högl, O., 89, 226, 227
Hollander, E., 435
Holly, O. M., 305, 380
Holm, G. E., 158, 326
Holman, R. T., 352
Holmes, A. D., 364
Holmes, H. N., 509
Holt, L. E., Jr., 426
Holton, W. B., 94, 222
Holwerda, B. J., 158
Hongo, S., 440
Hopff, H., 23
Hoppe-Seyler, F., 82, 84, 191, 214
Hopper, T. H., 487
Horall, B. E., 159, 175, 326
Horecker, B. L., 180
Horel, J., 220
Hori, T., 321
Horiuchi, Y., 271

Horowitz, N. H., 176, 415, 418
Horrall, B. E., 324
Horsfall, F. L., Jr., 448
Hortenstine, J. C., 430
Horvat, V., 55, 238
Horvath, A. A., 76, 89, 490
Horwitt, M. K., 453
Hotchkiss, R. D., 89
Houget, J., 178
Hove, E. L., 455
Hove, Z., 455
Howard, C. P., 182
Howell, W. H., 443, 446
Hughes, A., 70, 107
Hughes, R. H., 348
Humiston, C. G., 41
Hundeshagen, F., 10, 121
Hunt, R., 419
Hunter, F. E., 46, 171, 267, 277, 288, 293, 295, 296, 309, 310, 315, 376, 377, 388, 392
Hunter, I. R., 119, 126
Huntsman, M. E., 411, 413, 415
Hurtley, W. H., 359
Hurxthal, L. M., 441
Huseby, R. A., 344
Hynd, A., 357

Icke, R. N., 31
Ide, S., 439
Iguchi, T., 74
Ihde, A. J., 233
Imhaüser, K., 51
Imrie, C. G., 435
Inaba, T., 77, 79, 519
Ingersoll, A. W., 209
Ingvaldsen, T., 176, 177, 285
Inoue, R., 516
Inouye, T., 345
Inukai, F., 410
Ionesco-Mihaiesti, C., 450
Iosifova, M. A., 308
Irish, O. J., 180
Irvin, J. L., 297, 298
Irving, E., 289
Issekutz, B. V., Jr., 363
Iveson, H. T., 64, 496, 505
Ivy, A. C., 349
Iwasa, Y., 221
Iwata, M., 104, 106, 422
Izzo, R. A., 267, 378, 438

Jack, E. L., 324
Jackson, A. H., 239
Jacobi, H. P., 174, 415
Jacobs, B. R., 511
Jacobs, J. J., Jr., 514
Jacobs, W. A., 39
Jacobson, H., 191, 192, 238
Jacobson, O., 297
Jacobson, S. A., 428
James, M. S., 362
Jamieson, G. S., 94, 156, 162, 220, 222, 230, 326, 508
Januschke, E., 303
Januszkiewicz, M., 87
Javillier, M., 439
Jeker, L., 347
Jeney, A. v., 121, 123
Jervis, G. A., 427

Jesser, H., 511
Joannovics, G., 348, **367**
Johansen, A. H., **433**
Johnson, A. C., 274, **276**, 279
Johnson, C. S., 58, **223**
Johnson, **S. E., 180**
Johnston, C. G., 297, 298
Jokivartio, E., 434
Jona, B., 319
Jones, H. B., 387, 437
Jones, K. K., 297
Jones, N. W. V., 494
Jones, R., 72, 96
Jones, T. S. G., 402
Jong, H. G. B., de, 72, 74, 75, 76, 85
Jordan, R. C., 237, 405
Jordan, S., 498, 505, 507, 511, 512, 513
Jorpes, E., 306
Jorre, F., 522
Josephson, B., 349
Josephson, D. V., 510
Joslin, E. P., 435
Jost, H., 398
Joukovsky, N. I., 76
Jowett, M., 359, 393
Jozsa, S., 516
Jukes, T. H., 12, 13, 33, 84, 415, 416, 417, 418
Julian, P. L., 64, 489, 496, 500, 505, 514
Just, E., 161

Kabat, E. A., 448, 451
Kabashima, I., 119, 120, 122, 125
Kafka, F., 54
Kahane, E., 24, 34
Kahane, M., 34
Kahn, R. L., 451
Kakiuchi, S., 74
Kalabankoff, L., 99
Kalashnikov, E., 156
Kan, S., 411
Kapfhammer, J., 174
Kaplan, A., 435
Kaplan, N. O., 408
Karczag, L., 20, 411
Karlina, M. I., 72
Karpov, M. F., 505
Karr, W. G., 27, 29
Karrer, P., 16, 19
Kartin, B. L., 378
Kassell, B., 31
Kates, M., 10, 15, 16, 17, 95, 116, 123
Kato, J., 221, 490
Katsura, S., 161
Kaucher, M., 256, 277, 285, 292, 295, 306, 308, 310, 315, 321
Kaufmann, C., 302, 381
Kaufmann, H. P., 219, 220, 353
Kawai, K., 14
Kay, H. D., 17, 19, 20, 84, 105, 110, 112, 113, 402
Kazita, T., 516
Keesé, C., 23
Keeser, E., 72
Keevil, N. B., 414
Kehar, N. D., 442
Keiser, B., 503
Keller, E. B., **416**

Kellner, A., 380
Kemp, I., 14, 45
Kenyon, A. E., 174, 175, 176
Kern, C. J., 510
Kerr, R. H., 364
Kerson, M., 439
Kesten, H. D., 433
Kester, E. B., 119, 126
Keston, A. S., 372, 410
Kiessling, W., 18, 19
Kik, M. C., 378
Kimbara, R., 502
Kimizura, K., 448
King, A., 80
King, E. J., 17, 19, 47, 104, 105, 112, 122, 452, 453
King, H., 19, 105, 112
King, S. E., 430, 438
Kinney, T. D., 426
Kirby, W. G., 518
Kirchhoff, H., 402
Kirk, E., 149, 152, 160, 162, **165**, 169, 175, 177, 181, 261, 262, **264**, 266, 272, 430, 432
Kirkman, H., 86
Kitagawa, K., 77, 79, 519
Klein, G., 491, 513
Klein, G. I., 491
Klemperer, G., 435
Klenk, E., 22, 35, 37, 38, 39, 40, 43, 44, 47, 52, 53, 54, 55, 64, 66, 74, 176, 179, 221, 222, 258, 281, 282, 283, 289, 291, 296, 306, 312, 426, 427, 428
Kleppel, B., 396
Kline, B. E., 453
Klinghoffer, K. A., 391
Klumpp, T. G., 345
Knauer, 279
Kniga, A. G., 79
Knight, B. C. J. G., 112, 113
Knoop, F., 358, 359
Knop, W., 191
Knouff, R. A., 305
Knowles, F., 225
Knox, W. E., 361
Knudson, A., 180
Koch, F., 169
Koch, J., 215
Koch, K., 181, 438, 442
Koch, W., 25, 30, 214, 320, 326, 452
Kochakian, C. D., 396
Kochendorfer, E. W., 454
Köchling, J., 508
Koganei, R., 202
Kögl, G., 411
Kohl, M. F. F., 350
Kolmer, J. A., 451
Komatsu, S., 48, 54, 95
Kooyman, D. J., 315
Koppenhoefer, R. M., 314, 521
Kornerup, V., 425
Kornov, I. S., 220, 222
Korrodi, H., 298
Kosterlitz, H. W., 389
Koyanagi, H., 318
Kraay, G. M., 239
Krahl, M. E., 96
Krainick, H. G., 180
Krampitz, L. O., 88
Krasnow, F., 180, 439, 441

Krause, A. C., 316
Krause, R. F., 256, 298, 299
Kraybill, H. R., 56, 230, 489, 491, 492, 508
Kremers, R. E., 78, 84, 323, 513
Kresling, K., 202
Krieger, C. H., 440
Kritchevsky, W., 520
Kroeker, E. H., 161, 217
Kröper, H., 520
Kruft, H., 503
Krüger, M., 23
Kruse, N. F., 487
Kruyt, H. R., 75
Kudicke, R., 107
Kudrajawzewa, A., 440
Kugler, O. E., 341, 398
Kühl, H., 226, 511
Kuhn, R., 13
Kumagawa, M., 148
Kumler, W. D., 18
Kummer, H., 221
Kummerow, F. A., 239
Kunzer, H., 497
Kurahashi, K., 518
Kurosawa, T., 446
Kurtz, F. E., 181, 326
Kutscher, F., 110
Kuttner, T., 180
Kuwashima, K., 420
Kyes, P., 99, 107, 421, 422

LaBarre, J., 446
Ladd, A. T., 380
Landau, A. L., 418
Landsteiner, K., 447, 448
Lang, A., 283, 286, 342, 386, 436
Langwill, K. E., 505, 512
Lapworth, A., 39
Lardy, H. A., 397
Laszt, L., 347, 363
Lathrop, W. C., 204, 212
Latzer, P., 21, 95, 103, 107, 108, 110, 122
Laudenslager, H., 521
Lauffer, M. A., 213
Lausten, A., 84, 85, 323
Lawrence, J. H., 387, 437
Lea, C. H., 352
Leary, T., 433
Leathes, J. B., 4, 5, 69, 71, 340, 443
LeBreton, E., 109, 161, 260
Ledebt, E., 100, 107, 422
Lederer, E. L., 515, 520
Lee, W. Y., 223
Lefèvre-Lebeau, Y., 505
Legault-Demare, J., 13
Lehnherr, E. R., 380, 429
Lehninger, A. L., 344
Lehrman, L., 94
Leinfelder, P. J., 316
Leites, S., 298, 383
Leites, S. M., 355
Leloir, L. F., 359, 361
Lembke, A., 453
Leone, E., 301
Lepeshkin, V. V., 75
Lepper, H. A., 158, 159
Lerner, S. R., 370
Lesch, W., 406
Lesnick, G., 439

Lesser, M. A., 520
Lesuk, A., 16, 42, 53, 54, 257, 318
Letonoff, T. V., 450
Leuchs, H., 31
Leulier, A., 305
Levene, P. A., 11, 12, 16, 21, 27, 37, 39, 40, 43, 44, 46, 48, 54, 58, 59, 60, 61, 62, 63, 64, 95, 102, 103, 107, 108, 176, 177, 192, 219, 222, 257, 281, 282, 285, 289, 320, 321, 322, 422, 446
Levi, H. B., 401
Levin, B. S., 412
Levine, C., 177
Levine, M., 197, 198, 407
Levis, I. B., 503
Lévy, J., 24
Levy, S. R., 377, 388, 392, 436
Lewis, W. C. M., 12, 13, 14, 72, 78, 96
Li, S. L., 223
Libet, B., 453
Lichtenstein, L., 430
Lieb, H., 153, 275
Liebermann, L., 82
Lieboff, S. L., 181
Liebrecht, A., 96, 503
Liebreich, O., 23
Lignac, G. O. E., 426
Likiernik, A., 191
Limpächer, R., 12, 59, 108, 112, 122
Linden, G. M. von, 96, 503
Linderstrøm-Lang, K., 404
Lindgren, F. T., 88
Linnert, K., 54
Lintzel, W., 169, 176, 402
Lipmann, F., 113, 115
Lippmann, E. O., 238
Lishkevich, M. I., 219, 228, 229
Lison, L., 183, 507
Little, J. M., 348
Little, L., 507
Loane, C. M., 500, 514
Lobstein, J. E., 324
Lockwood, H. C., 93
Loeb, H. G., 379
Loeb, J., 341
Loew, O., 339
Loewe, S., 81, 98
Lohmann, Z., 110
Löhr, G., 288
Lombroso, U., 362
Long, C. N. H., 434
Long, J. H., 72, 74, 297
Longenecker, H. E., 230, 327, 350, 351
Looney, J. M., 379
Lorenz, F. W., 287, 386, 399, 401
Lorenz, K., 425, 426
Löwe, S., 68
Lowrimore, B., 510
Lucas, C. C., 36, 174, 413, 418
Lüdecke, H., 406
Lüdecke, K., 16, 59, 96, 99, 103
Ludewig, S., 426, 429, 430, 439
Ludwig, H., 508
Lukens, F. D. W., 359
Lund, A. A., 502, 516
Lundberg, W. O., 507
Lundsgaard, E., 374, 381
Lustig, B., 300

Lyons M. A., 441
Lyons, R. E., 196

Ma, T. S., 180
Ma, W., 442
MacArthur, C. G., 15, 27, 29, 37, 281
McArthur, C. S., 418, 433
McCalla, A. G., 224, 226
McCay, C. M., 402
McClenahan, F. M., 235, 405
McClendon, J. F., 82, 347
McCollum, E. V., 322, 400
McConnell, K. P., 283, 367, 395, 397
McDermott, E. B., 451
McDougall, E. J., 391
McEwen, H. D., 97, 396
McFarlane, A. S., 88, 213
Macfarlane, M. G., 112, 113, 213
Macfarlane, R. G., 444
McGavack, T. H., 435
McGuire, T. A., 181, 230
Macheboeuf, M. A., 81, 84, 86, 87, 91, 92, 93, 207, 274, 449
McHenry, E. W., 286, 295, 356, 393, 414
McKay, E. M., 359, 360, 363
McKee, S. H., 436
McKibben, J. M., 79, 153, 173
McKinney, R. S., 94, 156, 162, 220, 222
MacLachlan, P. L., 97, 182, 286, 305, 351, 378, 386, 396
MacLaren, F. H., 522
Maclean, H., 4, 5, 7, 11, 15, 25, 26, 28, 38, 54, 55, 57, 58, 59, 95, 150, 192, 320
MacLean, I. S., 4, 5, 7, 28, 38, 55, 150, 192, 214
McLean, J., 446
McLeod, J., 446
McNabb, A. R., 274, 276, 279
MacPherson, D. J., 432
Macpherson, L. B., 36
McQuarrie, I., 434, 441
Macy, J., 267
Maddison, L., 326
Magat, J., 453
Magendantz, H., 424, 425
Magistris, H., 55, 78, 103, 217, 236, 237, 238, 422
Magnant, C., 71
Mahler, A., 380
Maiese, M. R., 510
Majmin, R., 94
Malesani, S., 448
Malquori, G., 74
Maltaner, E., 90, 446, 448, 451
Maltaner, F., 58, 62, 90, 446, 448, 451
Man, E. B., 149, 152, 162, 377, 378, 379, 429, 430, 431, 434, 435, 441
Man, J., 502
Manasse, A., 322
Manceau, 406
Mandler, E., 300
Manery, J. F., 394
Mann, G. V., 513
Manwaring, W. H., 100
Manzi, G., 301

Marchenko, V. F., 451
Marenzi, A. D., 167, 171, 172, 175, 264, 267, 292, 378, 438
Markley, K. S., 483, 504
Markley, M. C., 501, 507
Markman, A., 496
Marmor, R. A., 496
Marquet, F., 274
Marrack, J. R., 477
Marshall, P. G., 20
Martin, H., 497, 499
Marziani, R., 387
Masai, Y., 399
Mashino, M., 490
Masoro, E. J., 353
Masuda, Y., 321
Masurovsky, B. I., 512, 513
Matagrin, A., 520
Materna, A., 303
Matthews, V. J., 314, 436
Mattikow, M., 493, 500
Mattill, H. A., 455
Mattson, R., 77
Maurukas, J., 119, 120
Maxwell, W., 192
May, A., 506
May, R. M., 161, 284
Mayer, A., 82, 270, 341, 342
Mayer, F., 55, 93, 321, 511
Mayer, F. M., 220, 224, 226, 227
Mayer, P., 93, 99
Maynard, L. A., 152, 402
Mazzoco, P., 380
Mecham, D. K., 89
Mecheels, O., 515
Medes, G., 354, 359
Meek, W. J., 174
Mehltretter, C. L., 103
Meier, R., 97
Meigs, E. B., 402
Meinertz, J., 54
Meissen, E., 96, 503
Melin, M., 88
Mellanby, J., 443
Memelsdorff, I., 408
Menke, W., 89
Menten, M. L., 427
Menzel, A. E. O., 94, 449
Merz, O., 517
Merz, W., 44, 53, 64, 65
Meserve, E. R., 175
Mesrobeanu, L., 449, 450
Meyer, E. W., 64, 500, 505, 514
Meyer, K., 448
Meyer, K. H., 23
Meyerhof, O., 19, 452, 453, 454
Migliacci, D., 182
Mihalik, I., 121, 123
Miles, A. A., 110, 450
Miles, E. M., 110
Miller, E. S., 363, 366, 369
Miller, E. v. O., 351
Miller, J. A., 453
Millican, R. C., 289
Mills, C. A., 86, 443, 444
Milner, R. T., 78, 156, 220
Milskii, A., 156
Minatoya, S., 518
Miner, I., 442
Minor, G. R., 430
Mitchell, H. S., 509
Mitimoto, H., 440

Mitolo, M., 278
Miura, K., 437
Moberly, C. W., 521
Modern, F., 448
Moggi, D., 346
Mojonnier, T., 326
Molines, J., 69, 180, 486
Möller, F. A., 522
Monasterio, G., 155, 169, 176
Montezomolo, R., 398
Montgomery, M. L., 356, 416
Moore, D. H., 86, 92
Moosnick, F. B., 415
Moraczewski, W. v., 77
Morávek, V., 77
Morawitz, P., 444
Morehead, R. P., 31, 357
Morehouse, M. G., 354
Morgan, R. H., 505
Morgan, W. T. J., 449, 450
Morgulis, S., 296, 309, 394
Mori, S., 490
Morris, C. E., 507
Morse, W. J., 221
Moruzzi, G., 15
Mossini, A., 499
Mottram, V. H., 387
Moussa, A., 407
Moyer, A. W., 416
Moyer, L. S., 88
Moyer, W. W., 496
Mueller, G. C., 453
Mühlbock, O., 381
Mukherjee, L. N., 80
Müller, E., 281
Müller, E. F. W., 297
Müller, F., 364
Muller, G. L., 432
Müller, J. H., 347, 349
Munk, I., 345, 348
Munoz, J. M., 361, 380
Muntoni, E., 436
Murlin, J. R., 407
Murphy, A. J., 441
Murti, K. S., 299
Musher, S., 509, 514, 522

Nachmann, M., 18
Nagai, M., 522
Nagel, R. H., 78
Nagler, F. P. O., 13
Nagy, J. J., 508
Nair, J. H., 159, 326
Nakahara, W., 410
Nakamoto, T., 422
Nakamura, M., 508
Narat, J. K., 431
Nartsisov, N. V., 451
Near, C., 225, 226
Nedswedsky, S. W., 383
Needham, J., 398
Nerking, J., 161, 313, 317
Neubauer, E., 72, 74
Neuberg, C., 20, 100, 411
Neumann, W., 230
Neuschlosz, S. M., 72
Newman, M. S., 208, 213, 214, 216
Newton, J. K., 314, 436
Nichols, P. L., Jr., 40
Nicolle, M., 196
Nielsen, J. P., 158
Nielson, P. E., 397

Niemann, C., 40, 42, 43
Niemierko, W., 319
Niescher, M. F., 511
Nikuni, J., 106
Ninomiya, M., 234
Nishimoto, U., 17, 222, 320, 322
Nishimura, T., 196
Noguchi, H., 99, 106, 422
Norberg, B., 153
Norbury, F. G., 27, 29
Nord, F. F., 420
Norris, W. P., 42, 116
North, G. C., 325, 507, 512
Nottbohm, F. E., 55, 93, 220, 224,
    226, 227, 321, 511
Noyce, B. N., 361
Nussbaumer, T., 505
Nyman, M. A., 89

Obata, Y., 19, 121
O'Connell, P. W., 454
Oehme, H., 60
Offenkrantz, F. M., 441
Ogawa, K., 101, 108
Ohara, I., 221, 490
Ohl, F., 515
Öhman, L. O., 115, 398
Okano, K., 221, 490
Okey, R., 287, 302, 342, 381
Okonogi, T., 378
Okunev, N., 73
Olcott, H. S., 36, 89, 227, 223,
    455
Oleson, M. C., 303, 305
Olley, J., 351, 356
Olsen, A. G., 78, 84, 323, 513
Olsen, C., 404
Olson, F. B., 395
Olson, K. B., 362, 368, 376, 388,
    392, 394
Oncley, J. L., 87, 88
Oosterhout, J. C. D., 514, 515
Osborne, T. B., 82, 84, 325
Ose, K., 221
Osterberg, A. E., 364
Othmer, D. F., 514
Otoslki, S. W., 298
Outhouse, E. L., 410, 420
Overman, R. S., 447

Paal, C., 60
Paal, H., 59
Pachur, R., 315
Page, I. H., 11, 12, 22, 27, 28, 32,
    33, 37, 59, 62, 100, 105, 112, 149,
    152, 160, 162, 168, 169, 181, 266,
    273, 282, 354, 378, 380, 385, 394,
    420, 430, 431, 452, 454
Palladin, A., 440
Palladin, A. V., 278
Palmer, K. J., 71, 73, 85, 91
Palmer, L. S., 88, 324
Pangborn, M. C., 15, 50, 58, 59,
    199, 451
Pantaleon, J., 109
Paquin, F., 438
Paris, J., 202
Paris, R., 17
Parnas, J., 25, 26, 37, 48
Parpart, A. K., 85
Parsons, T. R., 90

Partington, P. F., 362, 368, 376,
    388, 392, 394, 395
Partridge, S. M., 450
Pascal, J., 422, 423
Passino, H. J., 493
Pässler, J., 77, 513
Pasternak, L., 273, 378, 380, 394
Patek, A. J., Jr., 451
Patterson, J. M., 286, 295, 356,
    393, 414
Paul, H. E., 315
Paul, M. F., 315
Paul, S., 455
Pauli, W., 411
Pauling, L., 447
Pearson, R. W., 230, 239, 406
Peck, R. L., 211, 212, 217, 218
Pedelty, W. H., 22, 222, 231, 351,
    352
Pederson, K. D., 87
Pelkan, K. F., 149
Pelou, A., 176
Pelzman, O., 115
Peretti, G., 348, 369, 377
Peritz, G., 442
Perlman, E., 450
Perlman, I., 362, 373, 374, 376,
    387, 389, 390, 392, 394, 395, 401,
    408, 419
Perlman, J. L., 159, 323, 324, 326
Perrier, C., 374, 403
Petermann, M. L., 113
Peters, B. A., 453
Peters, J. P., 259, 345, 360, 377,
    407, 430, 431, 434, 435, 441
Petersen, W. E., 326, 415
Peterson, W. H., 161, 217
Pfähler, E., 18, 19
Pfennenger, U., 55
Pfützer, G., 405
Phelps, I. K., 158
Phillips, P. H., 397
Pick, E. P., 348, 367
Pick, L., 78, 425, 426
Pico, C. E., 448
Pierre, W. H., 230, 239, 406
Piettre, 16, 148
Piffault, C., 412
Pighini G., 104, 442
Pihl, A., 340
Pike, F., 30
Pillet, J., 97
Pinner, M., 447
Piper, C. V., 221
Pirie, H. W., 450
Pirosky, I., 450
Pisarev, N. S., 505
Pischinger, A., 53
Piskur, M. M., 508
Platt, A. P., 419
Plaut, F., 447
Plimmer, R. H. A., 18, 399
Poetsch, W., 215
Poindexter, C. A., 439
Polgar, N., 211
Pollack, A., 387
Pollak, J. E., 497
Ponticorvo, L., 352
Pool, W. O., 349
Popják, G., 295, 401
Poptzova, A., 229
Porges, O., 72, 74

Porter, A. E., 110
Porter, R. R., 419
Power, F. B., 16
Pratt, D. B., Jr., 511
Pratt, J. H., 362
Pratt, J. P., 301
Pregl, F., 181, 261
Present, C. H., 288, 386
Price, C. W., 14, 97
Price, H. I., 12, 13, 14
Proell, W. A., 514
Prohaska, J. V., 356
Prokopchuk, A., 439
Prout, F. S., 209, 211
Przylecki, S. J., 84, 94
Puchkovskiĭ, B. S., 79
Pyenson, H., 78
Pyman, F. L., 19

Quastel, J. H., 359, 393
Quimby, W. S., 514, 515

Raab, W., 380
Rabinowitch, I. M., 436
Rachelle, J. R., 416
Rae, J. J., 17, 19
Raeth, K., 302
Raistrick, H., 449
Ralli, E. P., 288, 355, 386
Ramsay, W. N. M., 165, 167, 170, 171, 178, 262, 263, 264, 265, 267
Randall, L. O., 276, 277, 279, 436
Randles, F. S., 180
Ranney, R. E., 273, 379, 387
Rapaport, G. H., 513
Raper, H. S., 349, 359, 370, 387, 392, 395
Rapp, 520
Rashba, E. I., 278
Rask, O. S., 158
Raspopina, A., 232
Rathbun, R. B., 515
Ravazzoni, C., 110, 121, 123
Ravdin, I. S., 347
Ravich-Shcherbo, M. I., 451
Raymond, M. J., 355
Rebbe, O. H., 401
Redemann, C. E., 31
Redgrove, H. S., 520
Rees, H. V., 515
Reeves, R. E., 88
Reichel, C., 446
Reichel, M., 43, 45, 47
Reineke, E. P., 403
Reiner, M., 347
Reinhardt, W. O., 349, 383
Reinstein, H., 165, 167, 171, 174, 264, 265, 385
Reiser, R., 157, 315, 390
Remezov, I., 14, 72, 74, 75
Renall, M. H., 26, 62
Renfrew, A. G., 212
Rennkamp, F., 64
Rering, C. M., 76
Reuland, K., 455
Reverey, G., 494, 499, 506
Revol, L., 305
Rewald, B., 4, 157, 158, 193, 215, 216, 220, 221, 222, 223, 225, 226, 227, 228, 229, 230, 232, 234, 235,

238, 239, 240, 241, 242, 314, 318, 323, 326, 405, 486, 487, 492, 497, 498, 504, 505, 506, 511, 513, 515, 516, 517, 518, 521
Reynolds, M. C., 506
Rezek, A., 109, 110
Reznichenko, M., 229
Rhoden, E., 387
Rhodes, E., 239, 240
Rhymer, I., 421
Rich, A. R., 414
Rich, J. R., 512
Richards, A. G., Jr., 279
Richardson, A. S., 510
Richardson, G. A., 509
Richter, G., 61, 502
Riddell, C. B., 442
Riddle, O., 399
Rideal, E. K., 70
Ridout, J. H., 357, 358, 370, 389, 418
Rieckehoff, I. G., 352
Riede, W., 220, 223, 405
Riedel, J. D., 60
Riegel, C., 347
Riemenschneider, R. W., 179, 320, 322, 508, 509
Riley, R. F., 410
Rimpila, C. E., 88
Rittenberg, D., 168, 170, 279, 280, 288, 292, 293, 312, 320, 350, 352, 354, 360
Ritter, F., 60
Ritter, W., 505
Rivas, L., 433
Rivers, T. M., 213
Roberts, E. G., 193, 205, 206, 208, 212
Roberts, R. L., 119, 126
Robertson, T. B., 398
Robinson, A., 407
Robinson, C. S., 348
Robinson, R., 211
Roche, A., 274
Rockwell, H. E., 116
Rodzevich, V., 320
Roe, J. H., 180
Roeder, F., 434, 448
Roehrig, P., 291, 292, 310, 341
Roffo, A., 411
Rogers, H. T., 230, 239, 406
Rogers, L. A., 327
Rohdewald, M., 81
Rolf, I. P., 12, 16, 21, 37, 58, 59, 60, 61, 62, 95, 102, 107, 108, 219, 222, 257, 281, 282, 320, 321, 322, 422
Rollett, A., 59
Rollman, H. S., 345
Roman, W., 175, 176
Romanoff, E. B., 379
Romieu, M., 183
Rona, P., 74, 75, 76
Rony, H. R., 379
Rosahn, P. D., 430
Rose, C. S., 419
Rose, W. G., 110, 116, 119, 120, 125, 508
Rosen, I., 439, 441
Rosenberg, A. A., 451
Rosenberg, D. H., 451
Rosenberg, E., 100

Rosenberg, H. R., 413
Rosenbloom, J., 97
Rosenbusch, R., 494, 498, 499, 501, 506, 520
Rosenheim, O., 54
Rosenstein, A., 348
Rosenthal, C., 353
Rosenthal, S. R., 433
Rosenthal, W., 502
Rossinskaya, I. M., 355
Rossiter, R. J., 274, 276, 279
Roth, H., 157, 405
Roth, M. H., 516
Rothwell, C. S., 349
Rotter, D. L., 357
Rousseau, E., 422, 423
Rowland, B. W., 522
Rowland, R. S., 425
Roy, A. C., 180
Royce, H. D., 508, 510
Ruben, S., 362, 364, 373, 374, 376, 387, 389, 390, 392, 395
Rubin, S. H., 288, 356, 386
Rückert, W., 403
Rudy, H., 12, 22, 27, 28, 32, 33, 37, 62, 168, 282, 447
Ruppert, A., 215
Rusch, H. P., 453
Rusoff, I. I., 363
Russell, M., 119, 120
Russell, M. A., 149, 429, 430
Rybak, B., 97
Rydin, A., 349

Sabin, F. R., 208, 210, 438, 449
Sachs, H., 99, 107, 448
Sadowski, T., 77
Sagara, J., 216
Sahyun, M., 31, 420
Saidel, L. J., 31
Sakai, R., 35, 221, 222
Sakaki, C., 301
Sakakibara, I., 450
Salcedo, J., Jr., 356, 357
Salis, T. v., 520
Salisbury, L. F., 63, 155, 215, 258, 318
Salit, P. W., 316
Salmoiraghi, E., 490
Salmon, W. D., 414
Salomon, H., 16
Sammartino, U., 292
Sammet, K., 406
Samuelson, E., 324
Sandelin, A. E., 513
Sandholzer, L. A., 197
Sandor, G., 84, 87, 92, 274, 449
Sarciron, R., 450
Sarzana, G., 388, 389, 390, 395
Sato, K., 522
Sato, M., 59, 60, 74, 77, 79, 491, 495, 502, 519
Saubert, S. S. P., 76
Saunders, H. F., 517
Schachner, H., 396, 408
Schaefer, W., 200, 449
Schaeffer, G., 270, 341, 342
Schäfer, P., 55, 237, 238
Schäffner, A., 20
Schaible, P. J., 273
Schantz, E. J., 513
Scharf, A., 440, 508

Schauenstein, E., 179
Scheff, G. J., 106
Scheidegger, S., 426
Schick, B. 425
Schlack, P., 517
Schlagdenhauffen, F., 191
Schleicher, E. M., 415
Schloemer, A., 182
Schmalfuss, K., 230
Schmidt, C. L. A., 420
Schmidt, E., 59, 105
Schmidt, G., 4, 16, 46, 67, 109, 172
Schmidt, G. A., 210
Schmidt, L. H., 149, 268, 380, 387, 394
Schmidt, R., 110
Schmidt, W., 179, 225, 226, 227, 233, 234, 513
Schmidt-Nielsen, K., 347, 390
Schmitt, F. O., 71, 73, 85, 91
Schmitz, E., 169, 440
Schneider, A. K., 211
Schneider, H. A., 5, 29, 168, 169, 256
Schneider, W. C., 344, 361
Schoeller, W., 503
Schoenbeck, O. v., 423
Schoenheimer, R., 343, 350, 352, 354, 357, 359, 360, 425, 433
Schofield, M., 490
Scholfield, C. R., 36, 222, 230
Schönfeld, H., 493
Schramme, A., 157
Schrauth, W., 503
Schuette, H. A., 233
Schulman, J. H., 70, 346
Schultz, A. S., 513
Schulze, E., 55, 93, 191, 192, 193, 224, 235, 238
Schulze, O., 29, 34, 176, 177
Schumann, E., 52, 66, 428
Schumoff-Simonowski, C., 110
Schuster, P., 157
Schuwirth, K., 274, 275, 279, 283
Schwab, E., 448
Schwarz, E. W. K., 515
Schwarz, G., 411
Schwarz, H., 520
Schwarzkopf, H., 520
Schweiger, A., 235, 241, 314, 496, 497, 499, 500, 511, 516, 521
Scott, E. L., 94
Scott, F. H., 399
Scudi, J. V., 357
Sedlmayr, T., 214
Seegers, W. H., 443
Segré, E., 388, 389, 390, 395
Seibert, F. B., 449
Seifriz, W., 78
Sell, H. M., 78, 84, 323, 513
Selle, W. A., 438
Serantes, M. E., 272, 277, 287, 292, 293, 294, 296, 308, 310, 379
Serono, C., 398
Setz, P., 44, 65, 150, 264, 265, 274
Severinghaus, A. E., 86
Shabanov, I. M., 234
Shaffer, P. A., 359, 360
Shapiro, A., 364
Shapiro, S., 183
Sharpless, G. R., 414

Shear, M. J., 450
Sheehy, E. J., 403
Shepardson, H. C., 436
Sherbakov, A. P., 406
Sherberg, R. O., 297
Shinowara, G. Y., 60, 305
Shinozaki, S., 60
Shinozaki, Y., 502
Shipley, R. A., 419
Shirley, D. A., 210
Shollenberger, J. H., 221
Shorey, E. C., 243
Shorland, F. B., 287, 290, 291
Shreder, V. N., 433
Sieber, N., 110
Siegel, L., 177
Sifferd, R. H., 489
Sigurdsson, B., 85
Silbowitz, R., 433
Simms, H. S., 12, 21, 59, 95, 102, 107, 108, 257, 289, 422
Simms, S., 448
Simon, F. P., 453
Simone, R. M., 510
Sinclair, A. T., 224, 226
Sinclair, R. G., 21, 58, 165, 262, 263, 264, 268, 273, 283, 291, 294, 300, 312, 315, 317, 342, 343, 346, 347, 350, 351, 357, 362, 364, 366, 367, 368, 369, 381, 388, 389, 390, 393, 394, 395, 396, 397, 452
Singer, K., 442
Singer, P. A., 490, 491
Sisley, J. P., 516
Sjölin, S., 71
Sjövall, A., 427
Skipin, A. I., 232
Slanetz, C. A., 440
Slight, D., 434
Slotta, K. H., 106, 108
Slowtzoff, B. J., 105
Smadel, J. E., 213
Small, C. W., 47
Smedley-MacLean, I., 4, 395
Smit, B. J., 327
Smith, A. K., 491
Smith, C., 347, 367, 389
Smith, C. C., 439
Smith, H. G., 454
Smith, J. A. B., 195, 240, 242, 289, 402
Smith, J. H. C., 405
Smith, J. L., 276
Smithburn, K. C., 449
Smolenski, K., 224
Snell, A. M., 431
Snider, R. H., 21, 289, 307, 308, 311, 312, 342, 454
Snyder, W. E., 512
Sobotka, H., 378, 409, 425, 440
Soden, O. v., 215
Sokolov, A. V., 156
Solandt, D. Y., 420
Solandt, O. M., 176
Sollmann, E. I., 514
Sommer, H. H., 325, 327
Sonol, J., 520
Sorenson, S. O., 487
Sörensen, S. P. L., 87
Sorg, K., 300, 309, 398
Soru, E., 450
Soskin, S., 354, 413, 431, 432, 451

Sosman, M. C., 425
Soule, M. H., 196
Sowden, J. C., 116
Sperry, W. M., 287, 364, 365, 368, 370, 395, 396, 425, 426, 427, 428, 432
Spiegel-Adolf, M., 72, 73, 74, 76, 90
Spielman, M. A., 208, 209, 210, 211
Spielmeyer, W., 428
Sprague, B. S., 503
Spranger, W., 79
Sprinsky, P., 438
Srere, P. A., 408, 433
Stadie, W. C., 345, 359, 360
Ställberg, S., 211
Stalmann, G., 522
Stamm, W., 110
Stanley, J., 77, 504, 506, 512
Stanley, W. M., 213
Stanley-Brown, M., 213, 446
Stare, F. J., 513
Stassano, H., 99
Stegmann, L., 48, 238
Steiger, A., 71
Steiger, E., 192, 224
Steiner, L. F., 521
Steinert, J., 450
Steinle, L. E., 518
Stenhagen, E., 211
Stephenson, M., 406
Stephenson, R. E., 406
Stepp, W., 51
Stern, B., 439
Stern, M., 25, 48
Stetten, D., Jr., 343, 350, 352, 353, 356, 357, 359, 371, 411, 416, 417, 419, 420
Stewart, C. P., 149, 161, 165, 167, 170, 171, 178, 180, 261, 262, 263, 264, 265, 267
Stewart, H. C., 346
Stewart, W. C., 350
Stieg, F. B., 517
Stiemans, H., 412
Stillman, N., 363, 389, 391, 419
Stirton, A. J., 509
Stodola, F. H., 88
Stoesser, A. V., 441
Stoneburg, C. A., 85
Stonecipher, W. D., 403
Stoop, F., 31
Storgårds, T., 510
Storm van Leeuwen, W., 103
Stotz, W., 454
Stoyanoff, V. A., 368, 370, 395, 396
Strauch, G., 501
Strauss, A., 96, 503
Strecker, A., 10, 21, 23, 95, 96, 297
Street, H. E., 174, 175, 176
Strickler, A., 439
Strohecker, R., 455
Strong, F. M., 161, 217
Strukova, J. P., 79
Sturgis, B. M., 521
Subbarow, Y., 180, 261
Sueyoshi, Y., 14, 320, 321, 378, 437, 440
Sullivan, B., 225, 226, 227

Sullivan, F. M., 493
Süllmann, H., 347, 349, 509
Sulze, W., 348
Sumrell, G., 211
Supplee, G. C., 327
Sure, B., 378, 414
Susaki, R., 327
Suto, K., 148
Suzuki, B., 17, 119, 222, 283
Svensson, H., 87
Swanson, A. M., 327
Swanson, M. A., 346, 372, 391
Sweany, H. C., 438
Swift, C. E., 508
Szent-György, A. v., 103, 454
Szyszka, G., 106

Tait, H., 452, 453
Tajima, K., 161, 349
Takata, R., 216
Talalay, J. A., 518
Tamamushi, B., 522
Tammelander, R., 59
Tamura, S., 55
Tanaka, I., 406
Taniguchi, T., 448
Tashiro, S., 380
Tatu, H., 515
Taub, A., 510
Tauboeck, K., 491
Täufel, K., 182, 508
Taurog, A., 148, 153, 169, 175, 266, 268, 287, 372, 387, 408, 410
Taveau, R., 419
Tayeau, F., 88, 92, 324, 429
Taylor, A. R., 213
Taylor, H. E., 173
Taylor, J. D., 315
Taylor, T. C., 94
Taylor, W. E., 153, 173
Tebb, M. C., 54
Tennant, R., 115, 438
Teorell, T., 70, 153
Tepperman, J., 434
Terroine, E. F., 82, 99, 291, 292, 310, 341, 342
Teunissen, P. H., 75, 296, 426
Thaler, H., 161
Thannhauser, S. J., 4, 16, 21, 42, 43, 44, 45, 46, 47, 53, 54, 65, 67, 109, 150, 165, 167, 171, 172, 173, 174, 257, 264, 265, 274, 276, 280, 285, 288, 292, 293, 294, 296, 310, 318, 385, 424, 425, 426, 429
Theis, E. R., 284, 285, 430
Thiele, F. H., 110
Thiele, F. W., 511
Thiele, M., 516
Thierfelder, H., 25, 29, 34, 38, 39, 48, 54, 55, 74, 176, 177
Thomae, E., 520
Thomas, A., 73
Thomas, E. M., 430
Thomas, K., 39
Thomas, R. C., 216
Thornley, B. D., 494
Thornton, M. H., 56, 58, 223, 230, 491, 492
Thudichum, J. L. W., 5, 6, 9, 11, 20, 23, 25, 38, 39, 43, 44, 46, 48, 182, 275, 276
Thunberg, T., 421, 453

Thurman, B. H., 227, 228, 230, 490, 492, 496, 498, 499, 507, 508, 513, 521
Thurston, L. M., 327, 510
Tidwell, H. C., 346
Timbres, H. G., 426
Tischer, A. O., 493
Tiselius, A., 87
Titus, H. W., 179, 320, 322
Tocantins, L. M., 447
Tomita, S., 508
Tompkins, E. H., 427, 438
Tompsett, S. L., 96
Töpler, 9, 191, 238
Topley, W. W. C., 449, 450
Torboli, A., 109
Tore, D., 348
Towne, C. C., 514
Trager, A., 115
Trautmann, A., 402
Treadwell, C. R., 355
Trevan, J. W., 444
Trier, G., 15, 23, 26, 235, 237, 420
Trifanowsky, D., 297
Tristram, G. R., 78, 240
Trotskiǐ, N. V., 243
Tropp, C., 43, 64, 293, 427
Troy, H. C., 326
Trueger, E., 503, 514
Trusler, R. B., 520
Tsujimoto, M., 37, 318
Tucker, H. F., 356, 415
Turer, J., 509
Turner, C. E., 403
Turner, H. A., 69
Turner, K., 70, 87, 294
Turner, M. E., 274
Turpeinen, O., 216
Tutin, F., 16, 18, 19
Tyrén, H., 368, 376

Udagawa, H., 101, 113
Uhnoo, B., 316
Ulpiani, C., 16, 95
Ulrich, R., 405
Umber, H., 435
Urban, F. F., 313
Urbanic, A., 77
Uri, W. J., 121, 123
Uyei, N., 201

Valdiguié, P., 279
Valencienne, 9
Valette, G., 75
Van der Waarden, 510
Van Slyke, D. D., 149, 152, 160, 162, 166, 169, 181, 259, 261, 266, 267, 345, 360, 377, 407, 430, 431
Van Voorhis, S. N., 197
Vaughan, J. A., 521
Vauquelin, 9, 255
Velick, S. F., 198, 209
Verberg, H. G., 72, 74
Verkade, P. E., 126, 359
Verna, L. C., 200
Verzár, F., 347, 363, 391
Vibrans, F. C., 508
Vigne, H., 326
Virtanen, A. L., 59
Vischer, E., 359

Vishnevskaya, G. R., 79
Vita, G., 59
Voit, K., 51, 183
Volkin, E., 451
von Euler, H., 236
von Schoenbeck, O., 22, 289, 291
von Zeynek, R., 297
Voris, L., 402
Voroshilova, L. A., 505
Voss, H., 502
Vuishnepolskaya, F., 496

Wachstein, M., 429, 451
Wacker, L., 434
Wada, N., 59
Wade, N. J., 414
Wadsworth, A., 90, 446, 448
Waelsch, H., 173, 368, 370, 395, 396
Wagner, F., 517
Wagner, H. H., 498
Wagner, R., 90
Wagner-Jauregg, T., 90, 125
Wakeman, A. J., 325
Waksman, S. A., 446
Walter, G., 320
Walters, A., 229
Walton, C., 297, 298
Warburg, O., 453
Wasteneys, H., 398
Watanabe, J., 301
Watkin, J. E., 225
Watson, G. M., 174, 175, 176
Watson, M. M., 70
Wayne, E. T., 359
Webster, J. E., 220, 225, 227, 229, 230, 233, 234, 237
Weeks, M. E., 229
Weetman, B., 522
Weidlein, E. R., Jr., 36
Weil, A. J., 442, 450
Weil, L., 149, 429, 430
Weill, J., 341
Weil-Malherbe, H., 438
Weineck, E., 213
Weinhouse, S., 303, 354, 359, 433
Weinstein, H. R., 396
Weiss, K., 231, 238, 508
Weissberger, L. H., 341, 391, 393
Weissman, N., 97
Weitkamp, A. W., 514
Welch, A. D., 418, 419
Welch, E. A., 96
Weller, A., 359
Weltman, W. C., 519
Welton, J. P., 427
Wendt, H., 377
Wenslow, A., 300
Went, I., 86
Wertheimer, D., 449
West, C. J., 27, 37, 39, 40, 43, 60, 63, 64, 95
West, H. D., 31
Westerkamp, R. F., 72, 75
Westphal, K., 438, 442
Weyl, Th., 82
Wheatley, A. H. M., 359
Wheeler, P., 442
Whetham, M. D., 406
White, M. F., 306
White, P., 431

White, P. B., 450
White, R. H., Jr., 521
Whitehead, R., 303, 305
Whitehead, W., 516
Whitehorn, J. C., 180
Wick, A. N., 360
Wiczer, S. B., 515
Widenbauer, F., 446
Wiedersheim, V., 43
Wieland, H., 353
Wiese, H. F., 88, 159, 326
Wiesehahn, G. A., 501, 504
Wilber, C. G., 318
Wilbrandt, W., 347, 349
Wilbur, K. M., 422
Wile, U. J., 313, 314, 412, 425
Wille, O., 317
Williams, C. H., 197
Williams, H. H., 169, 174, 265, 268, 344, 386, 394, 403, 432, 435
Williams, K. T., 510
Williamson, M. B., 31
Willius, F. A., 439
Willstätter, R., 16, 59, 81, 90
Wilson, J., 450
Wilson, K. M., 397, 398
Wilson, W. R., 273
Wimmer, J. E., 348
Winkler, A. W., 431
Winston, J. J., 511
Winter, I. C., 348

Winterstein, E., 48, 93, 193, 221, 224, 238
Winzler, R. J., 175
Wishart, G. M., 84
Wissner, B., 450
Witanowski, W. R., 64
Wittcoff, H., 501, 503
Witzemann, E. J., 353, 359
Wohlgemuth, J., 100, 110
Wolff, E., 431
Wolff, F., 522
Wolff, G., 512
Wollaeger, E. E., 364
Wolter, E., 522
Wood, J. L., 31
Woodman, R. M., 79, 521
Woods, H. S., 25, 320, 326
Wooldridge, L. C., 444
Woolley, D. W., 5, 35, 36, 88, 193, 217, 222, 228, 257, 280
Working, E. B., 226, 243, 504, 505, 507, 511
Worm, M., 297
Wörner, E., 39
Wornum, W. E., 494
Wright, I. S., 447
Wright, P. A., 158, 326
Wurtz, A., 23, 34

Yamasaki, M., 449
Yamamoto, R., 234

Yasuda, M., 182, 276, 291, 342, 434, 436
Yokela, E., 287
Yokoyama, Y., 17, 283, 321
Yoshinaga, T., 17, 110
Yosida, N., 411
Yosida, T., 319
Young, F. G., 354
Youngburg, G. E., 316
Yriart, M., 354
Yumikura, S., 78

Zacherl, M. K., 153, 275
Zain, H., 74
Zaky, Y. A. H., 22, 228, 231, 232, 234
Zamecnik, P. C., 113, 115
Zapp, J. A., Jr., 359
Zehner, L., 411
Ziegelmayer, W., 511
Ziesset, A., 158
Zietzsche, F., 18
Ziff, D., 288
Ziff, M., 91, 92, 98, 168, 170, 256, 279, 280, 292, 293, 312, 320, 445
Zilversmit, D. B., 347, 372, 382, 383, 384, 385, 388, 390, 391, 394
Zinsser, H. H., 443
Zlataroff, S., 405
Zorabyan, A. I., 232
Zunz, E., 446

Subject Index

Absorption
  of lipides, 346–348, 390–392
  of phosphatides, 346–348
Acetal phosphatides, 51, 52
  aldehydes in, 51, 53
  analysis of, 173, 174
  classification of, 7, 8
  distribution in animal organs, 257
  hydrolysis, 51, 52
  in brain, 280
  in cardiac muscle, 256, 310
  in liver, 256, 284–288
  properties of, 51, 52, 66, 67
  purification of, 52, 66, 67
  sources, 53
  structure proof, 51, 52
  synthesis of, 124
Acetylcholine, 419, 420
Acid-base relationships
  of cephalin phosphatides, 32–34
  of lecithin, 12–15
  of phosphatidylaminoethyl alcohol, 32–34
  of phosphatidylserine, 30, 31, 33
  of sphingomyelin, 45
Acids, mixtures with phosphatides, 500
Adhesives, 522
Adrenal gland
  phosphatides in, 303–306
  role in fat metabolism, 363
Adsorption of phosphatides, 56, 57, 491, 492
Alcohols (see also Glycerol, Inositol, Sphingosine), as constituents of phosphatides, 7
Alcoholysis, 59, 60
Aldehydes, in acetal phosphatides, 51, 53
Alfalfa, phosphatides in, 239, 242, 243
Alimentary paste, use of phosphatides in, 511
Alipotropism (see also Fatty livers, Lipotropism), 355–358, 414, 415
Alkaloids, 74, 97
Alkyd coatings, use of phosphatides in, 517, 518
Allergy, 442

Alumina, absorption of phosphatides on, 64
Amidomyelin, 38
Amines
  aminoethyl alcohol, 26, 34
  sphingosine, 7
Aminodihydroxyoctadecene (see Sphingosine)
Aminoethanol (see Aminoethyl alcohol)
Aminoethyl alcohol (see also Phosphatidylaminoethyl alcohol), 26, 34
  alcohol group, reactions of, 34
  amino group, reactions of, 34
  analysis by periodate oxidation, 170
  chloroplatinate of, 26
  classification of, 6
  determination of, 177
    as diiodosalicylate, 177
    as gold chloride salt, 177
    by distillation, 177
    by periodate oxidation, 170, 177
    by titration, 177
  gold chloride salt of, 26, 177
  in brain, 281
  isolation of as diiodosalicylate, 168
  metabolic functions of, 420, 421
  presence in cephalin fraction, 5
  properties of, 34
  salt formation, 34
  synthesis of, 34
Aminolipides, classification of, 6
Anemia, 432, 433
Animal oil, isolation of phosphatides from, 494
Animal organs, phosphatides in, 259 ff.
Animal tissue, phosphatides in, 9
Animals, phosphatides in, 255–258
Anticoagulants, 447
Antigens, 447–452
Antioxidants, 454, 455, 507–510
Apomyelin, 38
Arachidonic acid, 21, 281, 282
  in adrenal gland phosphatides, 305, 306
  in bone marrow phosphatides, 299
  in egg phosphatides, 321, 322
  in liver phosphatides, 289

547

Arachidonic acid, in muscle phosphatides, 312
  in pancreas phosphatides, 306
  in spleen phosphatides, 296
  in suprarenal gland phosphatides, 22
Arsenocholine, 418
Arteriosclerosis, 433
Arthritis, 442
Atherosclerosis (see also Arteriosclerosis), 433
Avitaminoses, phosphatide distribution during, 439–441

Bacillus albolactis, phosphatides in, 200
Bacillus Calmette-Guerin (see Calmette-Guerin bacteria)
Bacteria
  enteric, phosphatides of, 196, 197
  lipoproteins in, 88, 89
  phosphatides in, 196–212
    as antigens, 449, 450
Bacteriostasis, inhibition by phosphatides, 88, 89
Bacterium tumefaciens, 407
Baked goods, use of phosphatides in, 510, 511, 513
Barley, phosphatides in, 233
Bases (see also Aminoethyl alcohol, Choline, Serine, Sphingosine)
  classification of, 6
  mixture with phosphatides, 500
Beans, phosphatides in, 237
Beets, phosphatides in, 238
Behenic acid, in brain phosphatides, 22
Betaine, 417
  in phosphatides, 55
  lipotropic action of, 355
Bile, phosphatides in, 297, 298
Bile acids, role in absorption, 347
Bile ducts, diseases of, 428–430
Bile salts, 97
Blastomyces dermatiditis, phosphatides in, 217
Bleaching of phosphatides, 495, 496
Blood
  coagulation of, 340, 443–447
  diseases of, 432, 433
  phosphatides in
    absence of cephalin fraction in, 268
    determination of individual constituents of, 261–267
    determination of total, 261
    distribution of, 256, 259, 261–269
    effect of diet on, 377–379
    effect of drugs on, 379–380
    effect of heparin on, 268–270

effect of menstruation on, 380–381
    effect of oxalate on, 268, 270
    effect of pregnancy on, 380, 381
    fatty acids of, 273, 274
    metabolic activity of, 377–385
    occurrence as complexes, 274
    of animals, distribution of, 270–273
    of children, 267
    of humans, isolation of, 259–261
    origin of, 383, 384
    P^{32} experiments on, 381–384
    turnover of, 381, 382
Blood cells
  red, 259, 262, 272, 273
  white, 259, 267
Blood plasma, phosphatides in, 259, 272
Blood platelets, phosphatides in, 267
Blood serum
  lipoprotein in, 86, 87, 259
  phosphatides in, 259
Blood vessels, diseases of, 433, 434
Bollmann process, 486–488
Bone marrow, phosphatides in, 298–300
Brain
  metabolic activity of phosphatides of, 395, 396
  phosphatides in, 255, 256, 274–284
    acetal, structure of, 280
    configuration of, 17
    distribution of, 256, 257, 274, 276–278
    fatty acids of, 22, 281–283
    hydrolecithin, 280
    incorporation of deuterium into, 395
    incorporation of elaidic acid into, 395
    inositol-containing, 280
    isolation of, 9, 275
    metabolic activity of, 395, 396
    phosphatidylserine in, 279, 280
    synthesis of, 396
    variation with age of, 283, 284
  phosphorus in, 9
  role in fat metabolism, 364
Bromination of phosphatides, 12, 112
Butter, phosphatides in, 323–325
Butterflies, phosphatides in, 319
Buttermilk, phosphatides in, 323–325

Cabbage, phosphatides of, 238, 239
Cacao bean, phosphatides of, 235
Cactus, phosphatides of, 243
Cadmium chloride
  complex with lecithin, 26, 57, 58, 95
  complex with phosphatides, 95
  complex with sphingomyelin, 64
  salt with cephalin fraction, 26
  salt with lecithin, 26

Calcium
  activation of lecithinase A by, 107
  activation of lecithinase B by, 109
  activation of lecithinase D by, 113
Calmette-Guerin bacteria
  as antigen, 449
  phosphatides in, 200, 201
Candy, use of phosphatides in, 512
Carbohydrate complexes, as antigens, 449, 450
Carbohydrate esters in bacterial lipides, 199, 201, 202, 205, 208
Carbohydrates
  classification of, 3
  complexes with phosphatides, 93, 94
  conversion to lipides, 351–354
  in phosphatides, 15
  mixture with phosphatides, 497, 498
  solubility of, 3
Carcinoma 256, 369
Carcinosarcoma, 436, 437
Cardiac muscle, phosphatides in, 256, 310
Cardiolipin, 50
  as antigen, 451
Carnaubon, 54
Carrots, phosphatides in, 336
Castor seeds, phosphatides of, 235
Cell particulates
  lipoproteins in, 86
  phosphatides in, 343, 344
Cell permeability, relation of phosphatides to, 341
Cénapse, 81
Central nervous system
  diseases of, 434, 435
  metabolic activity of phosphatides of, 395, 396
Cephalin (*see also* Cephalin fraction, Cephalin phosphatides, Inositol Phosphatides, Phosphatidylaminoethyl alcohol, Phosphatidylserine), definition of, 5, 28
Cephalin fraction (*see also* Cephalin, Cephalin phosphatides, Inositol Phosphatides, Phosphatidylserine)
  acid-binding power of, 13
  antioxidant activity of, 454, 455
  bases in, 5
  classification of, 8
  inositol in, 5, 35
  inositolmonophosphoric acid in, 35
  reaction with diazomethane, 64
  reaction with formaldehyde, 64
  separation of inositol-containing phosphatides from, 35
  titration of, 12, 13, 33

Cephalin phosphatides (*see also* Cephalin, Cephalin fraction, Inositol Phosphatides, Phosphatidylaminoethyl alcohol, Phosphatidylserine)
  acid-base relationships, 32–34
  action of lecithinase D on, 113
  alcohol solubility of, 28
  amino acid constituents, evidence for, 5, 26, 28, 29
  analysis of, 168–170
  as protective colloid, 76, 77
  bases in impure mixture, 26
  bases of, 28, 29
  buffering capacity of, 33
  cadmium chloride complex of, 26, 58
  complexes (*see* Phosphatide complexes)
  composition of, 31, 32, 35
  distribution in animal organs, 256, 257
  electrophoresis of, 29
  fatty acids of, 37
  historical, 25
  hydrogenation of, 27, 63, 64
  hydrolysis of, 36
  hydrolysis products of, 36, 37
  identity as a mixture, 26
  in blood, 256, 259, 261–269
  in brain, 256, 257, 274, 276–278
  in cardiac muscle, 310
  in kidney, 256, 294, 295
  in liver, 256, 284–288
  in lung, 256, 293–294
  in spleen, 256, 296
  metallic complexes of, 58
  monomolecular film, effect of electrolytes on, 70, 71
  origin of name, 25
  properties of, 63
  purification of, 27, 28, 61, 62, 63
  reaction with isocyanates, 27, 64
  reaction with ninhydrin, 29
  separation into components, 62
  serine in, 29
  sol formation, 71, 72
  sols, x-ray diffraction of, 73
  solubility of, 25
  source of, 25
  structure of, 25–28
  structure proof, initial work on impure mixture, 26
  structure, Thudichum's contribution to, 25
  thromboplastic action of, 443, 444
  titration of, 29
  urea, contamination with, 28
Cephalinic acid, 25, 37
Cereals, phosphatides in, 219 ff.

Cerebrosides
  association with sphingomyelin, 38, 54
  classification, 6
  phrenosin, 39
Cheese, use of phosphatides in, 513
Chewing gum, use of phosphatides in, 513
Chloroplatinic acid
  salt with aminoethyl alcohol, 26
  salt with choline, 10
Chocolate, use of phosphatides in, 504, 505
Cholesterol
  as emulsifying agent, 78, 79
  effect on rate of diffusion in gels, 77, 78
  in blood, 256
  in muscles, 309
  in nervous system, 279
  inhibition of lecithinase A by, 107
  monomolecular film, 70
  role in absorption of lipides, 347
  sols, coagulation of, 74
Cholesterol complex
  with lecithin, 96, 97
  with phosphatides, 96, 97
Choline, 23, 24
  acetylation of, 419, 420
  analysis of, 174–177
  chloroplatinate of, 10
  classification of, 6
  confusion with neurine, 23
  determination
    as enneaiodide, 175, 176
    as insoluble salts, 174–176
    as mercuric chloride double salt, 176
    as reineckate, 174
    as salts, 176
    by microbiological methods, 176
    by oxidation, 176
    by photoelectrical methods, 175
    in phosphatide mixtures, 169
  from sphingomyelin, 38
  hydrolysis of
    from phosphatides, 167, 168
    from sphingomyelin, 38
  in brain, 281
  isolation as mercuric chloride double salt, 168
  lipotropic action of, 355, 413
  metabolism of, 413–420
  origin of name, 10, 23
  properties of, 23
  salts of, 23, 24
  structure, 23
  synthesis of, 23
    in vitro, 417

Choline analogs, as phosphatide labels, 370, 371
Choline deficiency, effect of, 414, 415
Cholinephosphatase (see Lecithinase C)
Chorea, 435
Cirrhosis, 429, 430
Clupanodonic acid
  in egg phosphatides, 321, 322
  in liver phosphatides, 290
"Cobralecithid", 99, 100
Cocoa powder, use of phosphatides in, 512
Coffee bean, phosphatides in, 235
Colamine (see Aminoethyl alcohol)
Color tests, 183
Commercial phosphatides, 485
Complex coacervation, 75, 76
Complexes (see Phosphatide complexes)
Compound lipides, classification of, 6
Configuration, of natural lecithin, 10
Conjugated acids, as phosphatide labels, 369, 370
Corn, phosphatides in, 229, 230
Corn oil, isolation of phosphatides from, 494
Corpus luteum, phosphatides in, 300, 302, 303
Corynin, 200
Cottonseed, phosphatides in, 227–229
Cottonseed Oil, isolation of phosphatides from, 494
Cream, phosphatides in, 323–325
Crown gall disease, 197
Crystallization of phosphatides, 58
Cuorin, 54
Currant seeds, phosphatides in, 235
Cysticercus fasciolaris
  hydrophosphatides in, 53
  phosphatides in, 318, 319

Deodorization of phosphatides, 494, 495
Depot fat
  composition of, 350, 351
  selectivity of, 351
Derived lipides, classification of, 6
Deuterium, as phosphatide label, 370
Diabetes, 435, 436
Dialectric constant, 13
Digestion
  of lipides, 345, 346
  of phosphatides, 345, 346
Diglyceride, preparation from glycidol, 119
Dihydrosphingosine, 39, 40, 41, 42
  N-acyl, reaction with periodic acid, 41
  occurrence of, 42

Dihydrosphingosine, oxidation of, 40
  periodic acid oxidation of, 41
  source of, 42
  synthesis of, 116
  triacetyl, 42
  tribenzoyl, 42
1, 3-Dihydroxy-2-aminoöctadecene-4 (*see*
  Sphingosine)
Dipalmityllecithin (*see* Hydrophosphatides)
Diphosphoinositide (*see also* Inositol
  phosphatides), 35, 62
Diphtheria, 442
Diphtheria bacteria, phosphatides in, 200
Diseases, effects on phosphatides, 424 ff.
Docosapentenoic acid, 282
Docosatetrenoic acid, 282

Egg
  absence of lecithin in, 9
  metabolism of phosphatides of, 397–
    401
  origin of phosphatides of, 400, 401
  phosphatides in, 9, 320–323
    configuration of, 17
    content of, 320, 321
    distribution of, 320, 321
    effect of diet on fatty acids of, 322
    extraction of, 320
    fatty acids of, 321, 322
    metabolism of, 397–401
    occurrence as complexes, 322, 323
Egg Yolk
  lipoprotein in, 84, 85
  phosphatides in, 9, 255
    origin of, 400, 401
Elaidic acid
  as phosphatide label, 367–369
  metabolic studies with, 367–369
Electrophoresis, 14, 87, 93
Élément constant, 341, 342
Élément variable, 341, 342
Embryo
  metabolism of phosphatides of, 397–399
  origin of phosphatides of, 400, 401
Emulsifying Agents, 78, 79, 80, 345, 346,
  504
"Endo" structure, 12, 13
Enteric bacteria, phosphatides in, 196, 197
Enzymes (*see also* Lecithinases), 50
  glycerophosphatases, 20
  in muscle press juice, resolution of α-
    glycerophosphoric acid with, 19
Epididymis, phosphatides in, 300
Epilepsy, 434, 435
Epoxides, reaction with phosphatides, 503

Erucic acid, 22, 195
Esters of higher alcohols, classification, 6
Esters of higher fatty acids, classification,
  6
Ethanolaimine (*see* Aminoethyl alcohol)
Euglobulin, 86
Excretion of lipides, 364, 365
Eyes, phosphatides in, 316, 317

Fat (*see* Lipides)
Fat absorption, role of phosphatides in,
  390–392
Fat depots, 350, 351
Fatty acids (*see also* Lecithin, Phosphatides, etc.)
  classification of, 6
  degradation of by liver, 358, 359
  determination of, 178, 179
  hydrolysis of, from lecithin, 20
  in brain phosphatides, 22, 281–283
  in cephalin fraction, 37
  in hydrophosphatides, 54
  in lecithin, 20–22
  in liver phosphatides, 289–291
  in phosphatides of animal origin, 257,
    258
  in phosphatidic acid, 49
  in phosphatidylaminoethyl alcohol, 37
  in phosphatidylserine, 30
  in sphingomyelin, 43
  oxidation of, 360, 361
    by liver, 358–361
  relation to lipides, 3, 4
  removal from intestines, 346–348
  separation of, 178, 179
  transport of by phosphatides, 384, 385
Fatty livers (*see also* Lipotropism), 355–
  358
Feces, lipides in, 364, 365
Fibrin, 443
Fibrinogen, 443
Flaxseed, phosphatides of, 234
Fluidization, 501
Flowers, phosphatides of, 240, 241
Foods, use of phosphatides in, 504 ff.
Forssman antigen, 448
Fruits, phosphatides of, 241
Fungi, phosphatides of, 214–218
Furfural, use in oil refining, 493

Galactosides (*see* Cerebrosides)
Gall bladder, phosphatides in, 297, 298
Gangliosides, 38, 39
Gasoline, use of phosphatides in, 514, 515
Gastric, mucosa, phosphatides in, 316

Gastrointestinal tract
  diseases of, 431, 432
  metabolic activity of phosphatides of, 389–392
Gaucher's disease, 295, 428
Glands, phosphatides in, 303–307
Globulin, 86
Glyceraldehyde, 19
Glycerides, classification of, 6
Glycerol
  determination of, 177, 178
  in phosphatide hydrolysate, 166
  in phosphatide technology, 489, 490
  in phosphatides, 7
  mixture with phosphatides, 498
Glycerophosphatase (*see* Lecithinase D)
Glycerophosphatides (*see* Acetal phosphatides, Cephalin phosphatides, Hydrophosphatides, Lecithin, Lysophosphatides, Phosphatides, Phosphatidylaminoethyl alcohol, Phosphatidylserine)
Glycerophosphoric acid, acid strength, 18
  α-configuration, 16
  α-isomer, absolute configuration of enantiomorphs, 19
    barium salt, 18, 19
    calcium salt, 18
    diethyl ether diethyl ester, 20
    dimethyl ether dimethyl ester, 19
    optical activity of, 19
    quinine salt of, 19
    resolution of, 19
    strychnine salt of, 19
    synthesis of, 18, 19
  analysis of isomers with enzymes, 20
  analysis of mixtures of α and β, 17
  β-configuration, 16
  β-isomer
    barium salt, 18
    calcium salt, 18
    synthesis of, 19
  choline ester (*see* Glycerylphosphorylcholine)
  configuration of, 16
  hydrogen bonding, effect on strength, 18
  hydrolysis of, 18, 20
  in egg lecithin, 9
  isolation of, 16, 18
  isomers in natural product, 18
  metabolic functions of, 421
  migration of phosphoric group, 17
  optical activity of, 19
  properties of, 18
  racemization of α-isomer, 17

  relation to urinary phosphorus, 20
  separation of isomers, 18
  synthesis of, 18, 19
Glycerylphosphorylaminoethyl alcohol, production by lecithinases, 109
Glycerylphosphorylcholine, migration of phosphoric group of, 17
  production by lecithinases, 109
  synthesis, 123, 124
  synthesis of enantiopmorphs, 123, 124
  synthetic, properties of, 124
Glycolipides (*see also* Cerebrosides)
  classification, 6, 7
  sphingosine in, 7
Gold chloride, salt with aminoethyl alcohol, 26
Grain sorghum, phosphatides in, 233, 234
Grains, phosphatides in, 219 ff.
Grass, phosphatides in, 242
Groundnuts (*see* Peanuts)
Gums, phosphatides in, 315

Hair, phosphatides in, 314
Halogenation, of phosphatides, 12, 21, 61, 502
Hand syndrome, 425
Hanger test, 451
Haptens, 447–449
Heart
  diseases of, 439
  phosphatides of, 256, 310
Heparin, 92, 268–270
Hepatitis, 451
Hevea latex, phosphatides in, 239, 240
Hydration, of phosphatides, 502, 503
Hydrocarbons, relationship to lipides, 6
Hydrogenation
  of cephalin phosphatides, 27
  of phosphatides, 60, 502
Hydrohalogenation of phosphatides, 61
Hydrolecithin
  determination of, 173
  effect of lecithinase A on, 108
  in brain, 280
  in *Cysticercus fasciolaris*, 318
  in lung, 256, 293, 294
  monomolecular films of, 69
  optical activity of, 67
  properties of, 60, 67
  purification of, 67
  sol, coagulation of, 74
Hydrolysis of carbohydrate-containing phosphatide, 15
  of lecithin, mechanism of, 15, 59
  of phosphatides, 15, 166, 167, 168
  of sphingomyelin, 15

Hydrophosphatides (*see also* Hydrogenation; Hydrolecithin; Hydrophosphatidylaminoethyl alcohol; Phosphatides, hydrogenation of, synthesis of; Sphingomyelin, hydrogenation of)
  distribution in animal organs, 257
  fatty acids of, 54
  hydrolysis of, 54
  isolation of, 54
  occurrence of, 53
  properties of, 67
  purification of, 67
  solubility of, 53
  source of, 53, 54
  structure proof of, 54
Hydrophosphatidylaminoethyl alcohol, 63, 64
Hydrosphingomyelin, acetylation of, 65
Hydroxylation, of phosphatides, 503
Hypercholesterolemia, in xanthomatosis, 425
Hypertension, 433, 434
Hypothyroidism, 441

Ice cream, use of phosphatides in, 512
Inositol (*see also* Cephalin fraction, Cephalin phosphatides, Inositol Phosphatides)
  in cephalin fraction, 5, 35
  in phosphatides of tubercle bacillus, 35, 36
  lipotropic action of, 355
Inositol Phosphatides (*see also* Cephalin fraction, Cephalin phosphatides, Inositol), 35, 62
  classification, 7, 8
  distribution of in animal organs, 257
  elementary analysis of, 35
  evidence for chemical union of inositol, 35
  hydrolysis of, 35
  in brain, 256, 257, 274, 276–278, 280
  in cephalin fraction, 7
  in soybeans, hydrolysis of, 36
  isolation of, 62
  metabolic functions of, 421
  separation from cephalin fraction, 35
  solubility of, 63
  sources, 36
Inositolmonophosphoric acid, in phosphatides of tubercle bacillus, 35
Intermediates, phosphatides as, 340
Intestinal mucosa, phosphatides in, 315, 316
Intestine, phosphatides in, 315, 316
  distribution of, 315, 386

  metabolic activity of, 389–391
Iodinated acids, as phosphatide labels, 369
Iodine number, determination of in phosphatides, 182
Isocyanates, reaction with cephalin phosphatides, 27, 64
Isoelectric point
  of lecithin, 14, 33
  of phosphatide mixtures, 14
  of phosphatidylaminoethyl alcohol, 33
Isotope dilution, 168
Isotopic phosphorus, as phosphatide label, 371–377

Jecorin, 54

Kahn test, 450, 451
Ketone bodies
  consumption of, 359, 360
  formation of, 359, 360
Kidney
  diseases of, 430, 431
  metabolism of phosphatides of, 392, 393
  phosphatides in, 256, 294, 295
    distribution of, 256, 294, 295
    fatty acids of, 21, 294
    iodine number of fatty acids of, 294
    metabolic activity of, 392, 393
    turnover of, 393
  role in fat metabolism, 362, 363
  synthesis of phosphatides by, 393
  turnover of phosphatides of, 393

Lacquer, use of phosphatides in, 517
Lactic acid, mixture with phosphatides, 498
Lactobacillus acidophilus, phosphatides in, 199, 200
Leather, use of phosphatides in processing, 516, 517
Leaves, phosphatides in, 243
Lecithalbumin, 86
Lecithin
  acid-base relationships of, 12–15
  acid binding power of, 13
  alcoholysis of, 59, 60
  α-configuration of, 10
  α-isomer, evidence for, 10
  antioxidant activity of, 454, 455
  as emulsifying agent, 78, 79, 80
  as protective colloid, 76, 77
  bleaching of, 495, 496
  brominated, action of lecithinase D on, 112
  bromination, 12, 21

Lecithin, cadmium chloride complex of, 26, 57, 58, 95
  choline in, 23
    ease of hydrolysis of, 168
  classification of, 7, 8
  color improvement of, 495, 496
  commercial isolation of, 486 ff.
  complex with cadmium chloride, 95
    effect of lecithinase A on, 107
  complex with cholesterol, 96, 97
  complexes (*see* Phosphatide complexes)
  configuration of natural, 10
  crystallization of, 58
  dehydration with glycerol, 489, 490
  deodorization of, 494, 495
  determination of from choline content, 166
  dialectric constant of, 13
  distribution of in animal organs, 256, 257
  effect on rate of diffusion in gels, 77, 78
  effect on swelling capacity of gels, 77, 78
  electrophoretic mobility of, 14
  emulsifying properties of, 78, 79, 80
  "endo" structure of, 12, 13
  extraction of
    with adsorbents, 491, 492
    with alcohol, 490, 491
  fatty acids of, 20
    contribution to isomers, 21
    determination of, 20
    distribution of, 20, 21
    ratio of saturated to unsaturated, 21
  fluidization of, 501
  glycerophosphoric acid in, 9
  halogenation of, 61, 502
  hydration of, 502, 503
  hydrogenation of (*see also* Hydrophosphatides), 60, 502
  hydrohalogenation of, 61
  hydrolysis of, 15, 59
    alcoholic, 15
    at various pH's, 59
    with acid, 59
    with alkali, 59
    mechanism of, 15
  hydrolysis products of, 15
  hydrolytic agents for, 15
  hydroxylation of, 503
  in bile, 297
  in blood, 256, 259, 262–269
  in cardiac muscle, 310
  in Cysticercus fasciolarus, configuration of, 16

  in eggs, 9
  in kidney, 256, 294, 295
  in liver, 256, 284–287
  in lung, 256, 292–294
  in spleen, 256, 296
  inner anhydride, structure of, 12
  interaction with water, 69
  isoelectric point of, 14, 33
  isolation of from animal oil, 494
    from animal tissue and organs, 255 ff., 494
    from corn oil, 494
    from cottonseed oil, 494
    from linseed oil, 494
    from oil residues, 488–490
    from peanut oil, 494
    from rapeseed oil, 494
    from soapstock, 490, 491
    from soybean oil, 493
  isomers due to configuration of glycerophosphoric acid, 10
  isomers due to fatty acids, 10
  light absorption of a solution of, 73
  mercuration of, 503
  metallic complexes of, 57, 58, 503
  migration of phosphoric group in, 17
  miscellaneous non-food uses, 521, 522
  mixture of with acids, 500
    with bases, 500
    with carbohydrates, 497, 498
    with glycerol, 498
    with lactates, 498
    with miscellaneous substances, 498, 499
    with organic carriers, 497, 498
    with salts, 499, 500
  molecular weight of, 12, 13
  monomolecular films, 69
    compressibility of, 70
    effect of cholesterol on area, 69, 70
  myelin forms of, 71
  open-dipole structure of, 12
  optical activity of, 59
  origin of name, 9
  phosphoric acid as salt in, 10
  polymerized structure of, 11, 12, 13
  precipitation from oils, 492
  properties of, 58, 59
  protective colloid,
    for gold sol, 77
    for homogenized milk, 77
    for leaded gasoline, 77
    in organosols, 77
  purification of, 57, 58
  reaction of,
    with epoxides, 503

Lecithin, reaction of, with hydroxylating agents, 503
  with 2-nitrobutan-1-ol, 503
refining of, 494 ff.
removal of during oil refining, 492, 493
removal of oil from, 496, 497
sol
  Brownian movement in, 72
  coagulation of, 73, 74
  discharge concentration of, 75
  effect of alcohol on, 75
  effect of alkaloids on, 74
  effect of electrolytes on, 74
  effect of on dialysis rate, 73
  formation of, 71, 72
  hydrotropic action of, 75
  osmotic pressure of, 73
  participation in complex coacervation of, 75, 76
  particle size of, 72
  precipitation of with electrolytes, 72
  properties of, 72, 73
  surface tension of, 72
  x-ray diffraction of, 73
solubility of, 3, 58
specifications of commercial product, 485
structure of, 9–24
sulfonation of, 61, 501, 502
surface tension of film of, 71
synthesis of, 119, 120, 121, 122
synthesis of enantiomorphs of, 116, 117
synthetic, action of lecithinase D on, 112
  action of lecithinases on, 122
  configuration of, 16
  effect of cobra venom on, 108
  properties of, 121
  properties of enantiomorphs of, 116
taste improvement of, 494, 495
thromboplastic action of, 443, 444
titration of, 12, 13, 33, 168
use as antioxidants, 507–510
use in bakery goods, 510, 511
use in candy, 512
use in cheese, 513
use in chewing gum, 513
use in chocolate, 504, 505
use in cocoa powder, 512
use in foods, 504 ff.
use in gasoline, 514, 515
use in ice cream, 512
use in leather processing, 516, 517
use in lubricating oil, 514
use in macaroni, 511
use in margarine, 505–507

use in mayonnaise, 513
use in miscellaneous foods, 512, 513
use in noodles, 511
use in paints, 517, 518
use in petroleum products, 514, 515
use in pharmaceuticals, 520
use in protective coatings, 517, 518
use in resin technology, 518, 519
use in rubber technology, 518
use in shortening, 507
use in soaps, 519, 520
use in textiles, 515, 516
use in winterization of oils, 512
uses of, 504 ff.
zwitterion form of, 12, 13
Lecithinase A (*see also* Lecithinases), 105–108
  action of, 105
  action on metallic complexes of lecithin, 107
  activation by calcium, 107
  calcium activation of, 107
  cholesterol inhibition of, 107
  crystallization of, 108
  detection of, 108
  effect of various substances on, 107, 108
  inhibition of, 107, 108
  isolation of, 108
  pH sensitivity of, 108
  preparation of, 108
  properties of, 106, 107
  source of, 105, 106
Lecithinase B (*see also* Lecithinases), 108, 109
  action of, 105, 109
  activation of by calcium, 109
  calcium activation of, 109
  production of glycerylphosphorylcholine by, 109
  properties of, 109
  source of, 109
Lecithinase C (*see also* Lecithinases), 110, 111
  action of, 105
  effect of pH on, 111
  isolation of, 110, 111
  properties of, 110, 111
  source of, 110
Lecithinase D (*see also* Lecithinases), 110–113
  action of, 105, 111
  action of calcium on, 113
  action on lysolecithin, 111
  action on cephalin phosphatides, 113
  action on sphingomyelin, 113

Lecithinase D, effect on blood serum, 113
  effect of pH on, 112, 113
  measurement of activity of, 113
  possible identity with diphosphatase, 113
  properties of, 111, 112, 113
  source of, 112
Lecithinases, 99 ff.
  action of, 101
  biological significance of, 115
  diagram of activity of, 114
  differentiation from lipases, 100
  historical, 99, 100
  nomenclature, 100, 101
  relation of to snake poisoning, 99
Lentils, phosphatides in, 239
Leprosy bacteria, phosphatides in, 201
Lettuce, phosphatides in, 239
Leucocytes, phosphatides in, 259, 267
Lignoceric acid, 43, 44, 45, 258, 274
Lignocerylsphingosine (*see also* Sphingosine), 43
  esters of, 47
  production of by enzymes, 113
Linoleic acid, 21
  in phosphatidic acids, 49
Linolenic acid, in phosphatidic acids, 49
Linseed oil, isolation of phosphatides from, 494
Lipase, 346
Lipemia retinalis, 436
Lipide, pronunciation of, 4
Lipides
  absorption of, 346–348
    role of phosphorylation in, 390, 391
  Bloor's classification of, 3, 4, 6
  catabolism of, 351–354
  characteristics of, 3, 4
  classification of, 3–8
  degradation of by liver, 358, 359
  degradation of *in vivo*, 353, 354
  digestion of, 345, 346
  disposition of after absorption, 348–350
  elements in, 3
  emulsification of in intestines, 345, 346
  excretion of, 364, 365
  functional groups of, 3
  in fat depots, 350, 351
  in feces, 364, 365
  metabolic synthesis of, 351–354
  metabolism of, 345 ff.
    role of liver in, 354 ff.
  nomenclature of, 3–8
  oxidation of, 360, 361
  solubility of, 3

  storage of, 350, 351
  synthesis of from carbohydrates, 351–354
  synthesis of from proteins, 351–354
  synthesis of *in vivo*, 351–354
  transport of, by phosphatides, 384, 385
  transportation of absorbed, 348–350
Lipidosis, 424–428
Lipocaic, 356
Lipoids (*see* Lipides)
Lipoprotein, 82 ff.
  as blood-clotting agent, 445
  β_1, from serum, composition of, 87
  dissociation of, 91, 92
    with alcohol, 91, 92
    with heparin, 92
  electrophoresis of, 87, 93
  in bacteria, 88, 89
  in blood serum, 86, 87
  in cell parts, 85, 86
  in egg yolk, 84, 85
  in lung, 86
  in milk, 88
  in mitochondria, 86, 343, 344
  in plants, 89
  in serum, properties of, 86, 87
  in tissue, 86
  in wheat germ, 89
  in yeast, 88, 89
  properties of, 91, 92
  reactions with solvents, 84
  source, 82, 84
  synthesis of, 90, 91
  types of linkages in, 82, 83
  with albumen, 90, 91
  with caseinogen, 90
  with clupein, 90
  with globin, 91
  with globulin, 90
  with histone, 91
  with pseudoglobulin, 90
  with salmine, 90
  with zein, 90
  x-ray diffraction of, 91
Lipositol (*see also* Inositol Phosphatides), 36
Lipotropic factors, 355–358
Lipotropism, 355–358, 413, 414, 418, 419
Lipovitellinin, 84, 85, 494
Liver
  diseases of, 428–430
    detection by antigens, 451
  distribution of phosphatides of, 386
  fat deposition in, 355–358
  phosphatides in, 256, 284–291
    configuration of, 17

Liver, phosphatides in, content of, 284–288
   distribution of, 256, 284–288
   effect of fasting on, 386
   effect of hormones on, 387
   effect of maturity on, 386
   fatty acids of, 21, 22, 289–291
   incorporation of P^{32} by, 387, 388
   iodine number of fatty acids of, 291
   isolation of, 284–288
   metabolic functions of, 385–389
   precursors of, 388
   turnover of, 389
   precursors of phosphatides of, 388
   role in fat disposition, 354, 355
   role in fat transportation, 354, 355
   role in metabolism, 354 ff.
   synthesis of phosphatides by, 388
   turnover of phosphatides of, 389
Lubricating oil, use of phosphatides in, 514
Lung, phosphatides in, 256, 292–294
Lupines, phosphatides in, 238
Lysocephalin (*see also* Lysophosphatides), preparation of, 102, 103
Lysocithin (*see also* Lysolecithin), 100
Lysocytin (*see also* Lysolecithin), 100
Lysolecithin (*see also* Lysophosphatides)
   biological significance of, 115
   classification of, 7, 8
   fatty acids of, 104
   in wheat, 227
   metallic complexes of, 107
   monomolecular films of, 70
   preparation of, 101, 102, 103
   properties of, 102
   source of, 104, 106
   structure of, 100, 103, 104
   synthetic, properties of, 122–124
Lysophosphatides (*see also* Enzymes, Lysolecithin, Lysophosphatidylaminoethyl alcohol, Lysosphingomyelin), 55, 99 ff.
   classification of, 7, 8
   hemolytic activity of, 421, 422
   historical, 99, 100
   in mitochondria, 343, 344
   metabolic functions of, 421–423
   nomenclature of, 100
   preparation of, 101, 102, 103
   relation of to snake poisoning, 99
   source of, 104
   structure of, 103, 104
   synthesis of, 122–124
Lysophosphatidylaminoethyl alcohol (*see also* Enzymes, Lysophosphatides)

classification of, 8
   preparation of, 102, 103
   properties of, 102
Lysosphingomyelin, 103
Lysozithin (*see also* Lysolecithin), 100

Macaroni, use of phosphatides in, 511
Magnesium chloride, precipitation of phosphatides with, 148, 161
Malaria, 442
Margaric acid, in phosphatides from egg, 9
Margarine, use of phosphatides in, 505–507
Marine animals, phosphatides in, 317, 318
Mayonnaise, use of phosphatides in, 513
Mechanism, of formation of phosphatides *in vivo*, 408–411
Mercuration, of phosphatides, 503
Metabolism
   of blood phosphatides, 377–385
   of lipides, 345 ff.
   of phosphatides, 366 ff.
   studies with radioactive P, 371–377
Metabolites, phosphatides as, 339–341
Metallic complexes, 94, 95, 96, 503
Methionine, 415
   lipotropic action of, 355
Methyl glycerophosphate, migration of phosphate group in, 17
Methyl groups, relation of to choline deficiency, 415–418
Microorganisms, phosphatides in, 196–218
Milk
   fatty acids of phosphatides in, 402, 403
   lipoproteins in, 88
   metabolism of phosphatides in, 401–403
   origin of phosphatides in, 402, 403
   phosphatides in, 323–327
Mitochondria
   lipoproteins in, 86
   lysophosphatides in, 343, 344
   phosphatides in, 343, 344
Molds, phosphatides in, 216, 217, 218
Monilia albicans, phosphatides in, 218
Monose, characterization of, 3
Monomolecular films, 69, 70, 71
Multiple sclerosis, 442
Muscle
   acetal phosphatides in, 51
   metabolic activity of phosphatides of, 393–395
   phosphatides in, 256, 307–313
   distribution of, 308–310
   fatty acids of, 21, 310–312

Muscle, phosphatides in, iodine number of fatty acids of, 310–312
  metabolic activity of, 393–395
  turnover of, 394, 395
  variation of with activity, 307, 308
  variation of with type, 307, 308
  turnover of phosphatides of, 394, 395
Myelin forms, 71

Naphthyl isocyanate, reaction with cephalin phosphatides, 27
Neoplasms (*see also* Tumors), 436–438
Nephritis, 430
Nerve cells, electrolytic equilibria of, 30
Nerves, phosphatides in, 278, 279
Nervonic acid, 44
Nervous system
  diseases of, 434, 435
  phosphatides in, 274–284
Neuraminic acid, 428
Neurine (*see also* Choline, Vinyltrimethylammonium hydroxide), 23, 38
Niemann-Pick's disease, 64, 295, 426–428
Ninhydrin, reaction with cephalin phosphatides, 29
2-Nitrobutan-1-ol, reaction with phosphatides, 503
Nitrogen, determination of in phosphatides, 181, 182
Nomenclature, of lipides, 3–8
Noodles, use of phosphatides in, 511
Nucleic acid, lipotropic action of, 355

Oats, phosphatides in, 234
Oil refining, 492, 493
Oil-producing plants, phosphatides in, 219 ff.
Oils, vegetable,
  phosphatides in, 219, 220
  stabilization of by phosphatides, 508, 509
Oleic acid, 21
  in egg lecithin, 9
  in phosphatidic acids, 49
Ovary, phosphatides in, 300, 301, 302
Oxalate, 268, 270
Oxidation
  beta-, 358, 359
  omega-, 359
  relation of phosphatides to, 452–455
  role of phosphatides in, 340, 452–455

Paint, use of phosphatides in, 517, 518
Palmitic acid, 21
  in phosphatidic acids, 49
  in sphingomyelin, 45

Palmitoleic acid, from liver phosphatides, 290
Pancreas
  diseases of, 431, 432
  phosphatides in, 306
  role in fat metabolism, 362
Pantothenic acid deficiency, 440
Paralysis, 442
Pathological conditions, effect on phosphatides, 424 ff.
Peanut oil, isolation of phosphatides in, 494
Peanuts, phosphatides in, 231, 232
Peas, phosphatides in, 237
Periodate oxidation, 170, 177
Petroleum products, use of phosphatides in, 514, 515
pH, regulation of by phosphatides, 341
Pharmaceuticals, use of phosphatides in, 520
Phenyl isocyanate, reaction with cephalin phosphatides, 27
Phosphatidates, *see* Phosphatidic acid
Phosphatide complexes (*see also* Lipoproteins), 81 ff., 257
  as emulsifying agents, 78
  in blood, 274
  in brain, 283
  in egg phosphatides, 322, 323
  in soybeans, 221, 222
  linkages in, 81, 83
  with alkaloids, 97
  with bile salts, 97
  with cadmium chloride, 95
  with carbohydrates, 93, 94
  with cholesterol, 96, 97
  with creatine, 97
  with creatinine, 97
  with digitonin, 97
  with dyes, 98
  with glycosides, 97
  with metallic salts, 94, 95, 96
  with miscellaneous substances, 97, 98
  with oleic acid, 97
  with platinum chloride, 96
  with proteins (*see also* Lipoproteins), 82
  with quaternary salts, 97
  with salicin, 97
  with salts, 95, 96, 97
  with streptomycin, 97
  with urea, 97
Phosphatides (*see also* individual phosphatides, e.g., Cephalin, Glycerophosphatides, Hydrophosphatides, Lecithin, Lysophosphatides, Phos-

phatidic acids, Phosphatidylaminoethyl alcohol, Phosphatidylserine,
Sphingomyelin, etc.)
alleged, 54
analysis of mixtures
  by isotope dilution, 168
  by preferential hydrolysis, 167, 168
  from hydrolysis products, 165, 166,
    167
analytical determination of, 147 ff.
antioxidant activity of, 454, 455, 507–
  510
as structural elements, 341–343
as transport agents, 340, 346, 347, 384,
  385
bacterial oxidation of, 453
biochemistry of, 339 ff.
chemistry of, 3 ff., 58, 59
choline in, 23
classification of, 6, 7, 8, 11
colloidal solutions of, 72
color improvement of, 495, 496
color tests for, 183
complex coacervates with, 33
complexes of (*see* Lipoproteins, Phosphatide complexes)
content of in oil seeds, 483
control of manufacture of, 484
crystallization of, 58
definition of, 5–7
dehydration of with glycerol, 489, 490
deodorization of, 494, 495
determination of
  by oxidative methods, 160, 161
  from fatty acid content, 162
  from phosphorus content, 161, 162
  in blood, by microprocedures, 262–
    267
determination of individual compounds
  in, 164 ff.
determination of iodine number, 182
determination of nitrogen in, 181, 182
determination of phosphorus in, 180,
  181
determination of total, 147, 159 ff.
diamino-, classification of, 7, 11
digestion of, 345, 346
distribution of in animal organs, 256,
  257
effect of diet on unsaturation of, 342,
  343
effect of radiation on, 411, 412
effect on motility of spermatozoa,
  397
emulsification of, 68
emulsifying properties of, 78, 79

enzymatic hydrolysis of, 105
enzymatic oxidation of, 453
extraction of, 56, 486 ff.
  for analysis, 147 ff.
  with adsorbents, 56, 57, 491, 492
  with alcohol, 56, 490, 491
factor for conversion of phosphorus
  content to total, 162
fatty acids (*see also* Fatty acids), 20–
  22
  degree of unsaturation of, 22
  distribution of, 20
  of brain, 22
  ratio of saturated to unsaturated, 21
fluidization of, 501
formation in intestine, 390
functions of, 339–343
halogenation of, 502
histochemical reactions of, 183
hydration of, 502–503
hydro (*see* Hydrolecithin, Hydrophosphatides)
hydrogenation of, 53, 502
hydroxylation of, 503
identification of by stain tests, 183
in vitro syntheses, 407, 408
industrial aspects of, 483 ff.
inositol-containing (*see also* Inositol
  phosphatides), sources of, 62, 150,
  488–494
"labeling" of, 367
macroextraction of, 154–159
mechanism of formation of, 408–411
mercuration of, 503
metallic complexes of, 57, 58, 64, 503
microextraction of, 147–158
miscellaneous non-food uses, 521, 522
mixtures
  with acids, 500
  with bases, 500
  with carbohydrates, 497, 498
  with glycerol, 498
  with lactates, 498
  with miscellaneous substances, 498–
    499
  with organic carriers, 497, 498
  with salts, 499, 500
monoamino-, classification of, 7, 11
myelin forms of, 71
natural configuration of, 17
nitrogen-to-phosphorus ratio in, 7
occurrence of, 9
oxidation of, 452–455
phosphorus-to-nitrogen ratio in, 7
physiology of, 339 ff.
physical chemistry of, 68 ff.

Phosphatides, polymeric structure of, 11, 12
  precipitation of, from oils, 492
    by salts, 161
    with acetone, 148
    with inorganic salts, 148
  production of, 483 ff.
  purification of, 56, 57, 58
  qualitative tests for, 182
  radioactive, extraction of, 153
  reaction with epoxides, 503
  reaction with 2-nitrobutan-1-ol, 503
  refining of, 494 ff.
  removal of during oil refining, 492, 493
  removal of oil from, 496, 497
  separation of
    by alcohol solubility, 27
    by solvents, 57, 58
    for analysis by absorption, 169
    into isomers, 17
    for analysis, 164, 165
  serological functions of, 443–452
  sols, 71–75
  solvent extract for analysis, purification of, 151
  specifications of commercial products, 485
  sulfonation of, 501, 502
  synthesis of, 116 ff.
    by isolated tissues, 407, 408
    by kidney, 393
    by liver, 388
  taste improvement of, 494, 495
  thromboplastic action of, 444
  Thudichum's identity of, 11
  uses of, 504–522
  water-soluble, 55
Phosphatide turnover, 372
Phosphatide turnover rate, 372
Phosphatidic acids, 48
  classification of, 6, 7, 8
  fatty acids of, 49
  from enzymic cleavage of glycerophosphatides, 50
  historical, 48
  hydrolysis products of, 49
  isolation of, 65, 66
  migration of phosphoric group of, 17
  origin of, 49, 110–111
  properties of, 66
  purification of, 66
  quinolium salt of, 126
  salts of, 66
  solubility of, 66
  structure proof of, 48
  synthesis of, 125, 126

Phosphatidylaminoethyl alcohol (*see also* Aminoethyl alcohol, Cephalin fraction, Phosphatides), 32–34
  acid-base relationships of, 32–34
  alcohol solubility of, 28
  buffering action of, 13, 33
  classification of, 7, 8
  determination of, 266, 267
    from aminoethyl alcohol content, 166
  dinitrobenzamide of, 118
  fatty acids of, 37
  hydrolysis of, 28, 63
  in blood, 268
  in brain, 274, 280
  in cephalin fraction, 5, 7
  isoelectric point of, 33
  isolation of, 27, 28, 32, 62
  properties of, 62
  purification of, 62
  reaction of
    with formaldehyde, 64
    with isocyanates, 64
  solubility in alcohol, 32
  structure of, 32
  synthesis of, 116–120, 122
  synthetic properties of, 118, 119, 120
  titration of, 12, 13, 28, 33, 118, 168
  ureido derivatives of, 64
  zwitterion formation in, 33
Phosphatidylethanolamine (*see* Phosphatidylaminoethyl alcohol)
Phosphatidylserine (*see also* Cephalin fraction, Serine), 28–30
  acid-base relationships of, 30, 31, 33
  alkali metal in, 30
  alkali metal salt of, 29, 30
  analysis of, 170
  classification of, 7, 8
  decarboxylation of, 31
  determination of, 170, 267
    from serine content, 166
  distribution of in animal organs, 256, 257
  elementary analysis of, 31
  enzymatic hydrolysis of, 110
  fatty acids of, 30
  hydrolysis of, 29
  hydrolysis products of, 30
  in blood, 268
  in brain, 256, 274, 279, 280
  in cephalin fraction, 5, 7
  in kidney, 295
  in liver, 284, 288
  in lung, 293
  isolation of, 62
  properties of, 62, 63

Phosphatidylserine, purification of, 62
    reaction of with nitrous acid, 30
    separation of from cephalin fraction, 29
    solubility of, 29
    structure of, 30
    titration of, 33
Phospholipides (see Phosphatides)
Phospholipins (see Phosphatides)
Phospholipine (see Phosphatides)
Phosphoric acid, production of by enzymatic hydrolysis of phosphatides, 111, 112
Phosphorus
    bone, phosphatides as source of, 341
    determination of in phosphatides, 180, 181
    presence in brain, 9
Phosphorylation, during lipide absorption, 391
Phrenosin (see also Cerebrosides), 39
Phthiocol, 213
Phthioic acid, 194, 210, 211
Phytomonas tumefaciens, phosphatides in, 197, 198
Phytomonic acid, 198
Pine seeds, 235
Pineal gland, 306
Pituitary gland, 306
Placenta, 301, 302
Plants
    effect of growth on phosphatide content of, 405
    lipoproteins in, 89
    metabolism of phosphatides of, 404–407
    phosphatides in, 191 ff.
        characterization of, 194
        concentration of, 192
        distribution of, 195
        early investigations of, 9, 191, 192
        fatty acids, 194, 195
        identity of with animal phosphatides, 9, 192
        metabolism of, 404–407
        nature of carbohydrates associated with, 193
        occurrence as complexes, 192, 193
        solubilization of carbohydrates by, 192, 193
Plasma, phosphatides in, 149, 150, 259, 272
Plasmal (see also Acetal phosphatides), 51
Plasmalogen (see also Acetal phosphatides), 51, 52

Plasmalogenic acid (see also Acetal phosphatides), 52
Plastic technology, use of phosphatides in, 518, 519
Platinum chloride, complex of with phosphatides, 96
Plum seeds, phosphatides in, 235
Pneumonia, 441
Polydiaminophosphatides, 65
Polymonoaminophosphatides, 11, 12, 13
Polyhydric alcohols (see Glycerol, Inositol, Sphingosine)
Polylecithins, 11, 12
Portal blood, lipides in, 348, 349
Potato, phosphatides in, 239
Propane, use in oil refining, 493
Protagon, 38, 54
Protective coatings, use of phosphatides in, 517, 518
Protective colloid
    cephalin phosphatides as, 76, 77
    lecithin as, 76, 77
Proteins
    characterization of, 3
    conversion to lipides, 351–354
    solubility of, 3
Prothrombin, 443
Psoriasis, 439
Psychosis, 434
P^{32} (see also Radioactive phosphorus)
    experiments with
        on blood phosphatides, 381–384
        on bone phosphatides, 403
        on brain phosphatides, 395, 396
        on egg phosphatides, 400, 401
        on gastrointestinal phosphatides, 389–392
        on heart phosphatides, 403
        on kidney phosphatides, 392, 393
        on liver phosphatides, 387, 388
        on lung phosphatides, 403
        on milk phosphatides, 402, 403
        on muscle phosphatides, 394, 395
        on nervous system phosphatides, 395, 396
        on pancreas phosphatides, 403
        on plant phosphatides, 404, 405
        on spleen phosphatides, 403
        on testes phosphatides, 397
        on tumors, 437, 438
    metabolic studies with, 371–377

Radiation, effect of on phosphatides, 411, 412
Radioactive atoms, as phosphatide labels, 370 ff.

Radioactive carbon, as phosphatide label, 370

Radioactive hydrogen, as phosphatide label, 370

Radioactive phosphorus (*see also* P^{32}), 381–384
  as phosphatide label, 371–377
  metabolic studies with, 371–377

Rapeseed, phosphatides in, 230, 231, 488, 494

Raspberry seeds, phosphatides in, 235

Reinecke acid, reaction with sphingomyelin, 65

Reinecke salt, precipitate with sphingomyelin, 171

Reproductive system
  metabolism of phosphatides of, 396, 397
  phosphatides in, 300–303

Resin technology, use of phosphatides in, 518, 519

Rubber latex, phosphatides in, 239, 240

Rubber technology, use of phosphatides in, 518

Rye, phosphatides in, 232, 233

Salt formation, with choline, 10

Salts
  complex with phosphatides, 94, 95, 96
  mixture with phosphatides, 95, 96, 97, 499, 500

Sarcoma, 436–438

Saturated phosphatides, analysis of, 173

Schüller-Christian disease, 425, 426

Serine (*see also* Phosphatidylserine), 31
  analysis of by periodate oxidation, 170
  classification of, 6
  in cardiac muscle, 310
  metabolic functions of, 420, 421
  presence of in cephalin fraction, 5, 29
  source of, 31
  structure of, 31
  synthesis of, 31

Serology, 443–452

Serum, 259

Sesame seed, phosphatides in, 235

Shortening, use of phosphatides in, 507

Silicates, adsorption of phosphatides by, 56, 57

Silkworm pupa, phosphatides in, 319

Simple lipides, classification of, 6

Skin
  diseases of, 439
  phosphatides in, 313–315

Smegma bacteria, phosphatides in, 201

Soap, use of phosphatides in, 519, 520

Soapstock, 490, 491

Sols, 71–76

Soybean oil, isolation of phosphatides in, 486 ff.

Soybeans, phosphatides in, 220–223

Spermatozoa, 397

Sphingol, 38

Sphingolipides (*see also* Cerebrosides, Gangliosides, Sphingomyelin, Sphingosine), 38, 39, 43, 64
  classification of, 7
  isolation of, 46

Sphingomyelin (*see also* Sphingosine), 38, 43
  acid-base relationships of, 45
  action of lecithinase D on, 113
  analysis of, 171
  cadmium chloride complex of, 64, 65
  choline in, 168
  complexes of (*see* Phosphatide complexes)
  determination of, 171
    as reineckate, 166, 171
    from choline content, 166
    in mixtures by selective hydrolysis, 172
  dielectric behavior of, 45
  distribution of in animal organs, 256, 257
  fatty acids of, 43, 44
  historical, 38
  hydrogenation of, 65
  hydrolysis of, 15, 46
  hydrolysis products of, 38, 43
  in bile, 297
  in blood, 256, 259, 262–269
  in brain, 256, 274, 276–278
  in brain of foetus, 275
  in intestines, 256
  in kidney, 256, 294, 295
  in liver, 256, 284–288
  in lung, 256, 292–294
  isoelectric point of, 45
  isolation of, 46
  metallic complexes of, 64
  monomolecular films of, 70
  optical activity of, 46
  origin of name of, 38
  properties of, 46, 65
  purification of, 64, 65
  reineckate of, 46, 65
  salts of, 46
  solubility of, 3, 46
  source of, 46, 64
  structure of, 38, 43

Sphingomyelin, Thudichum's investigations of, 38
  titration of, 45
  x-ray diffraction of sols of, 73
  zwitterionic structure of, 45
Sphingosine (*see also* Sphingomyelin), 39–41
  amides of, 39
  analysis of, 173
  anhydro form of, 43
  classification of, 6
  configuration of, 41, 43
  diacetyl derivative of, 41
  dibromo derivative of, 43
  dihydro derivative of, 39, 41, 116
  ethers of, 42
  hydrolysis product of sphingomyelin, 38
  lignoceryl derivative of, 43
  metabolic functions of, 420, 421
  N-benzoyl derivative, oxidation of, 41
  oxidation of, 39, 40
  ozonolysis of, 40
  properties of, 43
  structure of, 39, 40, 41
  sulfate of, 43
  triacetyl derivative of, 39, 40
    hydrogenation of, 40, 41
    optical activity of, 42
    ozonolysis of, 40
  tribenzoyl derivative of, 42
Sphingosine-containing phosphatides (*see also* Sphingolipides), classification of, 7, 8
Sphingosinephosphoric acid, choline ester of, 47
Spinal cord, phosphatides in, 278
Spleen, phosphatides in, 256, 295, 296
Spruce seeds, 235
Stearic acid, 21
  in phosphatidic acids, 49
  in sphingomyelin, 44
Steatorrhea, 431
Sugar, mixtures with phosphatides, 497, 498
Sugar cane, phosphatides in, 243
Sulfolipides, classification of, 6
Sulfonation, of phosphatides, 61, 501, 502
Sunflower seeds, phosphatides in, 232
Surface tension, 71
Symplex, 81
Synapse, 81
Synthesis of phosphatides, 116, 117, 119–126, 340, 351–354, 388, 393, 407, 408
Syphilis, 441, 450, 451

Takaphosphatase, resolution of α-glycerophosphoric acid with, 19
Tay Sach's disease, 428
Testes
  metabolism of phosphatides in, 396, 397
  phosphatides in, 300
  role of in fat metabolism, 364
Textiles, use of phosphatides in, 515, 516
Thoracic duct lymph, lipides in, 348, 349
Thrombin, 443
Thrombogen, 443
Thromboplastin
  composition of, 444, 445
  inhibitors of, 446, 447
  isolation of, 444, 445
  lipoprotein nature of, 444–446
Thymus, phosphatides in, 306
Thyroid gland
  diseases of, 441
  phosphatides in, 306
Timothy bacillus
  phophatides in, 199
  hydrolysis of, 15
Tissue, drying of, prior to phosphatide extraction, 150
Tissues, synthesis of phosphatides in, 407, 408
Tobacco, phosphatides in, 234
Tomato, phosphatides in, 239
Tooth pulp, 317
Transmethylation, 415–418
Triethyl-β-hydroxyethylammonium hydroxide, 418
Triglycerides, monomolecular films of, 70
Trimethyl-β-hydroxyethylammonium hydroxide (*see also* choline), 23
Tubercle bacillus
  phosphatides in, 202–213
    avian species, 205
    bovine species, 206
    carbohydrates associated with, 211–213
    characterization of, 207, 208
    classification of, 7, 8
    effect of culture medium on, 202, 203, 205
    fatty acids of, 208–11
    human species, 205
    hydrolysis products of, 204, 205
    in tuberculous tissue, 205
    inositol in, 35
    isolation of, 203, 204
    lack of organic base in, 204
Tuberculin, 449
Tuberculosis, 438, 439

Tuberculostearic acid, 194, 201, 206, 208–210
Tumors, phosphatides of, 436–438
Turtle bacteria, phosphatides in, 201

Unsaturated acids, as phosphatide label, 369, 370
Urea, 28, 97, 152
Uses, of phosphatides, 504 ff.

Varnish, use of phosphatides in, 517
Vegetable oils, stabilization of by phosphatides, 508, 509
Vegetables, phosphatides in, 236 ff.
Venom, lecithinase A in, 105, 106
Vertebrates, phosphatides in, 317–319
Vetch seeds, phosphatides in, 235
Vinyltrimethylammonium hydroxide (see also Neurine), 23
Virus, phosphatides in, 213
Vitamin A deficiency, phosphatide distribution during, 439, 440
Vitamin B deficiency, phosphatide distribution during, 440
Vitamin C deficiency, phosphatide distribution during, 440
Vitamin D deficiency, phosphatide distribution during, 440

Vitamin deficiency, phosphatide distribution during, 439–441
Vitamin K deficiency, phosphatide distribution during, 440, 441
Von Gierke's disease, 426

Walnuts, phosphatides in, 235
Wassermann antigen, 450, 451
Wassermann test, 450, 451
Waxes, classification of, 6
Wheat, phosphatides in, 224–227
Winterization of oils, use of phosphatides in, 512

Xanthoma disseminata, 425
Xanthomatosis, 425, 426
X-rays, effect of on phosphatides, 412

Yeast
   lipoproteins in, 88, 89
   phosphatide in, 214–216

Zwitterion
   in lecithin, 12, 13
   in phosphatides, 13
   in phosphatidylaminoethyl alcohol, 33
   in sphingomyelin, 45